COTTON IS KING,

AND

PRO-SLAVERY ARGUMENTS:

COMPRISING THE WRITINGS OF
HAMMOND, HARPER, CHRISTY, STRINGFELLOW, HODGE, BLEDSOE,
AND CARTWRIGHT,
ON THIS IMPORTANT SUBJECT.

BY

E. N. ELLIOTT, L.L.D.,

PRESIDENT OF PLANTERS' COLLEGE, MISSISSIPPI.

WITH AN ESSAY ON SLAVERY IN THE LIGHT OF INTERNATIONAL LAW,
BY THE EDITOR.

E. N. Elliott

Contents

INTRODUCTION

THERE is now but one great question dividing the American people, and that, to the great danger of the stability of our government, the concord and harmony of our citizens, and the perpetuation of our liberties, divides us by a geographical line. Hence estrangement, alienation, enmity, have arisen between the North and the South, and those who, from "the times that tried men's souls," have stood shoulder to shoulder in asserting their rights against the world; who, as a band of brothers, had combined to build up this fair fabric of human liberty, are now almost in the act of turning their fratricidal arms against each other's bosoms. All other parties that have existed in our country, were segregated on questions of policy affecting the whole nation and each individual composing it alike; they pervaded every section of the Union, and the acerbity of political strife was softened by the ties of blood, friendship, and neighborhood association. Moreover, these parties were constantly changing, on account of the influence mutually exerted by the members of each; the Federalist of yesterday becomes the Republican of to-day, and Whigs and Democrats change their party allegiance with every change of leaders. If the republicans mismanaged the government, they suffered the consequences alike with the federalists; if the democrats plunged our country into difficulties, they had to abide the penalty as well as the whigs. All parties alike had to suffer the evils, or enjoy the advantages of bad or good government. But it has been reserved to our own times to witness the rise, growth, and prevalence of a party confined exclusively to one section of the Union, whose fundamental principle is opposition to the rights and interests of the other section; and this, too, when those rights are most sacredly guaranteed, and those interests protected, by that compact under which we became a united nation. In a free government like ours, the eclecticism of parties—by which we mean the affinity by which the members of a party unite on questions of national policy, by which all sections of the country are alike affected—has always been considered as highly conducive to the purity and integrity of the government, and one of the causes most promotive of its perpetuity. Such has been the case, not only in our own country, but also in England, from whom we have mainly derived our ideas of civil and religious liberty, and even, to some extent, our form of government. But there, the case of oppressed and down-trodden Ireland, bears witness to the baneful effects of geographical partizan government and legislation.

In our own country this same spirit, which had its origin in the Missouri contest, is now beginning to produce its legitimate fruits: witness the growing distrust with which the people of the North and the South begin to regard each other; the diminution of

Southern travel, either for business or pleasure, in the Northern States; the efforts of each section to develop its own resources, so as virtually to render it independent of the other; the enactment of "unfriendly legislation," in several of the States, towards other States of the Union, or their citizens; the contest for the exclusive possession of the territories, the common property of the States; the anarchy and bloodshed in Kansas; the exasperation of parties throughout the Union; the attempt to nullify, by popular clamor, the decision of the supreme tribunal of our country; the existence of the "underground railroad," and of a party in the North organized for the express purpose of robbing the citizens of the Southern States of their property; the almost daily occurrence of fugitive slave mobs; the total insecurity of slave property in the border States;[1] the attempt to circulate incendiary documents among the slaves in the Southern States, and the flooding of the whole country with the most false and malicious misrepresentations of the state of society in the slave States; the attempt to produce division among us, and to array one portion of our citizens in deadly hostility to the other; and finally, the recent attempt to excite, at Harper's Ferry, and throughout the South, an insurrection, and a civil and servile war, with all its attendant horrors.

All these facts go to prove that there is a great wrong somewhere, and that a part, or the whole, of the American people are demented, and hurrying down to swift destruction. To ascertain where this great wrong and evil lies, to point out the remedy, to disabuse the public mind of all erroneous impressions or prejudices, to combat all false doctrines on *this* subject, and to establish the truth, shall be the aim of the following pages. In preparing them we have consulted the works of most of the writers on both sides of this question, as well as the statistics and history tending to throw light upon the subject. To this we would invite the candid and dispassionate attention of every patriot and philanthropist. To all such we would say, in the language of the Roman bard,

"Si quid novisti vectius istis,
Candidus imperti; si non,
His utere mecum."

In the following pages, the words slave and slavery are not used in the sense commonly understood by the abolitionists. With them these terms are contradistinguished from servants and servitude. According to their definition, a slave is merely a "chattel" in a human form; a *thing* to be bought and sold, and treated worse than a brute; a being without rights, privileges, or duties. Now, if this is a correct definition of the word, we totally object to the term, and deny that we have any such institution as *slavery* among us. We recognize among us no class, which, as the abolitionists falsely assert, that the Supreme Court decided "had no rights which a white man was bound to respect." The words *slave* and *servant* are perfectly synonymous, and differ only in being derived from different languages; the one from Sclavonic, the other from the Latin, just as feminine and womanly are respectively of Latin and Saxon origin. The Saxon synonym *thrall* has become

2

obsolete in our language, but some of its derivations, as thralldom, are still in use. In Greek the same idea was expressed by *doulos*, and in Hebrew by *ebed*. The one idea of servitude, or of obedience to the will of another, is accurately expressed by all these terms. He who wishes to see this topic thoroughly examined, may consult "Fletcher's Studies on Slavery."

The word *slavery* is used in the following discussions, to express the condition of the *African race* in our Southern States, as also in other parts of the world, and in other times. This word, as defined by most writers, does not truly express the relation which the African race in our country, *now* bears to the white race. In some parts of the world, the relation has essentially changed, while the word to express it has remained the same. In most countries of the world, especially in former times, the *persons* of the slaves were the absolute property of the master, and might be used or abused, as caprice or passion might dictate. Under the Jewish law, a slave might be beaten to death by his master, and yet the master go entirely unpunished, unless the slave died outright under his hand. Under the Roman law, slaves had no rights whatever, and were scarcely recognized as human beings; indeed, they were sometimes drowned in fish-ponds, to feed the eels. Such is not the labor system among us. As an example of faulty definition, we will adduce that of Paley: "Slavery," says he, "is an obligation to labor for the benefit of the master, without the contract or consent of the servant." Waiving, for the present, the accuracy of this definition, as far as it goes, we would remark that it is only half of the definition; the only idea here conveyed is that of compulsory and unrequited labor. Such is not our labor-system. Though we prefer the term slave, yet if this be its true definition, we must protest against its being applied to our system of African servitude, and insist that some other term shall be used. The true definition of the term, as applicable to the domestic institution in the Southern States, is as follows: Slavery is the duty and obligation of the slave to labor for the mutual benefit of both master and slave, under a warrant to the slave of protection, and a comfortable subsistence, under all circumstances. The person of the slave is not property, no matter what the fictions of the law may say; but the right to his labor is property, and may be transferred like any other property, or as the right to the services of a minor or an apprentice may be transferred. Nor is the labor of the slave solely for the benefit of the master, but for the benefit of all concerned; for himself, to repay the advances made for his support in childhood, for present subsistence, and for guardianship and protection, and to accumulate a fund for sickness, disability, and old age. The master, as the head of the system, has a right to the obedience and labor of the slave, but the slave has also his mutual rights in the master; the right of protection, the right of counsel and guidance, the right of subsistence, the right of care and attention in sickness and old age. He has also a right in his master as the sole arbiter in all his wrongs and difficulties, and as a merciful judge and dispenser of law to award the penalty of his misdeeds. Such is American slavery, or as Mr. Henry Hughes happily terms it, "Warranteeism."

In order that the subject of American slavery may be thoroughly discussed, we have availed ourselves of the labors of several of the ablest writers in the Union. These have been taken, not from one section only, but from both sections of our country. It is true, most of them are citizens of the Southern States, and for this there is a good and obvious reason; no one can correctly discuss this subject, or any other, who is practically unacquainted with it. This was the error of the French nation, when they undertook to legislate the African savages of St. Domingo into free citizens of the model republic; of the English nation when they undertook to interfere in the internal affairs of their colonies; and thus must it always be, when men undertake to think or write, or act, in reference to any subject, of whose fundamental truths, they are profoundly ignorant. It is true, that in every part of the civilized world there are noble minds, rising superior to the prejudices of education, and the influence of the society in which they are placed, and defending the truth for its own sake; to all such we render their due homage.

It is objected to the defenders of American slavery, that they have changed their ground; that from being apologists for it as an inevitable evil, they have become its defenders as a social and political good, morally right, and sanctioned by the Bible and by God himself. This charge is unjust, as by reference to a few historical facts will abundantly appear. The present slave States had little or no agency in the first introduction of Africans into this country; this was achieved by the Northern commercial States and by Great Britain. Wherever the climate suited the negro constitution, slavery was profitable and flourished; where the climate was unsuitable, slavery was unprofitable, and died out. Most of the slaves in the Northern States were sent southward to a more congenial clime. Upon the introduction into Congress of the first abolition discussions, by John Quincy Adams, and Joshua Giddings, Southern men altogether refused to engage in the debate, or even to receive petitions on the subject. They averred that no good could grow out of it, but only unmitigated evil.

The agitation of the abolition question had commenced in France during the horrors of her first revolution, under the auspices of the Red Republicans; it had pervaded England until it achieved the ruin of her West India colonies, and by anti-slavery missionaries it had been introduced into our Northern States. During all this agitation the Southern States had been quietly minding their own business, regardless of all the turmoil abroad. They had never investigated the subject theoretically, but they were well acquainted with all its practical workings. They had received from Africa a few hundred thousand pagan savages, and had developed them into millions of civilized Christians, happy in themselves, and useful to the world. They had never made the inquiry whether the system were fundamentally wrong, but they judged it by its fruits, which were beneficent to all. When therefore they were charged with upholding a moral, social, and political evil; and its immediate abolition was demanded, as a matter not only of policy, but also of justice and right, their reply was, we have never investigated the subject. Our fathers left it to us as a legacy, we have grown up with it; it has grown with our growth, and strengthened

4

with our strength, until it is now incorporated with every fibre of our social and political existence. What you say concerning its evils *may* be true or false, but we clearly see that your remedy involves a vastly greater evil, to the slave, to the master, to our common country, and to the world. We understand the nature of the negro race; and in the relation in which the providence of God has placed them to us, they are happy and useful members of society, and are fast rising in the scale of intelligence and civilization, and the time may come when they will be capable of enjoying the blessings of freedom and self-government. We are instructing them in the principles of our common Christianity, and in many instances have already taught them to read the word of life. But we know that the time has not yet come; that this liberty which is a blessing to *us*, would be a curse to *them*. Besides, to us and to you, such a violent disruption would be most disastrous, it would topple to its foundations the whole social and political edifice. Moreover, we have had warning on this subject. God, in his providence, has permitted the emancipation of the African race in a few of the islands contiguous to our shores, and far from being elevated thereby to the condition of Christian freemen, they have rapidly retrograded to the state of pagan savages. The value of property in those islands has rapidly depreciated, their production has vastly diminished, and their commerce and usefulness to the world is destroyed. We wish not to subject either ourselves or our dependents to such a fate. God has placed them in our hands, and he holds us responsible for our course of policy towards them.

This courteous, common-sense, and practical reply, far from closing the mouths of the agitators, only encouraged them to redouble their exertions, and to imbitter the epithets which they hurled at the slave-holders. They exhausted the vocabulary of billingsgate in denouncing those guilty of this most henious of all sins, and charged them in plain terms, with being *afraid* to investigate or to discuss the subject. Thus goaded into it, many commenced the investigation. Then for the first time did the Southern people take a position on this subject. It is due to a citizen of this State, the Rev. J. Smylie, to say that he was the first to promulgate the truth, as deduced from the Bible, on the subject of slavery. He was followed by a host of others, who discussed it not only in the light of revelation and morals, but as consistent with the Federal Constitution and the Declaration of Independence; until many of those who had commenced their career of abolition agitation by reasoning from the Bible and the Constitution, were compelled to acknowledge that they both were hopelessly pro-slavery, and to cry: "give us an anti-slavery constitution, an anti-slavery Bible, and an anti-slavery God." To such straits are men reduced by fanaticism. It is here worthy of remark, that most of the early abolition propagandists, many of whom commenced as Christian ministers, have ended in downright infidelity. Let us then hear no more of this charge, that the defenders of slavery have changed their ground; it is the abolitionists who have been compelled to appeal to "a higher law," not only than the Federal Constitution, but also, than the law of God. This is the inevitable result when men undertake to be "wise above what is written." The Apostle, in the Epistle to Timothy, has

5

not only explicitly laid down the law on the subject of slavery, but has, with prophetic vision, drawn the exact portrait of our modern abolitionists.

"Let as many servants as are under the yoke count their own masters worthy of all honor, that the name of God and his doctrine be not blasphemed. And they that have believing masters, let them not despise them, because they are brethren; but rather do them service, because they are faithful and beloved, partakers of the benefit. These things teach and exhort. If any man teach otherwise, and consent not to wholesome words, even the words of our Lord Jesus Christ, and to the doctrine which is according to godliness, he is proud, knowing nothing, but doting about questions and strifes of words, whereof cometh envy, strife, railings, evil surmisings, perverse disputings, of men of corrupt minds and destitute of the truth, supposing that gain is godliness; from such withdraw thyself."

Can any words more accurately and vividly portray the character and conduct of the abolitionists, or more plainly point out the results of their efforts? Is it any wonder that after having received such a castigation, they should totally repudiate the authority of God's law, and say, "Not *thy* will, but *mine* be done." It is here explicitly declared that this doctrine, the obedience of slaves to their masters, are the words of our Lord Jesus Christ; and the arguments of its opposers are characterized as doting sillily about questions and strifes of words, and therefore unworthy of reply and refutation. But the consequences are more serious; look at the catalogue. Envy, the root of the evil; strife, see the divisions in our churches, and in our political communities; railings, their calling slaveholders robbers, thieves, murderers, outlaws; evil surmisings, can any good thing come out of Nazareth, or from the Slave States? Perverse disputings of men of corrupt minds, their wresting the Scriptures from their plain and obvious meaning to compel them to teach abolitionism. Finally; the duty of all Christians: from such withdraw thyself.

The monographs embraced in this compendium of discussions on slavery, were written at different periods; some of them several years ago, and some of them were prepared expressly for this work, and some have been re-written in order to continue the subject down to the present time. There is this further advantage in combining works of different dates, that by comparing them it is evident that the earlier and later writers both stood on, substantially, the same ground, and take the same general views of the institution. The charge of inconsistency must, therefore, fall to the ground. To the reading public, most of the matter contained in these pages will be new; as, though some of them have been before the public for several years, they have had but a limited circulation, no efforts having been made by the Southern people to scatter them broadcast throughout the land, in the form of *Sunday school books*, or *religious tracts*. Nor will it be expected by the reader, that the authors of the works on the different topics embraced in this discussion, should have been able to confine their arguments strictly within the assigned limits. The subjects themselves so inosculate, that it would be strange indeed if the writers should not occasionally encroach upon each other's province; but even this, from the variety of argument, and mode of illustration, will be found interesting.

The work of Professor Christy, on the Economical Relations of Slavery, contains a large amount of the most accurate, valuable and well arranged statistical matter, and his combinations and deductions are remarkable for their philosophical accuracy. He spent several years in the service of the American Colonization Society, as agent for Ohio, and made himself thoroughly acquainted with the results, both to the blacks and whites, both of slavery and emancipation.

Governor Hammond is too well known, as an eminent statesman and political writer, to require notice here. His letters are addressed to Mr. Clarkson, of England, who, in conjunction with Wilberforce, after a long struggle, at last secured the passage, by the Parliament of Great Britain, of acts to abolish the slave trade and slavery, in the British West India colonies. The results of this are vividly portrayed by the author, and his predictions are now history.

Chancellor Harper, with a master hand, draws a parallel between the social condition of communities where slave labor exists and where it does not, and vindicates the South from the aspersions cast upon her.

Dr. Bledsoe's "Liberty and Slavery," or Slavery in the Light of Moral Science, discusses the right or wrong of slavery, exposes the fallacies, and answers the arguments of the abolitionists. His established reputation as an accurate reasoner, and a forcible writer, guarantees the excellence of this work.

Dr. Stringfellow's Slavery in the Light of Divine Revelation, and Dr. Hodge's Bible Argument on Slavery, form a synopsis of the whole theological argument on the subject. The plain and obvious teachings, of both Old and New Testament, are given with such irresistible force as to carry conviction to every mind, except those wedded to the theory of a "Higher Law" than the Law of God.

Dr. Cartwright's "Ethnology of the African Race," are the results of the observation and experience of a lifetime, spent in an extensive practice of medicine in the midst of the race. He has had the best of opportunities for becoming intimately acquainted with all the idiosyncrasies of this race, and he has well improved them. That the negro is *now* an inferior species, or at least variety of the human race, is well established, and must, we think, be admitted by all. That by himself he has never emerged from barbarism, and even when partly civilized under the control of the white man, he speedily returns to the same state, if emancipated, are now indubitable truths. Whether or not, under our system of slavery, he can ever be so elevated as to be worthy of freedom, time and the providence of God alone can determine. The most encouraging results have already been achieved by American slavery, in the elevation of the negro race in our midst; as they are now as far superior to the natives of Africa, as the whites are to them. In a religious point of view, also, there is great encouragement, as there are twice as many communicants of Christian churches among our slaves, as there are among the heathen at all the missionary stations in the world. (See Prof. Christy's statistics in this volume.) What the negroes might have been, but for the interference of the abolitionists, it is impossible to conjecture. That their influence has only been unmitigated evil, we have the united testimony, both of themselves and of the slave holders. (See Dr. Beecher's late sermon on the Harper's Ferry trials.)

To show what has been the uniform course of Christians in the South towards the slaves, we will quote from the first pastoral letter of the Synod of the Carolinas and Georgia, to the churches under their care.

After addressing husbands and wives, parents and children, on their relative duties, the Synod continues, "But parents and heads of families, think it not surprising that we inform you that God has committed others to your care, besides your natural offspring, in the welfare of whose souls you are also deeply interested, and whose salvation you are bound to endeavor to promote—we mean your slaves; poor creatures! shall they be bound for life, and their owners never once attempt to deliver their souls from the bondage of sin, nor point them to eternal freedom through the blood of the Son of God! On this subject we beg leave to submit to your consideration the conduct of Abraham, the father of the faithful, through whose example is communicated unto you the commandment of God (Gen. xviii: 19); 'For I know him,' says God, 'that he will command his children and his household after him, that they shall keep the ways of the Lord, to do justice and judgment.'

"Masters and servants, attend to your duty—in the express language of the Holy Ghost—'servants, obey your masters in all things; not with eye service, as men-pleasers, but in singleness of heart, fearing God; and whatsoever you do, do it heartily, as to the Lord, and not to man. And you, masters, render to your servants their due, knowing that your master is also in heaven, neither is there respect of persons with Him.' And let those who govern, and those who are governed, make the object of living in this world be, to prepare to meet your God and judge, when all shall stand on a level before His bar, and receive their decisive sentence according to the deeds done in the body.

"Servants, be willing to receive instruction, and discourage not your masters by your stubbornness or aversion. Remember, the interest is your own, and if you be wise, it will be for your own good; *spend the Sabbath in learning to read, and in teaching your young ones*, instead of rambling abroad from place to place; a few years will give you many Sabbaths, which, if rightly improved, will be sufficient for the purpose. Attend, also, on public worship, when you have opportunity, and behave there with decency and good order.

"Were these relative duties conscientiously practiced, by husbands and wives, parents and children, masters and servants, how pleasing would be the sight; expressing by your conduct pious Joshua's resolution, as for me and my house, we will serve the Lord."

The argument on slavery, deduced from the law of nations, we commend to the special attention of the candid reader. Indeed, it is from the recognition of the duty of the various races and nations composing the human family, to contribute their part for the advancement and good of the whole, not only that slavery has existed in all ages, but also that efforts have been, and are now being made, to extend the benefits of civilization and religion to the benighted races of the earth. This has been done in two different ways; one by sending the teacher forth to the heathen, the other by bringing the heathen to the teacher. Both have achieved great good, but the latter has been the more successful. Though the principles embraced in this general law of nations have been acknowledged and acted out in all times, it is due to J. Q. Adams, to state that he first gave a clear elucidation of those principles, so far as they apply to commerce.

Commending these arguments to the candid consideration of every friend to his country, we may be permitted to express the hope that they will redound, not only to the perpetuity of our blood-bought liberties, but to the glory of God, and the good of all men.

PORT GIBSON, MISS., Jan. 1, 1860.

COTTON IS KING:

OR,
SLAVERY IN THE LIGHT OF
POLITICAL ECONOMY.

BY

DAVID CHRISTY, ESQ.
OF CINCINNATI.

David Christy.

PREFACE TO THE THIRD EDITION.

THE first edition of COTTON IS KING was issued as an experiment. Its favorable reception led to further investigation, and an enlargement of the work for a second edition.

The present publishers have bought the copyright of the third edition, with the privilege of printing it in the form and manner that may best suit their purposes. This step severs the author from all further connection with the work, and affords him an opportunity of stating a few of the facts which led, originally, to its production. He was connected with the newspaper press, as an editor, from 1824 till 1836. This included the period of the tariff controversy, and the rise of the anti-slavery party of this country. After resigning the editorial chair, he still remained associated with public affairs, so as to afford him opportunities of observing the progress of events. In 1848 he accepted an appointment as Agent of the American Colonization Society, for Ohio; and was thus brought directly into contact with the elements of agitation upon the slavery question, in the aspect which that controversy had then assumed. Upon visiting Columbus, the seat of government of the State, in January, 1849, the Legislature, then in session, was found in great, agitation about the repeal of the Black Laws, which had originally been enacted to prevent the immigration of colored men into the State. The abolitionists held the balance of power, and were uncompromising in their demands. To escape from the difficulty, and prevent all future agitation upon the subject, politicians united in erasing this cause of disturbance from the statute book. The colored people had been in convention at the capitol; and felt themselves in a position, as they imagined, to control the legislation of the State. They were encouraged in this belief by the abolitionists, and proceeded to effect an organization by which black men were to *stump* the State in advocacy of their claims to an equality with white men.

At this juncture the Colonization cause was brought before the Legislature, by a memorial asking aid to send emigrants to Liberia. An appointment was also made, by the agent, for a Lecture on Colonization, to be delivered in the hall of the House of Representatives; and respectful notices sent to the African churches, inviting the colored people to attend. This invitation was met by them with the publication of a call for an indignation meeting; which, on assembling, denounced both the agent and the cause he advocated, in terms unfitted to be copied into this work. One of the resolutions, however, has some significance, as foreshadowing the final action they contemplated, and which has shown itself so futile, as a means of redress, in the recent Harper's Ferry Tragedy. That resolution reads as follows:

"*Resolved,*—That we will never leave this country while one of our brethren groans in slavish fetters in the United States, but will remain on this soil and contend for our rights, and those of our enslaved race—upon the rostrum—in the pulpit—in the social circle, and upon the field, if necessary, until liberty to the captive shall be proclaimed throughout the length and breadth of this great Republic, or we called from time to eternity."

In the winter of 1850, Mr. Stanley's proposition, to Congress, for the appropriation of the last installment of the Surplus Revenue to Colonization, was laid before the Ohio Legislature for approval. The colored people again held meetings, denouncing this proposition also, and the following resolutions, among others, were adopted—the first at Columbus and the second at Cincinnati:

"*Resolved,*—That it is our unalterable and eternal determination, as heretofore expressed, to remain in the United States at all hazards, and to 'buffet the withering flood of prejudice and misrule,' which menaces our destruction until we are exalted, to ride triumphantly upon its foaming billows, or honorably sink into its destroying vortex: although inducements may be held out for us to emigrate, in the shape of odious and oppressive laws, or liberal appropriations."

"*Resolved,*—That we should labor diligently to secure—first, the abolition of slavery, and, failing in this, the separation of the States; one or the other event being necessary to our ever enjoying in its fullness and power, the privilege of an American citizen."

Again, some three or four years later, on the occasion of the formation of the Ohio State Colonization Society, another meeting was called, in opposition to Colonization, in the city of Cincinnati, which, among others, passed the following resolution:

"*Resolved,*—That in our opinion the emancipation and elevation of our enslaved brethren depends in a great measure upon their brethren who are free, remaining in the country; and we will remain to be that 'agitating element' in American politics, which Mr Wise, in a late letter, concludes, has done so much for the slave."

Many similar resolutions might be quoted, all manifesting a determination, on the part of the colored people, to maintain their foothold in the United States, until the freedom of the slave should be effected; and indicating an expectation, on their part, that this result would be brought about by an insurrection, in which they expected to take a prominent part. In this policy they were encouraged by nearly all the opponents of Colonization, but especially by the active members of the organizations for running off slaves to Canada.

To meet this state of things, COTTON IS KING was written. The mad folly of the Burns' case, at Boston, in 1854, proved, conclusively, that white men, by the thousand, stood prepared to provoke a collision between the North and the South. The eight hundred men who volunteered at Worcester, and proceeded to Boston, on that occasion, with banner flying, showed that such a condition of public sentiment prevailed; while, at the same time, the sudden dispersion of that valorous army, by a single officer of the general government, who, unaided, captured their leader and bore off their banner, proved, as conclusively, that such philanthropists are not soldiers—that promiscuous crowds of undisciplined men are wholly unreliable in the hour of danger.

The author would here repeat, then, that the main object he had in view, in the preparation of COTTON IS KING, was to convince the abolitionists of the utter failure of their plans, and that the policy they had adopted was productive of results, the opposite of what they wished to effect;—that British and American abolitionists, in destroying tropical cultivation by emancipation in the West Indies, and opposing its promotion in Africa by Colonization, had given to slavery in the United States its prosperity and its power;—that the institution was no longer to be controlled by moral or physical force, but had become wholly subject to the laws of Political Economy;—and that, therefore, labor in tropical countries, to supply tropical products to commerce, and not insurrection in the United States, was the agency to be employed by those who would successfully oppose the extension of American Slavery: for, just as long as the hands of the free should persist in refusing to supply the demands of commerce for cotton, just so long it would continue to be obtained from those of the slave.

It will be seen in the perusal of the present edition, that Great Britain, in her efforts to promote cotton cultivation in India and Africa, now acts upon this principle, and that she thereby acknowledges the truth of the views which the author has advanced. It will be seen also, that to check American slavery and prevent a renewal of the slave trade by American planters, she has even determined to employ the slaves of Africa in the production of cotton: that is to say, the slavery of America is to be opposed by arraying against it the slavery of Africa—the petty chiefs there being required to force their slaves to the cotton patches, that the masters here may find a diminishing market for the products of their plantations.

In this connection it may be remarked, that the author has had many opportunities of conversing with colored men, on the subject of emigration to Africa, and they have almost uniformly opposed it on the ground that they would be needed here. Some of them, in defending their conduct, revealed the grounds of their hopes. But details on this point are unnecessary. The subject is referred to, only as affording an illustration of the extent to which ignorant men may become the victims of dangerous delusions. The sum of the matter was about this: the colored people, they said, had organizations extending from Canada to Louisiana, by means of which information could be communicated throughout the South, when the blow for freedom was to be struck. Philanthropic white men were expected to take sides against the oppressor, while those occupying neutral ground would offer no resistance to the passage of forces from Canada and Ohio to Virginia and Kentucky. Once upon slave territory, they imagined the work of emancipation would be easily executed, as every slave would rush to the standard of freedom.

These schemes of the colored people were viewed, at the time, as the vagaries of over excited and ignorant minds, dreaming of the repetition of Egyptian miracles for their deliverance; and were subjects of regret, only because they operated as barriers to Colonization. But when a friend placed in the author's hand, a few days since, a copy of the *Chatham* (Canada West) *Weekly Pilot*, of October 13, he could see that the seed sown at Columbus in 1849, had yielded its harvest of bitterness and disappointment at Harper's Ferry in 1859. That paper contained the proceedings and resolutions of the colored men, at Chatham, on the 3d of that month, in which the annexed resolution was included:

"*Resolved*,—That in view of the fact that a crisis will soon occur in the United States to affect our friends and countrymen there, we feel it the duty of every colored person to make the Canadas their homes. The temperature and salubrity of the climate, and the productiveness and fertility of the soil afford ample field for their encouragement. To hail their enslaved bondmen upon their deliverance, in the glorious kingdom of British Liberty, in the Canadas, we cordially invite the free and the bond, the noble and the ignoble— we have no 'Dred Scott Law.'"

The occasion which called out this resolution, together with a number of others, was the delivery of a lecture, on the 3d of October last, by an agent from Jamaica, who urged them to emigrate to that beautiful island. The import of this resolution will be better understood, when it is remembered, that the organization of Brown's insurrectionary scheme took place, in this same city of Chatham, on the 8th of May last. The "crisis" which was soon to occur in the United States, and the importance of every colored man remaining at his post, at that particular juncture, as urged by the resolutions, all indicate, very clearly, that Brown's movements were known to the leaders of the meeting, and that they desired to co-operate in the movement. The spirit breathed by the whole series of the Chatham resolutions, is so fully in accord with those passed from time to time in the United States, that there is no difficulty in perceiving that the views, expectations, and hopes of the colored people of both countries have been the same. The Chatham meeting was on the night of the 3d October, and the outbreak of Brown on that of the 16th.

But the failure of the Harper's Ferry movement should now serve as convincing proof, that nothing can be gained, by such means, for the African race. No successful organization, for their deliverance, can be effected in this country; and foreign aid is out of the question, not only because foreign nations will not wage war for a philanthropic object, but because they cannot do without our cotton for a single year. They are very much in the condition of our Northern politicians, since the old party landmarks have been broken down. The slavery question is the only one left, upon which any enthusiasm can be awakened among the people. The negro is to American politics what cotton is to European manufactures and commerce—the controlling element. As the overthrow of American slavery, with the consequent suspension of the motion of the spindles and looms of Europe, would bring ruin upon millions of its population; so the dropping of the negro question, in American politics, would at once destroy the prospects of thousands of aspirants to office. In ninety-nine cases out of a hundred, the clamor against slavery is made only for effect; and there is not now, nor has there been at any other period, any intention on the part of political agitators to wage actual war against the slave States themselves. But while the author believes that no intention of exciting to insurrection ever existed among leading politicians at the North, he must express the opinion that evil has grown out of the policy they have pursued, as it has excited the free negro to attempts at insurrection, by leading him to believe that they were in earnest in their professions of prosecuting the "irrepressible conflict," between freedom and slavery, to a termination destructive to the South; and, lured by this hope, he has been led to consider it his duty, as a man, to stand prepared for Mr Jefferson's crisis, in which Omnipotence would be arrayed upon his side. This stand he has been induced to take from principles of honor, instead of seeking new fields of enterprise in which to better his condition.

But there is another evil to the colored man, which has grown out of northern agitation on the question of slavery. The controversy is one of such a peculiar nature, that any needed modification of it can be made, by politicians, to suit whatever emergency may arise. The Burns' case convinced them that many men, white and black, were then prepared for treason. This was a step, however, that voters at large disapproved; and, not only was it unpopular to advocate the forcing of emancipation upon the slave States, but it seemed equally repugnant to the people to have the North filled with free negroes. The free colored man was, therefore, given to understand, that slavery was not to be disturbed in the States where it had been already established. But this was not all. He had to have another lesson in the philosophy of *dissolving scenes*, as exhibited in the great political magic lantern. Nearly all the Western States had denied him an equality with the white man, in the adoption or modification of their constitutions. He looked to Kansas for justice, and lo! it came. The first constitution, adopted by the free State men of that territory, excluded the free colored man from the rights of citizenship! "Why is this," said the author, to a leading German politician of Cincinnati: "why have the free State men excluded the free colored people from the proposed State?" "Oh," he replied, "we want it for our sons—for white men,—and we want the *nigger* out of our way: we neither want him there as a slave or freeman, as in either case his presence tends to degrade labor." This is not all. Nearly every slave State is legislating the free colored men out of their bounds, as a "disturbing element" which their people are determined no longer to tolerate. Here, then, is the result of the efforts of the free colored man to sustain himself in the midst of the whites; and here is the evil that political agitation has brought upon him.

Under these circumstances, the author believes he will be performing a useful service, in bringing the question of the economical relations of American slavery, once more, prominently before the public. It is time that the true character of the negro race, as compared with the white, in productive industry, should be determined. If the negro, as a voluntary laborer, is the equal of the white man, as the abolitionists contend, then, set him to work in tropical cultivation, and he can accomplish something for his race; but if he is incapable of competing with the white man, except in compulsory labor,—as slaveholders most sincerely believe the history of the race fully demonstrates—then let the truth be understood by the world, and all efforts for his elevation be directed to the accomplishment of the separation of the races. Because, until the colored men, who are now free, shall afford the evidence that freedom is best for the race, those held in slavery cannot escape from their condition of servitude.

Some new and important facts in relation to the results of West India emancipation are presented, which show, beyond question, that the advancing productiveness, claimed for these islands, is not due to any improvement in the industrial habits of the negroes, but is the result, wholly, of the introduction of immigrant labor from abroad. No advancement, of any consequence, has been made where immigrants have not been largely imported; and in Jamaica, which has received but few, there is a large decline in production from what existed during even the first years of freedom.

The present edition embraces a considerable amount of new matter, having a bearing on the condition of the cotton question, and a few other points of public interest. Several new Statistical Tables have been added to the appendix, that are necessary to the illustration of the topics discussed; and some historical matter also, in illustration of the early history of slavery in the United States.

CINCINNATI, JANUARY 1, 1860.

17

PREFACE TO THE SECOND EDITION

"COTTON IS KING" has been received, generally, with much favor by the public. The author's name having been withheld, the book was left to stand or fall upon its own merits. The first edition has been sold without any special effort on the part of the publishers. As they did not risk the cost of stereotyping, the work has been left open for revision and enlargement. No change in the matter of the first edition has been made, except a few verbal alterations and the addition of some qualifying phrases. Two short paragraphs only have been omitted, so as to leave the public documents and abolitionists, only, to testify as to the moral condition of the free colored people. The matter added to the present volume equals nearly one-fourth of the work. It relates mainly to two points: *First*, The condition of the free colored people; *Second*, The economical and political relations of slavery. The facts given, it is believed, will completely fortify all the positions of the author, on these questions, so far as his views have been assailed.

The field of investigation embraced in the book is a broad one, and the sources of information from which its facts are derived are accessible to but few. It is not surprising, then, that strangers to these facts, on first seeing them arranged in their philosophical relations and logical connection, should be startled at their import, and misconceive the object and motives of the author.

For example: One reviewer, in noticing the first edition, asserts that the writer "endeavors to prove that slavery is a great blessing in its relations to agriculture, manufactures, and commerce." The candid reader will be unable to find any thing, in the pages of the work, to justify such an assertion. The author has proved that the products of slave labor are in such universal demand, through the channels named by the reviewer, that it is impracticable, in the existing condition of the world, to overthrow the system; and that as the free negro has demonstrated his inability to engage successfully in cotton culture, therefore American slavery remains immovable, and presents a standing monument of the folly of those who imagined they could effect its overthrow by the measures they pursued. This was the author's aim.

Another charges, that the whole work is based on a fallacy, and that all its arguments, therefore, are unsound. The fallacy of the book, it is explained, consists in making cotton and slavery indivisible, and teaching that cotton can not be cultivated except by slave labor; whereas, in the opinion of the objector, that staple can be grown by free labor. Here, again, the author is misunderstood. He only teaches what is true beyond all question: not that free labor is incapable of producing cotton, but that it does not produce it so as to affect the interests of slave labor; and that the American planter, therefore, still finds himself in the possession of the monopoly of the market for cotton, and unable to meet the demand made upon him for that staple, except by a vast enlargement of its cultivation, requiring the employment of an increased amount of labor in its production.

Another says: "The real object of the work is an apology for American slavery. Professing to repudiate extremes, the author pleads the necessity for the present continuance of slavery, founded on economical, political, and moral considerations." The dullest reader can not fail to perceive that the work contains not one word of apology for the institution of slavery, nor the slightest wish for its continuance. The author did not suppose that Southern slave holders would thank any Northern man to attempt an apology for their maintaining what they consider their rights under the constitution; neither did he imagine that any plea for the continuance of American slavery was needed, while the world at large is industriously engaged in supporting it by the consumption of its products. He, therefore, neither attempted an apology for its existence nor a plea for its continuance. He was writing history and not recording his own opinions, about which he never imagined the public cared a fig. He was merely aiming at showing, how an institution, feeble and ill supported in the outset, had become one of the most potent agents in the advancement of civilization, notwithstanding the opposition it has had to encounter; and that those who had attempted its overthrow, in consequence of a lack of knowledge of the plainest principles of political economy and of human nature in its barbarous state, had contributed, more than any other class of persons, to produce this result.

Another charges the author with ignorance of the recent progress making in the culture of cotton, by free labor, in India and Algeria; and congratulates his readers that, "on this side of the ocean, the prospects of free soil and free labor, and of free cotton as one of the products of free soil and free labor, were never so fair as now." This is a pretty fair example of one's "whistling to keep his courage up," while passing, in the dark, through woods where he thinks ghosts are lurking on either side. Algeria has done nothing, yet, to encourage the hope that American slavery will be lessened in value by the cultivation of cotton in Africa. The British custom-house reports, as late as September, 1855, instead of showing any increase of imports of cotton from India, it will be seen, exhibit a great falling off in its supplies; and, in the opinion of the best authorities, extinguishes the hope of arresting the progress of American slavery by any efforts made to render Asiatic free labor more effective. As to the prospects on this side of the ocean, a glance at the map will show, that the chances of growing cotton in Kansas are just as good, and only as good as in Illinois and Missouri, from whence not a pound is ever exported. Texas was careful to appropriate nearly all the cotton lands acquired from Mexico, which lie on the eastern side of the Rocky Mountains; and, by that act, all such lands, mainly, have been secured to slavery. Where, then, is free labor to operate, even were it ready for the task?

Another alleges that the book is "a weak effort to slander the people of color." This is a charge that could have come only from a careless reader. The whole testimony, embraced in the first edition, nearly, as to the economical failure of West India Emancipation, and the moral degradation of the free colored people, generally, is quoted from abolition authorities, as is expressly stated; not to slander the people of color, but to show them what the world is to think of them, on the testimony of their particular friends and self-constituted guardians.

Another objects to what is said of those who hold the opinion that slavery is *malum in se*, and who yet continue to purchase and use its products. On this point it is only necessary to say, that the logic of the book has not been affected by the sophistry employed against it; and that if those who hold the *per se* doctrine, and continue to use slave labor products, dislike the charge of being *participes criminis* with robbers, they must classify slavery in some other mode than that in which they have placed it in their creeds. For, if they are not partakers with thieves, then slavery is not a system of robbery; but if slavery be a system of robbery, as they maintain, then, on their own principles, they are as much partakers with thieves as any others who deal in stolen property.

The severest criticism on the book, however, comes from one who charges the author with a "disposition to mislead, or an ignorance which is inexcusable," in the use of the statistics of crime, having reference to the free colored people, from 1820 to 1827. The object of the author, in using the statistics referred to, was only to show the reasons why the scheme of colonization was then accepted, by the American public, as a means of relief to the colored population, and not to drag out these sorrowful facts to the disparagement of those now living. But the reviewer, suspicious of every one who does not adopt his abolition notions, suspects the author of improper motives, and asks: "Why go so far back, if our author wished to treat the subject fairly?" Well, the statistics on this dismal topic have been brought up to the latest date practicable, and the author now leaves it to the colored people themselves to say, whether they have gained any thing by the reviewer's zeal in their behalf. He will learn one lesson at least, we hope, from the result: that a writer can use his pen with greater safety to his reputation, when he knows something about the subject he discusses.

But this reviewer, warming in his zeal, undertakes to philosophise, and says, that the evils existing among the free colored people, will be found in exact proportion to the slowness of emancipation; and complains that New Jersey was taken as the standard, in this respect, instead of Massachusetts, where, he asserts, "all the negroes in the commonwealth, were, by the new constitution, liberated in a day, and none of the ill consequences objected followed, either to the commonwealth or to individuals." The reviewer is referred to the facts, in the present edition, where he will find, that the amount of crime, at the date to which he refers, was *six times* greater among the colored people of Massachusetts, in proportion to their numbers, than among those of New Jersey. The next time he undertakes to review KING COTTON, it will be best for him not to rely upon his imagination, but to look at the facts. He should be able at least, when quoting a writer, to discriminate between evils resulting from insurrections, and evils growing out of common immoralities. Experience has taught, that it is unsafe, when calculating the results of the means of elevation employed, to reason from a civilized to a half civilized race of men.

The last point that needs attention, is the charge that the author is a slaveholder, and governed by mercenary motives. To break the force of any such objection to the work, and relieve it from prejudices thus created, the veil is lifted, and the author's name is placed upon the title page.

The facts and statistics used in the first edition, were brought down to the close of 1854, mainly, and the arguments founded upon the then existing state of things. The year 1853 was taken as best indicating the relations of our planters and farmers to the manufactures and commerce of the country and the world; because the exports and imports of that year were nearer an average of the commercial operations of the country than the extraordinary year which followed; and because the author had nearly finished his labors before the results of 1854 had been ascertained. In preparing the second edition for the press, many additional facts, of a more recent date, have been introduced: all of which tend to prove the general accuracy of the author's conclusions, as expressed in the first edition.

Tables IV and V, added to the present edition, embrace some very curious and instructive statistics, in relation to the increase and decrease of the free colored people, in certain sections, and the influence they appear to exert on public sentiment.

PREFACE TO THE FIRST EDITION.

In the preparation of the following pages, the author has aimed at clearness of statement, rather than elegance of diction. He sets up no claim to literary distinction; and even if he did, every man of classical taste knows, that a work, abounding in facts and statistics, affords little opportunity for any display of literary ability.

The greatest care has been taken, by the author, to secure perfect accuracy in the statistical information supplied, and in all the facts stated.

The authorities consulted are Brande's Dictionary of Science, Literature and Art; Porter's Progress of the British Nation; McCullough's Commercial Dictionary; Encyclopædia Americana; London Economist; De Bow's Review; Patent Office Reports; Congressional Reports on Commerce and Navigation; Abstract of the Census Reports, 1850; and Compendium of the Census Reports. The extracts from the Debates in Congress, on the Tariff Question, are copied from the *National Intelligencer.*

The tabular statements appended, bring together the principal facts, belonging to the questions examined, in such a manner that their relations to each other can be seen at a glance.

The first of these Tables, shows the date of the origin of cotton manufactories in England, and the amount of cotton annually consumed, down to 1853; the origin and amount of the exports of cotton from the United States to Europe; the sources of England's supplies of cotton, from countries other than the United States; the dates of the discoveries which have promoted the production and manufacture of cotton; the commencement of the movements made to meliorate the condition of the African race; and the occurrence of events that have increased the value of slavery, and led to its extension.

The second and third of the tables, relate to the exports and imports of the United States; and illustrate the relations sustained by slavery, to the other industrial interests and to the commerce of the country.

CHAPTER I

INTRODUCTORY STATEMENTS.

Character of the Slavery controversy in the United States—In Great Britain—Its influence in modifying the policy of Anti-Slavery men in America—Course of the Churches—Political Parties—Result, COTTON IS KING—Necessity of reviewing the policy in relation to the African race—Topics embraced in the discussion.

THE controversy on SLAVERY, in the United States, has been one of an exciting and complicated character. The power to emancipate existing, in fact, in the States separately and not in the general government, the efforts to abolish it, by appeals to public opinion, have been fruitless except when confined to single States. In Great Britain the question was simple. The power to abolish slavery in her West Indian colonies was vested in Parliament. To agitate the people of England, and call out a full expression of sentiment, was to control Parliament and secure its abolition. The success of the English abolitionists, in the employment of moral force, had a powerful influence in modifying the policy of American anti-slavery men. Failing to discern the difference in the condition of the two countries, they attempted to create a public sentiment throughout the United States adverse to slavery, in the confident expectation of speedily overthrowing the institution. The issue taken, that slavery is *malum in se*—a sin in itself—was prosecuted with all the zeal and eloquence they could command. Churches adopting the *sin per se* doctrine, inquired of their converts, not whether they supported slavery by the use of its products, but whether they believed the institution itself sinful. Could public sentiment be brought to assume the proper ground; could the slaveholder be convinced that the world denounced him as equally criminal with the robber and murderer; then, it was believed, he would abandon the system. Political parties, subsequently organized, taught, that to vote for a slaveholder, or a pro-slavery man, was sinful, and could not be done without violence to conscience; while, at the same time, they made no scruples of using the products of slave labor—the exorbitant demand for which was the great bulwark of the institution. This was a radical error. It laid all who adopted it open to the charge of practical inconsistency, and left them without any moral power over the consciences of others. As long as all used their products, so long the slaveholders found the *per se* doctrine working them no harm; as long as no provision was made for supplying the demand for tropical products by free labor, so long there was no risk in extending the field of operations. Thus, the very things necessary to the overthrow of American slavery, were left undone, while those essential to its prosperity, were continued in the most active operation; so that, now, after more than a thirty years' war, we may say, emphatically, COTTON IS KING, and his enemies are vanquished.

Under these circumstances, it is due to the age—to the friends of humanity—to the cause of liberty—to the safety of the Union—that we should review the movements made in behalf of the African race, in our country; so that errors of principle may be abandoned; mistakes in policy corrected; the free colored people taught their true relations to the industrial interests of the world; the rights of the slave as well as the master secured; and the principles of the constitution established and revered. It is proposed, therefore, to examine this subject in the light of the social, civil, and commercial history of the country; and, in doing this, to embrace the facts and arguments under the following heads:

1. The early movements on the subject of slavery; the circumstances under which the Colonization Society took its rise; the relations it sustained to slavery and to the schemes projected for its abolition; the origin of the elements which have given to American slavery its commercial value and consequent powers of expansion; and the futility of the means used to prevent the extension of the institution.

2. The relations of American slavery to the industrial interests of our own country; to the demands of commerce; and to the present political crisis.

3. The industrial, social, and moral condition of the free colored people in the British colonies and in the United States; and the influence they have exerted on public sentiment in relation to the perpetuation of slavery.

4. The moral relations of persons holding the *per se* doctrine, on the subject of slavery, to the purchase and consumption of slave labor products.

CHAPTER II

THE EARLY MOVEMENTS ON THE SUBJECT OF SLAVERY; THE CIRCUMSTANCES UNDER WHICH THE COLONIZATION SOCIETY TOOK ITS RISE; THE RELATIONS IT SUSTAINED TO SLAVERY AND TO THE SCHEMES PROJECTED FOR ITS ABOLITION; THE ORIGIN OF THE ELEMENTS WHICH HAVE GIVEN TO AMERICAN SLAVERY ITS COMMERCIAL VALUE AND CONSEQUENT POWERS OF EXPANSION; AND THE FUTILITY OF THE MEANS USED TO PREVENT THE EXTENSION OF THE INSTITUTION.

Emancipation in the United States begun—First Abolition Society organized—Progress of Emancipation—First Cotton Mill—Exclusion of Slavery from N. W. Territory—Elements of Slavery expansion—Cotton Gin invented—Suppression of the Slave Trade—Cotton Manufactures commenced in Boston—Franklin's Appeal—Condition of the Free Colored People—Boston Prison-Discipline Society—Darkening Prospects of the Colored People.

FOUR years after the Declaration of American Independence, Pennsylvania and Massachusetts had emancipated their slaves; and, eight years thereafter, Connecticut and Rhode Island followed their example.

Three years after the last named event, an *abolition society* was organized by the citizens of the State of New York, with John Jay at its head. Two years subsequently, the Pennsylvanians did the same thing, electing Benjamin Franklin to the presidency of their association. The same year, too, slavery was forever excluded, by act of Congress, from the Northwest Territory. This year is also memorable as having witnessed the erection of the first cotton mill in the United States, at Beverley, Massachusetts.

During the year that the New York Abolition Society was formed, Watts, of England, had so far perfected the *steam engine* as to use it in propelling machinery for spinning cotton; and the year the Pennsylvania Society was organized witnessed the invention of the *power loom*. The *carding machine* and the *spinning jenny* having been invented twenty years before, the power loom completed the machinery necessary to the indefinite extension of the manufacture of cotton.

The work of emancipation, begun by the four States named, continued to progress, so that in seventeen years from the adoption of the constitution, New Hampshire, Vermont,

New York, and New Jersey, had also enacted laws to free themselves from the burden of slavery.

As the work of manumission proceeded, the elements of slavery expansion were multiplied. When the four States first named liberated their slaves, no regular exports of cotton to Europe had yet commenced; and the year New Hampshire set hers free, only 138,328 lbs. of that article were shipped from the country. Simultaneously with the action of Vermont, in the year following, the *cotton gin* was invented, and an unparalleled impulse given to the cultivation of cotton. At the same time, Louisiana, with her immense territory, was added to the Union, and room for the extension of slavery vastly increased. New York lagged behind Vermont for six years, before taking her first step to free her slaves, when she found the exports of cotton to England had reached 9,500,000 lbs.; and New Jersey, still more tardy, fell five years behind New York; at which time the exports of that staple—so rapidly had its cultivation progressed—were augmented to 38,900,000 lbs.

Four years after the emancipations by States had ceased, the slave trade was prohibited; but, as if each movement for freedom must have its counter-movement to stimulate slavery, that same year the manufacture of cotton goods was commenced in Boston. Two years after that event, the exports of cotton amounted to 93,900,000 lbs. War with Great Britain, soon afterward, checked both our exports and her manufacture of the article; but the year 1817, memorable in this connection, from its being the date of the organization of the Colonization Society, found our exports augmented to 95,660,000 lbs., and her consumption enlarged to 126,240,000 lbs. Carding and spinning machinery had now reached a good degree of perfection, and the power loom was brought into general use in England, and was also introduced into the United States. Steamboats, too, were coming into use, in both countries; and great activity prevailed in commerce, manufactures, and the cultivation of cotton.

But how fared it with the free colored people during all this time? To obtain a true answer to this question we must revert to the days of the Pennsylvania Abolition Society.

With freedom to the slave, came anxieties among the whites as to the results. Nine years after Pennsylvania and Massachusetts had taken the lead in the trial of emancipation, Franklin issued an appeal for aid to enable his society to form a plan for the promotion of industry, intelligence, and morality among the free blacks; and he zealously urged the measure on public attention, as essential to their well-being, and indispensable to the safety of society. He expressed his belief, that such is the debasing influence of slavery on human nature, that its very extirpation, if not performed with care, may sometimes open a source of serious evils; and that so far as emancipation should be promoted by the society, it was a duty incumbent on its members to instruct, to advise, to qualify those restored to freedom, for the exercise and enjoyment of civil liberty.

How far Franklin's influence failed to promote the humane object he had in view, may be inferred from the fact, that forty-seven years after Pennsylvania passed her act of emancipation, and thirty-eight after he issued his appeal, *one-third* of the convicts in her penitentiary were colored men; though the preceding census showed that her slave population had almost wholly disappeared—there being but *two hundred and eleven* of them remaining, while her free colored people had increased in number to more than *thirty thousand*. Few of the other free States were more fortunate, and some of them were even in a worse condition—*one-half* of the convicts in the penitentiary of New Jersey being colored men.

But this is not the whole of the sad tale that must be recorded. Gloomy as was the picture of crime among the colored people of New Jersey, that of Massachusetts was vastly worse. For though the number of her colored convicts, as compared with the whites, was as *one to six*, yet the proportion of her colored population in the penitentiary was *one* out of *one hundred and forty*, while the proportion in New Jersey was but *one* out of *eight hundred and thirty-three*. Thus, in Massachusetts, where emancipation had, in 1780, been *immediate* and unconditional, there was, in 1826, among her colored people, about six times as much crime as existed among those of New Jersey, where *gradual* emancipation had not been provided for until 1804.

The moral condition of the colored people in the free States, generally, at the period we are considering, may be understood more clearly from the opinions expressed, at the time, by the *Boston Prison Discipline Society*. This benevolent association included among its members, Rev. Francis Wayland, Rev. Justin Edwards, Rev. Leonard Woods, Rev. William Jenks, Rev. B. B. Wisner, Rev. Edward Beecher, Lewis Tappan, Esq., John Tappan, Esq., Hon. George Bliss, and Hon. Samuel M. Hopkins.

In the First Annual Report of the Society, dated June 2, 1826, they enter into an investigation "of the progress of crime, with the causes of it," from which we make the following extracts:

"DEGRADED CHARACTER OF THE COLORED POPULATION.—The first cause, existing in society, of the frequency and increase of crime is the degraded character of the colored population. The facts, which are gathered from the penitentiaries, to show how great a proportion of the convicts are colored, even in those States where the colored population is small, show, most strikingly, the connection between ignorance and vice."

The report proceeds to sustain its assertions by statistics, which prove, that, in Massachusetts, where the free colored people constituted *one seventy-fourth* part of the population, they supplied *one-sixth* part of the convicts in her penitentiary; that in New York, where the free colored people constituted *one thirty-fifth* part of the population, they supplied more than *one-fourth* part of the convicts; that, in Connecticut and Pennsylvania, where the colored people constituted *one thirty-fourth* part of the population, they supplied more than *one-third* part of the convicts; and that, in New Jersey, where the colored people constituted *one-thirteenth* part of the population, they supplied more than *one-third* part of the convicts.

"It is not necessary," continues the report, "to pursue these illustrations. It is sufficiently apparent, that one great cause of the frequency and increase of crime, is neglecting to raise the character of the colored population.

"We derive an argument in favor of education from these facts. It appears from the above statement, that about *one-fourth* part of all the expense incurred by the States above mentioned, for the support of their criminal institutions, is for the colored convicts. * * Could these States have anticipated these surprising results, and appropriated the money to raise the character of the colored population, how much better would have been their prospects, and how much less the expense of the States through which they are dispersed for the support of their colored convicts! * * If, however, their character can not be raised, where they are, a powerful argument may be derived from these facts, in favor of colonization, and civilized States ought surely to be as willing to expend money on any given part of its population, to prevent crime, as to punish it.

"We can not but indulge the hope that the facts disclosed above, if they do not lead to an effort to raise the character of the colored population, will strengthen the hands and encourage the hearts of all the friends of colonizing the free people of color in the United States."

The Second Annual Report of the Society, dated June 1, 1827, gives the results of its continued investigations into the condition of the free colored people, in the following language and figures:

"CHARACTER OF THE COLORED POPULATION.—In the last report, this subject was exhibited at considerable length. From a deep conviction of its importance, and an earnest desire to keep it ever before the public mind, till the remedy is applied, we present the following table, showing, in regard to several States, the whole population, the colored population, the whole number of convicts, the number of colored convicts, proportion of convicts to the whole population, proportion of colored convicts:

	Whole Pop- ulation.	Colored Population.	Whole number of Convicts.	Number of Colored Convicts.	Proportion of Colored People.	Proportion of Colored Con- victs.
Mass.	523,000	7,000	314	50	1 to 74	1 to 6
Conn.	275,000	8,000	117	39	1 to 34	1 to 3
N. York	1,372,000	39,000	637	154	1 to 35	1 to 4
N. Jersey	277,000	20,000	74	24	1 to 13	1 to 3
Penn.	1,049,000	30,000	474	165	1 to 34	1 to 3

"Or,

	Proportion of the Population sent to Prison.	Proportion of the Colored Popu'n sent to Prison.
In Massachusetts,	1 out of 1665	1 out of 140
In Connecticut,	1 out of 2350	1 out of 205
In New York,	1 out of 2153	1 out of 253
In New Jersey,	1 out of 3743	1 out of 833
In Pennsylvania,	1 out of 2191	1 out of 181

EXPENSE FOR THE SUPPORT OF COLORED CONVICTS.
In Masachusetts, in 10 years, $17,734
In Connecticut, in 15 years, 37,166
In New York, in 27 years, 109,166
Total $164 066

"Such is the abstract of the information presented last year, concerning the degraded character of the colored population. The returns from several prisons show, that the white convicts are remaining nearly the same, or are diminishing, while the colored convicts are increasing. At the same time, the white population is increasing, in the Northern States, much faster than the colored population."

	Whole No. of Convicts.	Colored Convicts.	Proportion.
In Massachusetts,	313	50	1 to 6
In New York,	381	101	1 to 4
In New Jersey,	67	33	1 to 2

Such is the testimony of men of unimpeachable veracity and undoubted philanthrophy, as to the early results of emancipation in the United States. Had the freedmen, in the

Northern States, improved their privileges; had they established a reputation for industry, integrity, and virtue, far other consequences would have followed their emancipation. Their advancement in moral character would have put to shame the advocate for the perpetuation of slavery. Indeed, there could have been no plausible argument found for its continuance. No regular exports of cotton, no cultivation of cane sugar, to give a profitable character to slave labor, had any existence when Jay and Franklin commenced their labors, and when Congress took its first step for the suppression of the slave trade.

Unfortunately, the free colored people persevered in their evil habits. This not only served to fix their own social and political condition on the level of the slave, but it reacted with fearful effect upon their brethren remaining in bondage. Their refusing to listen to the counsel of the philanthropists, who urged them to forsake their indolence and vice, and their frequent violations of the laws, more than all things else, put a check to the tendencies, in public sentiment, toward general emancipation. The failure of Franklin to obtain the means of establishing institutions for the education of the blacks, confirmed the popular belief that such an undertaking was impracticable, and the whole African race, freedmen as well as slaves, were viewed as an intolerable burden, such as the imports of foreign paupers are now considered. Thus the free colored people themselves, ruthlessly threw the car of emancipation from the track, and tore up the rails upon which, alone, it could move.

CHAPTER III

State of public opinion in relation to colored population—Southern views of Emancipation—Influence of Mr. Jefferson's opinions—He opposed Emancipation except
connected with Colonization—Negro equality not contemplated by the Father's of the
Revolution—This proved by the resolutions of their conventions—The true objects of the
opposition to the slave trade—Motives of British Statesmen in forcing Slavery on the colonies—Absurdity of supposing negro equality was contemplated.

THE opinion that the African race would become a growing burden had its origin before the revolution, and led the colonists to oppose the introduction of slaves; but failing
in this, through the opposition of England, as soon as they threw off the foreign yoke
many of the States at once crushed the system—among the first acts of sovereignty by
Virginia, being the prohibition of the slave trade. In the determination to suppress this
traffic all the States united—but in emancipation their policy differed. It was found easier
to manage the slaves than the free blacks—at least it was claimed to be so—and, for this
reason, the slave States, not long after the others had completed their work of manumission, proceeded to enact laws prohibiting emancipations, except on condition that the
persons liberated should be removed. The newly organized free States, too, taking alarm
at this, and dreading the influx of the free colored people, adopted measures to prevent
the ingress of this proscribed and helpless race.

These movements, so distressing to the reflecting colored man, be it remembered,
were not the effect of the action of colonizationists, but took place, mostly, long before
the organization of the American Colonization Society; and, at its first annual meeting,
the importance and humanity of colonization was strongly urged, on the very ground that
the slave States, as soon as they should find that the persons liberated could be sent to
Africa, would relax their laws against emancipation.

The slow progress made by the great body of the free blacks in the North, or the absence, rather, of any evidences of improvement in industry, intelligence, and morality,
gave rise to the notion, that before they could be elevated to an equality with the whites,
slavery must be wholly abolished throughout the Union. The constant ingress of liberated
slaves from the South, to commingle with the free colored people of the North, it was
claimed, tended to perpetuate the low moral standard originally existing among the
blacks; and universal emancipation was believed to be indispensable to the elevation of
the race. Those who adopted this view, seem to have overlooked the fact, that the Africans, of savage origin, could not be elevated at once to an equality with the American

people, by the mere force of legal enactments. More than this was needed, for their elevation, as all are now, reluctantly, compelled to acknowledge. Emancipation, unaccompanied by the means of intellectual and moral culture, is of but little value. The savage, liberated from bondage, is a savage still.

The slave States adopted opinions, as to the negro character, opposite to those of the free States, and would not risk the experiment of emancipation. They said, if the free States feel themselves burdened by the few Africans they have freed, and whom they find it impracticable to educate and elevate, how much greater would be the evil the slave States must bring upon themselves by letting loose a population nearly twelve times as numerous. Such an act, they argued, would be suicidal—would crush out all progress in civilization; or, in the effort to elevate the negro with the white man, allowing him equal freedom of action, would make the more energetic Anglo-Saxon the slave of the indolent African. Such a task, onerous in the highest degree, they could not, and would not undertake; such an experiment, on their social system, they dared not hazard; and in this determination they were encouraged to persevere, not only by the results of emancipation, then wrought out at the North, but by the settled convictions which had long prevailed at the South, in relation to the impropriety of freeing the negroes. This opinion was one of long standing, and had been avowed by some of the ablest statesmen of the Revolution. Among these Mr. Jefferson stood prominent. He was inclined to consider the African inferior "in the endowments both of body and mind" to the European; and, while expressing his hostility to slavery earnestly, vehemently, he avowed the opinion that it was impossible for the two races to live equally free in the same government—that "nature, habit, opinion, had drawn indelible lines of distinction between them"—that, accordingly, emancipation and "deportation" (colonization) should go hand in hand—and that these processes should be gradual enough to make proper provisions for the blacks in a new country, and fill their places in this with free white laborers.[2]

Another point needs examination. Notwithstanding the well-known opinions of Mr. Jefferson, it has been urged that the Declaration of Independence was designed, by those who issued it, to apply to the negro as well as to the white man; and that they purposed to extend to the negro, at the end of the struggle, then begun, all the privileges which they hoped to secure for themselves. Nothing can be further from the truth, and nothing more certain than that the rights of the negro never entered into the questions then considered. That document was written by Mr. Jefferson himself, and, with the views which he entertained, he could not have thought, for a moment, of conferring upon the negro the rights of American citizenship. Hear him further upon this subject and then judge:

"It will probably be asked, why not retain and incorporate the blacks into the State, and thus save the expense of supplying by importation of white settlers, the vacancies they will leave? Deep-rooted prejudices entertained by the whites; ten thousand recollections, by the blacks, of the injuries they have sustained; new provocations; the real distinctions which nature has made; and many other circumstances, will divide us into parties, and produce convulsions, which will probably never end, but in the extermination of the one or the other race. To these objections, which are political, may be added others, which are physical and moral"[3]

Now it is evident, from this language, that Mr. Jefferson was not only opposed to allowing the negroes the rights of citizenship, but that he was opposed to emancipation also, except on the condition that the freedmen should be removed from the country. He could, therefore, have meant nothing more by the phrase, "all men are created equal," which he employed in the Declaration of Independence, than the announcement of a general principle, which, in its application to the colonists, was intended most emphatically to assert their equality, before God and the world, with the imperious Englishmen who claimed the divine right of lording it over them. This was undoubtedly the view held by Mr. Jefferson, and the extent to which he expected the language of the Declaration to be applied.[4] Nor could the signers of that instrument, or the people whom they represented, ever have intended to apply its principles to any barbarous or semi-barbarous people, in the sense of admitting them to an equality with themselves in the management of a free government. Had this been their design, they must have enfranchised both Indians and Africans, as both were within the territory over which they exercised jurisdiction.

But testimony of a conclusive character is at hand, to show that quite a different object was to be accomplished, than negro equality, in the movements of the colonists which preceded the outbreak of the American Revolution. They passed resolutions upon the subject of the slave trade, it is true, but it was to oppose it, because it increased the colored population, a result they deprecated in the strongest language. The checking of this evil, great as the people considered it, was not the principal object they had in view, in resolving to crush out the slave trade. It was one of far greater moment, affecting the prosperity of the mother country, and designed to force her to deal justly with the colonies.

This point can only be understood by an examination of the history of that period, so as to comprehend the relations existing between Great Britain and her several colonies. Let us, then, proceed to the performance of this task.

The whole commerce of Great Britain, in 1704, amounted, in value, to thirty-two and a half millions of dollars. In less than three quarters of a century thereafter, or three years preceding the outbreak of the American Revolution, it had increased to eighty millions annually. More than thirty millions of this amount, or over one-third of the whole, consisted of exports to her West Indian and North American colonies and to Africa. The yearly trade with Africa, alone, at this period—1772—was over four and a third millions of dollars: a significant fact, when it is known that this African traffic was in slaves.

But this statement fails to give a true idea of the value of North America and the West Indies to the mother country. Of the commodities which she imported from them—tobacco, rice, sugar, rum—ten millions of dollars worth, annually, were re-exported to her other dependencies, and five millions to foreign countries—thus making her indebted to these colonies, directly and indirectly, for more than one-half of all her commerce.

If England was greatly dependent upon these colonies for her increasing prosperity, they were also dependent upon her; and upon each other, for the mutual promotion of their comfort and wealth. This is easily understood. The colonies were prohibited from manufacturing for themselves. This rendered it necessary that they should be supplied with linen and woolen fabrics, hardware and cutlery, from the looms and shops of Great Britain; and, in addition to these necessaries, they were dependent upon her ships to furnish them with slaves from Africa. The North American colonies were dependent upon the West Indies for coffee, sugar, rum; and the West Indies upon North America, in turn, for their main supplies of provisions and lumber. The North Americans, if compelled by necessity, could do without the manufacures of England, and forego the use of the groceries and rum of the West Indies; but Great Britain could not easily bear the loss of half her commerce, nor could the West India planters meet a sudden emergency that would cut off their usual supplies of provisions.

Such were the relations existing between Great Britain and the colonies, and between the colonies themselves, when the Bostonians cast the tea overboard. This act of resistance to law, was followed by the passage, through Parliament, of the Boston Port Bill, closing Boston Harbor to all commerce whatsoever. The North American colonies, conscious of their power over the commerce of Great Britain, at once obeyed the call of the citizens of Boston, and united in the adoption of peaceful measures, to force the repeal of the obnoxious act. Meetings of the people were held throughout the country, generally, and resolutions passed, recommending the non-importation and non-consumption of all British manufactures and West India products; and resolving, also, that they would not export any provisions, lumber, or other products, whatever, to Great Britain or any of her colonies. These resolutions were accompanied by another, in many of the counties of Virginia, in some of the State conventions, and, finally, in those of the Continental Congress, in which the slave trade, and the purchase of additional slaves, were specially referred to as measures to be at once discontinued. These resolutions, in substance, declare, as the sentiment of the people: That the African trade is injurious to the colonies; that it obstructs the population of them by freemen; that it prevents the immigration of manufacturers and other useful emigrants from Europe from settling among them; that it is dangerous to virtue and the welfare of the population; that it occasions an annual increase of the balance of trade against them; that they most earnestly wished to see an entire stop put to such a wicked, cruel, and unlawful traffic; that they would not purchase any slaves hereafter to be imported, nor hire their vessels, nor sell their commodities or manufactures to those who are concerned in their importation.

From these facts it appears evident, that the primary object of all the resolutions was to cripple the commerce of England. Those in relation to the slave trade, especially, were expected, at once, when taken in connection with the determination to withhold all supplies of provisions from the West India planters—to stop the slave trade, and deprive the British merchants of all further profits from that traffic. But it would do more than this, as it would compel the West India planters, in a great degree, to stop the cultivation of sugar and cotton, for export, and force them to commence the growing of provisions for food— thus producing ruinous consequences to British manufactures and commerce.[5] But, in the opposition thus made to the slave trade, there is no act warranting the conclusion that the negroes were to be admitted to a position of equality with the whites. The sentiments expressed, with a single exception,[6] are the reverse, and their increase viewed as an evil. South Carolina and Georgia did not follow the example of Virginia and North Carolina in resolving against the slave trade, but acquiesced in the non-intercourse policy, until the grievances complained of should be remedied. Another reason existed for opposing the slave trade; this was the importance of preventing the increase of a population that might be employed against the liberties of the colonies. That negroes were thus employed, during the Revolution, is a matter of history; and that the British hoped to use that population for their own advantage, is clearly indicated by the language of the Earl of Dartmouth, who declared, as a sufficient reason for turning a deaf ear to the remonstrances of the colonists against the further importation of slaves, that "Negroes cannot become Republicans—they will be a power in our hands to restrain the unruly colonists."

And, now, will any one say, that the fathers of the Revolution ever intended to declare the negro the equal of the white man, in the sense that he was entitled to an equality of political privileges under the constitution of the United States!

CHAPTER IV

Dismal condition of Africa—Hopes of Wilberforce disappointed—Organization of the American Colonization Society—Its necessity, objects, and policy—Public sentiment in its favor—Opposition developes itself—Wm. Lloyd Garrison, James G. Birney, Gerrit Smith—Effects of opposition—Stimulants to Slavery—Exports of Cotton—England sustaining American Slavery—Failure of the Niger Expedition—Strength of Slavery—Political action—Its failure—Its fruits.

ANOTHER question, "How shall the slave trade be suppressed?" began to be agitated near the close of the last century. The moral desolation existing in Africa, was without a parallel among the nations of the earth. When the last of our Northern States had freed its slaves, not a single Christian Church had been successfully established in Africa, and the slave trade was still legalized to the citizens of every Christian nation. Even its subsequent prohibition, by the United States and England, had no tendency to check the traffic, nor ameliorate the condition of the African. The other Europeon powers, having now the monopoly of the trade, continued to prosecute it with a vigor it never felt before. The institution of slavery, while lessened in the United States, where it had not yet been made profitable, was rapidly acquiring an unprecedented enlargement in Cuba and Brazil, where its profitable character had been more fully realized. How shall the slave trade be annihilated, slavery extension prevented, and Africa receive a Christian civilization? were questions that agitated the bosom of many a philanthropist, long after Wilberforce had achieved his triumphs. It was found, that the passage of laws prohibiting the slave trade, and the extermination of that traffic, were two distinct things—the one not necessarily following the other. The success of Wilberforce with the British Parliament, only increased the necessity for additional philanthropic efforts; and a quarter of a century afterwards found the evil vastly increased which he imagined was wholly destroyed.

It was at the period in the history of Africa, and of public sentiment on slavery, which we have been considering, that the American Colonization Society was organized. It began its labors when the eye of the statesman, the philanthropist, and the Christian, could discover no other plan of overcoming the moral desolation, the universal oppression of the colored race, than by restoring the most enlightened of their number to Africa itself. Emancipation, by States, had been at an end for a dozen of years. The improvement of the free colored people, in the presence of the slave, was considered impracticable. Slave labor had become so profitable, as to leave little ground to expect general emancipation, even though all other objections had been removed. The slave trade had increased twenty-five per cent. during the preceding ten years. Slavery was rapidly extending itself in the tropics, and could not be arrested but by the suppression of the slave trade. The foothold of the Christian missionary was yet so precarious in Africa, as to leave it doubtful whether he could sustain his position.

The colonization of the free colored people in Africa, under the teachings of the Christian men who were prepared to accompany them, it was believed, would as fully meet all the conditions of the race, as was possible in the then existing state of the world. It would separate those who should emigrate from all further contact with slavery, and from its depressing influences; it would relax the laws of the slave States against emancipation, and lead to the more frequent liberation of slaves; it would stimulate and encourage the colored people remaining here, to engage in efforts for their own elevation; it would establish free republics along the coast of Africa, and drive away the slave trader; it would prevent the extension of slavery, by means of the slave trade, in tropical America; it would introduce civilization and Christianity among the people of Africa, and overturn their barbarism and bloody superstitions; and, if successful, it would react upon slavery at home, by pointing out to the States and General Government, a mode by which they might free themselves from the whole African race.

The Society had thus undertaken as great an amount of work as it could perform. The field was broad enough, truly, for an association that hoped to obtain an income of but five to ten thousand dollars a year, and realized annually an average of only $3,276 during the first six years of its existence. It did not include the destruction of American slavery among the objects it labored to accomplish. That subject had been fully discussed; the ablest men in the nation had labored for its overthrow; more than half the original States of the Union had emancipated their slaves; the advantages of freedom to the colored man had been tested; the results had not been as favorable as anticipated; the public sentiment of the country was adverse to an increase of the free colored population; the few of their number who had risen to respectability and affluence, were too widely separated to act in concert in promoting measures for the general good; and, until better results should follow the liberation of slaves, further emancipations, by the States, were not to be expected. The friends of the Colonization Society, therefore, while affording every encouragement to emancipation by individuals, refused to agitate the question of the general abolition of slavery. Nor did they thrust aside any other scheme of benevolence in behalf of the African race. Forty years had elapsed from the commencement of emancipation in the country, and thirty from the date of Franklin's Appeal, before the society sent off its first emigrants. At that date, no extended plans were in existence, promising relief to the free colored man. A period of lethargy, among the benevolent, had succeeded the State emancipations, as a consequence of the indifference of the free colored people, as a class, to their degraded condition. The public sentiment of the country was fully prepared, therefore, to adopt colonization as the best means, or, rather, as the only means for accomplishing any thing for them or for the African race. Indeed, so general was the sentiment in favor of colonization, somewhere beyond the limits of the United States, that those who disliked Africa, commenced a scheme of emigration to Hayti, and prosecuted it, until eight thousand free colored persons were removed to that island—a number nearly equaling the whole emigration to Liberia up to 1850. Haytien emigration, however, proved a most disastrous experiment.

But the general acquiescence in the objects of the Colonization Society did not long continue. The exports of cotton from the South were then rapidly on the increase. Slave labor had become profitable, and slaves, in the cotton-growing States, were no longer considered a burden. Seven years after the first emigrants reached Liberia, the South exported 294,310,115 lbs. of cotton; and, the year following, the total cotton crop reached 325,000,000 lbs. But a great depression in prices had occurred,[7] and alarmed the planters for their safety. They had decided against emancipation, and now to have their slaves rendered valueless, was an evil they were determined to avert. The Report of the Boston Prison Discipline Society, which appeared at this moment, was well calculated, by the disclosures it made, to increase the alarm in the South, and to confirm slaveholders in their belief of the dangers of emancipation.

At this juncture, a warfare against colonization was commenced at the South, and it was pronounced an abolition scheme in disguise. In defending itself, the society re-asserted its principles of neutrality in relation to slavery, and that it had only in view the colonization of the free colored people. In the heat of the contest, the South were reminded of their former sentiments in relation to the whole colored population, and that colonization merely proposed removing one division of a people they had pronounced a public burden.[8]

The emancipationists at the North had only lent their aid to colonization in the hope that it would prove an able auxiliary to abolition; but when the society declared its unalterable purpose to adhere to its original position of neutrality, they withdrew their support, and commenced hostilities against it. "The Anti-Slavery Society," said a distinguished abolitionist, "began with a declaration of war against the Colonization Society."[9] This feeling of hostility was greatly increased by the action of the abolitionists of England. The doctrine of "Immediate, not Gradual Abolition," was announced by them as their creed; and the anti-slavery men of the United States adopted it as the basis of their action. Its success in the English Parliament, in procuring the passage of the Act for West India emancipation, in 1833, gave a great impulse to the abolition cause in the United States.

In 1832, William Lloyd Garrison declared hostilities against the Colonization Society; in 1834, James G. Birney followed his example; and, in 1836 Gerritt Smith also abandoned the cause. The North everywhere resounded with the cry of "Immediate

Abolition;" and, in 1837, the abolitionists numbered 1,015 societies; had seventy agents under commission, and an income, for the year, of $36,000.[10] The Colonization Society, on the other hand, was greatly embarrassed. Its income, in 1838, was reduced to $10,000; it was deeply in debt; the parent society did not send a single emigrant, that year, to Liberia; and its enemies pronounced it bankrupt and dead.[11]

But did the abolitionists succeed in forcing emancipation upon the South, when they had thus rendered colonization powerless? Did the fetters fall from the slave at their bidding? Did fire from heaven descend, and consume the slaveholder at their invocation? No such thing! They had not touched the true cause of the extension of slavery. They had not discovered the secret of its power; and, therefore, its locks remained unshorn, its strength unabated. The institution advanced as triumphantly as if no opposition existed. The planters were progressing steadily, in securing to themselves the monopoly of the cotton markets of Europe, and in extending the area of slavery at home. In the same year that Gerritt Smith declared for abolition, the title of the Indians to fifty-five millions of acres of land, in the slave States, was extinguished, and the tribes removed. The year that colonization was depressed to the lowest point, the exports of cotton, from the United States, amounted to 595,952,297 lbs., and the consumption of the article in England, to 477,206,108 lbs.

When Mr. Birney seceded from colonization, he encouraged his new allies with the hope, that West India free labor would render our slave labor less profitable, and emancipation, as a consequence, be more easily effected. How stood this matter six years afterward? This will be best understood by contrast. In 1800, the West Indies exported 17,000,000 lbs. of cotton, and the United States, 17,789,803 lbs. They were then about equally productive in that article. In 1840, the West India exports had dwindled down to 427,529 lbs., while those of the United States had increased to 743,941,061 lbs.

And what was England doing all this while? Having lost her supplies from the West Indies, she was quietly spinning away at American slave labor cotton; and to ease the public conscience of the kingdom, was loudly talking of a free labor supply of the commodity from the banks of the Niger! But the expedition up that river failed, and 1845 found her manufacturing 626,496,000 lbs. of cotton, mostly the product of American slaves! The strength of American slavery at that moment may be inferred from the fact, that we exported that year 872,905,996 lbs. of cotton, and our production of cane sugar had reached over 200,000,000 lbs.; while, to make room for slavery extension, we were busied in the annexation of Texas and in preparations for the consequent war with Mexico!

But abolitionists themselves, some time before this, had, mostly, become convinced of the feeble character of their efforts against slavery, and allowed politicians to enlist them in a political crusade, as the last hope of arresting the progress of the system. The cry of "Immediate Abolition" died away; reliance upon moral means was mainly abandoned; and the limitation of the institution, geographically, became the chief object of effort. The results of more than a dozen years of political action are before the public, and what has it accomplished! We are not now concerned in the inquiry of how far the strategy of politicians succeeded in making the votes of abolitionists subservient to slavery extension. That they did so, in at least one prominent case, will never be denied by any candid man. All we intend to say, is, that the cotton planters, instead of being crippled in their operations, were able, in the year ending the last of June, 1853, to export 1,111,570,370 lbs. of cotton, beside supplying near 300,000,000 lbs. for home consumption; and that England, the year ending the last of January, 1853, consumed the unprecedented quantity of 817,998,048 lbs. of that staple.[12] The year 1854, instead of finding slavery perishing under the blows it had received, has witnessed the destruction of all the old barriers to its extension, and beholds it expanded widely enough for the profitable employment of the slave population, with all its natural increase, for a hundred years to come!!

If political action against slavery has been thus disastrously unfortunate, how is it with anti-slavery action, at large, as to its efficiency at this moment? On this point, hear the testimony of a correspondent of Frederick Douglass' Paper, January 26, 1855:

"How gloriously did the anti-slavery cause arise . . . . . . in 1833-4! And now what is it, in our agency! . . . . . . What is it, through the errors or crimes of its advocates variously—probably quite as much as through the brazen, gross, and licentious wickedness of its enemies. Alas! what is it but a mutilated, feeble, discordant, and half-expiring instrument, at which Satan and his children, legally and illegally, scoff! Of it I despair."

Such are the crowning results of both political and anti-slavery action, for the overthrow of slavery! Such are the demonstrations of their utter impotency as a means of relief to the bond and free of the colored people!

Surely, then, if the negro is capable of elevation, it is time that some other measures should be devised, than those hitherto adopted, for the melioration of the African race! Surely, too, it is time for the American people to rebuke that class of politicians, North and South, whose only capital consists in keeping up a fruitless warfare upon the subject of slavery—nay! abundant in fruits to the poor colored man; but to him, "their vine is of the vine of Sodom, and of the fields of Gomorrah; their grapes are grapes of gall, their clusters are bitter; their vine is the poison of dragons, and the cruel venom of asps."[13]

The application of this language, to the case under consideration, will be fully justified when the facts, in the remaining pages of this work, are carefully studied.

CHAPTER V

THE RELATIONS OF AMERICAN SLAVERY TO THE INDUSTRIAL INTERESTS OF OUR COUNTRY; TO THE DEMANDS OF COMMERCE; AND TO THE PRESENT POLITICAL CRISIS.

Present condition of Slavery—Not an isolated system—Its relations to other industrial interests—To manufactures, commerce, trade, human comfort—Its benevolent aspect—The reverse picture—Immense value of tropical possessions to Great Britain—England's attempted monopoly of Manufactures—Her dependence on American Planters—Cotton Planters attempt to monopolize Cotton markets—*Fusion* of these parties—Free Trade essential to their success—Influence on agriculture, mechanics—Exports of Cotton, Tobacco, etc.—Increased production of Provisions—Their extent—New markets needed.

THE institution of slavery, at this moment, gives indications of a vitality that was never anticipated by its friends or foes. Its enemies often supposed it about ready to expire, from the wounds they had inflicted, when in truth it had taken two steps in advance, while they had taken twice the number in an opposite direction. In each successive conflict, its assailants have been weakened, while its dominion has been extended.

This has arisen from causes too generally overlooked. Slavery is not an isolated system, but is so mingled with the business of the world, that it derives facilities from the most innocent transactions. Capital and labor, in Europe and America, are largely employed in the manufacture of cotton. These goods, to a great extent, may be seen freighting every vessel, from Christian nations, that traverses the seas of the globe; and filling the warehouses and shelves of the merchants over two-thirds of the world. By the industry, skill, and enterprise employed in the manufacture of cotton, mankind are better clothed; their comfort better promoted; general industry more highly stimulated; commerce more widely extended; and civilization more rapidly advanced than in any preceding age.

To the superficial observer, all the agencies, based upon the sale and manufacture of cotton, seem to be legitimately engaged in promoting human happiness; and he, doubtless, feels like invoking Heaven's choicest blessings upon them. When he sees the stockholders in the cotton corporations receiving their dividends, the operatives their wages, the merchants their profits, and civilized people everywhere clothed comfortably in cottons, he can not refrain from exclaiming: The lines have fallen unto them in pleasant places; yea, they have a goodly heritage!

But turn a moment to the source whence the raw cotton, the basis of these operations, is obtained, and observe the aspect of things in that direction. When the statistics on the subject are examined, it appears that nine-tenths of the cotton consumed in the Christian world is the product of the slave labor of the United States.[14] It is this monopoly that has given to slavery its commercial value; and, while this monopoly is retained, the institution will continue to extend itself wherever it can find room to spread. He who looks for any other result, must expect that nations, which, for centuries, have waged war to extend their commerce, will now abandon that means of aggrandizement, and bankrupt themselves to force the abolition of American slavery!

This is not all. The economical value of slavery, as an agency for supplying the means of extending manufactures and commerce, has long been understood by statesmen.[15] The discovery of the power of steam, and the inventions in machinery, for preparing and manufacturing cotton, revealed the important fact, that a single island, having the monopoly secured to itself, could supply the world with clothing. Great Britain attempted to gain this monopoly; and, to prevent other countries from rivaling her, she long prohibited all emigration of skillful mechanics from the kingdom, as well as all exports of machinery. As country after country was opened to her commerce, the markets for her manufactures were extended, and the demand for the raw material increased. The benefits of this enlarged commerce of the world, were not confined to a single nation, but mutually enjoyed by all. As each had products to sell, peculiar to itself, the advantages often gained by one were no detriment to the others. The principal articles demanded by this increasing commerce have been coffee, sugar, and cotton, in the production of which slave labor has greatly predominated. Since the enlargement of manufactures, cotton has entered more extensively into commerce than coffee and sugar, though the demand for all three has advanced with the greatest rapidity. England could only become a great commercial nation, through the agency of her manufactures. She was the best supplied, of all the nations, with the necessary capital, skill, labor, and fuel, to extend her commerce by this means. But, for the raw material, to supply her manufactories, she was dependent upon other countries. The planters of the United States were the most favorably situated for the cultivation of cotton; and while Great Britain was aiming at monopolizing its manufacture, they attempted to monopolize the markets for that staple. This led to a fusion of interests between them and the British manufacturers; and to the adoption of principles in political economy, which, if rendered effective, would promote the interests of this coalition. With the advantages possessed by the English manufacturers, "Free Trade" would render all other nations subservient to their interests; and, so far as their operations should be increased, just so far would the demand for American cotton be extended. The details of the success of the parties to this combination, and the opposition they have had to encounter, are left to be noticed more fully hereafter. To the cotton planters, the co-partnership has been eminently advantageous.

How far the other agricultural interests of the United States are promoted, by extending the cultivation of cotton, may be inferred from the Census returns of 1850, and the Congressional Reports on Commerce and Navigation, for 1854.[16] Cotton and tobacco, only, are largely exported. The production of sugar does not yet equal our consumption of the article, and we import, chiefly from slave labor countries, 445,445,680 lbs. to make up the deficiency.[17] But of cotton and tobacco, we export more than *two-thirds* of the amount produced; while of other products of the agriculturists, less than the *one forty-sixth* part is exported. Foreign nations, generally, can grow their provisions, but can not grow their tobacco and cotton. Our surplus provisions, not exported, go to the villages, towns, and cities, to feed the mechanics, manufacturers, merchants, professional men, and others; or to the cotton and sugar districts of the South, to feed the planters and their slaves. The increase of mechanics and manufacturers at the North, and the expansion of slavery at the South, therefore, augment the markets for provisions, and promote the prosperity of the farmer. As the mechanical population increases, the implements of industry and articles of furniture are multiplied, so that both farmer and planter can be supplied with them on easier terms. As foreign nations open their markets to cotton fabrics, increased demands for the raw material are made. As new grazing and grain-growing States are developed, and teem with their surplus productions, the mechanic is benefited, and the planter, relieved from food-raising, can employ his slaves more extensively upon cotton. It is thus that our exports are increased; our foreign commerce advanced; the home markets of the mechanic and farmer extended, and the wealth of the nation promoted. It is thus, also, that the free labor of the country finds remunerating markets for its products—though at the expense of serving as an efficient auxiliary in the extension of slavery!

But more: So speedily are new grain-growing States springing up; so vast is the territory owned by the United States, ready for settlement; and so enormous will soon be the amount of products demanding profitable markets, that the national government has been seeking new outlets for them, upon our own continent, to which, alone, they can be advantageously transported. That such outlets, when our vast possessions Westward are brought under cultivation, will be an imperious necessity, is known to every statesman. The farmers of these new States, after the example of those of the older sections of the country, will demand a market for their products. This can be furnished, only, by the extension of slavery; by the acquisition of more tropical territory; by opening the ports of Brazil, and other South American countries, to the admission of our provisions; by their free importation into European countries; or by a vast enlargement of domestic manufactures, to the exclusion of foreign goods from the country. Look at this question as it now stands, and then judge of what it must be twenty years hence. The class of products under consideration, in the whole country, in 1853, were valued at $1,551,176,490; of which there were exported to foreign countries, to the value of only $33,809,126.[18] The planter will not assent to any check upon the foreign imports of the country, for the benefit of the farmer. This demands the adoption of vigorous measures to secure a market for his products by some of the other modes stated. Hence, the orders of our executive, in 1851, for the exploration of the valley of the Amazon; the efforts, in 1854, to obtain a treaty with Brazil, for the free navigation of that immense river; the negotiations for a military foothold in St. Domingo; and the determination to acquire Cuba. But we must not anticipate topics to be considered at a later period in our discussion.

CHAPTER VI

Foresight of Great Britain—Hon. George Thompson's predictions—Their failure—England's dependence on Slave labor—Blackwood's Magazine—London Economist—McCullough—Her exports of cotton goods—Neglect to improve the proper moment for Emancipation—Admission of Gerrit Smith—*Cotton*, its exports, its value, extent of crop, and cost of our cotton fabrics—*Provisions*, their value, their export, their consumption—*Groceries*, source of their supplies, cost of amount consumed—Our total indebtedness to Slave labor—How far Free labor sustains Slave labor.

ANTECEDENT to all the movements noticed in the preceding chapter, Great Britain had foreseen the coming increased demand for tropical products. Indeed, her West Indian policy, of a few years previous, had hastened the crisis; and, to repair her injuries, and meet the general outcry for cotton, she made the most vigorous efforts to promote its cultivation in her own tropical possessions. The motives prompting her to this policy, need not be referred to here, as they will be noticed hereafter. The Hon. George Thompson, it will be remembered, when urging the increase of cotton cultivation in the East Indies, declared that the scheme must succeed, and that, soon, all slave labor cotton would be repudiated by the British manufacturers. Mr Garrison indorsed the measure, and expressed his belief that, with its success, the American slave system must inevitably perish from starvation! But England's efforts signally failed, and the golden apple, fully ripened, dropped into the lap of our cotton planters.[19] The year that heard Thompson's pompous predictions,[20] witnessed the consumption of but 445,744,000 lbs. of cotton, by England; while, fourteen years later, she used 817,998,048 lbs., nearly 700,000,000 lbs. of which were obtained from America!

That we have not overstated her dependence upon our slave labor for cotton is a fact of world-wide notoriety. *Blackwood's Magazine*, January, 1853, in referring to the cultivation of the article, by the United States, says:

"With its increased growth has sprung up that mercantile navy, which now waves its stripes and stars over every sea, and that foreign influence, which has placed the internal peace—we may say the subsistence of millions in every manufacturing country in Europe—within the power of an oligarchy of planters."

In reference to the same subject, the *London Economist* quotes as follows:

"Let any great social or physical convulsion visit the United States, and England would feel the shock from Land's End to John O'Groats. The lives of nearly two millions of our countrymen are dependent upon the cotton crops of America; their destiny may be said, without any kind of hyperbole, to hang upon a thread. Should any dire calamity befall the land of cotton, a thousand of our merchant ships would rot idly in dock; ten thousand mills must stop their busy looms; two thousand thousand mouths would starve, for lack of food to feed them."

A more definite statement of England's indebtedness to cotton, is given by McCullough; who shows that as far back as 1832, her exports of cotton fabrics were equal in value to about two-thirds of all the woven fabrics exported from the empire. The same state of things, nearly, existed in 1849, when the cotton fabrics exported, according to the *London Economist*, were valued at about $140,000,000, while all the other woven fabrics exported did not quite reach to the value of $68,000,000. On consulting the same authority, of still later dates, it appears, that the last four years has produced no material change in the relations which the different classes of British fabrics, exported, bear to each other. The present condition of the demand and supplies of cotton, throughout Europe, and the extent to which the increasing consumption of that staple must stimulate the American planters to its increased production, will be noticed in the proper place.[21]

There was a time when American slave labor sustained no such relations to the manufactures and commerce of the world as it now so firmly holds; and when, by the adoption of proper measures, on the part of the free colored people and their friends, the emancipation of the slaves, in all the States, might, possibly, have been effected. But that period has passed forever away, and causes, unforeseen, have come into operation, which are too powerful to be overcome by any agencies that have since been employed.[22] What Divine Providence may have in store for the future, we know not; but, at present, the institution of slavery is sustained by numberless pillars, too massive for human power and wisdom to overthrow.

Take another view of this subject. To say nothing now of the tobacco, rice, and sugar, which are the products of our slave labor, we exported raw cotton to the value of $109,456,404 in 1853. Its destination was, to Great Britain, 768,596,498 lbs.; to the Continent of Europe, 335,271,434 lbs.; to countries on our own Continent, 7,702,438 lbs.; making the total exports, 1,111,570,370 lbs. The entire crop of that year being 1,305,152,800 lbs., gives, for home consumption, 268,403,600 lbs.[23] Of this, there was manufactured into cotton fabrics to the value of $61,869,274;[24] of which there was retained, for home markets, to the value of $53,100,290. Our imports of cotton fabrics from Europe, in 1853, for consumption, amounted in value to $26,477,950:[25] thus making our cottons, foreign and domestic, for that year, cost us $79,578,240.

In bringing down the results to 1858, it will be seen that the imports of foreign cotton goods has fluctuated at higher and lower amounts than those of 1853; and that an actual decrease of our exports of cotton manufactures has taken place since that date.[26] But in the exports of raw cotton there has been an increase of nearly a hundred millions of pounds over that of 1853—the total exports of 1859 being 1,208,561,200 lbs. The total crop of 1859, in the United States, was 1,606,800,000 lbs., and the amount taken for consumption 371,060,800 lbs.[27]

Thus, while our consumption of foreign cotton goods is not on the increase, the foreign demand for our raw cotton is rapidly augmenting; and thus the American planter is becoming more and more important to the manufactures and commerce of the world.

This, now, is what becomes of our cotton; this is the way in which it so largely constitutes the basis of commerce and trade; and this is the nature of the relations existing between the slavery of the United States and the economical interests of the world.

But have the United States no other great leading interests, except those which are involved in the production of cotton? Certainly, they have. Here is a great field for the growth of provisions. In ordinary years, exclusive of tobacco and cotton, our agricultural property, when added to the domestic animals and their products, amounts in value $1,551,176,490. Of this, there is exported only to the value of $33,809,126; which leaves for home consumption and use, a remainder to the value of $1,517,367,364.[28] The portions of the property represented by this immense sum of money, which pass from the hands of the agriculturists, are distributed throughout the Union, for the support of the day laborers, sailors, mechanics, manufacturers, traders, merchants, professional men, planters, and the slave population. This is what becomes of our provisions.

Besides this annual consumption of provisions, most of which is the product of free labor, the people of the United States use a vast amount of groceries, which are mainly of slave labor origin. Boundless as is the influence of cotton, in stimulating slavery extension, that of the cultivation of groceries falls but little short of it; the chief difference being, that they do not receive such an increased value under the hand of manufacturers. The cultivation of coffee, in Brazil, employs as great a number of slaves as that of cotton in the United States.

But, to comprehend fully our indebtedness to slave labor for groceries, we must descend to particulars. Our imports of coffee, tobacco, sugar, and molasses, for 1853, amounted in value to $38,479,000; of which the hand of the slave, in Brazil and Cuba, mainly, supplied to the value of $34,451,000.[29] This shows the extent to which we are sustaining foreign slavery, by the consumption of these four products. But this is not our whole indebtedness to slavery for groceries. Of the domestic grown tobacco, valued at $19,975,000, of which we retain nearly one-half, the Slave States produce to the value of $16,787,000; of domestic rice, the product of the South, we consume to the value of

$7,092,000; of domestic slave grown sugar and molasses, we take, for home consumption, to the value of $34,779,000; making our grocery account, with domestic slavery, foot up to the sum of $50,449,000. Our whole indebtedness, then, to slavery, foreign and domestic, for these four commodities, after deducting two millions of re-exports amounts to $82,607,000.

The exports of tobacco are on the increase, as appears from Table VIII of Appendix, showing an extension of its cultivation; but the exports of rice are not on the increase, from which it would appear that its production remains stationary.

By adding the value of the foreign and domestic cotton fabrics, consumed annually in the United States, to the yearly cost of the groceries which the country uses, our total indebtedness, for articles of slave labor origin, will be found swelling up to the enormous sum of $162,185,240.[30]

We have now seen the channels through which our cotton passes off into the great sea of commerce, to furnish the world its clothing. We have seen the origin and value of our provisions, and to whom they are sold. We have seen the sources whence our groceries are derived, and the millions of money they cost. To ascertain how far these several interests are sustained by one another, will be to determine how far any one of them becomes an element of expansion to the others. To decide a question of this nature with precision is impracticable. The statistics are not attainable. It may be illustrated, however, in various ways, so as to obtain a conclusion proximately accurate. Suppose, for example, that the supplies of food from the North were cut off, the manufactories left in their present condition, and the planters forced to raise their provisions and draught animals: in such circumstances, the export of cotton must cease, as the lands of these States could not be made to yield more than would subsist their own population, and supply the cotton demanded by the Northern States. Now, if this be true of the agricultural resources of the cotton States—and it is believed to be nearly the full extent of their capacity—then the surplus of cotton, to the value of more than a hundred millions of dollars, now annually sent abroad, stands as the representative of the yearly supplies which the cotton planters receive from the farmers north of the cotton line. This, therefore, as will afterward more fully appear, may be taken as the probable extent to which the supplies from the North serve as an element of slavery expansion in the article of cotton alone.

CHAPTER VII

Economical relations of Slavery further considered—System unprofitable in grain growing, but profitable in culture of Cotton—Antagonism of Farmer and Planter—"Protection," and, "Free Trade" controversy—Congressional Debates on the subject—Mr. Clay—Position of the South—"Free Trade," considered indispensable to its prosperity.

BUT the subject of the relations of American slavery to the economical interests of the world, demands a still closer scrutiny, in order that the causes of the failure of abolitionism to arrest its progress, as well as the present relations of the institution to the politics of the country, may fully appear.

Slave labor has seldom been made profitable where it has been wholly employed in grazing and grain growing; but it becomes remunerative in proportion as the planters can devote their attention to cotton, sugar, rice, or tobacco. To render Southern slavery profitable in the highest degree, therefore, the slaves must be employed upon some one of these articles, and be sustained by a supply of food and draught animals from Northern agriculturists; and before the planter's supplies are complete, to these must be added cotton gins, implements of husbandry, furniture, and tools, from Northern mechanics. This is a point of the utmost moment, and must be considered more at length.

It has long been a vital question to the success of the slaveholder, to know how he could render the labor of his slaves the most profitable. The grain growing States had to emancipate their slaves, to rid themselves of a profitless system. The cotton-growing States, ever after the invention of the cotton gin, had found the production of that staple highly remunerative. The logical conclusion, from these different results, was, that the less provisions, and the more cotton grown by the planter, the greater would be his profits. This must be noted with special care. *Markets* for the surplus products of the farmer of the North, were equally as important to him as the supply of *Provisions* was to the planter. But the planter, to be eminently successful, must purchase his supplies at the lowest possible prices; while the farmer, to secure his prosperity, must sell his products at the highest possible rates. Few, indeed, can be so ill informed, as not to know, that these two topics, for many years, were involved in the "Free Trade" and "Protective Tariff" doctrines, and afforded the *materiel* of the political contests between the North and the South—between free labor and slave labor. A very brief notice of the history of that controversy, will demonstrate the truth of this assertion.

The attempt of the agricultural States, thirty years since, to establish the protective policy, and promote "Domestic Manufactures," was a struggle to create such a division of labor as would afford a "Home Market" for their products, no longer in demand abroad. The first decisive action on the question, by Congress, was in 1824; when the distress in these States, and the measures proposed for their relief, by national legislation, were discussed on the passage of the "Tariff Bill" of that year. The ablest men in the nation were engaged in the controversy. As provisions are the most important item on the one hand, and cotton on the other, we shall use these two terms as the representatives of the two classes of products, belonging, respectively, to free labor and to slave labor.

Mr. Clay, in the course of the debate, said: "What, again, I would ask, is the cause of the unhappy condition of our country, which I have fairly depicted? It is to be found in the fact that, during almost the whole existence of this government, we have shaped our industry, our navigation, and our commerce, in reference to an extraordinary war in Europe, and to foreign markets which no longer exist; in the fact that we have depended too much on foreign sources of supply, and excited too little the native; in the fact that, while we have cultivated, with assiduous care, our foreign resources, we have suffered those at home to wither, in a state of neglect and abandonment. The consequence of the termination of the war of Europe, has been the resumption of European commerce, European navigation, and the extension of European agriculture, in all its branches. Europe, therefore, has no longer occasion for any thing like the same extent as that which she had during her wars, for American commerce, American navigation, the produce of American industry. Europe in commotion, and convulsed throughout all her members, is to America no longer the same Europe as she is now, tranquil, and watching with the most vigilant attention, all her own peculiar interests, without regard to their operation on us. The effect of this altered state of Europe upon us, has been to circumscribe the employment of our marine, and greatly to reduce the value of the produce of our territorial labor. . . . . The greatest want of civilized society is a market for the sale and exchange of the surplus of the products of the labor of its members. This market may exist at home or abroad, or both, but it must exist somewhere, if society prospers; and, wherever it does exist, it should be competent to the absorption of the entire surplus production. It is most desirable that there should be both a home and a foreign market. But with respect to their relative superiority, I can not entertain a doubt. The home market is first in order, and paramount in importance. The object of the bill under consideration, is to create this home market, and to lay the foundation of a genuine American policy. It is opposed; and it is incumbent on the partisans of the foreign policy (terms which I shall use without any invidious intent) to demonstrate that the foreign market is an adequate vent for the surplus produce of our labor. But is it so? 1. Foreign nations can not, if they would, take our surplus produce. . . . . 2. If they could, they would not. . . . . We have seen, I think, the causes of the distress of the country. We have seen that an exclusive dependence upon the foreign market must lead to a still severer distress, to impoverishment, to ruin. We must, then, change somewhat our course. We must give a new direction to some portion of our industry. We must speedily adopt a genuine American policy. Still cherishing a foreign market, let us create also a home market, to give further scope to the consumption of the produce of American industry. Let us counteract the policy of foreigners, and withdraw the support which we now give to their industry, and stimulate that of our own country. . . . . The creation of a home market is not only necessary to procure for our agriculture a just reward of its labors, but it is indispensable to obtain a supply of our necessary wants. If we can not sell, we can not buy. That portion of our population (and we have seen that it is not less than four-fifths) which makes comparatively nothing that foreigners will buy, has nothing to make purchases with from foreigners. It is in vain that we are told of the amount of our exports, supplied by the planting interest. They may enable the planting interest to supply all its wants; but they bring no ability to the interests not planting, unless, which can not be pretended, the planting interest was an adequate vent for the surplus produce of all the labor of all other interests. . . . . But this home market, highly desirable as it is, can only be created and cherished by the protection of our own legislation against the inevitable prostration of our industry, which must ensue from the action of FOREIGN policy and legislation. . . . . The sole object of the tariff is to tax the produce of foreign industry, with the view of promoting American industry. . . . . But it is said by the honorable gentleman from Virginia, that the South, owing to the character of a certain portion of its population, can not engage in the business of manufacturing. . . . . The circumstances of its degradation unfits it for manufacturing arts. The well-being of the other, and the larger part of our population, requires the introduction of those arts.

"What is to be done in this conflict? The gentleman would have us abstain from adopting a policy called for by the interests of the greater and freer part of the population. But is that reasonable? Can it be expected that the interests of the greater part should be made to bend to the condition of the servile part of our population? That, in effect, would be to make us the slaves of slaves. . . . . I am sure that the patriotism of the South may be exclusively relied upon to reject a policy which should be dictated by considerations altogether connected with that degraded class, to the prejudice of the residue of our population. But does not a perseverance in the foreign policy, as it now exists, in fact, make all parts of the Union, not planting, tributary to the planting parts? What is the argument? It is, that we must continue freely to receive the produce of foreign industry, without regard to the protection of American industry, that a market may be retained for the sale abroad of the produce of the planting portion of the country; and that, if we lessen the consumption, in all parts of America, those which are not planting, as well as the planting sections, of foreign manufactures, we diminish to that extent the foreign market for the planting produce. The existing state of things, indeed, presents a sort of tacit compact between the cotton-grower and the British manufacturer, the stipulations of which are, on the part of the cotton-grower, that the whole of the United States, the other portions as well as the cotton-growing, shall remain open and unrestricted in the consumption of British manufactures; and, on the part of the British manufacturer, that, in consideration thereof, he will continue to purchase the cotton of the South. Thus, then, we perceive that the proposed measure, instead of sacrificing the South to the other parts of the Union, seeks only to preserve them from being actually sacrificed under the operation of the tacit compact which I have described."

The opposition to the Protective Tariff, by the South, arose from two causes: the first openly avowed at the time, and the second clearly deducible from the policy it pursued: the one to secure the foreign market for its cotton, the other to obtain a bountiful supply of provisions at cheap rates. Cotton was admitted free of duty into foreign countries, and Southern statesmen feared its exclusion, if our government increased the duties on foreign fabrics. The South exported about twice as much of that staple as was supplied to Europe by all other countries, and there were indications favoring the desire it entertained of monopolizing the foreign markets. The West India planters could not import food, but at such high rates as to make it impracticable to grow cotton at prices low enough to suit the English manufacturer. To purchase cotton cheaply, was essential to the success of his scheme of monopolizing its manufacture, and supplying the world with clothing. The close proximity of the provision and cotton-growing districts in the United States, gave its planters advantages over all other portions of the world. But they could not monopolize the markets, unless they could obtain a cheap supply of food and clothing for their negroes, and raise their cotton at such reduced prices as to undersell their rivals. A manufacturing population, with its mechanical coadjutors, in the midst of the provision-growers, on a scale such as the protective policy contemplated, it was conceived, would create a permanent market for their products, and enhance the price; whereas, if this manufacturing could be prevented, and a system of free trade adopted, the South would constitute the principal provision market of the country, and the fertile lands of the North supply the cheap food demanded for its slaves. As the tariff policy, in the outset, contemplated the encouragement of the production of iron, hemp, whisky, and the establishment of woolen manufactories, principally, the South found its interests but slightly identified with the system—the coarser qualities of cottons, only, being manufactured in the country, and, even these, on a diminished scale, as compared with the cotton crops of the South. Cotton, up to the date when this controversy had been fairly commenced, had been worth, in the English market, an average price of from $29^7/_{10}$ to $48^4/_{10}$ cents per lb.[31] But at this period, a wide spread and ruinous depression both in the culture and manufacture of the article, occurred—cotton, in 1826, having fallen, in England, as low as $11^9/_{10}$ to $18^9/_{10}$ cents per lb. The home market, then, was too inconsiderable to be of much importance, and there existed little hope of its enlargement to the extent demanded by its increasing cultivation. The planters, therefore, looked abroad to the existing markets, rather than to wait for tardily creating one at home. For success in the foreign markets, they relied, mainly, upon preparing themselves to produce cotton at the reduced prices then prevailing in Europe. All agricultural products, except cotton, being excluded from foreign markets, the planters found themselves almost the sole exporters of the country; and it was to them a source of chagrin, that the North did not, at once, co-operate with them in augmenting the commerce of the nation.

At this point in the history of the controversy, politicians found it an easy matter to produce feelings of the deepest hostility between the opposing parties. The planters were led to believe that the millions of revenue collected off the goods imported, was so much deducted from the value of the cotton that paid for them, either in the diminished price they received abroad, or in the increased price which they paid for the imported articles. To enhance the duties, for the protection of our manufacturers, they were persuaded, would be so much of an additional tax upon themselves, for the benefit of the North; and, beside, to give the manufacturer such a monopoly of the home market for his fabrics, would enable him to charge purchasers an excess over the true value of his stuffs, to the whole amount of the duty. By the protective policy, the planters expected to have the cost of both provisions and clothing increased, and their ability to monopolize the foreign markets diminished in a corresponding degree. If they could establish free trade, it would insure the American market to foreign manufacturers; secure the foreign markets for their leading staple; repress home manufactures; force a large number of the Northern men into agriculture; multiply the growth, and diminish the price of provisions; feed and clothe their slaves at lower rates; produce their cotton for a third or fourth of former prices; rival all other countries in its cultivation; monopolize the trade in the article throughout the whole of Europe; and build up a commerce and a navy that would make us ruler of the seas.

CHAPTER VIII

Tariff controversy continued—Mr. Hayne—Mr. Carter—Mr. Govan—Mr. Martindale—Mr. Buchanan—Sugar Planters invoked to aid Free Trade—The West also invoked—Its pecuniary embarrassments for want of markets—Henry Baldwin—Remarks on the views of the parties—State of the world—Dread of the Protective policy by the Planters—Their schemes to avert its consequences, and promote Free Trade.

To understand the sentiments of the South, on the Protective Policy, as expressed by its statesmen, we must again quote from the Congressional Debates of 1824:

Mr. Hayne, of South Carolina, said: "But how, I would seriously ask, is it possible for the home market to supply the place of the foreign market, for our cotton? We supply Great Britain with the raw material, out of which she furnishes the Continent of Europe, nay, the whole world, with cotton goods. Now, suppose our manufactories could make every yard of cloth we consume, that would furnish a home market for no more than 20,000,000 lbs. out of the 180,000,000 lbs. of cotton now shipped to Great Britain; leaving on our hands 160,000,000 lbs., equal to two-thirds of our whole produce. . . . . Considering this scheme of promoting certain employments, at the expense of others, as unequal, oppressive, and unjust—viewing prohibition as the *means*, and the destruction of all foreign commerce as the *end* of this policy—I take this occasion to declare, that we shall feel ourselves, justified in embracing the very first opportunity of repealing all such laws as may be passed for the promotion of these objects."

Mr. Carter, of South Carolina, said: "Another danger to which the present measure would expose this country, and one in which the Southern States have a deep and vital interest, would be the risk we incur, by this system of exclusion, of driving Great Britain to countervailing measures, and inducing all other countries, with whom the United States have any considerable trading connections, to resort to measures of retaliation. There are countries possessing vast capacities for the production of rice, of cotton, and of tobacco, to which England might resort to supply herself. She might apply herself to Brazil, Bengal, and Egypt, for her cotton; to South America, as well as to her colonies, for her tobacco; and to China and Turkey for her rice."

Mr. Govan, of South Carolina, said: "The effect of this measure on the cotton, rice, and tobacco-growing States, will be pernicious in the extreme:—it will exclude them from those markets where they depended almost entirely for a sale of those articles, and force Great Britain to encourage the cottons, (Brazil, Rio Janeiro, and Buenos Ayres,) which, in a short time, can be brought in competition with us. Nothing but the consumption of British goods in this country, received in exchange, can support a command of the cotton market to the Southern planter. It is one thing very certain, she will not come here with her gold and silver to trade with us. And should Great Britain, pursuing the principles of her reciprocal duty act, of last June, lay three or four cents on our cotton, where would, I ask, be our surplus of cotton? It is well known that the United States can not manufacture one-fourth of the cotton that is in it; and should we, by our imprudent legislative enactments, in pursuing to such an extent this restrictive system, force Great Britain to shut her ports against us, it will paralyze the whole trade of the Southern country. This export trade, which composes five-sixths of the export trade of the United States, will be swept entirely from the ocean, and leave but a melancholy wreck behind."

It is necessary, also, to add a few additional extracts, from the speeches of Northern statesmen, during this discussion.

Mr. Martindale, of New York, said: "Does not the agriculture of the country languish, and the laborer stand still, because, beyond the supply of food for his own family, his produce perishes on his hands, or his fields lie waste and fallow; and this because his accustomed market is closed against him? It does, sir. . . . . A twenty years' war in Europe, which drew into its vortex all its various nations, made our merchants the carriers of a large portion of the world, and our farmers the feeders of immense belligerent armies. An unexampled activity and increase in our commerce followed—our agriculture extended itself, grew and nourished. An unprecedented demand gave the farmer an extraordinary price for his produce. . . . . Imports kept pace with exports, and consumption with both. . . . . Peace came into Europe, and shut out our exports, and found us in war with England, which almost cut off our imports. . . . . Now we felt how *comfortable* it was to have plenty of food, but no clothing. . . . . Now we felt the imperfect organization of our system. Now we saw the imperfect distribution and classification of labor. . . . . Here is the explanation of our opposite views. It is employment, after all, that we are all in search of. It is a market for our labor and our produce, which we all want, and all contend for. 'Buy foreign goods, that we may import,' say the merchants: it will make a market for importations, and find employment for our ships. Buy English manufactures, say the cotton planters; England will take our cotton in exchange. Thus the merchant and the cotton planter fully appreciate the value of a market when they find their own encroached upon. The farmer and manufacturer claim to participate in the benefits of a market for their labor and produce; and hence this protracted debate and struggle of contending interests. It is a contest for a market between the *cotton-grower and the merchant* on the one side, and the *farmer and the manufacturer* on the other. That the manufacturer would furnish this market to the farmer, admits no doubt. The farmer should reciprocate the favor; and government is now called upon to render this market accessible to foreign fabrics for the mutual benefit of both. . . . . This, then, is the remedy we propose, sir, for the evils which we suffer. Place the mechanic by the side of the farmer, that the manufacturer who makes our cloth, should make it from *our* farmers' wool, flax, hemp, etc., and be fed by our farmers' provisions. Draw forth our iron from our own mountains, and we shall not drain our country in the purchase of the foreign. . . . . We propose, sir, to supply our own wants from our own resources, by the means which God and Nature have placed in our hands. . . . . But here is a question of sectional interest, which elicits unfriendly feelings and determined hostility to the bill. . . . . The cotton, rice, tobacco, and indigo-growers of the Southern States, claim to be deeply affected and injured by this system. . . . . Let us inquire if the Southern planter does not demand what, in fact, he denies to others. And now, what does he request? That the North and West should buy—what? Not their cotton, tobacco, etc., for that we do already, to the utmost of our ability to consume, or pay, or vend to others; and that is to an immense amount, greatly exceeding what they purchase of us. But they insist that we should buy English wool, wrought into cloth, that they may pay for it with their cotton; that we should buy Russia iron, that they may sell their cotton; that we should buy Holland gin and linen, that they may sell their tobacco. In fine, that we should not grow wool, and dig and smelt the iron of the country; for, if we did, they could not sell their cotton." (On another occasion, he said:) "Gentlemen say they *will* oppose every part of the bill. They will, therefore, move to strike out every part of it. And, on every such motion, we shall hear repeated, as we have done already, the same objections: that it will ruin trade and commerce; that it will destroy the revenue, and prostrate the navy; that it will enhance the prices of articles of the first necessity, and thus be taxing the poor; and that it will destroy the cotton market, *and stop the future growth of cotton.*"

Mr. Buchanan, of Pennsylvania, said: "No nation can be perfectly independent which depends upon foreign countries for its supply of iron. It is an article equally necessary in peace and in war. Without a plentiful supply of it, we cannot provide for the common defense. Can we so soon have forgotten the lesson which experience taught us during the late war with Great Britain? Our foreign supply was then cut off, and we could not manufacture in sufficient quantities for the increased domestic demand. The price of the article became extravagant, and both the Government and the agriculturist were compelled to pay double the sum for which they might have purchased it, had its manufacture, before that period, been encouraged by proper protecting duties."

Sugar cane, at that period, had become an article of culture in Louisiana, and efforts were made to persuade her planters into the adoption of the Free Trade system. It was urged that they could more effectually resist foreign competition, and extend their business, by a cheap supply of food, than by protective duties. But the Louisianians were too wise not to know, that though they would certainly obtain cheap provisions by the destruction of Northern manufactures, still, this would not enable them to compete with the cheaper labor supplied by the slave trade to the Cubans.

The West, for many years, gave its undivided support to the manufacturing interests, thereby obtaining a heavy duty on hemp, wool, and foreign distilled spirits: thus securing encouragement to its hemp and wool-growers, and the monopoly of the home market for its whisky. The distiller and the manufacturer, under this system, were equally ranked as public benefactors, as each increased the consumption of the surplus products of the farmer. The grain of the West could find no remunerative market, except as fed to domestic animals for droving East and South, or distilled into whisky which would bear transportation. Take a fact in proof of this assertion. Hon. Henry Baldwin, of Pittsburgh, at a public dinner given him by the friends of General Jackson, in Cincinnati, May, 1828, in referring to the want of markets, for the farmers of the West, said, "He was certain, the aggregate of their agricultural produce, finding a market in Europe, would not pay for the pins and needles they imported."

The markets in the Southwest, now so important, were then quite limited. As the protective system, coupled with the contemplated internal improvements, if successfully accomplished, would inevitably tend to enhance the price of agricultural products; while the free trade and anti-internal improvement policy, would as certainly reduce their value; the two systems were long considered so antagonistic, that the success of the one must sound the knell of the other. Indeed, so fully was Ohio impressed with the necessity of promoting manufactures, that all capital thus employed, was for many years entirely exempt from taxation.

It was in vain that the friends of protection appealed to the fact, that the duties levied on foreign goods did not necessarily enhance their cost to the consumer; that the competition among home manufacturers, and between them and foreigners, had greatly reduced the price of nearly every article properly protected; that foreign manufacturers always had, and always would advance their prices according to our dependence upon them; that domestic competition was the only safety the country had against foreign imposition; that it was necessary we should become our own manufacturers, in a fair degree, to render ourselves independent of other nations in times of war, as well as to guard against the vacillations in foreign legislation; that the South would be vastly the gainer by having the market for its products at its own doors, to avoid the cost of their transit across the Atlantic; that, in the event of the repression or want of proper extension of our manufactures, by the adoption of the free trade system, the imports of foreign goods, to meet the public wants, would soon exceed the ability of the people to pay, and, inevitably, involve the country in bankruptcy.

Southern politicians remained inflexible, and refused to accept any policy except free trade, to the utter abandonment of the principle of protection. Whether they were jealous of the greater prosperity of the North, and desirous to cripple its energies, or whether they were truly fearful of bankrupting the South, we shall not wait to inquire. Justice demands, however, that we should state that the South was suffering from the stagnation in the cotton trade existing throughout Europe. The planters had been unused to the low prices, for that staple, they were compelled to accept. They had no prospect of an adequate home market for many years to come, and there were indications that they might lose the one they already possessed. The West Indies was still slave territory, and attempting to recover its early position in the English market. This it had to do, or be forced into emancipation. The powerful Viceroy of Egypt, Mehemet Ali, was endeavoring to compel his subjects to grow cotton on an enlarged scale. The newly organized South American republics were assuming an aspect of commercial consequence, and might commence its cultivation. The East Indies and Brazil were supplying to Great Britain from one-third to one-half of the cotton she was annually manufacturing. The other half, or two-thirds, she might obtain from other sources, and repudiate all traffic with our planters. Southern men, therefore, could not conceive of any thing but ruin to themselves, by any considerable advance in duties on foreign imports. They understood the protective policy as contemplating the supply of our country with home manufactured articles to the exclusion of those of foreign countries. This would confine the planters, in the sale of their cotton, to the American market mainly, and leave them in the power of moneyed corporations; which, possessing the ability, might control the prices of their staple, to the irreparable injury of the South. With slave labor they could not become manufacturers, and must, therefore, remain at the mercy of the North, both as to food and clothing, unless the European markets should be retained. Out of this conviction grew the war upon Corporations; the hostility to the employment of foreign capital in developing the mineral, agricultural, and manufacturing resources of the country; the efforts to destroy the banks and the credit system; the attempts to reduce the currency to gold and silver; the system of collecting the public revenues in coin; the withdrawal of the public moneys from all the banks as a basis of paper circulation; and the sleepless vigilance of the South in resisting all systems of internal improvements by the General Government. Its statesmen foresaw that a paper currency would keep up the price of Northern products one or two hundred per cent. above the specie standard; that combinations of capitalists, whether engaged in manufacturing wool, cotton, or iron, would draw off labor from the cultivation of the soil, and cause large bodies of the producers to become consumers; and that roads and canals, connecting the West with the East, were effectual means of bringing the agricultural and manufacturing classes into closer proximity, to the serious limitation of the foreign commerce of the country, the checking of the growth of the navy, and the manifest, injury of the planters.

CHAPTER IX

Character of the Tariff controversy—Peculiar condition of the people—Efforts to enlist the West in the interest of the South—Mr. McDuffie—Mr. Hamilton—Mr. Rankin—Mr. Garnett—Mr. Cuthbert—the West still shut out from market—Mr. Wickliffe—Mr. Benton—Tariff of 1828 obnoxious to the South—Georgia Resolutions—Mr. Hamilton—Argument to Sugar Planters.

THE Protective Tariff and Free Trade controversy, at its origin, and during its progress, was very different in its character from what many now imagine it to have been. People, on both sides, were often in great straits to know how to obtain a livelihood, much less to amass fortunes. The word *ruin* was no unmeaning phrase at that day. The news, now, that a bank has failed, carries with it, to the depositors and holders of its notes, no stronger feelings of consternation, than did the report of the passage or repeal of tariff laws, then, affect the minds of the opposing parties. We have spoken of the peculiar condition of the South in this respect. In the West, for many years, the farmers often received no more than *twenty-five cents*, and rarely over *forty cents*, per bushel for their wheat, after conveying it, on horseback, or in wagons, not unfrequently, a distance of fifty miles, to find a market. Other products were proportionally low in price; and such was the difficulty in obtaining money, that people could not pay their taxes but with the greatest sacrifices. So deeply were the people interested in these questions of national policy, that they became the basis of political action during several Presidential elections. This led to much vacillation in legislation on the subject, and gave alternately, to one and then to the other section of the Union, the benefits of its favorite policy.

The vote of the West, during this struggle, was of the first importance, as it possessed the balance of power, and could turn the scale at will. It was not left without inducements to co-operate with the South, in its measures for extending slavery, that it might create a market among the planters for its products. This appears from the particular efforts made by the Southern members of Congress, during the debate of 1824, to win over the West to the doctrines of free trade.

Mr. McDuffie, of South Carolina, said: "I admit that the Western people are *embarrassed*, but I deny that they are *distressed*, in any other sense of the word. . . . . I am well assured that the permanent prosperity of the West depends more upon the improvement of the means of transporting their produce to market, and of receiving the returns, than upon every other subject to which the legislation of this government can be directed. . . . . Gentlemen (from the West) are aware that a very profitable trade is carried on by their constituents with the Southern country, in *live stock* of all descriptions, which they drive over the mountains and sell for cash. This extensive trade, which, from its peculiar character, more easily overcomes the difficulties of transportation than any that can be substituted in its place, is about to be put in jeopardy for the conjectural benefits of this measure. When I say this trade is about to be put in jeopardy, I do not speak unadvisedly. I am perfectly convinced that, if this bill passes, it will have the effect of inducing the people of the South, partly from the feeling and partly from the necessity growing out of it, to raise within themselves, the live stock which they now purchase from the West. . . . . If we cease to take the manufactures of Great Britain, she will assuredly cease to take our cotton to the same extent. It is a settled principle of her policy—a principle not only wise, but essential to her existence—to purchase from those nations that receive her manufactures, in preference to those who do not. We have, heretofore, been her best customers, and, therefore, it has been her policy to purchase our cotton to the full extent of our demand for her manufactures. But, say gentlemen, Great Britain does not purchase your cotton from affection, but from interest. I grant it, sir; and that is the very reason of my decided hostility to a system which will make it her interest to purchase from other countries in preference to our own. It *is* her interest to purchase cotton, even at a higher price, from those countries which receive her manufactures in exchange. It is better for her to give a little more for cotton, than to obtain nothing for her manufactures. It will be remarked that the situation of Great Britain is, in this respect, widely different from that of the United States. The powers of her soil have been already pushed very nearly to the maximum of their productiveness. The productiveness of her manufactures on the contrary, is as unlimited as the demand of the whole world. . . . . In fact, sir, the policy of Great Britain is not, as gentlemen seem to suppose, to secure the *home*, but the *foreign* market for her manufactures. The former she has without an effort. It is to attain the latter that all her policy and enterprise are brought into requisition. The manufactures of that country are *the basis of her commerce;* our manufactures, on the contrary are to be *the destruction of our commerce.* . . . . It can not be doubted that, in pursuance of the policy of forcing her manufactures into foreign markets, she will, if deprived of a large portion of our custom, direct all her efforts to South America. That country abounds in a soil admirably adapted to the production of cotton, and will, for a century to come, import her manufactures from foreign countries."

Mr. Hamilton, of South Carolina, said: "That the planters in his section shared in that depression which is common in every department of the industry of the Union, *excepting those from which we have heard the most clamor for relief.* This would be understood when it was known that sea-island cotton had fallen from 50 or 60 cents, to 25 cents—a fall even greater than that which has attended wheat, of which we had heard so much—as if the grain-growing section was the only agricultural interest which had suffered. . . . . While the planters of this region do not dread competition in the foreign markets on equal terms, from the superiority of their cotton, they entertain a well-founded apprehension, that the restrictions contemplated will lead to retaliatory duties on the part of Great Britain, which must end in ruin. . . . . In relation to our upland cottons, Great Britain may, without difficulty, in the course of a very short period, supply her wants from Brazil. . . . . How long the exclusive production, even of the sea-island cotton, will remain to our country, is yet a doubtful and interesting problem. The experiments that are making on the Delta of the Nile, if pushed to the Ocean, may result in the production of this beautiful staple, in an abundance which, in reference to other productions, has long blest and consecrated Egyptian fertility. . . . . We are told by the honorable Speaker (Mr. Clay,) that our manufacturing establishments will, in a very short period, supply the place of the foreign demand. The futility, I will not say mockery of this hope, may be measured by one or two facts. First, the present consumption of cotton, by our manufactories, is about equal to one-sixth of our whole production. . . . . How long it will take to increase these manufactories to a scale equal to the consumption of this production, he could not venture to determine; but that it will be some years after the epitaph will have been written on the fortunes of the South, there can be but little doubt.". . . . [After speaking of the tendency of increased manufactures in the East, to check emigration to the West, and thus to diminish the value of the public lands and prevent the growth of the Western States, Mr. H. proceeded thus:] "That portion of the Union could participate in no part of the bill, except in its burdens, in spite of the fallacious hopes that were cherished, in reference to cotton bagging for Kentucky, and the woolen duty for Steubenville, Ohio. He feared that to the entire region of the West, no 'cordial drops of comfort' would come, even in the duty on foreign spirits. To a large portion of our people, who are in the habit of solacing themselves with Hollands, Antigua, and Cogniac, whisky would still have 'a most villainous twang.' The cup, he feared, would be refused, though tendered by the hand of patriotism as well as conviviality. No, the West has but one interest, and that is, that its best customer, the South, should be prosperous."

Mr. Rankin, of Mississippi, said: "With the West, it appears to me like a rebellion of the members against the body. It is true, we export, but the amount received from those exports is only apparently, largely in our favor, inasmuch as we are the consumers of your produce, dependent on you for our implements of husbandry, the means of sustaining life, and almost every thing except our lands and negroes; all of which draws much from the apparent profits and advantages. In proportion as you diminish our exportations, you diminish our means of purchasing from you, and destroy your own market. You will compel us to use those advantages of soil and of climate which God and Nature have placed within our reach, and to live, as to you, as you desire us to live as to foreign nations—dependent on our own resources."

Mr. Garnett, of Virginia, said: "The Western States can not manufacture. The want of capital (of which they, as well as the Southern States, have been drained by the policy of government,) and other causes render it impossible. The Southern States are destined to suffer more by this policy than any other—the Western next; but it will not benefit the aggregate population of any State. It is for the benefit of capitalists only. If persisted in, it will drive the South to ruin and resistance."

Mr. Cuthbert, of Georgia, said: "He hoped the market for the cotton of the South was not about to be contracted within a little miserable sphere, (the home market,) instead of being spread throughout the world. If they should drive the cotton-growers from the only source from whence their means were derived, (the foreign market,) they would be unable any longer to take their supplies from the West—they must contract their concerns within their own spheres, and begin to raise flesh and grain for their own consumption. The South was already under a severe pressure—if this measure went into effect, its distress would be consummated."

In 1828, the West found still very limited means of communication with the East. The opening of the New York canal, in 1825, created a means of traffic with the seaboard, to the people of the Lake region; but all of the remaining territory, west of the Alleghanies, had gained no advantages over those it had enjoyed in 1824, except so far as steamboat navigation had progressed on the Western rivers. In the debate preceding the passage of the tariff in 1828, usually termed the "Woolens' Bill," allusion is made to the condition of the West, from which we quote as follows:

Mr. Wickliffe, of Kentucky, said: "My constituents may be said to be a grain-growing people. They raise stock, and their surplus grain is converted into spirits. Where, I ask, is our market?. . . . Our market is where our sympathies should be, in the South. Our course of trade, for all heavy articles, is down the Mississippi. What breadstuffs we find a market for, are principally consumed in the States of Mississippi, Louisiana, South Alabama, and Florida. Indeed, I may say, these States are the consumers, at miserable and ruinous prices to the farmers of my State, of our exports of spirits, corn, flour, and cured provisions. . . . . We have had a trade of some value to the South in our stock. We still continue it under great disadvantages. It is a ready-money trade—I may say it is the only money trade in which we are engaged. . . . . Are the gentlemen acquainted with the extent of that trade? It may be fairly stated at three millions per annum."

Mr. Benton urged the Western members to unite with the South, "for the purpose of enlarging the market, increasing the demand in the South, and its ability to purchase the horses, mules, and provisions, which the West could sell nowhere else."

The tariff of 1828, created great dissatisfaction at the South. Examples of the expressions of public sentiment, on the subject, adopted at conventions, and on other occasions, might be multiplied indefinitely. Take a case or two, to illustrate the whole. At a public meeting in Georgia, held subsequently to the passage of the "Woolens' Bill," the following resolution was adopted:

Resolved, That to retaliate as far as possible upon our oppressors, our Legislature be requested to impose taxes, amounting to prohibition, on the hogs, horses, mules, and cotton-bagging, whisky, pork, beef, bacon, flax, and hemp cloth, of the Western, and on all the productions and manufactures of the Eastern and Northern States.

Mr. Hamilton, of South Carolina, in a speech at the Waterborough Dinner, given subsequently to the passage of the tariff of 1828, said:

"It becomes us to inquire what is to be our situation under this unexpected and disastrous conjunction of circumstances, which, in its progress, will deprive us of the benefits of a free trade with the rest of the world, which formed one of the leading objects of the Union. Why, gentlemen, ruin, unmitigated ruin, must be our portion, if this system continues. . . . . From 1816 down to the present time, the South has been drugged, by the slow poison of the miserable empiricism of the prohibitory system, the fatal effects of which we could not so long have resisted, but for the stupendously valuable staples with which God has blessed us, and the agricultural skill and enterprise of our people."

In further illustration of the nature of this controversy, and of the arguments used during the contest, we must give the substance of the remarks of a prominent politician, who was aiming at detaching the sugar planters from their political connection with the manufacturers. We have to rely on memory, however, as we can not find the record of the language used on the occasion. It was published at the time, and commented on, freely, by the newspapers at the North. He said: "We must prevent the increase of manufactories, force the surplus labor into agriculture, promote the cultivation of our unimproved western lands, until provisions are so multiplied and reduced in price, that the slave can be fed so cheaply as to enable us to grow our sugar at *three cents a pound*. Then, without protective duties, we can rival Cuba in the production of that staple, and drive her from our markets."

CHAPTER X

Tariff controversy continued—Tariff of 1832—The crisis—*Secession* threatened—
Compromise finally adopted—Debates—Mr. Hayne—Mr. McDuffie—Mr. Clay—
Adjustment of the subject.

THE opening of the year 1832, found the parties to the Tariff controversy once more
engaged in earnest debate, on the floor of Congress; and midsummer witnessed the passage of a new Bill, including the principle of protection. This Act produced a crisis in the
controversy, and led to the movements in South Carolina toward secession; and, to avert
the threatened evil, the Bill was modified, in the following year, so as to make it acceptable to the South; and, so as, also, to settle the policy of the Government for the
succeeding nine years. A few extracts from the debates of 1832, will serve to show what
were the sentiments of the members of Congress, as to the effects of the protective policy
on the different sections of the Union, up to that date:

Mr. Hayne, of South Carolina, said: "When the policy of '24 went into operation, the
South was supplied from the West, through a single avenue, (the Saluda Mountain Gap,)
with live stock, horses, cattle, and hogs, to the amount of considerably upward of a million of dollars a year. Under the pressure of the system, this trade has been regularly
diminishing. It has already fallen more than one-half. . . . . In consequence of the dire calamities which the system has inflicted on the South—blasting our commerce, and
withering our prosperity—the West has been very nearly deprived of her best customer. . . . . And what was found to be the result of four years' experience at the South? Not a
hope fulfilled; not one promise performed; and our condition infinitely worse than it had
been four years before. Sir, the whole South rose up as one man, and protested against
any further experiment with this system. . . . . Sir, I seize the opportunity to dispel forever
the delusion that the South can find any compensation, in a home market, for the injurious operation of the protective system. . . . . What a spectacle do you even now exhibit
to the world? A large portion of your fellow-citizens, believing themselves to be griev-
ously oppressed by an unwise and unconstitutional system, are clamoring at your doors
for justice: while another portion, supposing that they are enjoying rich bounties under it,
are treating their complaints with scorn and contempt. . . . . This system may destroy the
South, but it will not permanently advance the prosperity of the North. It may depress us,
but can not elevate them. Beside, sir, if persevered in, it must annihilate that portion of
the country from which the resources are to be drawn. And it may be well for gentlemen
to reflect whether adhering to this policy would not be acting like the man who 'killed the

goose which laid the golden eggs.' Next to the Christian religion, I consider *Free Trade*, in its largest sense, as the greatest blessing that can be conferred on any people."

Mr. McDuffie, of South Carolina, said: "At the close of the late war with Great Britain, every thing in the political and commercial changes, resulting from the general peace, indicated unparalleled prosperity to the Southern States, and great embarrassment and distress to those of the North. The nations of the Continent had all directed their efforts to the business of manufacturing; and all Europe may be said to have converted their swords into machinery, creating unprecedented demand for cotton, the great staple of the Southern States. There is nothing in the history of commerce that can be compared with the increased demand for this staple, notwithstanding the restrictions by which this Government has limited that demand. As cotton, tobacco, and rice, are produced only on a small portion of the globe, while all other agricultural staples are common to every region of the earth, this circumstance gave the planting States very great advantages. To cap the climax of the commercial advantages opened to the cotton planters, England, their great and most valued customer, received their cotton under a mere nominal duty. On the other hand, the prospects of the Northern States were as dismal as those of the Southern States were brilliant. They had lost the carrying trade of the world, which the wars of Europe had thrown into their hands. They had lost the demand and the high prices which our own war had created for their grain and other productions; and, soon afterward, they also lost the foreign market for their grain, owing, partly, to foreign corn laws, but still more to other causes. Such were the prospects, and such the well-founded hope of the Southern States at the close of the late war, in which they bore so glorious a part in vindicating the freedom of trade. But where are now these cheering prospects and animating hopes? Blasted, sir—utterly blasted—by the consuming and withering course of a system of legislation which wages an exterminating war against the blessings of commerce and the bounties of a merciful Providence; and which, by an impious perversion of language, is called 'Protection.'. . . . I will not add, sir, my deep and deliberate conviction, in the face of all the miserable cant and hypocrisy with which the world abounds on the subject, that any course of measures which shall hasten the abolition of slavery, by destroying the value of slave labor, will bring upon the Southern States the greatest political calamity with which they can be afflicted; for I sincerely believe, that when the people of those States shall be compelled, by such means, to emancipate their slaves, they will be but a few degrees above the condition of slaves themselves. Yes, sir, mark what I say: when the people of the South cease to be masters, by the tampering influence of this Government, direct or indirect, they will assuredly be slaves. It is the clear and distinct perception of the irresistible tendency of this protective system to precipitate us upon this great moral and political catastrophe, that has animated me to raise my warning voice, that my fellow-citizens may foresee, and foreseeing, avoid the destiny that would otherwise befall them. . . . . And here, sir, it is as curious as it is melancholy and distressing, to see how striking is the analogy between the colonial vassalage to which the manufacturing States have reduced the planting States, and that which formerly bound the Anglo-American colonies to the British Empire. . . . England said to her American colonies 'You shall not trade with the rest of the world for such manufactures *as are produced in the mother country*.' The manufacturing States say to their Southern colonies, 'You shall not trade with the rest of the world for such manufactures as *we produce*, under a penalty of forty per cent. upon the value of every cargo detected in this illicit commerce; which penalty, aforesaid, shall be levied, collected, and paid out of the products of your industry, to nourish and sustain ours.'"

Mr. Clay, in referring to the condition of the country at large, said: "I have now to perform the more pleasing task of exhibiting an imperfect sketch of the existing state of the unparalleled prosperity of the country. On a general survey, we behold cultivation extended; the arts flourishing; the face of the country improved; our people fully and profitably employed, and the public countenance exhibiting tranquillity, contentment, and happiness. And, if we descend into particulars, we have the agreeable contemplation of a people out of debt; land rising slowly in value, but in a secure and salutary degree; a ready, though not an extravagant market for all the surplus productions of our industry; innumerable flocks and herds browsing and gamboling on ten thousand hills and plains, covered with rich and verdant grasses; our cities expanded, and whole villages springing up, as it were, by enchantment; our exports and imports increased and increasing; our tonnage, foreign and coastwise, swelled and fully occupied; the rivers of our interior animated by the perpetual thunder and lightning of countless steamboats; the currency sound and abundant; the public debt of two wars nearly redeemed; and, to crown all, the public treasury overflowing, embarrassing Congress, not to find subjects of taxation, but to select the objects which shall be liberated from the impost. If the term of seven years were to be selected, of the greatest prosperity which this people have enjoyed since the establishment of their present Constitution, it would be exactly that period of seven years which immediately followed the passage of the tariff of 1824.

"This transformation of the condition of the country from gloom and distress to brightness and prosperity, has been mainly the work of American legislation, fostering American industry, instead of allowing it to be controlled by foreign legislation, cherishing foreign industry. The foes of the American system, in 1824, with great boldness and confidence, predicted, first, the ruin of the public revenue, and the creation of a necessity to resort to direct taxation. The gentleman from South Carolina, (General Hayne,) I believe, thought that the tariff of 1824 would operate a reduction of revenue to the large amount of eight millions of dollars; secondly, the destruction of our navigation; thirdly, the desolation of commercial cities; and, fourthly, the augmentation of the price of articles of consumption, and further decline in that of the articles of our exports. Every prediction which they made has failed—utterly failed. . . . . It is now proposed to abolish the system to which we owe so much of the public prosperity. . . . . Why, sir, there is scarcely an interest—scarcely a vocation in society—which is not embraced by the beneficence of this system. . . . . The error of the opposite argument, is in assuming one thing, which, being denied, the whole fails; that is, it assumes that the *whole* labor of the United States would be profitably employed without manufactures. Now, the truth is, that the system *excites* and *creates* labor, and this labor creates wealth, and this new wealth communicates additional ability to consume; which acts on all the objects contributing to human comfort and enjoyment. . . . . I could extend and dwell on the long list of articles—the hemp, iron, lead, coal, and other items—for which a demand is created in the home market by the operation of the American system; but I should exhaust the patience of the Senate. *Where, where* should we find a market for all these articles, if it did not exist at home? What would be the condition of the largest portion of our people, and of the territory, if this home market were annihilated? How could they be supplied with objects of prime necessity? What would not be the certain and inevitable decline in the price of all these articles, but for the home market?"

But we must not burden our pages with further extracts. What has been quoted affords the principal arguments of the opposing parties, on the points in which we are interested, down to 1832. The adjustment, in 1833, of the subject until 1842, and its subsequent agitation, are too familiar, or of too easy access to the general reader, to require a notice from us here.

CHAPTER XI

Results of the contest on Protection and Free Trade—More or less favorable to all—Increased consumption of Cotton at home—Capital invested in Cotton and Woolen factories—Markets thus afforded to the Farmer—South successful in securing the monopoly of the Cotton markets—Failure of Cotton cultivation in other countries—Diminished prices destroyed Household Manufacturing—Increasing demand for Cotton—Strange Providences—First efforts to extend Slavery—Indian lands acquired—No danger of over-production—Abolition movements served to unite the South—Annexation of territory thought essential to its security—Increase of Provisions necessary to its success—Temperance cause favorable to this result—The West ready to supply the Planters—It is greatly stimulated to effort by Southern markets—*Tripartite Alliance* of Western Farmers, Southern Planters, and English Manufacturers—The East competing—The West has a choice of markets—Slavery extension necessary to Western progress—Increased price of Provisions—More grain growing needed—Nebraska and Kansas needed to raise food—The Planters stimulated by increasing demand for Cotton—Aspect of the Provision question—California gold changed the expected results of legislation—Reciprocity Treaty favorable to Planters—Extended cultivation of Provisions in the Far West essential to Planters—Present aspect of the Cotton question favorable to Planters—London Economist's statistics and remarks—Our Planters must extend the culture of Cotton to prevent its increased growth elsewhere.

THE results of the contest, in relation to Protection and Free Trade, have been more or less favorable to all parties. This has been an effect, in part, of the changeable character of our legislation; and, in part, of the occurrence of events in Europe, over which our legislators had no control. The manufaturing States, while protection lasted, succeeded in placing their establishments upon a comparatively permanent basis; and, by engaging largely in the manufacture of cottons, as well as woolens, have rendered home manufactures, practically, very advantageous to the South. Our cotton factories, in 1850, consumed as much cotton as those of Great Britain did in 1831; thus affording indications, that, by proper encouragement, they might, possibly, be multiplied so as to consume the whole crop of the country. The cotton and woolen factories, in 1850, employed over 130,000 work hands, and had $102,619,581 of capital invested in them. They thus afford an important market to the farmer, and, at the same time, have become an equally important auxiliary to the planter. They may yet afford him the only market for his cotton.

The cotton planting States, toward the close of the contest, found themselves rapidly accumulating strength, and approximating the accomplishment of the grand object at which they aimed—the monopoly of the cotton markets of the world. This success was due, not so much to any triumph over the North—to any prostration of our manufacturing interests—as to the general policy of other nations. All rivalry to the American planters from those of the West Indies, was removed by emancipation; as, under freedom, the cultivation of cotton was nearly abandoned. Mehemet Ali had become imbecile, and the indolent Egyptians neglected its culture. The South Americans, after achieving their independence, were more readily enlisted in military forays, than in the art of agriculture, and they produced little cotton for export. The emancipation of their slaves, instead of increasing the agricultural products of the Republics, only supplied, in ample abundance, the elements of promoting political revolutions, and keeping their soil drenched with human blood. Such are the uses to which degraded men may be applied by the ambitious demagogue. Brazil and India both supplied to Europe considerably less in 1838 than they had done in 1820; and the latter country made no material increase afterward, except when her chief customer, China, was at war, or prices were above the average rates in Europe. While the cultivation of cotton was thus stationary or retrograding, everywhere outside of the United States, England and the Continent were rapidly increasing their consumption of the article, which they nearly doubled from 1835 to 1845; so that the demand for the raw material called loudly for its increased production. Our planters gathered a rich harvest of profits by these events.

But this is not all that is worthy of note, in this strange chapter of Providences. No prominent event occurred, but conspired to advance the prosperity of the cotton trade, and the value of American slavery. Even the very depression suffered by the manufacturers and cultivators of cotton, from 1825 to 1829, served to place the manufacturing interests upon the broad and firm basis they now occupy. It forced the planters into the production of their cotton at lower rates; and led the manufacturers to improve their machinery, and reduce the price of their fabrics low enough to sweep away all household manufacturing, and secure to themselves the monopoly of clothing the civilized world. This was the object at which the British manufacturers had aimed, and in which they had been eminently successful. The growing manufactures of the United States, and of the Continent of Europe, had not yet sensibly affected their operations.

There is still another point requiring a passing notice, as it may serve to explain some portions of the history of slavery, not so well understood. It was not until events diminishing the foreign growth of cotton, and enlarging the demand for its fabrics, had been extensively developed, that the older cotton-growing States became willing to allow slavery extension in the Southwest; and, even then, their assent was reluctantly given—the markets for cotton, doubtless, being considered sufficiently limited for the territory under cultivation. Up to 1824, the Indians held over thirty-two millions of acres of land in Georgia, Mississippi, and Alabama, and over twenty millions of acres in Florida, Missouri and Arkansas; which was mostly retained by them as late as 1836. Although the States interested had repeatedly urged the matter upon Congress, and some of them even resorted to forcible means to gain possession of these Indian lands, the Government did not fulfill its promise to remove the Indians until 1836; and even then, the measure met with such opposition, that it was saved but by one vote—Mr. Calhoun and six other Southern Senators voting against it.[32] In justice to Mr. Calhoun, however, it must be stated that his opposition to the measure was based on the conviction that the treaty had been fraudulently obtained.

The older States, however, had found, by this time, that the foreign and home demand for cotton was so rapidly increasing that there was little danger of over-production; and that they had, in fact, secured to themselves the monopoly of the foreign markets. Beside this, the abolition movement at that moment, had assumed its most threatening aspect, and was demanding the destruction of slavery or the dissolution of the Union. Here was a double motive operating to produce harmony in the ranks of Southern politicians, and to awaken the fears of many, North and South, for the safety of the Government. Here, also, was the origin of the determination, in the South, to extend slavery, by the annexation of territory, so as to gain the political preponderance in the National Councils, and to protect its interests against the interference of the North.

It was not the increased demand for cotton, alone, that served as a protection to the older States. The extension of its cultivation, in the degree demanded by the wants of commerce, could only be effected by a corresponding increased supply of provisions. Without this, it could not increase, except by enhancing their price to the injury of the older States. This food did not fail to be in readiness, so soon as it was needed. Indeed, much of it had long been awaiting an outlet to a profitable market. Its surplus, too, had been somewhat increased by the Temperance movement in the North, which had materially checked the distillation of grain.

The West, which had long looked to the East for a market, had its attention now turned to the South, as the most certain and convenient mart for the sale of its products— the planters affording to the farmers the markets they had in vain sought from the manufacturers. In the meantime, steamboat navigation was acquiring perfection on the Western rivers—the great natural outlets for Western products—and became a means of communication between the Northwest and the Southwest, as well as with the trade and commerce of the Atlantic cities. This gave an impulse to industry and enterprise, west of the Alleghanies, unparalleled in the history of the country. While, then, the bounds of slave labor were extending from Virginia, the Carolinas, and Georgia, Westward, over Tennessee, Alabama, Mississippi and Arkansas, the area of free labor was enlarging, with equal rapidity, in the Northwest, throughout Ohio, Indiana, Illinois and Michigan. Thus, within these provision and cotton regions, were the forests cleared away, or the prairies broken up, simultaneously by those old antagonistic forces, opponents no longer, but harmonized by the fusion of their interests—the connecting link between them being the steamboat. Thus, also, was a *tripartite alliance* formed, by which the Western Farmer, the Southern Planter, and the English Manufacturer, became united in a common bond of interest: the whole giving their support to the doctrine of Free Trade.

This active commerce between the West and South, however, soon caused a rivalry in the East, that pushed forward improvements, by States or Corporations, to gain a share in the Western trade. These improvements, as completed, gave to the West a choice of markets, so that its Farmers could elect whether to feed the slave who grows the cotton, or the operatives who are engaged in its manufacture. But this rivalry did more. The competition for Western products enhanced their price, and stimulated their more extended cultivation. This required an enlargement of the markets; and the extension of slavery became essential to Western prosperity.

We have not reached the end of the alliance between the Western Farmer and Southern Planter. The emigration which has been filling Iowa and Minnesota, and is now rolling like a flood into Kansas and Nebraska, is but a repetition of what has occurred in the other Western States and Territories. Agricultural pursuits are highly remunerative, and tens of thousands of men of moderate means, or of no means, are cheered along to where none forbids them land to till. For the last few years, public improvements have called for vastly more than the usual share of labor, and augmented the consumption of provisions. The foreign demand added to this, has increased their price beyond what the planter can afford to pay. For many years free labor and slave labor maintained an even race in their Western progress. Of late the freemen have begun to lag behind, while slavery has advanced by several degrees of longitude. Free labor must be made to keep pace with it. There is an urgent necessity for this. The demand for cotton is increasing in a ratio greater than can be supplied by the American planters, unless by a corresponding increased production. This increasing demand must be met, or its cultivation will be facilitated elsewhere, and the monopoly of the planter in the European markets be interrupted. This can only be effected by concentrating the greatest possible number of slaves upon the cotton plantations. Hence they must be supplied with provisions.

This is the present aspect of the Provision question, as it regards slavery extension. Prices are approximating the maximum point, beyond which our provisions can not be fed to slaves, unless there is a corresponding increase in the price of cotton. Such a result was not anticipated by Southern statesmen, when they had succeeded in overthrowing the protective policy, destroying the United States Bank, and establishing the Sub-Treasury system. And why has this occurred? The mines of California prevented both the Free-Trade Tariff,[33] and the Sub-Treasury scheme from exhausting the country of the precious metals, extinguishing the circulation of Bank Notes, and reducing the prices of agricultural products to the specie value. At the date of the passage of the Nebraska Bill, the multiplication of provisions, by their more extended cultivation, was the only measure left that could produce a reduction of prices, and meet the wants of the planters. The Canadian Reciprocity Treaty, since secured, will bring the products of the British North American colonies, free of duty, into competition with those of the United States, when prices, with us, rule high, and tend to diminish their cost; but in the event of scarcity in Europe, or of foreign wars, the opposite results may occur, as our products, in such times, will pass, free of duty, through these colonies, into the foreign market. It is apparent, then, that nothing short of extended free labor cultivation, far distant from the seaboard, where the products will bear transportation to none but Southern markets, can fully secure the cotton interests from the contingencies that so often threaten them with ruinous embarrassments. In fact, such a depression of our cotton interests has only been averted by the advanced prices which cotton has commanded, for the last few years, in consequence of the increased European demand, and its diminished cultivation abroad.

On this subject, the *London Economist*, of June 9, 1855, in remarking on the aspects of the cotton question, at that moment says:

"Another somewhat remarkable circumstance, considering we are at war, and considering the predictions of some persons, is the present high price and consumption of cotton. The crop in the United States is short, being only 1,120,000,000 or 1,160,000,000 lbs., but not so short as to have a very great effect on the markets had consumption not increased. Our mercantile readers will be well aware of this fact, but let us state here that the total consumption between January 1st and the last week in May was:

CONSUMPTION OF COTTON.

	1853.	1854.	1855.
Pounds,	331,708,000	295,716,000	415,648,000
Less than 1855,	83,940,000	119,932,000	
Average consumption of lbs. per week,	15,600,000	14,000,000	19,600,000

"Though the crop in the United States is short up to this time, Great Britain has received 12,400,000 lbs. more of the crop of 1854 than she received to the same period of the crop of 1853. Thus, in spite of the war, and in spite of a short crop of cotton, in spite of dear corn and failing trade to Australia and the United States, the consumption of cotton has been one-fourth in excess of the flourishing year of 1853, and more than a third in excess of 1854. These facts are worth consideration.

"It is reasonably expected that the present high prices will bring cotton forward rapidly; but as yet this effect has not ensued. . . . . Thus, it will be seen that, notwithstanding the short crop in the States, (at present, they have sent us more in 1855 than in 1854, but not so much as in 1853,) the supply from other sources, except Egypt, has been smaller in 1855 than in either of the preceding years, and the supply from Egypt, though greater than in 1854, is less than in 1853." [From India, the principal hope of increased supplies, the imports for 1855, in the first four months of the year, were less by 47,960,000 lbs. than in 1854, and less by 64,000,000 lbs. than in 1853.[34]] "We may infer, therefore, that the rise in price hitherto, has not been sufficient to bring increased supplies from India and other places; but these will, no doubt, come when it is seen that the rise will probably be permanent in consequence of the enlarged consumption, and the comparative deficiency in the crop of the United States."

After noticing the increasing exports of raw cotton from both England and the United States to France and the other countries of the Continent, from which it is inferred that the consumption is increasing in Europe, generally, as well as in Great Britain, the *Economist* proceeds to remark:

"A rapidly increasing consumption of cotton in Europe has not been met by an equally rapidly increasing supply, and the present relative condition of the supply to the demand seems to justify an advance of price, unless a greatly diminished consumption can be brought about. What supplies may yet be obtained from India, the Brazils, Egypt, etc., we know not; but, judging from the imports of the three last years, they are not likely to supply the great deficiency in the stocks just noticed. A decrease in consumption, which is recommended, can only be accomplished by the state of the market, not by the will of individual spinners; for if some lessen their consumption of the raw material while the demand of the market is for more cloth, it will be supplied by others, either here or abroad; and the only real solution of the difficulty or means of lowering the price, is an increased supply. This points to other exertions than those which have been latterly directed to the production of fibrous materials to be converted directly into paper. Exertions ought rather to be directed to the production of fibrous materials which shall be used for textile fabrics, and so much larger supplies of rags—the cheapest and best material for making paper will be obtained. But theoretical production, and the schemers who propose it, not guided by the market demands, are generally erroneous, and what we now require is more and cheaper material for clothing as the means of getting more rags to make paper.

"Another important deduction may be made from the state of the cotton market. It has not been affected, at least the production of cotton with the importation into Europe has not been disturbed by the war, and yet it seems not to have kept pace with the consumption. From this we infer that legislative restrictions on traffic, permanently affecting the habits of the people submissive to them, and of all their customers, have a much more pernicious effect on production and trade than national outpourings in war of indignation and anger—which, if terrible in their effects, are of short duration. These are in the order of nature, except as they are slowly corrected and improved by knowledge; while the restrictions—the offspring of ignorance and misplaced ambition—are at all times opposed to her beneficent ordinances."

The *Economist* of June 30, in its Trade Tables, sums up the imports for the 5th month of the year 1855; from which it appears, that instead of any increase of the imports of cotton having occurred, they had fallen off to the extent of 43,772,176 lbs. below the quantity imported in the corresponding month of 1854.

The *Economist* of September 1, 1855, in continuing its notices of the cotton markets, and stating that there is still a falling off in its supplies, says:

"The decline in the quantity of cotton imported is notoriously the consequence of the smallness of last year's crops in the United States. . . . . It is remarkable that the additional supply which has made up partly for the shortness of the American crop comes from the Brazils, Egypt, and other parts. From British India the supply is relatively shorter than from the United States. It fails us more than that of the States, and the fact is rather unfavorable to the speculations of those who wish to make us independent of the States, and dependent chiefly on our own possessions. The high freights that have prevailed, and are likely to prevail with a profitable trade, would obviously make it extremely dangerous for our manufacturers to increase their dependence on India for a supply of cotton. In 1855, when we have a short supply from other quarters, India has sent us one-third less than in 1853."

The *Economist* of February 23, 1856, contains the Annual Statement of Imports for 1855, ending December 31, from which it appears that the supplies of cotton from India, for the whole year, were only 145,218,976 lbs., or 35,212,520 lbs. less than the imports for 1853. Of these imports 66,210,704 lbs. were re-exported; thus leaving the British manufacturers but 79,008,272 lbs. of the free labor cotton of India, upon which to employ their looms.[35]

This increasing demand for cotton beyond the present supplies, if not met by the cotton growers of the United States, must encourage its cultivation in countries which now send but little to market. To prevent such a result, and to retain in their own hands the monopoly of the cotton market, will require the utmost vigilance on the part of our planters. That vigilance will not be wanting.

CHAPTER XII

Consideration of foreign cultivation of Cotton further considered—Facts and opinions slated by the London Economist—Consumption of Cotton tending to exceed the production—India affords the only field of competition with the United States—Its vast inferiority—Imports from India dependent upon price—Free Labor and Slave Labor cannot be united on the same field—Supply of the United States therefore limited by natural increase of slaves—Limited supply of labor tends to renewal of slave trade—Cotton production in India the only obstacle which Great Britain can interpose against American Planters—Africa, too, to be made subservient to this object—Parliamentary proceedings on this subject—Successful Cotton culture in Africa—Slavery to be permanently established by this policy—Opinions of the *American Missionary*—Remarks showing the position of the Cotton question in its relations to slavery—Great Britain building up slavery in Africa to break it down in America.

THE remark which closes the preceding chapter was made in 1856. An opportunity is now offered for recording the results of the movements of Great Britain to promote cotton culture in her own possessions between that and 1859. The results will be startling. Few anti-slavery men in the United States expected that Great Britain would so soon be engaged zealously in establishing slave labor in Africa, or that Lord Palmerston should publicly commend the measure. The question is one of so much importance as to demand a full examination. The extracts are taken, mainly, from the *London Economist*, a periodical having the highest reputation for candor and fair dealing. On Feb. 12, 1859, the *Economist* said:

"We are not surprised that the future supply of cotton should have engaged the attention of Parliament on an early night of the Session. It is a question the importance of which can not well be overrated, if we refer only to the commercial interests which it involves, or to the social comfort or happiness of the millions who are now dependent upon it for their support. But it has an aspect far loftier and even more important. At its root lies the ultimate success of a policy for which England has made great struggles and great sacrifices—the maintaining of existing treaties, and perhaps the peace of the world. Every year as it passes, proves more and more that the question of slavery, and even of the slave trade, is destined to be materially affected, if not ultimately governed, by considerations arising out of the cultivation of this plant. It is impossible to observe the tendency of public opinion throughout America, not even excepting the Free States, with relation to the slave trade, without feeling conscious that it is drifting into indifference, and even laxity. In every light, then, in which this great subject can be viewed, it is one which well deserves the careful attention equally of the philanthropist and the statesman.

"It has been said, that in the case of cotton we have found an exception to the great commercial principle of supply and demand. Is this so? We doubt it. We doubt if, on the contrary, we shall not find, upon investigation, that it presents one of the strongest examples of the struggle of that principle to maintain its conclusions. No doubt the conditions of its production have made that struggle a severe one; but, nevertheless, it has not been altogether unsuccessful. Eighteen years ago, (in 1840) the total supply of cotton imported into this country was 592,488,000 lbs.: with temporary fluctuations, it had steadily grown until it had reached, in the last three years, upwards of 900,000,000 lbs., showing an increase of more than fifty per cent. Nevertheless, the demand had been constantly pressing upon the supply, the consumption has always shown a tendency to exceed the production, and the consequent result of a high price has, during a majority of those years, acted as a powerful stimulant to cultivation. But, practically speaking, we possess but two sources of supply, and both present such powerful obstacles to extended cultivation, that we are not surprised at the habitual uneasiness of those whose interests demand a continually increasing quantity. Those two sources are the United States and British India. It is true that Brazil, Egypt, the West Indies, and some other countries, furnish small quantities of cotton; but when we state that of the 931,847,000 lbs., imported into the United Kingdom in 1858, the proportion furnished by America and India was 870,656,000 lbs., leaving for all other places put together, a supply of only 61,191,000 lbs., notwithstanding the many laudable efforts, both on the part of Government, and of the mercantile community, to encourage its growth in new countries, it will be admitted that, as an *immediate* and practical question, it is confined to those two sources. They are not only the sources from whence the largest supplies are received, but they are also those where the chief increase has taken place.

"In 1840 the supply received from the United States was 487,856,000 lbs. Since that time, with some considerable fluctuations, it has steadily increased, until in 1858 it rose to 732,403,000 lbs.—the maximum quantity having reached in 1856, 780,040,000 lbs. Yet, great as this increase has been, it appears that it has not been equal to the increased demand, if we may judge from the price, at the two periods.[36] The large supplies of the last three years have commanded prices at least *sixteen per cent.* higher than the smaller supplies from 1840 to 1842. Every encouragement, therefore, which high and remunerative prices could give to increased cultivation has been liberally afforded to the cotton-growing States of America.

"But whatever the price, there is a condition which places an absolute limit upon the growth. Land in every way suited for the purpose, is abundant and cheap. Means of transport is of the cheapest and best kind, and is without limit. The limit lies in the necessary ingredient of labor. If cotton had been the produce of free labor, no doubt the principle of supply and demand would have solved the difficulty. The surplus of the Old World would have steadily maintained the balance between the two in the New World. Ireland, Germany, Switzerland, the Southern parts of France, and Portugal, would have sent their surplus labor to the best market. As it is, the two kinds of labor—that of the freeman and that of the slave—can not be united in the same cultivation. The slave States of America are, therefore, dependent for any increase of labor only upon themselves. The consuming States can draw supplies only from the breeding States. It is, therefore, exactly in proportion as the slave population increases that the cotton crop becomes larger. Taking the average of three or four years at any period of the history of the United States for the last forty years, it will be found that the growth of cotton is equal to one bale for each person of the slave population. The calculation is well known. When the slave population was two millions, the average produce of cotton was two millions of bales:—as the one rose the other increased. The slave population is now about three millions and a half; the cotton crop of the present year is computed at from 3,500,000 to 3,700,000 bales. The high price of cotton, and the great profit attached to its cultivation, have no doubt furnished the greatest stimulant to an increase of that part of the population. In the competition for more labor, the price of slaves was enormously increased. Some years ago the price of a slave was about £100; now they are worth from £200 to £400. But what must be the tendency of this fearful competition for a limited supply of human labor—limited as long as the slave trade is prohibited—unlimited as soon as the slave trade is legalized? What is the actual condition of the Southern States at this moment? There is on the ground and being secured, according to computation, the largest cotton crop ever known. The last estimates vary from 3,550,000 bales to 3,700,000 bales. A very few years ago it was calculated that cotton at any thing above *four cents* the pound for "middling quality" on the spot was a profitable crop. Now, the price for the same quality on the spot is fully *ten cents* the pound;—and it has been about the same or higher for a long time. What is the consequence? A correspondent writing by the last mail says: 'The people of this section of the country feel *made of gold*, and every thing here is, of course, going at full cry—*every planter wants to open more land and buy more negroes.*' What do these facts suggest? Do they furnish no explanation of the strong desire in the Southern States to possess Cuba? Do they furnish no explanation of the exaggerated irritation got up last year in respect to the West India squadron, and the demand of the American Government, we fear too successfully made, that the right of search in the mitigated form in which it existed should be altogether abandoned? A people familiarized not only with slavery, but also with the slave trade as between one class of States and another, can hardly be expected to entertain a very strong repugnance to a slave trade from beyond the seas. That cargoes of imported slaves have recently been landed in the United States is not denied:—that vessels fitted out as slavers have recently been seized in American ports, we know upon official authority. The same correspondent whom we have already quoted, says there are two great questions which occupy the Southern States at this moment. The one is the acquisition of Cuba. 'The other,' he says, 'is one which has been presented to me forcibly during my sojourn in the South, and that is the increase of slave population. You must have noticed an illicit importation of negroes from Africa landed in Georgia. This has undoubtedly been done, and I doubt not also that other negroes have been landed. It is of course the desire of every honest man that the whole force of the government should be used to put down such a trade, and punish the offenders; but I fear the profits of the trade are so enormous that it will be carried on in the face of all opposition. Negroes are now worth here from 1,000 to 2,000 dollars a-piece. The subject of their being introduced is being openly discussed, and the propriety of the trade being again legalized. It is plain this discussion will by and by take shape. Will not the government be obliged to listen to it, and what will be the result? When labor is so profitable it will be obtained. How? I confess to looking upon this subject with great anxiety. The feeling with regard to slavery both in the North and South has undergone a material change in the last four years. It is now looked upon with far less abhorrence.' Is it possible to separate the danger which is here presented so forcibly from the question of the high price of cotton? We know by experience the influence which the Southern States can exercise upon the election of a President. . . . . . . If the free States are indifferent, we know that, at whatever risk, the slave States will have their own way; and with them it is plain that much must depend upon the price of cotton and the motives which it furnishes to 'open more land and buy more negroes.'

"But with what an enormous interest does this view of the case invest the cultivation of cotton in India. It is the only real obstacle that we can interpose to the growing feeling in favor of slavery, to the diminishing abhorrence of the slave trade in the United States. It is the only field, competition with which can, for many years to come, redress the undue stimulant which high prices are giving to slave labor in America. Nor do the facts as regard the past discourage the hope that it may be successfully used for that purpose. In 1840 the supply of cotton from India was 77,011,000 lbs.;—in 1858 it had risen to 138,253,000 lbs.: having been in the immediately preceding year no less than 250,338,000 lbs. The average importation for four years from 1840 to 1843 amounted to 83,300,000 lbs.:—the average importation for the last four years has been 178,000,000 lbs. or somewhat more than double that of the former period. In some important respects the conditions of supply from India differ very much from those which attach to and determine the supply from America. In India there is no limit to the quantity of labor. There may be said to be little or none to the quantity of land. The obstacle is of another kind; it lies almost exclusively in the want of cheap transit. Our supplies of India cotton are not even determined by the quantity produced, but by that which, when produced, can profitably be forwarded to England. It is, therefore, a question of price whether we obtain more or less. A rise in the price of *one penny* the pound in 1857, suddenly increased the supply from 180,000,000 lbs. in 1856 to 250,000,000 lbs. in 1857. A fall in the price in 1858 again suddenly reduced it to 138,000,000 lbs. It was not that the production of cotton varied in these proportions in those years, but that at given prices it was possible to incur more cost in the transit than at others. The same high price, therefore, which at present renders a large supply possible from India, creates an unusual demand for slaves in the United States. But would not the same corrective consequence be produced if we could diminish the cost of transit in India? Every farthing a pound saved in carriage is equivalent to so much added to the price of cotton. Four-pence the pound in the Liverpool market for good India cotton, with a cost of two-pence from the spot of production, would command just as great a supply as a price of five-pence the pound if the intermediate cost were three-pence. The whole question resolves itself into one of good roads and cheap conveyance. Labor in India is infinitely more abundant than in the United States, and much cheaper; land is at least as cheap; the climate is as good;—but the bullock trains on the miserable roads of Hindostan cannot compete with the steamers and other craft on the Mississippi. No doubt we have new hopes in the district of Scinde, and in the aid of the Indus. We have new hopes in the railways which are being constructed,—not only in cheapening transit, but even more in improving the condition in which native produce will be brought to market. Whatever, therefore, be the financial sacrifice which in the first place must be made for the purpose of opening the interior of India, it should be cheerfully made, as the only means by which we can hope permanently to improve the revenues of India, to increase and cheapen the supply of the most important raw material of our own industry, and to bring in the abundant labor of the millions of our fellow-subjects in India, to redress the deficiency in the slave States of America, and thus to give the best practical check to the growing attractions of slavery and the slave trade."

On March 5, 1859, the editor resumes the subject, and discusses the bearing which the movements making in Africa are likely to have upon these interests.

"We pointed out in a recent number the very close connection between the traditional policy of England in resisting the slave trade, and the efforts which are now making to find other sources of cotton supply besides the United States. We showed that a cry is now arising in the United States, for the renewal of the slave trade—a cry stimulated principally by the high price of cotton. We showed that for every slave in the Southern States there is on the average a bale of cotton produced annually, and that as the demand for cotton, and consequently the price of cotton rises, the demand for slaves and the price of slaves rises with it. In the words of a correspondent whom we then quoted, 'every planter wants to open more land and buy more negroes.' Hence the demand in the South for the recently successful attempt to smuggle slave-cargoes into Georgia. If, then, either in India or any other quarter of the world, it be possible either to cheapen the carriage or facilitate the growth of cotton, so as to bring it into the English markets at a price that can compete successfully with the American cotton, we are conferring a double benefit on mankind—we are increasing the supply of one of the most necessary, and, relatively to the demand, one of the least abundant, articles of commerce, on the steady supply of which the livelihood of millions, and the comfort of almost every civilized nation on the face of the earth, depends, and by means of the increased competition we are diminishing the force of the motive which is now threatening the United States with a renewal of the slave trade. We cannot, therefore, well conceive of stronger considerations than those which are now urging Englishmen to do what may be in their power for the promotion of an increased supply from cotton-growing countries other than the States of America.

"Besides these reasons which apply to the promotion of the cotton-supply in India, or in our own West Indian islands, there is one peculiar to the case of Africa which makes it important that no opportunities of encouraging the cotton-growth of that continent should be neglected. The African supply, if ever it become large, will not only check the rise in the price of cotton, and therefore of slaves in America,—but it will diminish the profits of slave exportation on the coast of Africa. Experience has now sufficiently proved to us, that no one agency has been so effective in paralyzing the slave trade as the growth of any branch of profitable industry which convinces the native African chiefs that they can get a surer and, in the long run, larger profit by employing their subjects in peaceful labor, than they can even get from the large but uncertain gains of the slave trade. . . . . Once let the African chiefs find out, as in many instances they have already found out, that the sale of the laborer can be only a source of profit *once*, while his labor may be a source of constant and increasing profit, and we shall hear no more of their killing the hen which may lay so many golden eggs, for the sake only of a solitary and final prize."

The *American Missionary*, of April, 1859, gives a condensed statement of a discussion in the British Parliament, last summer, in which the condition of cotton culture in Africa was brought out, and its encouragement strongly urged as a means of suppressing the slave trade, and of increasing the supplies of that commodity to the manufacturers of England. S. Fitzgerald, Under Secretary of State, said:

"He did not scruple to say that, looking at the papers which he had perused, it was to the West Coast of Africa that we must look for that large increase in our supply of cotton which was now becoming absolutely necessary, and without which he and others who had studied this subject foresaw grave consequences to the most important branch of the manufactures of this country. Our consul at Lagos reported:

"The whole of the Yoruba and other countries south of the Niger, with the Houssa and the Nuffe countries on the north side of that river, have been, from all time, cotton-growing countries; and notwithstanding the civil wars, ravages, disorders and disruptions caused by the slave trade, more than sufficient cotton to clothe their populations has always been cultivated, and their fabrics have found markets and a ready sale in those countries where the cotton plant is not cultivated, and into which the fabrics of Manchester and Glasgow have not yet penetrated. The cultivation of cotton, therefore, in the above-named countries is not new to the inhabitants; all that is required is to offer them a market for the sale of as much as they can cultivate, and by preventing the export of slaves from the seaboard render some security to life, freedom, property, and labor." Another of our consuls, speaking of the trade in the Bight of Benin in 1856, said:

"'The readiness with which the inhabitants of the large town of Abbeokuta have extended their cultivation of the cotton plant merits the favorable notice of the manufacturer and of the philanthropist, as a means of supplanting the slave trade.'"

"It was worthy of notice that while the quantity of cotton obtained from America between 1784 and 1791, the first seven years of the importation into this country was only 74 bales; during the years 1855 and 1856 the town of Abbeokuta alone exported nearly twenty times that quantity. He thought he might fairly say that if we succeed in repressing the slave-trade, as he believed we should, we should in a few years receive a very large supply of this most important article from the West Coast of Africa."

"Mr. J. H. Gurney said he had received from Mr. Thomas Clegg, of Manchester, a few figures, from which it appeared that while in 1852 only 1800 lbs. of cotton had been brought into Great Britain from Africa, in the first five months of the present year it was 94,400 lbs.

"Mr. Buxton said: 'There was no question now, that any required amount of cotton, equal to that of New Orleans in quality, might be obtained. A very short time ago Mr. Clegg, of Manchester, aided by the Rev. H. Venn, and a few other gentlemen, trained and sent out two or three young negroes as agents to Abbeokuta. These young men taught the natives to collect and clean their cotton, and sent it home to England. The result was, that the natives had actually purchased 250 cotton-gins for cleaning their cotton. Mr. Clegg stated that he was in correspondence with seventy-six natives and other African traders, twenty-two of them being chiefs. With one of them Mr. Clegg had a transaction, by which he (the African) received £3500. And the amount of cotton received at Manchester had risen, hand over hand, till it came last year to nearly 100,000 lbs.' Well might Mr. Clegg say, that this was 'a rare instance of the rapid development of a particular trade, and the more so because every ounce of cotton had been collected, all labor performed, and the responsibility borne by native Africans alone.' The fact was, that the West African natives were not mere savages. In trade no men could show more energy and quickness. And a considerable degree of social organization existed. He could give a thousand proofs of this, but he would only quote a word or two from Lieutenant May's despatch to Lord Clarendon, dated the 24th of November, 1857. Lieutenant May crossed overland from the Niger to Lagos, and he says:

"A very pleasing and hopeful part of my report lies in the fact, that certainly three-quarters of the country was under cultivation. Nor was this the only evidence of the industry and peace of the country; in every hut is cotton spinning; in every town is weaving, dyeing; often iron smelting, pottery works, and other useful employments are to be witnessed; while from town to town, for many miles, the entire road presents a continuous file of men, women, and children carrying these articles of their production for sale. I entertain feelings of much increased respect for the industry and intellect of these people, and admiration for their laws and manners."

"Lord Palmerston said: 'I venture to say that you will find on the West Coast of Africa a most valuable supply of cotton, so essential to the manufactures of this country. The cotton districts of Africa are more extensive than those of India. The access to them is more easy than to the Indian cotton district; and I venture to say that your commerce with the Western Coast of Africa, in the article of cotton, will, in a few years, prove to be far more valuable than that of any other portion of the world, the United States alone excepted.'"

The *London Anti-Slavery Reporter*, as quoted by the *American Missionary* of March, 1859, says:

"A few days ago, Mr. Consul Campbell addressed us, saying: 'African cotton is no myth. A vessel has just arrived from Lagos with 607 bales on board, *on native account*. Several hundred bales more have been previously shipped this year.'

"In order to afford our readers some idea of the extraordinary development of this branch of native African industry and commerce, we append a statement which will exhibit it at a single glance. We have only to observe that we are indebted to Mr. Thomas Clegg, of Manchester, for these interesting particulars, and that the quantities ordered have been obtained from Abbeokuta alone. He is about to extend the field of his operations. Four Europeans have gone out, expressly to trade in native cotton; and several London houses, encouraged by the success which has attended Mr. Clegg's experiment, are about to invest largely in the same traffic. The quantity of raw cotton which has already been imported into England, from Abbeokuta, since 1851, is 276,235 lbs., and the trade has developed itself as follows:

1851-52	9	Bags or Bales lbs.	1810
1853	37	ditto	4617
1854	7	ditto	1588
1855	14	ditto	1651
1856	103	ditto	11,492
1857	283	ditto	35,419
1858	1819	ditto	220,099

"The last importation includes advices from Lagos up to the 1st of last November. Since that time, the presses and other machinery sent out, have been got into full work, and the quantity of the raw staple in stock has rapidly accumulated, the bulk shipped being on 'native account.' Each bag or bale weighs about 120 lbs. Let it be borne in mind that the whole of this quantity has been collected, all the labor performed and the responsibility borne by native Africans; while the cost of production, Mr. Clegg informs us, does not exceed one half-penny a pound in the end. It can be laid down in England at about $4^{1}/_{4}d.$ a pound, and sells at from $7d.$ to $9d.$"

The great point of interest in this movement consists in the fact, that in promoting the production of cotton in Africa, Englishmen are giving direct encouragement to the employment of slave labor. It is an undeniable fact, that from eight-tenths to nine-tenths of the population of Africa are held as slaves by the petty kings and chiefs; and that, more especially, the women, under the prevailing system of polygamy, are doomed to outdoors' labor for the support of their indolent and sensual husbands. Hitherto the labor of the women has, in general, been comparatively light, as the preparation of food and clothing limited the extent of effort required of them; but now, the cotton mills of England must be supplied by them, and the hum of the spindles will sound the knell of their days of ease. That we are not alone in this view of the question, will appear from the opinions expressed by the *American Missionary*, when referring to this subject. It says:

"An encouraging feature in this movement is, that the men engaged in it all feel that the suppression of the slave trade is absolutely essential to its success. The necessity of this is the great burden of all their arguments in its behalf. It thus acts with a double force. There can be no question that the development of the resources of Africa will be an effectual means, in itself, of discouraging the exportation of slaves, while at the same time those who would encourage this development are seeking the overthrow of that infamous traffic as the necessary removal of an obstacle to their success.

"There is, however, one danger connected with all this that can not be obviated by any effort likely to be put forth under the stimulus of commerce, or the spirit of trade. This danger can be averted only by sending the missionaries of a pure gospel, a gospel of equal and impartial love, into Africa, in numbers commensurate with the increase of its agricultural resources and its spirit of general enterprise.

"The danger to which we allude is not merely that of worldliness, such as in a community always accompanies an increase of wealth, but that the slavery now existing there may be strengthened and increased by the rapid rise in the value of labor, and thus become so firmly rooted that the toil of ages may be necessary for it removal. All this might have been prevented if the spirit of Christian enterprise had gone ahead of that of commerce, and thus prepared the way for putting commerce, under the influence of Christianity. For years Africa has been open to the missionary of the cross, to go everywhere preaching love to God and man, with nothing to hinder except the sickliness of the climate. This evil, and the dangers arising from it, business men are willing to risk, and within the next ten years there will be thousands, and tens of thousands, looking to Africa for the means of increasing their riches."

From all this it appears, that the question of slavery is becoming more intimately blended with cotton culture than at any former period; and that the urgent demand for its increased production must establish the system permanently, under the control of Great Britain, in Africa itself. Look at the facts, and especially at the position of Great Britain. The supply of cotton is inadequate to the demands of the manufacturing nations. Great Britain stands far in advance of all others in the quantity consumed. The ratio of increased production in the United States cannot be advanced except by a renewal of the slave trade, or a resort to the scheme of immigration on the plan of England and France. It is thought by English writers, that the renewal of the slave trade by the United States is inevitable, as a consequence of the present high prices of cotton and slaves, unless the slave traders can be shut out from the slave markets of Africa. They assume it as a settled principle, that the immigration system is impracticable wherever slavery exists; and that the American planter can only succeed in securing additional labor by means of the slave trade. Then, according to this theory, to prevent an increased production of cotton in the United States, it is only necessary to make it impracticable for us to renew that traffic.

The supply of cotton from India is not on the increase, nor can be, except when prices rule high in England, or until rail roads shall be constructed into the interior, a work requiring much time and money. The renewal of the slave trade by the United States, on a large scale, would, of course, cheapen cotton in the proportion of the amount of labor supplied. In this view the writers referred to are correct. They are right also in supposing that a reduction below present prices, of a cent or two per pound, would be ruinous to India in the present condition of her inland transportation. They desire, very naturally, therefore, that prices should be kept up for the advantage of India, so that its cotton can bear export. But while high prices benefit India, they also enrich the American planter, and afford him inducements to renew the slave trade.

Here Great Britain is thrown into a dilemma. The slave trade to America must be prevented, in her opinion, or it will ruin the East Indies. To prevent the renewal of this traffic—to keep up the price of cotton as long as may be necessary, for the benefit of India, and prevent a supply of African slaves from reaching the American planter—is a problem that requires more than an ordinary amount of skill to solve. That skill, if it exists any where, is possessed by British statesmen, and they are now employed in the execution of this difficult task. They are convinced that free labor cannot be found, at this moment, any where in the world, to meet the growing demands for cotton. To supply this increasing demand, a new element must be brought into requisition; or rather old elements must be employed anew. Her cotton spindles must not cease to whir, or millions of the people of Great Britain will starve at home, or be forced into emigration, to the weakening of her strength. The old sources of supply being inadequate, a new field of operations must be opened up—new forces must be brought into requisition in the cultivation of cotton. Slave labor and free labor, both combined, are not now able to furnish the quantity needed. Free labor cannot be increased, at present, in this department of production. Slave labor, therefore, is the only means left by which the work can be accomplished—not slave labor to the extent now employed, but to the extent to which it may be increased from the ranks of the scores of millions of the population of Africa.

This is the true state of the case; and the important question now agitated is: Who shall have the advantages of this labor? Two fields, only, present themselves in which this additional labor can be employed—Africa and America. Great Britain is deeply interested in limiting it to Africa, which she can only do by preventing a renewal of the slave trade to America: for she takes it for granted that we will renew the slave trade if we can make money by the operation. South Africa is unavailable for this purpose, as it is under British rule, and slavery abolished within its limits by law. Nothing can be done there, as it is filling up with English emigrants who will not toil, under a burning sun, in the cotton fields; and they can not be permitted to reduce the natives again to slavery. West Africa alone, affords the climate, soil, and population, necessary to success in cotton culture. To this point the attention of Englishmen is now mainly directed. One feature in the civil condition of West Africa must be specially noticed, as adapting it to the purposes to which it is to be devoted. The territory has not been seized by the British crown, as in South Africa, and British law does not bear rule within its limits. The tribes are treated as independent sovereignties, and are governed by their own customs and laws. This is fortunate for the new policy now inaugurating, as the native chiefs and kings hold the population at large as slaves. Heretofore they have sold their slaves at will, as well as their captives taken in war, to the slave traders. Now they are to be taught a different policy by Englishmen; and the African slaveholders are to be convinced that they will make more money by employing their slaves in growing cotton, than in selling them to be carried off to the American planters. This done, and the transportation of laborers to the United States will be prevented. This will put it out of the power of our planters, to increase their production of cotton so as to reduce prices; and this will enable India to complete her rail roads, so as to be able to compete with American cotton at any price whatever.

But this new policy, if successful, will do more than stop the slave trade, to the supposed injury of the American planter. England will thereby have the benefit of the labor of Africa secured to herself. With its scores of millions of population under her direction, she hopes to compete with American slavery in the production of cotton; and not only to compete with it, but to surpass it altogether, and, in time, to render it so profitless as to force emancipation upon us. She will there have access to a population ten fold greater than that of the slave population of the United States; and the only doubt of success exists in the question, as to whether the negro master in Africa can make the slave work as well there as the white master in America has done here.

But how shall England, in this measure, preserve her "traditional policy," in which she pledged herself no longer to cherish slave labor. This will be very easily done. She need not authorize slavery in Western Africa; but as it already exists among all the tribes "by local law," she has only to recognize their independence, and bargain with the chiefs for all the cotton they can force their slaves to produce. This has already been done, by Englishmen, at several points in Africa, and will doubtless be resorted to in many other porportions of that country. The moral responsibility of establishing slavery permanently in Africa, will thus be thrown upon the chiefs and kings, as it has heretofore been upon the American planter; and Great Britain can reap all the advantages of the increased production of slave labor cotton, while her moralists can easily satisfy the conscience of the people at home, by declaiming against the system which secures to them their bread.

Here now the policy of British statesmen can be comprehended. They must have cotton. The products of free labor would be preferred, but as it can not be had, in sufficient quantities, they must take that of slave labor. To allow the American planter to supply this want, by renewing the slave trade, would ruin India and benefit America. To save India, and, at the same time, to secure the cotton demanded by the manufacturers, slavery is to be encouraged in Africa; and this is to be done as a means not only of preventing the slave trade, and checking the extension of slavery in America, but of multiplying the fields of cotton cultivation—a policy very essential to the wants of the British nation. Thus, slavery is to be promoted in Africa as an effectual means of checking it in America; it is to be converted into a blessing there, and made instrumental in wiping out its curse here!

And this, now, is the result of England's philanthropic efforts for African freedom. Her economical errors, in West Indian emancipation, are to be repaired by the permanent establishment of slavery in Africa! But what must be the practical moral effect of her policy? What must be the opinion entertained of the negro race, when Great Britain abandons her policy in reference to them? This is not hard to divine. It will wipe out the odium she has managed to cast upon the system; and, so far as her example is concerned, will justify the American planter in refusing to emancipate his slaves. Her conduct is a practical acknowledgment of the Southern theory of the African race—that slavery is their normal condition, otherwise she must have adopted the same policy in West Africa that she has in South Africa.

But before closing this part of our investigations, it may be well to examine the claims of Great Britain in relation to her humanity towards the African, or any of the inferior races doomed to lives of toil—such as the coolies of India and the laborers of China.

The contest for the advantages of supplying the increasing demands for cotton, is between Great Britain operating in India and Africa, and the American planter operating by an increased amount of labor furnished by means of the slave trade. The contest between the parties may be imagined as assuming this form: A portion of the American planters insist, that they should be allowed to manage this matter; but Great Britain says, nay: my subjects can do it better than you can. You Americans are governed by mercenary motives: we Britons by philanthropic intentions. You Americans have made no sacrifices for the cause of humanity: we Britons have emancipated our West India slaves.

Aye, aye, replies the American planter; we understand all about the humanity of which you boast. Your special type of philanthropy is fully displayed in the history of your West Indies. Look at it. The total importation of slaves from Africa into your West Indian Islands, was 1,700,000 persons; of whom and their descendants, in 1833, only 660,000 remained for emancipation; we had less than 400,000 imported Africans, of whom and their descendants there existed among us, in 1850, more than 3,600,000 persons of African descent; that is to say, the number of Africans and their descendants in the United States, is nearly eight or ten to one of those that were imported, whilst in the British West Indies there are not two persons remaining for every five imported.[37] And besides, we have 500,000 free colored persons among us, a number nearly equal to that which your emancipation act set at liberty, and more than the whole number imported. Your slavery seems to have been a system of wholesale slaughter: ours the reverse.

All true, says Britain: but then we have ceased to do evil, and are learning to do well. We found "that slavery was bearing our colonies down to ruin with awful speed; that had it lasted but another half century, they must have sunk beyond recovery."[38]

What! says the planter; sunk beyond recovery! why, we find our slaves rapidly increasing, and ourselves almost "made of gold." Be pleased to explain, why slavery in the hands of Englishmen should be so destructive, while with the American it is not only profitable to the slaveholder himself, but the comfort of the slaves has been so well secured, from the first, that their natural increase has been about equal to that of any other people in the full enjoyment of the necessaries of life.

Certainly, says Britain: having done our duty, we are free to confess, that "what gave the death blow to slavery, in the minds of English statesmen, was the population returns, which showed the fact, 'the appalling fact,' that although only eleven out of the eighteen islands had sent them in, yet in those eleven islands the slaves had decreased in twelve years, by no less than 60,219, namely: from 558,194 to 497,975!"[39] Had similar returns been procured from the other seven colonies (including Mauritius, Antigua, Barbadoes, and Granada,) the decrease must have been little, if at all, less than 100,000! Now it was plain to every one that if this were really so, the system could not last. The driest economist would allow that it would not pay, to let the working classes be slaughtered. To work the laboring men of our West Indies to death, might bring in a good return for a while, but could not be a profitable enterprise in the long run. Accordingly, this was the main, we had almost said the only, topic of the debates on slavery in 1831 and 1832. Is slavery causing a general massacre of the working classes in our sugar islands, or is it not, was a question worth debating, in the pounds, shillings, and pence view, as well as in the moral one. And debated it was, long and fiercely. The result was the full establishment of the dreadful fact. The slaves, as Mr. Marryatt said, were 'dying like rotten sheep.' Whatever then may be said for West Indian slavery, this damning thing must be said of it, that *the slaves were dying of it*. Then came emancipation."[40] And in performing this act—in demonstrating to the world the destructive character of slavery—Englishmen expected America to follow their example, and to emancipate her slaves also.

And thereby deceived yourselves, says the planter, into the ruin of your islands, without effecting any good for the Africans at large, and but little for those upon whom your bounties were bestowed. And, then, we cannot see the vastness of your philanthropy, in allowing such destructive cruelties to prevail so long, and in only emancipating your slaves when it was apparent they must soon become extinct under the lash, as applied by the hands of Britons. We know that you claimed that slavery was the same everywhere, and that humane men in our country were deceived into the belief that American slavery was as ruinous to life as British West Indian slavery. We know that the elder Mr. Buxton, in 1831, used this language, "where the blacks are free they increase. But let there be a change in only one circumstance, let the population be the same in every respect, only let them be slaves instead of freemen, and the current is immediately stopped;" and, in support of this, his biographer adds: "This appalling fact was never denied, that at the time of the abolition of the slave trade, the number of slaves in the West Indies was 800,000; in 1830 it was 700,000; that is to say, in twenty-three years it had diminished by 100,000."[41] This assertion, that slavery is always destructive of life, was made by Mr. Buxton, in the face of the fact, that ten distinct sets of our *Census tables* were then accessible to him, in each one of which he had the evidence that American slavery, instead of reducing the number of our slave population, tended to its rapid increase. From this and kindred acts of that gentleman, we came to the conclusion, that, though he might be very benevolent, he was not very truthful; and was, therefore, a very unsafe guide to follow, as you must now acknowledge; unsafe, because your emancipation on a small scale, before securing a general emancipation by other countries, has thrown you under the necessity of now attempting to establish slavery elsewhere on a large scale; unsafe, because your negro population have not made half the moral progress under freedom, that ours have done under slavery; and because, that, where cultivation has depended upon the emancipated negro alone, with a single exception, the islands have almost gone to ruin.[42]

You misinterpret facts, says Britain: our islands are not ruined; no, by no means. Under slavery they would have been totally ruined; but emancipation has placed them in a position favorable to a full development of all their resources. "It is to be borne in mind that the influx of free labor is exactly one of those advantages of which a land is debarred by slavery. It is a part of the curse of slavery that it repels the freeman. When we are told that to judge of the effect of emancipation we must exclude those colonies that imported coolies, we reply at once that this useful importation has been one of the many blessings that freedom has brought in her train."[43]

I understand your views now, says the planter: but for emancipation, your colonies would have sunk to irretrievable destruction. That measure has prepared the way for the coolie system; and under its operations the prosperity of your islands is on the increase. But what is the character of this coolie system, that is working such wonders? In what does it differ from the slave trade, of which you desire to deprive us? And what must be its effects upon the colored population, which have received their freedom at your hands, and whose moral elevation your Christian missionaries are laboring to promote? On this point I would not multiply testimony. The character of the coolie traffic is but too well understood, and is now believed by all intelligent men to be the slave trade in disguise. A writer, representing the anti-slavery society of Great Britain, makes these statements.[44]

"I am prepared to show, that fraud, misrepresentation, and actual violence are the constituent elements of the immigration system, even as it is now conducted, and that no vigilance on the part of the government which superintends its prosecution can prevent the abuses incidental to it. . . . . In China, especially, this is notoriously the case, and I refer you to Sir John Bowring's despatches on Immigration from China, for the fullest revelations. I need only add, that he designates the Chinese coolie traffic as being in every essential particular 'as bad as the African slave trade,' and that he recommends its entire prohibition. . . . . The mortality during the sea-voyage is so great, that the Emigration Commissioners declare 'these results to be shocking to humanity, and disgraceful to the manner in which the traffic is carried on.' I beg to call your special attention to the term 'traffic,' and to refer you for particulars of the mortality, to the Emigration Commissioners' Report for 1858. They may be briefly summarised. During the season 1856-57 the deaths at sea amounted to $17.^{26}/_{100}$ per cent. on 4,094 coolies shipped from Calcutta— a rate which, if computed for the whole year, instead of 90 days, the term of the voyage, would average upwards of 70 per cent. The rate of mortality on shipments of Chinese bound to British Guiana, varied from 14 per cent. to 50. . . . . On shipments of Chinese bound to Havanna, on board British vessels, the death-rate fluctuated between 20 per cent. and 60. Yet, sir, immigration is said, by its advocates, to be now conducted on an improved system. . . . . We come now to the treatment of the coolie, as soon as he is discharged from the ship. There is no official evidence, that I am yet aware of, to show what abuses of authority he is subjected to, but the Jamaica Immigration Bill, now awaiting the sanction of Her Majesty's Government, proves that the imported laborer is, during his term of service, subject to conditions quite incompatible with a system of free labor, and the same remark applies to other colonies. That the immigrants are liable to ill usage and neglect, may be gathered from the reports of travelers who have seen them in every stage of destitution and misery; and that they are peculiarly affected by the kind of service they contract to render, and by climate, is sufficiently proved by the awful mortality during industrial residence, which we are assured the Immigration Agent General's returns for Jamaica show to be equal to 50 per cent. Sir E. B. Lytton admits it to be 33 per cent. But if we accept his correction—which I confess I am not prepared to do without knowing upon what evidence he makes it—I maintain that even this death-rate establishes the startling fact, that coolie labor in Jamaica is proportionately more destructive to human life than slave labor in Cuba."

On the question of the influence that the coolie immigration exerts upon the emancipated blacks in the West Indies, the Editor of the *London Economist* very justly remarks:

"Bringing with them depraved heathen habits, and the detestable traditions of the worst forms of idolatry, and always looking forward to their return as the epoch when they will renew their heathen worship and find themselves again among heathen standards of action,—they are almost proof against the best influences which can be brought to bear upon them, and, what is worse, they are not only proof against the good, but missionaries for evil. They are closely associated in their labor with a race that is just emerging out of barbarism with the fostering care of Christianity, and we need not say that their social influence on such a race is deteriorating in the extreme. The difficulty would be indefinitely diminished, were the new immigrants a permanent addition to the population. By careful regulations for that purpose, they might, in that case, be subdued by the higher influences of their English teachers; but the prospect of speedy restoration to the country and habits of their birth, entirely foils such attempts as these. How far this great difficulty can be overcome; and if it cannot, how far it may more than balance the moral and physical advantages of a fuller labor market,—it requires the most careful inquiry to determine." Here now are four distinct points upon which the testimony shows, conclusively, that the coolie system is worse than ever the slave trade has been represented to be; and that as the slave trade is opposed on the ground of the destruction of human life which attends it, so the coolie system should be abandoned upon the same grounds. The points are these: 1st, the frauds and cruelties incident to the procuring of immigrants; 2d, the mortality during the middle passage; 3d, the mortality in the islands where they are employed; 4th, the influence of the heathen coolies in demoralizing the emancipated blacks among whom they are intermingled. These points demand serious consideration by Britons, as well as Americans—by those who would reopen the slave trade, as well as those who would substitute for that traffic the immigration system.

And now, in conclusion, says the planter, I must beg to demur to Britain's claiming a monopoly of all the philanthropy in the world toward the African race; and upon that claim founding another which, if granted, will secure to her the monopoly of all the labor of Africa itself; and I would beg, further, that myself and my fellow planters may be excused, if we cannot see any thing more in all her movements than a determination to have a full supply of cotton, even at the risk of dooming Africa to become one vast slave plantation.

While a faithful view of the plans and expectations of the British, in relation to the production of cotton in Africa, has been presented, it would be doing injustice to the reader not to give a few facts, in closing, which indicate that their success, after all, may not equal their anticipations. The Rev. T. J. Bowen,[45] says of African cotton generally, that "the staple is good, but the yield can not be more than one-fourth of what it was on similar lands in the Southern States;" and of Yoruba, in particular, he says, that "both upland and sea island cotton are planted; but neither produces very well, owing to the extreme and constant heat of the climate." Of this, Mr. Bowen, who is a native of Georgia, must be regarded as a good judge. He spent six years as a missionary of the Baptist Church in exploring the Abbeokuta and Yoruba country. This cause of short crops in Yoruba is evidently incurable. It does not exist in equal force in Liberia and its vicinity. Mr. Bowen says: "The average in the dry season is about 80 degrees at Ijaye, and 82 at Ogbomoshaw, and a few degrees lower during the rains. I have never known the mercury to rise higher than 93 degrees in the shade, at Ijaye. The highest reading at Ogbomoshaw was 97.5." These places are from 100 to 150 miles inland.[46]

Another remark. The confidence with which it is asserted, that immigration is impracticable as a means of obtaining labor, wherever slavery prevails, will remind the reader of another theory to which Englishmen long tried to make us converts: that slave labor is necessarily unprofitable and should be abandoned on economical grounds. Now they are forced to admit that our planters seem to "be made of gold." Perhaps these same planters can use immigrant labor as successfully as slave labor. If necessary, doubtless, they will make the attempt, notwithstanding the opinions entertained beyond the sea.

CHAPTER XIII

Rationale of the Kansas-Nebraska movement—Western Agriculturists merely Feeders of Slaves—Dry goods and groceries nearly all of Slave labor origin—Value of Imports—How paid for—Planters pay for more than three-fourths—Slavery intermediate between Commerce and Agriculture—Slavery not self-sustaining—Supplies from the North essential to its success—Proximate extent of those supplies—Slavery the central power of the industrial interests depending on Manufactures and Commerce—Abolitionism contributing to this result—Protection prostrate—Free Trade dominant—The South triumphant—Country ambitious of territorial aggrandizement—The world's peace disturbed—our policy needs modifying to meet contingencies—Defeat of Mr. Clay—War with Mexico—Results unfavorable to renewal of Protective policy—Dominant political party at the North gives its adhesion to Free Trade—Leading Abolition paper does the same—Ditches on the wrong side of breastworks—Inconsistency—Free Trade the main element in extending Slavery—Abolition United States Senators' voting with the South—North thus shorn of its power—*Home Market* supplied by Slavery—People acquiesce—Despotism and Freedom—Preservation of the Union paramount—Colored people must wait a little—Slavery triumphant—People at large powerless—Necessity of severing the Slavery question from politics—Colonization the only hope—Abolitionism prostrate—Admissions on this point, by Parker, Sumner, Campbell—Other dangers to be averted—Election of Speaker Banks a Free Trade triumph—Neutrality necessary—Liberia the colored man's hope.

FROM what has been said, the dullest intellect can not fail, now, to perceive the *rationale* of the Kansas-Nebraska movement. The political influence which these Territories will give to the South, if secured, will be of the first importance to perfect its arrangements for future slavery extension—whether by divisions of the larger States and Territories, now secured to the institution, its extension into territory hitherto considered free, or the acquisition of new territory to be devoted to the system, so as to preserve the balance of power in Congress. When this is done, Kansas and Nebraska, like Kentucky and Missouri, will be of little consequence to slaveholders, compared with the cheap and constant supply of provisions they can yield. Nothing, therefore, will so exactly coincide with Southern interests, as a rapid emigration of freemen into these new Territories. White free labor, doubly productive over slave labor in grain-growing, must be multiplied within their limits, that the cost of provisions may be reduced and the extension of slavery and the growth of cotton suffer no interruption. The present efforts to plant them with slavery, are indispensable to produce sufficient excitement to fill them speedily with a free population; and if this whole movement has been a Southern scheme to cheapen provisions, and increase the ratio of the production of sugar and cotton, as it most unquestionably will do, it surpasses the statesman-like strategy which forced the people into an acquiescence in the annexation of Texas.

And should the anti-slavery voters succeed in gaining the political ascendency in these Territories, and bring them as free States triumphantly into the Union; what can they do, but turn in, as all the rest of the Western States have done, and help to feed slaves, or those who manufacture or who sell the products of the labor of slaves. There is no other resource left, either to them or to the older free States, without an entire change in almost every branch of business and of domestic economy. Reader, look at your bills of dry goods for the year, and what do they contain? At least three-fourths of the amount are French, English, or American cotton fabrics, woven from slave labor cotton. Look at your bills for groceries, and what do they contain? Coffee, sugar, molasses, rice—from Brazil, Cuba, Louisiana, Carolina; while only a mere fraction of them are from free labor countries. As now employed, our dry goods' merchants and grocers constitute an immense army of agents for the sale of fabrics and products coming, directly or indirectly, from the hand of the slave; and all the remaining portion of the people, free colored, as well as white, are exerting themselves, according to their various capacities, to gain the means of purchasing the greatest possible amount of these commodities. Nor can the country, at present, by any possibility, pay the amount of foreign goods consumed, but by the labor of the slaves of the planting States. This can not be doubted for a moment. Here is the proof:

Commerce supplied us, in 1853, with foreign articles, for consumption, to the value of $250,420,187, and accepted, in exchange, of our provisions, to the value of but $33,809,126; while the products of our slave labor, manufactured and unmanufactured, paid to the amount of $133,648,603, on the balance of this foreign debt. This, then, is the measure of the ability of the Farmers and Planters, respectively, to meet the payment of the necessaries and comforts of life, supplied to the country by its foreign commerce. The farmer pays, or seems only to pay, $33,800,000, while the planter has a broad credit, on the account, of $133,600,000.

This was true in 1853: is it so in 1859? The amounts are not now the same, but the proportions have not varied materially. Reference to Table VIII, in the Appendix, will show, that while the provisions exported, for the three years preceding 1859, amounted to a yearly average of $67,512,812, the value of the cotton and tobacco exported, during the same period, amounted to an annual average of $147,079,647.

But is this seeming productiveness of slavery real, or is it only imaginary? Has the system such capacities, over the other industrial interests of the nation, in the creation of wealth, as these figures indicate? Or, are these results due to its intermediate position between the agriculture of the country and its foreign commerce? These are questions worthy of consideration. Were the planters left to grow their own provisions, they would, as already intimated, be unable to produce any cotton for export. That their present ability to export so extensively, is in consequence of the aid they receive from the North, is proved by facts such as these:

In 1820, the cotton-gin had been a quarter of a century in operation, and the culture of cotton was then nearly as well understood as at present. The North, though furnishing the South with some live stock, had scarcely begun to supply it with provisions, and the planters had to grow the food, and manufacture much of the clothing for their slaves. In that year the cotton crop equaled 109 lbs. to each slave in the Union, of which 83 lbs. per slave were exported. In 1830 the exports of the article had risen to 143 lbs., in 1840 to 295 lbs., and in 1853 to 337 lbs. per slave. The total cotton crop of 1853 equaled 395 lbs. per slave—making both the production and export of that staple, in 1853, more than four times as large, in proportion to the slave population, as they were in 1820.[47] Had the planters, in 1853, been able to produce no more cotton, per slave, than in 1820, they would have grown but 359,308,472 lbs., instead of the actual crop of 1,305,152,800 lbs.; and would not only have failed to supply any for export, but have barely supplied the home demand, and been *minus* the total crop of that year, by 945,844,328 lbs.

In this estimate, some allowance, perhaps, should be made, for the greater fertility of the new lands, more recently brought under cultivation; but the difference, on this account, can not be equal to the difference in the crops of the several periods, as the lands, in the older States, in 1820, were yet comparatively fresh and productive.

Again, the dependence of the South upon the North, for its provisions, may be inferred from such additional facts as these: The "Abstract of the Census," for 1850, shows, that the production of wheat, in Florida, Alabama, Mississippi, Louisiana, Arkansas, and Texas, averaged, the year preceding, very little more than a peck, (it was $^{27}/_{100}$ of a bushel,) to each person within their limits. These States must purchase flour largely, but to what amount we can not determine. The shipments of provisions from Cincinnati to New Orleans and other down river ports, show that large supplies leave that city for the South; but what proportion of them is taken for consumption by the planters, must be left, at present, to conjecture. These shipments, as to a few of the prominent articles, for the four years ending August 31, 1854, averaged annually the following amounts:

Wheat flour	brls.	385,204
Pork and Bacon	lbs.	43,689,000
Whisky	gals.	8,115,360

Cincinnati also exports eastward, by canal, river and railroad, large amounts of these productions. The towns and cities westward send more of their products to the South, as their distance increases the cost of transportation to the East. But, in the absence of full statistics, it is not necessary to make additional statements.

From this view of the subject, it appears that slavery is not a self-sustaining system, independently remunerative; but that it attains its importance to the nation and to the world, by standing as an agency, intermediate, between the grain-growing States and our foreign commerce. As the distillers of the West transformed the surplus grain into whisky, that it might bear transport, so slavery takes the products of the North, and metamorphoses them into cotton, that they may bear export.

It seems, indeed, when the whole of the facts brought to view are considered, that American slavery, though of little force unaided, yet properly sustained, is the great central power, or energizing influence, not only of nearly all the industrial interests of our own country, but also of those of Great Britain and much of the Continent; and that, if stricken from existence, the whole of these interests, with the advancing civilization of the age, would receive a shock that must retard their progress for years to come.

This is no exaggerated picture of the present imposing power of slavery. It is literally true. Southern men, at an early day, believed that the Protective Tariff would have paralyzed it—would have destroyed it. But the abolitionists, led off by their sympathies with England, and influenced by American politicians and editors, who advocated free trade, were made the instruments of its overthrow. No such extended mining and manufacturing, as the Protective system was expected to create, has now any existence in the Union. Under it, according to the theory of its friends, more than one hundred and sixty millions in value, of the foreign imports for 1853, would have been produced in our own country. But free trade is dominant: the South has triumphed in its warfare with the North: the political power passed into its hands with the defeat of the Father of the Protective Tariff, ten years since, in the last effort of his friends to elevate him to the Presidency: the slaveholding and commercial interests then gained the ascendency, and secured the power of annexing territory at will: the nation has become rich in commerce, and unbounded in ambition for territorial aggrandizement: the people acquiesce in the measures of Government, and are proud of the influence it has gained in the world: nay, more, the peaceful aspect of the nations has been changed, and the policy of our own country must be modified to meet the exigencies that may arise.

One word more on the point we have been considering. With the defeat of Mr. Clay, came the immediate annexation of Texas, and, as he predicted, the war with Mexico. The results of these events let loose from its attachments a mighty avalanche of emigration and of enterprise, under the rule of the free trade policy, then adopted, which, by the golden treasures it yields, renders that system, thus far, self-sustaining, and able to move on, as its friends believe, with a momentum that forbids any attempt to return again to the system of protection. Whether the Tariff controversy is permanently settled, or not, is a question about which we shall not speculate. It may be remarked, however, that one of the leading parties in the North gave its adhesion to free trade many years since, and still continues to vote with the South. The leading abolition paper, too, ever since its origin, has advocated the Southern free trade system; and thus, in defending the cause it has espoused, as was said of a certain general in the Mexican war, its editors have been digging their ditches on the wrong side of their breastworks. To say the least, their position is a very strange one, for men who profess to labor for the subversion of American slavery. It would be as rational to pour oil upon a burning edifice, to extinguish the fire, as to attempt to overthrow that system under the rule of free trade. For, whatever differences of opinion may exist on the question of free trade, as applied to the nations at large, there can be no question that it has been the main element in promoting the value of slave labor in the United States; and, consequently, of extending the system of slavery, vastly, beyond the bounds it would otherwise have reached. But the editors referred to, do not stand alone. More than one United States Senator, after acquiring notoriety and position by constant clamors against slavery at home, has not hesitated to vote for free trade at Washington, with as hearty a good will as any friend of the extension of slavery in the country!

All these things together have paralyzed the advocates of the protection of free labor, at present, as fully as the North has thereby been shorn of its power to control the question of slavery. Indeed, from what has been said of the present position of American slavery, in its relation to the other industrial interests of the country, and of the world, there is no longer any doubt that it now supplies the complement of that *home market*, so zealously urged as essential to the prosperity of the agricultural population of the country: and which, it was supposed, could only be created by the multiplication of domestic manufactures. This desideratum being gained, the great majority of the people have nothing more to ask, but seem desirous that our foreign commerce shall be cherished; that the cultivation of cotton and sugar shall be extended; that the nation shall become cumulative as well as progressive; that, as despotism is striving to spread its raven wing over the earth, freedom must strengthen itself for the protection of the liberties of the world; that while three millions of Africans, only, are held to involuntary servitude for a time, to sustain the system of free trade, the freedom of hundreds of millions is involved in the preservation of the American Constitution; and that, as African emancipation, in every experiment made, has thrown a dead weight upon Anglo-Saxon progress, the colored people must wait a little, until the general battle for the liberties of the civilized nations is gained, before the universal elevation of the barbarous tribes can be achieved. This work, it is true, has been commenced at various outposts in heathendom, by the missionary, but is impeded by numberless hindrances; and these obstacles to the progress of Christian civilization, doubtless will continue, until the friends of civil and religious liberty shall triumph in nominally Christian countries; and, with the wealth of the nations at command, instead of applying it to purposes of war, shall devote it to sweeping away the darkness of superstition and barbarism from the earth, by extending the knowledge of science and revelation to all the families of man.

But we must hasten.

There are none who will deny the truth of what is said of the present strength and influence of slavery, however much they may have deprecated its acquisition of power. There are none who think it practicable to assail it, successfully, by political action, in the States where it is already established by law. The struggle against the system, therefore, is narrowed down to an effort to prevent its extension into territory now free; and this contest is limited to the people who settle the territories. The question is thus taken out of the hands of the people at large, and they are cut off from all control of slavery both in the States and Territories. Hence it is, that the American people are considering the propriety of banishing this distracting question from national politics, and demanding of their statesmen that there shall no longer be any delay in the adoption of measures to sustain the Constitution and laws of our glorious Union, against all its enemies, whether domestic or foreign.

The policy of adopting this course, may be liable to objection; but it does not appear to arise from any disposition to prove recreant to the cause of philanthropy, that a large portion of the people of the free States are desirous of divorcing the slavery question from all connection with political movements. It is because they now find themselves wholly powerless, as did the colonizationists, forty years since, in regard to emancipation, and are thus forced into a position of neutrality on that subject.

A word on this point. The friends of colonization, in the outset of that enterprise, found themselves shut up to the necessity of creating a Republic on the shores of Africa, as the only hope for the free colored people—the further emancipation of the slaves, by State action, having become impracticable. After nearly forty years of experimenting with the free colored people, by others, colonizationists still find themselves circumscribed in their operations, to their original design of building up the Republic of Liberia, as the only rational hope of the elevation of the African race—the prospects of general emancipation being a thousand-fold more gloomy in 1859 than they were in 1817.

Abolitionists, themselves, now admit that slavery completely controls all national legislation. This is equivalent to admitting that all their schemes for its overthrow have failed. Theodore Parker, of Boston, in a sermon before his congregation, recently, is reported as having made the following declaration: "I have been preaching to you in this city for ten years; and beside the multitudes addressed here, I have addressed a hundred thousand annually in excursions through the country; and in that time the area of slavery has increased a hundred fold." Gerrit Smith, in his late speech in Congress, said, that cotton is now the dominant interest of the country, and sways Church, and State, and commerce, and compels all of them to go for slavery. Mr. Sumner, in his thrice repeated lecture, in New York, in May, 1855, declared, that, "notwithstanding all its excess of numbers, wealth, and intelligence, the North is now the vassal of an oligarchy, whose single inspiration comes from slavery.". . . . . It "now dominates over the Republic, determines its national policy, disposes of its offices, and sways all to its absolute will.". . . . "In maintaining its power, the slave oligarchy has applied a new test for office"—. . . . "Is he faithful to slavery?". . . . "With arrogant ostracism, it excludes from every national office all who can not respond to this test." Hon. L. D. Campbell, in a letter to the Cincinnati Convention of Colored Freemen, January 5, 1852, said: "I regard the *present position* of your race in this country as infinitely worse than it was ten years ago. The States which were *then* preparing for gradual emancipation, are *now* endeavoring to extend, perpetuate, and strengthen slavery!. . . . A vast amount of territory which was *then* free is *now* everlastingly dedicated to slavery. . . . . From the lights of the past, I confess, I see nothing to justify a promise of much to your *future prospects.*"

That these gentlemen state a great truth, as to the present position of the slavery question, and the darkening prospects of emancipation, will be denied by no man of intelligence and candor. Doubtless, a certain class of politicians, because of the present dearth of political capital, of any other kind, will continue to agitate this subject. But, sooner or later, it must take the form we have stated, and become a question of minor importance in politics. This result is inevitable, because the people at large are beginning to realize their want of power over the institution of slavery, and the futility of any measures hitherto adopted to arrest its progress, and elevate the free colored people on terms of equality among the whites.

But, I am told that the North has recently achieved a great victory over the South, in the election of Mr. Banks, as Speaker.[48] Time was when such a result would have been considered far otherwise than a Northern triumph. Mr. Banks is an ultra free trade man, and his sentiments will assuredly work no ill to the commercial interests of the South. His election provoked no threats of secession. What, then, has been gained to the North, in the wild excitement consequent upon the controversy relative to the Speakership? The opponents of slavery are further than ever from accomplishing any thing practicable in checking the demand for the great staple of the South. Cotton is King still.

In such a crisis as this, shall the friends of the Union be rebuked, if they determine to take a position of neutrality, in politics, on the subject of slavery; while, at the same time, they offer to guarantee the free colored people a Republic of their own, where they may equal other races, and aid in redeeming a Continent from the woes it has suffered for thousands of years!

CHAPTER XIV

THE INDUSTRIAL, SOCIAL, AND MORAL CONDITION OF THE FREE PEOPLE OF COLOR IN THE BRITISH COLONIES, HAYTI, AND IN THE UNITED STATES; AND THE INFLUENCE THEY HAVE EXERTED ON PUBLIC SENTIMENT IN RELATION TO SLAVERY, AND TO THEIR OWN PROSPECTS OF EQUALITY WITH THE WHITES.

Effects of opposition to Colonization on Liberia—Its effects on free colored people—Their social and moral condition—Abolition testimony on the subject—American Missionary Association—Its failure in Canada—Degradation of West India free colored people—American and Foreign Anti-Slavery Society—Its testimony on the dismal condition of West India free negroes—London Times on same subject—Mr. Bigelow on same subject—Effect of results in West Indies on Emancipation—Opinion of Southern Planters—Economical failure of West India Emancipation—Ruinous to British Commerce—Similar results in Hayti—Extent of diminution of exports from West Indies resulting from Emancipation—Results favorable to American Planter—Moral condition of Hayti—Later facts in reference to the West Indies—Negro free labor a failure—Necessity of education to render freedom of value—Franklin's opinion confirmed—Colonization essential to promote Emancipation.

WE have noticed the social and moral condition of the free colored people, from the days of Franklin, to the projection of colonization. We have also glanced at the main facts in relation to the abolition warfare upon colonization, and its success in paralyzing the enterprise. This subject demands a more extended notice. The most serious injury from this hostility, sustained by the cause of colonization, was the prejudice created, in the minds of the more intelligent free colored men, against emigration to Liberia. The Colonization Society had expressed its belief in the natural equality of the blacks and whites; and that there were a sufficient number of educated, upright, free colored men, in the United States, to establish and sustain a Republic on the coast of Africa, "whose citizens, rising rapidly in the scale of existence, under the stimulants to noble effort by which they would be surrounded, might soon become equal to the people of Europe, or of European origin—so long their masters and oppressors." These were the sentiments of the first Report of the Colonization Society, and often repeated since. Its appeals were made to the moral and intelligent of the free colored people; and, with their co-operation, the success of its scheme was considered certain. But the very persons needed to lead the enterprise, were, mostly, persuaded to reject the proffered aid, and the society was left to prosecute its plans with such materials as offered. In consequence of this opposition, it was greatly embarrassed, and made less progress in its work of African redemption, than it must have done under other circumstances. Had three-fourths of its emigrants been the enlightened, free colored men of the country, a dozen Liberias might now gird the coast of Africa, where but one exists; and the slave trader be entirely excluded from its shores. Doubtless, a wise Providence has governed here, as in other human affairs, and may have permitted this result, to show how speedily even semi-civilized men can be elevated under American Protestant free institutions. The great body of emigrants to Liberia, and nearly all the leading men who have sprung up in the colony, and contributed most to the formation of the Republic, went out from the very midst of slavery; and yet, what encouraging results! It has been a sad mistake to oppose colonization, and thus to retard Africa's redemption!

But how has it fared with the free colored people elsewhere? The answer to this question will be the solution of the inquiry, What has abolitionism accomplished by its hostility to colonization, and what is the condition of the free colored people, whose interests it volunteered to promote, and whose destinies it attempted to control?

The abolitionists themselves shall answer this question. The colored people shall see what kind of commendations their tutors give them, and what the world is to think of them, on the testimony of their particular friends.

The concentration of a colored population in Canada, is the work of American abolitionists. *The American Missionary Association*, is their organ for the spread of a gospel untainted, it is claimed, by contact with slavery. Out of four stations under its care in Canada, at the opening of 1853, but one school, that of Miss Lyon, remained at its close. All the others were abandoned, and all the missionaries had asked to be released,[49] as we are informed by its Seventh Annual Report, chiefly for the reasons stated in the following extract, page 49:

"The number of missionaries and teachers in Canada, with which the year commenced, has been greatly reduced. Early in the year, Mr. Kirkland wrote to the committee, that the opposition to white missionaries, manifested by the colored people of Canada, had so greatly increased, by the interested misrepresentations of ignorant colored men, pretending to be ministers of the gospel, that he thought his own and his wife's labors, and the funds of the association, could be better employed elsewhere."

This Mission seems never to have been in a prosperous condition. Passing over to the Eleventh Annual Report, 1857, it is found that the Association had then but one missionary, the Rev. David Hotchkiss, in that field. In relation to his prospects, the Report says:

"It has, however, happened to him, as it frequently did to Paul and his fellow-laborers, that his faithfulness and his success have been the occasion of stirring up certain lewd fellows of the baser sort, so that at one time it was thought by some lookers-on that his life was in danger, and that he might be compelled to leave the scene of his present labors." He had succeeded, however, in gathering a church of 28 members, but "on the 21st of June, the house in which the little church worshiped was burned to the ground. This was undoubtedly the work of an incendiary, as there had been no fire in it for more than two weeks. Threats now were freely used against Mr. Hotchkiss and the church, but he continued his labors, and procured another house, and had it fitted up for worship. On the 24th of August, this also was burned down. They have since had to meet in private houses, and much doubt has been felt relative to ultimate duty. At later dates, however, the opposition was more quiet, and hopes revived. This field is emphatically a hard one, and requires much faith and patience from those who labor there."[50]

On the 30th of August, 1858, Mr. Hotchkiss writes: "My wife's school is in a prosperous condition. She has had nearly forty scholars, and they learn well. There are numbers who can not come to school for want of suitable clothing. They are nearly naked."[51]

On a late occasion it is remarked, that "this society seems to meet with the trouble which accompanies the efforts of other missionary societies in their endeavors to 'to seek and to save that which was lost.' They say they find it 'extremely difficult to win the confidence of the colored people of Canada.'"[52]

But we have a picture of a different kind to present, and one that proves the capacity of the free colored people for improvement—not when running at large and uncared for, but when subjected to wholesome restraint. This is as essential to the progress of the blacks as the whites, while they are in the course of intellectual, moral and industrial training:

"Some years ago the Rev. William King, a slave owner in Louisiana, manumitted his slaves and removed them to Canada. They now, with others, occupy a tract of land at Buxton and the vicinity, called the Elgin Block, where Mr. King is stationed as a Presbyterian missionary.

"A recent general meeting there was attended by Lord Althorp, son of Earl Spencer, and J. W. Probyn, Esq., both members of the British Parliament, who made addresses. The whole educational and moral machinery is worked by the presiding genius of the Rev. W. King, to whom the entire settlement are under felt and acknowledged obligations. He teaches them agriculture and industry. He superintends their education, and preaches on the Lord's day. He regards the experiment as highly successful."[53]

It is not our purpose to multiply testimony on this subject, but simply to afford an index to the condition of the colored people, as described by abolition pens, best known to the public. We turn, therefore, from the British colonies in the North, to her possessions in the Tropics.

West India emancipation, under the guidance of English abolitionists, has always been viewed as the grand experiment, which was to convince the world of the capacity of the colored man to rise, side by side, with the white man. We shall let the friends of the system, and the public documents of the British Government, testify as to its results, both morally and economically. Opening, again, the Seventh Annual Report of the *American Missionary Association*, page 30, where it speaks of their moral condition, we find it written:

"One of our missionaries, in giving a description of the moral condition of the people of Jamaica, after speaking of the licentiousness which they received as a legacy from those who denied them the pure joys of holy wedlock, and trampled upon and scourged chastity, as if it were a fiend to be driven out from among men—that enduring legacy, which, with its foul, pestilential influence, still blights, like the mildew of death, every thing in society that should be lovely, virtuous, and of good report; and alluding to their intemperance, in which they have followed the example set by the governor in his palace, the bishop in his robes, statesmen and judges, lawyers and doctors, planters and overseers, and even professedly Christian ministers; and the deceit and falsehood which oppression and wrong always engender, says: 'It must not be forgotten that we are following in the wake of the accursed system of *slavery*—a system that *unmakes man*, by warring upon his conscience, and crushing his spirit, leaving naught but the shattered wrecks of humanity behind it. If we may but gather up some of these floating fragments, from which the image of God is well nigh effaced, and pilot them safely into that better land, we shall not have labored in vain. But we may *hope to do more*. The chief fruit of our labors is to be sought in the *future*, rather than in the *present*.' It should be remembered, too, (continues the Report,) that there is but a small part of the population yet brought within the reach of the influence of enlightened Christian teachers, while the great mass by whom they are surrounded are but little removed from actual heathenism." Another missionary, page 33, says, it is the opinion of all intelligent Christian men, that "nothing save the furnishing of the people with ample means of education and religious instruction will save them from relapsing into a state of barbarism." And another, page 36, in speaking of certain cases of discipline, for the highest form of crime, under the seventh commandment, says: "There is *nothing* in public sentiment to save the youth of Jamaica in this respect."

The missions of this Association, in Jamaica, differ scarcely a shade from those among the actual heathen. On this point, the Report, near its close, says:

"For most of the adult population of Jamaica, the unhappy victims of long years of oppression and degradation, our missionaries have great fear. Yet for even these there may be hope, even though with trembling. But it is around the youth of the island that their brightest hopes and anticipations cluster; from them they expect to gather their principal sheaves for the great Lord of the harvest."

The *American Missionary*, a monthly paper, and organ of this Association, for July, 1855, has the following quotation from the letters of the missionaries, recently received. It is given, as abolition testimony, in further confirmation of the moral condition of the colored people of Jamaica:

"From the number of churches and chapels in the island, Jamaica ought certainly to be called a Christian land. The people may be called a church-going people. There are chapels and places of worship enough, at least in this part of the island, to supply the people if every station of our mission were given up. And there is no lack of ministers and preachers. As far as I am acquainted, almost the entire adult population profess to have a hope of eternal life, and I think the larger part are connected with churches. In view of such facts some have been led to say, 'The spiritual condition of the population is very satisfactory.' But there is another class of facts that is perfectly astounding. With all this array of the externals of religion, one broad, deep wave of moral death rolls over the land. A man may be a drunkard, a liar, a Sabbath-breaker, a profane man, a fornicator, an adulterer, and such like—and be known to be such—and go to chapel, and hold up his head there, and feel no disgrace from these things, because they are so common as to create a public sentiment in his favor. He may go to the communion table, and cherish a hope of heaven, and not have his hope disturbed. I might tell of persons guilty of some, if not all, these things, ministering in holy things."

What motives can prompt the American Missionary Association to cast such imputations upon the missions of the English and Scotch Churches, in Jamaica, we leave to be determined by the parties interested. Few, indeed, will believe that the English and Scotch Churches would, for a moment, tolerate such a condition of things, in their mission stations, as is here represented.

Next we turn to the Annual Report of the American and Foreign Anti-Slavery Society, 1853, which discourses thus, in its own language, and in quotations which it indorses:[54]

"The friends of emancipation in the United States have been disappointed in some respects at the results in the West Indies, because they expected too much. A nation of slaves can not at once be converted into a nation of intelligent, industrious, and moral freemen.".... "It is not too much, even now, to say of the people of Jamaica,.... their condition is exceedingly degraded, their morals woefully corrupt. But this must, by no means, be understood to be of universal application. With respect to those who have been brought under a healthful educational and religious influence, *it is not true*. But as respects the great mass, whose humanity has been ground out of them by cruel oppression—whom no good Samaritan hand has yet reached—how could it be otherwise? We wish to turn the tables; to supplant oppression by righteousness, insult by compassion and brotherly kindness, hatred and contempt by love and winning meekness, till we allure these wretched ones to the hope and enjoyment of manhood and virtue."[55] . . . . "The means of education and religious instruction are better enjoyed, although but little appreciated and improved by the great mass of the people. It is also true, that the moral sense of the people is becoming somewhat enlightened. . . . . But while this is true, yet their moral condition is very far from being what it ought to be. . . . . It is exceedingly dark and distressing. Licentiousness prevails to a most alarming extent among the people. . . . . The almost universal prevalence of intemperance is another prolific source of the moral darkness and degradation of the people. The great mass, among all classes of the inhabitants, from the governor in his palace to the peasant in his hut—from the bishop in his gown to the beggar in his rags—are all slaves to their cups."[56]

This is the language of American abolitionists, going out under the sanction of their Annual Reports. Lest it may be considered as too highly colored, we add the following from the *London Times*, of near the same date. In speaking of the results of emancipation, in Jamaica, it says:

"The negro has not acquired, with his freedom, any habits of industry or morality. His independence is but little better than that of an uncaptured brute. Having accepted few of the restraints of civilization, he is amenable to few of its necessities; and the wants of his nature are so easily satisfied, that at the present rate of wages, he is called upon for nothing but fitful or desultory exertion. The blacks, therefore, instead of becoming intelligent husbandmen, have become vagrants and squatters, and it is now apprehended that with the failure of cultivation in the island will come the failure of its resources for instructing or controlling its population. So imminent does this consummation appear, that memorials have been signed by classes of colonial society hitherto standing aloof from politics, and not only the bench and the bar, but the bishop, clergy, and ministers of all denominations in the island, without exception, have recorded their conviction, that, in the absence of timely relief, the religious and educational institutions of the island must be abandoned, and the masses of the population retrograde to barbarism."

One of the editors of the *New York Evening Post*, Mr. Bigelow, a few years since, spent a winter in Jamaica, and continues to watch, with anxious solicitude, as an anti-slavery man, the developments taking place among its colored population. In reviewing the returns published by the Jamaica House of Assembly, in 1853, in reference to the ruinous decline in the agriculture of the island, and stating the enormous quantity of lands thrown out of cultivation, since 1848, the *Post* says:

"This decline has been going on from year to year, daily becoming more alarming, until at length the island has reached what would appear to be the last profound of distress and misery,. . . . when thousands of people do not know, when they rise in the morning, whence or in what manner they are to procure bread for the day."

We must examine, more closely, the economical results of emancipation, in the West Indies, before we can judge of the effects, upon the trade and commerce of the world, which would result from general emancipation in the United States. We do this, not to afford an argument in behalf of the perpetuation of slavery, because its abolition might injuriously affect the interests of trade and commerce; but because the whole of these results have long been well known to the American planter, and serve as conclusive arguments, with him, against emancipation. He believes that, in tropical cultivation, African free labor is worthless; that the liberation of the slaves in this country, must, necessarily, be followed with results similar to what has occurred in the West Indies; and, for this reason, as well as on account of the profitable character of slavery, he refuses to give freedom to his slaves. We repeat, we do not cite the fact of the failure, economically, of free labor in Jamaica, as an argument for the perpetuation of slavery. Not at all. We allude to the fact, only to show that emancipation has greatly reduced the commerce of the colonies, and that the logic of this result militates against the colored man's prospects of advancement in the scale of political and social equality. But to the facts:

The British planters, up to 1806, had received from the slave traders an uninterrupted supply of laborers, and had rapidly extended their cultivation as commerce increased its demands for their products. Let us take the results in Jamaica as an example of the whole of the British West India islands. She had increased her exports of sugar from a yearly average of 123,979,000 lbs. in 1772-3, to 234,700,000 lbs. in 1805-6. No diminution of exports had occurred, as has been asserted by some anti-slavery writers, before the prohibition of the slave trade. The increase was progressive and undisturbed, except so far as affected by seasons, more or less favorable. But no sooner was her supply of slaves cut off, by the act of 1806, which took effect in 1808, than the exports of Jamaica began to diminish, until her sugar had fallen off from 1822 to 1832, to an annual average of 131,129,000 lbs., or nearly to what they had been sixty years before. It was not until 1833 that the Emancipation Act was passed; so that this decline in the exports of Jamaica, took place under all the rigors of West India slavery. The exports of rum, coffee, and cotton, were diminished in nearly the same ratio.

To arrest this ruinous decline in the commercial prosperity of the islands, emancipation was adopted in 1833 and perfected in 1838. This policy was pursued under the plea, that free labor is doubly as productive as slave labor; and, that the negroes, liberated, would labor twice as well as when enslaved. But what was the result? Ten years after final emancipation was effected, the exports of sugar from Jamaica were only 67,539,200 lbs. a year, instead of 234,700,000 lbs., as in 1805-6. The exports of coffee, during the same year, were reduced to 5,684,921 lbs., instead of 23,625,377 lbs., as in 1805-6; and the extinction of the cultivation of cotton, for export, had become almost complete, though in 1800, it had nearly equaled that of the United States. These are no fancy sketches, drawn for effect, but sober realities, attested by the public documents of the British government.[57] The Jamaica negro, ignorant and destitute of forethought, disappointed the English philanthropists.

In Hayti, emancipation had been productive of results, fully as disastrous to its commerce, as it had been to that of Jamaica. There was an almost total abandonment of the production of sugar, soon after freedom was declared. This took place in 1793. In 1790 the island exported 163,318,810 lbs. of sugar. But in 1801 its export was reduced to 18,534,112 lbs., in 1818, to 5,443,765 lbs., and in 1825 to 2,020 lbs.;[58] since which time its export has nearly ceased. Indeed, it is asserted, that, "at this moment there is not one pound of sugar exported from the island, and all that is used is imported from the United States."[59]

The exports of coffee, from Hayti, in 1790, were 76,835,219 lbs.; and of cotton, 7,004,274 lbs. But the exports of the former article, in 1801, were reduced to 43,420,270 lbs., and the latter to 474,118 lbs.[60] The exports of coffee have varied, annually, since that period, from thirty to forty million pounds; and the cotton exported has rarely much exceeded one million pounds.[61] At present, "with the exception of Gonaives, there is not a pound of cotton produced, and only a very limited quanity there, barely sufficient for consumption; and instead of exporting indigo, as formerly, they import all they use from the United States."[62]

According to the authorities before cited, the deficit of free labor tropical cultivation, as compared with that of slave labor, while sustained by the slave trade, including the British West Indies and Hayti, stands as follows:—a startling result, truly, to those who expected emancipation to work well for commerce, and supersede the necessity of employing slave labor:

Contrast of Slave Labor and Free Labor Exports from the West Indies.

SLAVE LABOR.

	Years.	lbs. Sugar.	lbs. Coffee.	lbs. Cotton.
British West Indies,	1807,	636,025,643	31,610,764	17,000,000[63]
Hayti,	1790,	163,318,810	76,835,219	7,286,126
Total		809,344,453	108,245,983	24,286,126

FREE LABOR.

	Years.	lbs. Sugar.	lbs. Coffee.	lbs. Cotton.
British West Indies,	1848,	313,306,112	6,770,792	427,529[64]
Hayti	1848,	very little.	34,114,717[65]	1,591,454[65]
Total		313,306,112	40,885,509	2,018,983
Free Labor Deficit		496,038,341	67,360,474	22,267,143

To understand the bearing which this decrease of production, by free labor, has upon the interests of the African race, it must be remembered, that the consumption of cotton and sugar has not diminished, but increased, vastly; and that for every bale of cotton, or hogshead of sugar, that the free labor production is diminished, an equal amount of slave labor cotton and sugar is demanded to supply its place; and, more than this, for every additional bale or hogshead required by their increased consumption, an additional one must be furnished by slave labor, because the world will not dispense with their use. As no material change has occurred, for several years, in the commercial condition of the islands, it is not necessary to bring this statement down to a later date than 1848. The causes operating to encourage the American planters, in extending their cultivation of cotton and sugar, can now be understood.

In relation to the moral condition of Hayti, we need say but little. It is known that a great majority of the children of the island are born out of wedlock, and that the Christian Sabbath is the principal market day in the towns. The *American and Foreign Christian Union*, a missionary paper of New York, after quoting the report of one of the missionaries in Hayti, who represents his success as encouraging, thus remarks: "This letter closes with some singular incidents not suitable for publication, showing the deplorable state of community there, both morally and socially. There seems to be a mixture of African barbarism with the sensuous civilization of France. . . . . That dark land needs the light which begins to dawn thereon."

Thus matters stood when the second edition of this work went to press. An opportunity is now afforded, of embracing the results of emancipation to a later date, and of forming a better judgment of the effects of that policy on the question of freedom in the

United States. For, if the negro, with full liberty, in the West Indies, has proved himself unreliable in voluntary labor, the experiment of freeing him here will not be attempted by our slaveholders.

Much has been said, recently, about British emancipation, and the returning commercial prosperity of her tropical islands. The American Missionary Association[66] gives currency to the assertion, that "they yield more produce than they ever did during the existence of slavery." It is said, also, in the *Edinburgh Review*, that existing facts "show that slavery was bearing our colonies down to ruin with awful speed; that had it lasted but another half century, they must have sunk beyond recovery. On the other hand, that now, under freedom and free trade, they are growing day by day more rich and prosperous; with spreading trade, with improving agriculture, with a more educated, industrious and virtuous people; while the comfort of the quondam slaves is increased beyond the power of words to portray."[67]

Now all this seems very encouraging; but how such language can be used, without its being considered as flatly contradicting well known facts, and what the American Missionary Association, Mr. Bigelow, and others, have heretofore said, will seem very mysterious to the reader. And yet, the assertions quoted would seem to be proved, by taking the aggregate production of the whole British West India islands and Mauritius, as the index to their commercial prosperity. But if the islands be taken separately, and all the facts considered, a widely different conclusion would be formed, by every candid man, than that the improvement is due to the increased industry of the negroes. On this subject the facts can be drawn from authorities which would scorn to conceal the truth with the design of sustaining a theory of the philanthropist. This question is placed in its true light by the *London Economist*, July 16, 1859, in which it is shown that the apparent industrial advancement of the islands is due to the importation of immigrants from India, China, and Africa, by the "coolie traffic," and not to the improved industry of the emancipated negroes. Says the *Economist*:

"We find one of the Emigration Commissioners, Mr. Murdock,[68] in an interesting memorandum on this subject, giving us the following comparison between the islands which have been recently supplied with immigrants, and those which have not:

	Number of Immigrants.	Sugar, pounds. The three years before Immigration.	Sugar, pounds. The last three years.
Mauritius	209,490	217,200,256	469,812,784
British Guiana	24,946	173,626,208	250,715,584
Trinidad	11,981	91,110,768	150,579,072

"With these are contrasted the results in Jamaica and Antigua, where there has been very little immigration:—

	Sugar, pounds. *The three years* *after apprenticeship.*[69]	*Sugar, pounds.* *The last three years.*
Jamaica	202,973,568	139,369,776
Antigua	63,824,656	70,302,736

Here, now, is presented the key to the mystery overhanging the British West Indies. Men, high in station, have asserted that West India emancipation has been an economic success; while others, equally honorable, have maintained the opposite view. Both have presented figures, averred to be true, that seemed to sustain their declarations. This apparent contradiction is thus explained. The first take the aggregate production in the whole of the islands, which, they say, exceeds that during the existence of slavery;[70] the second take the production in Jamaica alone, as representing the whole; and, thus, the startling fact appears, that the sugar crop of the last three years in Jamaica, has fallen 63,603,000 lbs., below what it was during the first three years of freedom. This argues badly for the free negroes; but it must be the legitimate fruits of emancipation, as no exterior force has been brought into that island to interfere, materially, with its workings. In Mauritius, Trinidad, and British Guiana, it will be seen that the production has greatly increased; but from a very different cause than any improvement in the industry of the blacks who had received their freedom—the increase in Mauritius having been more than double what it had been when the production depended upon them. The sugar crop, in this island, for the three years preceding the introduction of immigrant labor, was but 217,200,000 lbs.; while, during the last three years, by the aid of 210,000 immigrants, it has been run up to 469,812,000 lbs.

Taking all these facts into consideration, it is apparent that West India emancipation has been a failure, economically considered. The production in Jamaica, when it has depended upon the labor of the free blacks alone, has materially declined in some of the islands, since the abandonment of slavery, and is not so great now as it was during the first years of freedom; and, so far is it from being equal to what it was while slavery prevailed, and especially while the slave trade was continued, that it now falls short of the production of that period by an immense amount. In no way, therefore, can it be claimed, that the cultivation of the British West India islands is on the increase, except by resorting to the pious fraud of crediting the products of the immigrant labor to the account of emancipation—a resort to which no conscientious Christian man will have recourse, even to sustain a philanthropic theory.

But the Island of Barbadoes is an exception. It is said to have suffered no diminution in its production since emancipation, and that this result was attained without the aid of immigrant labor. The *London Economist* must be permitted to explain this phenomenon;

109

and must also be allowed to give its views on the subject of the effects of emancipation, after the lapse of a quarter of a century from the date of the passage of the Emancipation Act:

"We are no believers in Mr. Carlyle's gospel of the 'beneficent whip' as the bearer of salvation to tropical indolence. But we can not for a moment doubt that the first result of emancipation was, in most of the islands, to substitute for the worst kind of moral and political evil, one of a less fatal but still of a very pernicious kind. The negroes had been treated as mere machines for raising sugar and coffee. They were suddenly liberated from that mechanical drudgery; they became free beings—but without the discipline needful to use freedom well, and unfortunately with a larger amount of practical freedom than the laboring class of any Northern or temperate climate could by any possibility enjoy. They suddenly found themselves, in most of the islands, in a position in many respects analagous to that of a people possessed of a moderate property in England, who can supply their principal wants without any positive labor, and have no ambition to rise into any higher sphere than that into which they were born. The only difference was, that the negroes in most of the West India islands wanted vastly less than such people as these in civilized States,—wanted nothing in fact, but the plantains they could grow almost without labor, and the huts which they could build on any waste mountain land without paying rent for it. The consequence naturally was, that when the spur of physical tyranny was removed, there was no sufficient substitute for it, in most of the islands, in the wholesome hardships of natural exigencies. The really beneficent 'whip' of hunger and cold was not substituted for the human cruelty from which they had escaped. In Barbadoes alone, perhaps, the pressure of a dense population, with the absence of any waste mountain lands on which the negroes could squat, rent free, was an efficient substitute for the terrors of slavery. And, consequently, in Barbadoes alone, has the Emancipation Act produced unalloyed and conspicuous good. The natural spur of competition for the means of living, took the place there of the artificial spur of slavery, and the slow, indolent temperament of the African race was thus quickened into a voluntary industry essential to its moral discipline, and most favorable to its intellectual culture."

In further commenting on the figures quoted, the *Economist* remarks:

"These results, do not of course, necessarily represent in any degree the fresh spur to diligence on the part of the old population, caused by the new labor. In islands like Trinidad, where the amount of unredeemed land suited for such production is almost unlimited, the new labor introduced cannot for a long time press on the old labor at all. But wherever the amount of land fitted for this kind of culture is nearly exhausted, the presence of the new competition will soon be felt. And, in any case, it is only through this gradual supply of the labor market that we can hope to bring the wholesome spur of necessity to act eventually on the laboring classes. Englishmen, indeed, may well think that at times the good influences of this competitive jostling for employment are overrated and its evil underrated. But this is far from true of the negro race. To their slow and un-ambitious temperament, influences of this kind are almost unalloyed good, as the great superiority in the population of Barbadoes to that of the other islands sufficiently shows."

The *Economist*, in further discussing this question, favors the introduction of a perma-nent class of laborers, not only that the cultivation may be increased, but because there is "no doubt at all that if a larger supply of labor could be attained in the West Indies, with-out any very great incidental evils, the benefit experienced even by the planters would be by no means so great as that of the negro population themselves;" and thinks that "the philanthropic party, in their tenderness for the emancipated Africans, are sometimes not a little blind to the advantages of stern industrial necessities;" and that, "what the accident of population and soil has done for Barbadoes, it cannot be doubted that a stream of im-migration, if properly conducted, might do in some degree for the other islands."

Lest it should be thought that the *Economist* stands alone in its representations in rela-tion to the failure of negro free labor in Jamaica, we quote a statement of the Colonial Minister, which recently appeared in the *New York Tribune*, and was thence transferred to the *American Missionary*, February, 1859:

"The Colonial Minister says: 'Jamaica is now the only important sugar producing co-lony which exports a considerable smaller quantity of sugar than was exported in the time of slavery, while some such colonies since the passage of the Emancipation Act have largely increased their product.'"

Time is thus casting light upon the question of the capacity of the African race for vo-luntary labor. Jamaica included 311,692 negroes, at the time of emancipation, out of the 660,000 who received their freedom in the whole of the West Indian islands. This was but little less than half of the whole number. It was a fair field to test the question of the willingness of the free negro to work. But what is the result? We have it admitted by both the *Economist* and the Colonial Minister, that there has been a vast falling off in the ex-ports from Jamaica, and that a spur of some kind must be applied to secure their adopting habits of industry. The spur of the "whip" having been thrown away, the remedy pro-posed is to press them into a corner, by immigration from India and China, so that the securing of bread shall become the great necessity with them, and they be compelled to labor or starve, as has been the case in Barbadoes. This is the opinion of the *Economist*, always opposed to slavery, but now convinced that the "slow, indolent temperament of the African race" needs such a "spur" to quicken it "into a voluntary industry essential to its moral discipline, and most favorable to its intellectual culture."

The West India emancipation experiments have demonstrated the truth of a few prin-ciples that the world should fully understand. It must now be admitted that mere personal liberty, even connected with the stimulus of wages, is insufficient to secure the industry of an ignorant population. It is intelligence, alone, that can be acted upon by such motives. Intelligence, then, must precede voluntary industry. And, hereafter, that man, or nation, may find it difficult to command respect, or succeed in being esteemed wise, who will not, along with exertions to extend personal freedom to man, intimately blend with their efforts adequate means for intellectual and moral improvement. The results of West India emancipation, it must be further noticed, fully confirm the opinions of Franklin, that freedom, to unenlightened slaves, must be accompanied with the means of intellectual and moral elevation, otherwise it may be productive of serious evils to themselves and to society. It also sustains the views entertained by Southern slaveholders, that emancipation, unaccompanied by the colonization of the slaves, could be of little value to the blacks, while it would entail a ruinous burden upon the whites. These facts must not be overlooked in the projection of plans for emancipation, as none can receive the sanction of Southern men, which does not embrace in it the removal of the colored people. With the example of West India emancipation before them, and the results of which have been closely watched by them, it can not be expected that Southern statesmen will ever risk the liberation of their slaves, except on these conditions.

CHAPTER XV

Moral condition of the free colored people in United States—What have they gained by refusing to accept Colonization?—Abolition testimony on the subject—Gerrit Smith—New York Tribune—Their moral condition as indicated by proportions in Penitentiaries—Census Reports—Native whites, foreign born, and free colored, in Penitentiaries—But little improvement in Massachusetts in seventy years—Contrasts of Ohio with New England—Antagonism of Abolitionism to free negroes.

In turning to the condition of our own free colored people, who rejected homes in Liberia, we approach a most important subject. They have been under the guardianship of their abolition friends, ever since that period, and have cherished feelings of determined hostility to colonization. What have they gained by this hostility? What has been accomplished for them by their abolition friends, or what have they done for themselves? Those who took refuge in Liberia have built up a Republic of their own; and with the view of encouraging them to laudable effort, have been recognized as an independent nation, by five of the great governments of the earth. But what has been the progress of those who remained behind, in the vain hope of rising to an equality with the whites, and of assisting in abolishing American slavery?

We offer no opinion, here, of our own, as to the present social and moral condition of the free colored people in the North. What it was at the time of the founding of Liberia, has already been shown. On this subject we might quote largely from the proceedings of the Conventions of the colored people, and the writings of their editors, so as to produce a dark picture indeed; but this would be cruel, as their voices are but the wailings of sensitive and benevolent hearts, while weeping over the moral desolations that, for ages, have overwhelmed their people. Nor shall we multiply testimony on the subject; but in this, as in the case of Canada and the West Indies, allow the abolitionists to speak of their own schemes. The Hon. Gerrit Smith, in his letter to Governor Hunt, of New York, in 1852, while speaking of his ineffectual efforts, for fifteen years past, to prevail upon the free colored people to betake themselves to mechanical and agricultural pursuits, says:

"Suppose, moreover, that during all these fifteen years, they had been quitting the cities, *where the mass of them rot, both physically and morally,* and had gone into the country to become farmers and mechanics—suppose, I say, all this—and who would have the hardihood to affirm that the Colonization Society lives upon the malignity of the whites—but it is true that it lives upon *the voluntary degradation of the blacks.* I do not say that the colored people are more debased than the white people would be if persecuted, oppressed and outraged as are the colored people. But I do say that they are debased, deeply debased; and that to recover themselves they must become heroes, self-denying heroes, capable of achieving a great moral victory—a two-fold victory—a victory over themselves and a victory over their enemies."

The *New York Tribune*, September 22, 1855, in noticing the movements of the colored people of New York, to secure to themselves equal suffrage, thus gives utterance to its views of their moral condition:

"Most earnestly desiring the enfranchisement of the Afric-American race, we would gladly wean them, at the cost of some additional ill-will, from the sterile path of political agitation. They can help win their rights if they will, but not by jawing for them. One negro on a farm which he has cleared or bought patiently hewing out a modest, toilsome independence, is worth more to the cause of equal suffrage than three in an Ethiopian (or any other) convention, clamoring against white oppression with all the fire of a Spartacus. It is not logical conviction of the justice of their claims that is needed, but a prevalent belief that they would form a wholesome and desirable element of the body politic. Their color exposes them to much unjust and damaging prejudice; but if their degradation were but skin-deep, they might easily overcome it. . . . . Of course, we understand that the evil we contemplate is complex and retroactive—that the political degradation of the blacks is a cause as well as a consequence of their moral debasement. Had they never been enslaved, they would not now be so abject in soul; had they not been so abject, they could not have been enslaved. Our aborigines might have been crushed into slavery by overwhelming force; but they could never have been made to live in it. The black man who feels insulted in that he is called a 'nigger,' therein attests the degradation of his race more forcibly than does the blackguard at whom he takes offense; for negro is no further a term of opprobrium than the character of the blacks has made it so. . . . . If the blacks of to-day were all or mainly such men as Samuel R. Ward or Frederick Douglass, nobody would consider 'negro' an invidious or reproachful designation.

"The blacks of our State ought to enjoy the common rights of man; but they stand greatly in need of the spirit in which those rights have been won by other races. They will never win them as white men's barbers, waiters, ostlers and boot blacks; that is to say, the tardy and ungracious concession of the right of suffrage, which they may ultimately wrench from a reluctant community, will leave them still the political as well as social inferiors of the whites—excluded from all honorable office, and admitted to white men's tables only as waiters and plate-washers—unless they shall meantime have wrought out, through toil, privation and suffering, an intellectual and essential enfranchisement. At present, white men dread to be known as friendly to the black, because of the never-ending, still-beginning importunities to help this or that negro object of charity or philanthrophy to which such a reputation inevitably subjects them. Nine-tenths of the free blacks have no idea of setting themselves to work except as the hirelings and servitors of white men; no idea of building a church, or accomplishing any other serious enterprise, except through beggary of the whites. As a class, the blacks are indolent, improvident, servile and licentious; and their inveterate habit of appealing to white benevolence or compassion whenever they realize a want or encounter a difficulty, is eminently baneful and enervating. If they could never more obtain a dollar until they shall have earned it, many of them would suffer, and some perhaps starve; but, on the whole, they would do better and improve faster than may now be reasonably expected."

In tracing the causes which led to the organization of the American Colonization Society, the statistics of the penitentiaries down to 1827, were given, as affording an index to the moral condition of the free colored people at that period. The facts of a similar kind, for 1850, are added here, to indicate their present moral condition. The statistics are compiled from the Compendium of the Census of the United States, for 1850, and published in 1854.

Tabular Statement of the number of the native and foreign white population, the colored population, the number of each class in the Penitentiaries, the proportion of the convicts to the whole number of each class, the proportion of colored convicts over the foreign and also over the native whites, in the four States named, for the year 1850:

Classes, etc.	Mass.	N. York.	Penn.	Ohio.
NATIVE WHITES,	819,044	2,388,830	1,953,276	1,732,698
In the Penitentiary,	264	835	205	291
Being 1 out of	3,102	2,860	9,528	5,954
				218,099
FOREIGN WHITES,	163,598	655,224	303,105	
In the Penitentiary,	125	545	123	71
Being 1 out of	1,308	1,202	2,464	3,077
	9,064	49,069	53,626	25,279
COLORED POPULATION,				
In the Penitentiary,	47	257	109	44
Being 1 out of	192	190	492	574
Colored convicts over foreign,	6.8 times	6.3 times	5 times	5.3 times
Colored convicts over native whites,	16.1 times	15 times	19.3 times	10.3 times

It appears from these figures, that the amount of crime among the colored people of Massachusetts, in 1850, was $6^8/_{10}$ times greater than the amount among the foreign born population of that State, and that the amount, in the four States named, among the free colored people, averages *five-and-three-quarters* times more, in proportion to their numbers, than it does among the foreign population, and over *fifteen* times more than it does among the native whites. It will be instructive, also, to note the *moral condition* of the free colored people in Massachusetts, the great center of abolitionism, where they have enjoyed equal rights ever since 1780. Strange to say, there is nearly three times as much among them, in that State, as exists among those of Ohio! More than this will be useful to note, as it regards the direction of the *emigration* of the free colored people. Massachusetts, in 1850, had but 2,687 colored persons born out of the State, while Ohio had 12,662 born out of her limits. Take another fact: the increase, *per cent.*, of the colored population, in the whole New England States, was, during the ten years, from 1840 to 1850, but $1^{71}/_{100}$, while in Ohio, it was, during that time, $45^{76}/_{100}0$.

There is another point worthy of notice. Though the New England abolition States have offered equal political rights to the colored man, it has afforded him little temptation to emigrate into their bounds. On the contrary, several of these States have been diminishing their free colored population, for many years past, and none of them can have had accessions of colored immigrants; as is abundantly proved by the fact, that their additions, of this class of persons, have not exceeded the natural increase of the resident colored population.[71] Another fact is equally as instructive. It will be noted, that, in Ohio, the largest increase of the free colored population, is in the anti-abolition counties—the abolition counties, often, having increased very little, indeed, between 1840 and 1850. But the most curious fact is, that the largest majorities for the abolition candidate for governor, in 1855, were in the counties having the fewest colored people, while the largest majorities against him, were in those having the largest numbers of free negroes and mullatoes.[72] From these facts, both in regard to New England and Ohio, one of two conclusions may be logically deduced: Either the colored people find so little sympathy from the abolitionists, that they will not live among them; or else their presence, in any community, in large numbers, tends to cure the whites of all tendencies toward practical abolitionism!

CHAPTER XVI

Disappointment of English and American Abolitionists—Their failure attributed to the inherent evils of Slavery—Their want of discrimination—The differences in the system in the British Colonies and in the United States—Colored people of United States vastly in advance of all others—Success of the Gospel among the Slaves—*Democratic Review* on African civilization—Vexation of Abolitionists at their failure—Their apology not to be accepted—Liberia attests its falsity—The barrier to the colored man's elevation removable only by Colonization—Colored men begin to see it—Chambers, of Edinburgh—His testimony on the crushing effects of New England's treatment of colored people—Charges Abolitionists with insincerity—Approves Colonization—Abolition violence rebuked by an English clergyman.

THE condition of the free colored people can now be understood. The results, in their case, are vastly different from what was anticipated, when British philanthropists succeeded in West India emancipation. They are very different, also, from what was expected by American abolitionists: so different, indeed, that their disappointment is fully manifested, in the extracts made from their published documents. As an apology for the failure, it seems to be their aim to create the belief, that the dreadful moral depravation, existing in the West Indies, is wholly owing to the demoralizing tendencies of slavery. They speak of this effect as resulting from laws inherent in the system, which have no exceptions, and must be equally as active in the United States as in the British colonies. But in their zeal to cast odium on slavery, they prove too much—for, if this be true, it follows, that the slave population of the United States must be equally debased with that of Jamaica, and as much disqualified to discharge the duties of freemen, as both have been subjected to the operations of the same system. This is not all. The logic of the argument would extend even to our free colored people, and include them, according to the American Missionary Association, in the dire effects of "that enduring legacy which, with its foul, pestilential influences, still blights, like the mildew of death, every thing in society that should be lovely, virtuous, and of good report." Now, were it believed, generally, that the colored people of the United States are equally as degraded as those of Jamaica, upon what grounds could any one advocate the admission of the blacks to equal social and political privileges with the whites? Certainly, no Christian family or community would willingly admit such men to terms of social or political equality! This, we repeat, is the logical conclusion from the Reports of the American Missionary Association and the American and Foreign Anti-Slavery Society—a conclusion, too, the more certain, as it makes no exceptions between the condition of the colored people under the slavery of Jamaica and under that of the United States.

But in this, as in much connected with slavery, abolitionists have taken too limited a view of the subject. They have not properly discriminated between the effects of the original barbarism of the negroes, and those produced by the more or less favorable influences to which they were afterward subjected under slavery. This point deserves special notice. According to the best authorities, the colored people of Jamaica, for nearly three hundred years, were entirely without the gospel; and it gained a permanent footing among them, only at a few points, at their emancipation, twenty-five years ago; so that, when liberty reached them, the great mass of the Africans, in the British West Indies, were heathen.[73] Let us understand the reason of this. Slavery is not an element of human progress, under which the mind necessarily becomes enlightened; but Christianity is the *primary* element of progress, and can elevate the savage, whether in bondage or in freedom, if its principles are taught him in his youth. The slavery of Jamaica began with savage men. For three hundred years, its slaves were destitute of the gospel, and their barbarism was left to perpetuate itself. But in the United States, the Africans were brought under the influence of Christianity, on their first introduction, over two hundred and thirty years since, and have continued to enjoy its teachings, in a greater or less degree, to the present moment. The disappearance from among our colored people, of the savage condition of the human mind—the incapacity to comprehend religious truths— and its continued existence among those of Jamaica, can now be understood. The opportunities enjoyed by the former, for advancement, over the latter, have been *six* to *one*. With these facts before the mind, it is not difficult to perceive that the colored population of Jamaica can not but still labor under the disadvantages of hereditary barbarism and involuntary servitude, with the superadded misfortune of being inadequately supplied with Christian instruction, along with their recent acquisition of freedom. But while all this must be admitted, of the colored people of Jamaica, it is not true of those of our own country; for, long since, they have cast off the heathenism of their fathers, and have become enlightened in a very encouraging degree. Hence it is, that the colored people of the United States, both bond and free, have made vastly greater progress, than those of the British West Indies, in their knowledge of moral duties and the requirements of the gospel; and hence, too, it is, that Gerrit Smith is right, in asserting that the demoralized condition of the great mass of the free colored people, in our cities, is inexcusable, and deserving of the utmost reprobation, because it is *voluntary*—they knowing their duty but abandoning themselves to degrading habits.

This brings us to another point of great moment. It will be denied by but few—and by none maintaining the natural equality of the races—that the free colored people of the United States are sufficiently enlightened, to be elevated by education, in an encouraging degree, where proper restraints from vice, and encouragements to virtue prevail. A large portion, even, of the slave population, are similarly enlightened. We speak not of the state of the morals of either class.

As the public are not well informed, in relation to the extent to which the religious instruction of the slaves at the South prevails, the following information will prove interesting, and show that a good work has long been in progress, and has been producing its fruits:

"The South Carolina Methodist Conference have a missionary committee devoted entirely to promoting the religious instruction of the slave population, which has been in existence twenty-six years. The Report[74] of the last year shows a greater degree of activity than is generally known. They have twenty-six missionary stations in which thirty-two missionaries are employed. The Report affirms that public opinion in South Carolina is decidedly in favor of the religious instruction of slaves, and that it has become far more general and systematic than formerly. It also claims a great degree of success to have attended the labors of the missionaries."

The Report of the Missionary Board, of the Louisiana Conference, of the Methodist Episcopal Church, 1855, says:[75]

"It is stated upon good authority, that the number of colored members in the Church South, exceeds that of the entire membership of all the Protestant missions in the world. What an enterprise is this committed to our care! The position we, of the Methodist Church South, have taken for the African, has, to a great extent, cut us off from the sympathy of the Christian Church throughout the world; and it behooves us to make good this position in the sight of God, of angels, of men, of churches, and to our own consciences, by presenting before the throne of His glory multitudes of the souls of these benighted ones abandoned to our care, as the seals of our ministry. Already Lousiana promises to be one vast plantation. Let us—we must gird ourselves for this Heaven-born enterprise of supplying the pure gospel to the slave. The great question is, How can the greatest number be preached to?—The building roadside chapels is as yet the best solution of it. In some cases planters build so as to accommodate adjoining plantations, and by this means the preacher addresses three hundred or more slaves, instead of one hundred or less. Economy of this kind is absolutely essential where the labor of the missionary is so much needed and demanded.

"On the Lafourche and Bayou Black Missionwork, several chapels are in process of erection, upon a plan which enables the slave, as his master, to make an offering towards building a house of God. Instead of money, the hands subscribe labor. Timber is plenty; many of the servants are carpenters. Upon many of the plantations are saw mills. Here is much material; what hindereth that we should build a church on every tenth plantation? Let us maintain our policy steadily. Time and diligence are required to effect substantial good, especially in this department of labor. Let us continue to ask for buildings adapted to the worship of God, and set apart; to urge, when practicable, the preaching to blacks in the presence of their masters, their overseers, and the neighbors generally."

"One of the effects of the great revival among colored people has been the establishment of a regular system of prayer-meetings for their benefit. Meetings are held every night during the week at the tobacco factories, the proprietors of which have been kind enough to place those edifices at the disposal of the colored brethren. The owners of the several factories preside over these meetings, and the most absolute good conduct is exhibited."[76]

"In Newbern, N. C., the slaves have a large church of their own, which is well attended. They pay a salary of $500 per annum to their white minister. They have likewise a negro preacher in their employ, whom they purchased from his master.[77]

And Newbern in this respect is not isolated. For in nearly every town of any size in the Southern States, the colored people have their churches, and what is more than is always known at the North, *they sustain their churches and pay their ministers,*[78]

"*Resolved,* that the religious instruction of our *colored population* be affectionately and earnestly commended to the ministry and eldership of our churches generally, as opening to us a field of most obligatory and interesting Christian effort, in which we are called to labor more faithfully and fully, by our regard for our social interests, as well as by the higher considerations of duty to God and the souls of our fellow men.[79]

The following extracts are copied from the *New York Observer*, of the present year:

The Presbytery of Roanoke, Virginia, (O. S.) has addressed a Pastoral letter, on the instruction of the colored people, to the churches under its care, and ordered the same to be read in all the churches of the Presbytery, in those that are vacant, as well as where there are pastors or stated supplies. It commences by saying: "Among the important interests of the kingdom of our Lord Jesus Christ, which have claimed our special attention since the organization of the Presbytery in April last,—that the work of the Lord may be vigorously and efficiently carried forward within our bounds,—*the religious instruction of the colored people*, is hardly to be placed second to any other." After speaking of the obstacles and encouragements to the work, it gives the following statistics:

"In the Presbytery of Charleston, S. C., 1637 out of 2889 members, or considerably over one-half, are colored. In the whole Synod of South Carolina, 5,009 out of 13,074, are colored members. The Presbyteries of Mississippi and Central Mississippi, of Tuscaloosa and South Alabama, of Georgia, of Concord, and Fayetteville, also show many churches with large proportions of colored communicants, from one-third to one-seventh of the whole. Our own Presbytery reports 276 out of 1737 members. In the whole of the above mentioned bodies, there are 9,076 colored, out of 33,667 communicants. Among the churches of these Presbyteries, we find twenty with an aggregate colored membership of 3,600, or an average of 130 to each. We find also, such large figures as these, 260, 333, 356, 525! These facts speak for themselves and forbid discouragement."

Speaking of the obligations to instruct this class, the letter says:

"But these people are *among* us, at our doors, in our own fields, and around our firesides! If they need instruction, then the command of our Lord, and every obligation of benevolence, call us to the work of teaching them, with all industry, the doctrines of Christ. The *first and kindest* outgoings of our Christian compassion should be toward them. They are not only near us, but are also entirely *dependent* upon us. As to all means of securing religious privileges for themselves, and as to energy and self-directing power, they are but children,—forced to look to their masters for every supply. From this arises an obligation, at once imperative, and of most solemn and momentous significance to us, to make thorough provision for their religious instruction, to the full extent that we are able to provide it for ourselves. This obligation acquires great additional force when it is further considered, that besides proximity and dependence, they are indeed *members of our 'households*.' As the three hundred and eighteen 'trained servants' of Abraham were 'born in his own house;' i. e., were born and bred as members of his *household*, so are our servants. Of course no argument is needed, to show that every man is bound by high and sacred obligations, for the discharge of which he must give account, to provide his *family* suitably, or to the extent of his ability, with the means of grace and salvation.

After dwelling on the duties of the ministry, the letter goes on:

"But the work of Christianizing our colored population can never be accomplished by the labors of the ministry alone, unaided by the hearty co-operation of families, by carrying on a system of *home instruction. We must begin with the children.* For if the children of our servants be left to themselves during their early years, this neglect must of necessity beget two enormous evils. Evil habits will be rapidly acquired and strengthened; since if children are not learning good, they will be learning what is bad. And having thus grown up both ignorant and vicious, they will have no inclination to go to the Lord's house; or if they should go, their minds will be found so dark, so entirely unacquainted with the rudimental language and truths of the gospel, that much of the preaching must at first prove unintelligible, unprofitable at the time, and so uninteresting as to discourage further attendance. In every regard, therefore, masters are bound to see that religious instruction is provided at home for their people, especially for the young.

"If there be no other to undertake the work, (the mistress, or the children of the family,) the master is bound to deny himself and discharge the duty. It is for him to see that the thing is properly done; for the whole responsibility rests on him at last. It usually, however, devolves upon the mistress, or upon the younger members of the family, where there are children qualified for it, to perform this service. Some of our young men, and, *to their praise be it spoken*, still more of our young women, have willingly given themselves to this self-denying labor; in aid of their parents, or as a duty which they themselves owe to Christ their Redeemer, and to their fellow creatures. We take this occasion, gladly, to bid all these 'God speed' in their work of love. Co-workers together with us, we praise you for this. We bid you take courage. Let no dullness, indifference, or neglect, weary out your patience. You are laboring for Christ, and for precious souls. You are doing a work the importance of which *eternity* will fully reveal. You will be blessed, too, in your deed even now. This labor will prove to you an important means of grace. You will have something to pray for, and will enjoy the pleasing consciousness, that you are not idlers in the Lord's vineyard. You will be winning stars for your crowns of rejoicing through eternity. Grant that it will cost you much self-denial. Can you, notwithstanding, consent to see these immortal beings growing up in ignorance and vice, at your very doors?

"The methods of carrying on the home instruction are various, and we are abundantly supplied with the needful facilities. We need not name the reading of the Bible; and judiciously selected sermons, to be read to the adults when they cannot attend preaching, should not be omitted. Catechetical instruction, by means of such excellent aids as our own 'Catechism for young children,' and 'Jones' Catechism of Scripture doctrine and practice,' will of course be resorted to; together with teaching them *hymns* and *singing with them*. The reading to them, for variety, such engaging and instructive stories as are found in the 'Children's column' of some of our best religious papers; and suitable Sabbath school, or other juvenile books, such as 'The Peep of Day,' 'Line upon Line,' etc., will, in many cases, prove an excellent aid, in imbuing their minds with religious truth. *Masters should not spare expense or trouble*, to provide liberally these various helps to those who take this work in hand, to aid and encourage them to the utmost in their self-denying toil.

"Brethren, the time is propitious to urge your attention to this important duty. A deep and constantly increasing interest in the work, is felt throughout the South. Just at this time, also, extensively throughout portions of our territory, an unusual awakening has been showing itself among the colored people. It becomes us, and it is of vital importance on every account, by judicious instruction, both to guide the movement, and to improve the opportunity.

"We commend this whole great interest to the Divine blessing; and, under God, to your conscientious reflection, to devise the proper ways; and to your faithful Christian zeal, to accomplish whatever your wisdom may devise and approve."

The *Mobile Daily Tribune*, in referring to the religious training of the slaves, says:[80]

"Few persons are aware of the efforts that are continually in progress, in a quiet way, in the various Southern States, for the moral and religious improvement of the negroes—of the number of clergymen of good families, accomplished education, and often of a high degree of talent, who devote their whole time and energies to this work; or of the many laymen—almost invariably slaveholders themselves—who sustain them by their purses and by their assistance as catechists, Sunday school teachers, and the like. These men do not make platform speeches, or talk in public on the subject of their 'mission,' or theorize about the 'planes' on which they stand: they are too busy for this, but they work on quietly in labor and self-denial, looking for a sort of reward very different from the applause bestowed upon stump agitators. Their work is a much less noisy one, but its results will be far more momentous.

"We have very limited information on this subject, for the very reasons just mentioned, but enough to give some idea of the zeal with which these labors are prosecuted by the various Christian denominations. Thus, among the Old School Presbyterians it is stated that about one hundred ministers are engaged in the religious instruction of the negroes exclusively. In South Carolina alone there are forty-five churches or chapels of the Episcopal Church, appropriated exclusively to negroes; thirteen clergymen devote to them their whole time, and twenty-seven a portion of it; and one hundred and fifty persons of the same faith are engaged in imparting to them catechetical instruction. There are other States which would furnish similar statistics if they could be obtained.

"It is in view of such facts as these, that one of our cotemporaries, (the *Philadelphia Inquirer,*) though not free from a certain degree of anti-slavery proclivity, makes the following candid admission:

"'The introduction of African slavery into the colonies of North America, though doubtless brought about by wicked means, may in the end accomplish great good to Africa; a good, perhaps, to be effected in no other way. Hundreds and thousands have already been saved, temporally and spiritually, who otherwise must have perished. Through these and their descendants it is that civilization and Christianity have been sent back to the perishing millions of Africa.'"

The Fourteenth Annual Report of the Missionary Society of the Methodist Episcopal Church South, 1859, says:

"In our colored missions great good has been accomplished by the labors of the self-sacrificing and zealous missionaries.

"This seems to be at home our most appropriate field of labor. By our position we have direct access to those for whom these missions are established. Our duty and obligation in regard to them are evident. Increased facilities are afforded us, and open doors invite our entrance and full occupancy. The real value of these missions is often overlooked or forgotten by *Church census-takers* and statistic-reporters of our benevolent associations. We can but repeat that this field, which seems almost, by common consent, to be left for our occupancy, is one of the most important and promising in the history of missions. At home even its very humility obscures, and abroad a mistaken philanthropy repudiates its claims. But still the fact exists; and when we look at the large number of faithful, pious, and self-sacrificing missionaries engaged in the work, the wide field of their labors, and the happy thousands who have been savingly converted to God through their instrumentality, we can but perceive the propriety and justice of assigning to these missions the prominence we have. Indeed, the subject assumes an importance beyond the conception even of those more directly engaged in this great work, when it is remembered that these missions absolutely number more converts to Christianity, according to statistics given, than all the members of all other missionary societies combined."

The Tennessee Conference of the Methodist Episcopal Church South, in their Report for 1859, says:

"It is gratifying that so much has been done for the evangelization of this people. In addition to the missions presented in our report, thousands of this people are served by preachers in charge of circuits and stations. But still a great work remains to be accomplished among the negroes within your limits. New missions are needed, and increased attention to the work in this department generally demanded. Heaven devolves an immense responsibility upon us with reference to these sable sons of Ham. Providence has thrown them in our midst, not merely to be our household and agricultural servants, but to be served by us with the blessed gospel of the Son of God. Let us then, in the name of Him who made it a special sign of his Messiahship that the poor had the gospel preached unto them—let us in his name go forth, bearing the bread of life to these poor among us, and opening to them all the sources of consolation and encouragement afforded by the religion of Jesus."

The Texas Conference of the Methodist Episcopal Church South, in their Report for 1859, say:

"At the last Conference, Gideon W. Cottingham and David W. Fly were appointed Conference African missionaries, whose duties were to travel throughout the Conference, visit the planters in person, and organize missions in regions unsupplied. They report an extensive field open, and truly white unto the harvest, and have succeeded in organizing several important missions. All the planters, questioned upon the subject, were willing to give the missionary access to their servants, to preach and catechize, not only on the Sabbath, but during the week. And this willingness was not confined to the professors alone, but the deepest interest was displayed by many who make no pretensions to religion whatever. An interest shown not merely by giving the missionary access to their servants, but by their pledging their prompt support. The servants themselves receive the word with the utmost eagerness. They are hungering for the bread of life; our tables are loaded. Shall not these starving souls be fed? Cases of appalling destitution are found: numbers who heard for the first time the word of life listened eagerly to the wonders it unfolded. The Greeks are truly at our doors, heathens growing up in our midst, revival fire flames around them, a polar frost within their hearts. God help the Church to take care of these perishing souls! Our anniversaries are usually scenes of unmingled joy. With our sheaves in our hands, we come from the harvest field, and though sad that so little has been done, yet rejoicing that we have the privilege of laying any pledge of devotion upon the altar."

The Mississippi Conference of the Methodist Episcopal Church, in their Report for 1859, say:

"We are cheered to see a growing interest among our planters and slave-owners in our *domestic missions*. Still that interest is not what the importance of the subject demands. While few are willing to bar their servants all gospel privileges, there is a great want in many places of suitable houses for public worship. Too many masters think that to permit the missionary to come on the plantation, and preach in the gin, or mill, or elsewhere, as circumstances may dictate, is their only duty, especially if the missionary gets his bread. None of the attendant circumstances of a neat church, and suitable Sunday apparel, etc., to cheer and gladden the heart on the holy Sabbath, and cause its grateful thanksgiving to go up as clouds of incense before Him, are thought necessary by many masters.

"Notwithstanding, we are cheered by a brightening prospect. Christian masters are building churches for their servants. Owners in many places are adopting the wise policy of erecting their churches so as to bring two, three, or more plantations together for preaching. This plan is so consonant with the gospel economy, and so advantageous every way, that it must become the uniform practice of all our missionary operations among the slaves. Our late Conference wisely adopted a resolution, encouraging the building of churches for the accommodation of several plantations together, wherever it can be done."

The South Carolina Conference of the Methodist Episcopal Church, in their Report for 1859, say:

"Meanwhile the increasing claims of the destitute colored population must not be ignored. New fields are opening before us, the claims of which are pressed with an earnestness which nothing but deeply-felt necessity could dictate. And the question is pressed upon us, What shall we do? Must not the contributions of the Church be more liberal and more systematic? Must not the friends of the enterprise become more zealous? Will not the wealthy patrons of our society, whose people are served, contribute a sum equal in the aggregate to the salary of the missionaries who serve their people? This done, and every claim urged upon your Board shall be honored.

"This is wondrous work! God loves it, honors it, blesses it! He has crowned it with success. The old negro has abandoned his legendary rites, and has sought and found favor with God through Jesus Christ. The catechumens have received into their hearts the gracious instructions given by the missionary, and scores of them are converted annually, and become worthy members of the Church. Here lies the most inviting field of labor. To instruct these children of Ham in the plan of salvation, to preoccupy their minds with "the truth as it is in Jesus," to see them renounce the superstitions of their forefathers, and embrace salvation's plan, would make an angel's heart rejoice."

Failing in securing the Reports of the Baptists at the South, we are unable to exhibit in detail, their operations among the slave population. The same failure has also occurred in reference to the Cumberland Presbyterians, and some of the other denominations at the South. The statistics, taken from the *Southern Baptist Register*, will indicate the extent of their success. The following statement made up from the Annual Reports of the Churches named, or from the *Register*, shows the extent to which the slave population, in the entire South, have been brought under the influence of the gospel, and led to profess their faith in the Saviour:

Methodist Episcopal Church South,	188,000
Methodist Episcopal Church North,[81] in Va. and Md.,	15,000
Missionary and Anti-Missionary Baptist,	175,000
General Assembly Presbyterian, (O. S.,)	12,000
General Assembly Presbyterian, (N. S.,) estimated	6,000
Cumberland Presbyterians,	20,000
Protestant Episcopal Church, estimated	7,000
Christian Church,	10,000
All other denominations,	20,000
Total	453,000

The remark has been made, in two of the reports quoted, that the number of slaves brought into the Christian Church, as a consequence of the introduction of the African race into the United States, exceeds all the converts made, throughout the heathen world, by the whole missionary force employed by Protestant Christendom. Newcomb's Encyclopedia of Missions, 1856, gives the whole number of converts in the Protestant Christian missions in Asia, Africa, Pacific islands, West Indies, and North American Indians at 211,389; but more recent estimates make the number approximate 250,000: thus showing that the number of African converts in the Southern States, is almost double the whole number of heathen converts. It is well enough to observe here, that these facts are not given to prove that slavery should be adopted as a means of converting the heathen, but to call attention to the mode in which Divine Providence is working for the salvation of the African race.

Our opinion as to the advancement of the free colored people of the United States, in general intelligence, does not stand alone. It is sustained by high authority, not of the abolition school. The *Democratic Review*, of 1852,[82] when discussing the question of their ability to conquer and civilize Africa, says:

"The negro race has, among its freemen in this country, a mass of men who are eminently fitted for deeds of daring. They have generally been engaged in employments which give a good deal of leisure, and stimulus toward improvement of the mind. They have associated much more freely with the cultivated and intelligent white than even with their own color of the same humble station; and on such terms as to enable them to acquire much of his spirit, and knowledge, and valor. The free blacks among us are not only confident and well informed, but they have almost all seen something of the world. They are pre-eminently locomotive and perambulating. In rail roads, and hotels, and stages, and steamers, they have been placed incessantly in contact with the news, the views, the motives, and the ideas of the day. Compare the free black with ordinary white men without advantages, and he stands well. Add to this cultivation, that the negro body is strong and healthy, and the negro mind keen and bright, though not profound nor philosophical, and you have at once a formidable warrior, with a little discipline and knowledge of weapons. There is no doubt that the picked American free blacks, would be five times, ten times as efficient in the field of battle as the same number of native Africans."

Why is it then, that the efforts for the moral elevation of the free colored people, have been so unsuccessful? Before answering this question, it is necessary to call attention to the fact, that abolitionists seem to be sadly disappointed in their expectations, as to the progress of the free colored people. Their vexation at the stubborness of the negroes, and the consequent failure of their measures, is very clearly manifested in the complaining language, used by Gerrit Smith, toward the colored people of the eastern cities, as well as by the contempt expressed by the American Missionary Association, for the colored preachers of Canada. They had found an apology, for their want of success in the United States, in the presence and influence of colonizationists; but no such excuse can be made for their want of success in Canada and the West Indies. Having failed in their anticipations, now they would fain shelter themselves under the pretense, that a people once subjected to slavery, even when liberated, can not be elevated in a single generation; that the case of adults, raised in bondage, like heathen of similar age, is hopeless, and their children, only, can make such progress as will repay the missionary for his toil. But they will not be allowed to escape the censure due to their want of discrimination and foresight, by any such plea; as the success of the Republic of Liberia, conducted from infancy to independence, almost wholly by liberated slaves, and those who were born and raised in the midst of slavery, attests the falsity of their assumption.

But to return. Why have the efforts for the elevation of the free colored people, not been more successful? On this point our remarks may be limited to our own free colored people. The barrier to their progress here, exists not so much in their want of capacity, as in the absence of the incitements to virtuous action, which are constantly stimulating the white man to press onward and upward in the formation of character and the acquisition of knowledge. There is no position in church or state, to which the poorest white boy, in the common school, may not aspire. There is no post of honor, in the gift of his country, that is legally beyond his reach. But such encouragements to noble effort, do not and cannot reach the colored man, and he remains with us a depressed and disheartened being. Persuading him to remain in this hopeless condition, has been the great error of the abolitionists. They accepted Jefferson's views in relation to emancipation, but rejected his opinions as to the necessity of separating the races; and thus overlooked the teachings of history, that two races, differing so widely as to prevent their amalgamation by marriage, can never live together, in the same community, but as superiors and inferiors—the inferior remaining subordinate to the superior. The encouraging hopes held out to the colored people, that this law would be inoperative upon them, has led only to disappointment. Happily, this delusion is nearly at an end; and some of them are beginning to act on their own judgments. They find themselves so scattered and peeled, that there is not another half a million of men in the world, so enlightened, who are accomplishing so little for their social and moral advancement. They perceive that they are nothing but branches, wrenched from the great African *banyan*, not yet planted in genial soil, and affording neither shelter nor food to the beasts of the forest or the fowls of the air—their roots unfixed in the earth, and their tender shoots withering as they hang pendent from their boughs.

That this is no exaggerated picture of the discouragements surrounding our free colored people, is fully confirmed by the testimony of impartial witnesses. Chambers, of Edinburgh, who recently made the tour of the United States, investigated this point very carefully. His opinions on the subject have been published, and are so discriminating and truthful, that we must quote the main portion of them. In speaking of the agitation of the question of slavery, he says:

"For a number of years, as is well known, there has been much angry discussion on the subject between the Northern and Southern States; and at times the contention has been so great, as to lead to mutual threats of a dismemberment of the Union. A stranger has no little difficulty in understanding how much of this war of words is real, and how much is merely an explosion of *bunkum*. . . . . I repeat, it is difficult to understand what is the genuine public feeling on this entangled question; for with all the demonstrations in favor of freedom in the North, there does not appear in that quarter to be any practical relaxation of the usages which condemn persons of African descent to an inferior social status. There seems, in short, to be a fixed notion throughout the whole of the States, whether slave or free, that the colored is by nature a subordinate race; and that, in no circumstances, can it be considered equal to the white. Apart from commercial views, this opinion lies at the root of American slavery; and the question would need to be argued less on political and philanthropic than on physiological grounds. . . . . I was not a little surprised to find, when speaking a kind word for at least a very unfortunate, if not brilliant race, that the people of the Northern States, though repudiating slavery, did not think more favorably of the negro character than those further South. Throughout Massachusetts, and other New England States, likewise in the States of New York, Pennsylvania, etc., there is a rigorous separation of the white and black races. . . . . The people of England, who see a negro only as a wandering curiosity, are not at all aware of the repugnance generally entertained toward persons of color in the United States: it appeared to amount to an absolute monomania. As for an alliance with one of the race, no matter how faint the shade of color, it would inevitably lead to a loss of caste, as fatal to social position and family ties as any that occurs in the Brahminical system. . . . .

"Glad to have had an opportunity of calling attention to many cheering and commendable features in the social system of the Americans, I consider it not less my duty to say, that in their general conduct toward the colored race, a wrong is done which can not be alluded to except in terms of the deepest sorrow and reproach. I can not think without shame of the pious and polished New Englanders adding to their offenses on this score the guilt of hypocrisy. Affecting to weep over the sufferings of imaginary dark-skinned heroes and heroines; denouncing, in well-studied platform oratory, the horrid sin of reducing human beings to the abject condition of chattels; bitterly scornful of Southern planters for hard-hearted selfishness and depravity; fanatical on the subject of abolition; wholly frantic at the spectacle of fugitive slaves seized and carried back to their owners—these very persons are daily surrounded by manumitted slaves, or their educated descendants, yet shrink from them as if the touch were pollution, and look as if they would expire at the bare idea of inviting one of them to their house or table. Until all this is changed, the Northern abolitionists place themselves in a false position, and do damage to the cause they espouse. If they think that negroes are MEN, let them give the world an evidence of their sincerity, by moving the reversal of all those social and political arrangements which now, in the free States, exclude persons of color, not only from the common courtesies of life, but from the privileges and honors of citizens. I say, until this is done, the uproar about abolition is a delusion and a snare. . . . .

"While lamenting the unsatisfactory condition, present and prospective, of the colored population, it is gratifying to consider the energetic measures that have been adopted by the African Colonization Society, to transplant, with their own consent, free negroes from America to Liberia. Viewing these endeavors as, at all events, a means of encouraging emancipation, checking the slave trade, and, at the same time, of introducing Christianity and civilized usages into Africa, they appear to have been deserving of more encouragement than they have had the good fortune to receive. Successful only in a moderate degree, the operations of this society are not likely to make a deep impression on the numbers of the colored population; and the question of their disposal still remains unsettled."

That the Christian churches of the South are pursuing the true policy for the moral welfare of the slave population, will be admitted by every right minded man. The present chapter cannot be more appropriately closed, than by quoting the language of Rev. J. Waddington, of England, at a meeting in behalf of the American Missionary Association, held in Boston, July, 1859. The speakers had been very violent in their denunciations of slavery, and when Mr. Waddington came to speak, he thus rebuked their unchristian spirit:

"I have," said Mr. Waddington, "a strong conviction, that freedom can never come but of vital Christianity. It is not born of the intellect, it is not the product of the conscience; it can never be the result of the sword. It was with extreme horror that I heard the assertion made last night, that it must be through a baptism of blood that freedom must come. Never! never! The sword can destroy, it can never create. What do we want for freedom? Expansion of the heart. That we should honor other men; that we should be concerned for other men. What is it that causes slavery and oppression? Selfishness, intense, self-destroying selfishness if you will. Nothing can exorcise that selfishness but the constraining love of Christ. The gospel alone, by the Spirit of God, can waken freedom in men, in families, in nations."

Mr. Waddington, also remarked, that "every thing in America was extremely wonderful and surprising to him; and nothing more surprised him than the burning words with which his ministerial friends pelted each other; yet he had no doubt they were the kindest men in the world. He thought it was not intended that any harm should be done, but only that the cause of truth should be advanced."[83]

CHAPTER XVII

Failure of free colored people in attaining an equality with the whites—Their failure also in checking Slavery—Have they not aided in its extension? Yes—Facts in proof of this view—Abolitionists bad Philosophers—Colored men's influence destructive of their hopes—Summary manner in which England acts in their removal—Lord Mansfield's decision—Granville Sharp's labors and their results—Colored immigration into Canada—Information supplied by Major Lachlan—Demoralized condition of the blacks as indicated by the crimes they committed—Elgin Association—Public meeting protesting against its organization—Negro meeting at Toronto—Memorial of municipal council—Negro riot at St. Catherines—Col. Prince and the Negroes—Later cases of presentation by Grand Jury—Opinion of the Judge—Darkening prospects of the colored race—Views of Rev. Henry Ward Beecher—Their accuracy—The lesson they teach.

BUT little progress, it will be seen, has been made, by the free colored people, toward an approximation of equality with the whites. Have they succeeded better in aiding in the abolition of slavery? They have not, as is abundantly demonstrated by the triumph of the institution. This is an important point for consideration, as the principal object influencing them to remain in the country, was, that they might assist in the liberation of their brethren from bondage. But their agency in the attempts made to abolish the institution having failed, a more important question arises, as to whether the free colored people, by refusing to emigrate, may not have contributed to the advancement of slavery? An affirmative answer must be given to this inquiry. Nor is a protracted discussion necessary to prove the assertion.

One of the objections urged with the greatest force against colonization, is, its tendency, as is alleged, to increase the value of slaves by diminishing their numbers. "Jay's Inquiry," 1835, presents this objection at length; and the Report of the "Anti-Slavery Society of Canada," 1853, sums it up in a single proposition thus:

"The first effect of beginning to reduce the number of slaves, by colonization, would be to increase the market value of those left behind, and thereby increase the difficulty of setting them free."

The practical effect of this doctrine, is to discourage all emancipations; to render eternal the bondage of each individual slave, unless all can be liberated; to prevent the benevolence of one master from freeing his slaves, lest his more selfish neighbor should be thereby enriched; and to leave the whole system intact, until its total abolition can be effected. Such philanthropy would leave every individual, of suffering millions, to groan out a miserable existence, because it could not at once effect the deliverance of the whole. This objection to colonization can be founded only in prejudice, or is designed to mislead the ignorant. The advocates of this doctrine do not practice it, or they would not promote the escape of fugitives to Canada.

But abolitionists object not only to the colonization of liberated slaves, as tending to perpetuate slavery; they are equally hostile to the colonization of the free colored people, for the same reason. The "American Reform Tract and Book Society," the organ of the abolitionists, for the publication of anti-slavery works, has issued a Tract on "Colonization," in which this objection is stated as follows:

"The Society perpetuates slavery, by removing the free laborer, and thereby increasing the demand for, and the value of, slave labor."

The projectors and advocates of such views may be good philanthropists, but they are bad philosophers. We have seen that the power of American slavery lies in the demand for its products; and that the whole country, North of the sugar and cotton States, is actively employed in the production of provisions for the support of the planter and his slaves, and in consuming the products of slave labor. This is the constant vocation of the whites. And how is it with the blacks? Are they competing with the slaves, in the cultivation of sugar and cotton, or are they also supporting the system, by consuming its products? The latitudes in which they reside, and the pursuits in which they are engaged, will answer this question.

The census of 1850, shows but 40,900 free colored persons in the nine sugar and cotton States, including Texas, Louisiana, Arkansas, Tennessee, Mississippi, Alabama, Georgia, Florida, and South Carolina, while 393,500 are living in the other States. North Carolina is omitted, because it is more of a tobacco and wool-growing, than cotton-producing State.

Of the free colored persons in the first-named States, 19,260 are in the cities and larger towns; while, of the remainder, a considerable number may be in the villages, or in the families of the whites. From these facts it is apparent, that less than 20,000 of the entire free colored population (omitting those of North Carolina,) are in a position to compete with slave labor, while all the remainder, numbering over 412,800, are engaged, either directly or indirectly, in supporting the institution. Even the fugitives escaping to Canada, from having been producers necessarily become consumers of slave-grown products; and, worse still, under the Reciprocity Treaty, they must also become growers of provisions for the planters who continue to hold their brothers, sisters, wives and children, in bondage.

These are the practical results of the policy of the abolitionists. Verily, they, also, have dug their ditches on the wrong side of their breastworks, and afforded the enemy an easy entrance into their fortress. But, "Let them alone; they be blind leaders of the blind. And if the blind lead the blind, both shall fall into the ditch."[84]

But we are not yet prepared to estimate the full extent of the influence, for ill, exerted by the free colored people upon public sentiment. The picture of their degraded moral condition, drawn by the abolitionists, is a dark one indeed, and calculated to do but little toward promoting emancipation, or in placing themselves in a position of equality with the whites. According to their testimony, the condition of the slave, under the restraints of Christian masters, must be vastly more favorable to moral progress, than that of the majority of those who have received their freedom. While they have all the animal appetites and passions fully developed, they seem to remain, intellectually, child-like, with neither the courage nor the foresight enabling them to seize upon fields of enterprise that would lead to wealth and fame. Look at the facts upon this point. They were offered a home and government of their own in Africa, with the control of extensive tropical cultivation; but they rejected the boon, and refused to leave the land of their birth, in the vain belief that they could, by remaining here, assist in wrenching the chains from the slaves of the South. They expected great aid, too, in their work, from the moral effect of West Indian emancipation; but that has failed in the results anticipated, and the free colored laborer is about to be superseded there by imported coolie labor from abroad. They expected, also, that the emigrants and fugitives to Canada, rising into respectability under British laws, would do the race much honor, and show the value of emancipation; but even there the hope has not been realized, and it will be no uncommon thing should the Government set its face against them as most unwelcome visitors. A few scraps of history will be of service, in illustrating the feeling of the subjects of the British North American colonies, in relation to the inroads made upon them by the free colored people.

In 1833, an English military officer, thus wrote:

"There is a settlement of negroes a few miles from Halifax, Nova Scotia, at Hammond's Plains. Any one would have imagined that the Government would have taken warning from the trouble and expense it incurred by granting protection to those who emigrated from the States during the Revolution; 1200 of whom were removed to Sierra Leone in 1792 by their own request. Again when 600 of the insurgent negroes—the Maroons of Jamaica—were transported to Nova Scotia in 1796, and received every possible encouragement to become good subjects, by being granted a settlement at Preston, and being employed upon the fortifications at Halifax; yet they, too, soon became discontented, and being unwilling to earn a livelihood by labor, were, in 1800, removed to the same colony, after costing the island of Jamaica more than $225,000, and a large additional expense to the Province, i. e. Nova Scotia. Notwithstanding which, when the runaway slaves were received on board the fleet, off the Chesapeake, during the late war, permission was granted to them to form a settlement at Hammond's Plains, where the same system of discontent arose—many of the settlers professing that they would prefer their former well-fed life of slavery, in a more congenial climate, and earnestly petitioning to be removed, were sent to Trinidad in 1821. Some few of those who remained are good servants and farmers, disposing of the produce of their lands in the Halifax market; but the majority are idle, roving, and dirty vagabonds."[85]

Thus it appears, that as late as 1821, the policy of the British colonies of North America, was to remove the fugitive negroes from their territories. The 1200 exported from Halifax, in 1792, were fugitive slaves who had joined the English during the American Revolutionary war, and had been promised lands in Nova Scotia; but the Government having failed to meet its pledge, and the climate proving unfavorable, they sought refuge in Africa. These shipments of the colored people, from the British colonies at the North to those of the Tropics, was in accordance with the plan that England had adopted at home, in reference to the same class of persons—that of removing a people who were a public burden, to where they could be self-supporting. This is a matter of some interest, and is deserving of notice in this connection. On the 22d of May, 1772, Lord Mansfield decided the memorable Somerset case, and pronounced it unlawful to hold a slave in Great Britain. The close of that decision reads thus:

"Immemorial usage preserves a positive law, after the occasion or accident which gave rise to it, has been forgotten; and tracing the subject to natural principles, the claim of slavery never can be supported. The power claimed was never in use here, or acknowledged by the law. Upon the whole, we can not say the cause returned is sufficient by the law; therefore the man must be discharged."

Previous to this date, many slaves had been introduced into English families, and, on running away, the fugitives had been delivered up to their masters, by order of the Court of King's Bench, under Lord Mansfield; but now the poor African, no longer hunted as a beast of prey, in the streets of London, slept under his roof, miserable as it might be, in perfect security.[86]

To Granville Sharp belonged the honor of this achievement. By the decision, about 400 negroes were thrown upon their own resources. They flocked to Mr. Sharp as their patron; but considering their numbers, and his limited means, it was impossible for him to afford them adequate relief. To those thus emancipated, others, discharged from the army and navy, were afterward added, who, by their improvidence, were reduced to extreme distress. After much reflection, Mr. Sharp determined to colonize them in Africa; but this benevolent scheme could not be executed at once, and the blacks—indigent, unemployed, despised, forlorn, vicious—became such nuisances, as to make it necessary they should be sent somewhere, and no longer suffered to infest the streets of London.[87]

Private benevolence could not be sufficiently enlisted in their behalf, and fifteen years passed away, when Government, anxious to remove what it regarded as injurious, at last came to the aid of Mr. Sharp, and supplied the means of their transportation and support. In April, 1787, these colored people, numbering over 400, were put on shipboard for Africa, and in the following month were landed in Sierra Leone.[88]

But to return to Canada. We have at hand a flood of information, to enable us to present a true picture of the colored population of that Province, and to discern the feelings entertained toward them by the white inhabitants. On the 27th April, 1841, the Assistant Secretary to Government, addressed MAJOR ROBERT LACHLAN, Chairman of the Quarter Sessions for the Western District, requesting information relating to the colored immigrants in that quarter. Major Lachlan replied at length to the inquiries made, and kept a record of his Report. This volume he has had the goodness to place in our hands, from which to make such extracts as may be necessary to a true understanding of this question.

The Major entered the public service of the British Government in 1805, and was connected with the army in India for twenty years. Having retired from that service, he settled in Canada in 1835, with the intention of devoting himself to agriculture; but he was again called into public life, as sheriff, magistrate, colonel of militia, Chairman of the Quarter Sessions, and Associate Judge at the Assizes. In 1857 he removed to Cincinnati, where he now resides. A true Briton, he is an enemy of the system of slavery; but having been a close observer of the workings of society, under various circumstances, systems of law, degrees of intelligence, and moral conditions, he is opposed to placing two races, so widely diverse as the blacks and whites, upon terms of legal equality; not that he is opposed to the elevation of the colored man, but because he is convinced that, in his present state of ignorance and degradation, the two races cannot dwell together in peace and harmony. This opinion, it will be seen, was the outgrowth of his experience and observation in Canada, and not the result of a prejudice against the African race. The Western District, the field of his official labors, is the main point toward which nearly all the emigration from the States is directed; and the Major had, thus, the best of opportunities for studying this question. Besides the facts of an official nature, in the volume from which we quote, it has a large amount of documentary testimony, from other sources, from which liberal extracts have also been made.

To the Honorable S. B. Harrison, Secretary, etc., etc.

COLCHESTER, 28th *May*, 1841.

"SIR:—I have to apologize for being thus late in acknowledging the receipt of Mr. Assistant Secretary Hopkirk's letter of the 27th ult., requesting me to furnish Government with such information as I might be able to afford, 'respecting the colored people settled in the Western District;'[89] and beg to assure you that the delay has neither arisen from indifference to the task, nor indisposition to comply with the wishes of Government upon the subject—being one upon which I have long and anxiously bent my most serious reflections,—but owing to bad health, and want of leisure, coupled with the difficulty I have experienced, (without entering into an extended correspondence,) in arriving at any thing like a correct account of the gradual *increase* of these people, or even a fair estimate of their present numbers. I trust, therefore, that should the particulars furnished by me upon these heads, be found more meager and defective than might be expected, it will either be assigned to these causes, or to others which may be given in the course of the following remarks: and if these remarks, themselves, be found to be drawn up with more of loose unmethodical freedom than official conciseness, I trust that that feature will rather be regarded in their favor than otherwise.

"The exact period at which the colored people began to make their appearance in the Western District, *as settlers*, I have not been able to ascertain to my satisfaction; but it is generally believed to have been about the time of the War with the Americans, in 1812. Before then, however, there had been a few scattered about, who, generally speaking, had, prior to the passing of the Emancipation Bill, been slaves to different individuals in the District. From 1813 to 1821, the increase was very trifling; and they were generally content to hire themselves out as domestic or farm servants; but about the latter period the desire of several gentlemen residing near Sandwich and Amherstburgh to place settlers on their lands, induced them, in the absence of better, to resort to the unfortunate, impolitic expedient of leasing out or selling small portions of land to colored people on such inviting conditions as not only speedily allowed many of those who had already settled in the country to undertake 'farming on their own account,' but encouraged many more to escape from their American masters, to try their fortunes in this now far-famed 'land of liberty and promise.' The stream having thus begun to flow, the secret workings of the humane, but not unexceptionable abolitionist societies, existing in the American States, speedily widened and deepened the channel of approach, until a flood of colored immigrants, of the very worst classes, has been progressively introduced into the District, which had, last year, reached an aggregate of about 1500 souls, and which threatens to be doubled in the course of a very short time, unless it be within the power of the Government to counteract it;—but which, *if suffered to roll on unchecked*, will sooner or later lead to the most serious, if not most lamentable consequences.

"From my making so strong an observation at the very threshold of my remarks, it will be readily perceived that my opinion of these unfortunate people is unfavorable. I am therefore anxious, before proceeding further, to shield myself from the imputation of either groundless antipathy or pre-indisposition toward men of color, and to have it thoroughly understood that, as far as I can judge of my own feelings, *they* are the very reverse, having not only been warmly in favor of the poor enslaved negro, but having for near twenty years of my life been surrounded by free colored people, and retained my favorable leaning toward even the African race, till some time after my arrival in this Province. Unfortunately, however, for this pre-disposition, as well as for the character of this ill-fated race, my attention was shortly after directed by particular circumstances to the quiet study of their disposition and habits, and ended in a thorough conviction that without a radical change they would ere long, like the snake in the bosom of the husbandman, prove a curse, instead of a benefit to the country which fosters and protects them.

"The first time that I had occasion to express myself thus strongly on the subject, in an official way, was less than two years after my arrival in the District, while holding the office of sheriff,—when, in corresponding with Mr. Secretary Joseph, during the troubles in January, 1838, I, in a postscript to a letter in which I expressed unwillingness to call in aid from other quarters, while our own population were allowed to remain inactive, was led to add the following remarkable words: 'My vote has been equally decided against employing the colored people, except on a similar emergency;—in fact, though a cordial friend to the emancipation of the poor African, I regard the rapidly increasing population rising round us, as destined to be a bitter curse to the District; and do not think our employing them as our *defenders* at all likely to retard the progress of such an event;'—an opinion which all my subsequent observation and experience, whether as a private individual, as Sheriff of the District, as a local Magistrate, as Chairman of the Quarter Sessions, or as an anxious friend to pure British immigration, have only the more strongly confirmed."

After these preliminary remarks, the Records of Major Lachlan, proceed to the details of the various points upon which he was required by Government to report. Much of this, though the whole is interesting, must be omitted in our extracts. In speaking of the several townships to which the colored immigration was directed, he says of Amherstburgh:

"That place may now be regarded as the Western rendezvous of the colored race,—being the point to which all the idle and worthless, as well as the well disposed, first direct their steps, before dispersing over other parts of the District,—a distinction of which it unfortunately bears too evident marks in the great number of petty crimes committed by or brought home to these people,—to the great trouble of the investigating local magistrates, and the still greater annoyance of the inhabitants generally,—arising from the constant nightly depredations committed on their orchards, barns, granaries, sheep-folds, fowl-yards, and even cellars.".... "In Gosfield, I am given to understand their general character is rather above par;.... while in the next adjoining township of Mersea, so much are they disliked by the inhabitants, that they are, in a manner, proscribed by general consent—a colored man being there scarcely suffered to travel along the highroads unmolested.

"The first thing that forcibly struck me, in these people, was a total absence of that modest and unpresuming demeanor which I had been some how led to expect, and the assumption, instead, of a 'free and easy' independence of manner as well as language toward all white inhabitants, except their immediate employers, together with an apparent utter indifference to being hired on reasonable average wages, though, as already stated, seemingly without any visible means of a livelihood, and their also, at all times, estimating the value of their labor on a par, if not above that of the white man. And I had scarcely recovered from my surprise, at such conduct, as a private individual, when, as a magistrate, I was still more astonished at the great amount of not only petty offenses, but of crime of the most atrocious dye, perpetrated by so small a body of strangers compared with the great bulk of the white population: and such still continuing to be the unabating case, Session after Session, Assize after Assize, it at length became so appalling to my feelings, that on being placed in the chair of the Quarter Sessions, I could not refrain from more than once pointing to it in strong language in my charges to the Grand Juries. In July last year, for instance, I was led, in connection with a particular case of larceny, to observe . . . . 'The case itself will, I trust, involve no difficulty so far as the Grand Jury is concerned; but it affords the magistrates another opportunity of lamenting that there should so speedily be furnished no less than five additional instances of the rapid increase of crime in this (hitherto in that respect highly fortunate) District, arising solely from the recent great influx of colored people into it from the neighboring United States,—and who unfortunately not only furnish the major part of the crime perpetrated in the District, but also thereby a very great portion of its rapidly increasing debt,—from the expense attending their maintenance in jail before trial, as well as after conviction!. . . .

"In spite of these solemn admonitions, a large proportion of the criminals tried at the ensuing September Assizes were colored people; and among them were two aggravated cases of rape and arson; the former wantonly perpetrated on a respectable farmer's wife, in this township, to whom the wretch was a perfect stranger; the latter recklessly committed at a merchant's store in the vicinity of Sandwich, for the mere purpose of opening a hole through which to convey away his plunder. And, notwithstanding 'the general jail delivery' that then took place, the greater part of the crimes brought before the following mouth's Quarter Sessions (chiefly larceny and assaults) were furnished by the same people!—a circumstance of so alarming and distressing a character, that I was again led to comment upon it in my charge to the Grand Jury in the following terms. 'Having disposed of the law relating to these offenses, I arrive at a very painful part of nay observations, in once more calling the particular attention of the Grand Jury, as well as the public at large, to the remarkable and appalling circumstance that among a population of near 20,000 souls, inhabiting this District, the greater portion of the crime perpetrated therein should be committed by less than 2,000 refugees from a life of *abject slavery*, to a land of *liberty, protection and comfort*,—and from whom, therefore, if there be such generous feelings as thankfulness and gratitude, a far different line of conduct might reasonably be expected. I allude to the alarming increase of crime still perpetrated by the colored settlers, and who, in spite of the late numerous, harrowing, *convicted examples*, unhappily furnish *the whole of the offenses now likely to be brought before you!*. . . . .

"But, sir, the wide spreading current of crime among this unfortunate race was not to be easily arrested;—and I had long become so persuaded that it must sooner or later force itself upon the notice of the Legislature, that on feeling it my duty to draw the attention of my brother magistrates to the embarrassed state of the District finances, and to the greater portion of its expenses arising from this disreputable source, I was led, in framing the report of a special committee (of which I was chairman) appointed to investigate our pecuniary difficulties, to advert once more to the great undue proportion of our expenses arising from crime committed by so small a number of colored people, compared with the great body of the inhabitants, in the following strong but indisputable language: 'It is with pain and regret that your committee, in conclusion, feel bound to recur to the great additional burthen thrown upon the District, as well as the undeserved stigma cast upon the general character of its population, whether native or immigrant British, by the late great influx of colored people of the worst description from the neighboring States—a great portion of whom appear to have no visible means of gaining a livelihood,—and who, therefore, not only furnish a large proportion of the basest crimes perpetrated in the country, such as murder, rape, arson, burglary, and larceny, besides every other description of minor offense,—untraceable to the *color* of the perpetrators in a miscellaneous published calendar; but also, besides the constant trouble they entail upon magistrates who happen to reside in their neighborhood, produce a large portion of the debt incurred by the District, from the great number committed to and subsisted in prison, etc.; and they would with all respect for the liberty of the subject, and the sincerest good will toward their African brethren generally,—whom they would wish to regard with every kindly feeling, venture to suggest, for the consideration of Government, whether any legislative check can possibly be placed upon the rapid importation of the most worthless of this unfortunate race, such, as the good among themselves candidly lament, has of late inundated this devoted section of the Province, to the great detriment of the claims of the poor emigrant from the mother country upon our consideration, the great additional and almost uncontrollable increase of crime, and the proportionate demoralization of principle among the inhabitants of the country.' . . . . . .

"Notwithstanding all these strenuous endeavors, added to the most serious and impressive admonitions to various criminals after conviction and sentence, no apparent change for the better occurred; for at the Quarter Sessions of last January, the usual preponderance of negro crime struck me so forcibly as again to draw from me, in my charge to the Grand Jury, the following observations: 'I am extremely sorry to be unable to congratulate you or the country on a light calendar, the matters to be brought before you embracing no less than three cases of larceny, and one of enticing soldiers to desert, besides several arising from that ever prolific source, assaults, etc. I cannot, however, pass the former by altogether without once more emphatically remarking, that it is as much to the disgrace of the free colored settlers in our District, as it is creditable to the rest of our population, that the greater part of the culprits to be brought before us are still men of color: and I lament this the more, as I was somewhat in hopes that the earnest admonitions that I had more than once felt it my duty to address to that race, would have been attended with some good effect.'. . . . .

"In spite of all these reiterated, anxious endeavors, the amount of crime exhibited in the Calendar of the following Quarter Sessions, in April last, consisted solely (I think) of five cases of larceny, perpetrated by negroes; and at the late Assizes, held on the 20th instant, out of five criminal cases, one of enticing soldiers to desert, and two of theft, were, as usual, committed by men of color!!!

"Having thus completed a painful retrospect of the appalling amount of crime committed by the colored population in the District at large, compared with the general mass of the white population, I now consider it my duty to advert more particularly to what has been passing more immediately under my own observation in the township of Colchester."

The record from which we quote, has, under this head, the statement of the township collector, as to the moral and social condition of the colored people of the township, in which he says, "that, in addition to the black women there were fourteen yellow ones, and fifteen *white* ones—that they run together like beasts, and that he did not suppose one third of them were married; and further, that they would be a curse to this part of Canada, unless there is something done to put a stop to their settling among the white people.'

In referring to the enlistment of the blacks as soldiers, to the prejudice of the legitimate prospects of the deserving European emigrants, the record says: "With regard to continuing to employ the colored race to discharge—in some instances exclusively, as is now the case at Chatham—the duties of regular soldiers, in such times as these, *in a country peopled by BRITONS*, I regard it as not only impolitic in the extreme, but even *dangerous* also,—besides throwing a stigma of degradation on the honorable profession of which I was for twenty-four years of my life a devoted member. And I even put it to yourself, sir, what would have been your feelings, if, amid the great political excitement prevalent during the late Kent election,[90] there had been a serious disturbance and some unthinking magistrate had called in 'the aid of the military' to quell it, and blood had been shed!—for the thing was within possibility, and for some time gave me much uneasiness. Had such been the case,—what would have been the appalling, and probable, nay, almost *certain* result,—if I may judge from the well known feelings of the white population generally,—*that that unfortunate company would have been instantly turned upon, by men of all parties, and massacred on the spot with their own weapons!*" . . . . . "Allow me, therefore, at all events briefly to remark, that before any thing can be accomplished connected with the moral and religious improvement of the negro settlers, they must be rescued from the hands of the utterly ignorant and uneducated, yet conceited coxcombs of their own color, who assume to themselves the grave character and holy office of ministers and preachers of the gospel, and lead their still more ignorant followers into all the extravagancies of 'Love Feasts' and 'Camp Meetings,' without at all comprehending their import, and at the same time utterly neglecting all other essentials!—an object well deserving of the most serious and anxious consideration of an enlightened Government, as far as those who are already settled in the country are concerned; while it would be a most sound and politic measure to take every lawful step to discourage as much as possible, if we can not altogether *prevent* the further introduction of so objectionable and deleterious a class of settlers into a BRITISH *colony*."... . "Perhaps one of the wisest measures that could be devised—(since our friends, the American abolitionists, will insist on peopling Canada with run-away negro slaves)—will be to throw every possible obstacle in the way of the sadly deteriorating *amalgamation of color* already in progress, by Government allotting, at least, a distinct and separate location to all negro settlers, except those who choose to occupy the humble but useful station of farm and domestic servants; and even, if possible, purchasing back at the public expense, on almost any terms, whatever scattered landed property they may have elsewhere acquired in different parts of the Province."

The Report of Major Lachlan is very extensive, and embraces many topics connected with the question of negro immigration into Canada. His response to Government led to further investigation, and to some legislative action in the Canadian Parliament. The latest recorded communications upon the subject, from his pen, are dated November 9th, 1849, and June 4th, 1850, from which it appears that up to that date, there had been no abatement of the hostile feeling of the whites toward the blacks, nor any improvement in the social and moral condition of the blacks themselves.

In 1849, the Elgin Association went into operation. Its object was to concentrate the colored people at one point, and thus have them in a more favorable position for intellectual and moral culture. A large body of land was purchased in the Township of Raleigh, and offered for sale in small lots to colored settlers. The measure was strongly opposed, and called out expressions of sentiment adverse to it, from the people at large. A public meeting, held in Chatham, August 18, 1849, thus expressed itself:

"The Imperial Parliament of Great Britain has forever banished slavery from the Empire. In common with all good men, we rejoice at the consummation of this immortal act; and we hope, that all other nations may follow the example. Every member of the human family is entitled to certain rights and privileges, and no where on earth are they better secured, enjoyed, or more highly valued, than in Canada. Nature, however, has divided the same great family into distinct species, for good and wise purposes, and it is no less our interest, than it is our duty, to follow her dictates and obey her laws. Believing this to be a sound and correct principle, as well as a moral and a Christian duty, it is with alarm we witness the fast increasing emigration, and settlement among us of the African race; and with pain and regret, do we view the establishment of an association, the avowed object of which is to encourage the settlement in old, well-established communities, of a race of people which is destined by nature to be distinct and separate from us. It is also with a feeling of deep resentment that we look upon the selection of the Township of Raleigh, in this District, as the first portion of our beloved country, which is to be cursed, with a systematic organization for setting the laws of nature at defiance. Do communities in other portions of Canada, feel that the presence of the negro among them is an annoyance? Do they feel that the increase of the colored people among them, and amalgamation its necessary and hideous attendant, is an evil which requires to be checked? With what a feeling of horror, would the people of any of the old settled townships of the eastern portion of this Province, look upon a measure which had for its avowed object, the effect of introducing several hundreds of Africans, into the very heart of their neighborhood, their families interspersing themselves among them, upon every vacant lot of land, their children mingling in their schools, and all claiming to be admitted not only to political, but to social privileges? and when we reflect, too, that many of them must from necessity, be the very worst species of that neglected race; the fugitives from justice; how much more revolting must the scheme appear? How then can you adopt such a measure? We beseech our fellow subjects to pause before they embark in such an enterprise, and ask themselves, 'whether they are doing by us as they would wish us to do unto them.'. . . . Surely our natural position is irksome enough without submitting to a measure, which not only holds out a premium for filling up our district with a race of people, upon whom we can not look without a feeling of repulsion, and who, having been brought up in a state of bondage and servility, are totally ignorant both of their social and political duties; but at the same time makes it the common receptable into which all other portions of the Province are to void the devotees of misery and crime. Look at your prisons and your penitentiary, and behold the fearful preponderance of their black over their white inmates in proportion to the population of each. . . . . We have no desire to show hostility toward the colored people, no desire to banish them from the Province. On the contrary, we are willing to assist in any well-devised scheme for their moral and social advancement. Our only desire is, that they shall be separated from the whites, and that no encouragement shall hereafter be given to the migration of the colored man from the United States, or any where else. The idea that we have brought the curse upon ourselves, through the establishment of slavery by our ancestors, is false. As Canadians, we have yet to learn that we ought to be made a vicarious atonement for European sins.

"Canadians: The hour has arrived when we should arouse from our lethargy; when we should gather ourselves together in our might, and resist the onward progress of an evil which threatens to entail upon future generations a thousand curses. Now is the day. A few short years will put it beyond our power. Thousands and tens of thousands of American negroes, with the aid of the abolition societies in the States, and with the countenance given them by our philanthropic institutions, will continue to pour into Canada, if resistance is not offered. Many of you who live at a distance from this frontier, have no con-conception either of the number or the character of these emigrants, or of their poisonous effect upon the moral and social habits of a community. You listen with active sympathy to every thing narrated of the sufferings of the poor African; your feelings are enlisted, and your purse strings unloosed, and this often by the hypocritical declamation of some self-styled philanthropist. Under such influences many of you, in our large cities and towns, form yourselves into societies, and, without reflection, you supply funds for the support of schemes prejudicial to the best interests of our country. Against such proceedings, and especially against any and every attempt to settle any township in this District with negroes, we solemnly protest, and we call upon our countrymen, in all parts of the Province, to assist in our opposition.

"Fellow Christians: Let us forever maintain the sacred dogma, that all men have equal, natural, and inalienable rights. Let us do every thing in our power, consistent with international polity and justice, to abolish the accursed system of slavery in the neighboring Republic. But let us not, through a mistaken zeal to abate the evil of another land, entail upon ourselves a misery which every enlightened lover of his country must mourn. Let the slaves of the United States be free, but let it be in their own country. Let us not countenance their further introduction among us; in a word, let the people of the United States bear the burthen of their own sins.

"What has already been done, can not now be avoided; but it is not too late to do justice to ourselves, and retrieve the errors of the past. Let a suitable place be provided by the Government, to which the colored people may be removed, and separated from the whites, and in this scheme we will cordially join. We owe it to them, but how much more do we owe it to ourselves? But we implore you that you will not, either by your counsel, or your pecuniary aid, assist those who have projected the association for the settlement of a horde of ignorant slaves in the town of Raleigh. It is one of the oldest and most densely settled townships, in the very center of our new and promising District of Kent, and we feel that this scheme, if carried into operation, will have the effect of hanging like a dead weight upn our rising prosperity. What is our case to-day, to-morrow may be yours; join us then, in endeavoring to put a stop to what is not only a general evil, but in this case an act of unwarrantable injustice; and when the time may come when you shall be similarly situated to us, we have no doubt that, like us, you will cry out, and your appeal shall not be in vain."

On the 3d of September, 1849, the colored people of Toronto, Canada, held a meeting, in which they responded at length to the foregoing address. The spirit of the meeting can be divined from the following resolutions, which were unanimously passed:

"1st. *Resolved*, That we, as a portion of the inhabitants of Canada, conceive it to be our imperative duty to give an expression of sentiment in reference to the proceedings of the late meeting held at Chatham, denying the right of the colored people to settle where they please.

"2d. *Resolved*, That we spurn with contempt and burning indignation, any attempt, on the part of any person, or persons, to thrust us from the general bulk of society, and place us in a separate and distinct classification, such as is expressly implied in an address issued from the late meeting above alluded to.

"3d. *Resolved*, That the principle of selfishness, as exemplified in the originators of the resolutions and address, we detest, as we do similar ones emanating from a similar source; and we can clearly see the workings of a corrupt and depraved heart, arranged in hostility to the heaven-born principle of *liberty*, in its broadest and most unrestricted sense."

On the 9th of October, 1849, the Municipal Council of the Western District, adopted a Memorial to His Excellency, the Governor General, protesting against the proposed Elgin Association, in which the following language occurs:

. . . . . "Clandestine petitions have been got up, principally, if not wholly, signed by colored people, in order to mislead Government and the Elgin Association. These petitions do not embody the sentiments or feelings of the respectable, intelligent, and industrious yeomanry of the Western District. We can assure your Excellency that any such statement is false, that there is but one feeling, and that is of disgust and hatred, that they, the negroes, should be allowed to settle in any township where there is a white settlement. Our language is strong; but when we look at the expressions used at a late meeting held by the colored people of Toronto, openly avowing the propriety of amalgamation, and stating that it must, and will, and shall continue, we cannot avoid so doing. . . . . . The increased immigration of foreign negroes into this part of the Province is truly alarming. We cannot omit mentioning some facts for the corroboration of what we have stated. The negroes, who form at least one-third of the inhabitants of the township of Colchester, attended the township meeting for the election of parish and township officers, and insisted upon their right to vote, which was denied them by every individual white man at the meeting. The consequence was, that the Chairman of the meeting was prosecuted and thrown into heavy costs, which costs were paid by subscription from white inhabitants. In the same township of Colchester, as well as in many others, the inhabitants have not been able to get schools in many school sections, in consequence of the negroes insisting on their right of sending their children to such schools. No white man will ever act with them in any public capacity; this fact is so glaring, that no sheriff in this Province would dare to summons colored men to do jury duty. That such things have been done in other quarters of the British dominions we are well aware of, but we are convinced that the Canadians will never tolerate such conduct."

A Toronto paper of December 24, 1847, says: "The white inhabitants are fast leaving the vicinity of the proposed colored settlement, for the United States."

The *St. Catharines Journal*, June, 1852, under the head of "the fruits of having colored companies and colored settlements," says: "On the occasion of the June muster of the militia, a pretty large turn out took place at St. Catharines. We regret exceedingly that the day did not pass over without a serious riot. It seems that on the parade ground some insult was offered to the colored company, which was very properly restrained by Colonel Clark, and others. If the affair had ended here, it would have been fortunate; but the bad feeling exhibited on the parade ground was renewed, by some evil-minded person, and the colored population, becoming roused to madness, they proceeded to wreak their vengeance on a company in Stinson's tavern, after which a general melee took place, in which several men were wounded, and it is likely some will die of the injuries received. The colored village is a ruin, and much more like a place having been beseiged by an enemy than any thing else. This is the reward which the colored men have received for their loyalty, and the readiness with which they turned out to train, and no doubt would if the country required their services. This is a most painful occurrence, and must have been originated by some very ignorant persons. How any man possessing the common feelings of humanity, to say nothing of loyalty, could needlessly offer insult to so many men, so cheerfully turning out in obedience to the laws of the country, exceeds belief, if it were not a matter of fact. Too much credit cannot be given to those worthy citizens who used their best efforts to restrain the excitement, and prevented any further blood-shedding."

But here we have testimony of a later date. Hon. Colonel Prince, member of the Canadian Parliament in 1857, had resided among the colored people of the Western District; and, like other humane men, had sympathized with them, at the outset, and shown them many favors. Time and observation changed his views, and, in the course of his parliamentary duties, we find him taking a stand adverse to the further increase of the negro population in Canada. Hear him, as reported at the time:

"On the order of the day for the third reading of the emigrants' law amendment bill being called, Hon. Col. Prince said he was wishful to move a rider to the measure. The black people who infested the land were the greatest curse to the Province. The lives of the people of the West were made wretched by the inundation of these animals, and many of the largest farmers in the county of Kent have been compelled to leave their beautiful farms, because of the pestilential swarthy swarms.—What were these wretches fit for? Nothing. They cooked our victuals and shampooed us; but who would not rather that these duties should be performed by white men? The blacks were a worthless, useless, thriftless set of beings—they were too indolent, lazy and ignorant to work, too proud to

145

be taught; and not only that, if the criminal calendars of the country were examined, it would be found that they were a majority of the criminals. They were so detestable that unless some method were adopted of preventing their influx into this country by the "underground rail road," the people of the West would be obliged to drive them out by open violence. The bill before the House imposed a capitation tax upon emigrants from Europe, and the object of his motion was to levy a similar tax upon blacks who came hither from the States. He now moved, seconded by Mr. Patton, that a capitation tax of 5s for adults, and 3s 9d for children above one year and under fourteen years of age, be levied on persons of color emigrating to Canada from any foreign country.

"Ought not the Western men to be protected from the rascalities and villainies of the black wretches? He found these men with fire and food, and lodging when they were in need; and he would be bound to say that the black men of the county of Essex would speak well of him in this respect. But he could not admit them as being equal to white men; and, after a long and close observation of human nature, he had come to the conclusion that the black man was born to and intended for slavery, and that he was fit for nothing else. [Sensation.] Honorable gentlemen might try to groan him down, but he was not to be moved by mawkish sentiment, and he was persuaded that they might as well try to change the spots of the leopard as to make the black a good citizen. He had told black men so, and the lazy rascals had shrugged their shoulders and wished they had never ran away from their "good old massa" in Kentucky. If there was any thing unchristian in what he had proposed, he could not see it, and he feared that he was not born a Christian."

The *Windsor Herald*, of July 3d, 1857, contains the proceedings of an indignation meeting, held by the colored people of Toronto, at which they denounced Colonel Prince in unmeasured terms of reproach. The same paper contains the reply of the Colonel, copied from the *Toronto Colonist*, and it is given entire, as a specimen of the spicy times they have, in Canada, over the negro question. The editor remarks, in relation to the reply of Colonel Prince, that it has given general satisfaction in his neighborhood. It is as follows:

"DEAR SIR:—Your valuable paper of yesterday has afforded me a rich treat and not a little fun in the report of an indignation meeting of 'the colored citizens' of Toronto, held for the purpose of censuring me. Perhaps I ought not to notice their proceedings—perhaps it would be more becoming in me to allow them to pass at once into the oblivion which awaits them; but as it is the fashion in this country not unfrequently to assume that to be true which appears in print against an individual, unless he flatly denies the accusation, I shall, at least, for once, condescend to notice these absurd proceedings. They deal in generalities, and so shall I. Of the colored citizens of Toronto I know little or nothing; no doubt, some are respectable enough in their way, and perform the inferior duties belonging to their station tolerably well. Here they are kept in order—in their proper place—but their 'proceedings' are evidence of their natural conceit, their vanity, and their ignorance; and in them the cloven foot appears, and evinces what they would do, if they could. I believe that in this city, as in some others of our Province, they are looked upon as necessary evils, and only submitted to because white servants are so scarce. But I now deal with these fellows as a body, and I pronounce them to be, as such, the *greatest curse* ever inflicted upon the two magnificent western counties which I have the honor to represent in the Legislative Council of this Province! and few men have had the experience of them that I have. Among the many *estimable* qualities they possess, a systematic habit of *lying* is not the least prominent; and the 'colored citizens' aforesaid seem to partake of that quality in an eminent degree, because in their famous *Resolutions* they roundly assert that during the Rebellion 'I walked arm and arm with colored men'— that 'I owe my election to the votes of colored men'—and that I have 'accumulated much earthly gains,' as a lawyer, among 'colored clients.' All Lies! Lies! Lies! from beginning to end. I admit that one company of blacks did belong to my contingent battalion, but they made the very worst of soldiers, and were, comparatively speaking, unsusceptible of drill or discipline, and were conspicuous for one act only—a stupid sentry shot the son of one of our oldest colonels, under a mistaken notion that he was thereby doing his duty. But I certainly never did myself the honor of 'walking arm in arm' with any of the colored gentlemen of that distinguished corps. Then, as to my election. Few, very few blacks voted for me. *I never canvassed them*, and hence, I suppose, they supported, as a body, my opponent. They took compassion upon '*a monument of injured innocence*,' and they sustained the monument for a while, upon the pedestal their influence erected. But the monument fell, and the fall proved that such influence was merely ephemeral, and it sank into insignificant nothingness, as it should, and I hope ever will do; or God help this noble land. Poor Blackies! Be not so bold or so conceited, or so insolent hereafter, I do beseech you.

"Then how rich I have become among my 'colored clients!' I assert, without the fear of contradiction, that I have been the friend—the steady friend of our western 'Darkies' for more than twenty years; and amidst difficulties and troubles innumerable, (for they are a litigious race,) I have been their adviser, and I never made twenty pounds out of them in that long period! The fact is that the poor creatures had never the ability to pay a lawyer's fee.

"It has been my misfortune, and the misfortune of my family, to live among those blacks, (and they have lived *upon* us,) for twenty-four years. I have employed *hundreds* of them, and, with the exception of one, (named Richard Hunter,) not one has ever done for us a week's honest labor. I have taken them into my service, have fed and clothed them, year after year, on their arrival from the States, and in return I have generally found them rogues and thieves, and a graceless, worthless, thriftless, lying set of vagabonds. That is my very plain and very simple description of the darkies as a body, and it would be indorsed by all the western white men with very few exceptions.

"I have had scores of their George Washingtons, Thomas Jeffersons, James Madisons, as well as their Dinahs, and Gleniras, and Lavinias, in my service, and I understand them thoroughly, and I include the whole batch (old Richard Hunter excepted) in the category above described. To conclude, you 'Gentlemen of color,' East and West, and especially you 'colored citizens of Toronto,' I thank you for having given me an opportunity to publish my opinion of your race. Call another indignation meeting, and there make greater fools of yourselves than you did at the last, and then 'to supper with what appetite you may.'

"Believe me to remain,
Mr. Editor,
Yours very faithfully,
JOHN PRINCE.

Toronto, 26th June, 1857."

It is impracticable to extract the whole of the important facts referred to in Maj. Lachlan's Report, as it would make a volume of itself. In many places he takes occasion to urge the necessity of education for the colored people, as the only possible means of their elevation; and also presses upon the attention of the better classes of that race, the duty of co-operating with the magistrates in their efforts for the suppression of crime, as well as the advantages to be derived from the formation of associations for their intellectual and moral advancement. On the 23d of May, 1847, he addressed the Right Honorable, the Earl of Elgin, the Governor of Canada, on the subject of the causes checking the prosperity of the Western District, the fourth one of which he states to be "the unfortunate influx into its leading townships of swarms of run-away negro slaves, of the worst description, from the American States." After referring to the facts contained in his report of 1841, a portion of which are presented in the preceding pages, he says: "I shall therefore rest content with stating, in connection with these extracts, the simple fact, that on the Province gradually recovering from the shock given to immigration by the late rebellion, and the stream of British settlers beginning once more to flow toward the Province, a considerable number of emigrants of the laboring classes made their way to the Western District, and for some time wandered about in search of employment; but with the exception of those who had come to join relations and friends, and a few others, the greater portion, finding themselves unable to obtain work, from the ground which they naturally expected to occupy being already monopolized by negroes, and there being no public works of any kind on which they could be engaged, became completely disheartened, and were ultimately forced to disperse themselves elsewhere; and, most generally, found a refuge in the neighboring States of Michigan and Ohio. And such, it may be added, has ever since continued to be the case; while, on the other hand, the influx of negroes has been greatly on the increase. . . . . Far, however, be it for me to suppose it possible to abridge for one moment that noble constitutional principle—that slavery and *British Rule* and *British feeling are incompatible;* but still I consider it no trifling evil that any part of an essentially *British* colony should be thereby exposed to be made the receptable of the worst portion of the lowest grade of the human race, from every part of the American Union, to the evident serious injury of its own inhabitants, and equally serious prejudice to the claims of more congenial settlers."

This statement shows, very clearly, how the negro immigration into Canada operates injuriously to its prosperity by repelling the white immigrants.

What was true of the colored population of the "Western District of Canada, in 1841, while Major Lachlan filled the chair of the Quarter Sessions, seems to be equally true in 1859. The *Essex Advocate*, contains the following extract from the Presentment of the Grand Jury, at the Essex Assizes, November 17, 1859, in reference to the jail: "We are sorry to state to your Lordship the great prevalence of the colored race among its occupants, and beg to call attention to an accompanying document from the Municipal Council and inhabitants of the Township of Anderdon, which we recommend to your Lordship's serious consideration.

"'*To the Grand Jury of the County of Essex, in Inquest assembled:* We, the undersigned inhabitants of the Township of Anderdon, respectfully wish to call the attention of the Grand Inquest of the County of Essex to the fearful state of crime in our township. That there exists organized bands of thieves, too lazy to work, who nightly plunder our property! That nearly all of us, more or less, have suffered losses; and that for the last two years the stealing of sheep has been most alarming, one individual having had nine stolen within that period. We likewise beg to call your attention to the fact, that seven colored persons are committed to stand trial at the present assizes on the charge of sheep stealing, and that a warrant is out against the eighth, all from the Town of Anderdon. We beg distinctly to be understood, that although we are aware that nine-tenths of the crimes committed in the County of Essex, according to the population, are so committed by the colored people, yet we willingly extend the hand of fellowship and kindness to the emancipated slave, whom Great Britain has granted an asylum to in Canada We therefore hope the Grand Jury of the County of Essex will lay the statement of our case before his Lordship, the Judge at the present assizes, that some measure may be taken by the Government to protect us and our property, or persons of capital will be driven from the country.'"

We find it stated in the *Cincinnati Daily Commercial*, that the "Court, in alluding to this presentment, remarked that 'he was not surprised at finding prejudice existing against them (the negroes) among the respectable portion of the people, for they were indolent, shiftless and dishonest, and unworthy of the sympathy that some mistaken parties extended to them; they would not work when opportunity was presented, but preferred subsisting by thieving from respectable farmers, and begging from those benevolently inclined.'"

In September, 1859, Mr. Stanley, a government agent from the West Indies, visited Canada with the view of inducing the colored people of that Province to emigrate to Jamaica. The *Windsor Herald*, in noticing the movement, gives the details of the arguments presented, at the meeting in Windsor, to influence them to accept the offer. To men of intelligence and foresight, the reasons would have been convincing; but upon the minds of the colored people, they seem to have had scarcely any weight whatever—only one man entering his name, as an emigrant, at the close of the lecture. They were assured that in Jamaica they could obtain employment at remunerative salaries, and in three years become owners of property, besides possessing all the advantages of British subjects. Only a stipulated number were called for at the present time, they were told, but if the experiment proved successful, the gates would be thrown open for a general emigration. The Governor of the Island guaranteed them occupations on their arrival, or a certain stipend until such were found, and also their passage thither gratis. Four hundred emigrants were wanted to commence the experiment, and if they succeeded in getting the number required, they designed starting for Jamaica in the space of a month.

The indisposition of the colored people to accept the liberal offer of the authorites of Jamaica, created some surprise among the whites; but the mystery was explained when the agent visited Chatham, and made similar offers to the colored people of that town. As already stated, in the Preface to this work, they not only rejected the offered boon with contempt, but gave as their reason, that events would shortly transpire in the United States, which would demand their aid in behalf of their fellow countrymen there.[91] This was thirteen days before the Harper's Ferry outbreak, and Chatham was the town in which John Brown and his associates concocted their insurrectionary movement. The chief reason why the Jamaica emigration scheme was rejected, must have been the determination of the blacks of Canada to co-operate in the Brown insurrection.

Here, now, are all the results of the Canada experiment, as presented by the official action of its civil officers and public men. Need it be said, that the prospects of the African race have only been rendered the more dark and gloomy, by the conduct of the free colored men of that Province. And when we couple the results there with those of the West Indies, it must be obvious to all, that what has been attempted for the colored race is wholly impracticable; that in its present state of advancement from barbarism, the attainment of civil and social equality, with the enlightened white races, is utterly impossible.

It would appear, then, that philanthropists have committed a grave error in their policy, and the sooner they retrace their steps the better for the colored people. The error to which we refer, is this: they found a small portion of colored men, whose intelligence and moral character equaled that of the average of the white population; and, considering it a great hardship that such men should be doomed to a degraded condition, they attempted to raise them up to the civil and social position which their merits would entitle them to occupy. But in attempting to secure equal rights to the enlightened negro, the philanthropists claimed the same privilege for the whole of that race. In this they failed to recognize the great truth, that free government is not adapted to men in a condition of ignorance and moral degradation. By taking such broad ground—by securing the largest amount of liberty for a great mass of the most degraded of humanity—they have altogether failed in convincing the world, that freedom is a boon worth the bestowal upon the African in his present condition. The intelligent colored man, who could have been lifted up to a suitable hight, and maintained his position, if he had been taken alone, could not be elevated at all when the whole race were fastened to his skirts. And this mistake was a very natural one for men who think but superficially. Despotic government is repugnant to enlightened men: hence, in rejecting it for themselves, they repudiate it as a form of rule for all others. This decision, plausible as it may appear, is not consistent with the philosophy of human nature as it now is; nor is it in accordance with the sentiments of the profound statesmen who framed the American Constitution. They held that only men of intelligence and moral principle were capable of self-government; and, hence, they excluded from citizenship the barbarous and semi-barbarous Indians and Africans, who were around them and in their midst.

In discussing the results of emancipation in the United States, in a preceding chapter, it is stated that one principal cause, operating to check the further liberation of the slaves, at an early day in our history, was, that freedom had proved itself of little value to the colored man, while the measure had greatly increased the burdens of the whites; and that until he should make such progress as would prove that freedom was the best condition for the race, while intermingled with the whites, any further movements toward general emancipation were not to be expected. This view is now indorsed by some of the most prominent abolitionists. Listen to the Rev. Henry Ward Beecher on this subject. In his sermon in reference to the Harper's Ferry affair, he says:

"If we would benefit the African at the South, we must *begin at home*. This is to some men the most disagreeable part of the doctrine of emancipation. It is very easy to labor for the emancipation of beings a thousand miles off; but when it comes to the practical application of justice and humanity to those about us, it is not so easy. The truths of God respecting the rights and dignities of men, are just as important to free colored men, as to enslaved colored men. It may seem strange for me to say that the lever with which to lift the load of Georgia is in New York; but it is. I do not believe the whole free North can tolerate grinding injustice toward the poor, and inhumanity toward the laboring classes, without exerting an influence unfavorable to justice and humanity in the South. No one can fail to see the inconsistency between our treatment of those among us, who are in the lower walks of life, and our professions of sympathy for the Southern slaves. How are the free colored people treated at the North? They are almost without education, with but little sympathy for their ignorance. They are refused the common rights of citizenship which the whites enjoy. They can not even ride in the cars of our city rail roads. They are snuffed at in the house of God, or tolerated with ill-disguised disgust. Can the black man be a mason in New York? Let him be employed as a journeyman, and every Irish lover of liberty that carries the hod or trowel, would leave at once, or compel him to leave! Can the black man be a carpenter? There is scarcely a carpenter's shop in New York in which a journeyman would continue to work, if a black man was employed in it. Can the black man engage in the common industries of life? There is scarcely one in which he can engage. He is crowded down, down, down through the most menial callings, to the bottom of society. We tax them and then refuse to allow their children to go to our public schools. We tax them and then refuse to sit by them in God's house. We heap upon them moral obloquy more atrocious than that which the master heaps upon the slave. And notwithstanding all this, we lift ourselves up to talk to the Southern people about the rights and liberties of the human soul, and especially the African soul! It is true that slavery is cruel. But it is not at all certain that there is not more love to the race in the South than in the North. . . . . . . Whenever we are prepared to show toward the lowest, the poorest, and the most despised, an unaffected kindness, such as led Christ, though the Lord of glory, to lay aside his dignities and take on himself the form of a servant, and to undergo an ignominious death, that he might rescue men from ignorance and bondage—whenever we are prepared to do such things as these, we may be sure that the example at the North will not be unfelt at the South. Every effort that is made in Brooklyn to establish churches for the free colored people, and to encourage them to educate themselves and become independent, is a step toward emancipation in the South. The degradation of the free colored men in the North will fortify slavery in the South!"

We think we may safely guarantee, that whenever Northern abolitionists shall carry out Mr. Beecher's scheme, of spending their time and money for the moral and intellectual culture of the free colored people, the South will at once emancipate every slave within her limits; because we will then be in the midst of the millenium. Intelligent free colored men will agree with us in opinion, as they have tested them upon this subject.

One point more remains to be noticed:—the influence which the results in Canada and Jamaica have exerted upon the prospects of the free colored man in the United States. We mean, of course, his prospects for securing the civil and social equality to which he has been aspiring. His own want of progress has been the main cause of checking the extension of emancipation. This is now admitted even by Rev. H. W. Beecher, himself. Then, again, the fact that much less advancement has been made by the negroes in the British Provinces, than by those in the United States, operates still more powerfully in preventing any further liberation of the slaves. These two causes, combined, have dealt a death-blow to the hope of emancipation, in the South, by any moral influence coming from that quarter; and has, in fact, put back that cause, so far as the moral power of the negro is concerned, to a period hopelessly distant. Loyal Britons may urge upon us the duty of emancipation as strongly as they please; but so long as they denounce the influx of colored men as a curse to Canada, just so long they will fail in persuading Americans that an increase of free negroes will be a blessing to the United States. The moral power of the free negro, in promoting emancipation, is at an end; but how is it with his prospects of success in the employment of force? The Harper's Ferry movement is pronounced, by anti-slavery men themselves, as the work of a madman; and no other attempt of that kind can be more successful, as none but the insane and the ignorant will ever enlist in such an enterprise. The power of the free colored people in promoting emancipation, say what they will, is now at an end.

But these are not all the results of the movements noticed. They have not only rendered the free colored people powerless in emancipation, but have acted most injuriously upon themselves, as a class, in both the free and the slave States. In the Northwestern free States, every new Constitution framed, and every old one amended, with perhaps one exception, exclude the free negroes from the privileges of citizenship. In the slave States, generally, efforts are making not only to prevent farther emancipations, but to drive out the free colored population from their territories.

Thus, at this moment, stands the question of the capacity of the free colored people of the United States, to influence public opinion in favor of emancipation. And where are their champions who kindled the flame which is now extinguished? Many of them are in their graves; and the Harper's Ferry act, but applied the match that exploded the existing organizations. One chieftain—always truthful, ever in earnest—is, alas, in the lunatic asylum; another—whose zeal overcomes his judgment, at times—backs down from the position he had taken, that rifles were better than bibles in the conflict with slavery; another—coveting not the martyr's crown, yet a little—has left his editorial chair, to put the line dividing English and American territory between himself and danger; another—whose life could not well be spared, as he, doubtless, thought—after helping to organize the conspiracy at Chatham, in Canada, immediately set out to explore Africa: perhaps to select a home for the Virginia slaves, and be ready to receive them when Brown should set them free. These forces can never be re-combined. As for others, so far as politicians are concerned, the colored race have nothing to hope. The battle for free territory, in the sense in which they design to be understood, is a contest to keep the blacks and whites entirely separate. It is a determination to carry out the policy of Jefferson, by separating the races where it can be accomplished—a policy that will be adhered to in the free States, and which the Canadians would gladly adopt, if the mother country would permit them to carry out their wishes.

Free colored men of the United States! "in the days of adversity consider." Are not the signs of the times indicative of the necessity of a change of policy?

CHAPTER XVIII

THE MORAL RELATIONS OF PERSONS HOLDING THE *PER SE* DOCTRINE, ON THE SUBJECT OF SLAVERY, TO THE PURCHASE AND CONSUMPTION OF SLAVE LABOR PRODUCTS.

Moral relations of Slavery—Relations of the consumer of Slave labor products to the system—Grand error of all Anti-Slavery effort—Law of *particeps criminis*—Daniel O'-Connell—*Malum in se* doctrine—Inconsistency of those who hold it—English Emancipationists—Their commercial argument—Differences between the position of Great Britain and the United States—Preaching versus practice by Abolitionists—Cause of their want of influence over the Slaveholder—Necessity of examining the question—Each man to be judged by his own standard—Classification of opinions in the United States, in regard to the morality of Slavery—Three Views—A case in illustration—Apology of *per se* men for using Slave grown products insufficient—Law relating to "confusion of goods"—*Per se* men *participes criminis* with Slaveholders—Taking Slave grown products under *protest* absurd—World's Christian Evangelical Alliance—Amount of Slave labor Cotton in England at that moment—Pharisaical conduct—The Scotchman taking his wife under protest—Anecdote—American Cotton more acceptable to Englishmen than Republican principles—Secret of England's policy toward American Slavery—The case of robbery again cited, and the English Satirized—A contrast—Causes of the want of moral power of Abolitionists—Slaveholders no cause to cringe—Other results—Effect of the adoption of the *per se* doctrine by ecclesiastical bodies—Slaves thus left in all their moral destitution—Inconsistency of *per se* men denouncing others—What the Bible says of similar conduct.

HAVING noticed the political and economical relations of slavery, it may be expected that we shall say something of its moral relations. In attempting this, we choose not to traverse that interminable labyrinth, without a thread, which includes the moral character of the system, as it respects the relation between the master and the slave. The only aspect in which we care to consider it, is in the moral relations which the consumers of slave labor products sustain to slavery: and even on this, we shall offer no opinion, our aim being only to promote inquiry.

This view of the question is not an unimportant one. It includes the germ of the grand error in nearly all anti-slavery effort; and to which, chiefly, is to be attributed its want of moral power over the conscience of the slaveholder. The abolition movement, was designed to create a public sentiment, in the United States, that should be equally as potent in forcing emancipation, as was the public opinion of Great Britain. But why have not the Americans been as successful as the English? This is an inquiry of great importance. When the Anti-Slavery Convention, which met, December 6, 1833, in Philadelphia, declared, as a part of its creed: "That there is no difference in principle, between the African slave trade, and American slavery," it meant to be understood as teaching, that the person who purchased slaves imported from Africa, or who held their offspring as slaves, was *particeps criminis*—partaker in the crime—with the slave trader, on the principle that he who receives stolen property, knowing it be such, is equally guilty with the thief.

On this point Daniel O'Connell was very explicit, when, in a public assembly, he used this language: "When an American comes into society, he will be asked, 'are you one of the thieves, or are you an honest man? If you are an honest man, then you have given liberty to your slaves; if you are among the thieves, the sooner you take the outside of the house, the better.'"

The error just referred to was this: they based their opposition to slavery on the principle, that it was *malum in se*—a sin in itself—like the slave trade, robbery and murder; and, at the same time, continued to use the products of the labor of the slave as though they had been obtained from the labor of freemen. But this seeming inconsistency was not the only reason why they failed to create such a public sentiment as would procure the emancipation of our slaves. The English emancipationists began their work like philosophers—addressing themselves, respectfully to the power that could grant their requests. Beside the moral argument, which declared slavery a crime, the English philanthropists labored to convince Parliament, that emancipation would be advantageous to the commerce of the nation. The commercial value of the Islands had been reduced one-third, as a result of the abolition of the slave trade. Emancipation, it was argued, would more than restore their former prosperity, as the labor of freemen was twice as productive as that of slaves. But American abolitionists commenced their crusade against slavery, by charging those who sustained it, and who alone, held the power to manumit, with crimes of the blackest dye. This placed the parties in instant antagonism, causing all the arguments on human rights, and the sinfulness of slavery, to fall without effect upon the ears of angry men. The error on this point, consisted in failing to discriminate between the sources of the power over emancipation in England and in the United States. With Great Britain, the power was in Parliament. The masters, in the West Indies, had no voice in the question. It was the voters in England alone who controlled the elections, and, consequently, controlled Parliament. But the condition of things in the United States is the reverse of what it was in England. With us, the power of emancipation is in the States, not in Congress. The slaveholders elect the members to the State Legislatures; and they choose none but such as agree with them in opinion. It matters not, therefore, what public sentiment may be at the North, as it has no power over the Legislatures of the South. Here, then, is the difference: with us the slaveholder controls the question of emancipation, while in England the consent of the master was not necessary to the execution of that work.

Our anti-slavery men seem to have fallen into their errors of policy, by following the lead of those of England, who manifested a total ignorance of the relations existing between our General Government and the State Governments. On the abolition platform, slaveholders found themselves placed in the same category with slave traders and thieves. They were told that all laws, giving them power over the slave, were void in the sight of heaven; and that their appropriation of the fruits of the labor of the slave, without giving him compensation, was robbery. Had the preaching of these principles produced conviction, it must have promoted emancipation. But, unfortunately, while these doctrines were held up to the gaze of slaveholders, in the one hand of the exhorter, they beheld his other hand stretched out, from beneath his cloak of seeming sanctity, to clutch the products of the very robbery he was professing to condemn! Take a fact in proof of this view of the subject.

At the date of the declarations of Daniel O'Connell, on behalf of the English, and by the Philadelphia Anti-Slavery Convention, on the part of Americans, the British manufacturers were purchasing, annually, about 300,000,000 lbs. of cotton, from the very men denounced as equally criminal with slave traders and thieves; and the people of the United States were almost wholly dependent upon slave labor for their supplies of cotton and groceries. It is no matter for wonder, therefore, that slaveholders, should treat, as fiction, the doctrine that slave labor products are the fruits of robbery, so long as they are purchased without scruple, by all classes of men, in Europe and America. The pecuniary argument for emancipation, that free labor is more profitable than slave labor, was also urged here, but was treated as the greatest absurdity. The masters had, before their eyes, the evidence of the falsity of the assertion, that, if emancipated, the slaves would be doubly profitable as free laborers. The reverse was admitted, on all hands, to be true in relation to our colored people.

But this question, of the moral relations which the consumers of slave labor products sustain to slavery, is one of too important a nature to be passed over without a closer examination; and, beside, it is involved in less obscurity than the morality of the relation existing between the master and the slave. Its consideration, too, affords an opportunity of discriminating between the different opinions entertained on the broad question of the morality of the institution, and enables us to judge of the consistency and conscientiousness of every man, by the standard which he himself adopts.

The prevalent opinions, as to the morality of the institution of slavery, in the United States, may be classified under three heads: 1. That it is justified by Scripture example and precept. 2. That it is a great civil and social evil, resulting from ignorance and degradation, like despotic systems of government, and may be tolerated until its subjects are sufficiently enlightened to render it safe to grant them equal rights. 3. That it is *malum in se*, like robbery and murder, and can not be sustained, for a moment, without sin; and, like sin, should be immediately abandoned.

Those who consider slavery sanctioned by the Bible, conceive that they can, consistently with their creed, not only hold slaves, and use the products of slave labor, without doing violence to their consciences, but may adopt measures to perpetuate the system. Those who consider slavery merely a great civil and social evil, a despotism that may engender oppression, or may not, are of opinion that they may purchase and use its products, or interchange their own for those of the slaveholder, as free governments hold commercial and diplomatic intercourse with despotic ones, without being responsible for the moral evils connected with the system, But the position of those who believe slavery *malum in se*, like the slave trade, robbery and murder, is a very different one from either of the other classes, as it regards the purchase and use of slave labor products. Let us illustrate this by a case in point.

A company of men hold a number of their fellow men in bondage under the laws of the commonwealth in which they live, so that they can compel them to work their plantations, and raise horses, cattle, hogs, and cotton. These products of the labor of the oppressed, are appropriated by the oppressors to their own use, and taken into the markets for sale. Another company proceed to a community of freemen, on the coast of Africa, who have labored voluntarily during the year, seize their persons, bind them, convey away their horses, cattle, hogs, and cotton, and take the property to market. The first association represents the slaveholders; the second a band of robbers. The commodities of both parties, are openly offered for sale, and every one knows how the property of each was obtained. Those who believe the *per se* doctrine, place both these associations in the same moral category, and call them robbers. Judged by this rule, the first band are the more criminal, as they have deprived their victims of personal liberty, forced them into servitude, and then "despoiled them of the fruits of their labor."[92] The second band have only deprived their victims of liberty, while they robbed them; and thus have committed but two crimes, while the first have perpetrated three. These parties attempt to negotiate the sale of their cotton, say in London. The first company dispose of their cargo without difficulty—no one manifesting the slightest scruple at purchasing the products of slave labor. But the second company are not so fortunate. As soon as their true character is ascertained, the police drag its members to Court, where they are sentenced to Bridewell. In vain do these robbers quote the Philadelphia Anti-Slavery Convention, and Daniel O'Connell, to prove that their cotton was obtained by means no more criminal than that of the slaveholders, and that, therefore, judgment ought to be reversed. The Court will not entertain such a plea, and they have to endure the penalty of the law. Now, why this difference, if slavery be *malum in se?* And if the receiver of stolen property is *particeps criminis* with the thief, why is it, that the Englishman, who should receive and sell the cotton of the robbers, would run the risk of being sent to prison with them, while if he acted as agent of the slaveholders, he would be treated as an honorable man? If the master has no moral right to hold his slaves, in what respect can the products of their labor differ from the property acquired by robbery? And if the property be the fruits of robbery, how can any one use it, without violating conscience?

We have met with the following sage exposition of the question, in justification of the use of slave labor products, by those who believe the *per se* doctrine: The master owns the lands, gives his skill and intelligence to direct the labor, and feeds and clothes the slaves. The slaves, therefore, are entitled only to a part of the proceeds of their labor, while the master is also justly entitled to a part of the crop. When brought into the market, the purchaser can not know what part belongs, rightfully, to the master, and what to his slaves, as the whole is offered in bulk. He may, therefore, purchase the whole, innocently, and throw the sinfulness of the transaction upon the master, who sells what belongs to others. But if the *per se* doctrine be true, this apology for the purchaser is not a justification. Where a "confusion of goods" has been made by one of the owners, so that they can not be separated, he who "confused" them can have no advantage, in law, from his own wrong, but the goods are awarded to the innocent party. On this well known principle of law, this most equitable rule, the master forfeits his right in the property, and the purchaser, knowing the facts, becomes a party in his guilt. But aside from this, the "confusion of goods," by the master, can give him no moral right to dispose of the interest of his slaves therein for his own benefit; and the persons purchasing such property, acquire no moral right to its possession and use. These are sound, logical views. The argument offered, in justification of those who hold that slavery is *malum in se*, is the strongest that can be made. It is apparent, then, from a fair analysis of their own principles, that they are *participes criminis* with slaveholders.

Again, if the laws regulating the institution of slavery, be morally null and void, and not binding on the conscience, then the slaves have a moral right to the proceeds of their labor. This right can not be alienated by any act of the master, but attaches to the property wherever it may be taken, and to whomsoever it may be sold. This principle, in law, is also well established. The recent decision on the "Gardiner fraud," confirms it; the Court asserting, that the money paid out of the Treasury of the United States, under such circumstances, continued its character as the money and property of the United States, and may be followed into the hands of those who cashed the orders of Gardiner, and subsequently drew the money, but who are not the true owners of the said fund; and decreeing that the amount of funds, thus obtained, be collected off the estate of said Gardiner, and off those who drew funds from the treasury, on his orders.

These principles of law are so well understood, by every man of intelligence, that we can not conceive how those advocating the *per se* doctrines, if sincere, can continue in the constant use of slave grown products, without a perpetual violation of conscience and of all moral law. Taking them under *protest*, against the slavery which produced them, is ridiculous. Refusing to fellowship the slaveholder, while eagerly appropriating the products of the labor of the slave, which he brings in his hand, is contemptible. The most noted case of the kind, is that of the British Committee, who had charge of the preliminary arrangements for the admission of members to the World's Christian Evangelical Alliance. One of the rules it adopted, but which the Alliance afterward modified, excluded all American clergymen, suspected of a want of orthodoxy on the *per se* doctrine, from seats in that body. Their language, to American clergymen, was virtually, "Stand aside, I am holier than thou;" while, at the same moment, their parishioners, the manufacturers, had about completed the purchase of 624,000,000 lbs. of cotton, for the consumption of their mills, during the year; the bales of which, piled together, would have reached mountain-high, displaying, mostly, the brands, "New Orleans," "Mobile," "Charleston."

As not a word was said, by the Committee, against the Englishmen who were buying and manufacturing American cotton, the case may be viewed as one in which the fruits of robbery were taken under *protest* against the robbers themselves. To all intelligent men, the conduct of the people of Britain, in protesting against slavery, as a system of robbery, while continuing to purchase such enormous quantities of the cotton produced by slaves, appears as Pharasaical as the conduct of the *conscientious* Scotchman, in early times, in Eastern Pennsylvania, who married his wife under protest against the constitution and laws of the Government, and especially, against the authority, power, and right of the magistrate who had just tied the knot.[93]

Such pliable consciences, doubtless, are very convenient in cases of emergency. But as they relax when selfish ends are to be subserved, and retain their rigidity only when judging the conduct of others, the inference is, that the persons possessing them are either hypocritical, or else, as was acknowledged by Parson D., in similar circumstances, they have mistaken their *prejudices* for their *consciences*.

So far as Britain is concerned, she is, manifestly, much more willing to receive American slave labor cotton for her factories, than American republican principles for her people. And why so? The profits derived by her, from the purchase and manufacture of slave labor cotton, constitute so large a portion of the means of her prosperity, that the Government could not sustain itself were the supplies of this article cut off. It is easy to divine, therefore, why the people of England are boundless in their denunciation of American slavery, while not a single remonstrance goes up to the throne, against the importation of American cotton. Should she exclude it, the act would render her unable to pay the interest on her national debt; and many a declaimer against slavery, losing his income, would have to go supperless to bed.

Let us contrast the conduct of a pagan government with that of Great Britain. When the Emperor of China became fully convinced of his inability to resist the prowess of the

British arms, in the famous "Opium War," efforts were made to induce him to legalize the traffic in opium, by levying a duty on its import, that should yield him a heavy profit. This he refused to do, and recorded his decision in these memorable words:

"It is true, I can not prevent the introduction of the flowing poison. Gain-seeking and corrupt men will, for profit and sensuality, defeat my wishes, but nothing will induce me to derive a revenue from the vice and misery of my people."[94]

Let us revert a moment to the case of robbery, before cited, in further illustration of this subject. The prisoners serve out their term in Bridewell, and, after a year or two, again visit London with a cargo of cotton. The police recognize them, and they are a second time arraigned before the court for trial. The judge demands why they should have dared to revisit the soil of England, to offer for sale the products of their robbery. The prisoners assure his honor that they have neither outraged the public sentiment of the kingdom, nor violated its laws. "While in your prison, sir," they go on to say, "we became instructed in the morals of British economics. Anxious to atone for our former fault, and to restore ourselves to the confidence and respect of the pious subjects of your most gracious Queen, no sooner were we released from prison, than we hastened to the African coast, from whence our former cargo was obtained, and seizing the self-same men whom we had formerly robbed, we bore them off, bodily, to the soil of Texas. They resisted sturdily, it is true, but we mastered them. We touched none of the fruits of their previous labors. Their cotton we left in the fields, to be drenched by the rains or drifted by the winds; because, to have brought it into your markets would have subjected us, anew, to a place in your dungeons. In Texas, we brought our prisoners under the control of the laws, which there give us power to hold them as slaves. Stimulated to labor, under the lash of the overseer, they have produced a crop of cotton, which is now offered in your markets as a lawful article of commerce. We are not subjects of your Government, and, therefore, not indictable under your laws against slave trading. Your honor, will perceive, then, that our moral relations are changed. We come now to your shores, not as dealers in stolen property, but as slaveholders, with the products of slave labor. We are aware that *bunkum* speakers, at your public assemblies, denounce the slaveholder as a thief, and his appropriation of the fruits of the labor of his slaves, as robbery. We comprehend the motives prompting such utterances. We come not to attend meetings of Ecclesiastical Conventions, representing the republican principles of America, to unsettle the doctrines upon which the throne of your kingdom is based. But we come as cotton planters, to supply your looms with cotton, that British commerce may not be abridged, and England, the great civilizer of the world, may not be forced to slack her pace in the performance of her mission. This is our character and position; and your honor will at once see that it is your duty, and the interest of your Government, to treat us as gentlemen and your most faithful allies." The judge at once admits the justice of their plea, rebukes the police, apologizes to the prisoners, assures them that they have violated no law of the realm; and that, though the public sentiment of the nation denounces the slaveholder as a thief, yet the public necessity demands a full supply of cotton from the planter. He then orders their immediate discharge, and invites them to partake of the hos-hospitalities of his house during their stay in London.

This is a fair example of British consistency, on the subject of slavery, so far as the supply of cotton is concerned. The English manufacturers are under the absolute necessity of procuring it; but as free labor is incapable of increasing its production, slave labor must be made to remedy the defect.

The reason can now be clearly comprehended, why abolitionists have had so little moral power over the conscience of the slaveholder. Their practice has been inconsistent with their precepts; or, at least, their conduct has been liable to this construction. Nor do we perceive how they can exert a more potent influence, in the future, unless their energies are directed to efforts such as will relieve them from a position so inconsistent with their professions, as that of constantly purchasing products which they, themselves, declare to be the fruits of robbery. While, therefore, things remain as they are, with the world so largely dependent upon slave labor, how can it be otherwise, than that the system will continue to flourish? And while its products are used by all classes, of every sentiment, and country, nearly, how can the slaveholder be brought to see any thing, in the practice of the world, to alarm his conscience, and make him cringe, before his fellow-men, as a guilty robber?

But, has nothing worse occurred from the advocacy of the *per se* doctrine, than an exhibition of inconsistency on the part of abolitionists, and the perpetuation of slavery resulting from their conduct? This has occurred. Three highly respectable religious denominations, now limited to the North, had once many flourishing congregations in the South. On the adoption of the *per se* doctrine, by their respective Synods, their congregations became disturbed, were soon after broken up, or the ministers in charge had to seek other fields of labor. Their system of religious instruction, for the family, being quite thorough, the slaves were deriving much advantage from the influence of these bodies. But when they resolved to withhold the gospel from the master, unless he would emancipate, they also withdrew the means of grace from the slave; and, so far as they were concerned, left him to perish eternally! Whether this course was proper, or whether it would have been better to have passed by the morality of the legal relation, in the creation of which the master had no agency, and considered him, under Providence, as the moral guardian of the slave, bound to discharge a guardian's duty to an immortal being, we shall not undertake to determine. Attention is called to the facts, merely to show the practical effects of the action of these churches upon the slave, and what the *per se* doctrine has done in depriving him of the gospel.

Another remark, and we have done with this topic. Nothing is more common, in certain circles, than denunciations of the Christian men and ministers, who refuse to adopt the *per se* principle. We leave others to judge whether these censures are merited. One thing is certain: those who believe that slavery is a great civil and social evil, entailed upon the country, and are extending the gospel to both master and slave, with the hope of removing it peacefully, can not be reproached with acting inconsistently with their principles; while those who declare slavery *malum in se*, and refuse to fellowship the Christian slaveholder, because they consider him a robber, but yet use the products of slave labor, may fairly be classified, on their own principles, with the hypocritical people of Israel, who were thus reproached by the Most High: "What hast thou to do to declare my statutes, or that thou shouldst take my covenant in thy mouth?. . . . . When thou sawest a thief, then thou consentedst with him."[95]

CONCLUSION

In concluding our labors, there is little need of extended observation. The work of emancipation, in our country, was checked, and the extension of slavery promoted:—first, by the neglect of the free colored people to improve the advantages afforded them; second, by the increasing value imparted to slave labor; third, by the mistaken policy into which the English and American abolitionists have fallen. Whatever reasons might now be offered for emancipation, from an improvement of our free colored people, is far more than counterbalanced by its failure in the West Indies, and the constantly increasing value of the labor of the slave. If, when the planters had only a moiety of the markets for cotton, the value of slavery was such as to arrest emancipation, how must the obstacles be increased, now, when they have the monopoly of the markets of the world? And, besides all this, a more deadly blow, than has been given by all other causes combined, is now levelled at negro freedom from a quarter the least suspected. The failure of the Canadian immigrants to improve the privileges afforded them under British law, proves, conclusively, that the true laws of progress for the African race, do not consist in a mere escape from slavery.

We propose not to speak of remedies for slavery. That we leave to others. Thus far this very perplexing question, has baffled all human wisdom. Either some radical defect must have existed, in the measures devised for its removal, or the time has not yet come for successfully assailing the institution. Our work is completed, in the delineation we have given of its varied relations to our agricultural, commercial, and social interests. As the monopoly of the culture of cotton, imparts to slavery its economical value, the system will continue as long as this monopoly is maintained. Slave labor products have now become necessities of human life, to the extent of more than half the commercial articles supplied to the Christian world. Even free labor, itself, is made largely subservient to slavery, and vitally interested in its perpetuation and extension.

Can this condition of things be changed? It may be reasonably doubted, whether any thing efficient can be speedily accomplished: not because there is lack of territory where freemen may be employed in tropical cultivation, as all Western and Central Africa, nearly, is adapted to this purpose; not because intelligent free labor, under proper incentives, is less productive than slave labor; but because freemen, whose constitutions are adapted to tropical climates, will not avail themselves of the opportunity offered for commencing such an enterprise.

KING COTTON cares not whether he employs slaves or freemen. It is the *cotton*, not the *slaves*, upon which his throne is based. Let freemen do his work as well, and he will not object to the change. The efforts of his most powerful ally, Great Britain, to promote that object, have already cost her people many hundreds of millions of dollars, with total failure as a reward for her zeal; and she is now compelled to resort to the expedient of employing the slave labor of Africa, to meet the necessities of her manufacturers. One-sixth of the colored people of the United States are free; but they shun the cotton regions, and have been instructed to detest emigration to Liberia. Their improvement has not been such as was anticipated; and their more rapid advancement can not be expected, while they remain in the country. The free colored people of the British West Indies, can no longer be relied on to furnish tropical products, for they are resting contented in a state of almost savage indolence; and the introduction of coolie labor has become indispensable as a means of saving the Islands from ruin, as well as of forcing the negro into habits of industry. Hayti is not in a more promising condition; and even if it were, its population and territory are too limited to enable it to meet the increasing demand. HIS MAJESTY, KING COTTON, therefore, is forced to continue the employment of his slaves; and, by their toil, is riding on, conquering and to conquer! He receives no check from the cries of the oppressed, while the citizens of the world are dragging forward his chariot, and shouting aloud his praise!

KING COTTON is a profound statesman, and knows what measures will best sustain his throne. He is an acute mental philosopher, acquainted with the secret springs of human action, and accurately perceives who can best promote his aims. He has no evidence that colored men can grow his cotton, except in the capacity of slaves. Thus far, all experiments made to increase the production of cotton, by emancipating the slaves employed in its cultivation, have been a total failure. It is his policy, therefore, to defeat all schemes of emancipation. To do this, he stirs up such agitations as lure his enemies into measures that will do him no injury. The venal politician is always at his call, and assumes the form of saint or sinner, as the service may demand. Nor does he overlook the enthusiast, engaged in Quixotic endeavors for the relief of suffering humanity, but influences him to advocate measures which tend to tighten, instead of loosing the bands of slavery. Or, if he can not be seduced into the support of such schemes, he is beguiled into efforts that waste his strength on objects the most impracticable; so that slavery receives no damage from the exuberance of his philanthropy. But should such a one, perceiving the futility of his labors, and the evils of his course, make an attempt to avert the consequences; while he is doing this, some new recruit, pushed forward into his former place, charges him with lukewarmness, or pro-slavery sentiments, destroys his influence with the public, keeps alive the delusions, and sustains the supremacy of KING COTTON in the world.

In speaking of the economical connections of slavery, with the other material interests of the world, we have called it a *tripartite alliance*. It is more than this. It is *quadruple*. Its structure includes four parties, arranged thus: The Western Agriculturists; the Southern Planters; the English Manufacturers; and the American Abolitionists! By this arrangement, the abolitionists do not stand in direct contact with slavery; they imagine, therefore, that they have clean hands and pure hearts, so far as sustaining the system is concerned. But they, no less than their allies, aid in promoting the interests of slavery. Their sympathies are with England on the slavery question, and they very naturally incline to agree with her on other points. She advocates *Free Trade*, as essential to her manufactures and commerce; and they do the same, not waiting to inquire into its bearings upon *American slavery*. We refer now to the people, not to their leaders, whose integrity we choose not to indorse. The free trade and protective systems, in their bearings upon slavery, are so well understood, that no man of general reading, especially an editor, or member of Congress, who professes anti-slavery sentiments, at the same time advocating free trade, will ever convince men of intelligence, pretend what he may, that he is not either woefully perverted in his judgment, or emphatically, a "dough-face" in disguise! England, we were about to say, is in alliance with the cotton planter, to whose prosperity free trade is indispensable. Abolitionism is in alliance with England. All three of these parties, then, agree in their support of the free trade policy. It needed but the aid of the Western farmer, therefore, to give permanency to this principle. His adhesion has been given, the *quadruple alliance* has been perfected, and slavery and free trade *nationalized!*

Slavery, thus intrenched in the midst of such powerful allies, and without competition in tropical cultivation, has become the sole reliance of KING COTTON. Lest the sources of his aggrandisement should be assailed, we can well imagine him as being engaged constantly, in devising new questions of agitation, to divert the public from all attempts to abandon free trade and restore the protective policy. He now finds an ample source of security, in this respect, in agitating the question of slavery extension. This exciting topic, as we have said, serves to keep politicians of the abolition school at the North in his constant employ. But for the agitation of this subject, few of these men would succeed in obtaining the suffrages of the people. Wedded to England's free trade policy, their votes in Congress, on all questions affecting the tariff, are always in perfect harmony with Southern interests, and work no mischief to the system of slavery. If Kansas comes into the Union as a slave State, he is secure in the political power it will give him in Congress; but if it is received as a free State, it will still be tributary to him, as a source from whence to draw provisions to feed his slaves. Nor does it matter much which way the controversy is decided, so long as all agree not to disturb slavery in the States where it is already established by law. Could KING COTTON be assured that this position will not be abandoned, he would care little about slavery in Kansas; but he knows full well that the public sentiment in the North is adverse to the system, and that the present race of politicians may readily be displaced by others who will pledge themselves to its overthrow in all the States of the Union, Hence he wills to retain the power over the question in his own hands.

The crisis now upon the country, as a consequence of slavery having become dominant, demands that the highest wisdom should be brought to the management of national affairs. Slavery, nationalized, can now be managed only as a national concern. It can now be abolished only with the consent of those who sustain it. Their assent can be gained only by employing other agents to meet the wants it now supplies. It must be superseded, then, if at all, by means that will not injuriously affect the interests of commerce and agriculture, to which it is now so important an auxiliary. None other will be accepted, for a moment, by the slaveholder. To supply the existing demand for tropical products, except by the present mode, is impossible. To make the change, is not the work of a day, nor of a generation. Should the influx of foreigners continue, such a change may, one day, be possible. But to effect the transition from slavery to freedom, on principles that will be acceptable to the parties who control the question; to devise and successfully sustain such measures as will produce this result; must be left to statesmen of broader views and loftier conceptions than are to be found among those at present engaged in this great controversy.

Take a more particular view of this subject, in the light of the commercial operations of the United States, for the year 1859, as best indicating the relations of the North and the South, and their mutual dependence upon each other. The total value of the imports of foreign commodities, including specie, was $338,768,130.[96] Of this $20,895,077 were re-exported, leaving for home consumption, $317,873,053—an amount more than eleven times greater than the whole foreign commerce of Great Britain one hundred and fifty-six years ago, and more than four times greater than her exports eighty-six years ago.[97]

Let us inquire how this immense foreign commerce is sustained; how these $317,873,000 of foreign imports are paid for by the American people; and how far the Northern and Southern States respectively have contributed to its payment. More than one-half the amount, or $161,434,923, was paid in raw cotton, and more than one-third of the remainder, or $57,502,305, in the precious metals; leaving less than $100,000,000 to be paid in the other productions of the country. More than one-third of this remainder was paid in cotton fabrics, tobacco, and rice; while the products of the forest, of the sea, and of various minor manufactures, swelled up our credits, so that the exports of breadstuffs and provisions, needed to liquidate the debt, only amounted to a little over $38,000,000.[98] Of this amount the exports, from the Northern States, of wheat and wheat flour, made up only $15,262,769, and the corn and corn meal but $2,206,396. "King Hay," so much lauded for his magnitude and money value, never once ventured on board a merchant vessel, to seek a foreign land, so as to aid in paying for the commodities which we imported.[99] In a word, the products of the forest and of agriculture, exported by the free States, amounted in value to about $45,300,000; while the same classes of products, supplied for export by the Slave States, amounted to more than $193,400,000.[100]

The economical relations of the North and the South can now be understood more clearly than they could be from the statistics referred to in the body of this work. The facts, in relation to the commerce of the United States, for 1859, were not accessible until after the stereotyping had been completed; and they are only crowded in here by omitting two or three pages of remarks of another kind, but of less importance, which closed the volume. By consulting Table XII, and two or three of the others, which contain similar facts, covering the commercial operations of the country since the year 1821, the whole question of the relations of the North and the South can be fully comprehended. It will be seen that the exports of tobacco, which are mainly from the South, have equaled in value considerably more than one-third the amount of that of breadstuffs and provisions; and that, in the same period, the exports of cotton have exceeded in value those of breadstuffs and provisions to the amount of $1,421,482,261.[101] Here, now, a just conception can be formed of the importance of cotton to the commerce of the country, as compared with our other productions. The amount exported, of that article, in the last thirty-nine years, has exceeded in value the exports of breadstuffs and provisions to the extent of *fourteen hundred and twenty-one millions of dollars!* Verily, Cotton is King!

Another point needs consideration. It is a fact, not to be questioned, that the productions of the Northern States amount to an immense sum, above those of the Southern States, when valued in dollars and cents; but the proportion of the products of the former; exported to foreign countries, is very insignificant, indeed, when compared with the value of the exports from the latter.[102] And, yet, the North is acquiring wealth with amazing rapidity. This fact could not exist, unless the Northern people produce more than they consume—unless they have a surplus to sell, after supplying their own wants. They must, therefore, find a permanent and profitable market, somewhere, for the surplus products that yield them their wealth. As that market is not in Europe, it must be in the Southern States. But the extent to which the South receive their supplies from the North, cannot be determined by any data now in the possession of the public. It must, however, be very large in amount, and, if withheld, would greatly embarrass the Southern people, by lessening their ability to export as largely as hitherto. So, on the other hand, if the Northern people were deprived of the markets afforded by the South, they would find so little demand elsewhere for their products, that it would have a ruinous effect upon their prosperity. All that can be safely said upon this subject is, that the interests of both sections of the country are so intimately connected, so firmly blended together, that a dissolution of the Union would be destructive to all the economical interests of both the North and the South. Cut off from the South all that the North supplies to the planters, in such articles as agricultural implements, furniture, clothing, provisions, horses, and mules, and cotton culture would at once have to be abandoned to a great extent. But would the South alone be the sufferer? Could the Northern agriculturist, manufacturer, and mechanic, remain prosperous, and continue to accumulate wealth, without a market for their products? Could Northern merchants dwell in their palaces, and roll in luxury, with a foreign commerce contracted to one-third of its present extent, and a domestic demand for merchandize reduced to one-half its present amount? Certainly not.

And if the mere necessity of self supply, of food and clothing, such as existed in 1820, would now be disastrous to the South, and react destructively upon the North, what would be the effect of emancipation upon the country at large? What would be the effect of releasing from restraint three and a half millions of negroes, to bask in idleness, under the genial sunshine of the South, or to emigrate hither and thither, at will, with none to control their actions? It is too late to insist that free labor would be more profitable than slave labor, when negroes are to be the operatives: Jamaica has solved that problem. It is too late to claim that white labor could be made to take the place of black labor, while the negroes remain upon the ground: Canada, and the Northern States, demonstrate that the two races cannot be made to labor together peacefully and upon terms of equality. Nothing is more certain, therefore, than that emancipation would inevitably place the Southern States in a similar position to that of Jamaica. On this point take a fact or two.

The *Colonial Standard*,[103] of the 13th January, 1859, in speaking of the present industrial condition of that Island, says, that there are not more than twenty thousand laborers who employ themselves in sugar cultivation for wages. This will seem astonishing to those who expected so much from emancipation, when it is stated that the black population of Jamaica, when liberated from slavery, numbered three hundred and eleven thousand, six hundred and ninety two; and that the exports of sugar from the Island, in 1805, before the slave trade was prohibited, amounted to 237,751,150 lbs.;[104] while, in 1859, the exports of that staple commodity, only amounted to 44,800,000 lbs.[105] It will thus be seen that the exports of sugar from Jamaica is now less than one-fifth of what it was in the prosperous days of slavery; and so it must be as to cotton, in the South, were emancipation forced upon this country. And what would be the condition of our foreign commerce, and what the effect upon the country, generally, were the exports of the South diminished to less than one-fifth of their present amount? Would the lands of the Northern farmers still continue to advance in price, if the markets for the surplus products of the soil no longer existed? Would those of the Southern planters rise in value, in the event of emancipation, to an equality with the lands at the North, when no laborers could be found to till the soil? No man entitled to the name of statesman—no man of practical common sense—could imagine that such a result would follow the liberation of the slaves in the Southern States. Under the philanthropic legislation of Great Britain, no such result followed the passage of the act for the abolition of slavery in her colonies; but, on the contrary, the value of their real estate soon became reduced to a most ruinous extent; and such must inevitably be the result under the adoption of similar measures in the United States. This is the conviction of the men of the South, and they will act upon their own judgment.

There are strong indications that the views presented in the first edition of this work, and reported in the subsequent issues, are rapidly becoming the views of intelligent and unprejudiced men everywhere. At a late date in the British Parliament, Lord Brougham made a strong anti-American cotton and anti-American slavery speech. The *London Times*, thus "takes the backbone all out of his argument, and leaves him nothing but his sophistries to stand on," thus:

"Lord Brougham and the veterans of the old Anti-Slavery Society do not share our delight at this great increase in the employment of our home population. Their minds are still seared by those horrible stories which were burnt in upon them in their youth, when England was not only a slave-owning, but even a slave-trading State. Their remorse is so great that the ghost of a black man is always before them. They are benevolent and excellent people; but if a black man happened to have broken his shin, and a white man were in danger of drowning, we much fear that a real anti-slavery zealot would bind up the black man's leg before he would draw the white man out of the water. It is not an inconsistency, therefore, that while we see only cause of congratulation in this wonderful increase of trade, Lord Brougham sees in it the exaggeration of an evil he never ceases to deplore.

"We, and such as we, who are content to look upon society as Providence allows it to exist—to mend it when we can, but not to distress ourselves immoderately for evils which are not of our creation—we see only the free and intelligent English families who thrive upon the wages which these cotton bales produce. Lord Brougham sees only the black laborers who, on the other side of the Atlantic, pick the cotton pods in slavery. Lord Brougham deplores that in this tremendous exportation of a thousand millions of pounds of cotton, the lion's share of the profits goes to the United States, and has been produced by slave labor. Instead of twenty-three millions, the United States now send us eight hundred and thirty millions, and this is all cultivated by slaves. It is very sad that this should be so, but we do not see our way to a remedy. There seems to be rather a chance of its becoming worse.

"If France, who is already moving onwards in a restless, purblind state, should open her eyes wide, should give herself fair-play, by accepting our coals, iron, and machinery, and, under the stimulus of a wholesome competition, should take to manufacturing upon a large scale, even these three millions of slaves will not be enough. France will be competing with us in the foreign cotton markets, stimulating still further the produce of Georgia and South Carolina. The jump which the consumption of cotton in England has just made is but a single leap, which may be repeated indefinitely. There are a thousand millions of mankind on the globe, all of whom can be most comfortably clad in cotton. Every year new tribes and new nations are added to the category of cotton-wearers. There is every reason to believe that the supply of this universal necessity will, for many years yet to come, fail to keep pace with the demand, and in the interest of that large class of our countrymen to whom cotton is bread, we must continue to hope that the United States will be able to supply us in years to come with twice as much as we bought of them in years past. 'Let us raise up another market,' says the anti-slavery people. So say we all. . . . . .

"But even Lord Brougham would not ask us to believe that there is any proximate hope that the free cotton raised in Africa will, within any reasonable time, drive out of culture the slave-grown cotton of America. If this be so, of what use can it be to make irritating speeches in the House of Lords against a state of things by which we are content to profit? Lord Brougham and Lord Grey are not men of such illogical minds as to be incapable of understanding that it is the demand of the English manufacturers which stimulates the produce of slave-grown American cotton. They are, neither of them, we apprehend, so reckless or so wicked as to close our factories and to throw some two millions of our manufacturing population out of bread. Why, then, these inconsequent and these irritating denunciations? Let us create new fields of produce of we can; but, meanwile, it is neither just nor dignified to buy the raw material from the Americans, and to revile them for producing it."

We have said that the more popular belief, in reference to the moral character of slavery, now prevailing throughout the world, ranks it as identical in principle with despotic forms of government. Here arises a question of importance. Can despotism be acknowledged by Christians as a lawful form of government? Those who hold the view of slavery under consideration, answer in the affirmative. The necessity of civil government, they say, is denied by none. Society can not exist in its absence. Republicanism can be sustained only where the majority are intelligent and moral. In no other condition can free government be maintained. Hence, despotism establishes itself, of necessity, more or less absolutely, over an ignorant or depraved people; obtaining the acquiescence of the enlightened, by offering them security to person and property. Few nations, indeed, possess moral elevation sufficient to maintain republicanism. Many have tried it, have failed, and relapsed into despotism. Republican nations, therefore, must forego all intercourse with despotic governments, or acknowledge them to be lawful. This can be done, it is claimed, without being accountable for moral evils connected with their administration. Elevated examples of such recognitions are on record. Christ paid tribute to Cæsar; and Paul, by appealing to Cæsar's tribunal, admitted the validity of the despotic government of Rome, with its thirty millions of slaves. To deny the lawfulness of despotism, and yet hold intercourse with such governments, is as inconsistent as to hold the *per se* doctrine, in regard to slavery, and still continue to use its products.

How far masters in general escape the commission of sin, in the treatment of their slaves, or whether any are free from guilt, is not the point at issue, in this view of slavery. The mere possession of power over the slave, under the sanction of law, is held not to be sinful; but, like despotism, may be used for the good of the governed. That Southern masters are laboring for the good of the slave, to an encouraging extent, is apparent from the missionary efforts they are sustaining among the slave population. And when it is considered that the African race, under American slavery, have made much greater progress than they have ever done in any other part of the world; and that the elevating influences are now greatly increased among them; it is to be expected that dispassionate men will be disposed to leave the present condition of things undisturbed, rather than to rush madly into the adoption of measures that may prove fatal to the existence of the Union.

APPENDIX

EARLY MOVEMENTS IN THE AMERICAN COLONIES ON THE SLAVERY QUESTION.

SENTIMENTS have been quoted from the proceedings of the public meetings held by the fathers of the Revolution, which, when taken in connection with the language of the Declaration of Independence, seem to favor the opinion that it was their purpose to extend to the colored people all the privileges to be secured by that struggle. An examination of the historical records, leads to the conclusion, that no such intention existed on the part of the statesmen and patriots of that day. The opinions expressed, with scarcely an exception, show that they viewed the slave trade and slavery as productive of evils to the colonies, and calculated to retard their prosperity, if not to prevent their acquisition of independence. The question of negro slavery was one of little moment, indeed, in the estimation of the colonists, when compared with the objects at which they aimed; and the resolutions adopted, which bound them not to import any more slaves, or purchase any imported by others, was a blow aimed at the commerce of the mother country, and designed to compel Parliament to repeal its obnoxious laws. But the resolutions themselves must be given, as best calculated to demonstrate what were the designs of those by whom they were adopted. Before doing this, however, it is necessary to ascertain what were the relations which the North American Colonies bore to the commerce of the British Empire, and why it was, that the refusal any longer to purchase imported slaves would be so ruinous to Great Britain, and her other colonies. When this is done, and not till then, can the full meaning of the resolutions be determined. Such were the links connecting these colonies with England—with the West Indies—and with the African slave trade, conducted by British merchants—that more than one-half of the commerce of the mother country was directly or indirectly under their control. The facts on this subject are extracted from the debates in the British Parliament, and especially from the speech of Hon. EDMUND BURKE, on his resolutions, of March 22d, 1775, for conciliation with America.[106] He said:—

"I have in my hand two accounts; one, a comparative statement of the export trade of England to its colonies, as it stood in the year 1704, and as it stood in the year 1772. The other, a state of the export trade of this country to its colonies alone, as it stood in 1772, compared with the whole trade of England to all parts of the world, (the colonies included,) in the year 1704. They are from good vouchers; the latter period from the accounts on your own table, the earlier, from an original manuscript of Davenant, who first established the Inspector General's Office, which has been, ever since his time, so abundant a source of Parliamentary information.

"The export trade to the colonies, consists of three great branches. The African, which, terminating almost wholly in the colonies, must be put to the account of their commerce; the West Indian, and the North American. All these are so interwoven, that the attempt to separate them would tear to pieces the contexture of the whole; and if not entirely destroy, would very much depreciate the value of all the parts. I, therefore, consider these three denominations to be, what in effect they are, one trade.

"The trade to the colonies, taken on the export side, at the beginning of this century, that is, in the year 1704, stood thus:

"Exports to North America and the West Indies	$2,416,325
To Africa	433,325
	$2,849,650

"In the year 1772, which I take as a middle year, between the highest and lowest of those lately laid on your table, the account was as follows:

"To North America and the West Indies	$23,958,670
To Africa	4,331,990
To which, if you add the export trade from Scotland, which had, in 1704, no existence	1,820,000
	$30,110,660

"From a little over two millions and three quarters, it has grown to over thirty millions.[107] It has increased no less than twelve fold. This is the state of the colony trade, as compared with itself at these two periods, within this century; and this is matter for meditation. But this is not all. Examine my second account. See how the export trade to the colonies alone, in 1772, stood in the other point of view, that is, as compared to the whole trade of England, in 1704.

"The whole trade of England, including that to the colonies, in 1704	$32,545,000
Export to the colonies alone, in 1772	30,120,000
Difference	$2,425,000

"The trade with America alone, is now within less than two millions and a half of being equal to what this great commercial nation, England, carried on at the beginning of this century with the whole world! If I had taken the largest year of those on your table, it would rather have exceeded. But, it will be said, is not this American trade an unnatural protuberance, that has drawn the juices from the rest of the body? The reverse. It is the very food that has nourished every other part into its present magnitude. Our general trade has been greatly augmented; and augmented more or less in almost every part to which it ever extended; but with this material difference, that of the thirty-two millions and a half, which, in the beginning of the century, constituted the whole mass of our export commerce, the colony trade was but one-twelfth part; it is now considerably more than a third of the whole—[which is $80,000,000.] This is the relative proportion of the importance of the colonies at these two periods; and all reasoning concerning our mode of treating them, must have this proportion as its basis; or it is a reasoning, weak, rotten, and sophistical."

It is easy to perceive, from what is said by Mr. Burke, the embarrassments that must fall upon the mother country, in the event of a rebellion in the North American colonies. Take another illustration of this point. More than one-third of the exports of Great Britain were made to North America, the West Indies, and Africa. They stood thus during the three years ending at Christmas, 1773:

Annual average exports to North America	$17,500,000
To the West Indies	6,500,000
To Africa	3,500,000
Total value of exports	$27,500,000

But this is not all. The total value of the exports of Great Britain to all the world, at this date, was $80,000,000. These exports were made up, in part, of colonial products, tobacco, rice, sugar, etc., to the amount of $15,000,000;—$5,000,000 to foreign countries, and $10,000,000 to Ireland,—which, when added to the $27,500,000, paid for by the colonies, exhibits them as sustaining more than one-half of the commerce of the mother country.[108]

The immediate cause of the alarm which led to the examination of this subject by the Hon. Edmund Burke, and others, of the British Parliament, was the adoption, by the North American colonies, of the policy of non-importation and non-consumption of all English products, whether from the mother country, or any of her colonies; and the non-exportation of any North American products to Great Britain, the West Indies, or any of the dependencies of the crown. This agreement was adopted as a measure of retaliation upon Parliament, for the passage of the Boston Port Bill, which ordered the closing of Boston harbor to all commerce. The measure was first proposed at a meeting of the citizens of Boston, held on May 13, 1774. It was soon seconded by all the principal cities, towns, and counties, throughout the colonies; and when the Continental Congress met at Philadelphia, the terms of the league were drawn up and adopted, October 20, 1774, and went into operation.

A few extracts from memorials to Parliament, praying that the difficulties with North America might be adjusted, and the threatened evils averted, will show how the slave trade was then interwoven with the commerce and national prosperity of Great Britain, and to what extent the American league could affect that prosperity.

In the House of Commons, January 23, 1775: "Mr. Burke then presented a petition of the Master, Wardens, and Commonalty, of the Society of Merchants Venturers of the city of Bristol, under their common seal; which was read, setting forth, That a very beneficial and increasing trade to the British colonies in America, has been carried on from the port of Bristol, highly to the advantage of the kingdom in general, and of the said city in particular; and that the exports from the said port to America, consist of almost every species of British manufactures, besides East India goods, and other articles of commerce; and the returns are made not only in many valuable and useful commodities from thence, but also, by a circuitous trade, carried on with Ireland, and most parts of Europe, to the great emolument of the merchant, and improvement of his Majesty's revenue; and that the merchants of the said port are also deeply engaged in the trade to the West India islands, which, by the exchange of their produce with America, for provisions, lumber, and other stores, are thereby almost wholly maintained, and consequently, become dependent upon North America for support; and that the trade to Africa, which is carried on from the said port to a very considerable extent, is also dependent upon the flourishing state of the West India islands, and America; and that these different branches of commerce give employment not only to a very numerous body of artists and manufacturers, but also to a great number of ships, and many thousand seamen, by which means a very capital increase is made to the naval strength of Great Britain. . . . . . The passing certain acts of Parliament, and other measures lately adopted, caused such a great uneasiness in the minds of the inhabitants of America, as to make the merchants apprehensive of the most alarming consequences, and which, if not speedily remedied, must involve them in utter ruin. And the petitioners, as merchants deeply interested in measures which so materially affect the commerce of this kingdom, and not less concerned as Englishmen, in every thing that relates to the general welfare, cannot look without emotion on the many thousands of miserable objects, who, by the total stop put to the export trade of America, will be discharged from their manufactories for want of employment, and must be reduced to great distress."[109]

January 26, 1775. A petition of the merchants and tradesmen of the port of Liverpool, was presented to the House, and read, setting forth: "That an extensive and most important trade has been long carried on, from said town to the continent and islands of America; and that the exports from thence infinitely exceed in value the imports from America, from whence an immense debt arises, and remains due to the British merchant; and that every article which the laborer, manufacturer, or more ingenious artist, can furnish for use, convenience, or luxury, makes a part in these exports, for the consumption of the American; and that those demands, as important in amount as various in quality, have for many seasons been so constant, regular, and diffusive, that they are now become essential to the flourishing state of all their manufactures, and of consequence to every ndividual in these kingdoms; and that the bread of thousands in Great Britain, principally and immediately depends upon this branch of commerce, of which a temporary interruption will reduce the hand of industry to idleness and want, and a longer cessation of it would sink the now opulent trader in indigence and ruin; and that at this particular season of the year, the petitioners have been accustomed to send to North America many ships wholly laden with the products of Britain; but by the unhappy differences at present subsisting, from whatever source they flow, the trade to these parts is entirely at a stand; and that the present loss, though great, is nothing, when compared with the dreadful mischiefs which will certainly ensue, if some effectual remedy is not speedily applied to this spreading malady, which must otherwise involve the West India islands, and the trade to Africa, in the complicated ruin; but that the petitioners can still, with pleasing hopes, look up to the British Parliament, from whom they trust that these unhappy divisions will speedily be healed, mutual confidence and credit restored, and the trade of Britain again flourishing with undecaying vigor."[110]

March 16, 1775. To the question "From what places do the sugar colonies draw food for subsistence?" the answer, given before Parliament, was, in part, as follows: "I confine myself at present to necessary food. Ireland furnishes a large quantity of salted beef, pork, butter, and herrings, but no grain. North America supplies all the rest, both corn and provisions. North America is truly the granary of the West Indies; from whence they draw the great quantities of flour and biscuit for the use of one class of people, and of Indian corn for the support of all the others; for the support, not of man only, but of every animal . . . . . . North America also furnishes the West Indies with rice . . . . . . North America not only furnishes the West Indies with bread, but with meat, with sheep, with poultry, and some live cattle; but the demand for these is infinitely short of the demand for the salted beef, pork, and fish. Salted fish, (if the expression may be permitted in contrast with bread,) is the meat of all the lower ranks in Barbadoes and the Leeward Islands. It is the meat of all the slaves in the West Indies. Nor is it disdained by persons in better condition. The North American colonies also furnishes the sugar colonies with salt from Turks' Island, Sal Tortuga, and Anguilla; although these islands are themselves a part of the West Indies. The testimony which some experience has enabled me to bear, you will find confirmed, Sir, by official accounts. The same accounts will distinguish the source of the principal, the great supply of corn and provisions. They will fix it precisely in the middle colonies of North America; in those colonies who have made a public agreement in their Congress, to withhold all their supplies after the tenth of next September. How far that agreement may be precipitated in its execution, may be retarded or frustrated, it is for the wisdom of Parliament to consider: but if it is persisted in, I am well founded to say, that nothing will save Barbadoes and the Leeward Islands from the dreadful consequences of absolute famine. I repeat, the famine will not be prevented. The distress will fall upon them suddenly; they will be overwhelmed with it, before they can turn themselves about to look for relief. What a scene! when rapine, stimulated by hunger, has broken down all screens, confounded the rich with the poor, and leveled the freeman with his slave! The distress will be sudden. The body of the people do not look forward to distant events; if they should do this, they will put their trust in the wisdom of Parliament. Suppose them to be less confident in the wisdom of Parliament, they are destitute of the means of purchasing an extraordinary stock. Suppose them possessed of the means; a very extraordinary stock is not to be found at market. There is a plain reason in the nature of the thing, which prevents any extraordinary stock at market, and which would forbid the planter from laying it in, if there was; it is, that the objects of it are perishable. In those climates, the flour will not keep over six or eight weeks; the Indian corn decays in three months; and all the North American provisions are fit only for present use."[111]

To the question, what are the advantages of the sugar colonies to Great Britain? it was answered: "The advantage is not that the profits all centre here; it is, that it creates, in the course of attaining those profits, a commerce and navigation in which multitudes of your people, and millions of your money are employed; it is that the support which the sugar colonies received in one shape, they give in another. In proportion to their dependence on North America, and upon Ireland, they enable North America and Ireland to trade with Great Britain. By their dependence upon Great Britain for hands to push the culture of the sugar-cane, they uphold the trade of Great Britain to Africa. A trade which in the pursuit of negroes, as the principal, if not the only intention of the adventurer, brings home ivory and gold as secondary objects. In proportion as the sugar colonies consume, or cause to be consumed, among their neighbors, Asiatic commodities, they increase the trade of the English East India Company. In this light I see the India goods which are carried to the coast of Guinea.[112]

To the question, what proportion of land in the Leeward Islands, being applied to raising provisions, would supply the negroes with provisions, on an estate of two hundred hogsheads, for instance? it was answered: "The native products of the Islands are very uncertain; all so, but Guinea corn; therefore, much more land would be applied to this purpose than would be necessary to raise the supply for the regular constant consumption. They must provide against accidents, such as hurricanes, excess of wet weather, or of dry weather, the climate being very uncertain; it is, therefore, impossible to answer this question precisely; but this I can say, that if they were obliged to raise their own food, that their food then must be their principal object, and sugar only a secondary object; it would be but the trifle, which provisions are now."[113]

The testimony in reference to Jamaica, was very similar to that quoted in relation to Barbadoes and the Leeward Islands; except that as Jamaica had more unimproved land, and greater diversity of soil and climate, it might, in time, stand prepared to meet the shock. But as the emergency was likely to be sudden and unexpected, much suffering must ensue in the outset of the non-intercourse policy.

It is only necessary to add a few remarks, from the speech of Mr. Glover, in summing up the testimony. He said: "From this ground see what is put in hazard; not merely a monied profit, but our bulwark of defense, our power in offense—the acts and industry of our Nation. Instead of thousands and tens of thousands of families in comfort, a navigation extensive and enlarging, the value and rents of lands yearly rising, wealth abounding, and at hand for further improvements, see or foresee, that this third of our whole commerce, that sole basis of our Empire, and this third in itself the best, once lost, carries with it a proportion of our national faculties, our treasure, our public revenue, and the value of land, succeeded in its fall by a multiplication of taxes to reinstate that revenue, an increasing burden on every increasing estate, decreasing by the reduced demand of its produce for the support of Manufactures, and menaced with a heavier calamity still—the diminution of our Marine, of our seamen, of our general population, by the emigration of useful subjects, strengthening that very country you wish to humble, and weakening this in the sight of rival powers, who wish to humble us.

"To recapitulate the heads of that material evidence delivered before you, would be tedious in me, unnecessary in itself. Leaving it, therefore, to its own powerful impression, I here add only, in a general mode of my own, that of the inhabitants of those Islands, above four hundred thousand are blacks, from whose labor the immense riches there, so distinctly proved at your bar, are derived, with such immense advantage to these kingdoms. How far these multitudes, if their intercourse with North America is stopped, may be exposed to famine, you have heard. One-half in Barbadoes and the Leeward Islands, say one hundred thousand negroes, in value at least twenty millions of dollars, possibly, it grieves me to say probably, may perish. The remainder must divert to provisions the culture of the produce so valuable to Great Britain. The same must be the practice in great part throughout Jamaica and the new settled acquisitions. They may feel a distress just short of destruction, but must divert for subsistence so much labor as, in proportion, will shorten their rich product."[114]

The North American colonies could not have devised a measure so alarming to Great Britain, and so well calculated to force Parliament into the repeal of her obnoxious laws, as this policy of non-intercourse. It would deprive the West Indies of their ordinary supplies of provisions, and force them to suspend their usual cultivation, to produce their own food. It would cause not only the cessation of imports from Great Britain into the West Indies, on account of the inability of its people to pay, but would, at once, check all demand for slaves, both in the sugar Islands and in North America—thus creating a loss, in the African trade alone, of three and a half millions of dollars, and putting in peril one-half of the commerce of England.

We are now prepared to introduce the resolutions, passed by the North American colonies, on the subject of the slave trade and slavery. It is not considered necessary to burden our pages with a repetition of the whole of the accompanying resolutions. They embraced every item of foreign commodities, excepting in a few instances where medicines, saltpetre, and other necessaries, were exempted from the prohibition. In a few counties, though they condemned the slave trade, they excepted negroes, and desired to retain the privilege of procuring them. This was in the early part of the movement. When the Continental Congress came to act upon it, no such exemption was made.

On May 17, 1774, the citizens of Providence, Rhode Island, met and acquiesced in the Boston resolutions. Their proceedings closed with this declaration: "Whereas, the inhabitants of America are engaged in the preservation of their rights and liberties; and as personal liberty is an essential part of the natural rights of mankind, the deputies of the town are directed to use their endeavors to obtain an act of the General Assembly, prohibiting the importation of negro slaves in this colony; and that all negroes born in the colony should be free at a certain age."

Prince George county, Virginia, June 1774, responded to Boston, and added this resolution: "*Resolved*, That the African trade is injurious to this colony, obstructs the population of it by freemen, prevents manufacturers and other useful emigrants from Europe from settling among us, and occasions an annual balance of trade against the colony."[115]

Culpepper County, Virginia, July 7, 1774 acquiesced in the non-intercourse policy, and added this resolution: "*Resolved*, That the importing slaves and convict servants, is injurious to this colony, as it obstructs the population of it with freemen and useful manufacturers, and that we will not buy such slave or convict hereafter to be imported."[116]

The Provincial Convention, at Charleston, South Carolina, July 6, 7, 8, 1774, resolved to acquiesce in the Boston non-intercourse measures, and the merchants agreed not to import goods or slaves, until the grievances were redressed.[117]

Nansemond County Virginia, July 11, 1774, gave full assent to the Boston measures, and also "*Resolved*, That the African trade is injurious to this colony, obstructs the population of it by freemen, prevents manufacturers and other useful emigrants from Europe from settling among us, and occasions an annual increase of the balance of trade against the colony ."[118]

Caroline County, Virginia, July 14, 1774, cordially acceded to the Boston policy, and also "*Resolved*, That the African trade is injurious to this colony, obstructs our population by freemen, manufacturers, and others, who would emigrate from Europe and settle here, and occasions a balance of trade against the country that ought to be associated against."[119]

Surry County, Virginia, July 6, 1774, decided to sustain the Bostonians and also "*Resolved*, That as the population of this colony, with freemen and useful manufacturers, is greatly obstructed by the importation of slaves and convict servants, we will not purchase any such slaves or servants, hereafter to be imported."[120]

Fairfax County, Virginia, July 18, 1774, took ground strongly with Boston, and further "*Resolved*, That it is the opinion of this meeting, that during our present difficulties and distress, no slaves ought to be imported into any of the British colonies on the continent; and we take this opportunity of declaring our most earnest wishes to see an entire stop forever put so such a wicked, cruel, and unnatural trade."[121]

Hanover county, Virginia, July 20, 1774, sustained the Boston resolutions, and also "*Resolved*, That the African trade for slaves, we consider as most dangerous to virtue and the welfare of this country; we therefore most earnestly wish to see it totally discouraged."[122]

Prince Ann County, Virginia, July 27, 1784, adopted the Boston policy, most distinctly, and also "*Resolved*, That our Burgesses be instructed to oppose the importation of slaves and convicts as injurious to this colony, by preventing the population of it by freemen and useful manufacturers."[123]

The Virginia Convention of Delegates, which met at Williamsburgh, August 1, 1774, fully indorsed the non-intercourse policy, medicines excepted, and in their resolutions declared: "We will neither ourselves import, nor purchase any slave or slaves imported by any other person, after the first day of November next, either from Africa, the West Indies, or any other place."[124]

The North Carolina Convention of Delegates, which met at Newbern, August 24, 1774, fully indorsed the non-intercourse policy, and also passed this among their other resolutions: "*Resolved*, That we will not import any slave or slaves, or purchase any slave or slaves, imported or brought into this Province by others, from any part of the world, after the first day of November next."[125]

And, finally, the Continental Congress, which met at Philadelphia, Sept. 5, 1774, in passing its non-importation, non-exportation, and non-consumption Agreement, included the following as the second article of that document:

"That we will neither import nor purchase any slave imported after the first day of December next; after which time we will wholly discontinue the slave trade, and will neither be concerned in it ourselves, nor will we hire our vessels, nor sell our commodities or manfactures to those who are concerned in it."[126]

To afford a clear view of the reasons which prompted the colonies to adopt such stringent measures to compel Parliament to repeal its oppressive acts, it is only necessary to quote the very brief summary of grievances of which they complained, as drawn up by the Pennsylvania Convention, which met in Philadelphia, July 15, 1774:

"The legislative authority claimed by Parliament over these colonies, consists of two heads: first, a general power of internal legislation; and, secondly, a power of regulating our trade; both, she contends, are unlimited. Under the first may be included, among other powers, those of forbidding us to worship our Creator in the manner we think most acceptable to him—imposing taxes on us—collecting them by their own officers—enforcing the collection by Admiralty Courts, or Courts Martial—abolishing trials by jury—establishing a standing army among us in time of peace, without consent of our Assemblies—paying them with our money—seizing our young men for recruits—changing constitutions of government—stopping the press—declaring any action, even a meeting of the smallest number, to consider of peaceable modes to obtain redress of grievances, high treason—taking colonists to Great Britain to be tried—exempting 'murderers' of colonists from punishment, by carrying them to England, to answer indictments found in the colonies—shutting up our ports—prohibiting us from slitting iron to build our houses, making hats to cover our heads, or clothing to cover the rest of our bodies, etc."[127]

It was in the midst of grievances such as these, and of efforts of redress such as the adoption of the Non-Intercourse Agreement was expected to afford, that the resolutions against the slave trade and slavery were passed. What, then, was their true import? Did the patriots of the Revolution contemplate the enfranchisement of the negro, in the event of securing their own independence? Did their views of free institutions include the idea that barbarism and civilization could coalesce and co-exist in harmony and safety? Or did they not hold, as a great fundamental truth, that a high degree of intelligence and moral principle was essential to the success of free government? And was it not on this very principle, that they opposed the further introduction of negroes from Africa, and afterwards, by a special clause in the Constitution, excluded the Indians from citizenship?

The resolutions which have been quoted, have given rise to much discussion, and have often been misrepresented. By severing them from their connection with the circumstances under which they were adopted, and associating them with the phrase in the Declaration of Independence, that "all men are created equal," the impression has been made that the negroes were to be included in the rights therein claimed. But as they have not been made participants in the benefits of the Revolution, it has been argued that the nation has broken its covenant engagements, and must expect that the judgments of Heaven will be poured out upon her.

Now, what are the facts? The colonists were aiming at a high degree of mental and moral culture, and were desirous of developing the resources of the country, by encouraging the influx of freemen from Europe, and especially of mechanics and manufacturers. They were anxiously looking forward to the time when they could cast off the yoke of oppression which the mother country had forced upon their necks. The multiplication of the negro population was considered as a barrier to the success of their measures, and as most dangerous to virtue and the welfare of the country. It was increasing the indebtedness of the citizens to foreign merchants, and augmenting the balance of trade against the colonies. But there was no settled policy in reference to the future disposition of the colored population. Feelings of pity were manifested toward them, and some expressed themselves in favor of emancipation. The Continental Congress, in addition to its action in the Non-Intercourse Agreement, *Resolved*, April 6, 1776, "That no slaves be imported into any of the thirteen United Colonies."[128] The Delaware Convention, August 27, 1776, adopted, as the 26th article of its Constitution, that "No person hereafter imported into this State from Africa, ought to be held in slavery on any pretense whatever; and no negro, Indian, or mulatto slave ought to be brought into this State, for sale, from any part of the world."[129]

There was more of meaning in this action, than the resolution, standing alone, would seem to indicate. On the 11th of July, preceding, Gen. Washington wrote to the Massachusetts Assembly, that the enemy had excited the slaves and savages to arms against him;[130] and on November 7th, 1775, Lord Dunmore had issued a proclamation, declaring the emancipation of all slaves "that were able and willing to bear arms, they joining his Majesty's troops, as soon as may be, for the more speedy reducing the colonists to their duty to his Majesty's crown and dignity."[131]

Previous to the commencement of hostilities, the resolutions of the colonists, adverse to the slave trade and slavery, were designed to operate against British commerce; but, after that event, the measures adopted had reference, mainly, to the prevention of the increase of a population that had been, and might continue to be, employed against the liberties of the colonies. That such a course formed a part of the policy of Great Britain, is beyond dispute; and that she considered the prosecution of the slave trade as necessary to her purposes, was clearly indicated by the Earl of Dartmouth, who declared, as a sufficient reason for turning a deaf ear to the remonstrances of the colonists against the further importation of slaves, that "Negroes cannot become republicans—they will be a power in our hands to restrain the unruly colonists." That such motives prompted England to prosecute the introduction of slaves into the colonies, was fully believed by American statesmen; and their views were expressed, by Mr. Jefferson, in a clause in the first draft of the Declaration of Independence, but which was afterward omitted.

That the emancipation of the negroes was not contemplated, by those in general, who voted for the resolutions quoted, is evident from the subsequent action of Virginia, where the greater portion of the meetings were held. They could not have intended to enfranchise men, whom they declared to be obstacles in the way of public prosperity, and as dangerous to the virtues of the people. Nor could the signers of the Declaration of Independence have designed to include the Indians and negroes in the assertion that all men are created equal, because these same men, in afterwards adopting the Constitution, deliberately excluded the Indians from citizenship, and forever fixed the negro in a condition of servitude, under that Constitution, by including him, as a slave, in the article fixing the ratio of Congressional representation on the basis of five negroes equaling three white men. The phrase—"all men are created equal"—could, therefore, have meant nothing more than the declaration of a general principle, asserting the equality of the colonists, before God, with those who claimed it as a divine right to lord it over them. The Indians were men as well as the negroes. Both were within the territory over which the United Colonies claimed jurisdiction. The exclusion of both from citizenship under the Constitution, is conclusive that neither were intended to be embraced in the Declaration of Independence.

That the colonists were determined, at any sacrifice, to achieve their own liberties, even at the sacrifice of their slave property, seems to have been the opinion of intelligent Englishmen. Burke, in his speech already quoted, thus dissipates the hopes of those who expected to find less resistance at the South than at the North.

"There is, however, a circumstance attending the [Southern] colonies, which, in my opinion, fully counterbalances this difference, and makes the spirit of liberty still more high and haughty than in those to the Northward. It is that in Virginia and the Carolinas, they have a vast multitude of slaves. Where this is the case, in any part of the world, those who are free, are by far the most proud and jealous of their freedom. Freedom is to them not only an enjoyment, but a kind of rank and privilege. Not seeing there that freedom, as in countries where it is a common blessing, and as broad and general as the air, may be united with much abject toil, with great misery with all the exterior of servitude, liberty looks, among them, like something that is more noble and liberal. I do not mean, sir, to commend the peculiar morality of this sentiment, which has at least as much pride as virtue in it; but I can not alter the nature of man. The fact is so; and these people of the Southern colonies are much more strongly, and with a higher and more stubborn spirit, attached to liberty, than those to the Northward. Such were all the ancient commonwealths; such were our Gothic ancestors; such in our days were the Poles; and such will be all masters of slaves, who are not slaves themselves. In such a people the haughtiness of domination combines with the spirit of freedom, fortifies it, and renders it invincible."

FREE COLORED POPULATION.

WHEN the author was carefully collating the facts from the Record of MAJOR LACHLAN, in reference to the fugitive slaves in Canada, he was not aware that he should be so fortunate as to obtain, from other sources, any testimony in their support. Canada has all along been a sealed book to the public of the States, so far as the condition of blacks, who had escaped thither, were concerned. Since the completion of the stereotyping of the volume, and just as it was about ready for the press, the *New York Herald*, of January 5, reached us. It embraces a detailed report on this important subject, which was prepared by a special agent, who visited the settlements he describes. It is very interesting to find, that the opinions and predictions of Major Lachlan, made in 1841 to 1850, as to the results of colored immigration into Canada, should be so fully sustained and fulfilled, by a report upon the actual facts in 1859.

It may be remarked, here, that we believe a crisis has arrived in the history of the free colored people of the United States, which demands the most calm and serious consideration; and we would remind the more intelligent colored men, that the honor of conducting their fellow-men in the road to a high civilization, will be as great as are the honors heaped upon the few of the white race, who have been the master spirits in bringing up their fellow-men to the pinnacle of greatness upon which they now stand. More than one field, for the accomplishment of this object, now presents itself; and, as the darkest hour is said to be that which immediately proceeds the dawn of day; it may be hoped that the lowering clouds now overshadowing their prospects, will soon be dissipated by a brighter sun, that shall reveal the highway of their deliverance.

But to the extracts from the *Herald*. After giving a detailed account of the whole subject of negro immigration into Canada, together with the particulars of the results of the several attempts at founding settlements for the refugees, the *Herald's* reporter sums up the whole matter thus:

"THE SOCIAL AND MORAL EFFECT OF THE IMPORTATION OF FUGITIVE SLAVES INTO CANADA.

"While, as we have seen, the British abolitionists in Canada are laboring with the republican abolitionists of America to entice away the slave property of the South, and to foment a servile insurrection in the Southern States, and a disruption of the Union, there are men of sense and of honor among our neighbors over the borders, who deplore this interference of their countrymen in the affairs of the republic, and appreciate the terrible catastrophe to which, if persevered in, it must eventually lead. I conversed with a prominent abolitionist in Chatham, holding a public position of trust and honor, who told me that the first suggestion of the Harper's Ferry attack was made to Brown by British abolitionists in Chatham, and who assured me that he had himself subscribed money to aid Brown in raising men for the service in Ohio and elsewhere in the States. In reply to some questions I put to him, he stated that he and his associates on the other side looked with expectation and hope to the day, not far distant, when a disruption of the Union would take place; for that, in that case, the British abolitionists would join the republican abolitionists of America in open warfare upon the slaveholding States. When I reminded him that the patriotic men of the North would raise a barrier of brave hearts, through which such traitors would find it difficult to reach the Southern States, he replied—'Oh, we have often talked over and calculated upon that; but you forget that we should have the negroes of the South to help us in their own homes against their oppressors, with the knife and the fire-brand.'

"I conversed on the other hand with conservative, high-minded men, who expressed the most serious apprehension that the bold and unjustifiable association of Canadian abolitionists with the negro stealers and insurrectionists of America would eventually plunge the two countries into war.

"We have seen that the immigration of fugitive slaves into Canada is unattended by any social or moral good to the negro. It is injurious, also, to the white citizens of Canada, inasmuch as it depresses the value of their property, diminishes their personal comfort and safety, and destroys the peace and good order of the community. Mr. Sheriff Mercer, of Kent county, assured me that the criminal statistics of that county prove that nine-tenths of the offenses against the laws are committed by colored persons. The same proportion holds good in Essex county, and the fact is the more startling when it is remembered that the blacks do not at present number more than one-fourth of the whole population.

"In the township of Anderdon, Essex county, this fall, nearly every sheep belonging to the white farmers has been stolen. The fact was presented in the return of the Grand Jury of the county, and some twelve negro families, men, women and children, were committed to jail on the charge of sheep stealing. The cases of petit larceny are incredibly numerous in every township containing negro settlements, and it is a fact that frequently the criminal calendars would be bare of a prosecution but for the negro prisoners.

"The offenses of the blacks are not wholly confined to those of a light character. Occasionally some horrible crime startles the community, and is almost invariably attended by a savage ferocity peculiar to the vicious negro. If a murder is committed by a black, it is generally of an aggravated and brutal nature. The offense of rape is unfortunately peculiarly prevalent among the negroes. Nearly every assize is marked by a charge of this character. A prominent lawyer of the Province, who has held the position of public prosecutor, told me that his greatest dread was of this offense, for that experience had taught him that no white woman was safe at all times, from assault, and those who were rearing daughters in that part of Canada, might well tremble at the danger by which they are threatened. He told me that he never saw a really brutal look on the human face until he beheld the countenances of the negroes charged with the crime of rape. When the lust comes over them they are worse than the wild beast of the forest. Last year, in broad daylight, a respectable white woman, while walking in the public road within the town of Chatham, was knocked down by a black savage and violated. This year, near Windsor, the wife of a wealthy farmer, while driving alone in a wagon, was stopped by a negro in broad daylight, dragged out into the road, and criminally assaulted in a most inhuman manner. It was impossible to hear the recital of these now common crimes without a shudder.

"The fugitive slaves go into Canada as beggars, and the mass of them commit larceny and lay in jail until they become lowered and debased, and ready for worse crimes. Nor does there seem at present a prospect of education doing much to better their condition, for they do not appear anxious to avail themselves of school privileges as a general rule. The worse class of blacks are too poor and too indolent to clothe their children in the winter, and their services are wanted at home in the summer. The better class affect airs as soon as they become tolerably well to do, and refuse to send their little ones to any but white schools. In Windsor there are two public colored schools, but the negroes of that place choose to refuse to allow their children to attend these institutions, and sent them to the schools for whites. They were not admitted, and two of the black residents, named Jones and Green, tested the question at law, to try whether the trustees or teachers had a right to exclude their children. It was decided that the trustees had such power, when separate schools were provided for colored persons.

"That property is seriously depreciated in all neighborhoods in which the negroes settle is a well known fact. Mr. S. S. Macdonnel, a resident of Windsor, and a gentleman of high social and political position, is the owner of a large amount of real estate in that place. The Bowyer farm, a large tract of land belonging to him, was partitioned into lots some few years since, and sold at auction. Some of the lots were bid in by negroes of means, among others, by a mulatto named De Baptiste, residing in Detroit. As soon as the white purchasers found that negroes were among the buyers, they threw up their lots, and since then the value of the property has been much depressed. In several instances Mr. Macdonnel paid premiums to the negroes to give up their purchases, where they had happened to buy in the midst of white citizens. At a subsequent sale of another property, cut up into very fine building lots, by the same gentleman, one of the conditions of sale announced was, that no bid should be received from colored persons. De Baptiste attended and bid in a lot. When his bid was refused, he endeavored to break up the auction in a row, by the aid of other negroes, and failing in this, brought an action at law against Mr. Macdonnel. This Mr. M. prepared to defend, but it was never pressed to a trial. These incidents, together with the attempt of the Windsor negroes to force their children into the schools for whites, illustrate the impudent assumption of the black, as soon as he becomes independent, and the deeply seated antipathy of the whites in Canada to their dark skinned neighbors. At the same time it is observable that the 'free negro' in Canada—that is, the black who was free in the States—endeavors to hold his head above the 'fugitive,' and has a profound contempt for the escaped slave.

"As I desired to obtain the views of intelligent Canadians upon the important questions before me, I requested a prominent and wealthy citizen of Windsor to favor me with a written statement of his observations on the effect of the negro immigration and received the following hastily prepared and brief communication, in reply. The opinions expressed are from one of the most accomplished gentlemen in the Province, and are worthy of serious consideration, although the public position he occupies renders it proper that I should not make public use of his name:—

"'WINDSOR, Dec. 23, 1859.

"'MY DEAR SIR—In reply to your request, I beg to say that I would cheerfully give you my views at length upon the important topics discussed at our interview, did not my pressing engagements just now occupy too much of my time to make it possible that I should do more than hastily sketch down such thoughts as occur to me in the few moments I can devote to the subject.

"'The constant immigration of fugitives from slavery into the two western counties of the Province of Canada, Kent and Essex, has become a matter for serious consideration to the landed proprietors in those counties, both as it effects the value and salability of real estate, and as rendering the locality an undesirable place of abode.

"'It is certain that ever since large numbers of fugitive slaves have, by means of the organization known here and in the States as "the Underground Railroad," and of such associations as the Dawn and Elgin Institutes and the Refugee Home Society, been annually introduced into these two counties, no settlers from the old country, from the States, or from the eastern part of Canada, have taken up lands there. And there is every reason to assign the fact of there being a large colored population, and that population constantly on the increase, as the chief cause why these counties do not draw a portion at least of the many seeking Western homes.

"'Kent and Essex have been justly styled "the Garden of Upper Canada." The soil in most parts of the counties cannot be excelled in richness and fertility, and the climate is mild and delightful. There are thousands of acres open for sale at a moderate price, but it now seldom happens that a lot of wild land is taken up by a new comer. The farmer who has achieved the clearing of the land that years ago was settled upon may wish to extend his possessions for the sake of his sons who are growing up, by the acquisition of an adjoining or neighboring piece of wild land; but seldom or never is the uncleared forest intruded upon now by the encampment of emigrant families.

"'It may be broadly asserted, first, in general, that the existence of a large colored population in Kent and Essex has prevented many white settlers from locating there who otherwise would have made a home in one of those counties; and, secondly, that in particular instances it constantly occurs that the sale of a lot of land is injuriously affected by reason of the near settlement of colored people.

"'Next, as to the general feeling of the gentry and farmers who live in the midst of this population: All regard it with dissatisfaction, and with a foreboding—an uncomfortable anticipation for the future, as they behold the annual inpouring of a people with whom they have few or no sympathies in common, many of whose characteristics are obnoxious and bad, and who have to make a commencement here, in the development of their better nature, should they possess any, from perhaps the lowest point to which the human mind can be degraded, intellectually and morally.

"'There is undoubtedly hardly a well thinking person whose heart is not touched with a feeling of pity for the unfortunates who present themselves as paupers, in the name of liberty, to become denizens of our country. And it would, doubtless, be a great moral spectacle to witness these escaped slaves, as they are sometimes pictured by professional philanthropists, rendering themselves happy in their freedom, acquiring property, surrounding themselves with the comforts, if not the elegancies of life, and advancing themselves intellectually, socially and politically. But, alas for human nature! If the negro is really fitted by the Creator to enjoy freedom as we enjoy it, the habits of mind and of action, however baneful they may be, that have been long exercised, are not to be suddenly broken or changed; and the slave who was idle, and lying, and thievish in the South, will not obtain opposite qualities forthwith by crossing the line that makes him free.

"'This is not said in a spirit of malevolence toward the colored people that are here and are brought here, but as presenting their case as it really is, and as explaining the position in which residents of these counties are placed, or will be placed, if this continuous flow from the slave States is poured in by means of the organizations and societies formed for that purpose in many of the Northern States of America, and fostered and aided by many indiscreet men in our own country.

"'The main argument in favor of the free school system is, that it is a benefit to all to be surrounded by an intelligent and moral community, and for such a benefit every property holder should be glad to contribute his quota. Is there, then, any need of asking the question, if the people of these counties desire the sort of population that comes to them from the Southern States?

"'What is the condition of the negroes on their arrival here? What their progress in the acquisition of property and knowledge, and their conduct as citizens?

"'There are very few indeed who arrive here with sufficient means at once to acquire a farm, or to enter into business of any kind. The great mass of them may be called paupers, claiming aid from the societies through whose agency they are brought out. Some of these societies hold large tracts of land, which they sub-divide and sell to new comers upon long time, but with conditions as to clearing, residence, etc., that are difficult of observance. I believe there is much trouble in carrying out this plan, arising in some measure from the peculiarities of negro character—a want of constancy or steadiness of purpose, as well as from a feeling of distrust as to their having the land secured to them. If the land is not purchased from any of these societies, a parcel of ten or fifteen colored families get together and purchase and settle upon some other spot.

"While there are instances of colored men accumulating property here, the great mass of them fail even in securing a living without charity or crime. They have but little forethought for the future, and care only to live lazily in the present. The criminal records of the county show that nine-tenths of the offenses are committed by the colored population, and I think the experience of every citizen who resides near a settlement will testify to their depredating habits.

"'I have given you thus hurriedly and disconnectedly my views on these subjects. They are important enough to demand more time and consideration in their discussion, but I believe the opinions I have advanced you will find shared in by a large proportion of the residents of the Province. I am, my dear sir, faithfully yours.'   —— ——.

"In addition to the testimony of the writer of the above communication, my views upon the subject under examination were confirmed by the valuable opinion of the Hon. Colonel Prince, the representative of the county in the Provincial Parliament for a long term of years. Colonel Prince has bestowed much consideration upon the negro question, and he has practical experience of the condition and conduct of the colored population. In June, 1858, in the course of a debate in the Legislative Council, Col. Prince was reported to have spoken as follows:

"'In the county of Essex the greatest curse that befell them was the swarm of blacks that infested that county. They were perfectly inundated with them. Some of the finest farmers of the county of Kent had actually left their beautiful farms, so as not to be near this terrible nuisance. If they looked over the criminal calendars of the country they would see that the majority of names were those of colored people. They were a useless, worthless, thriftless set of people, too lazy and indolent to work, and too proud to be taught. . . . . Were the blacks to swarm the country and annoy them with their rascalities? Honorable gentlemen might speak feelingly for the negroes, but they had never lived among them as he had done. Notwithstanding all that he said about them, they would say, if asked on the subject, that they had no better friend than Col. Prince. But there was no use in trying to get the white man to live with them. It was a thing they would not do. There was a great sympathy always expressed for the black man who escaped from the slave life; but he had lived with them twenty-five years, and had come to the conclusion that the black man was born for servitude, and was not fit for any thing else. He might listen to the morbid philanthropy of honorable gentlemen in favor of the negro; but they might as well try to change the spots of the leopard as to change the character of the blacks. They would still retain their idle and thievish propensities.'

"While Col. Prince claims that he was very inaccurately reported, and that he never said one word in favor of slavery, which he professes to abhor with a holy horror, he yet adheres to the opinion that the colored race is not fit to live and mix in freedom with the whites. He deplores deeply the action of such of his countrymen as improperly interfere in the affairs of the States, and condemns the lawless running off of slaves from the South, and the attempts to raise servile insurrection in the slaveholding States. As a con-stitutional British gentleman, he reveres the laws, and believes that where they are bad, or where the constitution of a country is unwise, the remedy lies in the power of the people by legal means. He sees the evil effect, morally and socially, of the influx of fugitive slaves into Canada, and would shut them out if he could. He knows that the negroes form an enormous portion of the criminals of his county, and the county of Kent, and he is doubly annoyed that men who come from servitude to freedom should abuse their privi-leges as the negroes do. He admits that every distinct attempt to make a settlement of negroes self-supporting and prosperous, has failed, and he believes that the negro is not yet fit for self-government, and requires over him a guiding, if not a master's hand.

Col. Prince is a gentleman of the old school—hale, hearty and whole-souled—and does not fear to express the sentiments he entertains.

"The lessons taught by an examination into the action of the Canadian abolitionists, and of the condition and prospects of the fugitive slaves in the Province, should be made useful to the American people. The history of the past proves that Great Britain would gladly destroy the Union of the States, which makes the American republic a leading power among nations. As in days past she sought to accomplish this object through the instrumentality of traitors and of the foes of the Union, so now she seeks aid in her de-signs from the republican abolition enemies of the confederacy in our own States. The intrigues of the British emissaries in Canada should stay the hand of every man who fan-cies that in helping to rob the South of its slaves he is performing an act of humanity; for they should teach him that he is but helping on the designs of those who look eagerly to the slavery agitation and the sectional passions engendered thereby, to accomplish a dis-ruption of the Union, and encompass the failure of our experiment of free government. . . . .

"Let our merchants and our farmers carefully consider these facts, and then reflect upon what they are required by the abolition agitators to do. To what end are the syste-matized negro stealing of the North, the attempts to incite insurrection at the South, and their natural results, a dissolution of the Union, to lead? Are we to render New York and the other free States subject to the same deplorable evils as afflict the western counties of

Canada? Are our Northern farmers willing to have the value of their lands depreciated, and to subject their crops and stock to constant depredations by inviting here the same class of neighbors that at present deplete whole Canadian townships of their sheep? Unless we desire to accomplish such results, why, under a mistaken idea of charity to the negro, do we take him from a life of usefulness and content at the South to plant him in freedom and suffering at the North? Why do we consent to help forward, directly or indirectly, an agitation that can only incite a disruption of the Union and bring upon us the very evils we deplore?"

IMPORTANT DECISIONS.

Since the volume was in type, the Supreme Court of Ohio has made a decision of great importance to the free colored people. We copy from the *Law Journal*, December, 1859:

"NEGROES AND THE COMMON SCHOOLS.

"The Supreme Court of Ohio, on Tuesday, on a question before them involving the right of *colored* children to be admitted into the Common Schools of the State, decided that the law of the State interfered with no right of colored children on the subject, and that they were not, therefore, entitled of *right* to the admission demanded. The following is the reported statement of the case:

"'Enos Van Camp *vs.* Board of Equalization of incorporated village of Logan, Hocking County, Ohio. Error to District Court of Hocking County.

"'Peck J. held:

"'1. That the statute of March 14, 1853, 'to provide for the reorganization, supervision, and maintenance of Common Schools, is a law of *classification* and not of *exclusion*, providing for the education of *all* youths within the prescribed ages, and that the words 'white' and 'colored,' as used in said act, are used in their popular and ordinary signification.

"'2. That children of three-eighths African and five-eighths white blood, but who are distinctly colored, and generally treated and regarded as colored children by the community where they reside, are not, *as of right*, entitled to admission into the Common Schools, set apart under said act, for the instruction of white youths.

"'Brinkherhoff, C. J., and Sutliff, J., dissented.'"

(From the Cincinnati Gazette.)

MASSACHUSETTS BLACK MILITIA.

Last Wednesday a bill passed by the Massachusetts Legislature authorizing colored persons to join military organizations, was vetoed by Gov. Banks, on the ground that he believed the chapter in the bill relating to the militia, in which the word "white" was stricken out, to be unconstitutional. In this opinion he is sustained by the Supreme Court and by the Attorney General.

The matter was discussed in the House at some length, and the veto sustained by a vote of 146 to 6.

A new chapter was then introduced on leave, and it being precisely the same as the other, except that the word "white" was restored, it passed the House with but one negative vote.

Under a suspension of the rules the new bill was then sent to the Senate, where, after debate, it was passed by a vote of 11 to 15.

The Governor signed the new bill, and the Legislature adjourned *sine die*.

SOUTH-SIDE VIEWS.

Rev. Dr. Fuller, of Baltimore, has written a long letter to Hon. Edward Everett, in regard to the present state of things as regards slavery. We subjoin two or three specimens:—*Cincinnati Gazette.*

"In June, 1845, there assembled in Charleston a body of men, representing almost all the wisdom and wealth of South Carolina. There were present, also, delegates from Georgia, and I believe from other States. It was a meeting of the association for the improvement, moral and religious, of the slave population. The venerable Judge Huger presided. Having been appointed to address that large and noble audience, I did not hesitate to speak my whole mind: appealing to masters to imitate the Antonines and other magnanimous Roman Emperors, to become the guardians of their slaves, to have laws enacted protecting them in their relations as husbands and wives and parents; to recognize the rights which the Gospel asserts for servants as well as masters. In a word, I pressed upon them the solemn obligations which their power over these human beings imposed upon them—obligations only the more sacred, because their power was so irresponsible.

"That august assembly not only honored me with their attention, but expressed their approval, the presiding officer concurring most emphatically in the views submitted.

"I need scarcely tell you that no such address would be regarded as wise or prudent at this time. It is not that masters are less engaged in seeking to promote the moral and religious well-being of their servants; but measures which once could have been adopted most beneficially would now only expose master and servant to the baneful influence of fanatical intermeddling.

"If any thing is certain, it is that the Gospel does not recognise hatred, abuse, violence and blood as the means by which good is to be done. The Gospel is a system of love. It assails no established social relations, but it infuses love into the hearts of those who are bound together, and thus unites them in affection."

Again he says:

"I think I speak accurately when I say, that hitherto every sacrifice for the emancipation of slaves has been made by Southern men; and many hundred thousand dollars have been expended in such liberations. The North has wasted large sums for abolition books and lectures; for addresses calculated to inflame the imaginations of women and children, and to mislead multitudes of men—most excellent and pious—but utterly ignorant as to the condition of things at the South. We now find, indeed, that money has been contributed even for the purchase of deadly weapons to be employed against the South, and to enlist the most ferocious passions in secret crusades, compared with which an open invasion by foreign enemies would be a blessing. I believe, however, that not one cent has yet been given to set on foot—or even encourage when proposed—any plausible enterprise for the benefit of the slave."

"I do now believe that the guardianship of a kind master is at this time a great blessing to the African. If emancipation is ever to take place, it will be gradually, and under the mild, but resistless influence of the Gospel. Whether slavery be an evil or not, we at the South did not bring these Africans here—we protested against their introduction. The true friend of the African is at the South, and thousands of hearts there are seeking to know what can be done for the race. There must be some limits to human responsibility, and a man in New England has no more right to interfere with the institutions of Virginia, than he has to interfere with those of England or France. All such interference will be repelled by the master, but it will prove injurious to the slave. Dr. Channing was regarded as a leading abolitionist in his day, but could that noble man now rise up, he would stand aghast at the madness which is rife everywhere on this subject. 'One great principle, which we should lay down as immovably true, is, that if a good work cannot be carried on by the calm, self-controlled, benevolent spirit of Christianity, then the time for doing it has not yet come.' Such was his language, when opposing slavery. Were he now living, the delirious spirit of the day would denounce him, as it denounced Mr. Webster, and now denounces you and every true patriot. Nay, even Mr. Beecher is abused as not truculent enough.

"Jesus saw slavery all around him. Did he seek to employ force? He said 'All power in heaven and earth is given unto me, therefore, go teach, go preach the Gospel.'"

COLORED PEOPLE EMIGRATING FROM LOUISIANA TO HAYTI.

The *New Orleans Picayune* notices that a vessel cleared from that port on the previous day, having on board eighty-one free colored persons, emigrating to Hayti. The *Picayune* says:

"These people are all from the Opelousas parishes, and all cultivators—well versed in farming, and in all the mechanical arts connected with a farm. Among them are brickmakers, blacksmiths, wheelwrights, carpenters, etc. Some of them are proficient weavers, who have long been employed making the stuff called Attakapas cottonade, so favorably known in the market. They take along with them the necessary machinery for that trade, and all sorts of agricultural and mechanical implements.

"These eighty-one persons—twenty-four adults and fifty-seven children and youths—compose fourteen families, or rather households, for they are all related, and the eighty-one may be called one family. They are all in easy circumstances, some even rich, one family being worth as much as $50,000. They were all land owners in this State, and have sold out their property with the intention of investing their capital in Hayti."—

Cincinnati Commercial, January, 1860.

THE COOLIE TRAFFIC.

It may be well to put upon record one of those extreme cases of hardship and cruelty which necessarily accompany the transportation of laborers to the West Indies, whether under the name of the slave trade, or coolie immigration. The China correspondent of the *New York Journal of Commerce*, of a recent date, says: The Flora Temple, an English vessel, had made all arrangements to secure a full cargo of coolies. They were cheated, inveigled, or stolen, and either taken directly to the ship or else confined in the barracoons in Macao till the ship was ready to sail for Havanna—the crew numbering fifty, and the coolies eight hundred and fifty. The vessel sailed October 8, 1859, when the coolies soon learned their destiny, and resolved to avert it at all hazards. On the morning of the 11th, without weapons of any kind, they rushed upon the guard and killed him. The noise brought the captain and his brother on deck, fully armed with revolvers, who by rapid firing and resolutely pressing forward, drove the miserable wretches below; where, without light and air, they were locked and barred like felons, in a space too limited to permit their living during the long voyage before them. Think of eight hundred and fifty human beings all full grown men, pressed into this contracted, rayless, airless dungeon, in which they were to be deported from China to Havana, all the long way over the China sea, the Indian ocean, and the Atlantic!

On the 14th, the vessel struck upon an unknown reef, a gale of wind in the meantime blowing, and the sea running high. Every effort was made to save the ship by the officers and crew; the poor coolies, battened down beneath the decks, being allowed no chance to aid in saving the ship or themselves. Although the yards were "braced around" and the ship "hove aback," she struck first slightly, and then soon after several times with a tremendous crash, the breakers running alongside very high. Pieces of her timbers and planking floated up on her port side, and after some more heavy thumps she remained apparently immovable. The water rapidly increased in the hold till it reached the "between-decks," where the eight hundred and fifty coolies were confined.

While this was going on, indeed, almost immediately after the ship first struck, the officers and crew very naturally became afraid of the coolies for the treatment they had received, and the captain ordered the boats to be lowered, not to save the coolies in whole or in part, but to preserve himself and crew. These boats, even under favorable circumstances, were not more than sufficient for the officers and crew, showing that no provision had been made for the poor coolies in case of disaster. The boats passed safely through the breakers, leaving the ship almost without motion, all her masts standing, her back broken, and the sea making a clear break over her starboard and quarter.

When the boats left the ship, and steered away, without making an effort to save the eight hundred and fifty coolies, or allowing them to do any thing themselves, with their last look toward the ship they saw that the coolies had escaped from their prison through doors which the concussion had made for them, and stood clustering together, helpless and despairing, upon the decks, and gazing upon the abyss which was opening its jaws to receive them. My friend assures me that he knows these poor creatures were completely imprisoned all the night these terrible occurences were going on, the hatches being "battened down," and made as secure as a jail door under lock and bars.

The ship was three hundred miles from land when it struck, and after fourteen days of toil and struggle, one of the boats only succeeded in reaching Towron, in Cochin-China. The three other boats were never heard of. Here the French fleet was lying; and the admiral at once sent one of his vessels to the fatal scene of the disaster, where some of the wreck was to be seen; but not a *single coolie!* Every one of the *eight hundred and fifty* had perished.

TABLE I.
FACTS IN RELATION TO COTTON—ITS GROWTH, MANUFACTURE, AND INFLUENCE ON COMMERCE, SLAVERY, EMANCIPATION, ETC., CHRONOLOGICALLY ARRANGED.

YEARS.	Great Britain Annual Import and Consumption of Cotton, from earliest dates to 1858, in lbs.	United States' Annual Exports Cotton to Great Britain and Europe generally.
1641	Cotton manufacture first named in English history.	
	TOTAL IMPORTS.	
1697	1,976,359	
1701	1,985,868	
1700	} 1,170,881	
to	715,008	
1705	1,972,805	
1710	1,545,472	1747-48, 7 bags of
1720	1,645,031	Cotton were shipped
1730	2,976,610	from Charleston, S. C.,
1741	3,870,392	to England.
1751	} 6,766,613	
1764	5,198,778	1770, 2,000 lbs. shipped
1771	11,828,039	from Charleston.
to	9,735,663	
1775	11,482,083	
1781	18,400,384	
1782	19,475,020	
1783	23,250,268	71 bags shipped
1784	20,467,436	and seized in
1785	32,576,023	England, on the
1786	31,447,605	ground that America
1787	28,706,675	could not produce
1788	34,907,497	so much.
1789	19,040,929	
1790	24,358,567	

	Total Consumption.	
1791	26,401,340	
1792	23,126,357	
1793	23,354,371	lbs. 189,316
1794	31,880,641	500,000
1795	43,379,278	1,601,760
1796	56,010,732	6,276,300
1797	56,004,305	6,100,000
1798	60,345,600	3,800,000
1799	53,812,284	9,330,000
1800	61,867,329	9,500,000
1801	59,682,406	17,789,803
1802	58,176,283	20,900,000
1803	74,925,306	27,500,000
1804	43,605,982	41,900,000
1805	92,812,282	38,900,000
1806	132,488,935	40,330,000
1807	91,576,535	37,500,000
1808	63,025,936	66,200,000
1809	50,966,000	12,000,000
1810	73,728,000	53,200,000
1811	96,200,000	93,900,000
1812	97,310,000	62,200,000
1813	126,240,000	29,000,000
1814		19,400,000
1815	Total Consumption.	17,800,000
1816	109,902,000	83,000,000
1817	109,518,000	81,800,000
	120,265,000	95,660,000
1818	129,029,000	
1819	145,493,000	
1820	154,146,000	92,500,000
1821	165,174,000	88,000,000
1822	166,831,000	127,800,000
1823	150,213,000	124,893,405
1824	197,200,000	144,675,095
1825	217,860,000	173,723,270
1826	219,200,000	142,369,663
1827	247,600,000	176,449,907
1828	262,700,000	204,535,415
1829	276,900,000	294,310,115
1830	287,000,000	210,590,463

1831	303,000,000	264,837,186
1832	326,407,692	298,459,102
1833	363,684,232	276,979,784
1834	367,564,752	322,215,122
1835	477,206,108	324,698,604
1836	445,744,000	384,717,907
1837	517,254,400	387,358,992
1838	460,387,200	423,631,307
1839	477,339,200	444,211,537
1840	555,214,400	595,952,297
1841	570,731,200	413,624,212
1842	626,496,000	743,941,061
1843	624,000,000	530,204,100
1844	442,416,000	584,717,017
1845	602,160,000	792,297,106
1846	624,000,000	663,633,455
1847	606,000,000	872,905,996
1848	648,000,000	547,558,055
1849	817,998,048	527,219,958
1850	746,376,848	814,274,431
1851	761,646,704	1,026,602,269
1852	775,814,112	635,381,604
1853	877,225,440	927,237,089
1854	837,406,300	1,093,230,639
1855	884,733,696	1,111,570,370
1856	. . . .	987,833,106
1857		1,008,424,601
1858		1,351,431,827
1859		1,048,282,475
		1,118,624,012
		1,372,755,006

Great Britain's sources of Cotton supplies other than the United States, with total Cotton crop of United States at intervals.

Previous to 1791 Great Britain obtained her supplies of Cotton from the West Indies and South America, and the countries around the eastern parts of the Mediterranean. From that date she began to receive supplies from the U. S.

Dates of Inventions promoting the growth and manufacture of Cotton, and of movements to elevate the African race.

Previous to the invention of the machinery named below, all carding, spinning, and weaving of wool and cotton had been done by the use of the hand-cards, one-spindle wheels, and common hand-looms. The work, for a long period, was performed in families; but the improved machinery propelled by steam power, has so reduced the cost of cotton manufactures, that all household manufacturing has long since been abandoned, and the monopoly yielded to capitalists, who now fill the world with their cheap fabrics.

1762. Carding machine invented.
1767. Spinning Jenny invented.
1769. Spinning Roller-frame invented.
  „   Cotton first planted in the United States.
  "   Watt's Steam Engine patented.
1775. Mule Jenny invented.
1776. Virginia forbids foreign slave trade.
1780. Emancipation by Pennsylvania and Massachusetts.
1781. Muslins first made in England.
1784. Emancipation by Connecticut and Rhode Island.
1785. Watts' Engine improved and applied to cotton machinery.
     First cotton mill erected, 1783.
1785. New York Abolition Society organized.
1786. Carding and spinning machines erected in Massachusetts.
1787. Power Loom invented.
  „   First Cotton mill erected in Beverly, Massachusetts.
  „   Pennsylvania Abolition Society formed.
     Slavery excluded from N. W. Territory, including Ohio, Indiana, Illinois, &c.
  "
1789. Franklin issues an appeal for aid to instruct the free blacks.

1792. Emancipation by New Hampshire.
1793. Cotton Gin invented.

1786. *Imports* by Great Britain from—
Br. W. Indies,   lbs. 5,800,000
Fr. and Spanish Colonies   5,500,000
Dutch   do.   1,600,000
Portuguese   do.   2,000,000
Turkey and Smyrna,   5,000,000
1789. Cotton crop of United States, 1,000,000 lbs.
1791. *Imports* by Great Britain from—
Br. West Indies,   lbs. 12,000,000
Brazil,   20,000,000
1794. Cotton crop of the U. S., 8,000,000 lbs.
1796. Cotton crop of the U. S., 10,000,000 lbs.
1798. India, the first imports from, 1,622,000 lbs.
1799. Cotton crop of the U. S., 20,000,000

lbs.
1800. *Exports* from—
India, lbs. 30,000,000
West Indies, 17,000,000 1799. Emancipation by New York.
Brazil, 24,000,000 1804. Do. New Jersey.
Elsewhere, 7,000,000 1800. Cotton consumed in the United
States, 200,000 lbs.
1801. United States exported to—
France, lbs. 750,000
England 19,000,000
1803. Louisiana Territory acquired, includ-
1806. Cotton crop of the U. S., 80,000,000 ing the region between the Mississippi
lbs. river (upper and lower) and the Mex-
ican line.
1805. United States export to France,
4,500,000 lbs.
1807. Fulton started his steamboat.
1808. Slave trade prohibited by United
States and England.
1808. Cotton manufacture established in
1812. War declared between the United Boston.
States and Great Britain. 1810. Cotton consumed in United States,
4,000,000 lbs.
1812. Two-thirds of steam engines in Great
1815. Peace proclaimed between the United Britain employed in cotton spinning,
States and Great Britain. etc.
1813. United States export to France,
10,250,000 lbs.
1815. Power Loom first used in United
States.
1818. Cotton crop of the U. S., 125,000,000 1816. First steamboat crossed the British
lbs. Channel.
1816. Power Loom brought into general
use in England.
1817. Colonization Society organized.
1821. *Exports* from— 1819. Florida annexed.
West Indies, lbs. 9,000,000 1820. Slave trade declared piracy by Con-
Brazil, 28,000,000 gress.
India, 50,000,000 1820. Emigrants to Liberia first sent.
Turkey and Egypt, 5,500,000 1821. Benjamin Lundy published his "Ge-
Elsewhere, 6,000,000 nius of Universal Emancipation."

1822. Cotton crop of the U. S., 210,000,000 lbs.

1828. Cotton crop of the U. S., 325,000,000 lbs.

1823. United States export to France, 25,000,000 lbs.

1824. Do. do. do. 40,500,000 lbs.

1825. New York and Erie Canal opened. Production and manufacture of cotton now greatly above the consumption, and prices fell so as to produce general distress and stagnation, which continued with more or less intensity throughout 1828 and 1829. The fall of prices was about 55 per cent.—*Encyc. Amer.*

Imports by Great Britain from West Indies,—

1829.	lbs. 4,640,414
1830,	3,449,249
1831,	2,401,685
1834,	2,296,525

1826. Creek Indians removed from Georgia.

1829. Emancipation in Mexico.

1830. United States export to France, 75,000,000 lbs.

1831. Slave Insurrection in Virginia.

1832. *Imports* by Great Britain from—

Brazil,	lbs. 20,109,560
Turkey and Egypt,	9,113,890
East Indies and Mauritius	5,178,625
British West Indies.	1,708,764
Elsewhere,	964,933

1832. Garrison declares war against the Colonization Society.

1832. Ohio Canal completed.

1833. Cotton consumption in France, 72,767,551 lbs.

1834. Emancipation in West Indies, commenced.

1834. Birney deserted the Colonization Society.

1835. United States export to France, 100,330,000 lbs.

1836. Gerrit Smith repudiates the Colonization Society.

1836. Cherokee and Choctaw Indians removed from Georgia, Mississippi, and Alabama.

1837. American Anti-Slavery Society had

1838. *Imports* by Great Britain from—

Brazil,	lbs. 24,464,505
East Indies and Mauritius	40,230,064
British West Indies,	928,425

1840. *Imports* by Great Britain from—

British West Indies,	lbs. 427,529

1841. *Imports* by Great Britain from India, 1835 to 1839, annual average, 57,600,000 lbs.

Imports by Great Britain, 1840 to 1844, during the Chinese war, 92,800,000 lbs.

1845.   Do. from Egypt, 32,537,600 lbs.

1848. *Imports* by Great Britain from—

West Indies and Demarara,	lbs. 3,155,600
Brazil and Portuguese Colonies	40,080,400
East Indies,	91,004,800

Imports by Great Britain from—

1849. East Indies,	lbs. 72,800,000
1850. Do.	123,200,000
1852. Do.	84,022,432
1853. Do.	180,431,496
1854. Do.	119,835,968
1855. Do.	145,218,976

1856. *Imports* by Great Britain from—

British East Indies,	lbs. 180,496,624
Brazil,	21,830,704

an income of $36,000, and 70 agents commissioned.

1838. Colonization Society had an income of only $10,900.

1840. Cotton consumed in the United States, 106,000,000 lbs.

Value of cotton goods imported into the United States $13,286,830.

1844.

1845. Texas annexed.

1846. Mexican War.

1847. Gold discovered in California.

1848. New Mexico and California annexed.

1849. United States export to France, 151,340,000 lbs.

Do. Other Continental countries, 128,800,000 lbs.

1850. Cotton consumed in United States, 256,000,000 lbs.

1851. Value of United States cotton fabrics, $61,869,184.

1853. Value of cottons imported, $27,675,000.

1853. United States export to England, 768,596,498 lbs.

1853.   Do.   do.   Continent, 335,271,064 lbs.

1855. United States export to Great Britain and North American Colonies, 672,409,874 lbs.

1855.   Do.   do.   Continent, 322,905,056 lbs.

1855. Value of Cottons imported, $21,655,624.

The remaining statistics of this column can be found in the other Tables.

Egypt,		34,399,008
1857. *Imports* from—		
Brazil,	lbs.	29,910,832
Egypt,		24,532,256
1858. *Imports* from Brazil,	lbs.	18,617,872
Do. Egypt,		38,232,320

NOTE.—Our commercial year ends June 30: that of England January 1. This will explain any seeming discrepancy in the imports by her from us, and our exports to her.

N. B.—In 1781 Great Britain commenced re-exporting a portion of her imports of Cotton to the Continent; but the amount did not reach a million of pounds, except in one year, until 1810, when it rose to over eight millions. The next year, however, it fell to a million and a quarter, and only rose, from near that amount, to six millions in 1814 and 1815. From 1818, her *consumption*, only, of cotton, is given, as best representing her relations to slave labor for that commodity. After this date her exports of cotton gradually enlarged, until, in 1853, they reached over one hundred and forty-seven millions of pounds. Of this, over eighty-two millions were derived from the United States, and over fifty-nine millions from India. That is to say, of her imports of 180,431,000 lbs. in 1853, from India, she re-exported 59,000,000.

We are enabled to add, for our second edition, that the imports of Cotton into Great Britain, from India, for 1854, amounted to 119,835,968 lbs., of which 66,405,920 lbs. were re-exported; and that her imports from the same for 1855 amounted to 145,218,976 lbs., of which 66,210,704 lbs. were re-exported; thus leaving, for the former year, but 53,430,048 lbs., and for the latter but 79,008,272 lbs. of East India Cotton for consumption in England. The present condition of cotton supplies from India up to 1859, will be seen in the extracts from the *London Economist*.

TABLE II.

TABULAR STATEMENT OF AGRICULTURAL PRODUCTS, DOMESTIC ANIMALS, ETC., EXPORTED FROM THE UNITED STATES: THE TOTAL VALUE OF PRODUCTS AND ANIMALS RAISED IN THE COUNTRY; AND THE VALUE OF THE PORTION THEREOF LEFT FOR HOME CONSUMPTION AND USE, FOR THE YEAR 1853. See Patent Office Report; Abstract of Census; Rep. Com. Nav., etc.

	Value of Exports.		Total Value of Products and Animals.	Value of portion left for home consumption.
Cattle, and their products,	$3,076,897	Catt.	$400,000,000	$396,923,103
Horses and Mules,	246,731		300,000,000	299,753,269
Sheep and Wool,	44,375	Sheep,	46,000,000	45,955,625
Hogs and their products,	6,202,324	Hogs,	160,000,000	153,797,676
Indian Corn and Meal,	2,084,051	Corn,	240,000,000	237,915,949
Wheat Flour and Biscuit,	19,591,817	Wheat,	100,000,000	80,408,183
Rye Meal,	34,186	Rye,	12,600,000	12,565,814
Other Grains, and Peas and Beans,	165,824		54,144,874	53,979,050
Potatoes,	152,569		42,400,00	42,247,431
Apples,	107,283	(1850)	7,723,326	7,616,043
Hay, averaged at $10 per ton,	—	(1850)	138,385,790	138,385,790
Hemp,	18,195		4,272,500	4,254,305
Sugar—Cane and maple, etc.,	427,216	(1850)	36,900,000	36,472,784
Rice,	1,657,658		8,750,000	7,092,342
Totals,	$33,809,126		$1,551,176,490	$1,517,367,364
Cotton,	$109,456,404		$128,000,000	$18,543,596
Tobacco, and its products,	11,319,319		19,900,000	8,580,681
Totals,	$120,775,723		$147,900,000	$27,124,277

NOTE.—This table is left as it was in the first edition. As the census tables supply a portion of its materials, a new statement cannot be made until after 1860.

TABLE III.

TOTAL IMPORTS OF THE MORE PROMINENT ARTICLES OF GROCERIES, FOR THE YEAR ENDING JUNE 30, 1853; SPECIFYING ALSO, THE RE-EXPORTS, AND THE PROPORTIONS FROM SLAVE-LABOR COUNTRIES. See Report on Commerce and Navigation.

Coffee,	Imported,	Value,	$15,525,954	lbs.	199,049,823
"	Re-Exported,		1,163,875	"	13,349,319
"	Slave-Labor production,		12,059,476	"	156,108,569
Sugar,	Imported,		$15,093,003	"	464,427,281
"	Re-Exported,		819,439	"	18,981,601
"	Slave-Labor production,		14,810,091	"	459,743,322
Molasses,	Imported,		$3,684,888	gals.	31,886,100
"	Re-Exported,		97,880	"	488,666
"	Slave-Labor production,		3,607,160	"	31,325,735
Tobacco, etc.,	Imported,		$4,175,238		
"	Re-Exported,		312,733		
"	Slave-Labor production,		3,674,402		

NOTE.—A part of the modifications necessary in this table to adopt it to 1859, can be inferred from some of the tables which follow.

TABLE IV.
FREE COLORED AND SLAVE POPULATION, OF THE STATES NAMED, IN THE PERIODS OF TEN YEARS, FROM 1790 TO 1850, WITH THE RATIO OF INCREASE OR DECREASE PER CENT. PER ANNUM, OF THE FORMER.

STATES AND CLASSES.	1790.	1800.	1810.	1820.	1830.	1840.	1850.
PENNSYLVANIA.							
Free Colored	6,537	14,561	22,492	30,202	37,930	47,854	53,626
Increase per cent. per annum	......	12.27	5.44	3.42	2.55	2.61	1.20
Slaves	3,737	1,706	795	211	403	64	......
MASSACHUSETTS.							
Free Colored	5,463	6,452	6,737	6,740	7,048	8,669	9,064
Increase per cent. per annum	......	1.81	.44	.004	.45	2.29	.45
Slaves	......	......	......	......	......	......	......
NEW YORK.							
Free Colored	4,654	10,374	25,333	29,279	44,870	50,027	49,069
Increase or decrease per cent. per annum	......	12.29	14.41	1.55	5.32	1.14	[132].19
Slaves	21,324	20,343	15,017	10,088	75	4	......
NEW JERSEY.							
Free Colored	2,762	4,402	7,843	12,460	18,303	21,044	23,810
Increase per cent. per annum	......	5.93	7.81	5.88	4.68	1.49	1.31
Slaves	11,423	12,422	10,851	7,557	2,254	674	236
RHODE ISLAND.							
Free Colored	3,469	3,304	3,609	3,554	3,561	3,238	3,670
Increase or decrease per cent. per annum	......	[132].47	.92	[132].15	.01	[132]90	1.33
Slaves	952	381	108	48	17	5	......
VERMONT.							
Free Colored	225	557	750	903	881	730	718
Increase or decrease per cent. per annum	......	11.84	3.46	2.04	[132].24	[132]1.71	[132]16
Slaves	17	......	......	......	......	......	......
MAINE.							
Free Colored	538	818	969	929	1,190	1,355	1,356
Increase or decrease per	......	5.20	1.84	[132].41	2.80	1.38	.007

cent. per annum							
Slaves	......	......	......	......	2	......	......
NEW HAMPSHIRE.							
Free Colored	630	856	970	786	604	537	520
Increase or decrease per cent. per annum	......	3.58	1.33	[132]1.89	[132]2.31	[132]1.10	[132].31
Slaves	158	8	......	......	3	1	......
CONNECTICUT.							
Free Colored	2,801	5,330	6,453	7,844	8,047	8,105	7,693
Increase or decrease per cent. per annum	......	9.02	2.10	2.15	.25	.07	[132].50
Slaves	2,759	951	310	97	25	17	......
OHIO.							
Free Colored	......	337	1,899	4,723	9,568	17,342	25,279
Increase per cent. per annum	......	......	46.35	14.87	10.25	8.12	4.57
Slaves	......	......	......	......	6	3	......
INDIANA.							
Free Colored	......	163	393	1,230	3,629	7,165	11,262
Increase per cent. per annum	......	......	14.11	21.29	19.50	9.74	5.75
Slaves	......	135	237	190	3	3	......
DELAWARE.							
Free Colored	3,899	8,268	13,163	12,958	15,855	16,919	18,073
Increase or decrease per cent. per annum	......	11.20	5.88	[132].13	2.23	.67	.68
Slaves	8,887	6,153	4,177	4,509	3,292	2,605	2,290
MARYLAND.							
Free Colored	8,043	19,587	33,927	39,730	52,938	62,078	74,723
Increase per cent. per annum	......	14.35	7.32	1.71	3.32	1.72	2.03
Slaves	103,036	105,635	111,502	107,397	102,994	89,737	90,368
VIRGINIA.							
Free Colored	12,766	20,124	30,570	36,889	47,348	49,852	54,333
Increase per cent. per annum	......	5.76	5.99	2.06	2.83	.52	.89
Slaves	293,427	345,796	392,518	425,153	469,757	449,087	472,528
NORTH CAROLINA.							
Free Colored	4,975	7,043	10,266	14,612	19,543	22,732	27,463

Increase per cent. per annum	. . . . . .	4.15	4.57	4.23	3.37	1.63	2.08
Slaves	100,572	133,296	168,824	205,017	245,601	245,817	288,548
SOUTH CAROLINA.							
Free Colored	1,801	3,185	4,554	6,826	7,921	8,276	8,960
Increase per cent. per annum	. . . . . .	7.68	4.29	4.98	1.60	.44	.82
Slaves	107,094	146,151	196,365	258,475	315,401	327,038	584,984
GEORGIA.							
Free Colored	398	1,019	1,801	1,763	2,486	2,753	2,931
Increase or decrease per cent. per annum	. . . . . .	15.60	7.67	[132].21	4.10	1.07	.64
Slaves	22,264	59,404	105,218	149,654	217,531	280,944	381,682
TENNESSEE.							
Free Colored	361	309	1,317	2,727	4,555	5,524	6,422
Increase or decrease per cent. per annum	. . . . . .	[132]1.44	32.62	10.70	6.70	2.12	1.62
Slaves	3,417	13,584	44,535	80,107	141,603	183,050	239,459
MISSISSIPPI.							
Free Colored	. . . . . .	182	240	458	519	1,366	930
Increase or decrease per cent. per annum	. . . . . .	. . . . . .	3.18	9.08	1.33	16.31	[132]3.19
Slaves	. . . . . .	3,489	17,088	32,814	65,659	195,211	309,878
ALABAMA.							
Free Colored	. . . . . .	. . . . . .	. . . . . .	517	1,572	2,039	2,265
Increase per cent. per annum	. . . . . .	. . . . . .	. . . . . .	. . . . . .	17.53	2.97	1.10
Slaves	. . . . . .	. . . . . .	. . . . . .	41,879	117,549	252,532	342,844
MISSOURI.							
Free Colored	. . . . . .	. . . . . .	607	347	596	1,574	2,618
Increase or decrease per cent. per annum	. . . . . .	. . . . . .	. . . . . .	[132]4.28	6.39	17.66	6.63
Slaves	. . . . . .	. . . . . .	3,011	10,222	25,091	58,240	87,422
KENTUCKY.							
Free Colored	114	741	1,713	2,759	4,917	7,317	10,011
Increase per cent. per annum	. . . . . .	55.00	13.11	6.10	7.82	4.88	3.68
Slaves	11,830	40,343	80,561	126,732	165,213	182,258	210,981
LOUISIANA.							

Free Colored	......	......	7,585	10,476	16,710	25,502	17,462
Increase or decrease per cent. per annum	......	......	......	3.81	5.95	5.26	[132]3.15
Slaves	......	......	34,660	69,064	109,588	168,452	244,809

ILLINOIS.

Free Colored	......	......	613	457	1,637	3,598	5,436
Increase or decrease per cent. per annum	......	......	......	[132]2.54	25.82	11.97	5.10
Slaves	......	......	168	917	747	331	......

FLORIDA.

Free Colored	......	......	......	......	844	817	932
Increase or decrease per cent. per annum	......	......	......	......	......	[132].31	1.40
Slaves	......	......	......	......	15,501	25,717	39,310

ARKANSAS.

Free Colored	......	......	......	59	141	465	608
Increase per cent. per annum	......	......	......	......	13.89	2.29	1.10
Slaves	......	......	......	1,617	4,576	19,935	47,100

MICHIGAN.

Free Colored	......	......	120	174	261	707	2,583
Increase per cent. per annum	......	......	......	4.50	5.00	17.08	25.53
Slaves	......	......	24	......	32	......	......

DISTRICT OF COLUMBIA.

Free Colored	......	783	2,549	4,048	6,152	8,361	10,059
Increase per cent. per annum	......	......	22.55	5.88	5.19	3.59	2.03
Slaves	......	3,244	5,395	6,377	6,119	4,694	3,687

TABLE V.
INFLUENCE OF THE COLORED POPULATION ON PUBLIC SENTIMENT.

TABLE SHOWING THE PROPORTION OF THE FREE COLORED POPULATION IN THE NORTHERN AND SOUTHERN PORTIONS OF THE STATE OF OHIO, BY COUNTIES, AS PRESENTED BY THE CENSUS OF 1840 AND 1850, TOGETHER WITH THE POPULAR VOTE FOR AND AGAINST THE ABOLITION CANDIDATE, HON. S. P. CHASE, AT THE ELECTION FOR GOVERNOR, OCTOBER, 1855.

SOUTHERN COUNTIES.			MR. CHASE.		NORTHERN COUNTIES.			MR. CHASE.	
COUNTIES.	1840.	1850.	FOR	AGAINST	COUNTIES.	1840.	1850.	FOR	AGAINST
Hamilton,	2,576	3,600	4,516	18,764	Ashtabula,	17	43	3,772	1,156
Clermont,	122	412	2,434	2,879	Lake,	21	38	1,640	521
Brown,	614	863	1,571	2,129	Geauga,	3	7	1,816	486
Adams,	63	55	1,139	1,629	Cuyahoga,	121	359	3,965	3,545
Scioto,	206	211	1,042	1,497	Trumbull,	70	65	3,109	1,505
Lawrence,	148	326	1,092	1,067	Portage,	39	58	2,660	1,871
Gallia,	799	1,198	344	1,972	Summit,	42	121	2,242	1,326
Meigs,	28	52	1,515	1,504	Medina,	13	35	2,032	1,526
Jackson,	315	391	714	906	Lorain,	62	264	2,693	919
Pike,	329	618	641	1,156	Huron,	106	39	2,295	1,411
Highland,	786	896	1,209	2,599	Erie,	97	202	1,564	1,191
Clinton,	377	598	1,640	964	Seneca,	65	151	2,332	1,976
Warren,	341	602	2,306	1,821	Sandusky,	41	47	1,382	1,509
Butler,	254	367	1,960	3,235	Ottawa,	5	1	369	406
Preble,	88	77	1,567	1,326	Lucas,	54	139	1,618	1,156
Montgomery,	376	249	2,746	3,830	Fulton,	133	1	715	453
Greene,	344	654	1,953	1,357	Williams,	2	0	890	878
Fayette,	239	291	909	757	Defiance,	133	19	592	626
Ross,	1,195	1,906	2,160	2,255	Henry,	6	0	440	511
Vinton,	133	107	722	901	Wood,	32	18	1,099	636
Hocking,	46	117	927	1,199	Paulding,	0	1	362	115
Pickaway,	333	412	1,521	1,862	Putnam,	133	11	528	858
Fairfield,	342	280	2,474	2,726	Hancock,	8	26	1,238	1,359
Perry,	47	29	1,772	1,540	Vanwert,	0	47	602	483

County					County				
Athens,	55	106	1,634	1,072	Allen,	23	27	1,235	929
Washington,	269	390	2,212	1,774	Wyandott,	[133]	49	1,143	1,106
Morgan,	68	90	1,776	1,235	Crawford,	5	10	1,449	1,753
Noble,	[133]	[134]	1,361	1,030	Richland,	65	67	2,220	2,329
Monroe,	13	69	1,451	1,901	Ashland,	[133]	3	1,580	1,660
Belmont,	742	778	1,755	2,856	Wayne,	41	28	2,421	2,585
Guernsey,	190	168	1,893	1,491	Starke,	204	159	3,343	3,044
Muskingum,	562	631	2,551	3,204	Mahoning,	[133]	90	1,592	1,552
Franklin,	805	1,607	2,487	4,033	Columbia-na,	417	182	3,118	2,170
Madison,	97	78	562	1,012	Carroll,	49	52	1,502	1,082
Clarke,	20	323	1,866	1,404	Tuscarawas,	71	89	2,552	2,179
Miami,	211	602	1,787	1,977	Coshocton,	38	44	2,064	2,014
Darke,	200	248	1,685	1,829	Holmes,	3	5	1,194	1,675
Champaigne,	328	494	1,353	1,463	Knox,	63	62	2,166	2,135
Union,	78	128	1,222	829	Morrow,	[133]	18	1,631	1,371
Delaware,	76	135	1,602	1,504	Marion,	52	21	1,220	1,184
Licking,	140	128	2,021	3,252	Hardin,	4	14	903	725
Harrison,	163	287	1,712	1,259	Logan,	407	536	1,424	1,119
Jefferson,	497	665	2,156	1,654	Mercer,	204	399	492	968
Shelby,	262	407	955	1,286	Auglaise,	[133]	87	643	1,286
Total, South,	14,924	21,745	72,915	95,941	Total, North,	2,450	3,524	73,877	59,319

TABLE VI.

TOTAL COTTON CROP OF THE UNITED STATES, WITH THE AMOUNTS EXPORTED, THE CONSUMPTION OF THE UNITED STATES, NORTH OF VIRGINIA, AND THE STOCK ON HAND, SEPTEMBER 1, OF EACH YEAR, FROM 1840 TO 1859, IN POUNDS.—*London Economist*, 1859.

YEARS.	TOTAL CROP.	EXPORTS TO VARIOUS PLACES.				CONSUMPTION OF U. S. NORTH OF VIRGINIA.	STOCK ON HAND 1ST SEPTEMBER.
		ENGLAND.	FRANCE.	OTHER POINTS.	TOTAL.		
1840	871,134,000	498,716,400	178,986,000	72,698,800	750,401,200	118,077,200	23,376,800
1841	653,978,000	343,496,800	139,510,400	42,303,600	525,290,800	118,915,200	28,991,600
1842	673,429,600	374,252,400	159,251,600	52,594,800	586,098,800	107,140,000	12,722,800
1843	551,550,000	587,884,400	138,455,600	77,714,800	804,052,000	130,051,600	37,794,400
1844	812,163,600	480,999,200	113,074,000	57,722,800	651,796,000	138,697,600	63,908,800
1845	957,801,200	575,722,400	143,742,800	114,037,200	433,502,400	155,602,400	39,368,000
1846	840,214,800	440,497,600	143,881,200	81,888,000	666,716,800	169,038,800	42,848,800
1847	711,460,400	332,363,600	96,594,400	67,530,800	496,488,800	171,186,800	85,934,800
1848	939,053,600	529,706,000	111,668,800	101,929,600	1,743,304,400	212,708,800	68,587,200
1849	1,091,437,600	615,160,400	147,303,600	128,672,400	891,141,600	207,215,600	61,901,200
1850	838,682,400	422,708,400	115,850,800	77,502,800	636,062,000	195,107,600	67,172,000
1851	942,102,800	565,306,000	120,534,200	107,634,800	795,484,000	161,643,200	51,321,600
1852	1,206,011,600	667,499,600	168,550,000	141,408,800	977,458,400	241,211,600	36,470,400
1853	1,305,152,800	694,744,000	170,691,200	145,924,800	1,011,360,000	268,403,600	54,257,200
1854	1,172,010,8	641,500,0	149,623,2	136,536,0	927,659,20	244,228,400	27,120,60

	00	00	00	00	0		0
1855	1,138,935,600	619,886,400	163,972,400	113,824,000	897,683,600	237,433,600	28,667,200
1856	1,411,138,000	768,554,400	192,254,800	221,033,200	1,181,842,400	261,091,600	25,668,400
1857	1,175,807,600	571,548,000	165,342,800	164,172,000	901,062,800	280,855,200	17,703,200
1858	1,245,584,800	723,986,400	153,600,800	158,594,800	1,036,181,000	184,692,800	40,410,000
1859	1,606,800,000	. . . .	. . . .	. . . .	1,208,561,200	304,087,200	. . . .

☞ Consumption for Virginia and South of that State, for 1859, is estimated at 66,973,600 lbs. The *crop* year closes, August 31st.

TABLE VII.

STATEMENT OF THE VALUE OF COTTON MANUFACTURES, OF FOREIGN PRODUCTION, WHICH WERE IMPORTED INTO THE UNITED STATES; AND THE VALUE OF THE COTTON GOODS MANUFACTURED IN THE UNITED STATES, AND EXPORTED, DURING THE YEARS STATED—THE YEAR ENDING JUNE 30.

YEARS.	FOREIGN IMPORTS.	DOMESTIC EXPORTS.	YEARS.	FOREIGN IMPORTS.	DOMESTIC EXPORTS.
1840.	$ 6,504,484	$3,549,607	1850.	$20,108,719	$4,734,424
1841.	11,757,036	3,122,546	1851.	22,164,442	7,241,205
1842.	9,578,515	2,970,690	1852.	19,689,496	7,672,151
1843.	2,958,796	3,223,550	1853.	27,731,313	8,768,894
1844.	13,641,478	2,898,780	1854.	33,949,503	5,535,516
1845.	13,863,282	4,327,928	1855.	17,757,112	5,857,181
1846.	13,530,625	3,545,481	1856.	25,917,999	6,967,309
1847.	15,192,875	4,082,523	1857.	28,685,726	6,115,177
1848.	18,421,589	5,718,205	1858.	17,965,130	5,651,504
1849.	15,754,841	4,933,129	1859.	26,026,140	8,316,222

NOTE. Of the goods imported, a part were re-exported, and the remainder was used in the United States. The re-exports stood as follows, beginning with 1840:—$1,103,489—$929,056—$836,892—$314,040—$404,648—$502,553—$673,203—$486,135—$1,216,172—$571,082—$427,107—$677,940—$977,030—$1,254,363—$1,468,179—$2,012,554—$1,580,495—$570,802—$390,988.—*Congress Report on Finances.*

STATEMENT SHOWING THE AMOUNT OF COFFEE IMPORTED INTO THE UNITED STATES ANNUALLY, WITH THE AMOUNT TAKEN FOR CONSUMPTION, DURING THE YEARS 1850 TO 1858, INCLUSIVE—THE YEAR ENDING DECEMBER 31.

YEARS.	RECEIPTS.	CONSUMPTION.
1850.	lbs. 152,580,310	lbs. 134,539,736
1851.	216,043,870	181,225,700
1852.	205,542,855	204,991,595
1853.	193,112,300	175,687,790
1854.	182,473,853	179,481,083
1855.	283,214,533	210,378,287
1856.	230,913,150	218,225,490
1857.	217,871,839	172,565,934
1858.	227,656,186	251,255,099

NOTE. The New York *Shipping and Commercial List*, to which we are indebted for these statements, says, that it includes the quantity withdrawn from our markets, and forwarded inland to Canada and the British Provinces; the amount of which is not ascertained, but will not vary greatly from 2,230,000 lbs., for the last year.

TABLE VIII.

STATEMENT EXHIBITING THE VALUE OF THE EXPORTS FROM THE UNITED STATES, OF BREADSTUFFS AND PROVISIONS; THE AMOUNT AND VALUE OF COTTON EXPORTED, WITH THE AVERAGE COST, IN CENTS, PER POUND; AND THE AMOUNT OF TOBACCO EXPORTED, FROM 1821 TO 1859 INCLUSIVE: THE YEAR FROM 1821 TO 1842 ENDING SEPTEMBER 30, AND FROM 1844 TO 1859 ENDING JUNE 30,—THE YEAR 1843 INCLUDING ONLY NINE MONTHS.

| YEARS | BREADSTUFFS AND PROVISIONS. | COTTON. | | AVERAGE COST PER lb. IN CENTS. | TOBACCO UNMANUFACTURED |
		POUNDS.	VALUE.		
1821	$12,341,901	124,893,405	$20,157,484	16.2	$5,648,962
1822	13,886,856	144,675,095	24,035,058	16.6	6,222,838
1823	13,767,847	173,723,270	20,445,520	11.8	6,282,672
1824	15,059,484	142,369,663	21,947,401	15.4	4,855,566
1825	11,634,449	176,449,907	36,846,649	20.9	6,115,623
1826	11,303,496	204,535,415	25,025,214	12.2	5,347,208
1827	11,685,556	294,310,115	29,359,545	10	6,577,123
1828	11,461,144	210,590,463	22,487,229	10.7	5,269,960
1829	13,131,858	264,837,186	26,575,311	10	4,982,974
1830	12,075,430	298,459,102	29,674,883	9.9	5,586,365
1831	17,538,227	276,979,784	25,289,492	9.1	4,892,388
1832	12,424,703	322,215,122	31,724,682	9.8	5,999,769
1833	14,209,128	324,698,604	36,191,105	11.1	5,755,968
1834	11,524,024	384,717,907	49,448,402	12.8	6,595,305
1835	12,009,399	387,358,992	64,961,302	16.8	8,250,577
1836	10,614,130	423,631,307	71,284,925	16.8	10,058,640
1837	9,588,359	444,211,537	63,240,102	14.2	5,795,647
1838	9,636,650	595,952,297	61,566,811	10.3	7,392,029
1839	14,147,779	413,624,212	61,238,982	14.8	9,832,943

1840	19,067,535	743,941,061	63,870,307	8.5	9,883,957
1841	17,196,102	530,204,100	54,330,341	10.2	12,576,703
1842	16,902,876	584,717,017	47,593,464	8.1	9,540,755
1843	11,204,123	792,297,106	49,119,806	6.2	4,650,979
1844	17,970,135	663,633,455	54,063,501	8.1	8,397,255
1845	16,743,421	872,905,996	51,739,643	5.92	7,469,819
1846	27,701,121	547,558,055	42,767,341	7.81	8,478,270
1847	68,701,921	527,219,958	53,415,848	10.34	7,242,086
1848	37,472,751	814,274,431	61,998,294	7.61	7,551,122
1849	38,155,507	1,026,602,269	66,396,967	6.4	5,804,207
1850	26,051,373	635,381,604	71,984,616	11.3	9,951,023
1851	21,948,651	927,237,089	112,315,317	12.11	9,219,251
1852	25,857,027	1,093,230,639	87,965,732	8.05	10,031,283
1853	32,985,322	1,111,570,370	109,456,404	9.85	11,319,319
1854	65,941,323	987,833,106	93,596,220	9.47	10,016,046
1855	38,895,348	1,008,424,601	88,143,844	8.74	14,712,468
1856	77,187,301	1,351,431,701	128,382,351	9.49	12,221,843
1857	74,667,852	1,048,282,475	131,575,859	12.55	20,662,772
1858	50,683,285	1,118,624,012	131,386,661	11.70	17,009,767
1859	38,171,881	1,372,755,006	161,434,923	11.75	21,074,038
	$961,545,275	$23,366,357,434	$2,383,027,536		$339,274,520

NOTE. The articles exported which are not included above, are as follows, for 1859:— product of the sea, $4,462,974; product of the forest, $14,489,406; cotton piece goods, manufactured tobacco, spirits, seeds, hemp, and various other articles, $31,579,008. The value of the manufactured tobacco, exported in 1859, and included in the last item, was over $3,334,401, which, added to the $21,074,038, of unmanufactured included above, makes the total exports of tobacco for that year amount to $24,408,439.

TABLE IX.

STATEMENT EXHIBITING THE VALUE OF FOREIGN GOODS IMPORTED AND TAKEN FOR CONSUMPTION, IN THE UNITED STATES; THE VALUE OF DOMESTIC PRODUCE OF THE UNITED STATES EXPORTED, EXCLUSIVE OF SPECIE; THE VALUE OF SPECIE AND BULLION IMPORTED, AND THE VALUE OF SPECIE AND BULLION EXPORTED, FROM 1821 TO 1859 INCLUSIVE: THE YEAR FROM 1821 TO 1842 ENDING SEPTEMBER 30, AND FROM 1844 TO 1859 ENDING JUNE 30,—THE YEAR 1843 INCLUDING ONLY NINE MONTHS.

YEARS.	IMPORTS ENTERED FOR CONSUMPTION, EXCLUSIVE OF SPECIE.	DOMESTIC PRODUCE EXPORTED, EXCLUSIVE OF SPECIE.	SPECIE AND BULLION.	
			IMPORTED.	EXPORTED.
1821	$43,696,405	$43,671,894	$8,064,890	$10,477,969
1822	68,367,425	49,874,079	3,369,846	10,810,180
1823	51,308,936	47,155,408	5,097,896	6,372,987
1824	53,846,567	50,649,500	8,379,835	7,014,552
1825	66,375,722	66,944,745	6,150,765	8,787,659
1826	57,652,577	52,449,855	6,880,966	4,704,533
1827	54,901,108	57,878,117	8,151,130	8,014,880
1828	66,975,475	49,976,632	7,489,741	8,243,476
1829	54,741,571	55,087,307	7,403,612	4,924,020
1830	49,575,009	58,524,878	8,155,964	2,178,773
1831	82,808,110	59,218,583	7,305,945	9,014,931
1832	75,327,688	61,726,529	5,907,504	5,656,340
1833	83,470,067	69,950,856	7,070,368	2,611,701
1834	86,973,147	80,623,662	17,911,632	2,076,758
1835	122,007,974	100,459,481	13,131,447	6,477,775
1836	158,811,392	106,570,942	13,400,881	4,324,336
1837	113,310,571	94,280,895	10,516,414	5,976,249
1838	86,552,598	95,560,880	17,747,116	3,508,046
1839	145,870,816	101,625,533	8,595,176	8,776,743
1840	86,250,335	111,660,561	8,882,813	8,417,014
1841	114,776,309	103,636,236	4,988,633	10,034,332
1842	87,996,318	91,798,242	4,087,016	4,813,539
1843	37,294,129	77,686,354	22,390,559	1,520,791
1844	96,390,548	99,531,774	5,830,429	5,454,214
1845	105,599,541	98,455,330	4,070,242	8,606,495
1846	110,048,859	101,718,042	3,777,732	3,905,268

1847	116,257,595	150,574,844	24,121,289	1,907,024
1848	140,651,902	130,203,709	6,360,224	15,841,616
1849	132,565,168	131,710,081	6,651,240	5,404,648
1850	164,032,033	134,900,233	4,628,792	7,522,994
1851	200,476,219	178,620,138	5,453,592	29,472,752
1852	195,072,695	154,931,147	5,505,044	42,674,135
1853	251,071,358	189,869,162	4,201,382	27,486,875
1854	275,955,893	215,156,304	6,958,184	41,436,456
1855	231,650,340	192,751,135	3,659,812	56,247,343
1856	295,650,938	266,438,051	4,207,632	45,745,485
1857	333,511,295	278,906,713	12,461,799	69,136,922
1858	242,678,413	251,351,033	19,274,496	52,633,147
1859	324,258,159	278,392,080	7,434,789	63,887,411
	$5,064,761,199	$4,540,620,945	$332,476,827	$522,100,369

NOTE. There is usually re-exported from twenty to thirty million dollars worth of the foreign articles imported. In 1859 the re-exports were to the value of $14,509,971; in 1858 they were $30,886,142; in 1857 they were $23,975,617; and in 1856, but $16,378,578. By adding the re-exports to the imports entered for consumption, the product will show the whole amount of the imports. The above figures are from the Congressional Report on Finances, 1857-8, and the Report on Commerce and Navigation, 1859.

TABLE X.

STATEMENT SHOWING THE AMOUNT OF CANE SUGAR CONSUMED IN THE UNITED STATES, ANNUALLY, WITH THE PROPORTIONS THAT ARE DOMESTIC OR FOREIGN, DURING THE YEARS STATED—THE YEAR ENDING DECEMBER 31.

YEARS.	FOREIGN.	DOMESTIC.	TOTAL.
1850.	lbs. 319,420,800	lbs. 283,183,040	lbs. 603,603,840
1851.	406,530,880	240,661,120	646,206,400
1852.	440,289,920	265,796,160	706,086,080
1853.	449,366,400	386,128,960	835,495,360
1854.	337,912,960	522,954,560	863,067,520
1855.	431,432,960	304,731,520	846,164,480
1856.	594,254,080	276,568,320	848,422,400
1857.	541,553,600	87,360,000	628,913,600
1858.	548,257,920	310,740,160	870,222,080

STATEMENT SHOWING THE AMOUNT, IN GALLONS, OF MOLASSES CONSUMED IN THE UNITED STATES, ANNUALLY, WITH THE PROPORTIONS WHICH ARE FOREIGN OR DOMESTIC, DURING THE YEARS STATED—THE YEAR ENDING DECEMBER 31.

YEARS.	FOREIGN.	DOMESTIC.	TOTAL.
1850.	Gals. 24,806,949	Gals. 12,202,300	Gals. 37,019,249
1851.	33,238,278	10,709,740	43,948,018
1852.	29,417,511	18,840,000	48,258,511
1853.	28,576,821	26,930,000	55,536,821
1854.	24,437,019	32,053,000	56,493,019
1855.	23,533,423	24,251,207	47,266,085
1856.	23,014,878	16,584,000	39,608,878
1857.	23,266,404	5,242,380	28,508,784
1858.	24,795,374	20,373,790	45,169,164

NOTE. The above table is taken from the *Shipping and Commercial List, and New York Price Current*, January 22, 1859. The sources of supply are the same as when the first edition went to press, and the proportions from slave labor and free labor countries respectively, has undergone very little change. The year ends December 31st, while the Congressional fiscal year ends June 30th.

The value of imports of Sugar, for the year ending June 30, 1858, from a few principal countries, stood thus: Cuba, $15,555,409; Porto Rico, $3,584,503; British West Indies, $386,546; British Guiana, $255,481; British Honduras, $26; Hayti, $851; San Domingo, $5,529.

TABLE XI.

COTTON IMPORTED INTO GREAT BRITAIN FROM VARIOUS COUNTRIES, QUANTITY RE-EXPORTED, AND STOCK ON HAND DECEMBER 31, FOR A SERIES OF YEARS, IN POUNDS. BY DEDUCTING THE EXPORTS AND THE STOCK ON HAND AT THE END OF EACH YEAR FROM THE WHOLE IMPORTS, THE REMAINDER IS THE QUANTITY TAKEN FOR CONSUMPTION.

Years	From United States.	From Brazil.	From Mediterranean.	From East Indies.	West Indies and Guiana.	Other Countries.	Total Imported.	Amount Exported.	Stocks, December 31.
1840.	487,856,504	14,779,171	8,324,937	77,011,839	866,157	3,649,402	592,488,010	38,673,229	233,600,000
1841.	358,240,964	16,671,348	9,097,180	97,388,153	1,533,197	5,061,513	487,992,355	37,673,586	247,760,000
1842.	414,030,779	15,222,828	4,489,017	92,972,609	593,603	4,441,250	531,750,086	45,251,248	269,760,000
1843.	574,738,520	18,675,123	9,674,076	65,709,729	1,260,444	3,135,224	673,193,116	39,620,000	368,280,000
1844.	517,218,662	21,084,744	12,406,327	88,639,776	1,707,194	5,054,641	646,111,304	47,222,560	414,760,000
1845.	626,650,412	20,157,633	14,614,699	58,437,426	1,394,447	725,336	721,979,953	42,916,384	478,160,000
1846.	401,949,393	14,746,321	14,278,447	34,540,143	1,201,857	1,140,113	467,856,274	65,930,704	263,520,000
1847.	364,599,291	19,966,922	4,814,268	83,934,614	793,933	598,587	474,707,615	74,954,320	204,760,000
1848.	600,247,488	19,971,378	7,231,861	84,101,961	640,437	827,036	713,020,161	74,019,792	239,440,000
1849.	634,504,050	30,738,133	17,369,843	70,838,515	944,307	1,074,164	755,469,012	98,893,536	263,760,000
1850.	493,153,112	30,299,982	18,931,414	118,872,742	228,913	2,090,698	663,576,861	102,469,696	248,960,000
1851.	596,638,962	19,339,104	16,950,525	122,626,976	446,529	1,377,653	757,379,749	111,980,400	237,600,000
1852.	765,630,544	26,506,144	48,058,640	84,922,432	703,696	3,960,992	929,782,448	111,894,303	322,960,000
1853	658,451,	24,190,	28,353,575	181,848,	350,42	2,084,1	895,278,7	148,596,	327,000,

	796	628		160	8	62	49	680	000
1854.	722,151,346	19,703,600	23,503,003	119,836,009	409,110	1,730,081	887,333,149	123,326,112	282,520,000
1855.	681,629,424	24,577,952	32,904,153	145,179,216	468,452	6,992,755	891,751,952	124,368,100	226,600,000
1856.	780,040,016	21,830,704	34,616,848	180,496,624	462,784	6,439,328	1,023,886,304	146,660,864	197,080,000
1857.	654,758,048	29,910,832	24,882,144	250,338,144	1,443,568	7,986,160	969,318,896	131,928,720	217,040,000
1858.	732,403,840	16,466,800	34,867,840	138,253,360	9,862,272	931,847,056		153,035,680	184,782,000

AVERAGE WEEKLY CONSUMPTION OF COTTON IN EUROPE, FOR A SERIES OF YEARS, IN POUNDS.[135]

COUNTRIES.	1850.	1851.	1852.	1853.	1854.	1855.	1856.	1857.	1858.
France	2,830,800	2,869,200	4,230,000	3,607,200	3,400,000	3,684,400	4,046,000	3,438,400	. . . .
Belgium	453,600	446,000	653,600	615,200	538,400	484,400	615,200	438,400	. . . .
Holland	415,200	415,200	546,000	469,200	661,200	684,400	761,200	753,200	. . . .
Germany	661,200	846,000	976,800	1,107,600	1,592,400	822,800	1,900,000	444,800	. . . .
Trieste	915,200	884,400	1,038,400	792,400	715,200	651,200	746,000	576,800	. . . .
Genoa, Naples, etc.	223,200	238,400	376,800	392,000	322,800	439,400	846,000	692,000	. . . .
Spain	592,400	707,200	730,400	653,600	715,200	876,800	938,400	692,000	. . . .
Russia, Norway, etc.	1,169,200	1,169,200	1,622,800	1,600,000	1,030,800	961,600	1,769,200	1,538,400	. . . .
Total on Continent	7,260,800	7,575,600	10,174,800	9,237,200	8,976,000	9,414,000	11,622,000	9,786,000	. . . .
Add Great Britain	11,650,000	12,795,200	14,316,000	14,545,200	15,131,600	16,161,200	16,794,800	15,626,000	16,533,200
Total weekly European Consumption	18,910,800	20,370,800	24,490,800	23,882,400	24,107,600	25,575,200	28,416,800	25,412,000	. . . .

TABLE XII.

SUMMARY STATEMENT OF THE VALUE OF EXPORTS OF THE GROWTH, PRODUCE, AND MANUFACTURE OF THE UNITED STATES, FOR THE YEAR ENDING JUNE 30, 1859; THE PRODUCTIONS OF THE NORTH AND OF THE SOUTH, RESPECTIVELY, BEING PLACED IN OPPOSITE COLUMNS; AND THE ARTICLES OF A MIXED ORIGIN BEING STATED SEPARATELY.—*Report on Com. and Nav.*, 1859.

EXPORTS OF THE NORTH. PRODUCT OF THE FOREST.		EXPORTS OF THE SOUTH. PRODUCT OF THE FOREST.	
Wood and its products,	$7,829,666	Wood and its products,	$2,210,884
Ashes, pot and pearl,	643,861	Tar and pitch	141,058
Ginseng,	54,204	Rosin and turpentine,	2,248,381
Skins and furs,	1,361,352	Spirits of turpentine,	1,306,035

PRODUCT OF AGRICULTURE.		PRODUCT OF AGRICULTURE.	
Animals and their products,	15,262,769	Animals and their products,	287,048
Wheat and wheat flour,	15,113,455	Wheat and wheat flour,	2,169,328
Indian corn and meal,	2,206,396	Indian corn and meal,	110,976
Other grains, biscuit, and vegetables,	2,226,585	Biscuit or ship bread,	12,864
		Rice,	2,207,148
Hemp, and Clover seed,	546,060	Cotton,	161,434,923
Flax seed,	8,177	Tobacco, in leaf,	21,074,038
Hops,	53,016	Brown sugar,	196,935
	$45,305,541		$193,399,618

ARTICLES OF MIXED ORIGIN.

Refined sugar, wax, chocolate, molasses,	$ 550,937
Spirituous liquors, ale, porter, beer, cider, vinegar, linseed oil,	1,370,787
Household furniture, carriages, rail-road cars, etc.	1,722,797
Hats, fur, silk, palm leaf, saddlery, trunks, valises,	317,727
Tobacco, manufactured and snuff,	3,402,491
Gunpowder, leather, boots, shoes, cables, cordage,	2,011,931
Salt, lead, iron and its manufactures,	5,744,952
Copper and brass, and manufactures of,	1,048,246
Drugs and medicines, candles and soap,	1,933,973
Cotton fabrics of all kinds,	8,316,222
Other products of manufactures and mechanics,	3,852,910
Coal and ice,	818,117
Products not enumerated,	4,132,857

Gold and silver, in coin and bullion,	57,502,305
Products of the sea, being oil, fish, whalebone, etc.	4,462,974
	$97,189,226
Add Northern exports,	45,305,541
Add Southern exports,	193,399,618
Total exports,	$335,894,385

EXPLANATORY NOTE.—The whole of the exports from the ports of Delaware, Baltimore, and New Orleans, are placed in the column of Northern exports, because there is no means of determining what proportion of them were from free or slave States, and it has been thought best to give this advantage to the North. Taking into the account only the heavier amounts, the exports from these ports foot up $11,287,898; of which near one-half consisted of provisions and lumber. The total imports for the year were $338,768,130. Of this $20,895,077 were re-exported, which, added to the domestic exports, makes the total exports $356,789,462, thus leaving a balance in our favor of $18,021,332.

LIBERTY AND SLAVERY:
OR, SLAVERY IN THE LIGHT OF MORAL AND POLITICAL PHILOSOPHY.

BY
ALBERT TAYLOR BLEDSOE, LL. D.,
PROFESSOR OF MATHEMATICS IN THE UNIVERSITY OF VIRGINIA.

INTRODUCTION.

THIS work has, for the most part, been thought out for several years, and various portions of it reduced to writing. Though we have long cherished the design of preparing it for the press, yet other engagements, conspiring with a spirit of procrastination, have hitherto induced us to defer the execution of this design. Nor should we have prosecuted it, as we have done, during a large portion of our last summer vacation, and the leisure moments of the first two months of the present session of the University, but for the solicitation of two intelligent and highly-esteemed friends. In submitting the work, as it now is, to the judgment of the truth-loving and impartial reader, we beg leave to offer one or two preliminary remarks.

We have deemed it wise and proper to notice only the more decent, respectable, and celebrated among the abolitionists of the North. Those scurrilous writers, who deal in wholesale abuse of Southern character, we have deemed unworthy of notice. Their writings are, no doubt, adapted to the taste of their readers; but as it is certain that no educated gentleman will tolerate them, so we would not raise a finger to promote their downfall, nor to arrest their course toward the oblivion which so inevitably awaits them.

In replying to the others, we are conscious that we have often used strong language; for which, however, we have no apology to offer. We have dealt with their arguments and positions rather than with their motives and characters. If, in pursuing this course, we have often spoken strongly, we merely beg the reader to consider whether we have not also spoken justly. We have certainly not spoken without provocation. For even these men—the very lights and ornaments of abolitionism—have seldom condescended to argue the great question of Liberty and Slavery with us as with equals. On the contrary, they habitually address us as if nothing but a purblind ignorance of the very first elements of moral science could shield our minds against the force of their irresistible arguments. In the overflowing exuberance of their philanthropy, they take pity of our most lamentable moral darkness, and graciously condescend to teach us the very A B C of ethical philosophy! Hence, if we have deemed it a duty to lay bare their pompous inanities, showing them to be no oracles, and to strip their pitiful sophisms of the guise of a profound philosophy, we trust that no impartial reader will take offense at such vindication of the South against her accusers and despisers.

In this vindication, we have been careful throughout to distinguish between the abolitionists, our accusers, and the great body of the people of the North. Against these we have said nothing, and we could say nothing; since for these we entertain the most profound respect. We have only assailed those by whom we have been assailed; and we have held each and every man responsible only for what he himself has said and done. We should, indeed, despise ourselves if we could be guilty of the monstrous injustice of denouncing a whole people on account of the sayings and doings of a portion of them. We had infinitely rather suffer such injustice—as we have so long done—than practice it toward others.

We cannot flatter ourselves, of course, that the following work is without errors. But these, whatever else may be thought of them, are not the errors of haste and inconsideration. For if we have felt deeply on the subject here discussed, we have also thought long, and patiently endeavored to guard our minds against fallacy. How far this effort has proved successful, it is the province of the candid and impartial reader alone to decide. If our arguments and views are unsound, we hope he will reject them. On the contrary, if they are correct and well-grounded, we hope he will concur with us in the conclusion, that the institution of slavery, as it exists among us at the South, is founded in political justice, is in accordance with the will of GOD and the designs of his providence, and is conducive to the highest, purest, best interests of mankind.

CHAPTER I.

THE NATURE OF CIVIL LIBERTY.

The commonly-received definition of Civil Liberty.—Examination of the commonly-received definition of Civil Liberty.—No good law ever limits or abridges the Natural Liberty of Mankind.—The distinction between Rights and Liberty.—The Relation between the State of Nature and Civil Society.—Inherent and Inalienable Rights.—Conclusion of the First Chapter.

FEW subjects, if any, more forcibly demand our attention, by their intrinsic grandeur and importance, than the great doctrine of human liberty. Correct views concerning this are, indeed, so intimately connected with the most profound interests, as well as with the most exalted aspirations, of the human race, that any material departure therefrom must be fraught with evil to the living, as well as to millions yet unborn. They are so inseparably interwoven with all that is great and good and glorious in the destiny of man, that whosoever aims to form or to propagate such views should proceed with the utmost care, and, laying aside all prejudice and passion, be guided by the voice of reason alone.

Hence it is to be regretted—deeply regretted—that the doctrine of liberty has so often been discussed with so little apparent care, with so little moral earnestness, with so little real energetic searching and longing after truth. Though its transcendent importance demands the best exertion of all our powers, yet has it been, for the most part, a theme for passionate declamation, rather than of severe analysis or of protracted and patient investigation. In the warm praises of the philosopher, no less than in the glowing inspirations of the poet, it often stands before us as a vague and ill-defined *something* which all men are required to worship, but which no man is bound to understand. It would seem, indeed, as if it were a mighty something not to be clearly seen, but only to be deeply felt. And felt it has been, too, by the ignorant as well as by the learned, by the simple as well as by the wise: felt as a fire in the blood, as a fever in the brain, and as a phantom in the imagination, rather than as a form of light and beauty in the intelligence. How often have the powers of darkness surrounded its throne, and desolation marked its path! How often from the altars of this *unknown idol* has the blood of human victims streamed! Even here, in this glorious land of ours, how often do the *too-religious* Americans seem to become deaf to the most appalling lessons of the past, while engaged in the frantic worship of this their tutelary deity! At this very moment, the highly favored land in which we live is convulsed from its centre to its circumference, by the agitations of these pious devotees of freedom; and how long ere scenes like those which called forth the celebrated exclamation of Madame Roland—"O Liberty, what crimes are perpetrated in thy name!" may be enacted among us, it is not possible for human sagacity or foresight to determine.

If no one would talk about liberty except those who had taken the pains to understand it, then would a perfect calm be restored, and peace once more bless a happy people. But there are so many who imagine they understand liberty as Falstaff knew the true prince, namely, by instinct, that all hope of such a consummation must be deferred until it may be shown that their instinct is a blind guide, and its oracles are false. Hence the necessity of a close study and of a clear analysis of the nature and conditions of civil liberty, in order to a distinct delineation of the great idol, which all men are so ready to worship, but which so few are willing to take the pains to understand. In the prosecution of such an inquiry, we intend to consult neither the pecuniary interests of the South nor the prejudices of the North; but calmly and immovably proceed to discuss, upon purely scientific principles, this great problem of our social existence and national prosperity, upon the solution of which the hopes and destinies of mankind in no inconsiderable measure depend. We intend no appeal to passion or to sordid interest, but only to the reason of the wise and good. And if justice, or mercy, or truth, be found at war with the institution of slavery, then, in the name of God, let slavery perish. But however guilty, still let it be tried, condemned, and executed according to law, and not extinguished by a despotic and lawless power more terrific than itself.

§ I. *The commonly-received definition of civil liberty.*

"Civil liberty," says Blackstone, "is no other than natural liberty so far restrained as is necessary and expedient for the general advantage." This definition seems to have been borrowed from Locke, who says that, when a man enters into civil society, "he is to part with so much of his *natural liberty*, in providing for himself, as the good, prosperity, and safety of the society shall require." So, likewise, say Paley, Berlamaqui, Rutherforth, and a host of others. Indeed, among jurists and philosophers, such seems to be the commonly-received definition of civil liberty. It seems to have become a political maxim that civil liberty is no other than a certain portion of our natural liberty, which has been carved therefrom, and secured to us by the protection of the laws.

But is this a sound maxim? Has it been deduced from the nature of things, or is it merely a plausible show of words? Is it truth—solid and imperishable truth—or merely one of those fair semblances of truth, which, through the too hasty sanction of great names, have obtained a currency among men? The question is not what Blackstone, or Locke, or Paley may have thought, but what is truth? Let us examine this point, then, in order that our decision may be founded, not upon the authority of man, but, if possible, in the wisdom of God.

§ II. *Examination of the commonly-received definition of civil liberty.*

Before we can determine whether such be the origin of civil liberty, we must first ascertain the character of that natural liberty out of which it is supposed to be reserved. What, then, is natural liberty? What is the nature of the material out of which our civil liberty is supposed to be fashioned by the art of the political sculptor? It is thus defined by Locke: "To understand political power right, and derive it from its original, we must consider what state all men are naturally in; and that is a state of perfect freedom to order their actions and dispose of their possessions and persons as they think fit, *within the bounds of the law of nature*, without asking leave or depending upon the will of any other man."[136] In perfect accordance with this definition, Blackstone says: "This natural liberty consists in a power of acting as one thinks fit, without any restraint or control, unless by the laws of nature, being a right inherent in us by birth, and one of the gifts of God to man at his creation, when he endowed him with the faculty of free-will." Such, according to Locke and Blackstone, is that natural liberty, which is limited and abridged, as they suppose, when we enter into the bonds of civil society.

Now mark its features: it is the gift of God to man at his creation; the very top and flower of his existence; that by which he is distinguished from the lower animals and raised to the rank of moral and accountable beings. Shall we sacrifice this divine gift, then, in order to secure the blessings of civil society? Shall we abridge or mutilate the image of God, stamped upon the soul at its creation, by which we are capable of knowing and obeying his law, in order to secure the aid and protection of man? Shall we barter away any portion of this our glorious birthright for any poor boon of man's devising? Yes, we are told—and why? Because, says Blackstone, "Legal obedience and conformity is infinitely more valuable than *the wild and savage liberty which is sacrificed to obtain it*."

But how is this? *Now* this natural liberty is a thing of light, and *now* it is a power of darkness. Now it is the gift of God, that moves within a sphere of light, and breathes an atmosphere of love; and anon, it is a wild and savage thing that carries terror in its train. It would be an angel of light, if it were not a power of darkness; and it would be a power of darkness, if it were not an angel of light. But as it is, it is both by turns, and neither long, but runs through its Protean changes, according to the exigencies of the flowing discourse of the learned author. Surely such inconsistency, so glaring and so portentous, and all exhibited on one and the same page, is no evidence that the genius of the great commentator was as steady and profound as it was elegant and classical.

The source of this vacillation is obvious. With Locke, he defines natural liberty to be a power of acting as one thinks fit, *within the limits prescribed by the law of nature;* but he soon loses sight of this all-important limitation, from which natural liberty derives its form and beauty. Hence it becomes in his mind a power to act as one pleases, without the restraint or control of any law whatever, either human or divine. The sovereign will and pleasure of the individual becomes the only rule of conduct, and lawless anarchy the condition which it legitimates. Thus, having loosed the bonds and marred the beauty of natural liberty, he was prepared to see it, now become so "wild and savage," offered up as a sacrifice on the altar of civil liberty.

This, too, was the great fundamental error of Hobbes. What Blackstone thus did through inadvertency, was knowingly and designedly done by the philosopher of Malmesbury. In a state of nature, says he, all men have a right to do as they please. Each individual may set up a right to all things, and consequently to the same things. In other words, in such a state there is no law, exept that of force. The strong arm of power is the supreme arbiter of all things. Robbery and outrage and murder are as lawful as their opposites. That is to say, there is no such thing as a law of nature; and consequently all things are, in a state of nature, equally allowable. Thus it was that Hobbes delighted to legitimate the horrors of a state of nature, as it is called, in order that mankind might, without a feeling of indignation or regret, see the wild and ferocious liberty of such a state sacrificed to despotic power. Thus it was that he endeavoured to recommend the "Leviathan," by contrasting it with the huger monster called Natural Liberty.

This view of the state of nature, by which all law and the great Fountain of all law are shut out of the world, was perfectly agreeable to the atheistical philosophy of Hobbes. From one who had extinguished the light of nature, and given dominion to the powers of darkness, no better could have been expected; but is it not deplorable that a Christian jurist should, even for a moment, have forgotten the great central light of his own system, and drawn his arguments from such an abyss of darkness?

Blackstone has thus lost sight of truth, not only in regard to his general propositions, but also in regard to particular instances. "The law," says he, "which restrains a man from doing mischief to his fellow-citizens diminishes the natural liberty of mankind." Now, is this true? The doing of mischief is contrary to the law of nature, and hence, according to the definition of Blackstone himself, the perpetration of it is not an exercise of any natural right. As no man possesses a natural right to do mischief, so the law which forbids it does not diminish the natural liberty of mankind. The law which forbids mischief is a restraint not upon the *natural liberty*, but upon the *natural tyranny*, of man.

Blackstone is by no means alone in the error to which we have alluded. By one of the clearest thinkers and most beautiful writers of the present age,[137] it is argued, "that as government implies restraint, it is evident we give up a certain portion of our liberty by entering into it." This argument would be valid, no doubt, if there were nothing in the world beside liberty to be restrained; but the evil passions of men, from which proceed so many frightful tyrannies and wrongs, are not to be identified with their rights or liberties. As government implies restraint, it is evident that something is restrained when we enter into it; but it does not follow that this something must be our natural liberty. The argument in question proceeds on the notion that government can restrain nothing, unless it restrain the natural liberty of mankind; whereas, we have seen, the law which forbids the perpetration of mischief, or any other wrong, is a restriction, not upon the *liberty*, but upon the *tyranny*, of the human will. It sets a bound and limit, not to any right conferred on us by the Author of nature, but upon the evil thoughts and deeds of which we are the sole and exclusive originators. Such a law, indeed, so far from restraining the natural liberty of man, recognizes his natural rights, and secures his freedom, by protecting the weak against the injustice and oppression of the strong.

The way in which these authors show that natural liberty is, and of right ought to be, abridged by the laws of society, is, by identifying this natural freedom, not with a power to act as God wills, but with a power in conformity with our own sovereign will and pleasure. The same thing is expressly done by Paley.[138] "To do what we will," says he, "is natural liberty." Starting from this definition, it is no wonder that he should have supposed that natural liberty is restrained by civil government. In like manner, Burke first says, "That the effect of liberty to individuals is, *that they may do what they please;*" and then concludes, that in order to "secure some liberty," we make "a surrender in trust of the whole of it."[139] Thus the natural rights of mankind are first caricatured, and then sacrificed.

If there be no God, if there be no difference between right and wrong, if there be no moral law in the universe, then indeed would men possess a natural right to do mischief or to act as they please. Then indeed should we be fettered by no law in a state of nature, and liberty therein would be coextensive with power. Right would give place to might, and the least restraint, even from the best laws, would impair our natural freedom. But we subscribe to no such philosophy. That learned authors, that distinguished jurists, that celebrated philosophers, that pious divines, should thus deliberately include the enjoyment of our natural rights and the indulgence of our evil passions in one and the same definition of liberty, is, it seems to us, matter of the most profound astonishment and regret. It is to confound the source of all tyranny with the fountain of all freedom. It is to put darkness for light, and light for darkness. And it is to inflame the minds of men with the idea that they are struggling and contending for liberty, when, in reality, they may be only struggling and contending for the gratification of their malignant passions. Such an offense against all clear thinking, such an outrage against all sound political ethics, becomes the more amazing when we reflect on the greatness of the authors by whom it is committed, and the stupendous magnitude of the interests involved in their discussions.

Should we, then, exhibit the fundamental law of society, and the natural liberty of mankind, as antagonistic principles? Is not this the way to prepare the human mind, at all times so passionately, not to say so madly, fond of freedom, for a repetition of those tremendous conflicts and struggles beneath which the foundations of society have so often trembled, and some of its best institutions been laid in the dust? In one word, is it not high time to raise the inquiry, Whether there be, in reality, any such opposition as is usually supposed to exist between the law of the land and the natural rights of mankind? Whether such opposition be real or imaginary? Whether it exists in the nature of things, or only in the imagination of political theorists?

§ III. *No good law ever limits or abridges the natural liberty of mankind*

By the two great leaders of opposite schools, Locke and Burke, it is contended that when we enter into society the natural rights of self-defense is surrendered to the government. If any natural right, then, be limited or abridged by the laws of society, we may suppose the right of self-defense to be so; for this is the instance which is always selected to illustrate and confirm the reality of such a surrender of our natural liberty. It has, indeed, become a sort of maxim, that when we put on the bonds of civil society, we give up the natural right of self-defense.

But what does this maxim mean? Does it mean that we transfer the right to repel force by force? If so, the proposition is not true; for this right is as fully possessed by every individual after he has entered into society as it could have been in a state of nature. If he is assailed, or threatened with immediate personal danger, the law of the land does not require him to wait upon the strong but slow arm of government for protection. On the contrary, it permits him to protect himself, to repel force by force, in so far as this may be necessary to guard against injury to himself; and the law of nature allows no more. Indeed, if there be any difference, the law of the land allows a man to go further in the defense of self than he is permitted to go by the law of God. Hence, in this sense, the maxim under consideration is not true; and no man's natural liberty is abridged by the State.

Does this maxim mean, then, that in a state of nature every man has a right to redress his own wrongs by the *subsequent* punishment of the offender, which right the citizen has transferred to the government? It is clear that this must be the meaning, if it have any correct meaning at all. But neither in this sense is the maxim or proposition true. The right to punish an offender must rest upon the one or the other of two grounds: either upon the ground that the offender deserves punishment, or that his punishment is necessary to prevent similar offenses. Now, upon neither of these grounds has any man, even in a state of nature, the right to punish an offense committed against himself.

First, he has no right to punish such an offense on the ground that it deserves punishment. No man has, or ever had, the right to wield the awful attribute of retributive justice; that is, to inflict so much pain for so much guilt or moral turpitude. This is the prerogative of God alone. To his eye, all secrets are known, and all degrees of guilt perfectly apparent; and to him alone belongs the vengeance which is due for moral ill-desert. His law extends over the state of nature as well as over the state of civil society, and calls all men to account for their evil deeds. It is evident that, in so far as the intrinsic demerit of actions is concerned, it makes no difference whether they be punished here or hereafter. And beside, if the individual had possessed such a right in a state of nature, he has not transferred it to society; for society neither has nor claims any such right. Blackstone but utters the voice of the law when he says: "The end or final cause of human punishment is not by way of atonement or expiation, for that must be left to the just determination of the supreme Being, but a precaution against future offenses of the same kind." The exercise of retributive justice belongs exclusively to the infallible Ruler of the world, and not to frail, erring man, who himself so greatly stands in need of mercy. Hence, the right to punish a transgressor on the ground that such punishment is deserved, has not been transferred from the individual to civil society: first, because he had no such natural right to transfer; and, secondly, because society possesses no such right.

In the second place, if we consider the other ground of punishment, it will likewise appear that the right to punish never belonged to the individual, and consequently could not have been transferred by him to society. For, by the law of nature, the individual has no right to punish an offense against himself *in order to prevent further offences of the same kind.* If the object of human punishment be, as indeed it is, to prevent the commission of crime, by holding up examples of terror to evil-doers, then, it is evidently no more the natural right of the party injured to redress the wrong, than it is the right of others. All men are interested in the prevention of wrongs, and hence all men should unite to redress them. All men are endowed by their Creator with a sense of justice, in order to impel them to secure its claims, and throw the shield of its protection around the weak and oppressed.

The prevention of wrong, then, is clearly the natural duty, and consequently the natural right, of all men.

This duty should be discharged by others, rather than by the party aggrieved. For it is contrary to the law of nature itself, as both Locke and Burke agree, that any man should be "judge in his own case;" that any man should, by an *ex post facto* decision, determine the amount of punishment due to his enemy, and proceed to inflict it upon him. Such a course, indeed, so far from preventing offenses, would inevitably promote them; instead of redressing injuries, would only add wrong to wrong; and instead of introducing order, would only make confusion worse confounded, and turn the moral world quite upside down.

On no ground, then, upon which the right to punish may be conceived to rest, does it appear that it was ever possessed, or could ever have been possessed, by the individual. And if the individual never possessed such a right, it is clear that he has never transferred it to society. Hence, this view of the origin of government, however plausible at first sight, or however generally received, has no real foundation in the nature of things. It is purely a creature of the imagination of theorists; one of the phantoms of that manifold, monstrous, phantom deity called Liberty, which has been so often invoked by the *pseudo* philanthropists and reckless reformers of the present day to subvert not only the law of capital punishment, but also other institutions and laws which have received the sanction of both God and man.

The simple truth is, that we are all bound by the law of nature and the law of God to love our neighbor as ourselves. Hence it is the duty of every man, in a state of nature, to do all in his power to protect the rights and promote the interests of his fellow-men. It is the duty of all men to consult together, and concert measures for the general good. Right here it is, then, that the law of man, the constitution of civil society, comes into contact with the law of God and rests upon it. Thus, civil society arises, not from a surrender of individual rights, but from a right originally possessed by all; nay, from a solemn duty originally imposed upon all by God himself—a duty which must be performed, whether the individual gives his consent or not. The very law of nature itself requires, as we have seen, not only the punishment of the offender, but also that he be punished acccording to a pre-established law, and by the decision of an impartial tribunal. And in the enactment of such law, as well as in the administration, the collective wisdom of society, or its agents, moves in obedience to the law of God, and not in pursuance of rights derived from the individual.

§ IV. *The distinction between rights and liberty.*

In the foregoing discussion we have, in conformity to the custom of others, used the terms *rights* and *liberty* as words of precisely the same import. But, instead of being convertible terms, there seems to be a very clear difference in their signification. If a man be taken, for example, and without cause thrown into prison, this deprives him of his *liberty*, but not of his *right*, to go where he pleases. The right still exists; and his not being allowed to enjoy this right, is precisely what constitutes the oppression in the case supposed. If there were no right still subsisting, then there would be no oppression. Hence, as the *right* exists, while the *liberty* is extinguished, it is evident they are distinct from each other. The liberty of a man in such a case, as in all others, would consist in an opportunity to enjoy his right, or in a state in which it might be enjoyed if he so pleased.

This distinction between rights and liberty is all-important to a clear and satisfactory discussion of the doctrine of human freedom. The great champions of that freedom, from a Locke down to a Hall, firmly and passionately grasping the natural rights of man, and confounding these with his liberty, have looked upon society as the restrainer, and not as the author, of that liberty. On the other hand, the great advocates of despotic power, from a Hobbes down to a Whewell, seeing that there can be no genuine liberty—that is, no secure enjoyment of one's rights—in a state of nature, have ascribed, not only our liberty, but all our existing rights also, to the State.

But the error of Locke is a noble and generous sentiment when compared with the odious dogma of Hobbes and Whewell. These learned authors contend that we derive all our existing rights from society. Do we, then, live and move and breathe and think and worship God only by rights derived from the State? No, certainly. We have these rights from a higher source. God gave them, and all the powers of earth combined cannot take them away. But as for our liberty, this we freely own is, for the most part, due to the sacred bonds of civil society. Let us render unto Cæsar the things that are Cæsar's, and unto God the things that are God's.

§ V. *The relation between the state of nature and of civil society.*

Herein, then, consists the true relation between the *natural* and the *social* states. Civil society does not abridge our natural rights, but secures and protects them. She does not assume our right of self-defense,—she simply discharges the duty imposed by God to defend us. The original right is in those who compose the body politic, and not in any individual. Hence, civil society does not impair our natural liberty, as actually existing in a state of nature, or as it might therein exist; for, in such a state, there would be no real liberty, no real enjoyment of natural rights.

Mr. Locke, as we have seen, defines the state of nature to be one of "perfect freedom." Why, then, should we leave it? "If man, in the state of nature, be so free," says he, "why will he part with his freedom? To which it is obvious to answer," he continues, "that though, in the state of nature, he hath such a right, *yet the enjoyment of it is very uncertain*, and constantly exposed to the invasion of others; for all being kings as much as he, every man his equal, and the greater part not strict observers of equity and justice, the enjoyment of the property he has in this state is very unsafe, very insecure. This makes him willing to quit a condition which, *however free, is full of fears and continual dangers;* and it is not without reason that he seeks out, and is willing to join in society with, others who are already united, or have a mind to unite, *for the mutual preservation of their lives, liberties, and estates*, which I call by the general name *property*."[140] What! can that be a state of perfect freedom which is subject to fears and perpetual dangers? In one word, can a reign of terror be the reign of liberty? It is evident, we think, that Locke has been betrayed into no little inaccuracy and confusion of thought from not having distinguished between rights and liberty.

The truth seems to be that, in a state of nature, we would possess rights, but we could not enjoy them. That is to say, notwithstanding all our rights, we should be destitute of freedom or liberty. Society interposes the strong arm of the law to protect our rights, to secure us in the enjoyment of them. She delivers us from the alarms, the dangers, and the violence of the natural state. Hence, under God, she is the mother of our peace and joy, by whose sovereign rule anarchy is abolished and liberty established. Liberty and social law can never be dissevered. Liberty, robed in law, and radiant with love, is one of the best gifts of God to man. But liberty, despoiled of law, is a wild, dark, fierce spirit of licentiousness, which tends "to uproar the universal peace."

Hence it is a frightful error to regard the civil state or government as antagonistic to the natural liberty of mankind; for this is, indeed, the author of the very liberty we enjoy. Good government it is that restrains the elements of tyranny and oppression, and introduces liberty into the world. Good government it is that shuts out the reign of anarchy, and secures the dominion of equity and goodness. He who would spurn the restraints of law, then, by which pride, and envy, and hatred, and malice, ambition, and revenge are kept within the sacred bounds of eternal justice,—he, we say, is not the friend of human liberty. He would open the flood-gates of tyranny and oppression; he would mar the harmony and extinguish the light of the world. Let no such man be trusted.

If the foregoing remarks be just, it would follow that the state of nature, as it is called, would be one of the most unnatural states in the world. We may conceive it to exist, for the sake of illustration or argument; but if it should actually exist, it would be at war with the law of nature itself. For this requires, as we have seen, that men should unite together, and frame such laws as the general good demands.

Not only the law, but the very necessities of nature, enjoin the institution of civil government. God himself has thus laid the foundations of civil society deep in the nature of man. It is an ordinance of Heaven, which no human decree can reverse or annul. It is not a thing of compacts, bound together by promises and paper, but is itself a law of nature as irreversible as any other. Compacts may give it one form or another, but in one form or another it must exist. It is no accidental or artificial thing, which may be made or unmade, which may be set up or pulled down, at the mere will and pleasure of man. It is a decree of God; the spontaneous and irresistible working of that nature, which, in all climates, through all ages, and under all circumstances, manifests itself in social organizations.

§ VI. *Inherent and inalienable rights.*

Much has been said about inherent and inalienable rights, which is either unintelligible or rests upon no solid foundation. "The inalienable rights of men" is a phrase often brandished by certain reformers, who aim to bring about "the immediate abolition of slavery." Yet, in the light of the foregoing discussion, it may be clearly shown that the doctrine of inalienable rights, if properly handled, will not touch the institution of slavery.

An inalienable right is either one which the possessor of it himself cannot alienate or transfer, or it is one which society has not the power to take from him. According to the import of the terms, the first would seem to be what is meant by an inalienable right; but in this sense it is not pretended that the right to either life or liberty has been transferred to society or alienated by the individual. And if, as we have endeavored to show, the right, or power, or authority of society is not derived from a transfer of individual rights, then it is clear that neither the right to life nor liberty is transferred to society. That is, if no rights are transferred, than these particular rights are still untransferred, and, if you please, untransferable. Be it conceded, then, that the individual has never transferred his right to life or liberty to society.

But it is not in the above sense that the abolitionist uses the expression, *inalienable rights*. According to his view, an inalienable right is one of which society itself cannot, without doing wrong, deprive the individual, or deny the enjoyment of it to him. This is evidently his meaning; for he complains of the injustice of society, or civil government, in depriving a certain portion of its subjects of civil freedom, and consigning them to a state of servitude. "Such an act," says he, "is wrong, because it is a violation of the inalienable rights of all men." But let us see if his complaint be just or well founded.

It is pretended by no one that society has the right to deprive any subject of either life or liberty, *without good and sufficient cause or reason*. On the contrary, it is on all hands agreed that it is only for good and sufficient reasons that society can deprive any portion of its subjects of either life or liberty. Nor can it be denied, on the other side, that a man may be deprived of either, or both, by a preordained law, in case there be a good and sufficient reason for the enactment of such law. For the crime of murder, the law of the land deprives the criminal of life: *à fortiori*, might it deprive him of liberty. In the infliction of such a penalty, the law seeks, as we have seen, not to deal out so much pain for so much guilt, nor even to deal out pain for guilt at all, but simply to protect the members of society, and *secure the general good*. The general good is the sole and sufficient consideration which justifies the State in taking either the life or the liberty of its subjects.

Hence, if we would determine in any case whether society is justified in depriving any of its members of civil freedom by law, we must first ascertain whether the general good demands the enactment of such a law. If it does, then such a law is just and good—as perfectly just and good as any other law which, for the same reason or on the same ground, takes away the life or liberty of its subjects. All this talk about the inalienable rights of men may have a very admirable meaning, if one will only be at the pains to search it out; but is it not evident that, when searched to the bottom, it has just nothing at all to do with the great question of slavery? But more of this hereafter.[141]

This great problem, as we have seen, is to be decided, not by an appeal to the inalienable rights of men, but simply and solely by a reference to the general good. It is to be decided, not by the aid of abstractions alone; a little good sense and *practical sagacity* should be allowed to assist in its determination. There are inalienable rights, we admit—

inalienable both because the individual cannot transfer them, and because society can never rightfully deprive any man of their enjoyment. But life and liberty are *not* "among these." There are inalienable rights, we admit, but then such abstractions are the edge-tools of political science, with which it is dangerous for either men or children to play. They may inflict deep wounds on the cause of humanity; they can throw no light on the great problem of slavery.

One thing seems to be clear and fixed; and that is, that the rights of the individual are subordinate to those of the community. *An inalienable right is a right coupled with a duty; a duty with which no other obligation can interfere.* But, as we have seen, it is the *duty*, and consequently, the *right*, of society to make such laws as the general good demands. This inalienable right is conferred, and its exercise enjoined, by the Creator and Governor of the universe. All individual rights are subordinate to this inherent, universal, and inalienable right. It should be observed, however, that in the exercise of this paramount right, this supreme authority, no society possesses the power to contravene the principles of justice. In other words, it should be observed that no unjust law can ever promote the public good. Every law, then, which is not unjust, and which the public good demands, should be enacted by society.

But we have already seen and shall still more fully see, that the law which ordains slavery is not unjust in itself, or, in other words, that it interferes with none of the inalienable rights of man. Hence, if it be shown that the public good, and especially the good of the slave, demands such a law, then the question of slavery will be settled. We purpose to show this before we have done with the present discussion. And if, in the prosecution of this inquiry, we should be so fortunate as to throw only one steady ray of light on the great question of slavery, by which the very depths of society have been so fearfully convulsed, we shall be more than rewarded for all the labor which, with no little solicitude, we have felt constrained to bestow upon an attempt at its solution.

§ VII. *Conclusion of the first chapter.*

In conclusion, we shall merely add that if the foregoing remarks be just, it follows that the great problem of political philosophy is not precisely such as it is often taken to be by statesmen and historians. This problem, according to Mackintosh and Macaulay, consists in finding such an adjustment of the antagonistic principles of public order and private liberty, that neither shall overthrow or subvert the other, but each be confined within its own appropriate limits. Whereas, if we are not mistaken, these are not *antagonistic*, but *co-ordinate*, principles. The very law which institutes public order is that which introduces private liberty, since no secure enjoyment of one's rights can exist where public order is not maintained. And, on the other hand, unless private liberty be introduced, public order cannot be maintained, or at least such public order as should be established; for, if there be not private liberty, if there be no secure enjoyment of one's rights, then the highest and purest elements of our nature would have to be extinguished, or else exist in perpetual conflict with the surrounding despotism. As license is not liberty, so despotism is not order, nor even friendly to that enlightened, wholesome order, by which the good of the public and the individual are at the same time introduced and secured. In other words, what is taken from the one of these principles is not given to the other; on the contrary, every additional element of strength and beauty which is imparted to the one is an accession of strength and beauty to the other. Private liberty, indeed, lives and moves and has its very being in the bosom of public order. On the other hand, that public order alone which cherishes the true liberty of the individual is strong in the approbation of God and in the moral sentiments of mankind. All else is weakness, and death, and decay.

The true problem, then, is, not how the conflicting claims of these two principles may be adjusted, (for there is no conflict between them,) but how a real public order, whose claims are identical with those of private liberty, may be introduced and maintained. The practical solution of this problem, for the heterogeneous population of the South imperatively demands, as we shall endeavor to show, the institution of slavery; and that without such an institution it would be impossible to maintain either a sound public order or a decent private liberty. We shall endeavor to show, that the very laws or institution which is supposed by fanatical declaimers to shut out liberty from the Negro race among us, really shuts out the most frightful *license* and disorder from society. In one word, we shall endeavor to show that in preaching up liberty *to and for* the slaves of the South, the abolitionist is "casting pearls before swine," that can neither comprehend the nature, nor enjoy the blessings, of the freedom which is so officiously thrust upon them. And if the Negro race should be moved by their fiery appeals, it would only be to rend and tear in pieces the fair fabric of American liberty, which, with all its shortcomings and defects, is by far the most beautiful ever yet conceived or constructed by the genius of man.

CHAPTER II.

THE ARGUMENTS AND POSITIONS OF ABOLITIONISTS.

The first fallacy of the Abolitionist.—The second fallacy of the Abolitionist.—The third fallacy of the Abolitionist.—The fourth fallacy of the Abolitionist.—The fifth fallacy of the Abolitionist.—The sixth fallacy of the Abolitionist.—The seventh fallacy of the Abolitionist.—The eighth fallacy of the Abolitionist.—The ninth fallacy of the Abolitionist.—The tenth, eleventh, twelfth, thirteenth, fourteenth, fifteenth, and sixteenth fallacies of the Abolitionist; or his seven arguments against the right of a man to hold property in his fellow-man.—The seventeenth fallacy of the Abolitionist; or, the Argument from the Declaration of Independence.

HAVING in the preceding chapter discussed and defined the nature of civil liberty, as well as laid down some of the political conditions on which its existence depends, we shall now proceed to examine the question of slavery. In the prosecution of this inquiry, we shall, in the first place, consider the arguments and positions of the advocates of immediate abolition; and, in the second, point out the reasons and grounds on which the institution of slavery is based and its justice vindicated. The first branch of the investigation, or that relating to the arguments and positions of the abolitionist, will occupy the remainder of the present chapter.

It is insisted by abolitionists that the institution of slavery is, in all cases and under all circumstances, morally wrong, or a violation of the law of God. Such is precisely the ground assumed by the one side and denied by the other.

Thus says Dr. Wayland: "I have wished to make it clear that slavery, or the holding of men in bondage, and 'obliging them to labor for our benefit, without their contract or consent,' is always and everywhere, or, as you well express it, *semper et ubique*, a moral wrong, a violation of the obligations under which we are created to our fellow-men, and a transgression of the law of our Creator."

Dr. Fuller likewise: "The simple question is, Whether it *is necessarily, and amid all circumstances, a crime to hold men in a condition where they labor for another without their consent or contract?* and in settling this matter all impertinences must be retrenched."

In one word, Dr. Wayland insists that slavery is condemned by the law of God, by the moral law of the universe. We purpose to examine the arguments which he has advanced in favor of this position. We select his arguments for examination, because, as a writer on moral and political science, he stands so high in the northern portion of the Union. His work on these subjects has indeed long since passed the fiftieth thousand; a degree of success which, in his own estimation, authorizes him to issue his letters on slavery over the signature of "THE AUTHOR OF THE MORAL SCIENCE." But the very fact that his popularity is so great, and that he is *the* author of *the* Moral Science, is a reason why his arguments on a question of such magnitude should be subjected to a severe analysis and searching scrutiny, in order that, under the sanction of so imposing a name, no error may be propagated and no mischief done.

Hence we shall hold Dr. Wayland amenable to all the laws of logic. Especially shall we require him to adhere to the point he has undertaken to discuss, and to retrench all irrelevancies. If, after having subjected his arguments to such a process, it shall be found that every position which is assumed on the subject is directly contradicted by himself, we shall not make haste to introduce anarchy into the Southern States, in order to make it answer to the anarchy in his views of civil and political freedom. But whether this be the case or not, it is not for us to determine; we shall simply proceed to examine, and permit the impartial reader to decide for himself.

§ I. *The first fallacy of the abolitionist.*

The abolitionists do not hold their passions in subjection to reason. This is not merely the judgment of a Southern man: it is the opinion of the more decent and respectable abolitionists themselves. Thus says Dr. Channing, censuring the conduct of the abolitionists: "They have done wrong, I believe; nor is their wrong to be winked at because done fanatically or with good intentions; for how much mischief may be wrought with good designs! They have fallen into the common error of enthusiasts—that of exaggerating their object, of feeling as if no evil existed but that which they opposed, and as if no guilt could be compared with that of countenancing or upholding it."[142] In like manner, Dr. Wayland says: "I unite with you and the lamented Dr Channing in the opinion that the tone of the abolitionists at the North has been frequently, I fear I must say generally, 'fierce, bitter, and abusive.' The abolitionist press has, I believe, from the beginning, too commonly indulged in *exaggerated statement*, in violent denunciation, and in coarse and lacerating invective. At our late Missionary Convention in Philadelphia, I heard many things from men who claim to be the exclusive friends of the slave, which pained me more than I can express. It seemed to me that the spirit which many of them manifested was very different from the spirit of Christ. I also cheerfully bear testimony to the general courtesy, the Christian urbanity, and the calmness under provocation which, in a remarkable degree, characterized the conduct of the members from the South."

In the flood of sophisms which the abolitionists usually pour out in their explosions of passion, none is more common than what is technically termed by logicians the *ignoratio elenchi*, or a mistaking of the point in dispute. Nor is this fallacy peculiar to the more vulgar sort of abolitionists. It glares from the pages of Dr. Wayland, no less than from the writings of the most fierce, bitter, and vindictive of his associates in the cause of abolitionism. Thus, in one of his letters to Dr. Fuller, he says: "To present this subject in a simple light. Let us suppose that your family and mine were neighbors. We, our wives and children, are all human beings in the sense that I have described, and, in consequence of that common nature, and by the will of our common Creator, are subject to the law, *Thou shalt love thy neighbor as thyself.* Suppose that I should set fire to your house, shoot you as you came out of it, and seizing your wife and children, 'oblige them to labor for my benefit without their contract or consent.' Suppose, moreover, aware that I could not thus oblige them, unless they were inferior in intellect to myself, I should forbid them to read, and thus consign them to intellectual and moral imbecility. Suppose I should measure out to them the knowledge of God on the same principle. Suppose I should exercise this dominion over them and their children as long as I lived, and then do all in my power to render it certain that my children should exercise it after me. *The question before us I suppose to be simply this: Would I, in so doing, act at variance with the relations existing between us as creatures of God?* Would I, in other words, violate the supreme law of my Creator, Thou shalt love thy neighbor as thyself? or that other, Whatsoever ye would that men should do unto you, do ye even so unto them? I do not see how any intelligent creature can give more than one answer to this question. Then I think that every intelligent creature must affirm that do this is wrong, or, in the other form of expression, that it is a great moral evil. Can we conceive of any greater?"

It was surely very kind in Dr. Wayland to undertake, with so much pains, to instruct us poor, benighted sons of the South in regard to the difference between right and wrong. We would fain give him full credit for all the kindly feeling he so freely professes for his "Southern brethren;" but if he really thinks that the question, whether arson, and murder, and cruelty are offenses against the "supreme law of the Creator," is still open for discussion among us, then we beg leave to inform him that he labors under a slight hallucination. If he had never written a word, we should have known, perhaps, that it is wrong for a man to set fire to his neighbor's house, and shoot him as he came out, and reduce his wife and children to a state of ignorance, degradation, and slavery. Nay, if we should find his house already burnt, and himself already shot, we should hardly feel justified in treating his wife and children in so cruel a manner. Not even if they were "guilty of a skin," or ever so degraded, should we deem ourselves justified in reducing them to a state of servitude. This is NOT "the question before us." We are quite satisfied on all such points. The precept, too, Thou shalt love thy neighbor as thyself, was not altogether unknown in the Southern States before his letters were written. A committee of very amiable philanthropists came all the way from England, as the agents of some abolition society there, and told us all that the law of God requires us to love our neighbor as ourselves. In this benevolent work of enlightenment they were, if we mistake not, several months in advance of Dr. Wayland. We no longer need to be enlightened on such points.

Being sufficiently instructed, we admit that we should love our neighbor as ourselves, and also that arson, murder, and so forth are violations of this law. But we want to know whether, *semper et ubique*, the institution of slavery is morally wrong. *This is the question*, and to this we intend to hold the author.

§ II. *The second fallacy of the abolitionist.*

Lest we should be suspected of misrepresentation, we shall state the position of Dr. Wayland in his own words. In regard to the institution of slavery, he says: "I do not see that it does not sanction the whole system of the slave-trade. *If I have a right to a thing after I have gotten it, I have a natural right to the means necessary for getting it.* If this be so, I should be as much justified in sending a vessel to Africa, murdering a part of the inhabitants of a village, and making slaves of the rest, as I should be in hunting a herd of wild animals, and either slaying them or subjecting them to the yoke."

Now mark the principle on which this most wonderful argument is based: "If I have a right to a thing after I have gotten it, I have a natural right to the means for getting it." That is to say, If I have the right to a slave, now that I have got him, then I may rightfully use all necessary means to reduce other men to slavery! I may shoot, burn, or murder, if by this means I can only get slaves! Was any consequence ever more wildly drawn? Was any *non sequitur* ever more glaring?

Let us see how this argument would apply to other things. If I have a right to a watch after I have gotten it, no matter how, then I have a right to use the means necessary to get watches; I may steal them from my neighbors! Or, if I have a right to a wife, provided I can get one, then may I shoot my friend and marry his widow! Such is the argument of one who seeks to enlighten the South and reform its institutions!

§ III. *The third fallacy of the abolitionist.*

Nearly allied to the foregoing argument is that of the same author, in which he deduces from the right of slavery, supposing it to exist, another retinue of monstrous rights. "This right also," says Dr. Wayland, referring to the right to hold slaves, "as I have shown, involves the right to use all the means necessary to its establishment and perpetuity, and, *of course, the right to crush his intellectual and social nature*, and to stupefy his conscience, in so far as may be necessary to enable me to enjoy this right with the least possible peril." This is a compound fallacy, a many-sided error. But we will consider only two phases of its absurdity.

In the first place, if the slaveholder should reason in this way, no one would be more ready than the author himself to condemn his logic. If any slaveholder should say, That because I have a right to my slaves, therefore I have the right to crush the intellectual and moral nature of men, in order to *establish* and perpetuate their bondage,—he would be among the first to cry out against such reasoning. This is evident from the fact that he everywhere commends those slaveholders who deem it their duty, as a return for the service of their slaves, to promote both their temporal and eternal good. He everywhere insists that such is the duty of slaveholders; and if such be their duty, they surely have no right to violate it, by crushing the intellectual and moral nature of those whom they are bound to elevate in the scale of being. If the slaveholder, then, should adopt such an argument, his logic would be very justly chargeable by Dr. Wayland with evidencing not so much the existence of a clear head as of a bad heart.

In the second place, the above argument overlooks the fact that the Southern statesman vindicates the institution of slavery on the ground that it finds the Negro race already so degraded as to unfit it for a state of freedom. He does not argue that it is right to seize those who, by the possession of cultivated intellects and pure morals, are fit for freedom, and debase them in order to prepare them for social bondage. He does not imagine that it is ever right to shoot, burn, or corrupt, in order to reduce any portion of the enlightened universe to a state of servitude. He merely insists that those only who are already unfit for a higher and nobler state than one of slavery, should be held by society in such a state. This position, although it is so prominently set forth by every advocate of slavery at the South, is almost invariably overlooked by the Northern abolitionists. They talk, and reason, and declaim, indeed, just as if we had caught a bevy of black angels as they were winging their way to some island of purity and bliss here upon earth, and reduced them from their heavenly state, by the most diabolical cruelties and oppressions, to one of degradation, misery, and servitude. They forget that Africa is not yet a paradise, and that Southern servitude is not quite a hell. They forget—in the heat and haste of their argument they forget—that the institution of slavery is designed by the South not for the enlightened and the free, but only for the ignorant and the debased. They need to be constantly reminded that the institution of slavery is not the mother, but the daughter, of ignorance and degradation. It is, indeed, the legitimate offspring of that intellectual and moral debasement which, for so many thousand years, has been accumulating and growing upon the African race. And if the abolitionists at the North will only invent some method by which all this frightful mass of degradation may be blotted out *at once*, then will we most cheerfully consent to "the *immediate* abolition of slavery." On this point, however, we need not dwell, as we shall have occasion to recur to it again when we come to consider the grounds and reasons on which the institution of slavery is vindicated.

Having argued that the right of slavery, if it exist, implies the right to shoot and murder an enlightened neighbor, with a view to reduce his wife and children to a state of servitude, as well as to crush their intellectual and moral nature in order to keep them in such a state, the author adds, "If I err in making these inferences, I *err innocently*." We have no doubt of the most perfect and entire innocence of the author. But we would remind him that innocence, however perfect or *childlike*, is not the only quality which a great reformer should possess.

§ IV. *The fourth fallacy of the abolitionist.*

He is often guilty of a *petitio principii*, in taking it for granted that the institution of slavery is an injury to the slave, which is the very point in dispute. Thus says Dr. Wayland: "If it be asked when, [slavery must be abandoned,] I ask again, when shall a man begin to cease doing wrong? Is not the answer *immediately?* If a man is injuring us, do we doubt as to the *time when* he ought to cease? There is, then, no doubt in respect to the time when we ought to cease inflicting injury upon others."[143] Here it is assumed that slavery is an *injury* to the slave: but this is the very point which is denied, and which he should have discussed. If a state of slavery be a greater injury to the slave than a state of freedom would be, then are we willing to admit that it should be abolished. But even in that case, not *immediately*, unless it could be shown that the remedy would not be worse than the evil. If, on the whole, the institution of slavery be a curse to the slave, we say let it be abolished; not suddenly, however, as if by a whirlwind, but by the counsels of wise, cautious, and far-seeing statesmen, who, capable of looking both before and after, can comprehend in their plans of reform all the diversified and highly-complicated interests of society.

"But it may be said," continues the author, "immediate abolition would be the greatest possible injury to the slaves themselves. They are not competent to self-government." True: this is the very thing which may be, and which is, said by every Southern statesman in his advocacy of the institution of slavery. Let us see the author's reply. "This is a question of fact," says he, "*which is not in the province of moral philosophy to decide.* It very likely may be so. So far as I know, the facts are not sufficiently known to warrant a full opinion on the subject. We will, therefore, suppose it to be the case, and ask, What is the duty of masters *under these circumstances?*" In the discussion of this question, the author comes to the conclusion that a master may hold his slaves in bondage, provided his intentions be good, and with a view to set them at liberty as soon as they shall be qualified for such a state.

Moral philosophy, then, it seems, when it closes its eyes upon facts, pronounces that slavery should be *immediately* abolished; but if it consider facts, which, instead of being denied, are admitted to be "very likely" true, it decides against its immediate abolition! Or, rather, moral philosophy looks at the fact that slavery is an *injury*, in order to see that it should be forthwith abolished; but closes its eyes upon the fact that its abolition may be a still greater injury, lest this foregone conclusion should be called in question! Has moral philosophy, then, an eye only for the facts which lie one side of the question it proposes to decide?

Slavery is an *injury*, says Dr. Wayland, and therefore it should be *immediately* abolished. But its abolition would be a still greater injury, replies the objector. This may be true, says Dr. Wayland: it is highly probable; but then this question of injury is one of fact, which it is not in the province of moral philosophy to decide! So much for the consistency and even-handed justice of the author.

The position assumed by him, that questions of fact are not within the province of moral philosophy, is one of so great importance that it deserves a separate and distinct notice. Though seldom openly avowed, yet is it so often tacitly assumed in the arguments and declamations of abolitionists, that it shall be more fully considered in the following section.

§ V. *The fifth fallacy of the abolitionist.*

"Suppose that A has a right to use the body of B according to his—that is, A's—will. Now if this be true, it is true universally; and hence, A has the control over the body of B, and B has control over the body of C, C of D, &c., and Z again over the body of A: that is, every separate will has the right of control over some other body besides its own, and has no right of control over its own body or intellect."[144] Now, if men were cut out of pasteboard, all exactly alike, and distinguished from each other only by the letters of the alphabet, then the reasoning of the author would be excellent. But it happens that men are not cut out of pasteboard. They are distinguished by differences of character, by diverse habits and propensities, which render the reasonings of the political philosopher rather more difficult than if he had merely to deal with or arrange the letters of the alphabet. In one, for example, the intellectual and moral part is almost wholly eclipsed by the brute; while, in another, reason and religion have gained the ascendency, so as to maintain a steady empire over the whole man. The first, as the author himself admits, is incompetent to self-government, and should, therefore, be held by the law of society in a state of servitude. But does it follow that "if this be true, it is true *universally?*" Because one man who can not govern himself may be governed by another, does it follow that every man should be governed by others? Does it follow that the one who has acquired and maintained the most perfect self-government, should be subjected to the control of him who is wholly incompetent to control himself? Yes, certainly, if the reasoning of Dr. Wayland be true; but, according to every sound principle of political ethics, the answer is, emphatically, No!

There is a difference between a Hottentot and a Newton. The first should no more be condemned to astronomical calculations and discoveries, than the last should be required to follow a plough. Such differences, however, are overlooked by much of the reasoning of the abolitionist. In regard to the question of fact, whether a man is really a man and not a mere thing, he is profoundly versed. He can discourse most eloquently upon this subject: he can prove, by most irrefragable arguments, that a Hottentot is a man as well as a Newton. But as to the differences among men, such nice distinctions are beneath his philosophy! It is true that one may be sunk so low in the scale of being that civil freedom would be a curse to him; yet, whether this be so or not, is a question of fact which his philosophy does not stoop to decide. He merely wishes to know what rights A can possibly have, either by the law of God or man, which do not equally belong to B? And if A would feel it an injury to be placed under the control of B, then, "there is no doubt" that it is equally wrong to place B under the control of A? In plain English, if it would be injurious and wrong to subject a Newton to the will of a Hottentot, then it would be equally injurious and wrong to subject a Hottentot to the will of a Newton! Such is the inevitable consequence of his very profound political principles! Nay, such is the identical consequence which he draws from his own principles!

If questions of fact are not within the province of the moral philosopher, then the moral philosopher has no business with the science of political ethics. This is not a pure, it is a mixed science. Facts can no more be overlooked by the political architect, than magnitude can be disregarded by the mathematician. The man, the political dreamer, who pays no attention to them, may be fit, for aught we know, to frame a government out of moonshine for the inhabitants of Utopia; but, if we might choose our own teachers in political wisdom, we should decidedly prefer those who have an eye for facts as well as abstractions. If we may borrow a figure from Mr. Macaulay, the legislator who sees no difference among men, but proposes the same kind of government for all, acts about as wisely as a tailor who should measure the Apollo Belvidere to cut clothes for all his customers—for the pigmies as well as for the giants.

§ VI. *The sixth fallacy of the abolitionist.*

It is asserted by Dr. Wayland that the institution of slavery is condemned as "a violation of the plainest dictates of natural justice," by "the natural conscience of man, from at least as far back as the time of Aristotle." If any one should infer that Aristotle himself condemned the institution of slavery, he would be grossly deceived; for it is known to every one who has read the Politics of Aristotle that he is, under certain circumstances, a strenuous advocate of the natural justice, as well as of the political wisdom, of slavery. Hence we shall suppose that Dr. Wayland does not mean to include Aristotle in his broad assertion, but only those who came after him. Even in this sense, or to this extent, his positive assertion is so diametrically opposed to the plainest facts of history, that it is difficult to conceive how he could have persuaded himself of its truth. It is certain that, on other occasions, he was perfectly aware of the fact that the natural conscience of man, from the time of Aristotle down to that of the Christian era, was in favor of the institution of slavery; for as often as it has served his purpose to assert this fact, he has not hesitated to do so. Thus, "the universal existence of slavery at the time of Christ," says he, "took its origin from the moral darkness of the age. The immortality of the soul was unknown. Out of the Hebrew nation not a man on earth had any true conception of the character of the Deity or of our relations and obligations to him. The law of universal love to man had never been heard of."[145] No wonder he here argues that *slavery received the universal sanction of the heathen world*, since so great was the moral darkness in which they were involved. This darkness was so great, if we may believe the author, that the men of one nation esteemed those of another "as by nature foes, whom they had a right" not only "to subdue or enslave," but also to murder "whenever and in what manner soever they were able."[146] The sweeping assertion, that such was the moral darkness of the heathen world, is wide of the truth; for, at the time of Christ, no civilized nation "esteemed it right to murder or enslave, whenever and in what manner soever they were able," the people of other nations. There were some ideas of natural justice, even then, among men; and if there were not, why does Dr. Wayland appeal to their ideas of natural justice as one argument against slavery? If the heathen world "esteemed it right" to make slaves, how can it be said that its conscience condemned slavery? Is it not evident that Dr. Wayland is capable of asserting either the one thing or its opposite, just as it may happen to serve the purpose of his anti-slavery argument? Whether facts lie within the province of moral philosophy or not, it is certain, we think, that the moral philosopher who may be pleased to set facts at naught has no right to substitute fictions in their stead.

§ VII. *The seventh fallacy of the abolitionist.*

"Thou shalt love thy neighbor as thyself," is the rule of action which, in the estimation of abolitionists, should at once and forever decide every good man against the institution of slavery. But when we consider the stupendous interests involved in the question, and especially those of an intellectual and moral nature, we dare not permit ourselves to be carried away by any form of mere words. We *must* pause and investigate. The fact that the dexterous brandishing of the beautiful precept in question has made, and will no doubt continue to make, its thousands of converts or victims, is a reason why its real import should be the more closely examined and the more clearly defined. The havoc it makes among those whose philanthropy is stronger than their judgment—or, if you please, whose judgment is weaker than their philanthropy—flows not from the divine precept itself, but only from human interpretations thereof. And it should ever be borne in mind that he is the real enemy of the great cause of philanthropy who, by absurd or overstrained applications of this sublime precept, lessens that profound respect to which it is so justly entitled from every portion of the rational universe.

It is repeatedly affirmed by Dr. Wayland that every slaveholder lives in the habitual and open violation of the precept which requires us to love our neighbor as ourselves. "The moral precepts of the Bible," says he, "are diametrically opposed to slavery. These are, 'Thou shalt love thy neighbor as thyself,' and 'All things whatsoever ye would that men should do unto you, do ye even so unto them.' Now, were this precept obeyed," he continues, "it is manifest that slavery could not in fact exist for a single instant. The principle of the precept is absolutely subversive of the principle of slavery." If strong assertion were argument, we should no doubt be overwhelmed by the irresistible logic of Dr. Wayland. But the assertion of no man can be accepted as sound argument. We want to know the very meaning of the words of the great Teacher, and to be guided by *that*, rather than by the fallible authority of an earthly oracle. What, then, is the meaning, the real meaning, of his inspired words?

Do they mean that whatsoever we might, in any relation of life, desire for ourselves, we should be willing to grant to others in the like relation or condition? This interpretation, we are aware, has been put upon the words by a very celebrated divine. If we may believe that divine, we cannot do as we would be done by, unless, when we desire the estate of another, we forthwith transfer our estate to him! If a poor man, for example, should happen to covet the estate of his rich neighbor, then he is bound by this golden rule of benevolence to give his little all to him, without regard to the necessities or wants of his own family! But this interpretation, though seriously propounded by a man of undoubted genius and piety, has not, so far as we know, made the slightest possible impression on the plain good sense of mankind. Even among his most enthusiastic admirers, it has merely excited a good-natured smile at what they could not but regard as the strange hallucination of a benevolent heart.

A wrong desire in one relation of life is not a reason for a wrong act in another relation thereof. A man may desire the estate, he may desire the man-servant, or the maid-servant, or the wife of his neighbor, but this is no reason why he should abandon his own man-servant, or his maid-servant, or his wife to the will of another. The criminal who trembles at the bar of justice may desire both judge and jury to acquit him, but this is no reason why, if acting in the capacity of either judge or juror, he should bring in a verdict of acquittal in favor of one justly accused of crime. If we would apply the rule in question aright, we should consider, not what we might wish or desire if placed in the situation of another, but what we *ought* to wish or desire.

If a man were a child, he might wish to be exempt from the wholesome restraint of his parents; but this, as every one will admit, is no reason why he should abandon his own children to themselves. In like manner, if he were a slave, he might most vehemently desire freedom; but this is no reason why he should set his slaves at liberty. The whole question of right turns upon what he *ought* to wish or desire if placed in such a condition. If he were an intelligent, cultivated, civilized man,—in one word, if he were fit for freedom,—then his desire for liberty would be a rational desire, would be such a feeling as he *ought* to cherish; and hence, he should be willing to extend the same blessing to all other intelligent, cultivated, civilized men, to all such as are prepared for its enjoyment. Such is the sentiment which he should entertain, and such is precisely the sentiment entertained at the South. No one here proposes to reduce any one to slavery, much less those who are qualified for freedom; and hence the inquiry so often propounded by Dr. Wayland and other abolitionists, how we would like to be subjected to bondage, is a grand impertinence. We should like it as little as themselves; and in this respect we shall do as we would be done by.

But suppose we were veritable slaves—slaves in character and in disposition as well as in fact—and as unfit for freedom as the Africans of the South—what *ought* we then to wish or desire? Ought we to desire freedom? We answer, no; because on that supposition freedom would be a curse and not a blessing. Dr. Wayland himself admits that "it is very likely" freedom would be "the greatest possible injury" to the slaves of the South. Hence, we cannot perceive that if we were such as they, we ought to desire so great an evil to ourselves. It would indeed be to desire "the greatest possible injury" to ourselves; and though, as ignorant and blind slaves, we might cherish so foolish a desire, especially if instigated by abolitionists, yet this is no reason why, as enlightened citizens, we should be willing to inflict the same great evil upon others. *A foolish desire, we repeat, in one relation of life, is not a good reason for a foolish or injurious act in another relation thereof.*

The precept which requires us to do as we would be done by, was intended to enlighten the conscience. It is used by abolitionists to hoodwink and deceive the conscience. This precept directs us to conceive ourselves placed in the condition of others, in order that we may the more clearly perceive what is due to them. The abolitionist employs it to convince us that, because we desire liberty for ourselves, we should extend it to all men, even to those who are not qualified for its enjoyment, and to whom it would prove "the greatest possible injury." He employs it not to show us what is due to others, but to persuade us to injure them! He may deceive himself; but so long as we believe what even he admits as highly probable—namely, that the "abolition of slavery would be the greatest possible injury to the slaves themselves"—we shall never use the divine precept as an instrument of delusion and of wrong. What! inflict the greatest injury on our neighbor, and that, too, out of pure Christian charity?

But we need not argue with the abolitionist upon his own admissions. We have infinitely stronger ground to stand on. The precept, "Thou shalt love thy neighbor as thyself," is to be found in the Old Testament as well as in the New. Thus, in the nineteenth chapter of Leviticus, it is said, "Thou shalt love thy neighbor as thyself;" and no greater love than this is any where inculcated in the New Testament. Yet in the twenty-fifth chapter of the same book, it is written, "Of the children of the strangers that do sojourn among you, of them shall ye buy, and of their families that are with you, which they begat in your land: and they shall be your possession. And ye shall take them as an inheritance for your children after you, to inherit them for a possession; they shall be your bondmen forever." This language is too plain for controversy. In regard to this very passage, in which the Hebrews are commanded to enter upon and take possession of the land of the Canaanites, Dr. Wayland himself is constrained to admit—"The authority to take them as slaves seems to be a part of this original, peculiar, and I may perhaps say, anomalous grant."[147] Now, if the principle of slavery, and the principle of the precept, Thou shalt love thy neighbor as thyself, be as Dr. Wayland boldly asserts, *always and everywhere* at war with each other, how has it happened that both principles are so clearly and so unequivocally embodied in one and the same code by the Supreme Ruler of the world? Has this discrepancy escaped the eye of Omniscience, and remained in the code of laws from heaven, to be detected and exposed by "the author of the Moral Science"?

We do not mean that Dr. Wayland sees any discrepancy among the principles of the divine legislation. It is true he sees there the precept, "Thou shalt love thy neighbor as thyself," and also this injunction, "Thou shalt buy them for a possession," and "They shall be your bondmen forever;" but although this looks very "anomalous" to him, he dare not pronounce it absurd or self-contradictory. It is true, he declares, that slavery is condemned *always and everywhere* by "the plainest dictates of natural justice;" but yet, although, according to his own admission,[148] it was instituted by Heaven, he has found out a method to save the character of the Almighty from the disgrace of such a law. He says, "I know the word '*shalt*' is used when speaking of this subject, but it is clearly used as *prophetic*, and not as *mandatory*." Ay, the words "thou shalt" are used in regard to the buying and holding of slaves, just as they are used in the commands which precede and follow this injunction. There is no change in the form of the expression. There is not, in any way, the slightest intimation that the Lawgiver is about to prophesy; all seems to be a series of commands, and is clothed in the same language of authority—"*thou shalt*." Yet in one particular instance, and in one instance only, this language seems "clearly" *prophetic* to Dr. Wayland, and not *mandatory*. Now, I submit to the candid and impartial reader, if this be not egregious trifling with the word of God.

Dr. Wayland forgets that he had himself admitted that the very passage in question clothed the Hebrews with "the authority to take slaves."[149] He now, in the face of his own admission, declares that this language "is clearly prophetic," and tells what *would* or what *might* be, and not what *should* or what *must* be." The poor Hebrews, however, when they took slaves by the authority of a "*thou shalt*" from the Lord, never imagined that they were merely fulfilling a prophecy, and committing an abominable sin.

This is clear to Dr. Wayland, if we may trust the last expression of his opinion. But it is to be regretted, that either the clearness of his perceptions, or the confidence of his assertions, is so often disproportioned to the evidence before him. Thus, he says with the most admirable modesty, "It *seems to me* that the soul is the most important part of a human being;"[150] and yet he peremptorily and positively declares that the very strongest language of authority ever found in Scripture "is *clearly* used as prophetic and not mandatory!" He may, however, well reserve the tone of dogmatic authority for such propositions, since, if they may not be carried by assertion, they must be left wholly without the least shadow of support. But one would suppose that strength of assertion in such cases required for its unembarrassed utterance no little strength of countenance.

"If any one doubts," says Dr. Wayland, "respecting the bearing of the Scripture precept upon this case, a few plain questions may throw additional light upon the subject."[151]

Now, if we mistake not, the few plain questions which he deems so unanswerable may be answered with the most perfect ease. "Would the master be willing," he asks, "that another person should subject him to slavery, for the same reasons and on the same grounds that he holds his slave in bondage?" We answer, No. If any man should undertake to subject Southern masters to slavery, on the ground that they are intellectually and morally sunk so low as to be unfit for freedom or self-control, we should certainly not like the compliment. It may argue a very great degree of self-complacency in us, but yet the plain fact is, that we really do believe ourselves competent to govern ourselves, and to manage our affairs, without the aid of masters. And as we are not willing to be made slaves of, especially on any such humiliating grounds, so we are not willing to see any other nation or race of men, whom we may deem qualified for the glorious condition of freedom, subjected to servitude.

"Would the gospel allow us," he also asks, "if it were in our power, to reduce our fellow-citizens of our own color to slavery?" Certainly not. Nor do we propose to reduce any one, either white or black, to a state of slavery. It is amazing to see with what an air of confidence such questions are propounded. Dr. Channing, no less than Dr. Wayland, seems to think they must carry home irresistible conviction to the heart and conscience of every man who is not irremediably blinded by the detestable institution of slavery. "Now, let every reader," says he, "ask himself this plain question: Could I, can I, be rightfully seized and made an article of property?" And we, too, say, Let every reader ask himself this plain question, and then, if he please, answer it in the negative. But what, then, should follow? Why, if you please, he should refuse to seize any other man or to make him an article of property. He should be opposed to the crime of kidnapping. But if, from such an answer, he should conclude that the institution of slavery is "everywhere and always wrong," then surely, after what has been said, not another word is needed to expose the ineffable weakness and futility of the conclusion.

This golden rule, this divine precept, requires us to conceive ourselves placed in the condition of our slaves, and then to ask ourselves, How should we be treated by the master? in order to obtain a clear and impartial view of our duty to them. This it requires of us; and this we can most cheerfully perform. We can conceive that we are poor, helpless, dependent beings, possessing the passions of men and the intellects of children. We can conceive that we are by nature idle, improvident, and, without a protector and friend to guide and control us, utterly unable to take care of ourselves. And, having conceived all this, if we ask ourselves, How should we be treated by the masters whom the law has placed over us, what is the response? Is it that they should turn us loose to shift for ourselves? Is it that they should abandon us to ourselves, only to fall a prey to indolence, and to the legion of vices and crimes which ever follow in its train? Is it that they should set us free, and expose us, without protection, to the merciless impositions of the worst portions of a stronger and more sagacious race? Is it, in one word, that we should be free from the dominion of men, who, as a general thing, are humane and wise in their management of us, only to become the victims—the most debased and helpless victims—of every evil way? We answer, No! Even the spirit of abolitionism itself has, in the person of Dr. Wayland, declared that such treatment would, in all probability, be the greatest of calamities. We feel sure it would be an infinite and remediless curse. And as we believe that, if we were in the condition of slaves, such treatment would be so great and so withering a curse, so we cannot, out of a feeling of love, proceed to inflict this curse upon our slaves. On the contrary, *we would do as we so clearly see we ought to be done by*, if our conditions were changed.

Is it not amazing, as well as melancholy, that learned divines, who undertake to instruct the benighted South in the great principles of duty, should entertain such superficial and erroneous views of the first, great, and all-comprehending precept of the gospel? If their interpretation of this precept were correct, then the child might be set free from the authority of the father, and the criminal from the sentence of the judge. All justice would be extinguished, all order overthrown, and boundless confusion introduced into the affairs of men. Yet, with unspeakable self-complacency, they come with such miserable interpretations of the plainest truths to instruct those whom they conceive to be blinded by custom and the institution of slavery to the clearest light of heaven. They tell us, "Thou shouldst love thy neighbor as thyself;" and they reiterate these words in our ears, just as if we had never heard them before. If this is all they have to say, why then we would remind them that the *meaning* of the precept is the precept. It is not a mere *sound*, it is *sense*, which these glorious words are intended to convey. And if they can only repeat the words for us, why then they might just as well send a host of free negroes with good, strong lungs to be our instructors in moral science.

§ VIII. *The eighth fallacy of the abolitionist.*

An argument is drawn from the divine attributes against the institution of slavery. One would suppose that a declaration from God himself is some little evidence as to what is agreeable to his attributes; but it seems that moral philosophers have, now-a-days, found out a better method of arriving at what is implied by his perfections. Dr. Wayland is one of those who, setting aside the word of God, appeal to his attributes in favor of the immediate and universal abolition of slavery. If slavery were abolished, says he, "the laborer would then work in conformity with the conditions which God has appointed, whereas he now works at variance with them; in the one case, we should be attempting to accumulate property under the blessing of God, whereas now we are attempting to do it under *his special and peculiar malediction*. How can we expect to prosper, when there is not, as Mr. Jefferson remarks, 'an attribute of the Almighty that can be appealed to in our favor'?"[152] If we may rely upon his own words, rather than upon the confident assertions of Dr. Wayland, we need not fear the curse of God upon the slaveholder. The readiness with which Dr. Wayland points the thunders of the divine wrath at our heads, is better evidence of the passions of his own heart than of the perfections of the Almighty.

Again he says: "If Jefferson trembled for his country when he remembered that God is just, and declared that, 'in case of insurrection, the Almighty has no attribute that can take part with us in the contest,' surely it becomes a *disciple of Jesus Christ* to pause and reflect." Now let it be borne in mind that all this proceeds from a man, from a professed disciple of Jesus Christ, who, in various places, has truly, as well as emphatically, said, "*The duty of slaves* is also explicitly made known in the Bible. They are bound to *obedience, fidelity, submission*, and respect to their masters,"[153] etc., etc.

Such, then, according to Dr. Wayland himself, is the clear and unequivocal teaching of revelation. And such being the case, shall the *real* "disciple of Jesus Christ" be made to believe, on the authority of Mr. Jefferson or of any other man, that the Almighty has no attribute which could induce him to take sides with his own law? If, instead of submission to that law, there should be rebellion,—and not only rebellion, but bloodshed and murder,—shall we believe that the Almighty, the supreme Ruler of heaven and earth, would look on well pleased? Since such is the express declaration of God himself respecting the duty of slaves, it surely becomes a disciple of Christ to pause and reflect whether he will follow his voice or the voice of man.

We owe at least one benefit to the Northern abolitionists. Ere the subject of slavery was agitated by them, there were many loose, floating notions among us, as well as among themselves, respecting the nature of liberty, which were at variance with the institution of slavery. But since this agitation began, we have looked more narrowly into the grounds of slavery, as well as into the character of the arguments by which it is assailed, and we have found the first as solid as adamant, the last as unsubstantial as moonshine. If Mr. Jefferson had lived till the present day, there can be no doubt, we think, that he would have been on the same side of this great question with the Calhouns, the Clays, and the Websters of the country. We have known many who, at one time, fully concurred with Mr. Jefferson on this subject, but are now firm believers in the perfect justice and humanity of negro slavery.

§ IX. *The ninth fallacy of the abolitionist.*

We have already seen that the abolitionist argues the question of slavery as if Southerners were proposing to catch freemen and reduce them to bondage. He habitually overlooks the fact, that slavery results, not from the action of the individual, but from an ordinance of the State. He forgets that it is a civil institution, and proceeds to argue as if it were founded in individual wrong. And even when he rises—as he sometimes does—to a contemplation of the real question in dispute, he generally takes a most narrow and one-sided view of the subject. For he generally takes it for granted that the legislation which ordains the institution of slavery is *intended* solely and exclusively for the benefit of the master, without the least regard to the interests of the slave.

Thus says Dr. Wayland: "Domestic slavery proceeds upon the principle that the master has a right to control the actions—physical and intellectual—of the slave for his own (that is, the master's) individual benefit,"[154] etc. And again: "It supposes that the Creator intended one human being to govern the physical, intellectual, and moral actions of as many other human beings as, by purchase, he can bring within his physical power; and that *one human being may thus acquire a right to sacrifice the happiness of any number of other human beings, for the purpose of promoting his own.*"[155] Now, surely, if this representation be just, then the institution of slavery should be held in infinite abhorrence by every man in Christendom.

But we can assure Dr. Wayland that, however ignorant or heathenish he may be pleased to consider the people of the Southern States, we are not so utterly lost to all reverence for the Creator as to suppose, even for a moment, that he *intended any one human being to possess the right of sacrificing the happiness of his fellow-men to his own.* We can assure him that we are not quite so dead to every sentiment of political justice, as to imagine that any legislation which intends to benefit the one at the expense of the many is otherwise than unequal and iniquitous in the extreme. There is some little sense of justice left among us yet; and hence we approve of no institution or law which proceeds on the monstrous principle that any one man has, or can have, the "*right to sacrifice the happiness of any number of other human beings for the purpose of promoting his own.*" We recognize no such right. It is as vehemently abhorred and condemned by us as it can be abhorred and condemned by the author himself.

In thus taking it for granted, as Dr. Wayland so coolly does, that the institution in question is "intended" to sacrifice the happiness of the slaves to the selfish interest of the master, he incontinently begs the whole question. Let him establish this point, and the whole controversy will be at an end. But let him not hope to establish any thing, or to satisfy any one, by assuming the very point in dispute, and then proceed to demolish what every man at the South condemns no less than himself. Surely, no one who has looked at both sides of this great question can be ignorant that the legislation of the South proceeds on the principle that slavery is beneficial, not to the master only, but also and *especially* to the slave. Surely, no one who has either an eye or an ear for facts can be ignorant that the institution of slavery is based on the ground, or principle, that it is beneficial, not only to the parts, but also to the whole, of the society in which it exists. This ground, or principle, is set forth in every defense of slavery by the writers and speakers of the South; it is so clearly and so unequivocally set forth, that he who runs may read. Why, then, is it overlooked by Dr. Wayland? Why is he pleased to imagine that he is combating Southern principles, when, in reality, he is merely combating the monstrous figment, the distorted conception of his own brain,—namely, the right of one man to sacrifice the happiness of multitudes to his own will and pleasure? Is it because facts do not lie within the province of the moral philosopher? Is it because fiction alone is worthy of his attention? Or is it because a blind, partisan zeal has so far taken possession of his very understanding, that he finds it impossible to speak of the institution of slavery, except in the language of the grossest misrepresentation?

§ X. *The tenth, eleventh, twelfth, thirteenth, fourteenth, fifteenth, and sixteenth fallacies of the abolitionist; or his seven arguments against the right of a man to hold property in his fellow-man.*

"This claim of property in a human being," says Dr. Channing, "is altogether false, groundless. No such right of man in man can exist. A human being cannot be justly owned." The only difficulty in maintaining this position is, according to Dr. Channing, "on account of its exceeding obviousness. It is too plain for proof. To defend it is like trying to confirm a self-evident truth," etc., etc. Yet he advances no less than seven "arguments," as he calls them, in order to establish this self-evident position. We shall examine these seven arguments, and see if his great confidence be not built on a mere abuse of words.

"The consciousness of our humanity," says he, "involves the persuasion that we cannot be owned as a tree or a brute." This, as every body knows, is one of the hackneyed commonplaces of the abolitionist. He never ceases to declaim about the injustice of slavery, because it regards, as he is pleased to assert, a man as a mere thing or a brute. Now, once for all, we freely admit that it were monstrously unjust to regard or treat a man otherwise than as a man. We freely admit that a human being "can not be owned as a tree or a brute."

A tree may be *absolutely* owned. That is to say, the owner of a tree may do what he pleases with his own, provided he do no harm or injury with it. He may cut it down; and, if he please, he may beat it as long as he has the power to raise an arm. He may work it into a house or into a piece of furniture, or he may lay it on the fire, and reduce it to ashes. He may, we repeat, do just exactly what he pleases with his own, if his own be such a thing as a tree, *for a tree has no rights*.

It is far otherwise with a brute. The owner of a horse, for example, may not do what he pleases with his own. Here his property is not *absolute;* it is *limited*. He may not beat his horse without mercy, "for a good man is merciful to his beast." He may not cut his horse to pieces, or burn him on the fire. For the horse has rights, which the owner himself is bound to respect. The horse has a right to food and kind treatment, and the owner who refuses these is a tyrant. Nay, the very worm that crawls beneath our feet has his rights as well as the monarch on his throne; and just in so far as these rights are disregarded by a man is that man a tyrant.

Hence even the brute may not be regarded or treated as a mere thing or a tree. He can be owned and treated no otherwise than as a brute. The horse, for example, may not be left, like a tree, without food and care; but he may be saddled and rode as a horse; or he may be hitched to the plough, and compelled to do his master's work.

In like manner, a man cannot be owned or treated as a horse. He cannot be saddled or rode, nor hitched to the plough and be made to do the work of a horse. On the contrary, he should be treated as a man, and required to perform only the work of a man. The right to such work is all the ownership which any one man can rightfully have in another; and this is all which any slaveholder of the South needs to claim.

The real question is, *Can one man have a right to the personal service or obedience of another without his consent?* We do not intend to let the abolitionist throw dust in our eyes, and shout victory amid a clamor of words. We intend to hold him to the point. Whether he be a learned divine, or a distinguished senator, we intend he shall speak to the point, or else his argument shall be judged, not according to the eloquent noise it makes or the excitement it produces, but according to the *sense* it contains.

Can a man, then, have a right to the labor or obedience of another without his consent? Give us this right, and it is all we ask. We lay no claim to the soul of the slave. We grant to the abolitionist, even more freely than he can assert, that the "soul of the slave is his own." Or, rather, we grant that his soul belongs exclusively to the God who gave it. The master may use him not as a tree or a brute, but only as a rational, accountable, and immortal being may be used. He may not command him to do any thing which is wrong; and if he should so far forget himself as to require such service of his slave, he would himself be guilty of the act. If he should require his slave to violate any law of the land, he would be held not as a *particeps criminis* merely, but as a criminal in the first degree. In like manner, if he should require him to violate the law of God, he would be guilty— far more guilty than the slave himself—in the sight of heaven. These are truths which are just as well understood at the South as they are at the North.

The master, we repeat, lays no claim to the soul of the slave. He demands no spiritual service of him, he exacts no divine honors. With his own soul he is fully permitted to serve his own God. With this soul he may follow the solemn injunction of the Most High, "Servants, obey your masters;" or he may listen to the voice of the tempter, "Servants, fly from your masters." Those only who instigate him to violate the law of God, whether at the North or at the South, are the men who seek to deprive him of his rights and to exercise an infamous dominion over his soul.

Since, then, the master claims only a right to the labor and lawful obedience of the slave, and no right whatever to his soul, it follows that the argument, which Dr. Channing regards as the strongest of his seven, has no real foundation. Since the master claims to have no property in the "rational, moral, and immortal" part of his being, so all the arguments, or rather all the empty declamation, based on the false supposition of such claim, falls to the ground. So the passionate appeals, proceeding on the supposition of such a monstrous claim, and addressed to the religious sensibilities of the multitude, are only calculated to deceive and mislead their judgment. It is a mere thing of words; and, though "full of sound and fury," it signifies nothing. "The traffic in human souls," which figures so largely in the speeches of the divines and demagogues, and which so fiercely stirs up the most unhallowed passions of their hearers, *is merely the transfer of a right to labor*.

Does any one doubt whether such a right may exist? The master certainly has a right to the labor of his apprentice for a specified period of time, though he has no right to his soul even for a moment. The father, too, has a right to the personal service and obedience of his child until he reach the age of twenty-one; but no one ever supposed that he owned the soul of his child, or might sell it, if he pleased, to another. Though he may not sell the soul of his child, it is universally admitted that he may, for good and sufficient reasons, transfer his right to the labor and obedience of his child. Why, then, should it be thought impossible that such a right to service may exist for life? If it may exist for one period, why not for a longer, and even for life? If the good of both parties and the good of the whole community require such a relation and such a right to exist, why should it be deemed so unjust, so iniquitous, so monstrous? This whole controversy turns, we repeat, not upon any consideration of abstract rights, but solely upon the highest good of all— upon the highest good of the slave as well as upon that of the community.

"It is plain," says Dr. Channing, in his first argument, "that if any one may be held as property, then any other man may be so held." This sophism has been already sufficiently refuted. It proceeds on the supposition that if one man, however incapable of self-government, may be placed under the control of another, then all men may be placed under the control of others! It proceeds on the idea that all men should be placed in precisely the same condition, subjected to precisely the same authority, and required to perform precisely the same kind of labor. In one word, it sees no difference and makes no distinction between a Negro and a Newton. But as an overstrained and false idea of equality lies at the foundation of this argument, so it will pass under review again, when we come to consider the great demonstration which the abolitionist is accustomed to deduce from the axiom that "all men are created equal."

The third argument of Dr. Channing is, like the first, "founded on the essential equality of men." Hence, like the first, it may be postponed until we come to consider the true meaning and the real political significancy of the natural equality of all men. We shall barely remark, in passing, that two arguments cannot be made out of one by merely changing the mode of expression.

The second argument of the author is as follows: "A man cannot be seized and held as property, because he has rights. . . . A being having rights cannot justly be made property, *for this claim over him virtually annuls all his rights*." This argument, it is obvious, is based on the arbitrary idea which the author has been pleased to attach to the term *property*. If it proves any thing, it would prove that a horse could not be held as property, for a horse certainly has rights. But, as we have seen, a limited property, or a right to the labor of a man, does not deny or annul all his rights, nor necessarily any one of them. This argument needs no further refutation. For we acknowledge that the slave has rights; and the limited or qualified property which the master claims in him, extending merely to his personal human labor and his lawful obedience, touches not one of these rights.

The fourth argument of Dr. Channing is identical with the second. "That a human being," says he, "cannot be justly held as property, is apparent from *the very nature of property*. Property is an exclusive right. It shuts out all claim but that of the possessor. What one man owns cannot belong to another." The only difference between the two arguments is this: in one the "*nature of* property" is said "to annul all rights;" and in the other it is said "to exclude all rights!" Both are based on the same idea of property, and both arrive at the same conclusion, with only a very slight difference in the mode of expression!

And both are equally unsound. True; "what one man owns cannot belong to another." But may not one man have a right to the labor of another, as a father to the labor of his son, or a master to the labor of his apprentice; and yet that other a right to food and raiment, as well as to other things? May not one have a right to the service of another, without annulling or excluding all the rights of that other? This argument proceeds, it is evident, on the false supposition that if any being be held as property, then he has no rights; a supposition which, if true, would exclude and annul the right of property in every living creature.

Dr. Channing's fifth argument is deduced from "the universal indignation excited toward *a man* who makes another his slave." "Our laws," says he, "know no higher crime than that of reducing a man to slavery. To steal or to buy an African on his own shores is piracy." "To steal a man," we reply, is one thing; and, by the authority of the law of the land, to require him to do certain labor, is, one would think, quite another. The first may be as high a crime as any known to our laws; the last is recognized by our laws themselves. Is it not wonderful that Dr. Channing could not see so plain a distinction, so broad and so glaring a difference? The father of his country held slaves; *he did not commit the crime of man-stealing.*

The sixth argument of Dr. Channing, "against the right of property in man," is "drawn from a very obvious principle of moral science. It is a plain truth, universally received, that every right supposes or involves a corresponding obligation. If, then, a man has a right to another's person or powers, the latter is under obligation to give himself up as a chattel to the former." Most assuredly, if one man has a right to the service or obedience of another, then that other is under obligation to render that service or obedience to him. But is such an obligation absurd? Is it inconsistent with the inherent, the inalienable, the universal rights of man that the "servant should obey his master?" If so, then we fear the rights of man were far better understood by Dr. Channing than by the Creator of the world and the Author of revelation.

Such are the seven arguments adduced by Dr. Channing to show that no man can rightfully hold property in his fellow-man. But before we quit this branch of the subject, we shall advert to a passage in the address of the Hon. Charles Sumner, before the people of New York, at the Metropolitan Theatre, May 9, 1855. "I desire to present this argument," says he, "on grounds above all controversy, impeachment, or suspicion, even from slave-masters themselves. Not on triumphant story, not even on indisputable facts, do I now accuse slavery, but on its character, as revealed in its own simple definition of itself. Out of its own mouth do I condemn it." Well, and why does he condemn it? Because, "by the law of slavery, man, created in the image of God, is *divested of his human character* and declared to be a *mere* chattel. That the statement may not seem to be put forward without precise authority, I quote the law of two different slave States." That is the accusation. It is to be proved by the law of slavery itself. It is to be proved beyond "all controversy," by an appeal to "indisputable facts." Now let us have the facts: here they are. "The law of another polished slave State, says Mr. Sumner, "gives this definition: 'Slaves shall be delivered, sold, taken, reputed, and adjudged in law to be chattels personal, in the hands of their owners and possessors, and their executors, administrators, and assignees, to all intents, constructions, and purposes whatsoever.'"

Now, *mark;* the learned Senator undertook to prove, beyond all doubt and controversy, that slavery *divests the slave of his human character*, and declares him to be a *mere* chattel. But he merely proves that it declares him to be a "chattel personal." He merely proves that the law of a Southern State regards the slave, not as real estate or landed property, but as a "chattel personal." Does this divest him of his human character? Does this make him a *mere* chattel? May the slave, in consequence of such law, be treated as a brute or a tree? May he be cut in pieces or worked to death at the will and pleasure of the master?

"We think that a learned Senator, especially when he undertakes to demonstrate, should distinguish between declaring a man to be "a chattel personal," and a *mere* chattel. No one doubts that a man is a thing; but is he therefore a *mere* thing, or nothing more than a thing? In like manner, no one doubts that a man is an animal; does it follow, therefore, that he is a *mere* animal, or nothing but an animal? It is clear, that to declare a man may be held as a "chattel personal," is a very different thing from declaring that he is a *mere* chattel. So much for his honor's "precise authority."

In what part of the law, then, is the slave "divested of his human character?" In no part whatever. If it had declared him to be a *mere* thing, or a *mere* chattel, or a *mere* animal, it would have denied his human character, we admit; but the law in question has done no such thing. Nor is any such declaration contained in the other law quoted by the learned Senator from the code of Louisiana. It is *merely* by the interpolation of this little word *mere*, that the Senator of Massachusetts has made the law of South Carolina divest an immortal being of his "human character." He is welcome to all the applause which this may have gained for him in the "Metropolitan Theatre."

The learned Senator adduces another authority. "A careful writer," says he, "Judge Stroud, in a work of juridical as well as philanthropic merit, thus sums up the laws: 'The cardinal principle of slavery—that the slave is not to be ranked among *sentient*[156] beings, but among things—as an article of property—a chattel personal—obtains as undoubted law in all these (the slave) States.'" We thus learn from this very "careful writer" that slaves among us are "not ranked among *sentient* beings," and that this is "the cardinal principle of slavery." No, they are not fed, nor clothed, nor treated as sentient beings! They are left without food and raiment, just as if they were stocks and stones! They are not talked to, nor reasoned with, as if they were rational animals, but only driven about, like dumb brutes beneath the lash! No, no, not the lash, for that would recognize them as "sentient beings!" They are only thrown about like stones, or boxed up like chattels; they are not set, like men, over the lower animals, required to do the work of men; the precise work which, of all others, in the grand and diversified economy of *human* industry, they are the best qualified to perform! So far, indeed, is this from being "the cardinal principle of slavery," that it is no principle of slavery at all. It bears not the most distant likeness or approximation to any principle of slavery, with which we of the South have any the most remote acquaintance.

That man may, in certain cases, be held as property, is a truth recognized by a higher authority than that of senators and divines. It is, as we have seen, recognized by the word of God himself. In that word, the slave is called the "possession"[157] of the master, and even "his money."[158] Now, is not this language as strong, if not stronger, than that adduced from the code of South Carolina? It certainly calls the "bondman" his master's "money." Why, then, did not the Senator from Massachusetts denounce this language, as divesting "a man of his human character," and declaring him to be *mere* money? Why did he not proceed to condemn the legislation of Heaven, as well as of the South, out of its own mouth? Most assuredly, if his principles be correct, then is he bound to pronounce the law of God itself manifestly unjust and iniquitous. For that law as clearly recognizes the right of property in man as it could possibly be recognized in words. But it nowhere commits the flagrant solecism of supposing that this right of the master annuls or excludes all the rights of the slave. On the contrary, the rights of the slave are recognized, as well as those of the master. For, according to the law of God, though "a possession," and an "inheritance," and "a bondman forever," yet is the slave, nevertheless, a man; and, as a man, is he protected in his rights; in his rights, not as defined by abolitionists, but as recognized by the word of God.

§ XI. *The seventeenth fallacy of the abolitionist; or the argument from the Declaration of Independence.*

This argument is regarded by the abolitionists as one of their great strongholds; and no doubt it is so in effect, for who can bear a superior? Lucifer himself, who fell from heaven because he could not acknowledge a superior, seduced our first parents by the suggestion that in throwing off the yoke of subjection, they should become "as gods." We need not wonder, then, if it should be found, that an appeal to the absolute equality of all men is the most ready way to effect the ruin of States. We can surely conceive of none better adapted to subvert all order among us of the South, involving the two races in a servile war, and the one or the other in utter extinction. Hence we shall examine this argument from the equality of all men, or rather this appeal to all men's abhorrence of inferiority. This appeal is usually based on the Declaration of Independence: "We hold these truths to be self-evident: that all men are created equal; that they are endowed by their Creator with certain inalienable rights; that among these are life, liberty, and the pursuit of happiness." We do not mean to play upon these words; we intend to take them exactly as they are understood by our opponents. As they are not found in a metaphysical document or discussion, so it would be unfair to suppose—as is sometimes done—that they inculcate the wild dream of Helvetius, that all men are created with equal natural capacities of mind. They occur in a declaration of independence; and as the subject is the doctrine of human rights, so we suppose they mean to declare that all men are created equal with respect to natural rights.

Nor do we assert that there is no truth in this celebrated proposition or maxim; for we believe that, if rightly understood, it contains most important and precious truth. It is not on this account, however, the less dangerous as a maxim of political philosophy. Nay, falsehood is only then the more dangerous, when it is so blended with truth that its existence is not suspected by its victims. Hence the unspeakable importance of dissecting this pretended maxim, and separating the precious truth it contains from the pernicious falsehood by which its followers are deceived. Its truth is certainly very far from being self-evident, or rather its truth is self-evident to some, while its falsehood is equally self-evident to others, according to the side from which it is viewed. We shall endeavor to throw some light both upon its truth and its falsehood, and, if possible, draw the line which divides them from each other.

This maxim does not mean, then, that all men have, by nature, an equal right to political power or to posts of honor. No doubt the words are often understood in this sense by those who, without reflection, merely echo the Declaration of Independence; but, in this sense, they are utterly untenable. If all men had, by nature, an equal right to any of the offices of government, how could such rights be adjusted? How could such a conflict be reconciled? It is clear that all men could not be President of the United States; and if all men had an equal natural right to that office, no one man could be elevated to it without a wrong to all the rest. In such case, all men should have, at least, an equal chance to occupy the presidential chair. Such equal chance could not result from the right of all men to offer themselves as candidates for the office; for, at the bar of public opinion, vast multitudes would not have the least shadow of a chance. The only way to effect such an object would be by resorting to the lot. We might thus determine who, among so many equally just claimants, should actually possess the power of the supreme magistrate. This, it must be confessed, would be to recognize in deed, as well as in word, the equal rights of all men. But what more absurd than such an equality of rights? It is not without example in history; but it is to be hoped that such example will never be copied. The democracy of Athens, it is well known, was, at one time, so far carried away by the idea of equal rights, that her generals and orators and poets were elected by the lot. This was an equality, not in theory merely, but in practice. Though the lives and fortunes of mankind were thus intrusted to the most ignorant and depraved, or to the most wise and virtuous, as the lot might determine, yet this policy was based on an equality of rights. It is scarcely necessary to add that this idea of equality prevailed, not in the better days of the Athenian democracy, but only during its imbecility and corruption.

If all men, then, have not a natural right to fill an office of government, who has this right? Who has the natural right, for example, to occupy the office of President of the United States? Certainly some men have no such right. The man, for example, who has no capacity to govern himself, but needs a guardian, has no right to superintend the affairs of a great nation. Though a citizen, he has no more right to exercise such power or authority than if he were a Hottentot, or an African, or an ape. Hence, in bidding such a one to stand aside and keep aloof from such high office, no right is infringed and no injury done. Nay, right is secured, and injury prevented.

Who has such a right, then?—such natural right, or right according to the law of nature or reason? The man, we answer, who, all things considered, is the best qualified to discharge the duties of the office. The man who, by his superior wisdom, and virtue, and statesmanship, would use the power of such office more effectually for the good of the whole people than would any other man. If there be one such man, and only one, he of *natural right* should be our President. And all the laws framed to regulate the election of President are, or should be, only so many means designed to secure the services of that man, if possible, and thereby secure the rights of all against the possession of power by the unworthy or the less worthy. This object, it is true, is not always attained, these means are not always successful; but this is only one of the manifold imperfections which necessarily attach to all human institutions; one of the melancholy instances in which natural and legal right run in different channels. All that can be hoped, indeed, either in the construction or in the administration of human laws, is an approximation, more or less close, to the great principles of natural justice.

What is thus so clearly true in regard to the office of President, is equally true in regard to all the other offices of government. It is contrary to reason, to natural right, to justice, that either fools, or knaves, or demagogues should occupy seats in Congress; yet all of these classes are sometimes seen there, and by the law of the land are entitled to their seats. Here, again, that which is right and fit in itself is different from that which exists under the law.

The same remarks, it is evident, are applicable to governors, to judges, to sheriffs, to constables, and to justices of the peace. In every instance, he who is best qualified to discharge the duties of an office, and who would do so with greatest advantage to all concerned, has the natural right thereto. And no man who would fill any office, or exercise any power so as to injure the community, has any right to such office or power.

There is precisely the same limitation to the exercise of the elective franchise. Those only should be permitted to exercise this power who are qualified to do so with advantage to the community; and all laws which regulate or limit the possession of this power should have in view, not the equal rights of all men, but solely and exclusively the public good. It is on this principle that foreigners are not allowed to vote as soon as they land upon our shores, and that native Americans can do so only after they have reached a certain age. And if the public good required that any class of men, such as free blacks or slaves, for example, should be excluded from the privilege altogether, then no doubt can remain the law excluding them would be just. It might not be equal, but would be *just*. Indeed, in the high and holy sense of the word, it would be equal; for, if it excluded some from a privilege or power which it conferred upon others, this is because they were not included within the condition on which alone it should be extended to any. Such is not an equality of rights and power, it is true; but it is an equality of justice, like that which reigns in the divine government itself. In the light of that justice, it is clear that no man, and no class of men, can have a natural right to exercise a power which, if intrusted to them, would be wielded for harm, and not for good.

This great truth, when stripped of the manifold sophistications of a false logic, is so clear and unquestionable, that it has not failed to secure the approbation of abolitionists themselves. Thus, after all his wild extravagancies about inherent, inalienable, and equal rights, Dr. Channing has, in one of his calmer moods, recognized this great fundamental truth. "The slave," says he, "cannot rightfully, and should not, be owned by the individual. But, like every citizen, *he is subject to the community*, AND THE COMMUNITY HAS A RIGHT AND IS BOUND TO CONTINUE ALL SUCH RESTRAINTS AS ITS OWN SAFETY AND THE WELL-BEING OF THE SLAVE DEMANDS." Now this is all we ask in regard to the question of equal rights. All we ask is, that each and every individual may be in such wise and so far restrained as the public good demands and no further. All we ask is, as may be seen from the first chapter of this Essay, that the right of the individual, whether real or imaginary, may be held in subjection to the undoubted right of the community to protect itself and to secure its own highest good. This solemn right, so inseparably linked to a sacred duty, is paramount to the rights and powers of the individual. Nay, as we have already seen,[159] the individual can have no right that conflicts with this; because it is his *duty* to co-operate in the establishment of the general good. Surely he can have no right which is adverse to duty. Indeed, if for the general good, he would not cheerfully lay down both liberty and life, then both may be rightfully taken from him. We have, it is true, inherent and *inalienable rights*, but among these is neither liberty nor life. For these, upon our country's altar, may be sacrificed; but conscience, truth, honor may not be touched by man.

Has the community, then, after all, the right to compel "a man," a "rational and immortal being," to work? Let Dr. Channing answer: "If he (the slave) cannot be induced to work by rational and natural motives, *he should be obliged to labor, on the same principle on which the vagrant in other communities is confined and compelled to earn his bread.*" Now, if a man be "confined, and compelled" to work in his confinement, what becomes of his "inalienable right to liberty?" We think there must be a slight mistake somewhere. Perhaps it is in the Declaration of Independence itself. Nay, is it not evident, indeed, that if all men have an inalienable right to liberty," then is this sacred right trampled in the dust by every government on earth? Is it not as really disregarded by the enlightened Commonwealth of Massachusetts, which "confines and compels" vagrants to earn their bread, as it is by the Legislature of Virginia, which has taken the wise precaution to prevent the rise of a swarm of vagrants more destructive than the locusts of Egypt? The plain truth is, that although this notion of the "inalienable right" of all to liberty may sound very well in a declaration of independence, and may be most admirably adapted to stir up the passions of men and produce fatal commotions in a commonwealth, yet no wise nation ever has been or ever will be guided by it in the construction of her laws. It may be a brand of discord in the hands of the abolitionist and the demagogue. It will never be an element of light, or power, or wisdom, in the bosom of the statesman.

"The gift of liberty," continues Dr. Channing, "would be a mere name, and worse than nominal, were he (the slave) to be let loose on society under circumstances driving him to commit crimes, for which he would be condemned to severer bondage than he had escaped." If then, after all, liberty may be worse than a mere name, is it not a pity that all men should have an "inalienable right" to it? If it may be a curse, is it not a pity that all men should be required to embrace it, and to be even ready to die for it, as an invaluable blessing? We trust that "no man," that "no rational and immortal being," will ever be so ungrateful as to complain of those who have withheld from him that which is "worse than nominal," and a curse. For if such, and such only, be his inalienable birthright, were it not most wisely exchanged for a mess of pottage? The vagrant, then, should not be consulted whether he will work or not. He should be "confined and compelled" to work, says Dr. Channing. Nor should the idle and the vicious, those who cannot be induced to work by rational motives, be asked whether they will remain pests to society, or whether they will eat their bread in the sweat of their brow. "For they, too," says Dr. Channing, "should be compelled to work." But how? "The slave should not have an owner," says Dr. Channing, "but he should have a guardian. He needs authority, to supply the lack of that discretion which he has not yet attained; but it should be the authority of a friend, an official authority, conferred by the State, and for which there should be responsibility to the State." Now, if all this be true, is not the doctrine of equal rights, as held by Dr. Channing, a mere dream? If one man may have "a guardian," "an official authority," appointed by the State, to compel him to work, why may not another be placed under the same authority, and subjected to the same servitude? Are not all equal? Have not all men an equal right to liberty and to a choice of the pursuits of happiness? Let these questions be answered by the admirers of Dr. Channing; and it will be found that they have overthrown all the plausible logic, and blown away all the splendid rhetoric, which has been reared, on the ground of equal rights, against the institution of slavery at the South.

We are agreed, then, that men may be compelled to work. We are also agreed that, for this purpose, the slaves of the South should be placed under guardians and friends by the authority of the State. Dr. Channing thinks, however, that the owner is not the best guardian or the best friend whom the State could place over the slave. On the contrary, he thinks his best friend and guardian would be an official overseer, bound to him by no ties of interest, and by no peculiar feelings of affection. In all this, we think Dr. Channing greatly mistaken; and mistaken because he is an utter stranger to the feelings usually called forth by the relation of master and slave. But, be this as it may, since such are the concessions made by Dr. Channing, it is no longer necessary to debate the question of slavery with him, on the high ground of abstract inalienable rights. It is brought down to one of practical utility, of public expediency.

And such being the nature of the question, we, as free citizens of the South, claim the right to settle the matter for ourselves. We claim the right to appoint such guardians and friends for this class of our population as we believe will be most advantageous to them, as well as to the whole community. We claim the right to impose such restraints, and such only, as the well-being of our own society seems to us to demand. This claim may be denied. The North may claim the right to think for us in regard to this question of expediency. But it cannot be denied that if liberty may be a curse, then no man can, in such case, have a right to it as a blessing.

If liberty would be an equal blessing to all men, then, we freely admit, all men would have an equal right to liberty. But to concede, as Dr. Channing does, that it were a curse to some men and yet contend that all men have an equal right to its enjoyment, is sheer absurdity and nonsense. But Dr. Channing, as we have seen, sometimes speaks a better sense. Thus, he has even said, "It would be cruelty, not kindness, to the latter (to the slave) to give him a freedom which he is unprepared to understand or enjoy. It would be cruelty to strike the fetters from a man whose first steps would infallibly lead him to a precipice." So far, then, according to the author himself, are all men from having an "inalienable right" to liberty, that some men have no right to it at all.

In like manner, Dr. Wayland, by his own admission, has overthrown all his most confident deductions from the notion of equal rights. He, too, quotes the Declaration of Independence, and adds, "That the equality here spoken of is not of the means of happiness, but in the right to use them as one wills, is too evident to need illustration." If this be the meaning, then the meaning is not so evidently true. On the contrary, the vaunted maxim in question, as understood by Dr. Wayland, appears to be pure and unmixed error. Power, for example, is one means of happiness; and so great a means, too, that without it all other means would be of no avail. But has any man a right to use this means of happiness as he wills? Most assuredly not. He has no right to use the power he may possess, nor any other means of happiness, as he will, but only as lawful authority has willed. If it be a power conferred by man, for example, such as that of a chief magistrate, or of a senator, or of a judge, he may use it no otherwise than as the law of the land permits, or in pursuance of the objects for which it was conferred. In like manner, if it proceed from the Almighty, it may be used only in conformity with his law. So far, then, is it from being true that all men possess an equal right to use the means of happiness as they please, that no man ever has, or ever will, possess any such right at all. And if such be the meaning of the Declaration of Independence, then the Declaration of Independence is too evidently erroneous to need any further refutation. Unless, indeed, man may put forth a declaration of independence which shall annul and destroy the immutable obligations of the moral law, and erect *one's will* as the rule of right. But is an equal exemption from the restraints of that law liberty, or is it universal anarchy and confusion?

It were much nearer the truth to say that all men have an equal right, not to act as "one wills," but to have their wills restrained by law. No greater want is known to man, indeed, than the restraints of law and government. Hence, all men have an equal right to these, but not to the same restraints, to the same laws and governments. All have an equal right to that government which is the best for them. But the same government is not the best for all. A despotism is best for some; a limited monarchy is best for others; while, for a third people, a representative republic is the best form of government.

This proposition is too plain for controversy. It has received the sanction of all the great teachers of political wisdom, from an Aristotle down to a Montesquieu, and from a Montesquieu down to a Burke. It has become, indeed, one of the commonplaces of political ethics; and, however strange the conjunction, it is often found in the very works which are loudest in proclaiming the universal equality of human rights. Thus, for example, says Dr. Wayland: "The best form of government for any people *is the best that its present moral condition renders practicable. A people may be so entirely surrendered to the influence of passion, and so feebly influenced by moral restraints, that a government which relied upon moral restraint could not exist for a day.* In this case, a subordinate and inferior principle remains—*the principle of fear, and the only resort is to a government of force* or a military despotism. And such do we see to be the fact." What, then, becomes of the equal and inalienable right of all men to freedom? Has it vanished with the occasion which gave it birth?

But this is not all. "Anarchy," continues Wayland, "always ends in this form of government. [A military despotism.] After this has been established, and habits of subordination have been formed, while the moral restraints are too feeble for self-government, an hereditary government, which addresses itself to the imagination, and strengthens itself by the influence of domestic connections, may be as good a form as a people can sustain. As they advance in intellectual and moral cultivation, it may advantageously become more and more elective, and, in a suitable moral condition, it may be wholly so. For beings who are willing to govern themselves by moral principles, there can be no doubt that a government relying upon moral principle is the true form of government. There is no reason why a man should be oppressed by taxation and subjected to fear who is willing to govern himself by the law of reciprocity. It is surely better for an intelligent and moral being to do right from his own will, than *to pay another to force him to do right*. And yet, as it is better that he should do right than wrong, even though he be forced to do it, it is well that he should pay others to force him, if there be no other way of insuring his good conduct. God has rendered the blessing of freedom inseparable from moral restraint to the individual; and hence it is vain for a people to expect to be free unless they are first willing to be virtuous." Again, "There is no self-sustaining power in any form of social organization. The only self-sustaining power is in individual virtue.

"And the form of a government will always adjust itself to the moral condition of a people. A virtuous people will, by their own moral power, frown away oppression, and, under any form of constitution, become essentially free. A people surrendered up to their own licentious passions must be held in subjection by force; for every one will find that force alone can protect him from his neighbors; and he will submit to be oppressed, if he can only be protected. Thus, in the feudal ages, the small independent landholders frequently made themselves slaves of one powerful chief to shield themselves from the incessant oppression of twenty."

Now all this is excellent sense. One might almost imagine that the author had been reading Aristotle, or Montesquieu, or Burke. It is certain he was not thinking of equal rights. It is equally certain that his eyes were turned away from the South; for he could see how even "independent landholders" might rightfully make slaves of themselves. After such concessions, one would think that all this clamor about inherent and *inalienable* rights ought to cease.

In a certain sense, or to a certain extent, all men have equal rights. All men have an equal right to the air and light of heaven; to the same air and the same light. In like manner, all men have an equal right to food and raiment, though not to the same food and raiment. That is, all men have an equal right to food and raiment, provided they will earn them. And if they will not earn them, choosing to remain idle, improvident, or nuisances to society, then they should be placed under a government of force, and compelled to earn them.

Again, all men have an equal right to serve God according to the dictates of their own consciences. The poorest slave on earth possesses this right—this inherent and inalienable right; and he possesses it as completely as the proudest monarch on his throne. He may choose his own religion, and worship his own God according to his own conscience, provided always he seek not in such service to interfere with the rights of others. But neither the slave nor the freeman has any right to murder, or instigate others to murder, the master, even though he should be ever so firmly persuaded that such is a part of his religious duty. He has, however, the most absolute and perfect right to worship the Creator of all men in all ways not inconsistent with the moral law. And wo be to the man by whom such right is denied or set at naught! Such a one we have never known; but whosoever he may be, or wheresoever he may be found, let all the abolitionists, we say, hunt him down. He is not fit to be a man, much less a Christian master.

But, it will be said, the slave has also a right to religious instruction, as well as to food and raiment. So plain a proposition no one doubts. But is this right regarded at the South? No more, we fear, than in many other portions of the so-called Christian world. Our children, too, and our poor, destitute neighbors, often suffer, we fear, the same wrong at our remiss hands and from our cold hearts. Though we have done much and would fain do more, yet, the truth must be confessed, this sacred and imperious claim has not been fully met by us.

It may be otherwise at the North. There, children and poor neighbors, too, may all be trained and taught to the full extent of the moral law. This godlike work may be fully done by our Christian brethren of the North. They certainly have a large surplus of benevolence to bestow on us. But if this glorious work has not been fully done by them, then let him who is without sin cast the first stone. This simple thought, perhaps, might call in doubt their right to rail at us, at least with such malignant bitterness and gall. This simple thought, perhaps, might save us many a pitiless pelting of philanthropy.

But here lies the difference—here lies our peculiar sin and shame. This great, primordial right is, with us, denied by law. The slave shall not be taught to read. Oh! that he might be taught! What floods of sympathy, what thunderings and lightnings of philanthropy, would then be spared the world! But why, we ask, should the slave be taught to read? That he might read the Bible, and feed on the food of eternal life, is the reply; and the reply is good.

Ah! if the slave would only read his Bible, and drink its very spirit in, we should rejoice at the change; for he would then be a better and a happier man. He would then know his duty, and the high ground on which his duty rests. He would then see, in the words of Dr. Wayland, "*That the duty of slaves is explicitly made known in the Bible. They are bound to obedience, fidelity, submission, and respect to their masters—not only to the good and kind, but also to the unkind and froward; not, however, on the ground of duty to man, but on the ground of duty to God.*" But, with all, we have some little glimpse of our dangers, as well as some little sense of our duties.

The tempter is not asleep. His eye is still, as ever of old, fixed on the forbidden tree; and thither he will point his hapless victims. Like certain senators, and demagogues, and doctors of divinity, he will preach from the Declaration of Independence rather than from the Bible. He will teach, not that submission, but that *resistance*, is a duty. To every evil passion his inflammatory and murder-instigating appeals will be made. Stung by these appeals and maddened, the poor African, it is to be feared, would have no better notions of equality and freedom, and no better views of duty to God or man, than his teachers themselves have. Such, then, being the state of things, ask us not to prepare the slave for his own utter undoing. Ask us not—O most kind and benevolent Christian teacher!—ask us not to lay the train beneath our feet, that *you* may no longer hold the blazing torch in vain!

Let that torch be extinguished. Let all incendiary publications be destroyed. Let no conspiracies, no insurrections, and no murders be instigated. Let the pure precepts of the gospel and its sublime lessons of peace be everywhere set forth and inculcated. In one word, let it be seen that in reality the eternal good of the slave is aimed at, and, by the co-operation of all, may be secured, and then may we be asked to teach him to read. But until then we shall refuse to head a conspiracy against the good order, the security, the morals, and against the very lives, of both the white and the black men of the South.

We might point out other respects in which men are essentially equal, or *have equal rights*. But our object is not to write a treatise on the philosophy of politics. It is merely to expose the errors of those who push the idea of equality to an extreme, and thereby unwisely deny the great differences that exist among men. For if the scheme or the political principles of the abolitionists be correct, then there is no difference among men, not even among the different races of men, that is worthy the attention of the statesman.

There is one difference, we admit, which the abolitionists have discovered between the master and the slave at the South. Whether this discovery be entirely original with them, or whether they received hints of it from others, it is clear that they are now fully in possession of it. The dazzling idea of equality itself has not been able to exclude it from their visions. For, in spite of this idea, they have discovered that between the Southern master and slave there is a difference of color! Hence, as if this were the only difference, in their political harangues, whether from the stump or from the pulpit, they seldom fail to rebuke the Southern statesman in the words of the poet: "He finds his fellow guilty of a skin not colored like his own;" and "for such worthy cause dooms and devotes him as his lawful prey." Shame and confusion seize the man, we say, who thus dooms and devotes his fellow-man, because he finds him "guilty of a skin!" If his sensibilities were only as soft as his philosophy is shallow, he would certainly cry, "Down with the institution of slavery!" For how could he tolerate an institution which has no other foundation than a difference of color? Indeed, if such were the only difference between the two races among us, we should ourselves unite with Mr. Seward of New York, and most "affectionately advise all men to be born white." For thus, the only difference having been abolished, all men would be equal in fact, and consequently entitled to become equal in political rights, and power, and position. But if such be not the only difference between the white and the black man of the South, then neither philosophy nor paint can establish an equality between them.

Every man, we admit, is a man. But this profound aphorism is not the only one to which the political architect should give heed. An equality of conditions, of political powers and privileges, which has no solid basis in an equality of capacity or fitness, is one of the wildest and most impracticable of all Utopian dreams. If in the divine government such an equality should prevail, it is evident that all order would be overthrown, all justice extinguished, and utter confusion would reign. In like manner, if in human government such equality should exist, it would be only for a moment Indeed, to aim at an equality of conditions, or of rights and powers except by first aming at an equality of intelligence and virtue, is not to reform—it is to demolish—the governments of society. It is, indeed, to war against the eternal order of divine Providence itself in which an immutable justice ever regins. "It is this aiming after an equality," says Aristotle, "which is the cause of seditions." But though seditions it may have stirred up, and fierce passions kindled, yet has it never led its poor deluded victims to the boon after which they have so fondly panted.

Equality is not liberty. "The French," said Napoleon, "love equality: they care little for liberty." Equality is plain, simple, easily understood. Liberty is complex, and exceedingly difficult of comprehension. The most illiterate peasant may, at a glance, grasp the idea of equality; the most profound statesman may not, without much care and thought, comprehend the nature of liberty. Hence it is that equality, and not liberty, so readily seizes the mind of the multitude, and so mightily inflames its passions. The French are not the only people who care but little for liberty, while they are crazy for equality. The same blind passion, it is to be feared, is possible even in this enlightened portion of the globe. Even here, perhaps, a man may rant and rave about equality, while, really, he may know but little more, and consequently care but little more, about that complicated and beautiful structure called civil liberty, than a horse does about the mechanism of the heavens.

Thus, for example, a Senator[160] of the United States declares that the democratic principle is "Equality of natural rights, guaranteed and secured to all by the laws of a just, popular government. For one, I desire to see that principle applied to every subject of legislation, no matter what that subject may be—to the great question involved in the resolution now before the Senate, and to every other question." Again, this principle is "the element and guarantee of liberty."

Apply this principle, then, to every subject, to every question, and see what kind of government would be the result. All men have an equal right to freedom from restraint, and consequently all are made equally free. All have an equal right to the elective franchise, and to every political power and privilege. But suppose the government is designed for a State in which a large majority of the population is without the character, or disposition, or habits, or experience of freemen? No matter: the equal rights of all are natural; and hence they should be applied in all cases, and to every possible "subject of legislation." The principle of equality should reign everywhere, and mold every institution. Surely, after what has been said, no comment is necessary on a scheme so wild, on a dream so visionary. "As distant as heaven is from earth," says Montesquieu, "so is the true spirit of equality from that of extreme equality." And just so distant is the Senator in question, with all his adherents, from the true idea of civil and political freedom.

The Senator thinks the conduct of Virginia "singular enough," because, in presenting a bill of rights to Congress, she omitted the provision of "her own bill of rights," "that all men are born[161] equally free and independent." We think she acted wisely. For, in truth and in deed, all men are born absolutely dependent and utterly devoid of freedom. What right, we ask, has the new born infant? Has he the right to go where he pleases? He has no power to go at all; and hence he has no more a right to go than he has to fly. Has he the right to think for himself? The power of thought is as yet wholly undeveloped. Has he the right to worship God according to his own conscience? He has no idea of God, nor of the duties due to him. The plain truth is, that no human being possesses a right until the power or capacity on which the enjoyment of that right depends is suitably developed or acquired. The child, for instance, has no right to think for himself, or to worship God according to the dictates of conscience, until his intellectual and moral powers are suitably developed. He is certainly not born with such rights. Nor has he any right to go where he pleases, or attempt to do so, until he has learned to walk. Nor has he the right then, for, according to the laws of all civilized nations, he is subject to the control of the parent until he reaches the lawful age of freedom. The truth is, that all men are born not equally free and independent, but equally without freedom and without independence. "All men are born equal," says Montesquieu; but he does not say they "are born equally free and independent." The first proposition is true: the last is diametrically opposed to the truth.

Another Senator[162] seems to entertain the same passion for the principle of equality. In his speech on the Compromise Bill of 1850, he says that "a statesman or a founder of States" should adopt as an axiom the declaration, "That all men are created equal, and have inalienable rights of life, liberty, and choice of pursuits of happiness." Let us suppose, then, that this distinguished statesman is himself about to establish a constitution for the people of Mississippi or Louisiana, in which there are more blacks than whites. As they all have a natural and "inalienable right" to liberty, of course he would make them all free. But would he confer upon all, upon black as well as upon white, the power of the elective franchise? Most certainly. For he has said, "We of New York are guilty of slavery still by withholding the *right of suffrage* from the race we have emancipated." Surely, if he had to found a State himself, he would not thus be guilty of slavery—of the one odious thing which his soul abhors. All would then be invested with the right of suffrage. A black legislature would be the consequence. The laws passed by such a body would, we fear, be no better than the constitution provided by the Senator—by the statesman—from New York.

"All men are born equal," says Montesquieu; but in the hands of such a thinker no danger need be apprehended from such an axiom. For having drank deeply of the true spirit of law, he was, in matters of government, ever ready to sacrifice abstract perfection to concrete utility. Neither the principle of equality, nor any other, would he apply in all cases or to every subject. He was no dreamer. He was a profound thinker and a real statesman. "Though real equality," says he, "be the very soul of a democracy, *it is so difficult to establish, that an extreme exactness in this respect is not always convenient.*"

Again, he says: "All inequalities in democracies ought to be derived from the nature of the government, and even from the principle of equality. For example, it may be apprehended that people who are obliged to live by labor would be too much impoverished by public employment, or neglect the duties of attending to it; that artisans would grow insolent; and that *too great a number of freemen would overpower the ancient citizens*. IN THIS CASE, THE EQUALITY IN A DEMOCRACY MAY BE SUPPRESSED FOR THE GOOD OF THE STATE."

Thus to give all men equal power where the majority is ignorant and depraved, would be indeed to establish equality, but not liberty. On the contrary, it would be to establish the most odious despotism on earth,—the reign of ignorance, passion, prejudice, and brutality. It would be to establish a mere nominal equality, and a real inequality. For, as Montesquieu says, by introducing "too great a number of freemen," the "ancient citizens" would be oppressed. In such case, the principle of equality, even in a democracy, should be "suppressed for the good of the State." It should be suppressed, in order to shut out a still greater and more tremendous inequality. The legislator, then, who aims to introduce an extreme equality, or to apply the principle of equality to every question, would really bring about the most frightful of all inequalities, especially in a commonwealth where the majority are ignorant and depraved.

Hence the principle of equality is merely a standard toward which an approximation may be made—an approximation always limited and controlled by the public good. This principle should be applied, not to every question, but only to such as the general good permits. For this good it "may be suppressed." Nay, it must be suppressed, if, without such suppression, the public order may not be sustained; for, as we have abundantly seen, it is only in the bosom of an enlightened public order that liberty can live, or move, or have its being. Thus, as Montesquieu advises, we deduce an inequality from the very principle of equality itself; since, if such inequality be not deduced and established by law, a still more terrific inequality would be forced upon us. Blind passion would dictate the laws, and brute force would reign, while innocence and virtue would be trampled in the dust. Such is the inequality to which the honorable senators would invite us; and that, too, by an appeal to our love of equality! If we decline the invitation, this is not because we are the enemies, but because we are the friends, of human freedom. It is not because we love equality less, but liberty more.

The legislators of the North may, if they please, choose the principle of equality as the very "element and guarantee" of their liberty; and, to make that liberty perfect, they may apply it to every possible "subject of legislation," and to "every question" under the sun. But, if we may be permitted to choose for ourselves, we should beg to be delivered from such an extreme equality. We should reject it as the very worst "element," and the very surest "guarantee" of an unbounded licentiousness and an intolerable oppression. As the "element and guarantee" of freedom for ourselves, and for our posterity, we should decidedly prefer the principle of an enlightened public order.

CHAPTER III.

THE ARGUMENT FROM THE SCRIPTURES.

The Argument from the Old Testament.—The Argument from the New Testament.

IN discussing the arguments of the abolitionists, it was scarcely possible to avoid intimating, to a certain extent, the grounds on which we intend to vindicate the institution of slavery, as it exists among us at the South. But these grounds are entitled to a more distinct enunciation and to a more ample illustration. In the prosecution of this object we shall first advert to the argument from revelation; and, if we mistake not, it will be found that in the foregoing discussion we have been vindicating against aspersion not only the peculiar institution of the Southern States, but also the very legislation of Heaven itself.

§ I. *The argument from the Old Testament.*

The ground is taken by Dr. Wayland and other abolitionists, that slavery is always and everywhere, *semper et ubique*, morally wrong, and should, therefore, be instantly and universally swept away. We point to slavery among the Hebrews, and say, There is an instance in which it was not wrong, because there it received the sanction of the Almighty. Dr. Wayland chooses to overlook or evade the bearing of that case upon his fundamental position; and the means by which he seeks to evade its force is one of the grossest fallacies ever invented by the brain of man.

Let the reader examine and judge for himself. Here it is: "Let us reduce this argument to a syllogism, and it will stand thus: Whatever God sanctioned among the Hebrews he sanctions for all men and at all times. God sanctioned slavery among the Hebrews; therefore God sanctions slavery for all men and at all times."

Now I venture to affirm that no man at the South has ever put forth so absurd an argument in favor of slavery,—not only in favor of slavery for the negro race so long as they may remain unfit for freedom, but in favor of slavery for all men and for all times. If such an argument proved any thing, it would, indeed, prove that the white man of the South, no less than the black, might be subjected to bondage. But no one here argues in favor of the subjection of the white man, either South or North, to a state of servitude. No one here contends for the subjection to slavery of any portion of the civilized world. We only contend for slavery in certain cases; in opposition to the thesis of the abolitionist, we assert that it is not always and everywhere wrong. For the truth of this assertion we rely upon the express authority of God himself. We affirm that since slavery has been ordained by him, it cannot be always and everywhere wrong. And how does the abolitionist attempt to meet this reply? Why, by a little legerdemain, he converts this reply from an argument against his position, that slavery is always and everywhere wrong, into an argument in favor of the monstrous dogma that it is always and everywhere right! If we should contend that, in some cases, it is right to take the life of a man, he might just as fairly insist that we are in favor of having every man on earth put to death! Was any fallacy ever more glaring? was any misrepresentation ever more flagrant?

Indeed we should have supposed that Dr. Wayland might have seen that his representation is not a fair one, if he had not assured us of the contrary. We should have supposed that he might have distinguished between an argument in favor of slavery for the lowest grade of the ignorant and debased, and an argument in favor of slavery for all men and all times, if he had not assured us that he possesses no capacity to make it. For after having twisted the plea of the most enlightened statesmen of the South into an argument in favor of the universal subjection of mankind to slavery, he coolly adds, "I believe that in these words I express the argument correctly. If I do not, it is solely because I do not know how to state it more correctly." Is it possible Dr. Wayland could not distinguish between the principle of slavery for some men and the principle of slavery for all men? between the proposition that the ignorant, the idle, and the debased may be subjected to servitude, and the idea that all men, even the most enlightened and free, may be reduced to bondage? If he had not positively declared that he possessed no such capacity, we should most certainly have entertained a different opinion.

It will not be denied, we presume, that the very best men, whose lives are recorded in the Old Testament, were the owners and holders of slaves. "I grant at once," says Dr. Wayland, "that the Hebrews held slaves from the time of the conquest of Canaan, and that Abraham and the patriarchs held them many centuries before. I grant also that Moses enacted laws with special reference to that relation. . . . . I wonder that any should have had the hardihood to deny so plain a matter of record. I should almost as soon deny the delivery of the ten commandments to Moses."

Now, is it not wonderful that directly in the face of "so plain a matter of record," a pious Presbyterian pastor should have been arraigned by abolitionists, not for holding slaves, but for daring to be so far a freeman as to express his convictions on the subject of slavery? Most abolitionists must have found themselves a little embarrassed in such a proceeding. For *there* was the fact, staring them in the face, that Abraham himself, "the friend of God" and the "father of the faithful," was the owner and holder of more than a thousand slaves. How, then, could these professing Christians proceed to condemn and excommunicate a poor brother for having merely approved what Abraham had practiced? Of all the good men of old, Abraham was the most eminent. The sublimity of his faith and the fervor of his piety has, by the unerring voice of inspiration itself, been held up as a model for the imitation of all future ages. How, then, could a parcel of poor common saints presume, without blushing, to cry and condemn one of their number because he was no better than "Father Abraham?" This was the difficulty; and, but for a very happy discovery, it must have been an exceedingly perplexing one. But "Necessity is the mother of invention." On this trying occasion she conceived the happy thought that the plain matter of record "was all a mistake;" that Abraham never owned a slave; that, on the contrary, he was "a prince," and the "men whom he bought with his money" were "his subjects" merely! If, then, we poor sinners of the South should be driven to the utmost extremity,—all honest arguments and pleas failing us,—may we not escape the unutterable horrors of civil war, by calling our masters princes, and our slaves subjects?

We shall conclude this topic with the pointed and powerful words of Dr. Fuller, in his reply to Dr. Wayland: "Abraham," says he, "was 'the friend of God,' and walked with God in the closest and most endearing intercourse; nor can any thing be more exquisitely touching than those words, 'Shall I hide from Abraham that thing which I do?' It is the language of a friend who feels that concealment would wrong the confidential intimacy existing. The love of this venerable servant of God in his promptness to immolate his son has been the theme of apostles and preachers for ages; and such was his faith, that all who believe are called 'the children of faithful Abraham.' This Abraham, you admit, held slaves. Who is surprised that Whitefield, with this single fact before him, could not believe slavery to be a sin? Yet if your definition of slavery be correct, holy Abraham lived all his life in the commission of one of the most aggravated crimes against God and man which can be conceived. His life was spent in outraging the rights of hundreds of human beings, as moral, intellectual, immortal, fallen creatures, and in violating their relations as parents and children, and husbands and wives. And God not only connived at this appalling iniquity, but, in the covenant of circumcision made with Abraham, expressly mentions it, and confirms the patriarch in it, speaking of those 'bought with his money,' and requiring him to circumcise them. Why, at the very first blush, every Christian will cry out against this statement. To this, however, you must come, or yield your position; and this is only the first utterly incredible and monstrous corollary involved in the assertion that slavery is essentially and always 'a sin of appalling magnitude.'"

Slavery among the Hebrews, however, was not left merely to a tacit or implied sanction. It was thus sanctioned by the express legislation of the Most High: "Both thy bondmen and thy bond-maids, which thou shalt have, shall be of the heathen that are round about you; of them shall ye buy bondmen and bond-maids. Moreover, of the children of the strangers that do sojourn among you, of them shall ye buy, and of their families that are with you, which they begat in your land; and they shall be your possession. And ye shall take them as an inheritance for your children after you, to inherit them for a possession; they shall be your bondmen forever."[163] Now these words are so perfectly explicit, that there is no getting around them. Even Dr. Wayland, as we have seen, admits that the authority to take slaves *seems* to be a part of "this original, peculiar," and perhaps "anomalous grant." No wonder it appeared *peculiar* and *anomalous*. The only wonder is, that it did not appear impious and absurd. So it has appeared to some of his co-agitators, who, because they could not agree with Moses, have denied his mission as an inspired teacher, and joined the ranks of infidelity.

Dr. Channing makes very light of this and other passages of Scripture. He sets aside this whole argument from revelation with a few bold strokes of the pen. "In this age of the world," says he, "and amid the light which has been thrown on the true interpretation of the Scriptures, such reasoning hardly deserves notice." Now, even if not for our benefit, we think there are two reasons why such passages as the above were worthy of Dr. Channing's notice. In the first place, if he had condescended to throw the light in his possession on such passages, he might have saved Dr. Wayland, as well as other of his admirers, from the necessity of making the very awkward admission that the Almighty had authorized his chosen people to buy slaves, and hold them as "bondmen forever." He might have enabled them to see through the great difficulty, that God has authorized his people to commit "a sin of apalling magnitude," to perpetrate as "great a crime as can be conceived;" which seems so clearly to be the case, if their views of slavery be correct. Secondly, he might have enabled his followers to espouse the cause of abolition without deserting, as so many of them have openly done, the armies of the living God. For these two reasons, if for no other, we think Dr. Channing owed it to the honor of his cause to notice the passages of Scripture bearing on the subject of slavery.

The Mosaic Institutes not only recognize slavery as lawful; they contain a multitude of minute directions for its regulation. We need not refer to all of them; it will be sufficient for our purpose if we only notice those which establish some of the leading characteristics of slavery among the people of God.

1. Slaves were regarded as property. They were, as we have seen, called a "possession" and an "inheritance."[164] They were even called the "money" of the master. Thus, it is said, "if a man smite his servant or his maid with a rod, and he die under his hand, he shall surely be punished. Notwithstanding, if he continue a day or two, he shall not be punished, for he is his money."[165] In one of the ten commandments this right of property is recognized: "Thou shalt not covet thy neighbor's house, thou shalt not covet thy neighbor's wife, nor *his* man-servant, nor *his* maid-servant, nor his ox, nor his ass, nor any thing that is thy neighbor's."

2. They might be sold. This is taken for granted in all those passages in which, for particular reasons, the master is forbidden to sell his slaves. Thus it is declared: "Thou shalt not make merchandise of her, because thou hast humbled her." And still more explicitly: "If a man sell his daughter to be a maid-servant, she shall not go out as the men-servants do. If she please not her master who hath betrothed her to himself, then shall he let her be redeemed: to sell her to a strange nation, he shall have no power, seeing he hath dealt deceitfully with her.[166]

3. The slavery thus expressly sanctioned was hereditary and perpetual: "Ye shall take them as an inheritance for your children after you, to inherit them for a possession; they shall be your bondmen forever." Even the Hebrew servant might, by his own consent, become in certain cases a slave for life: "If thou buy a Hebrew servant, six years shall he serve; and in the seventh shall he go out free for nothing. If he came in by himself, he shall go out by himself: if he were married, then his wife shall go out with him. If his master have given him a wife, and she have borne him sons or daughters, the wife and the children shall be her master's, and he shall go out by himself. And if the servant shall plainly say, I love my master, my wife, and my children; I will not go out free: then his master shall bring him unto the judges: he shall also bring him to the door or unto the door-post, and his master shall bore his ear through with an awl, and *he shall serve him forever*."

Now it is evident, we think, that the legislator of the Hebrews was not inspired with the sentiments of an abolitionist. The principles of his legislation are, indeed, so diametrically opposed to the political notions of the abolitionist, that the latter is sadly perplexed to dispose of them. While some deny the authority of these principles altogether, and of the very book which contains them, others are content to evade their force by certain ingenious devices of their own. We shall now proceed to examine some of the more remarkable of these cunningly-devised fables.

It is admitted by the inventors of these devices, that God expressly permitted his chosen people to buy and hold slaves. Yet Dr. Wayland, by whom this admission is made, has endeavored to weaken the force of it by alleging that God has been pleased to enlighten our race progressively. If, he argues, the institution of slavery among His people appears so very "peculiar and anomalous," this is because he did not choose to make known his whole mind on the subject. He withheld a portion of it from his people, and allowed them, by express grant, to hold slaves until the fuller revelation of his will should blaze upon the world. Such is, perhaps, the most plausible defense which an abolitionist could possibly set up against the light of revelation.

But to what does it amount? If the views of Dr. Wayland and his followers, respecting slavery, be correct, it amounts to this: The Almighty has said to his people, you may commit "a sin of appalling magnitude;" you may perpetrate "as great an evil as can be conceived;" you may persist in a practice which consists in "outraging the rights" of your fellow-men, and in "crushing their intellectual and moral" nature. They have a natural, inherent, and inalienable right to liberty as well as yourselves, but yet you may make slaves of them, and they may be your bondmen forever. In one word, *you*, my chosen people, may degrade "rational, accountable, and immortal beings" to the "rank of brutes." Such, if we may believe Dr. Wayland, is the first stage in the divine enlightenment of the human race! It consists in making known a part of God's mind, not against the monstrous iniquity of slavery, but in its favor! It is the utterance, not of a partial truth, but of a monstrous falsehood! It is the revelation of his will, not against sin, but in favor of as great a sin "as can be conceived." Now, we may fearlessly ask if the cause which is reduced to the necessity of resorting to such a defense may not be pronounced desperate indeed, and unspeakably forlorn?

It is alleged that polygamy and divorce, as well as slavery, are permitted and regulated in the Old Testament. This, we reply, proves, in regard to polygamy and divorce, exactly what it proves in regard to slavery,—namely, that neither is in itself sinful, that neither is *always* and *everywhere* sinful. In other words, it proves that neither polygamy nor divorce, as permitted in the Old Testament, is "*malum in se*," is inconsistent with the eternal and unchangeable principles of right. They are forbidden in the New Testament, not because they are in themselves absolutely and immutably wrong, but because they are inconsistent with the best interests of society; especially in civilized and Christian communities. If they had been wrong in themselves, they never could have been permitted by a holy God, who is of purer eyes than to behold iniquity, except with inifinite abhorrence.

Again, it is contended by Dr. Wayland that "Moses intended to abolish slavery," because he forbade the Jews "to deliver up a fugitive slave." The words are these: "Thou shalt not deliver unto his master the servant that is escaped from his master unto thee: "He shall dwell with thee, even among you, in that place which he shall choose in one of the gates where it liketh him best: thou shalt not oppress him."[167] "This precept, I think," says Dr. Wayland, "clearly shows that Moses intended to abolish slavery. How could slavery long continue in a country where every one was forbidden to deliver up a fugitive slave? How different would be the condition of slaves, and how soon would slavery itself cease, were this the law of compulsory bondage among us!"

The above passage of Scripture is a precious morsel with those who are opposed to a fugitive slave law. A petition from Albany, New York, from the enlightened seat of empire of the Empire State itself, signed, if we recollect right, by one hundred and fifty persons, was presented to the United States Senate by Mr. Seward, praying that no bill in relation to fugitive slaves might be passed, which should not contain that passage. Whether Mr. Seward was enlightened by his constituents, or whether he made the discovery for himself, it is certain that he holds an act for the reclamation of fugitive slaves to be "contrary to the divine law." It is certain that he agrees with his constituents, who, in the petition referred to, pronounced every such act "immoral," and contrary to the law of God. But let us look at this passage a little, and see if these abolitionists, who thus plant themselves so confidently upon "a higher law," even upon "the divine law" itself, be not as hasty and rash in their interpretation of this law as they are accustomed to be in their judgment respecting the most universal and long-established institutions of human society.

In the first place, if their interpretation be correct, we are at once met by a very serious difficulty. For we are required to believe that one passage of Scripture grants an "authority to take slaves," while another passage is designed to annul this authority. We are required to believe that, in one portion of the divine law, the right of the master to hold his slaves as "bondmen" is recognized, while another part of the same law denies the existence of such right. In fine, we are required to believe that the legislator of the Jews intended, in one and the same code, both to establish and to abolish slavery; that with one hand he struck down the very right and institution which he had set up with the other. How Dr. Channing and Mr. Sumner would have disposed of this difficulty we know full well, for they carry within their own bosoms a higher law than this higher law itself. But how Dr. Wayland, as an enlightened member of the good old orthodox Baptist Church, with whom the Scripture is really and in truth the inspired word of God, would have disposed of it, we are at some loss to conceive.

We labor under no such difficulty. The words in question do not relate to slaves owned by Hebrew masters. They relate to those slaves only who should escape from heathen masters, and seek an asylum among the people of God. "The first inquiry of course is," says a learned divine,[168] "in regard to those very words, 'Where does his master live?' Among the Hebrews, or among foreigners? The language of the passage fully develops this and answers the question. 'He has escaped from his master unto the Hebrews; (the text says—*thee, i. e.* Israel;) *he shall dwell with thee, even among you . . . in one of thy gates.*' Of course, then, he is an *immigrant*, and did *not dwell among them* before his flight. If he had been a Hebrew servant, belonging to a Hebrew, the whole face of the thing would be changed. Restoration, or restitution, if we may judge by the tenor of other property-laws among the Hebrews, would have surely been enjoined. But, be that as it may, the language of the text puts it beyond a doubt that the servant is a *foreigner*, and has fled from a *heathen master*. This entirely changes the complexion of the case. The Hebrews were God's chosen people, and were the only nation on earth which worshiped the only living and true God. . . . . In case a slave escaped from them (the heathen) and came to the Hebrews, two things were to be taken into consideration, according to the views of the Jewish legislator. The first was that the treatment of slaves among the heathen was far more severe and rigorous than it could lawfully be under the Mosaic law. The heathen master possessed the power of life and death, of scourging or imprisoning, or putting to excessive toil, even to any extent that he pleased. Not so among the Hebrews. *Humanity* pleaded there for the protection of the fugitive. The second and most important consideration was, that only among the Hebrews could the fugitive slave come to the knowledge and worship of the only living and true God."

Now this view of the passage in question harmonizes one portion of Scripture with another, and removes every difficulty. It shows, too, how greatly the abolitionists have deceived themselves in their rash and blind appeal to "the divine law" in question. "The reason of the law," says my Lord Coke, "is the law." It is applicable to those cases, and to those cases only, which come within the reason of the law. Hence, if it be a fact, and if our Northern brethren really believe that we are sunk in the darkness of heathen idolatry, while the light of the true religion is with them alone, why, then, we admit that the reason and principle of the divine law in question is in their favor. Then we admit that the return of our fugitive slaves is "contrary to the divine law." But if we are not heathen idolaters, if the God of the Hebrews be also the God of Southern masters, then the Northern States do not violate the precept in question—they only discharge a solemn constitutional obligation—in delivering up our "fugitives from labor."

§ II. *The argument from the New Testament.*

The New Testament, as Dr. Wayland remarks, was given, "not to one people, but to the whole race; not for one period, but for all time." Its lessons are, therefore, of universal and perpetual obligation. If, then, the Almighty had undertaken to enlighten the human race by degrees, with respect to the great sin of slavery, is it not wonderful that, in the very last revelation of his will, he has uttered not a single syllable in disapprobation thereof? Is it not wonderful, that he should have completed the revelation of his will,—that he should have set his seal to the last word he will ever say to man respecting his duties, and yet not one word about the great obligation of the master to emancipate his slaves, nor about the "appalling sin" of slavery? Such silence must, indeed, appear exceedingly peculiar and anomalous to the abolitionist. It would have been otherwise had he written the New Testament. He would, no doubt, have inserted at least one little precept against the sin of slavery.

As it is, however, the most profound silence reigns through the whole word of God with respect to the sinfulness of slavery. "It must be granted," says Dr. Wayland, "that the New Testament contains no *precept* prohibitory of slavery." Marvellous as such silence must needs be to the abolitionist, it cannot be more so to him than his attempts to account for it are to others. Let us briefly examine these attempts:

"You may give your child," says Dr. Wayland, "if he were approaching to years of discretion, permission to do an act, while you inculcate upon him principles which forbid it, for the sake of teaching him to be governed by principles, rather than by any direct enactment. In such case you would expect him to obey the principle, and not avail himself of the permission." Now we fearlessly ask every reader whose moral sense has not been perverted by false logic, if such a proceeding would not be infinitely unworthy of the Father of mercies? According to Dr. Wayland's view, he beholds his children living and dying in the practice of an abominable sin, and looks on without the slightest note of admonition or warning. Nay, he gives them permission to continue in the practice of this frightful enormity, to which they are already bound by the triple tie of habit, interest, and feeling! Though he gives them line upon line, and precept upon precept, in order to detach them from other sins, he yet gives them permission to live and die in this awful sin!

And why? To teach them, forsooth, not to follow his permission, but to be guided by his principles! Even the guilty Eli remonstrated with his sons. Yet if, instead of doing this, he had given them permission to practice the very sins they were bent upon, he might have been, for all that, as pure and faithful as the Father of mercies himself is represented to be in the writings of Dr. Wayland. Such are the miserable straits, and such the impious sophisms, to which even divines are reduced, when, on the supposition that slavery is a sin, they undertake to vindicate or defend the word which they themselves are ordained to preach!

Another reason, scarcely less remarkable than the one already noticed, is assigned for the omission of all precepts against slavery. "It was no part of the scheme of the gospel revelation," we are told by Dr. Wayland, (who quotes from Archbishop Whately,) "to lay down any thing approaching to a complete system of *moral precepts*—to enumerate every thing that is *enjoined* or *forbidden* by our religion." If this method of teaching had been adopted, "the New Testament would," says Dr. Wayland, "have formed a library in itself, more voluminous than the laws of the realm of Great Britain." Now, all this is very true; and hence the necessity of leaving many points of duty to the enlightened conscience, and to the application of the more general precepts of the gospel. But how has it happened that slavery is passed over in silence? Because, we are told; "every thing" could not be noticed. If, indeed, slavery be so great a sin, would it not have been easier for the divine teacher to say, Let it be abolished, than to lay down so many minute precepts for its regulation? Would this have tended to swell the gospel into a vast library, or to abridge its teachings? Surely, when Dr. Wayland sets up such a plea, he must have forgotten that the New Testament, though it cannot notice "every thing," contains a multitude of rules to regulate the conduct of the master and the slave. Otherwise he could scarcely have imagined that it was from an aversion to minuteness, or from an impossibility to forbid every evil, that the sin of slavery is passed over in silence.

He must also have forgotten another thing. He must have forgotten the colors in which he had painted the evils of slavery. If we may rely upon these, then slavery is no trifling offense. It is, on the contrary, a stupendous sin, overspreading the earth, and crushing the faculties—both intellectual and moral—of millions of human beings beneath its odious and terrific influence. Now, if this be so, then would it have been too much to expect that at least one little word might have been directed against so great, so tremendous an evil? The method of the gospel may be comprehensive, if you please; it may teach by great principles rather than by minute precepts. Still, it is certain that St. Paul could give directions about his cloak; and he could spend many words in private salutations. In regard to the great social evil of the age, however, and beneath which a large majority of even the civilized world were crushed to the earth, he said nothing, lest he should become too minute,—lest his epistles should swell into too large a volume! Such is one of Dr. Wayland's defences of the gospel. We shall offer no remark; we shall let it speak for itself.

A third reason for the silence in question is the alleged ease with which precepts may be evaded. "A simple precept or prohibition," says Dr. Wayland, "is, of all things, the easiest to be evaded. Lord Eldon used to say, that 'no man in England could construct an act of Parliament through which he could not drive a coach-and-four.' We find this to have been illustrated by the case of the Jews in the time of our Saviour. The Pharisees, who prided themselves on their strict obedience to the *letter*, violated the *spirit* of every precept of the Mosaic code."

Now, in reply to this most extraordinary passage, we have several remarks to offer. In the first place, perhaps every one is not so good a driver as Lord Eldon. It is certain, that acts of Parliament have been passed, through which the most slippery of rogues have not been able to make their escape. They have been caught, tried, and condemned for their offenses, in spite of all their ingenuity and evasion.

Secondly, a "principle" is just as easily evaded as a "precept;" and, in most cases, it is far more so. The great principle of the New Testament, which our author deems so applicable to the subject of slavery, is this: "Thou shalt love thy neighbor as thyself." Now, if this be the great principle intended to enlighten us respecting the sin of slavery, we confess it has been most completely evaded by every slave State in the Union. We have, indeed, so entirely deceived ourselves in regard to its true import, that it seems to us to have not the most remote application to such a subject. If any one will give our remarks on this great "principle" a candid examination, we think he will admit that we have deceived ourselves on very plausible, if not on unanswerable, grounds. If slavery be a sin,—*always and everywhere* a monstrous iniquity,—then we should have been far more thoroughly enlightened with respect to its true nature, and found evasion far more difficult, if the New Testament had explicitly declared it to be such, and commanded all masters everywhere to emancipate their slaves. We could have driven a coach-and-four neither through, nor around, any such express prohibition. It is indeed only in consequence of the default, or omission, of such precept or command, that the abolitionist appeals to what he calls the principles of the gospel. If he had only one such precept,—if he had only one such precise and pointed prohibition, he might then, and he *would*, most triumphantly defy evasion. He would say, There is *the word;* and none but the obstinate gainsayers, or unbelievers, would dare reply. But as it is, he is compelled to lose himself in vague generalities, and pretend to a certainty which nowhere exists, except in his own heated mind. This pretense, indeed, that an express precept, prohibitory of slavery, is not the most direct way to reveal its true nature, because a precept is so much more easily evaded than a principle, is merely one of the desperate expedients of a forlorn and hopeless cause. If the abolitionist would maintain that cause, or vindicate his principles, it will be found that he must retire, and hide himself from the light of revelation.

Thirdly, the above passage seems to present a very strange view of the Divine proceedings. According to that view, it appears that the Almighty tried the method of teaching by precept in the Old Testament, and the experiment failed. For precepts may be so easily evaded, that every one in the Mosaic code was violated by the Pharisees. Hence, the method of teaching by precept was laid aside in the New Testament, and the better method of teaching by principle was adopted. Such is the conclusion to which we must come, if we adopt the reasoning of Dr. Wayland. But we cannot adopt his reasoning; since we should then have to believe that the experiment made in the Old Testament proved a failure, and that its Divine Author, having grown wiser by experience, improved upon his former method.

The truth is, that the method of the one Testament is the same as that of the other. In both, the method of teaching by precept is adopted; by precepts of greater and of lesser generality. Dr. Wayland's principle is merely a general or comprehensive precept; and his precept is merely a specific or limited principle. The distinction he makes between them, and the use he makes of this distinction, only reflect discredit upon the wisdom and consistency of the Divine Author of revelation.

A third account which Dr. Wayland gives of the silence of the New Testament respecting the sin of slavery, is as follows: "If this form of wrong had been singled out from all the others, and had alone been treated preceptively, the whole system would have been vitiated. We should have been authorized to inquire why were not similar precepts in other cases delivered? and if they were not delivered, we should have been at liberty to conclude that they were intentionally omitted, and that the acts which they would have forbidden are innocent." Very well. But idolatry, polygamy, divorce, is each and every one singled out, and forbidden by precept, in the New Testament. Slavery alone is passed over in silence. Hence, according to the principle of Dr. Wayland himself, we are at liberty to conclude that a precept forbidding slavery was "intentionally omitted," and that slavery itself "is innocent."

Each one of these reasons is not only exceedingly weak in itself, but it is inconsistent with the others. For if a precept forbidding slavery were purposely omitted, in order to teach mankind to be governed by principle and to disregard permissions, then the omission could not have arisen from a love of brevity. Were it not, indeed, just as easy to give a precept forbidding, as to give one permitting, the existence of slavery? Again, if a great and world-devouring sin, such as the abolitionists hold slavery to be, has been left unnoticed, lest its condemnation should impliedly sanction other sins, then is it not worse than puerile to suppose that the omission was made for the sake of brevity, or to teach mankind that the permissions of the Most High may in certain cases be treated with contempt, may be set at naught, and despised as utterly inconsistent, as diametrically opposed to the principles and purity of his law?

If the abolitionist is so completely lost in his attempts to meet the argument from the silence of Scripture, he finds it still more difficult to cope with that from its express precepts and injunctions. *Servants, obey your masters*, is one of the most explicit precepts of the New Testament. This precept just as certainly exists therein as does the great principle of love itself. "The obedience thus enjoined is placed," says Dr. Wayland, "not on the ground of duty to man, but on the ground of duty to God." We accept the interpretation. It cannot for one moment disturb the line of our argument. It is merely the shadow of an attempt at an evasion. All the obligations of the New Testament are, indeed, placed on the same high ground. The obligation of the slave to obey his master could be placed upon no higher, no more sacred, no more impregnable, ground.

Rights and obligations are correlative. That is, every right implies a corresponding obligation, and every obligation implies a corresponding right. Hence, as the slave is under an obligation to obey the master, so the master has a right to his obedience. Nor is this obligation weakened, or this right disturbed, by the fact that the first is imposed by the word of God, and rests on the immutable ground of duty to him. If, by the divine law, the obedience of the slave is due to the master, then, by the same law, the master has a right to his obedience.

Most assuredly, the master is neither "a robber," nor "a murderer," nor "a manstealer," merely because he claims of the slave that which God himself commands the slave to render. All these epithets may be, as they have been, hurled at us by the abolitionist. His anathemas may thunder. But it is some consolation to reflect, that, as he was not consulted in the construction of the moral code of the universe, so, it is to be hoped, he will not be called upon to take part in its execution.

The most enlightened abolitionists are sadly puzzled by the precept in question; and, from the manner in which they sometimes speak of it, we have reason to fear it holds no very high place in their respect. Thus, says the Hon. Charles Sumner, "Seeking to be brief, I shall not undertake to reconcile texts of the Old Testament, which, whatever may be their import, are all absorbed in the New; nor shall I stop to consider the precise interpretation of the oft-quoted phrase, *Servants, obey your masters;* nor seek to weigh any such imperfect injunction in the scales against those grand commandments on which hang all the law and the prophets."[169] Now this is a very significant passage. The orator, its learned author, will not stop to consider the texts of the Old Testament bearing on the subject of slavery, because they are all merged in the New! Nor will he stop to consider any "such *imperfect injunction*" as those contained in the New, because they are all swallowed up and lost in the grand commandment, "Thou shalt love thy neighbor as thyself!"

If he had bestowed a little more attention on this grand commandment itself, he might have seen, as we have shown, that it in no wise conflicts with the precept which enjoins servants to obey their masters. He might have seen that it is not at all necessary to "weigh" the one of those precepts "in the scales against" the other, or to brand either of them as imperfect. For he might have seen a perfect harmony between them. It is no matter of surprise, however, that an abolitionist should find imperfections in the moral code of the New Testament.

It is certainly no wonder that Mr. Sumner should have seen imperfections therein. For he has, in direct opposition to the plainest terms of the gospel, discovered that it is the first duty of the slave to fly from his master. In his speech delivered in the Senate of the United States, we find among various other quotations, a verse from Sarah W. Morton, in which she exhorts the slave to fly from bondage. Having produced this quotation "as part of the testimony of the times," and pronounced it "a truthful homage to the inalienable rights" of the slave, Mr. Sumner was in no mood to appreciate the divine precept, "Servants, obey your masters." Having declared fugitive slaves to be "the heroes of the age," he had not, as we may suppose, any very decided taste for the commonplace Scriptural duties of submission and obedience. Nay, he spurns at and rejects such duties as utterly inconsistent with the "inalienable rights of man." He appeals from the oracles of eternal truth to "the testimony of the times." He appeals from Christ and his apostles to Sarah W. Morton. And yet, although he thus takes ground directly against the plainest precepts of the gospel, and even ventures to brand some of them as "imperfect," he has the hardihood to rebuke those who find therein, not what it really contains, but only a reflection of themselves!

The precept in question is not an isolated injunction of the New Testament. It does not stand alone. It is surrounded by other injunctions, equally authoritative, equally explicit, equally unequivocal. Thus, in Eph. vi. 5: "Servants, be obedient to them that are your masters according to the flesh." Precisely the same doctrine was preached to the Colossians: (iii. 22:) "Servants, obey in all things your masters according to the flesh; not with eye-service, as men-pleasers, but in singleness of heart, fearing God." Again, in St. Paul's Epistle to Timothy, he writes: "Let as many servants as are under the yoke count their own masters worthy of all honor, that the name of God and his doctrine be not blasphemed." Likewise, in Tit. ii. 9, 10, we read: "Exhort servants to be obedient to their own masters, and to please them well in all things; not answering again; not purloining, but showing all good fidelity, that they may adorn the doctrine of God our Saviour in all things." And in 1 Pet. ii. 18, it is written: "Servants, be subject to your masters with all fear; not only to the good and gentle, but also to the froward." Yet, in the face of these passages, Mr. Sumner declares that it is the duty of slaves to fly from bondage, and thereby place themselves among "the heroes of the age." He does not attempt to interpret or explain these precepts; he merely sets them aside, or passes them by with silent contempt, as "imperfect." Indeed, if his doctrines be true, they are not only imperfect—they are radically wrong and infamously vicious. Thus, the issue which Mr. Sumner has made up is not with the slaveholders of the South; it is with the word of God itself. The contradiction is direct, plain, palpable, and without even the decency of a pretended disguise. We shall leave Mr. Sumner to settle this issue and controversy with the Divine Author of revelation.

In the mean time, we shall barely remind the reader of what that Divine Author has said in regard to those who counsel and advise slaves to disobey their masters, or fly from bondage. "They that have believing masters," says the great Apostle to the Gentiles, "let them not despise them because they are brethren; but rather do them service, because they are faithful and beloved, partakers of the benefit. These things teach and exhort. If any man teach otherwise, and consent not to wholesome words, even the words of our Lord Jesus Christ, and to the doctrine which is according to godliness, *he is proud, knowing nothing.*" Mr. Sumner congratulates himself that he has stripped "from slavery the apology of Christianity." Let servants "count their own masters worthy of all honor," and "do them service," says St. Paul. "Let servants disobey their masters," says Mr. Sumner, "and cease to do them service." "These things teach and exhort," says St. Paul. "These things denounce and abhor," says Mr. Sumner. "If any man teach otherwise," says St. Paul, "he is proud, knowing nothing." "I teach otherwise," says Mr. Sumner. And is it by such conflict that he strips from slavery the sanction of Christianity? If the sheer *ipse dixit* of Mr. Sumner be sufficient to annihilate the authority of the New Testament, which he professes to revere as divine, then, indeed, has he stripped the sanction of Christianity from the relation of master and slave. Otherwise, he has not even stripped from his own doctrines the burning words of her condemnation.

Dr. Wayland avoids a direct conflict with the teachings of the gospel. He is less bold, and more circumspect, than the Senator from Massachusetts. He has honestly and fairly quoted most of the texts bearing on the subject of slavery. He shows them no disrespect. He pronounces none of them imperfect. But with this array of texts before him he proceeds to say: "Now, I do not see that the scope of these passages can be misunderstood." Nor can we. It would seem, indeed, impossible for the ingenuity of man to misunderstand the words, quoted by Dr. Wayland himself, "Servants, *obey* in all things your masters according to the flesh." Dr. Wayland does not misunderstand them. For he has said, in his Moral Science: "The *duty of slaves* is explicitly made known in the Bible. They are bound to obedience, fidelity, submission, and respect to their masters, not only to the good and kind, but also to the unkind and froward." But when he comes to reason about these words, which he finds it so impossible for any one to misunderstand, he is not without a very ingenious method to evade their plain import and to escape from their influence. Let the reader hear, and determine for himself.

"I do not see," says Dr. Wayland, "that the scope of these passages can be misunderstood. They teach patience, meekness, fidelity, and charity—duties which are obligatory on Christians toward all men, and, of course, toward masters. These duties are obligatory on us toward enemies, because an enemy, like every other man, is a moral creature of God." True. But is this all? Patience, meekness, fidelity, charity—duties due to all men! But what has become of the word *obedience?* This occupies a prominent—nay, the most prominent—place in the teachings of St. Paul. It occupies no place at all in the reasonings of Dr. Wayland. It is simply dropped out by him, or overlooked; and this was well done, for this word *obedience* is an exceedingly inconvenient one for the abolitionist. If Dr. Wayland had retained it in his argument, he could not have added, "duties which are obligatory on Christians toward all men, and, of course, toward masters." Christians are not bound to obey all men. But slaves are bound to obey "their own masters." It is precisely upon this injunction to obedience that the whole argument turns. And it is precisely this injunction to obedience which Dr. Wayland leaves out in his argument. He does not, and he cannot, misunderstand the word. But he can just drop it out, and, in consequence, proceed to argue as if nothing more were required of slaves than is required of all Christian men!

The only portion of Scripture which Mr. Sumner condescends to notice is the Epistle of St. Paul to Philemon. He introduces the discussion of this epistle with the remark that, "In the support of slavery, it is the habit to pervert texts and to invent authority. Even St. Paul is vouched for a wrong which his Christian life rebukes."[170] Now we intend to examine who it is that really perverts texts of Scripture, and invents authority. We intend to show, as in the clear light of noonday, that it is the conduct of Mr. Sumner and other abolitionists, and not that of the slaveholder, which is rebuked by the life and writings of the great apostle.

The epistle in question was written to a slaveholder, who, if the doctrine of Mr. Sumner be true, lived in the habitual practice of "a wrong so transcendent, so loathsome, so direful," that it "must be encountered *wherever it can be reached*, and the battle must be continued, without truce or compromise, until the field is entirely won." Is there any thing like this in the Epistle to Philemon? Is there any thing like it in any of the epistles of St. Paul? Is there anywhere in his writings the slightest hint that slavery is a sin at all, or that the act of holding slaves is in the least degree inconsistent with the most exalted Christian purity of life? We may safely answer these questions in the negative. The very epistle before us is from "Paul, a prisoner of Jesus Christ, and Timothy our brother, unto Philemon, *our dearly-beloved, and fellow-laborer*." The inspired writer then proceeds in these words: "I thank my God, making mention of thee always in my prayers. Hearing of thy love and faith, which thou hast toward the Lord Jesus, and toward all saints; that the communication of thy faith may become effectual by the acknowledging of every good thing which is in you in Christ Jesus. For we have great joy and consolation in thy love, because the bowels of the saints are refreshed by thee, brother."

Now if, instead of leaving out this portion of the epistle, Mr. Sumner had pronounced it in the hearing of his audience, the suspicion might have arisen in some of their minds that the slaveholder may not, after all, be so vile a wretch. It might even have occurred to some, perhaps, that the Christian character of Philemon, the slaveholder, might possibly have been as good as that of those by whom all slaveholders are excommunicated and consigned to perdition. It might have been supposed that a Christian man may possibly hold slaves without being as bad as robbers, or cut-throats, or murderers. We do not say that Mr. Sumner shrunk from the reading of this portion of the epistle in the hearing of his audience, lest it should seem to rebuke the violence and the uncharitableness of his own sentiments, as well as those of his brother abolitionists at the North. We do say, however, that Mr. Sumner had no sort of use for this passage. It could in no way favor the impression his oration was designed to make. It breathes, indeed, a spirit of good-will toward the Christian master as different from that which pervades the speeches of the honorable Senator, as the pure charity of Heaven is from the dire malignity of earth.

"It might be shown," says Mr. Sumner, "that the present epistle, when truly interpreted, is a protest against slavery, and a voice for freedom." If, instead of merely asserting that this "might be done," the accomplished orator had actually done it, he would have achieved far more for the cause of abolitionism than has been effected by all the splendors of his showy rhetoric. He has, indeed, as we shall presently see, made some attempt to show that the Epistle to Philemon is an emancipation document. When we come to examine this most extraordinary attempt, we shall perceive that Mr. Sumner's power "to pervert texts and to invent authority," has not been wholly held in reserve for what "might be done." If his view of this portion of Scripture be not very profound, it certainly makes up in originality what it lacks in depth. If it should fail to instruct, it will at least amuse the reader. It shall be noticed in due time.

The next point that claims our attention is the intimation that St. Paul's "real judgment of slavery" may be inferred "from his condemnation, on another occasion, of 'manstealers,' or, according to the original text, slave-traders, in company with murderers of fathers and murderers of mothers." Were we disposed to enter into the exegesis of the passage thus referred to, we might easily show that Mr. Sumner is grossly at fault in his Greek. We might show that something far more enormous than even trading in slaves is aimed at by the condemnation of the apostle. But we have not undertaken to defend "manstealers," nor "slave-traders," in any form or shape. Hence, we shall dismiss this point with the opinion of Macknight, who thinks the persons thus condemned in company with murderers of fathers and mothers, are "they who make war for the inhuman purpose of selling the vanquished as slaves, as is the practice of the African princes." To take any free man, whether white or black, by force, and sell him into bondage, is manstealing. To make war for such a purpose, were, we admit, wholesale murder and manstealing combined. This view of the passage in question agrees with that of the great abolitionist, Mr. Barnes, who holds that "the *essential* idea of the term" in question, "is *that of converting a free man into a slave*" . . . . the "changing of a freeman into a slave, especially by traffic, subjection, etc." Now, as we of the South, against whom Mr. Sumner is pleased to inveigh, propose to make no such changes of freemen into slaves, much less to wage war for any such purpose, we may dismiss his gross perversion of the text in question. He may apply the condemnation of the apostle to us now, if it so please the benignity of his Christian charity, but it will not, we assure him, enter into our consciences, until we shall not only become "slave-traders," but also, with a view to the gain of such odious traffic, make war upon freemen.

We have undertaken to defend, as we have said, neither "slave-traders," nor "manstealers." We leave them both to the tender mercies of Mr. Sumner. But we have undertaken to defend slavery, that is, *the* slavery of the South, and to vindicate the character of Southern masters against the aspersions of their calumniators. And in this vindication we shrink not from St. Paul's "real judgment of slavery." Nay, we desire, above all things, to have his real judgment. His judgment, we mean, not of manstealers or of murderers, but of slavery and slaveholders. We have just seen "his real judgment" respecting the character of one slaveholder. We have seen it in the very epistle Mr. Sumner is discussing. Why, then, does he fly from St. Paul's opinion of the slaveholder to what he has said of the manstealer and the murderer? We would gather an author's opinion of slavery from what he has said of slavery itself, or of the slaveholder. But this does not seem to suit Mr. Sumner's purpose quite so well. Entirely disregarding the apostle's opinion of the slaveholder contained in the passage right before him, as well as elsewhere, Mr. Sumner infers his "real judgment of slavery" from what he has said of manstealers and murderers! He might just as well have inferred St. Paul's opinion of Philemon from what he has, "on another occasion," said of Judas Iscariot.

Mr. Sumner contents himself with "calling attention to two things, apparent on the face" of the epistle itself; and which, in his opinion, are "in themselves an all-sufficient response." The first of these things is, says he: "While it appears that Onesimus had been in some way the servant of Philemon, it does not appear that he had ever been held as a slave, much less as a chattel." It does not appear that Onesimus was the slave of Philemon, is the position of the celebrated senatorial abolitionist. We cannot argue this position with him, however, since he has not deigned to give any reasons for it, but chosen to let it rest upon his assertion merely. We shall, therefore, have to argue the point with Mr. Albert Barnes, and other abolitionists, who have been pleased to attempt to bolster up so novel, so original, and so bold an interpretation of Scripture with exegetical reasons and arguments.

In looking into these reasons and arguments,—if reasons and arguments they may be called,—we are at a loss to conceive on what principle their authors have proceeded. The most plausible conjecture we can make is, that it was deemed sufficient to show that it is possible, by a bold stroke of interpretation, to call in question the fact that Onesimus was the slave of Philemon; since, if this may only be questioned by the learned, then the unlearned need not trouble themselves with the Scripture, but simply proceed with the work of abolitionism. Then may they cry, "Who shall decide when doctors disagree?"[171] and give all such disputings to the wind. Such seems to us to have been the principle on which the assertion of Mr. Sumner and Mr. Barnes has proceeded; evincing, as it does, an utter, total, and reckless disregard of the plainest teachings of inspiration. But let the candid reader hear, and then determine for himself.

The Greek word δοῦλος, applied to Onesimus, means, according to Mr. Barnes, either a slave, or a hired servant, or an apprentice. It is not denied that it means a *slave*. "The word," says Mr. Barnes himself, "is that which is commonly applied to a slave." Indeed, to assert that the Greek word δοῦλος does not mean *slave*, were only a little less glaringly absurd than to affirm that no such meaning belongs to the English term *slave* itself. If it were necessary, this point might be most fully, clearly, and conclusively established; but since is is not denied, no such work of supererogation is required at our hands.

But it is insisted, that the word in question has a more extensive signification than the English term *slave*. "Thus," says Mr. Barnes, "it is so extensive in its signification as to be applicable to any species of servitude, whether voluntary or involuntary." Again: "All that is necessairly implied by it is, that he was, in some way, the servant of Philemon—whether *hired or bought cannot be shown*." Once more, he says: "The word denotes *servant* of any kind, and it should never be assumed that those to whom it was applied were slaves." Thus, according to Mr. Barnes, the word in question denotes a slave, or a hired servant, or, as he has elsewhere said, an apprentice. It denotes "servant of *any* kind," whether "voluntary or involuntary."

Such is the positive assertion of Mr. Barnes. But where is the proof? Where is the authority on which it rests? Surely, if this word is applied to hired servants, either in the Greek classics or in the New Testament, Mr. Barnes, or Mr. Sumner, or some other learned abolitionist, should refer us to the passage where it is so used. We have Mr. Barnes' assertion, again and again repeated, in his very elaborate Notes on the Epistle to Philemon; but not the shadow of an authority for any such use of the word. But stop: in making this assertion, he refers us to his "Notes on Eph. vi 5, and 1 Tim. vi." Perhaps we may find his authority by the help of one of these references. We turn, then, to Eph. vi. 5; and we find the following note: "Servants. Οἱ δοῦλοι Hoi douloi]. The word here used denotes one who is bound to render service to another, whether that service be free or voluntary, and may denote, therefore, either a slave, or one who binds himself to render service to another. *It is often used in these senses in the New Testament, just as it is elsewhere.*"[172] Why, then, if it is so often used to denote a hired servant, or an apprentice, or a voluntary servant of any kind, in the New Testament, is not at least one such instance of its use produced by Mr. Barnes? He must have been aware that one such authority from the New Testament was worth more than his bare assertion, though it were a hundred times repeated. Yet no such authority is adduced or referred to; he merely supports his assertion in the one place by his assertion in the other?

Let us look, in the next place, to his other reference, which is to 1 Tim. vi. 1. Here, again, we find not the shadow of an authority that the word in question is applicable to "hired servants," or "apprentices." We simply meet the oft-repeated assertion of the author, that it is applicable to *any* species of servitude. He refers from assertion to assertion, and nowhere gives a single authority to the point in question. If we may believe him, such authorities are abundant, even in the New Testament; yet he leaves the whole matter to rest upon his own naked assertion! Yea, as Greek scholars, he would have us to believe that δοῦλος may mean a "hired servant," just as well as a slave; and he would have us to believe this, too, not upon the usage of Greek writers, but upon his mere assertion! We look for other evidence; and we intend to pin him down to proof, ere we follow him in questions of such momentous import as the one we have in hand.

Why is it, then, we ask the candid reader, if the term in question mean "a hired servant," as well as a slave, that no such application of the word is given? If such applications be as abundant as our author asserts they are, why not refer us to a single instance, that our utter ignorance may be at least relieved by one little ray of light? Why refer us from assertion to assertion, if authorities may be so plentifully had? We cannot conceive, unless the object be to deceive the unwary, or those who may be willingly deceived. An assertion merely, bolstered up with a "See note," here or there, may be enough for such; but if, after all, there be nothing but assertion on assertion piled, we shall not let it pass for proof. Especially, if such assertion be at war with truth, we shall track its author, and, if possible, efface his footprints from the immaculate word of God.

If the term δοῦλος signifies "a hired servant," or "an apprentice," it is certainly a most extraordinary circumstance that the best lexicographers of the Greek language have not made the discovery. This were the more wonderful, if, as Mr. Barnes asserts, the word "is often used in these senses" by Greek writers. We have several Greek lexicons before us, and in not one of them is there any such meaning given to the word. Thus, in Donnegan, for example, we find: "δοῦλος, a slave, a servant, as opposed to δεσπότης, a master." But we do not find from him that it is ever applied to hired servants or apprentices. In like manner, Liddell and Scott have "δοῦλος, a *slave*, *bondman*, strictly one born so, opposed to ανδραποδον." But they do not lay down "a hired servant," or "an apprentice," as one of its significations. If such, indeed, be found among the meanings of the word, these celebrated lexicographers were as ignorant of the fact as ourselves. Stephens also, as any one may see by referring to his "Thesaurus, Ling. Græc., Tom I. art. Δοῦλος," was equally ignorant of any such use of the term in question. Is it not a pity, then, that, since such knowledge rested with Mr. Barnes, and since, according to his own statement, proofs of its accuracy were so abundant, he should have withheld all the evidence in his possession, and left so important a point to stand or fall with his bare assertion? Even if the rights of mankind had not been in question, the interests of Greek literature were, one would think, sufficient to have induced him to enlighten our best lexicographers with respect to the use of the word under consideration. Such, an achievement would, we can assure him, have detracted nothing from his reputation for scholarship.

But how stands the word in the New Testament? It is certain that, however "often it may be applied" to hired servants in the New Testament, Mr. Barnes has not condescended to adduce a single application of the kind. This is not all. Those who have examined every text of the New Testament in which the word δοῦλος occurs, and compiled lexicons especially for the elucidation of the sacred volume, have found no such instance of its application.

Thus, Schleusner, in his Lexicon of the New Testament, tells us that it means slave as opposed to, λευθερος, *freeman*. His own words are: "Δοῦλος, ου, ὁ, (1) proprie: *servus, minister, homo non liber nec sui juris*, et opponitur τῶ ελευθερος. Matt. viii. 9; xiii. 27, 28; 1 Cor. vii. 21, 22; xii. 13; εἴτε δοῦλοι, εἴτε ἐλεύθεροι. Tit. ii. 9."

We next appeal to Robinson's Lexicon of the New Testament. We there find these words: "Δοῦλος, ου, ὁ, *a bondman, slave, servant, pr. by birth;* diff. from ανδραποδον, 'one enslaved in war,' comp. Xen. An., iv. 1, 12," etc. Now if, as Mr. Barnes asserts, the word in question is so often applied to hired servants in the New Testament, is it not passing strange that neither Schleusner nor Robinson should have discovered any such application of it? So far, indeed, is Dr. Robinson from having made any such discovery, that he expressly declares that the δοῦλος "WAS NEVER A HIRED SERVANT; *the latter being called* μισθιος, μισθωτος." "In a family," continues the same high authority, "the δοῦλος was *bound to serve, a slave*, and was the property of his master, 'a living possession,' as Aristotle calls him."

"The Greek δοῦλος," says Dr. Smith, in his Dictionary of Antiquities, "like the Latin *servus*, corresponds to the usual meaning of our word slave. . . . . Aristotle (Polit. i. 3.) says that a complete household is that which consists of slaves and freemen, (οικία δε τέλειος εκ δουλων καὶ ελευθερων,) and he defines a slave to be a living working-tool and possession. (Ὁ δοῦλος ἔμφυχον, ὄργανον, Ethic. Nicim. viii. 13; ὁ δοῦλος κτημα τι εμφυχον, Pol. i. 4.) Thus Aristotle himself defines the δοῦλος to be, not a "servant of any kind," but a slave; and we presume that he understood the force of this Greek word at least as well as Mr. Barnes or Mr. Sumner. And Dr. Robinson, as we have just seen, declares that it never means a hired servant.

Indeed, all this is so well understood by Greek scholars, that Dr. Macknight does not hesitate to render the term δοῦλος, applied to Onesimus in the Epistle to Philemon, by the English word *slave*. He has not even added a footnote, as is customary with him when he deems any other translation of a word than that given by himself at all worthy of notice. In like manner, Moses Stuart just proceeds to call Onesimus "the slave of Philemon," as if there could be no ground for doubt on so plain a point. Such is the testimony of these two great Biblical critics, who devoted their lives in great measure to the study of the language, literature, and interpretation of the Epistles of the New Testament.

Now, it should be observed, that not one of the authorities quoted by us had any motive "to pervert texts," or "to invent authorities," "in support of slavery." Neither Donnegan, nor Liddell and Scott, nor Stephens, nor Schleusner, nor Robinson, nor Smith, nor Macknight, nor Stuart, could possibly have had any such motive. If they were not all perfectly unbiassed witnesses, it is certain they had no bias in favor of slavery. It is, indeed, the abolitionist, and not the slaveholder, who, in this case, "has perverted texts;" and if he has not "invented authorities," it is because his attempts to do so have proved abortive.

Beside the clear and unequivocal import of the word applied to Onesimus, it is evident, from other considerations, that he was the slave of Philemon. To dwell upon all of these would, we fear, be more tedious than profitable to the reader. Hence we shall confine our attention to a single circumstance, which will, we think, be sufficient for any candid or impartial inquirer after truth. Among the arguments used by St. Paul to induce Philemon to receive his fugitive slave kindly, we find this: "For perhaps he therefore departed *for a season*, that thou shouldest receive him *forever*." This verse is thus paraphrased by Macknight: "To mitigate thy resentment, consider, that *perhaps also for this reason he was separated* from thee *for a little while*, (so πρὸς ὥραν signified, 1 | Thess. ii. 17, note 2,) *that thou mightest have him* thy slave *for life*." Dr. Macknight also adds, in a footnote: "By telling Philemon that he would now have Onesimus forever, the apostle intimates to him his firm persuasion that Onesimus would never any more run away from him." Such seems to be the plain, obvious import of the apostle's argument. No one, it is believed, who had no set purpose to subserve, or no foregone conclusion to support, would view this argument in any other light. Perhaps he was separated for a while as a slave, that "thou mightest have him forever," or for life. How have him? Surely, one would think, as a slave, or in the same capacity from which he was separated for a while. The argument requires this; the opposition of the words, and the force of the passage, imperatively require it. But yet, if we may believe Mr. Barnes, the meaning of St. Paul is, that perhaps Onesimus was separated for a while *as a servant*, that Philemon might never receive him again as a servant, but forever as a Christian brother! Lest we should be suspected of misrepresentation, we shall give his own words. "The meaning is," says he, "that it was possible that this was permitted in the providence of God, *in order* that Onesimus might be brought under the influence of the gospel, and be far more serviceable to Philemon as a Christian than he could have been in his former relation to him."

In the twelfth verse of the epistle, St. Paul says: "Whom I have sent again," or, as Macknight more accurately renders the words, "Him I have sent back," (ὃν ἀνέπεμψα.) | Here we see the great apostle *actually sending back a fugitive slave to his master*. That act of St. Paul is not, and cannot be, denied. The words are too plain for denial. Onesimus "*I have sent back*." Surely it cannot be otherwise than a most unpleasant spectacle to abolitionist eyes thus to see Paul, the aged—perhaps the most venerable and glorious hero

301

whose life is upon record—assume such an attitude toward the institution of slavery. Had he dealt with slavery as he always dealt with every thing which he regarded as sin; had he assumed toward it an attitude of stern and uncompromising hostility, and had his words been thunderbolts of denunciation, then indeed would he have been a hero after the very hearts of the abolitionists. But, as it is, they have to *apologize* for the great apostle, and try, as best they may, to deliver him from his *very equivocal position!* But if they are true apostles, and not false, then, we fear, the best apology for his conduct is that he had never read the Declaration of Independence, nor breathed the air of Boston.

This point, however, we shall not decide. We shall examine their apologies, and let the candid reader decide for himself. St. Paul, it is not denied, sent back Onesimus. But, says Mr. Barnes, he did not *compel* or *urge* him to go. He did not send him back against his will. Onesimus, no doubt, desired to return, and St. Paul was moved to send him by his own request. Now, in the first place, this apology is built on sheer assumption. There is not the slightest evidence that Onesimus requested St. Paul to send him back to his master. "There may have been many reasons," says Mr. Barnes, "why Onesimus desired to return to Colosse, and no one can prove that he did not express that desire to St. Paul, and that his 'sending' him was not in consequence of such request." True; even if Onesimus had felt no such desire, and had expressed no such desire to St. Paul, it would have been impossible, in the very nature of things, for any one to prove such negatives, unless he had been expressly informed on the subject by the writer of the epistle. But is it not truly wonderful, that any one should, without the least particle or shadow of evidence, be pleased to imagine a series of propositions, and then call upon the opposite party to disprove them? Is not such proceeding the very stuff that dreams are made of?

No doubt there may have been reasons why Onesimus should desire to return to his master. There were certainly reasons, and reasons of tremendous force, too, why he should have desired no such thing. The fact that Philemon, whom he had offended by running away, had, according to law, the power of life and death over him, is one of the reasons why he should have dreaded to return. Hence, unless required by the apostle to return, he *may* have desired no such thing, and no one can prove that an expression of such desire on his part was the ground of the apostle's action. It is certain, that he who affirms should prove.

In the second place, if St. Paul were an abolitionist at heart, he should have avoided the appearance of so great an evil. He should not, for a moment, have permitted himself to stand before the world in the simple and unexplained attitude of one who had sent back a fugitive slave to his master. No honest abolitionist would permit himself to appear in such a light. He would scorn to occupy such a position. Hence, we repeat, if St. Paul were an abolitionist at heart, he should have let it be known that, in sending Onesimus back, he was moved, not originally by the principles of his own heart, but by the desire and request of the fugitive himself. By such a course, he would have delivered himself from a false position, and spared his friends among the abolitionists the necessity of making awkward apologies for his conduct.

Thirdly, the positions of Mr. Barnes are not merely sheer assumptions; they are perfectly gratuitous. For it is easy to explain the determination of St. Paul to send Onesimus back, without having recourse to the supposition that Onesimus desired him to do so. Such determination was, indeed, the natural and necessary result of the well known principles of the great apostle. He had repeatedly, and most emphatically, inculcated the principle, that it is the duty of slaves to "obey their masters," and to "count them worthy of all honor." This duty Onesimus had clearly violated in running away from his master. If St. Paul, then, had not taught Onesimus a different doctrine from that which he had taught the churches, he must have felt that he had done wrong in absconding from Philemon, and desired to repair the wrong by returning to him. "It is," says Mr. Barnes, "by no means necessary to suppose that Paul felt that Onesimus was under *obligation* to return." But we must suppose this, unless we suppose that Paul felt that Onesimus was under no obligation to obey the precepts which he himself had delivered for the guidance and direction of all Christian servants.

We shall now briefly notice a few other of Mr. Barnes' arguments, and then dismiss this branch of the subject. "If St. Paul sent back Onesimus," says he, "this was, doubtless, at his own request; for there is not the slightest evidence that he *compelled* him, or even urged him, to go." We might just as well conclude that St. Paul first required Onesimus to return, because there is not the slightest evidence that Onesimus made any such request.

"Paul," says Mr. Barnes, "had no power to send Onesimus back to his master unless he chose to go." This is very true. But still Onesimus may have chosen to go, just because St. Paul, his greatest benefactor and friend, had told him it was his duty to do so. He may have chosen to go, just because the apostle had told him it is the duty of servants not to run away from their masters, but to obey them, and count them worthy of all honor. It is also true, that "there is not the slightest evidence that he *compelled* him, or even *urged* him, to go." It is, on the other hand, equally true, that there is not the slightest evidence that any thing more than a bare expression of the apostle's opinion, or a reiteration of his well-known sentiments, was necessary to induce him to return.

"The language is just as would have been used," says our author, "on the supposition, either that he requested him to go and bear a letter to Colosse, or that Onesimus desired to go, and that Paul sent him agreeably to his request. Compare Phil. ii. 25: 'Yet I suppose it necessary *to send* Epaphroditus, my brother, and companion in labor,' etc.; Col. iv. 7, 8: 'All my estate shall Tychicus declare unto you, who is a beloved brother, and a faithful minister and fellow-servant in the Lord: whom I have *sent* unto you for the same purpose, that he might know your estate.' But Epaphroditus and Tychicus were not sent against their own will,—nor is there any more reason to think that Onesimus was." Now there is not the least evidence that either Epaphroditus or Tychicus *requested* the apostle to *send* them as he did; and, so far as appears from his statements, the whole thing originated with himself. It is simply said that he *sent* them. It is true, they were "not sent against their own will," for they were ready and willing to obey his directions. We have good reason, as we have seen, to believe that precisely the same thing was true in regard to the sending of Onesimus.

But there is another case of *sending* which Mr. Barnes has overlooked. It is recorded in the same chapter of the same epistle which speaks of the sending of Epaphroditus. We shall adduce it, for it is a case directly in point. "But ye know the proof of him, (*i. e.* of Timothy,) that, as a son with the father, he hath served with me in the gospel. Him, therefore, I hope to *send* presently, so soon as I shall see how it will go with me." Now, here the apostle proposes to send Timothy, not so soon as Timothy should request to be sent, but so soon as he should see how it would go with himself as a prisoner at Rome. "As a son with the father," so Timothy, after his conversion, served with the great apostle, and, not against his own will, but most cheerfully, obeyed his directions. And in precisely the same ineffably endearing relation did Onesimus stand to the apostle. As a recent convert,—as a sincere and humble Christian,—he naturally looked to his great inspired teacher for advice, and was, no doubt, with more than filial affection, ready to obey.

Hence, we insist that Paul was responsible for the return of Onesimus to his master. He might have prevented his return, had he so desired; for he tells us so himself, (ver. 13.) But he chose to send him back. And why? Because Onesimus requested? The apostle says not so. "I would have retained him with me," says he to Philemon, "that in thy stead he might have ministered unto me in the bonds of the gospel. BUT WITHOUT THY MIND WOULD I DO NOTHING." Nay, whatever may have been his own desires, or those of Onesimus, he would do nothing without the mind of Philemon. Such is the reason which the apostle assigns for his own conduct, for his own determination not to retain the fugitive slave.

"What the apostle wrote to Philemon on this occasion is," says Dr. Macknight, "highly worthy of notice; namely, that although he had great need of an affectionate, honest servant to minister to him in his bonds, such as Onesimus was, who had expressed a great inclination to stay with him; and although, if Onesimus had remained with him, he would only have discharged the duty which Philemon himself owed to his spiritual father, yet the apostle would by no means detain Onesimus without Philemon's leave, because it belonged to him to dispose of his own slave in the way he thought proper. Such was the apostle's regard to justice, and to the rights of mankind!"

According to Mr. Barnes, however, the apostle was governed in this transaction, not by a regard to principle or the rights of mankind, but by a regard for the feelings of the master! Just listen, for one moment, to his marvellous discourse: "It is probable," says he, "that *if* Onesimus had proposed to return, it would have been easy for Paul to have retained him with him. He might have represented his own want of a friend. He might have appealed to his gratitude on account of his efforts for his conversion. He might have shown him that he was under no moral obligation to go back. He might have refused to give him this letter, and might have so represented to him the dangers of the way, and the probability of a harsh reception, as effectually to have dissuaded him from such a purpose. But, in that case, it is clear that this might have caused hard feeling in the bosom of Philemon, and rather than do that, he preferred to let him return to his master, and to plead for him that he might have a kind reception. It is, therefore, by no means necessary to suppose that Paul felt that Onesimus was under *obligation* to return, or that he was disposed to *compel* him, or that Onesimus was not inclined to return voluntarily; but all the circumstances of the case are met by the supposition that, if Paul had retained him, Philemon might conceive that he had injured *him*."

Alas! that so much truth should have been suppressed; and that, too, by the most glorious champion of truth the world has ever seen. He tells not his "son Onesimus" that he is under no moral obligation to return to his master. On the contrary, he leaves him ignorant of his rights—of his inherent, sacred, and eternal rights. He sees him blindly put off "the hero," and put on "the brute" again. And why? Because, forsooth, if he should only speak, *he might cause hard feeling in the bosom of his master!* Should he retain Onesimus, his son, he would not injure Philemon at all. But then Philemon "might *conceive*" that he had injured him. Ah! when will abolitionist again suppress such mighty truth, lest he disturb some *fancied* right, or absurd feeling ruffle? When the volcano of his mind suppress and keep its furious fires in, lest he consume some petty despot's despicable sway; or else, at least, touch his tender sensibilities with momentary pain? "*Fiat justitia, ruat cœlum,*" is a favorite maxim with other abolitionists. But St. Paul, it seems, could not assume quite so lofty a tone. He could not say, "Let justice be done, though the heavens should fall." He could not even say, "Let justice be done," though the feelings of Philemon should be hurt.

It is evident, we think, that St. Paul needs to be defended against Mr. Barnes' defenses of him, and vindicated against his apologies. If, indeed, he were so pitiful a pleader of "the innocent cause" as Mr. Barnes would have us to believe he is, then, we ask if those abolitionists are not in the right who despise both the apostle and his doctrine? No other abolitionist, it is certain, will ever imitate his example, as that example is represented by Mr. Barnes. No other abolitionist will ever suppress the great truths—as he conceives them to be—with which his soul is on fire, and which, in his view, lie at the foundation of human happiness, lest he should "cause hard feelings" in the bosom of a slaveholder.

It may be said, perhaps, that the remarks and apology of Mr. Barnes do not proceed on the supposition that Onesimus was a slave. If so, the answer is at hand. For surely Mr. Barnes cannot think it would have been dishonorable in the apostle to advise, or even to urge, "a hired servant," or "an apprentice," to return and fulfill his contract. It is evident that, although Mr. Barnes would have the reader to believe that Onesimus was merely a hired servant or an apprentice, he soon forgets his own interpretation, and proceeds to reason just as if he himself regarded him as a slave. This, if possible, will soon appear still more evident.

The apostle did not, according to Mr. Barnes, wholly conceal his abolition sentiments. He made them known to Philemon. Yes, we are gravely told, the letter which Onesimus carried in his pocket, as he wended his way back from Rome to Colosse, was and is an emancipation document! This great discovery is, we believe, due to the abolitionists of the present day. It was first made by Mr. Barnes, or Dr. Channing, or some other learned emancipationist, and after them by Mr. Sumner. Indeed, the discovery that it appears from the face of the epistle itself that it is an emancipation document, is the second of the two "conclusive things" which, in Mr. Sumner's opinion, constitute "an all-sufficient response" to anti-abolitionists.

Now supposing St. Paul to have been an abolitionist, such a disclosure of his views would, we admit, afford some little relief to our minds. For it would show that, although he did not provoke opposition by proclaiming the truth to the churches and to the world, he could at least run the risk of hurting the feelings of a slaveholder. But let us look into this great discovery, and see if the apostle has, in reality, whispered any such words of emancipation in the ear of Philemon.

In his note to the sixteenth verse of the epistle, Mr. Barnes says: "Not now as a servant. The adverb rendered 'not now,' (οὐκέτι) means *no more, no further, no longer*." So let it be. We doubt not that such is its meaning. Hence, we need not examine Mr. Barnes' numerous authorities, to show that such is the force of the adverb in question. He has, we admit, most abundantly established his point that οὐκέτι means *no longer*. But then this is a point which no anti-abolitionist has the least occasion to deny. We find precisely the same rendition in Macknight, and we are perfectly willing to abide by his translation. If Mr. Barnes had spared himself the trouble of producing these authorities, and adduced only one to show that δοῦλος means *a hired servant*, or *an apprentice*, his labor would have been bestowed where it is needed.

As the passage stands, then, St. Paul exhorts Philemon to receive Onesimus, "no longer as a servant." Now this, we admit, is perfectly correct *as far as it goes*. "It (*i. e.* this adverb) implies," says Mr. Barnes, "that he had been in this condition, *but was not to be now*." He was *no longer* to be a servant! Over this view of the passage, Mr. Sumner goes into quite a paroxysm of triumphant joy. "Secondly," says he, "in charging Onesimus with this epistle to Philemon, the apostle announces him as 'not now a servant, but above a servant,—a brother beloved;' and he enjoins upon his correspondent the hospitality due only to a freeman, saying expressly, 'If thou count me, therefore, as a partner, *receive him as myself;'* ay, sir, not as slave, not even as servant, but as a brother beloved, even as the apostle himself. Thus with apostolic pen wrote Paul to his disciple Philemon. Beyond all doubt, in these words of gentleness, benediction, and EMANCIPATION,[173] dropping with celestial, soul-awakening power, there can be no justification for a conspiracy, which, beginning with the treachery of Iscariot, and the temptation of pieces of silver, seeks by fraud, brutality, and violence, through officers of the law armed to the teeth like pirates, and amid soldiers who degrade their uniform, to hurl a fellow-man back into the lash-resounding den of American slavery; and if any one can thus pervert this beneficent example, allow me to say that he gives too much occasion to doubt his intelligence or his sincerity."

Now in regard to the spirit of this passage we have at present nothing to say. The sudden transition from the apostle's "words of blessing and benediction," to Mr. Sumner's words of railing and vituperation, we shall pass by unnoticed. Upon these the reader may make his own comments. It is our object simply to comment on the words of the great apostle. And, in the first place, we venture to suggest that there are several very serious difficulties in the way of Mr. Barnes' and Mr. Sumner's interpretation of the passage in question.

Let us, for the sake of argument, concede to these gentlemen that Onesimus was merely the hired servant, or apprentice, of Philemon. What then follows? If they are not in error, it clearly and unequivocally follows that St. Paul's "words of emancipation" were intended, not for slaves merely, but for hired servants and apprentices! For servants of any and every desrciption! Mr. Sumner expressly tells us that he was to return, "not as a slave, *not even as a servant*, but as a brother beloved." Now such a scheme of emancipation would, it seems to us, suit the people of Boston as little as it would those of Richmond. It would abolish every kind of "servitude, whether voluntary or involuntary," and release all hired servants, as well as apprentices, from the obligation of their contracts. Such is one of the difficulties in their way. It may not detract from the "sincerity," it certainly reflects no credit on the "intelligence," of Mr. Sumner, to be guilty of such an oversight.

There is another very grave difficulty in the way of these gentlemen. St. Paul writes that the servant Onesimus, who had been unprofitable to Philemon in times past, would now be profitable to him. But how profitable? As a servant? No! he was no longer to serve him at all. His "emancipation" was announced! He was to be received, not as a slave, not even as a servant, but *only* as a brother beloved! Philemon was, indeed, to extend to him the hospitalities due to a freeman, even such as were due to the apostle himself? Now, for aught we know, it may have been very agreeable to the feelings of Philemon, to have his former servant thus unceremoniously "emancipated," and quartered upon him as "a gentleman of elegant leisure;" but how this could have been so *profitable* to him is more than we can conceive.

It must be admitted, we think, that in a worldly point of view, all the profits would have been on the side of Onesimus. "But," says Mr. Barnes, "he would now be more profitable as a Christian brother." It is true, Onesimus had not been very profitable as a Christian brother before he ran away, for he had not been a Christian brother at all. But if he were sent back by the apostle, because he would be profitable merely as a Christian brother, we cannot see why any other Christian brother would not have answered the purpose just as well as Onesimus. If such, indeed, were the apostle's object, he might have conferred a still greater benefit upon Philemon by sending several Christian brethren to live with him, and to feast upon his good things.

Thirdly, the supposition that St. Paul thus announced the emancipation of Onesimus, is as inconsistent with the whole scope and design of the passage, as it is with the character of the apostle. If he would do nothing without the consent of Philemon, not even retain his servant to minister to himself while in prison, much less would he declare him emancipated, and introduce him to his former master as a freeman. We submit to the candid reader, we submit to every one who has the least perception of the character and spirit of the apostle, if such an interpretation of his words be not simply ridiculous.

It is certain that such an interpretation is peculiar to abolitionists. "Men," says Mr. Sumner, "are prone to find in uncertain, disconnected texts, a confirmation of their own personal prejudices or prepossessions. And I,"—he continues, "who am no divine, but only a simple layman—make bold to say, that whosoever finds in the gospel any sanction of slavery, finds there merely a reflection of himself." He must have been a very simple layman indeed, if he did not perceive how very easily his words might have been retorted. We venture to affirm that no one, except an abolitionist, has ever found the slightest tincture of abolitionism in the writings of the great apostle to the Gentiles.

The plain truth is, that Philemon is exhorted to receive Onesimus "no longer as a slave ONLY, but above a slave,—a brother beloved." Such is the translation of Macknight, and such, too, is the concurrent voice of every commentator to whom we have access. Pool, Clarke, Scott, Benson, Doddridge—all unite in the interpretation that Onesimus was, in the heaven-inspired and soul-subduing words of the loving apostle, commended to his master, not as a slave *merely*, but also as a Christian brother. The great fact—the "words of emancipation," which Mr. Sumner sees so clearly on "the face of the epistle,"—they cannot see at all. Neither sign nor shadow of any such thing can they perceive. It is a sheer reflection of the abolitionist himself. Thus, the Old Testament is not only merged in the New, but the New itself is merged in Mr. Charles Sumner, of Massachusetts.

We shall notice one passage more of Scripture. The seventh chapter of the Epistle to the Corinthians begins thus: "Now concerning the things whereof ye wrote unto me;" and it proceeds to notice, among other things, the relation of master and slave. This passage was designed to correct the disorders among the Christian slaves at Corinth, who, agreeably to the doctrine of the false teacher, *claimed their liberty, on pretense that, as breth-ren in Christ, they were on an equality with their Christian masters*." Here, then, St. Paul met abolitionism face to face. And how did he proceed? Did he favor the false teacher? Did he recognize the claim of the discontented Christian slaves? Did he even once hint that they were entitled to their freedom, on the ground that all men are equal, or on any other ground whatever? His own words will furnish the best answer to these questions.

"Let every man," says he, "abide in the same calling wherein he was called. Art thou called, being a servant? *care not for it.*" Thus, were Christian slaves exhorted to continue in that condition of life in which they were when converted to Christianity. This will not be denied. It is too plain for controversy. It is even admitted by Mr. Barnes himself. In the devout contemplation of this passage Chrysostom exclaims: "Hast thou been called, being a slave? Care not for it. Continue to be a slave. Hast thou been called, being in un-circumcision? Remain uncircumcised. Being circumcised, didst thou become a believer? Continue circumcised. For these are no hindrances to piety. Thou are called, being a slave; another, with an unbelieving wife; another, being circumcised. [Astonishing! Where has he put slavery?] As circumcision profits not, and uncircumcision does no harm, so neither doth slavery nor yet liberty."

"The great argument" against slavery is, according to Dr. Channing and other aboli-tionists, drawn from the immortality of the soul. "Into every human being," says he, "God has breathed an immortal spirit, more precious than the whole outward creation. No earthly nor celestial language can exaggerate the worth of a human being." The powers of this immortal spirit, he concludes, "reduce to insignificance all outward distinctions." Yea, according to St. Paul himself, they reduce to utter insignificance all outward distinc-tions, and especially the distinction between liberty and slavery. "Art thou called," says he, "being a slave? care not for it." Art thou, indeed, the Lord's freeman and *as such* des-tined to reign on a throne of glory forever? Oh, then, care not for the paltry distinctions of the passing world!

Now, whom shall the Christian teacher take for his model?—St. Paul, or Dr. Chan-ning? Shall he seek to make men contented with the condition in which God has placed them, or shall he stir up discontent, and inflame the restless passions of men? Shall he himself, like the great apostle, be content to preach the doctrines of eternal life to a pe-rishing world; or shall he make politics his calling, and inveigh against the domestic relations of society? Shall he exhort men not to continue in the condition of life in which God has placed them, but to take his providence out of his hands, and, *in direct opposi-tion to his word*, assert their rights? In one word, shall he preach the gospel of Christ and his apostles, or shall he preach the gospel of the abolitionist?

"Art thou called, being a servant? care not for it; but if thou mayest be made free, use it rather." The Greek runs thus: αλλ' εἰ καὶ δύνασαι ἐλεύθερος γενέσαι μᾶλλον χρῆσαι,—

309

literally, "but even if thou canst become free, rather make use of." Make use of what? The Greek verb is left without a case. How, then, shall this be applied? To what does the ambiguous *it* of our translation refer? "One and all of the native Greek commentators in the early ages," says Stuart, "and many expositors in modern times, say that the word to be supplied is δουλεία, i. e. *slavery, bondage.* The reason which they give for it is, that this is the only construction which can support the proposition the apostle is laboring to establish, viz.: 'Let every man abide in *statu quo.*' Even De Wette, (who, for his high liberty notions, was banished from Germany,) in his commentary on this passage, seems plainly to accede to the force of this reasoning; and with him many others have agreed. No man can look at the simple continuity of logic in the passage without feeling that there is force in the appeal." Yet the fact should not be concealed, that Stuart himself is "not satisfied with this exegesis of the passage;" which, according to his own statement, was the universal interpretation from "the early ages" down to the sixteenth century. This change, says he, "seems to have been the spontaneous prompting of the spirit of liberty, that beat high" in the bosom of its author.

Now have we not some reason to distrust an interpretation which comes not exactly from Heaven, but from a spirit beating high in the human breast? *That* is certainly not an unerring spirit. We have already seen what it can do with the Scriptures. But whether it has erred in this instance, or not, it is certain that it should never be permitted to beat so very high in any human breast as to annul the teachings of the apostle, or to make him contradict himself. This has been too often done. We too frequently hear those who admit that St. Paul exhorts "slaves to continue in slavery," still contend that "if they may be made free," they should move heaven and earth to attain so desirable an object. They "should continue in that state," and yet exert all their power to escape therefrom!

Conybeare and Howson, who are acknowledged to be among the best commentators of the Epistles of St. Paul, have restored "the continuity of his logic." They translate his words thus: "Nay, though thou have power to gain thy freedom, seek rather to remain content." This translation certainly possesses the advantage that it makes the doctrine of St. Paul perfectly consistent with itself.

But let us return to the point in regard to which there is no controversy. It is on all sides agreed, that St. Paul no less than three times exhorts every man to continue in the condition in which Providence has placed him. "And this rule," says he, "ordain I in all the churches." Yet—would any man believe it possible?—the very quintessence of abolitionism itself has been extracted from this passage of his writings! Let us consider for a moment the wonderful alchemy by which this has been effected.

We find in this passage the words: "Be not ye the servants of men." These words are taken from the connection in which they stand, dissevered from the words which precede and follow them, and then made to teach that slaves should not submit to the authority of their masters, should not continue in their present condition. It is certain that no one but an abolitionist, who has lost all respect for revelation except when it happens to square with his own notions, could thus make the apostle so directly and so flatly contradict himself and all his teaching. Different interpretations have been given to the words just quoted; but until abolitionism set its cloven foot upon the Bible, such violence had not been done to its sacred pages.

Conybeare and Howson suppose that the words in question are intended to caution the Corinthians against "their servile adherence to party leaders." Bloomfield, in like manner, says: "The best commentators are agreed," that they are "to be taken figuratively, in the sense, 'do not be blindly followers of men, conforming to their opinions,' etc." It is certain that Rosenmüller, Grotius, and we know not how many more, have all concurred in this interpretation. But be the meaning what it may, *it is not* an exhortation to slaves to burst their bonds in sunder, unless the apostle has, in one and the same breath, taught diametrically opposite doctrines.

Yet, in direct opposition to the plain words of the apostle, and to the concurrent voice of commentators and critics, is he made to teach that slaves should throw off the authority of their masters! Lest such a thing should be deemed impossible, we quote the words of the author by whom this outrage has been perpetrated. "The command of the 23d verse," says he, "'be not ye the servants of men,' is equally plain. There are no such commands uttered in regard to the relations of husband and wife, parent and child, as are here given in regard to slavery. *No one is thus urged to dissolve the marriage relation. No such commands are given to relieve children from obedience to their parents*," etc.[174] Nor is any such command, we repeat, given to relieve slaves from obedience to their masters, or to dissolve the relation between them.

If such violence to Scripture had been done by an obscure scribbler, or by an infidel quoting the word of God merely for a purpose, it would not have been matter of such profound astonishment. But is it not unspeakably shocking that a Christian man, nay, that a Christian minister and doctor of divinity, should thus set at naught the clearest, the most unequivocal, and the most universally received teachings of the gospel? If he had merely accused the Christian man of the South, as he has so often done in his two stupid volumes on slavery, of the crimes of "swindling," of "theft," of "robbing," and of "manstealing," we could have borne with him well; and, as we have hitherto done, continued to pass by his labors with silent contempt. But we have deemed it important to show in what manner, and to what extent, the spirit of abolitionism can wrest the pure word of God to its antichristian purpose.

We shall conclude the argument from scripture with the following just and impressive testimony of the Princeton Review: "The mass of the pious and thinking people in this country are neither abolitionists nor the advocates of slavery. They stand where they ever have stood—on the broad Scriptural foundation; maintaining the obligation of all men, in their several places and relations, to act on the law of love, and to promote the spiritual and temporal welfare of others by every means in their power. They stand aloof from the abolitionists for various reasons. In the first place, they disapprove of their principles. The leading characteristic doctrine of this sect is that slaveholding is in all cases a sin, and should, therefore, under all circumstances, be immediately abandoned. *As nothing can be plainer than that slaveholders were admitted to the Christian church by the inspired apostles, the advocates of this doctrine are brought into direct collision with the Scriptures. This leads to one of the most dangerous evils connected with the whole system, viz., a disregard of the authority of the word of God, a setting up a different and higher standard of truth and duty, and a proud and confident wresting of Scripture to suit their own purposes.* THE HISTORY OF INTERPRETATION FURNISHES NO EXAMPLES OF MORE WILLFUL AND VIOLENT PERVERSIONS OF THE SACRED TEXT THAN ARE TO BE FOUND IN THE WRITINGS OF THE ABOLITIONISTS. THEY SEEM TO CONSIDER THEMSELVES ABOVE THE SCRIPTURES; AND WHEN THEY PUT THEMSELVES ABOVE THE LAW OF GOD, IT IS NOT WONDERFUL THAT THEY SHOULD DISREGARD THE LAWS OF MEN. Significant manifestations of the result of this disposition to consider their own light a surer guide than the word of God, are visible in the anarchical opinions about human governments, civil and ecclesiastical, and on the rights of women, which have found appropriate advocates in the abolition publications. Let these principles be carried out, and there is an end to all social subordination, to all security for life and property, to all guarantee for public or domestic virtue. If our women are to be emancipated from subjection to the law which God has imposed upon them, if they are to quit the retirement of domestic life, where they preside in stillness over the character and destiny of society; if they are to come forth in the liberty of men, to be our agents, our public lecturers, our committee-men, our rulers; if, in studied insult to the authority of God, we are to renounce in the marriage contract all claim to obedience, we shall soon have a country over which the genius of Mary Wolstonecraft would delight to preside, but from which all order and all virtue would speedily be banished. There is no form of human excellence before which we bow with profounder deference than that which appears in a delicate woman, adorned with the inward graces and devoted to the peculiar duties of her sex; and there is no deformity of human character from which we turn with deeper loathing than from a woman forgetful of her nature, and clamorous for the vocation and rights of men. It would not be fair to object to the abolitionists the disgusting and disorganizing opinions of even some of their leading advocates and publications, did they not continue to patronize those publications, and were not these opinions the legitimate consequences of their own principles. Their women do but apply their own method of dealing with Scripture to another case. This no inconsiderable portion of the party have candor enough to acknowledge, and are therefore prepared to abide the result."

CHAPTER IV

THE ARGUMENT FROM THE PUBLIC GOOD.

The Question—Emancipation in the British Colonies—The manner in which Emancipation has ruined the British Colonies—The great benefit supposed, by American Abolitionists, to result to the freed Negroes from the British Act of Emancipation—The Consequences of Abolition to the South—Elevation of the Blacks by Southern Slavery.

WE have not shunned the abstractions of the abolitionist. We have, on the contrary, examined all his arguments, even the most abstract, and endeavored to show that they either rest on false assumptions, or consist in false deductions. While engaged in this analysis of his errors, we have more than once had occasion to remind him that the great practical problem of slavery is to be determined, if determined at all, not by an appeal to abstractions, but simply by a consideration of the public good. It is under this point of view, or with reference to the highest good of the governed, that we now proceed to consider the institution of slavery.

The way is open and clear for this view of the subject. For we have seen, we trust, that slavery is condemned neither by any principle of natural justice, nor by any precept of divine revelation. On the other hand, if we mistake not, it has been most clearly shown that the doctrines and practices of the abolitionist are at war with the most explicit words of God, as well as with the most unquestionable principles of political ethics. Hence, without the least disrespect to the eternal principles of right, we may now proceed to subject his doctrines to the only remaining test of political truth, namely, *to the test of experience*. Having examined the internal qualities of the tree and found them bad, we may now proceed to inquire if "its fruits" be not poison. And if the sober lessons of history, if the infallible records of experience, be found in perfect harmony with the conclusions of reason and of revelation, then shall we not be triply justified in pronouncing abolitionism a social and a moral curse?

§ I. *The Question.*

Here, at the outset, we may throw aside a mass of useless verbiage, with which our inquiry is usually encumbered. We are eternally told that Kentucky has fallen behind Ohio, and Virginia behind Pennsylvania, because their energies have been crippled, and their prosperity over-clouded, by the institution of slavery. Now, it is of no importance to our argument that we should either deny the fact, or the explanation which is given of it by abolitionists. If the question were, whether slavery should be introduced among us, or into any non-slaveholding State, then such facts and explanations would be worthy of our notice. Then such an appeal to experience would be relevant to the point in dispute. But such is not the question. We are not called upon to decide whether slavery shall be established in our midst or not. This question has been decided for us. Slavery—as every body knows—was forced upon the colonies by the arbitrary and despotic rule of Great Britain, and that, too, against the earnest remonstrances of our ancestors. The thing has been done. The past is beyond our control. It is fixed and unalterable. The only inquiry which remains for us now is, whether the slavery which was thus forced upon our ancestors shall be continued, or whether it shall be abolished? The question is not what Virginia, or Kentucky, or any other slave State, *might* have been, but what they would be in case slavery were abolished. If abolitionists would speak to the point, then let them show us some country in which slavery has been abolished, and we will abide by the experiment. Fortunately for us, we need not look far for such an experiment;—an experiment which has been made, not upon mere chattels or brutes, but upon the social and moral well-being of more than a million of human beings. We refer, of course, to the emancipation of the slaves in the British colonies. This work, as every one knows, was the great vaunted achievement of British abolitionists. Here, then, we may see their philosophy—if philosophy it may be called—"teaching by example." Here we may see and taste the fruits of abolitionism, ere we conclude to grow them upon our own soil.

§ II. *Emancipation in the British Colonies.*

It is scarcely in the power of human language to describe the enthusiastic delight with which the abolitionists, both in England and in America, were inspired by the spectacle of West India Emancipation. We might easily adduce a hundred illustrations of the almost frantic joy with which it intoxicated their brains. We shall, however, for the sake of brevity, confine our attention to a single example,—which will, at the same time, serve to show, not only how wild the abolitionist himself was, but also how indignant he became that others were not equally disposed to part with their sober senses. "The prevalent state of feeling," said Dr. Channing in 1840, "in the free States in regard to slavery is indifference—an indifference strengthened by the notion of great difficulties attending the subject. The fact is painful, but the truth should be spoken. The majority of the people, even yet, care little about the matter. A painful proof of this insensibility was furnished about a year and a half ago, when the English West Indies were emancipated. An event surpassing this in moral grandeur is not recorded in history. In one day, probably seven hundred thousand of human beings were rescued from bondage to full, unqualified freedom. The consciousness of wrongs, in so many breasts, was exchanged into rapturous, grateful joy. What shouts of thanksgiving broke forth from those liberated crowds! What new sanctity and strength were added to the domestic ties! What new hopes opened on future generations! The crowning glory of this day was the fact that the work of emancipation was wholly due to the principles of Christianity. The West Indies were freed, not by force, or human policy, but by the reverence of a great people for justice and humanity. The men who began and carried on this cause were Christian philanthropists; and they prevailed by spreading their own spirit through a nation. In this respect, the emancipation of the West Indies was a grander work than the redemption of the Israelites from bondage. This was accomplished by force, by outward miracles, by the violence of the elements. That was achieved by love, by moral power, by God, working, not in the stormy seas, but in the depths of the human heart. And how was this day of emancipation—one of the most blessed days that ever dawned upon the earth—received in this country? While in distant England a thrill of gratitude and joy pervaded thousands and millions, we, the neighbors of the West Indies, and who boast of our love of liberty, saw the sun of that day rise and set with hardly a thought of the scenes on which it was pouring its joyful light. The greater part of our newspapers did not refer to the event. The great majority of the people had forgotten it. Such was the testimony we gave to our concern for the poor slave; and is it from discussions of slavery among such a people that the country is to be overturned?"

Such were the glowing expectations of the abolitionists. It now remains to be seen whether they were true prophets, or merely "blind leaders of the blind." Be that as it may, for the present we cannot agree with Dr. Channing, that the good people of the free States were insincere in boasting of their "love of liberty," because they did not go into raptures over so fearful an experiment before they had some little time to see how it would work. They did, no doubt, most truly and profoundly love liberty. But then they had some reason to suspect, perhaps, that liberty may be one thing, and abolitionism quite another. Liberty, they knew, was a thing of light and love; but as for abolitionism, it was, for all they knew, a demon of destruction. Hence they would wait, and see. We do well to rejoice at once, exclaims Dr. Channing. If a man-child is born into the world, says he, do we wait to read his future life ere we rejoice at his birth? Ah, no! But then, perhaps, this offspring of abolitionism is no man-child at all. It may, for aught we know, be an abortion of night and darkness merely. Hence, we shall wait, and mark his future course, ere we rend the air with shouts that he is born at last.

This man-child, or this monster, is now seventeen years and four months old. His character is developed, and fixed for life. We may now read his history, written by impartial men, and determine for ourselves, whether it justifies the bright and boundless hopes of the abolitionists, or the "cold indifference," nay, the suspicions and the fears, of the good people of the free States.

We shall begin with Jamaica, which is by far the largest and most valuable of the British West Indies. The very first year after the complete emancipation of the slaves of this island, its prosperity began to manifest symptoms of decay. As long as it was possible, however, to find or invent an explanation of these fearful signs, the abolitionists remained absolutely blind to the real course of events. In 1839, the first year of complete emancipation, it appeared that the crop of sugar exported from the island had fallen off no less than eight thousand four hundred and sixty-six hogsheads. But, then, it was discovered that the hogsheads had been larger this year than the preceding! It is true, there was not exactly any proof that larger hogsheads had been used all over the island, but it was rumored; and the rumor was, of course, eagerly swallowed by the abolitionists.

And besides, it was quite certain that the free negroes had eaten more sugar than while they were slaves, which helped mightily to account for the great diminution in the exports of the article. No one could deny this. It is certain, that if the free negroes only devoured sugar as eagerly as such floating conjectures were gulped down by the abolitionists, the whole phenomenon needed no other cause for its perfect explanation. It never once occured, however, to these reasoners to imagine that the decrease in the amount of rum exported from another island *might* be owing to the circumstance that the free blacks had swallowed a little more of that article as well as of sugar. On the contrary, this fact was held up as a most conclusive and triumphant proof that the free negroes had not only become temperate themselves, but also so virtuous that they scorned to produce such an article to poison their fellow-men. The English abolitionists who rejoiced at such a reflection were, it must be confessed, standing on rather delicate ground. For if such an inference proved any thing, it proved that the blacks of the island in question had, at one single bound, passed from the depths of degradation to an exaltation of virtue far above their emancipators, the English people themselves; since these, as every reader of history knows, not only enforced the culture of opium in India, but also absolutely compelled the poor Chinese to receive it at the mouth of the cannon!

It also appears that, for 1839, the amount of coffee exported had fallen off 38,554 cwt., or about one third of the whole amount of the preceding year. "The coffee is a very uncertain crop," said a noted English emancipationist, in view of this startling fact, "and the deficiency, on the comparison of these two years, is not greater, I believe, than has often occurred before." This is true, for a drought or a hurricane had before created quite as great a deficiency. But while the fact is true, it only proves that the first year of emancipation was no worse on the coffee crop than a drought or a hurricane.

"We should also remember," says this zealous abolitionist, "that, both in sugar and coffee, the profit to the planter may be increased by the saving of expense, even where the produce is diminished." Such a thing, we admit, is possible; it *may* be true. But *in point of fact*, as we shall soon see, the expense was increased, while the crop was diminished.

But after every possible explanation, even Dr. Channing and Mr. Gurney were bound to admit "that some decrease has taken place in both the articles, in connection with the change of system." They also admitted that "so far as this decrease of produce is connected with the change of system, *it is obviously to be traced to a corresponding decrease in the quantity of labor.*"

May we not suppose, then, that here the ingenuity of man is at an end, and the truth begins to be allowed to make its appearance? By no means. For here "comes the critical question,"—says Mr. Gurney, "the real turning point. To what is this decrease in the quantity of labor owing? I answer deliberately but without reserve, '*Mainly* to causes which class under slavery and not under freedom.' It is, for the most part, the result of those impolitic attempts to force the labor of freemen which have disgusted the peasantry, and have led to the desertion of many of the estates."

Now suppose this were the case, is it not the business, is it not the duty, of the legislator to consider the passions, the prejudices, and the habits of those for whom he legislates? Indeed, if he overlook these, is he not a reckless experimenter rather than a wise statesman? If he legislates, not for man as he *is*, but for man as he *ought to be*, is he not a political dreamer rather than a sound philosopher?

The abolitionist not only closed his eyes on every appearance of decline in the prosperity of the West Indies, he also seized with avidity every indication of the successful operation of his scheme, and magnified it both to himself and to the world. He made haste, in particular, to paint in the most glowing colors the rising prosperity of Jamaica.[175] His narrative was hailed with eager delight by abolitionists in all parts of the civilized world. It is a pity, we admit, to spoil so fine a story, or to put a damper on so much enthusiasm. But the truth, especially in a case like the present, should be told. While, then, to the enchanted imagination of the abolitionist, the wonderful industry of the freed negroes and the exuberant bounty of nature were concurring to bring about a paradise in the island of Jamaica, the dark stream of emancipation was, in reality, undermining its prosperity and glory. We shall now proceed to adduce the evidence of this melancholy fact, which has in a few short years become so abundant and so overwhelming, that even the most blind and obstinate must feel its force.

After describing the immense sources of wealth to be found in Jamaica, an intelligent eye-witness says: "Such are some of the natural resources of this dilapidated and poverty-stricken country. Capable as it is of producing almost every thing, and actually producing nothing which might not become a staple with a proper application of capital and skill, its inhabitants are miserably poor, and daily sinking deeper into the utter helplessness of abject want.

"'Magnas inter opes inops.'

"Shipping has deserted her ports; her magnificent plantations of sugar and coffee are running to weeds; her private dwellings are falling to decay; the comforts and luxuries which belong to industrial prosperity have been cut off, one by one, from her inhabitants; and the day, I think, is at hand when there will be none left to represent the wealth, intelligence, and hospitality for which the Jamaica planter was once distinguished."[176]

"It is impossible," says Mr. Carey, "to read Mr. Bigelow's volume, without arriving at the conclusion that the freedom granted to the negro has had little effect except that of enabling him to live at the expense of the planter so long as any thing remained. Sixteen years of freedom did not appear to its author to have 'advanced the dignity of labor or of the laboring classes one particle,' while it had ruined the proprietors of the land, and thus great damage had been done to the one class without benefit of any kind to the other.

From a statistical table, published in August, 1853, it appears, says one of our northern journals, that, since 1846, "the number of sugar estates on the island that have been totally abandoned amounts to one hundred and sixty-eight, and the number partially abandoned to sixty-three; the value of which two hundred and thirty-one estates was assessed, in 1841, at £1,655,140, or nearly eight millions and a half of dollars. Within the same period two hundred and twenty-three coffee-plantations have been totally, and twenty partially, abandoned, the assessed value of which was, in 1841, £500,000, or two millions and a half of dollars; and of cattle-pens, (grazing farms,) one hundred and twenty-two have been totally, and ten partially, abandoned, the value of which was a million and a half of dollars. The aggregate value of these six hundred and six estates, which have been thus ruined and abandoned in the island of Jamaica, within the last seven or eight years, amounted by the regular assessments, ten years since, to the sum of nearly two and a half millions of pounds sterling, or twelve and a half millions of dollars."[177]

In relation to Jamaica, another witness says: "The marks of decay abound. Neglected fields, crumbling houses, fragmentary fences, noiseless machinery—these are common sights, and soon become familiar to observation. I sometimes rode for miles in succession over fertile ground, which used to be cultivated, and which is now lying waste. So rapidly has cultivation retrograded, and the wild luxuriance of nature replaced the conveniences of art, that parties still inhabiting these desolated districts have sometimes, in the strong language of a speaker at Kingston, 'to seek about the bush to find the entrance into their houses.'

"The towns present a spectacle no less gloomy. A great part of Kingston was destroyed, some years ago, by an extensive conflagration: yet multitudes of the houses which escaped that visitation are standing empty, though the population is little, if at all, diminished. The explanation is obvious. Persons who have nothing, and can no longer keep up their domestic establishments, take refuge in the abodes of others, where some means of subsistence are still left; and in the absence of any discernible trade or occupation, the lives of crowded thousands appear to be preserved from day to day by a species of miracle. The most busy thoroughfares of former times have now almost the quietude of a Sabbath.

"'The finest land in the world,' says Mr. Bigelow, 'may be had at any price, and almost for the asking.' Labor 'receives no compensation, and the product of labor does not seem to know how to find the way to market.'"[178]

From the report made in 1849, and signed by various missionaries, the moral and religious state of the island appears no less gloomy than its scenes of poverty and distress. The following extract from that report we copy from Mr. Carey's "Slave Trade, Domestic and Foreign:"—

"Missionary efforts in Jamaica are beset at the present time with many and great discouragements. Societies at home have withdrawn or diminished the amount of assistance afforded by them to chapels and schools throughout this island. The prostrate condition of its agriculture and commerce disables its own population from doing as much as formerly for maintaining the worship of God and the tuition of the young, and induces numbers of negro laborers to retire from estates which have been thrown up, to seek the means of subsistence in the mountains, where they are removed in general from moral training and superintendence. The consequences of this state of matters are very disastrous. Not a few missionaries and teachers—often struggling with difficulties which they could not overcome—have returned to Europe, and others are preparing to follow them. Chapels and schools are abandoned, or they have passed into the hands of very incompetent instructors."

We cannot dwell upon each of the West India Islands. Some of these have not suffered so much as others; but while some, from well-known causes, have been partially exempt from the evils of emancipation, all have suffered to a fearful extent. This, as we shall now show, is most amply established by English authorities.

Mr. Bigelow, whose "Notes on Jamaica in 1850" we have noticed, is an American writer; a Northern man; and, it is said, by no means a friend to the institution of slavery. It is certain that Mr. Robert Baird, from whom we shall now quote, is not only a subject of Great Britain, but also a most enthusiastic advocate of "the glorious Act of British Emancipation." But although he admires that act, yet, on visiting the West Indies for his health, he could not fail to be struck with the appalling scenes of distress there exhibited. In describing these, his object is not to reflect shame on the misguided philanthropy of Great Britain; but only to urge the adoption of other measures, in order to rescue the West Indies from the utter ruin and desolation which must otherwise soon overtake them. We might easily adduce many impressive extracts from his work; but, for the sake of brevity, we shall confine our attention to one or two passages.

"Hope," says Mr. Baird, "delights to brighten the prospects of the future; and thus it is that the British West Indian planter goes on from year to year, struggling against his downward progress, and still hoping that something may yet turn up to retrieve his ruined fortunes. But all do not struggle on. Many have given in, and many more can and will confirm the statement of a venerable friend of my own—a gentleman high in office in one of the islands above-mentioned—who, when showing me his own estate and sugar-works, assured me, that for above a quarter of a century they had yielded him nearly £2000 per annum; and that now, despite all his efforts and improvements, (which were many,) he could scarcely manage to make the cultivation pay itself. Instances of this kind might be multiplied till the reader was tired, and even heart-sick, of such details. But what need of such? Is it not notorious? Has it not been proved by the numerous failures that have taken place of late years among our most extensive West Indian merchants? Are not the reports of almost all the governors of our colonial possessions filled with statements to the effect that great depreciation of property has taken place in all and each of our West Indian colonies, and that great has been the distress consequent thereupon? These governors are, of course, all of them imbued, to some extent, with the ministerial policy—at least it is reasonable to assume that they are so. At all events, whether they are so or not, their position almost necessitates their doing their utmost to carry out, with success, the ministerial views and general policy. To embody the substance of the answer given by a talented lieutenant-governor, in my own hearing, to an address which set forth, somewhat strongly, the ruined prospects and wasted fortunes of the colonists under his government: 'It must, or it ought to be, the object and the desire of every governor or lieutenant-governor in the British West Indian Islands, to disappoint and stultify, if he can, the prognostications of coming ruin with which the addresses he receives from time to time are continually charged?' Yet what say these governors? Do not the reports of one and all of them confirm the above statement as to the deplorable state of distress to which the West Indian planters in the British colonies are reduced?"[179]

Again, he says: "That the British West Indian colonists have been loudly complaining that they are ruined, is a fact so generally acknowledged, that the very loudness and frequency of the complaint has been made a reason for disregarding or undervaluing the grounds of it. That the West Indians are always grumbling is an observation often heard; and, no doubt, it is very true that they are so. But let any one who thinks that the extent and clamor of the complaint exceeds the magnitude of the distress which has called it forth, go to the West Indies and judge for himself. Let him see with his own eyes the neglected and abandoned estates,—the uncultivated fields, fast hurrying back into a state of nature, with all the speed of tropical luxuriance—the dismantled and silent machinery, the crumbling walls, and deserted mansions, which are familiar sights in most of the British West Indian colonies. Let him, then, transport himself to the Spanish islands of Porto Rico and Cuba, and witness the life and activity which in these slave colonies prevail. Let him observe for himself the activity of the slavers—the improvements daily making in the cultivation of the fields and in the processes carried on at the Ingenios or sugar-mills—and *the general indescribable air of thriving and prosperity which surrounds the whole,*—and then let him come back to England and say, if he honestly can, that the British West Indian planters and proprietors are grumblers, who complain without adequate cause."[180]

Great Britain has shown no little solicitude to ascertain the real state of things in her West India colonies. For this purpose, she appointed, in 1842, a select committee, consisting of some of the most prominent members of Parliament, with Lord Stanley at their head. In 1848, another committee was appointed by her, with Lord George Bentinck as its chairman, to inquire into the condition of her Majesty's East and West India possessions and the Mauritius, and to consider whether any measures could be adopted for their relief. The report of both committees show, beyond all doubt, that unexampled distress existed in the colonies. The report of 1848 declares: "That many estates in the British West India colonies have been already abandoned, that many more are in the course of abandonment, and that from this cause a very serious diminution is to be apprehended in the total amount of production. That the first effect of this diminution will be an increase in the price of sugar, and the ultimate effect a greater extension to the growth of sugar in slave countries, and a greater impetus to slavery and the slave-trade." From the same report, we also learn that the prosperity of the Mauritius, no less than that of the West India Islands, had suffered a fearful blight, in consequence of the "glorious act of emancipation."

A third commission was appointed, in 1850, to inquire into the condition and prospects of British Guiana. Lord Stanley, in his second letter to Mr. Gladstone, the Secretary of the British colonies, has furnished us with the following extracts from the report of this committee:—

"Of Guiana generally they say—'It would be but a melancholy task to dwell upon the misery and ruin which so alarming a change must have occasioned to the proprietary body; but your commissioners feel themselves called upon to notice the effects which this wholsale abandonment of property has produced upon the colony at large. Where whole districts are fast relapsing into bush, and occasional patches of provisions around the huts of village settlers are all that remain to tell of once flourishing estates, it is not to be wondered at that the most ordinary marks of civilization are rapidly disappearing, and that in many districts of the colony all travelling communication by land will soon become utterly impracticable.'

"Of the Abary district:—'Your commission find that the line of road is nearly impassable, and that a long succession of formerly cultivated estates presents now a series of pestilent swamps, overrun with bush, and productive of malignant fevers.'

"Nor are matters," says Lord Stanley, "much better further south.

"'Proceeding still lower down, your commissioners find that the public roads and bridges are in such a condition that the few estates still remaining on the upper west bank of Mahaica Creek are completely cut off, save in the very dry season; and that with regard to the whole district, unless something be done very shortly, travelling by land will entirely cease. In such a state of things it cannot be wondered at that the herdsman has a formidable enemy to encounter in the jaguar and other beasts of prey, and that the keeping of cattle is attended with considerable loss from the depredations committed by these animals.'

"It may be worth noticing," continues Lord Stanley, "that this district—now overrun with wild beasts of the forest—was formerly the very garden of the colony. The estates touched one another along the whole line of the road, leaving no interval of uncleared land.

"The east coast, which is next mentioned by the commissioners, is better off. Properties, once of immense value, had there been bought at nominal prices; and the one railroad of Guiana passing through that tract, a comparatively industrious population—composed of former laborers on the line—enabled the planters still to work these to some profit. Even of this favored spot, however, they report that it 'feels most severely the want of continuous labor.'

"The commissioners next visit the east bank of the Demerara River, thus described:—

"'Proceeding up the east bank of the river Demerara, the generally prevailing features of ruin and distress are everywhere perceptible. Roads and bridges almost impassable are fearfully significant exponents of the condition of the plantations which they traverse; and Canal No. 3, once covered with plantains and coffee, presents now a scene of almost total desolation.'

"Crossing to the west side, they find prospects somewhat brighter: 'A few estates, are still 'keeping up a cultivation worthy of better times.' But this prosperous neighborhood is not extensive, and the next picture presented to our notice is less agreeable:—

"'Ascending the river still higher, your commissioners learn that the district between Hobaboe Creek and "Stricken Heuvel" contained, in 1829, eight sugar and five coffee and plantain estates, and now there remain but three in sugar, and four partially cultivated with plantains, by petty settlers; while the roads, with one or two exceptions, are in a state of utter abandonment. Here, as on the opposite bank of the river, hordes of squatters have located themselves, who avoid all communication with Europeans, and have seemingly given themselves up altogether to the rude pleasures of a completely savage life.'

"The west coast of Demerara—the only part of the country which still remains unvisited—is described as showing *only* a diminution of fifty per cent. upon its produce of sugar; and with this fact the evidence concludes as to one of the three sections into which the colony is divided. Does Demerara stand alone in its misfortunes?

"Again hear the report:—'If the present state of the county of Demerara affords cause for deep apprehension, your commissioners find that Essequibo has retrograded to a still more alarming extent. In fact, unless a large and speedy supply of labor be obtained to cultivate the deserted fields of this once flourishing district, there is great reason to fear that it will relapse into total abandonment.'

"Describing another portion of the colony—they say of one district, 'Unless a fresh supply of labor be very soon obtained, there is every reason to fear that it will become completely abandoned.' Of a second, 'speedy immigration alone can save this island from total ruin.' 'The prostrate condition of this once beautiful part of the coast,' are the words which begin another paragraph, describing another tract of country. Of a fourth, 'the proprietors on this coast seem to be keeping up a hopeless struggle against approaching ruin.' Again, 'the once famous Arabian coast, so long the boast of the colony, presents now but a mournful picture of departed prosperity. Here were formerly situated some of the finest estates in the country, and a large resident body of proprietors lived in the district, and freely expended their incomes on the spot whence they derived them.' Once more, 'the lower part of the coast, after passing Devonshire Castle, to the river Pomeroon, presents a scene of almost total desolation.' Such is Essequibo!

"Berbice," says Lord Stanley, "has fared no better. Its rural population amounts to 18,000. Of these, 12,000 have withdrawn from the estates, and mostly from the neighborhood of the white man, to enjoy a savage freedom of ignorance and idleness, beyond the reach of example and sometimes of control. But on the condition of the negro I shall dwell more at length hereafter; at present it is the state of property with which I have to do. What are the districts which together form the county of Berbice? The Corentyne coast—the Canje Creek—east and west banks of the Berbice River—and the west coast, where, however, cotton was formerly the chief article produced. To each of these respectively the following passages, quoted in order, apply:—

"'The abandoned plantations on this coast,[181] which, if capital and labor could be procured, might easily be made very productive, are either wholly deserted, or else appropriated by hordes of squatters, who of course are unable to keep up at their own expense the public roads and bridges; and consequently all communication by land between the Corentyne and New Amsterdam is nearly at an end. The roads are impassable for horses or carriages, while for foot passengers they are extremely dangerous. The number of villages in this deserted region must be upward of 2500, and as the country abounds with fish and game, they have no difficulty in making a subsistence. In fact, the Corentyne coast is fast relapsing into a state of nature.'

"'Canje Creek was formerly considered a flourishing district of the county, and numbered on its east bank seven sugar and three coffee estates, and on its west bank eight estates, of which two were in sugar and six in coffee, making a total of eighteen plantations. The coffee cultivation has long since been entirely abandoned, and of the sugar estates but eight still now remain. They are suffering severely for want of labor, and being supported principally by African and Coolie immigrants, it is much to be feared that if the latter leave and claim their return passages to India, a great part of the district will become abandoned.'

"Under present circumstances, so gloomy is the condition of affairs here,[182] that the two gentlemen whom your commissioners have examined with respect to this district, both concur in predicting "its slow but sure approximation to the condition in which civilized man first found it."'

"'A district[183] that in 1829 gave employment to 3635 registered slaves, but at the present moment there are not more than 600 laborers at work on the few estates still in cultivation, although it is estimated there are upward of 2000 people idling in villages of their own. The roads are in many parts several feet under water and perfect swamps, while in some places the bridges are wanting altogether. In fact the whole district is fast becoming a total wilderness, with the exception of the one or two estates which yet continue to struggle on, and which are hardly accessible now but by water.'

"'Except in some of the best villages,[184] they care not for back or front dams to keep off the water; their side-lines are disregarded, and consequently the drainage is gone, while in many instances the public road is so completely flooded that canoes have to be used as a means of transit. The Africans are unhappily following the example of the Creoles in this district, and buying land on which they settle in contented idleness; and your commissioners cannot view instances like these without the deepest alarm, for if this pernicious habit of squatting is allowed to extend to the immigrants also, there is no hope for the colony.'"[185]

We might fill a volume with extracts to the same effect. We might in like manner point to other regions, especially to Guatemala, to the British colony on the southern coast of Africa, and to the island of Hayti, in all of which emancipation has been followed by precisely similar results. But we must hasten to consider how it is that emancipation has wrought all this ruin and desolation. In the mean time, we shall conclude this section in the ever-memorable words of Alison, the historian: "The negroes," says he, "who, in a state of slavery, were comfortable and prosperous beyond any peasantry in the world, and rapidly approaching the condition of the most opulent serfs of Europe, *have been by the act of emancipation irretrievably consigned to a state of barbarism.*"

§ III. *The manner in which emancipation has ruined the British Colonies.*

By the act of emancipation, Great Britain paralyzed the right arm of her colonial industry. The laborer would not work except occasionally, and the planter was ruined. The morals of the negro disappeared with his industry, and he speedily retraced his steps toward his original barbarism. All this had been clearly foretold. "Emancipation," says Dr. Channing in 1840, "was resisted on the ground that the slave, if restored to his rights, *would fall into idleness and vagrancy, and even relapse into barbarism.*"

This was predicted by the West Indian planters, who certainly had a good opportunity to know something of the character of the negro, whether bond or free. But who could suppose for a moment that an enlightened abolitionist would listen to slaveholders? His response was, that "their unhappy position as slaveholders had robbed them of their reason and blunted their moral sense." Precisely the same thing had been foretold by the Calhouns and the Clays of this country. But they, too, were unfortunately slaveholders, and, consequently, so completely "sunk in moral darkness," that their testimony was not entitled to credit. The calmest, the profoundest, the wisest statesman of Great Britain likewise forewarned the agitators of the desolation and the woes they were about to bring upon the West Indies. But the madness of the day would confide in no wisdom except its own, and listen to no testimony except to the clamor of fanatics. Hence the frightful experiment was made, and, as we have seen, the prediction of the anti-abolitionist has been fulfilled to the very letter.

The cause of this downward tendency in the British colonies is now perfectly apparent to all who have eyes to see. On this point, the two committees above referred to both concur in the same conclusion. The committee of 1842 declare, "that the principal causes of this diminished production, and consequent distress, are the great difficulty which has been experienced by the planters in obtaining *steady* and *continuous* labor, and the high rate of remuneration which they give for even the *broken* and *indifferent* work which they are able to procure."

The cry of the abolitionist has been changed. At first—even before the experiment was more than a year old—he insisted that the industry of the freed black was working wonders in the British colonies. In the West Indies, in particular, he assured us that the freed negro would do "an infinity of work for wages."[186] Though he had been on the islands, and had had an opportunity to see for himself, he boasted that "the old notion that the negro is, by constitution, a lazy creature, who will do no work at all except by compulsion, *is now forever exploded.*"[187] He even declared, that the free negro "understands his interest as well as a Yankee."[188] These confident statements, made by an eye-witness, were hailed by the abolitionists as conclusive proof that the experiment was working admirably. "The great truth has come out," says Dr. Channing, "that the hopes of the most sanguine advocates of emancipation have been realized—if not surpassed—by the West Indies." What! the negro become idle, indeed! "He is more likely," says the enchanted doctor, "to fall into the civilized man's cupidity than into the filth and sloth of the savage." But all these magnificent boasts were quite premature. A few short years have suf-ficed to demonstrate that the deluded authors of them, who had so lamentably failed to predict the future, could not even read the present.

Their boasts are now exploded. Their former hopes are blasted; and their cry is changed. The song now is,—"Well, suppose the negroes will not work: they are FREE! They can now do as they list, and there is no man to hinder." Ah, yes! they can now, at their own sweet will, stretch themselves "under their gracefully-waving groves," and be lulled to sleep amid the sound of waterfalls and the song of birds.

Such, precisely, is the paradise for which the negro sighs, except that he does not care for the waterfalls and the birds. But it should be remarked, that when sinful man was dri-ven from the only Paradise that earth has ever seen, he was doomed to eat his bread in the sweat of his brow. This doom he cannot reverse. Let him make of life—as the Haytien negroes do—"one long day of unprofitable ease,"[189] and he may dream of Paradise, or the abolitionists may dream for him. But while he dreams, the laws of nature are sternly at their work. Indolence benumbs his feeble intellect, and inflames his passions. Poverty and want are creeping on him. Temptation is surrounding him; and vice, with all her mot-ley train, is winding fast her deadly coils around his very soul, and making him the devil's slave, to do his work upon the earth. Thus, the blossoms of his paradise are *fine words*, and its fruits are *death*.

"If but two hours' labor per day," says Theodore Parker, "are necessary for the support of each colored man, I know not why he should toil longer." You know not, then, why the colored man should work more than two hours a day? Neither does the colored man himself. You know not why he should have any higher or nobler aim in life than to supply his few, pressing, animal wants? Neither does he. You know not why he should think of the future, or provide for the necessities of old age? Neither does he. You know not why he should take thought for seasons of sickness? Neither does he; and hence his child often dies under his own eyes, for the want of medical attendance. You know not that the colored man, who begins with working only two hours a day, will soon end with ceasing from all regular employment, and live, in the midst of filth, by stealing or other nefarious means? In one word, you know not why the colored man should not live like the brute, in and for the present merely—blotting out all the future from his plans of life? If, indeed, you really know none of these things, then we beg you will excuse us, if *we* do not know why you should assume to teach our senators wisdom;—if we do not know why the cobbler should not stick to his last, and all such preachers to their pulpits.[190]

Abolitionism is decidedly progressive. The time was when Dr. Channing thought that men should work, and that, if they would not labor from rational motives, they should be compelled to labor.[191] The time was, when even abolitionists looked upon labor with respect, and regarded it as merely an obedience to the very first law of nature, or merely a compliance with the very first condition of all economic, social, and moral well-being. But the times are changed. The exigencies of abolitionism now require that *manual labor, and the gross material wealth* it produces, should be sneeringly spoken of, and great swelling eulogies pronounced on the infinite value of the negro's freedom. For this is all he has; and for this, all else has been sacrificed. Thus, since abolitionists themselves have been made to see that the freed negro—the pet and idol of their hearts—will not work from rational motives, then the principles of political economy, and the affairs of the world, all must be adjusted to the course *he* may be pleased to take.

In this connection we shall notice a passage from Montesquieu, which is exactly in point. He is often quoted by the abolitionists, but seldom fairly. It is true, he is exceedingly hostile to slavery *in general*, and very justly pours ridicule and contempt on some of the arguments used in favor of the institution. But yet, with all his enthusiastic love of liberty,—nay, with his ardent passion for equality,—he saw far too deeply into the true "Spirit of Laws" not to perceive that slavery is, in certain cases, founded on the great principles of political justice. It is precisely in those cases in which a race or a people will not work without being compelled to do so, that he justifies the institution in question. Though warmly and zealously opposed to slavery, yet he was not bent on sacrificing the good of society to abstractions or to prejudice. Hence, he could say: "But as all men are born equal, slavery must be accounted unnatural, THOUGH IN SOME COUNTRIES IT BE FOUNDED ON NATURAL REASON; and a wide difference ought to be made betwixt such countries, and those in which natural reason rejects it, as in Europe, where it has been happily abolished."[192] Now, if we inquire in what countries, or under what circumstances, he considered slavery founded on natural reason, we may find his answer in a preceding portion of the same page. It is in those "countries," says he, "where the excess of heat enervates the body, and renders men so slothful and dispirited, that nothing but the fear of chastisement can oblige them to perform any laborious duty," etc. Such, as we have seen, is precisely the case with the African race in its present condition.

"Natural slavery, then," he continues, "is to be limited to some particular parts of the world."[193] And again: "Bad laws have made lazy men—they have been reduced to slavery because of their laziness." The first portion of this remark—that bad laws have made lazy men—is not applicable to the African race. For they were made lazy, not by bad laws, but by the depravity of human nature, in connection and co-operation with long, long centuries of brutal ignorance and the most savage modes of life. But, be the cause of this laziness what it may, it is sufficient, according to the principles of this great advocate of human freedom and equality, to justify the servitude in which the providence of God has placed the African.

No doubt it is very hard on lazy men that they should be compelled to work. It is for this reason that Montesquieu calls such slavery "the most cruel that is to be found among men;" by which he evidently means that it is the most cruel, though necessary, because those on whom it is imposed are least inclined to work. If he had only had greater experience of negro slavery, the hardship would have seemed far less to him. For though the negro is naturally lazy, and too improvident to work for himself, he will often labor for a master with a right good will, and with a loyal devotion to his interests. He is, indeed, often prepared, and made ready for labor, because he feels that, in his master, he has a protector and a friend.

But whether labor be a heavy burden or a light, it must be borne. The good of the lazy race, and the good of the society into which they have been thrown, both require them to bear this burden, which is, after all and at the worst, far lighter than that of a vagabond life. "Nature cries aloud," says the abolitionist, "for freedom." Nature, we reply, demands that man shall work, and her decree must be fulfilled. For ruin, as we have seen, is the bitter fruit of disobedience to her will.

It is now high time that we should notice some of the exalted eulogies bestowed by abolitionists upon freedom; and also *the kind of freedom* on which these high praises have been so eloquently lavished. This, accordingly, we shall proceed to do in the following section.

§ IV. *The great benefit supposed by American abolitionists to result to the freed negroes from the British act of emancipation.*

We have, in the preceding sections, abundantly seen that the freed colored subjects of the British crown are fast relapsing into the most irretrievable barbarism, while the once flourishing colonies themselves present the most appalling scenes of desolation and distress. Surely it is no wonder that the hurrahing of the English people has ceased. "At the present moment," says the London Times for December 1st, 1852, "if there is one thing in the world that the British public do not like to talk about, or *even to think about*, it is the condition of the race for whom this great effort was made." Not so with the abolitionists of this country. They still keep up the annual celebration of that great event, the act of emancipation, by which, in the language of one of their number, more than half a million of human beings were "turned from brutes into freemen!"

It is the freedom of the negro which they celebrate. Let us look, then, for a few moments, into the mysteries of this celebration, and see, if we may, the nature of the praises they pour forth in honor of freedom, and *the kind of freedom on which* they are so passionately bestowed.

We shall not quote from the more insane of the fraternity of abolitionists, for their wild, raving nonsense would, indeed, be unworthy of serious refutation. We shall simply notice the language of Dr. Channing, the scholar-like and the eloquent, though visionary, advocate of British emancipation. Even as early as 1842, in an address delivered on the anniversary of that event, he burst into the following strain of impassioned eulogy: "Emancipation works well, far better than could have been anticipated. *To me it could hardly have worked otherwise than well.* It banished *slavery*, that wrong and curse not to be borne. It gave *freedom*, the dear birthright of humanity; and had it done nothing more, I should have found in it cause for joy. Freedom, simple freedom, is 'in my estimation just, far prized above all price.' *I do not stop to ask if the emancipated are better fed and clothed than formerly.* THEY ARE FREE; AND THAT ONE WORD CONTAINS A WORLD OF GOOD,[194] unknown to the most pampered slave." And again, he says, "Nature cries aloud for freedom as our proper good, our birthright and our end, and resents nothing so much as its loss."

In these high-sounding praises, which hold up personal freedom as "our proper good," as "our end," it is assumed that man was made for liberty, and not liberty for man. It is, indeed, one of the fundamental errors of the abolitionist to regard freedom as a great substantive good, or as in itself a blessing, and not merely as a relative good. It may be, and indeed often is, an unspeakable benefit, but then it is so only as a means to an end. The end of our existence, the *proper good*, is the improvement of our intellectual and moral powers, the perfecting of our rational and immortal natures. When freedom subserves this end, it is a good; when it defeats this end, it is an evil. Hence there may be a world of evil as well as a world of good in "this one word."

The wise man adapts the means to the end. It were the very hight of folly to sacrifice the end to the means. No man gives personal freedom to his child because he deems it always and in all cases a good. His heart teaches him a better doctrine when the highest good of his child is concerned. Should we not be permitted, then, to have something of the same feeling in regard to those whom Providence has placed under our care, especially since, having the passions of men, with only the intellects of children, they stand in utmost need of guidance and direction?

As it is their duty to labor, so the law which compels them to do so is not oppressive. It deprives them of the enjoyment of no right, unless, indeed, they may be supposed to have a right to violate their duty. Hence, in compelling the colored population of the South to work, the law does not deprive them of liberty, in the true sense of the word; that is, *it does not deprive them of the enjoyment of any natural right*. It merely requires them to perform a natural duty.

This cannot be denied. It has been, as we have shown, admitted both by Dr. Wayland and Dr. Channing.[195] But while the *end* is approved, the *means* are not liked. Few of the abolitionists are disposed to offer any substitute for our method. They are satisfied merely to pull down and destroy, without the least thought or care in regard to consequences.

Dr. Channing has, however, been pleased to propose another method, for securing the industry of the black and the prosperity of the State. Let us then, for a moment, look at this scheme.

The black man, says he, should not be owned. He should work, but not under the control of a master. His overseer should be appointed by the State, and be amenable to the State for the proper exercise of his authority. Now, if this learned and eloquent orator had only looked one inch beneath the surface of his own scheme, he would have seen that it is fraught with the most insuperable difficulties, and that its execution must needs be attended with the most ruinous consequences.

Emancipate the blacks, then, and let the State undertake to work them. In the first place, we must ignore every principle of political economy, and consent to the wildest and most reckless of experiments, ere we can agree that the State should superintend and carry on the agricultural interests of the country. But suppose this difficulty out of the way, on what land would the State cause *its slaves* to be worked? It would scarcely take possession of the plantations now under improvements; and, setting aside the owners, proceed to cultivate the land. But it must either do this, or else leave these plantations to become worthless for the want of laborers, and open new ones for the benefit of the State! In no point of view could a more utterly chimerical or foolish scheme be well conceived. If we may not be allowed to adhere to our own plan, we beg that some substitute may be proposed which is not fraught with such inevitable destruction to the whole South. Otherwise, we shall fear that these self-styled friends of humanity are more bent on carrying out their own designs than they are on promoting our good.

But what is meant by the freedom of the emancipated slaves, on which so many exalted eulogies have been pronounced? Its first element, it is plain, is a freedom from labor[196]—freedom from the very first law of nature. In one word, its sum and substance is a power on the part of the freed black to act pretty much as he pleases. Now, before we expend oceans of enthusiasm on such a freedom, would it not be well to see *how* he would be pleased to act?

Dr. Channing has told us, we are aware, of the "indomitable love of liberty," which had been infused into the breast of "fierce barbarians" by their native wildernesses.[197] But we are no great admirers of a liberty which knows no law except its own will, and seeks no end except the gratification of passion.[198] Hence, we have no very great respect for the liberty of fierce barbarians. It would make a hell on earth. "My maxim," exclaims Dr. Channing, "is anything but slavery!" Even slavery, we cry, before a freedom such as his!

This kind of freedom, it should be remembered, was born in France and cradled in the revolution. May it never be forgotten that the "Friends of the Blacks" at Boston had their exact prototypes in "*les Amis des Noirs*" of Paris. Of this last society Robespierre was the ruling spirit, and Brissot the orator. By the dark machinations of the one,[199] and the fiery eloquence of the other, the French people—*la grande nation*—were induced, in 1791, to proclaim the principle of equality to and for the free blacks of St. Domingo. This beautiful island, then the brightest and most precious jewel in the crown of France, thus became the first of the West Indies in which the dreadful experiment of a forced equality was tried. The authors of that experiment were solemnly warned of the horrors into which it would inevitably plunge both the whites and the blacks of the island. Yet, firm and immovable as death, Robespierre sternly replied, then "Perish the colonies rather than sacrifice one iota of our principles!"[200] The magnificent colony of St. Domingo did not quite perish, it is true; but yet, as every one, except the philanthropic "Ami des Noirs" of the present day, still remembers with a thrill of horror, the entire white population soon melted, like successive flakes of snow, in the furnace of that freedom which a Robespierre had kindled.

The atrocities of this awful massacre have had, as the historian has said,[201] no parallel in the annals of human crime. "The negroes," says Alison, "marched with spiked infants on their spears instead of colors; they sawed asunder the male prisoners, and violated the females on the dead bodies of their husbands." The work of death, thus completed with such outbursts of unutterable brutality, constituted and closed the first act in the grand drama of Haytien freedom.

But equality was not yet established. The colored men, or mulattoes, beheld, with an eye burning with jealousy, the superior power and ascendency of the blacks. Hence arose the horrors of a civil war. Equality had been proclaimed, and anarchy produced. In this frightful chaos, the ambitious mulattoes, whose insatiable desire of equality had first disturbed the peace of the island, perished miserably beneath the vengeance of the very slaves whom they had themselves roused from subjection and elevated into irresistible power. Thus ended the second act of the horrible drama.

This bloody discord, this wild chaos of disgusting brutalities, of course terminated not in freedom, but in a military despotism. With the subsequent wars and fearful destruction of human life our present inquiry has nothing to do. We must confine our attention to the point before us, namely, the kind of freedom achieved by the blacks of St. Domingo. We have witnessed the two great manifestations of that freedom; we shall now look at its closing scene. This we shall, for obvious reasons, present in the language of an English author.

"An independent negro state," says he, "was thus established in Hayti; but the people have not derived all the benefits which they sanguinely expected. Released from their compulsory toil, they have not yet learned to subject themselves to the restraints of regular industry. The first absolute rulers made the most extraordinary efforts to overcome the indolence which soon began to display itself. The *Code Rural* directed that the laborer should fix himself on a certain estate, which he was never afterward to quit without a passport from the government. His hours of labor and rest were fixed by statute. The whip, at first permitted, was ultimately prohibited; but as every military officer was allowed to chastise with a thick cane, and almost every proprietor held a commission, the laborer was not much relieved. By these means Mr. Mackenzie supposes that the produce of 1806 was raised to about a third of that of 1789. But such violent regulations could not continue to be enforced amid the succeeding agitations, and under a republican *régime*. Almost all traces of laborious culture were soon obliterated; large tracts, which had been one entire sugar garden, presented now only a few scattered plantations."[202]

Thus the lands were divided out among the officers of the army, while the privates were compelled to cultivate the soil under their former military commanders, clothed with more than "a little brief authority." No better could have been expected except by fools or fanatics. The blacks might preach equality, it is true, but yet, like the more enlightened ruffians of Paris, they would of course take good care not to practice what they had preached. Hence, by all the horrors of their bloody resolution, they only effected a change of masters. The white man had disappeared, and the black man, one of their own race and color, had assumed his place and his authority. And of all masters, it is well known, the naturally servile are the most cruel. "The earth," says Solomon, "cannot bear a servant when he reigneth."[203]

"The sensual and the dark rebel in vain:
Slaves by their own compulsion, in mad game
They burst their manacles, to wear the *name*
Of Freedom, graven on a heavier chain."

COLERIDGE.

Thus "the world of good" they sought was found, most literally, in "the word;" for the word, the name of freedom, was all they had achieved—at least of good. Poverty, want, disease, and crime, were the substantial fruits of their boasted freedom.

In 1789, the sugar exported was 672,000,000 pounds; in 1806, it was 47,516,531 pounds; in 1825, it was 2020 pounds; in 1832, it was 0 pounds. If history had not spoken, we might have safely inferred, from this astounding decline of industry, that the morals of the people had suffered a fearful deterioration. But we are not left to inference. We are informed, by the best authorities,[204] that their "morals are exceedingly bad;" and that under the reign of liberty, as it is called, their condition has, in all respects, become far worse than it was before. "There appears every reason to apprehend," says James Franklin, "that it will recede into irrecoverable insignificance, poverty, and disorder."[205]

Mr. T. Babington Macaulay has, we are aware, put forth certain notions on the subject of liberty, which are exactly in accordance with the views and the spirit of the abolitionists, as well as with the cut-throat philosophy of the Parisian philanthropists of the revolution. As these notions are found in one of his juvenile productions, and illustrated by "a pretty story" out of Ariosto, we should not deem it worth while to notice them, if they had not been retained in the latest edition of his Miscellanies. But for this circumstance, we should pass them by as the rhetorical flourish of a young man who, in his most mature productions, is often more brillant than profound.

"Ariosto," says he, "tells a pretty story of a fairy, who, by some mysterious law of her nature, was condemned to appear at certain seasons in the form of a foul and poisonous snake. Those who injured her during the period of her disguise were forever excluded from participation in the blessings which she bestowed. But to those who, in spite of her loathsome aspect, pitied and protected her, she afterward revealed herself in the beautiful and celestial form which was natural to her, accompanied their steps, granted all their wishes, filled their houses with wealth, made them happy in love, and victorious in war. Such a spirit is Liberty. At times she takes the form of a hateful reptile. She grovels, she hisses, she stings. But wo to those who in disgust shall venture to crush her! And happy are those who, having dared to receive her in her degraded and frightful shape, shall at length be rewarded by her in the time of her beauty and her glory."

For aught we know, all this may be very fine poetry, and may deserve the place which it has found in some of our books on rhetoric. But yet this beautiful passage will—like the fairy whose charms it celebrates—be so surely transformed into a hateful snake or venomous toad, that it should not be swallowed without an antidote. Robespierre, Danton, Marat, Barrière, and the black Dessalines, took this hateful, hissing, stinging, maddening reptile to their bosoms, and they are welcome to its rewards. But they mistook the thing: it was not liberty transformed; it was tyranny unbound, the very scourge of hell, and Satan's chief instrument of torture to a guilty world. It was neither more nor less than Sin, despising GOD, and warring against his image on the earth.

We do not doubt—nay, we firmly believe—that in the veritable history of the universe, *analogous* changes have taken place. But then these awful changes were not mere fairy tales. They are recorded in the word of God. When Lucifer, the great bearer of light, himself was *free*, he sought equality with God, and thence became a hateful, hissing serpent in the dust. But he was not fully cursed, until "by devilish art" he reached "the organs of man's fancy," and with them forged the grand illusion that equality alone is freedom.

For even sinless, happy Eve was made to feel herself oppressed, until, with keen desire of equality with gods, "forth reaching to the fruit, she plucked, she ate:"—

> "Earth felt the wound, and Nature from her seat,
> Sighing through all her works, gave signs of wo,
> That all was lost."

How much easier, then, to effect the ruin of poor, fallen man, by stirring up this fierce desire of equality with discontented thoughts and vain hopes of unattainable good! It is this dark desire, and not liberty, which, in its rage, becomes the "poisonous snake;" and, though decked in fine, allegoric, glowing garb, it is still the loathsome thing, the "false worm," that turned God's Paradise itself into a blighted world.

If Mr. Macaulay had only distinguished between liberty and license, than which no two things in the universe are more diametrically opposed to each other, his passion for fine rhetoric would not have betrayed him into so absurd a conceit respecting the diverse forms of freedom. Liberty is—as we have seen—the bright emanation of reason in the form of law; license is the triumph of blind passion over all law and order. Hence, if we would have liberty, the great deep of human passion must be restrained. For this purpose, as Mr. Burke has said, there must be power somewhere; and if there be not moral power within, there must be physical power without. Otherwise, the restraints will be too weak; the safeguards of liberty will give way, and the passions of men will burst into anarchy, the most frightful of all the forms of tyranny. Shall we call this liberty? Shall we seek the secure enjoyment of natural rights in a wild reign of lawless terror? As well might we seek the pure light of heaven in the bottomless pit. It is, indeed, a most horrible desecration of the sacred name of liberty, to apply it either to the butcheries and brutalities of the French Revolution, or to the more diabolical massacres of St. Domingo. If such were freedom, it would, in sober truth, be more fitly symbolized by ten thousand hissing serpents than by a single poisonous snake; and by all on earth, as in heaven, it should be abhorred. Hence, those pretended friends and advocates of freedom, who would thus fain transmute her form divine into such horribly distorted shapes, are with her enemies confederate in dark, misguided league.

§ V. *The consequences of abolition to the South.*

"We have had experience enough in our own colonies," says the *Prospective Review*, for November, 1852, "not to wish to see the experiment tried elsewhere on a larger scale." Now this, though it comes to us from across the Atlantic, really sounds like the voice of genuine philanthropy. Nor do we wish to see the experiment, which has brought down such wide-spread ruin on all the great interests of St. Domingo and the British colonies, tried in this prosperous and now beautiful land of ours. It requires no prophet to foresee the awful consequences of such an experiment on the lives, the liberties, the fortunes, and the morals, of the people of the Southern States. Let us briefly notice some of these consequences.

Consider, in the first place, the vast amount of property which would be destroyed by the madness of such an experiment. According to the estimate of Mr. Clay, "the total value of the slave property in the United States is twelve hundred millions of dollars," all of which the people of the South are expected to sacrifice on the altar of abolitionism. It only moves the indignation of the abolitionist that we should for one moment hesitate. "I see," he exclaims, "in the immenseness of the value of the slaves, the enormous amount of the robbery committed on them. I see 'twelve hundred millions of dollars' seized, extorted by unrighteous force."[206] But, unfortunately, his passions are so furious, that his mind no sooner comes into contact with any branch of the subject of slavery, than instantly, as if by a flash of lightning, his opinion is formed, and he begins to declaim and denounce as if reason should have nothing to do with the question. He does not even allow himself time for a single moment's serious reflection. Nay, resenting the opinion of the most sagacious of our statesmen as an insult to his understanding, he deems it beneath his dignity even to make an attempt to look beneath the surface of the great problem on which he condescends to pour the illuminations of his genius. Ere we accept his oracles as inspired, we beg leave to think a little, and consider their intrinsic value.

Twelve hundred millions of dollars extorted by unrighteous force! What enormous robbery! Now, let it be borne in mind, that this is the language of a man who, as we have seen, has—in one of his lucid intervals—admitted that *it is right to apply force* to compel those to work who will not labor from rational motives. Such is precisely the application of the force which now moves his righteous indignation!

This force, so justly applied, has created this enormous value of twelve hundred millions of dollars. It has neither seized, nor extorted this vast amount from others; it has simply created it out of that which, but for such force, would have been utterly valueless. And if experience teaches any thing, then, no sooner shall this force be withdrawn, than the great value in question will disappear. It will not be restored; it will be annihilated. The slaves—now worth so many hundred millions of dollars—would become worthless to themselves, and nuisances to society. No free State in the Union would be willing to receive them—or a considerable portion of them—into her dominions. They would be regarded as pests, and, if possible, everywhere expelled from the empires of freemen.

Our lands, like those of the British West Indies, would become almost valueless for the want of laborers to cultivate them. The most beautiful garden-spots of the sunny South would, in the course of a few years, be turned into a jungle, with only here and there a forlorn plantation. Poverty and distress, bankruptcy and ruin, would everywhere be seen. In one word, the condition of the Southern States would, in all material respects, be like that of the once flourishing British colonies in which the fatal experiment of emancipation has been tried.

Such are some of the fearful consequences of emancipation. But these are not all. The ties that would be severed, and the sympathies crushed, by emancipation, are not at all understood by abolitionists. They are, indeed, utter strangers to the moral power which these ties and sympathies now exert for the good of the inferior race. "Our patriarchal scheme of domestic servitude," says Governor Hammond, "is indeed well calculated to awaken the higher and finer feelings of our nature. It is not wanting in its enthusiasm and its poetry. The relations of the most beloved and honored chiefs, and the most faithful and admiring subjects, which, from the time of Homer, have been the theme of song, are frigid and unfelt, compared with those existing between the master and his slaves; who served his father, and rocked his cradle, or have been born in his household, and look forward to serve his children; who have been through life the props of his fortune, and the objects of his care; who have partaken of his griefs, and looked to him for comfort in their own; whose sickness he has so frequently watched over and relieved; whose holidays he has so often made joyous by his bounties and his presence; for whose welfare, when absent, his anxious solicitude never ceases, and whose hearty and affectionate greetings never fail to welcome him home. In this cold, calculating, ambitious world of ours, there are few ties more heart-felt, or of more benignant influence, than those which mutually bind the master and the slave, under our ancient system, handed down from the father of Israel."

Let the slaves be emancipated then, and, in one or two generations, the white people of the South would care as little for the freed blacks among us, as the same class of persons are now cared for by the white people of the North. The prejudice of race would be restored with unmitigated violence. The blacks are contented in servitude, so long as they find themselves excluded from none of the privileges of the condition to which they belong; but let them be delivered from the authority of their masters, and they will feel their rigid exclusion from the society of the whites and all participation in their government. They would become clamorous for "their inalienable rights." Three millions of freed blacks, thus circumstanced, would furnish the elements of the most horrible civil war the world has ever witnessed.

These elements would soon burst in fury on the land. There was no civil war in Jamaica, it is true, after the slaves were emancipated; but this was because the power of Great Britain was over the two parties, and held them in subjection. It would be far otherwise here. For here there would be no power to check—while there would be infernal agencies at work to promote—civil discord and strife. As Robespierre caused it to be proclaimed to the free blacks of St. Domingo that they were naturally entitled to all the rights and privileges of citizens; as Mr. Seward proclaimed the same doctrine to the free blacks of New York; so there would be kind benefactors enough to propagate the same sentiments among our colored population. They would be instigated, in every possible way, to claim their natural equality with the whites; and, by every diabolical art, their bad passions would be inflamed. If the object of such agitators were merely to stir up scenes of strife and blood, it might be easily attained; but if it were to force the blacks into a social and political equality with the whites, it would most certainly and forever fail. For the government of these Southern States was, by our fathers, founded on the VIRTUE and the INTELLIGENCE of the people, and there we intend it shall stand. The African has neither part nor lot in the matter.

We cannot suppose, for a moment, that abolitionists would be in the slightest degree moved by the awful consequences of emancipation. Poverty, ruin, death, are very small items with these sublime philanthropists. They scarcely enter into their calculations. The dangers of a civil war—though the most fearful the world has ever seen—lie quite beneath the range of their humanity.

Indeed, we should expect our argument from the consequences of emancipation to be met by a thorough-going abolitionist with the words,—"Perish the Southern States rather than sacrifice one iota of our principles!" We ask them not to sacrifice their principles to us; nor do we intend that they shall sacrifice us to their principles. For if perish we must, it shall be as a sacrifice to our own principles, and not to theirs.

NOTE.—It has not fallen within the scope of our design to consider the effects of emancipation, and of the consequent destruction of so large an amount of property, on the condition and prosperity of the world. Otherwise it might easily have been shown that every civilized portion of the globe would feel the shock. This point has been very happily, though briefly, illustrated by Governor Hammond, in his "Letters on Slavery."

Nor has it formed any part of our purpose, in the following section, to discuss the influence of American slavery on the future destiny and civilization of Africa. This subject has been ably discussed by various writers; and especially by an accomplished divine, the Rev. William N. Pendleton, in a discourse published in the "Virginian Colonizationist," for September, 1854.

§ VI. *Elevation of the Blacks by Southern slavery.*

The abolitionists, with the most singular unanimity, perseveringly assert that Southern slavery degrades its subjects "into brutes." This assertion fills us with amazement. If it were possible, we would suppose, in a judgment of charity, that its authors knew nothing of the history of Africa or of the condition of our slaves. But such ignorance is not possible. On the other hand, we find it equally impossible to believe that so many men and women—the very lights of abolitionism—could knowingly utter so palpable a falsehood. Thus we are forced to the conclusion, that the authors of this charge are so completely carried away by a blind hatred of slavery, that they do not care to keep their words within the sacred bounds of eternal truth. This seems to be the simple, melancholy fact. The great question with them seems to be, not what is true or what is false, but what will most speedily effect the destruction of Southern slavery. Any thing that seems to answer this purpose is blindly and furiously wielded by them. The Edinburgh Review, in a high-wrought eulogy on an American authoress, says that she assails slavery with arrows "poisoned by truth." Her words, it is true, are dipped in flaming poison; but *that* poison is not truth. The truth is never poison.

The native African could not be degraded. Of the fifty millions of inhabitants of the continent of Africa, it is estimated that forty millions were slaves. The master had the power of life and death over the slave; and, in fact, his slaves were often fed, and killed, and eaten, just as we do with oxen and sheep in this country. Nay, the hind and fore-quarters of men, women, and children, might there be seen hung on the shambles and exposed for sale! Their women were beasts of burden; and, when young, they were regarded as a great delicacy by the palate of their pampered masters. A warrior would sometimes take a score of young females along with him, in order to enrich his feasts and regale his appetite. He delighted in such delicacies. As to his religion, it was even worse than his morals; or rather, his religion was a mass of the most disgusting immoralities. His notion of a God, and the obscene acts by which that notion was worshiped, are too shocking to be mentioned. The vilest slave that ever breathed the air of a Christian land could not begin to conceive the horrid iniquities of such a life. And yet, in the face of all this, we are told—yea, we are perseveringly and eternally told—that "the African has been degraded into a brute" by American slavery! Indeed, if such creatures ever reach the level of simple brutality at all, is it not evident they must be elevated, and not degraded, to it?

The very persons who make the above charge know better. Their own writings furnish the most incontestable proof that they know better. A writer in the Edinburgh Review,[207] for example, has not only asserted that "slavery degrades its subjects into brutes," but he has the audacity to declare, in regard to slavery in the United States, that "we do not believe that such oppression is to be found in any other part of the world, civilized or uncivilized. We do not believe that such oppression ever existed before." Yet even this unprincipled writer has, in the very article containing this declaration, shown that he knows better. He has shown that he knows that the African has been elevated and improved by his servitude in the United States. We shall proceed to convict him out of his own mouth.

"The African slave-trade was frightful," says he; "but its prey were savages, accustomed to suffering and misery, and to endure them with patience almost amounting to apathy. The victims of the American slave-trade have been bred in a highly-cultivated community. Their dispositions have been softened, their intellects sharpened, and their sensibilities excited, by society, by Christianity, and by all the ameliorating but enervating influences of civilization. The savage submits to be enslaved himself, or have his wife or his child carried off by his enemies, as merely a calamity. His misery is not embittered by indignation. He suffers only what—if he could—he would inflict. He cannot imagine a state of society in which there shall not be masters and slaves, kidnapping and man-selling, coffles and slave-traders, or in which any class shall be exempt from misfortunes which appear to him to be incidental to humanity."

Thus, according to this very sagacious, honest, consistent writer, it matters little what you do with the native African: he has no moral sense; he feels no wrong; he suffers only what he would inflict. But when you come to deal with the American slave, or, as this writer calls him, "the civilized Virginian," it is quite another thing! His dispositions have been softened, his intellect sharpened, and his sensibilities roused to a new life, by society and by Christianity! And yet, according to this very writer, this highly civilized Virginian is the man who, by American slavery, has been degraded from the native African into a brute! We dismiss his lawless savage, and his equally lawless pen, from our further consideration.

We proceed, in like manner, to condemn Dr. Channing out of his own mouth. He has repeatedly asserted that slavery among us degrades its subjects into brutes. Now hear him on the other side of this question.

"The European race," says he, "have manifested more courage, enterprise, invention; but in the dispositions which Christianity particularly honors, how inferior are they to the African? When I cast my eyes over our Southern region,—the land of bowie-knives, lynch-law, and duels, of 'chivalry,' 'honor,' and revenge; and when I consider that Christianity is declared to be a spirit of charity, 'which seeketh not its own, is not easily provoked, thinketh no evil, and endureth all things,' and is also declared to be 'the wisdom from above,' which is 'first pure, then peaceable, gentle, easy to be entreated, full of mercy and good fruits;' can I hesitate in deciding to which of the races in that land Christianity is most adapted, and in which its noblest disciples are most likely to be reared?"[208]

It was by casting his eyes over "our Southern region" that Dr. Channing concluded "that we are holding in bondage one of the best races of the human family." If he had cast them over the appallingly dark region of Africa, he would have been compelled, in spite of the wonder-working power of his imagination, to pronounce it one of the very worst and most degraded races upon earth. If, as he imagines, this race among us is now nearer to the kingdom of heaven than we ourselves are, how dare he assert—as he so often has done—that our slavery has "degraded them into brutes?" If, indeed, they had not been elevated—both physically and morally—by their servitude in America, it would have been beyond the power of even Dr. Channing to pronounce such a eulogy upon them. We say, then, that he knew better when he asserted that we have degraded them into brutes. He spoke, not from his better knowledge and his conscience, but from blind, unreflecting passion. For he knew—if he knew any thing—that the blacks have been elevated and improved by their contact with the whites of this enlightened portion of the globe.

The truth is, the abolitionist can make the slave a brute or a saint, just as it may happen to suit the exigency of his argument. If slavery degrades its subjects into brutes, then one would suppose that slaves are brutes. But the moment you speak of selling a slave, he is no longer a brute,—he is a civilized man, with all the most tender affections, with all the most generous emotions. If the object be to excite indignation against slavery, then it always transforms its subjects into brutes; but if it be to excite indignation against the slaveholder, then he holds, not brutes, but a George Harris—or an Eliza—or an Uncle Tom—in bondage. Any thing, and every thing, except fair and impartial statement, are the materials with which he works.

No fact is plainer than that the blacks have been elevated and improved by their servitude in this country. We cannot possibly conceive, indeed, how Divine Providence could have placed them in a better school of correction. If the abolitionists can conceive a better method for their enlightenment and religious improvement, we should rejoice to see them carry their plan into execution. They need not seek to rend asunder our Union, on account of the three millions of blacks among us, while there are fifty millions of the same race on the continent of Africa, calling aloud for their sympathy, and appealing to their Christian benevolence. Let them look to that continent. Let them rouse the real, active, self-sacrificing benevolence of the whole Christian world in behalf of that most degraded portion of the human family; and, after all, if they will show us on the continent of Africa, or elsewhere, three millions of blacks in as good a condition—physically and morally—as our slaves, then will we most cheerfully admit that all other Christian nations, combined, have accomplished as much for the African race, as has been done by the Southern States of the Union.

CHAPTER V

THE FUGITIVE SLAVE LAW.

Mr. Seward's Attack on the Constitution of his Country—The Attack of Mr. Sumner on the Constitution of his Country—The Right of Trial by Jury not impaired by the Fugitive Slave Law—The Duty of the Citizen in regard to the Constitution of the United States.

WE have, under our present Union, advanced in prosperity and greatness beyond all former example in the history of nations. We no sooner begin to reason from the past to the future, than we are lost in amazement at the prospect before us. We behold the United States, and that too at no very distant period, the first power among the nations of the earth. But such reasoning is not always to be relied on. Whether, in the present instance, it points to a reality, or to a magnificent dream merely, will of course depend on the wisdom, the integrity, and the moderation, of our rulers.

It cannot be disguised that the Union, with all its unspeakable advantages and blessings, is in danger. It is the Fugitive Slave Law against which the waves of abolitionism have dashed with their utmost force and raged with an almost boundless fury. On the other hand, it is precisely the Fugitive Slave Law—that great constitutional guarantee of our rights—which the people of the South are, as one man, the most inflexibly determined to maintain. We are prepared, and we shall accordingly proceed, to show that, in this fearful conflict, the great leaders of abolitionism—the Chases, the Sewards, and the Sumners, of the day—are waging a fierce, bitter, and relentless warfare against the Constitution of their country.

§ I. *Mr. Seward's attack on the Constitution of his country.*

There is one thing which Mr. Seward's reasoning overlooks,—namely, that he has taken an oath to support the Constitution of the United States. We shall not lose sight of this fact, nor permit him to obscure it by his special pleadings and mystifications; since it serves to show that while, in the name of a "higher law," he denounces the Constitution of his country, he at the same time commits a most flagrant outrage against that higher law itself.

The clause of the Constitution which Mr. Seward denounces is as follows: "No person held to service or labor in one State, under the laws thereof, escaping into another, shall, in consequence of any law or regulation therein, be discharged from such service or labor, but shall be delivered up on claim of the party to whom such service or labor may be due." This clause, as Mr. Seward contemptuously says, is "from the Constitution of the United States in 1787." He knows of only one other compact like this "in diplomatic history;" and that was made between despotic powers "in the year of grace 902, in the period called the Dark Ages." But whether this compact made by the fathers of the Republic, or the sayings and doings of Mr. Seward in regard to it, are the more worthy of the Dark Ages, it is not for him alone to determine.

"The law of nature," says he, "disavows such compacts; the law of nature, written on the hearts and consciences of freemen, repudiates them." If this be so, then it certainly follows that in founding States no such compacts should be formed. For, as Mr. Seward says, "when we are founding States, all these laws must be brought to the standard of the laws of God, and must be tried by that standard, and must stand or fall by it." This is true, we repeat; but the Senator who uttered this truth was *not* founding States or forming a constitution. He was living and acting under a constitution already formed, and one which he had taken an oath to support. If, in the construction of this instrument, our fathers really followed "as precedents the abuses of tyrants and robbers," then the course of the Senator in question was plain: *he should have suffered martyrdom rather than take an oath to support it*. For the law of nature, it is clear, permits no man first to take an oath to support such compacts, and then repudiate them. If they are at war with his conscience, then, in the name of all that is sacred, let him repudiate them, but, by all means, without having first placed himself under the necessity of repudiating, at the same time, the obligation of his oath.

There is a question among casuists, whether an oath extorted by force can bind a man to act in opposition to his conscience. But this was not Mr. Seward's case. His oath was not extorted. If he had refused to take it, he would have lost nothing *except an office*.

"There was deep philosophy," says he, "in the confession of an eminent English judge. When he had condemned a young woman to death, under the late sanguinary code of his country, for her first theft, she fell down dead at his feet. 'I seem to myself,' said he, 'to have been pronouncing sentence, not against the prisoner, but against the law itself.'" Ay, there was something better than "deep philosophy" in that English judge; there was stern integrity; for, though he felt the law to be hard and cruel, yet, having taken an oath to support it, he hardly felt himself at liberty to dispense with the obligation of his oath. We commend his example to the Senator from New York.

But who is this Senator, or any other politician of the present day, that he should presume to pass so sweeping and so peremptory a sentence of condemnation on a compact made by the fathers of the Republic and ratified by the people of the United States? For our part, if we wished to find "the higher law," we should look neither into the Dark Ages nor into his conscience. We had infinitely rather look into the great souls of those by whom the Constitution was framed, and by every one of whom the very compact which Mr. Seward pronounces so infamous was cordially sanctioned.

"Your Constitution and laws," exclaims Mr. Seward, "convert hospitality to the refugee from the most degrading oppression on earth into a crime, but all mankind except you esteem that hospitality a virtue." Not content with thus denouncing the "Constitution and laws," he has elsewhere exhorted the people to an open resistance to their execution. "It is," says he, in a speech at a mass-meeting in Ohio, "written in the Constitution of the the United States," and "in violation to divine law,[209] that we shall surrender the fugitive slave who takes refuge at our fireside from his relentless pursuer." He then and there exhorts the people to resist the execution of this clear, this unequivocal, this *acknowledged*, mandate of the Constitution! "Extend," says he, a "cordial welcome *to the fugitive who lays his weary limbs at your door*, and DEFEND HIM AS YOU WOULD YOUR HOUSEHOLD GODS."

We shall not trust ourselves to characterize such conduct. In the calm, judicial language of the Chancellor of his own State such proceeding of Mr. Seward will find its most fitting rebuke. "Independent, however," says Chancellor Walworth, "*of any legislation on this subject either by the individual States or by Congress*, if the person whose services are claimed is in fact a fugitive from servitude under the laws of another State, *the constitutional provision is imperative that he shall be delivered up to his master upon claim made*." Thus far, Mr. Seward concurs with the chancellor in opinion; but the latter continues—"and any state officer or private citizen, who owes allegiance to the United States, and has taken the usual oath to support the Constitution thereof, cannot, WITHOUT INCURRING THE MORAL GUILT OF PERJURY, do any act to deprive the master of his right of recaption, when there is no real doubt that the person whose services are claimed is in fact the slave of the claimant."[210] Yet, regardless of the question whether the fugitive is a slave or not, the life and labors of Mr. Seward are, in a great measure, dedicated to a subversion of the constitutional clause and right under consideration. He counsels open resistance! Yea, he exhorts the people to protect and defend fugitive slaves *as such*, and though they had confessed themselves to have fled from servitude! But we doubt not that "the law of nature, written on the hearts and consciences of freemen," will reverse this advice of his, and reaffirm the decision of the chancellor of his own State. Nay, wherever there exists a freeman with a real heart and conscience, there that decision already stands affirmed.

As Mr. Seward's arguments are more fully elaborated by Mr. Sumner, of Massachusetts, so they will pass under review when we come to examine the speech of that Senator. In the mean time, we beg leave to lay before the reader a few living examples of the manner in which the law of nature, as written on the hearts and consciences of freemen, has expressed itself in regard to the points above considered.

"I recognize, indeed," says the Hon. R. C. Winthrop, of Boston, "a power above all human law-makers and a code above all earthly constitutions! And whenever I perceive a clear conflict of jurisdiction and authority between the Constitution of my country and the laws of my God, my course is clear. I shall resign my office, whatever it may be, and renounce all connection with public service of any sort. Never, never, sir, will I put myself under the necessity of calling upon God to witness my promise to support a constitution, any part of which I consider to be inconsistent with his commands.

"But it is a libel upon the Constitution of the United States—and, what is worse, sir, it is a libel upon the great and good men who framed, adopted, and ratified it; it is a libel upon Washington and Franklin, and Hamilton and Madison, upon John Adams, and John Jay, and Rufus King; it is a libel upon them all, and upon the whole American people of 1789, who sustained them in their noble work, and upon all who, from that time to this, generation after generation, in any capacity,—national, municipal, or state,—have lifted their hands to heaven in attestation of their allegiance to the government of their country;—it is a gross libel upon every one of them, to assert or insinuate that there is any such inconsistency! Let us not do such dishonor to the fathers of the Republic and the framers of the Constitution."

Mr. Ashman, of Massachusetts, after reciting the clause in the Constitution which demands the restoration of fugitive slaves, proceeds as follows: "This reads very plainly, and admits of no doubt but that, so far as fugitive slaves are concerned, the Constitution fully recognizes the right to reclaim them from within the limits of the free States. It is the Constitution which we have all sworn to support, and which I hope we all mean to support; and I have no mental reservation excluding any of its clauses from the sanction of that oath. It is too late now to complain that such a provision is there. Our fathers, who formed that entire instrument, placed it there, and left it to us as an inheritance; and nothing but an amendment of the Constitution, or a violation of our oaths, can tear it out. And, however much we may abhor slavery, there is no way for honorable, honest—nay, conscientious—men, who desire to live under our laws and our Constitution, but to abide by it in its spirit."

In like manner, the Hon. S. A. Douglas, of Illinois, declares: "All I have to say on that subject is this, that the Constitution provides that a fugitive from service in one State, escaping into another, 'shall be delivered up.' The Constitution also provides that no man shall be a Senator unless he takes an oath to support the Constitution. Then, I ask, how does a man acquire a right on this floor to speak, except by taking an oath to support and sustain the Constitution of the United States? And when he takes that oath, I do not understand that he has a right to have a mental reservation, or entertain any secret equivocation that he excepts that clause which relates to the surrender of fugitives from service. I know not how a man reconciles it to his conscience to take that oath to support the Constitution, when he believes that Constitution is in violation of the law of God. If a man thus believes, and takes the oath, he commits perfidy to his God in order that he may enjoy the temporary honors of a seat upon this floor. In this point of view, it is simply a question of whether Senators will be true to their oaths and true to the Constitution under which we live."

§ II. *The attack of Mr. Sumner on the Constitution of his country.*

If we have not noticed the arguments of Mr. Chase, of Ohio, it is because they are reproduced in the celebrated speech of Mr. Sumner, and because he has so fully indorsed the history and logic of this speech as to make it his own. Hence, in replying to the one of these Senators, we at the same time virtually reply to the other.

We select the speech of Mr. Sumner for examination, because it is generally considered the more powerful of the two. It is, indeed, the most elaborate speech ever made in the Senate of the United States, or elsewhere, on the subject of the Fugitive Slave Law. Even Mr. Weller found it "so handsomely embellished with poetry, both Latin and English, so full of classical allusions and rhetorical flourishes," as to make it more palatable than he supposed an abolition speech could possibly be made. As to the abolitionists themselves, they seem to know no bounds in their enthusiastic admiration of this sublime effort of their champion. We should not wonder, indeed, if many a female reformer had gone into hysterics over an oration which has received such violent bursts of applause from grave and dignified Senators. "By this effort," says Mr. Hale, he has placed "himself side by side with the first orators of antiquity, and as far ahead of any living American orator as freedom is ahead of slavery. I believe that he has formed to-day a new era in the history of the politics and of the eloquence of the country; and that in future generations the young men of this nation will be stimulated to effort by the record of what an American Senator has this day done," etc.

We have no doubt that young men may attempt to imitate the speech in question; but, as they grow older, it is to be hoped that their taste will improve. The speech in question will make a "new era" in the tactics of abolitionism, and that is all. We shall see this when we come to examine this wonderful oration, which so completely ravished *three Senators*, and called forth such wild shouts of applause from the whole empire of abolitionism.

Mr. Chase seems almost equally delighted with this marvellous effort. "I avow my conviction, now and here," says he, "that, logically and historically, his argument is impregnable—entirely impregnable." . . . . . . "In my judgment," he continues, "the speech of my friend from Massachusetts will make a NEW ERA in American history." Indeed, Mr. Sumner himself does not seem altogether dissatisfied with this effort, if we may judge from the manner in which it is referred to in his other speeches. We do not blame him for this. We can see no reason why he should be the only abolitionist in the universe who is not enraptured with his oration. But when he so "fearlessly asserts" that his speech "has *never been answered*," we beg leave to assure him that it *may* be refuted with the most perfect ease. For, indeed, its history is half fiction, and its logic wholly false: the first containing just enough of truth to deceive, and the last just enough of plansibility to convince those who are waiting, and watching, and longing to be convinced.

The first thing which strikes the mind, on reading the speech of Mr. Sumner, is the strange logical incoherency of its structure. Its parts are so loosely hung together, and appear so distressingly disjointed, that one is frequently at a loss to perceive the design of the oration. Its avowed object is to procure a repeal of the Fugitive Slave Law of 1850; but no one would ever imagine or suspect such a thing from the title of the speech, which is as follows: "Freedom, national; Slavery, sectional." It is difficult, at first view, to perceive what logical connection this title, or proposition, has with the repeal of the Fugitive Slave Law. But if there be little or no logical connection between these things, we shall soon see how the choice of such a title and topic of discourse opens the way for the rhetorician to make a most powerful appeal to the passions and to the prejudices of his readers. We say, of his readers, because it is evident that the speech was made for Buncombe, and not for the Senate of the United States.

Mr. Sumner deems it necessary to refute the position that slavery is a national institution, in order to set the world right with respect to the relations of the Federal Government to slavery. "The relations of the Government of the United States," says he,—"I speak of the National Government—to slavery, *though plain and obvious, are constantly misunderstood.*" Indeed, nothing in history seems more remarkable than the amount of ignorance and stupidity which prevailed in the world before the appearance of the abolitionists, except the wonderful illuminations which accompanied their advent. "A popular belief at this moment," continues Mr. Sumner, "makes slavery a national institution, and, of course, renders its support a national duty. The extravagance of this error can hardly be surpassed." In truth, it is so exceedingly extravagant, that we doubt if it really exists. It is certain, that we have no acquaintance, either historically or personally, with those who have fallen into so wild an absurdity.

It is true, there is "a popular belief"—nay, there is a deep-rooted national conviction—that the Government of the United States is bound to protect the institution of slavery, in so far as this may be done by the passage of a Fugitive Slave Law. This national conviction has spoken out in the laws of Congress; it has been ratified and confirmed by the judicial opinion of the Supreme Court of the United States, as well as by the decisions of the Supreme Courts of the three great non-slaveholding States of Massachusetts, New York, and Pennsylvania. But no one, so far as we know, has ever deduced this obligation to protect slavery, in this respect, from the absurd notion that "it is a national institution." No such deduction is to be found in any of the arguments of counsel before the courts above-mentioned, nor in the opinions of the courts themselves. We shrewdly suspect that it is to be found nowhere except in the fertile imagination of Mr. Sumner.

We concede that slavery is *not* "a national institution." In combating this position, Mr. Sumner is merely beating the air. We know that slavery is not national; it is local, being confined to certain States, and exclusively established by local or State laws. Hence, Mr. Sumner may fire off as much splendid rhetoric as he pleases at his men of straw. "Slavery national!" he indignantly exclaims: "Sir, this is all a mistake and absurdity, fit to take a place in some new collection of 'Vulgar Errors' by some other Sir Thomas Browne, with the ancient but exploded stories that the toad has a stone in its head and that ostriches digest iron." These may be very fine embellishments; they certainly have nothing to do with the point in controversy. The question is not whether slavery is a national institution, but whether the National Government does not recognize slavery as a local institution, and is not pledged to protect the master's right to reclaim the fugitive from his service. This is the question, and by its relevancy to this question the rhetoric of Mr. Sumner must be tried.

We do not say it has no such relevancy. Mr. Sumner beats the air, it is true, but he does not beat the air in vain. His declamation may have no logical bearing on the point in dispute, but, if you watch it closely, you will always find that it is most skillfully adapted to bring the prejudices and passions of the reader to bear on that point. Though he may not be much of a logician, yet, it must be admitted, he is "skillful of fence." We should do him great injustice as an antagonist, at least before the tribunal of human passion, if we should suppose that it is merely for the abstract glory of setting up a man of straw, and then knocking it down, that he has mustered all the powers of his logic and unfurled all the splendors of his rhetoric. He has a design in all this, which we shall now proceed to expose.

Here are two distinct questions. First, Is slavery a national institution? Secondly, Has Congress the power to pass a Fugitive Slave Law? These two questions are, we repeat, perfectly distinct; and hence, if Mr. Sumner wished to discuss them fairly and honestly, he should have argued each one by itself. We agree with him in regard to the first; we dissent *toto cœlo* from him in regard to the last. But he has not chosen to keep them separate, or to discuss each one by itself. On the contrary, he has, as we have seen, connected them together as premiss and conclusion, and he keeps them together through the first portion of his speech. Most assuredly Mr. Sumner knows that one of the very best ways in the world to cause a truth or proposition to be rejected is to bind it up with a manifest error or absurdity. Yet the proposition for which we contend—that Congress has the power to support slavery by the passage of a Fugitive Slave Law—is bound up by him with the monstrous absurdity that "slavery is a national institution;" and both are denounced together as if both were equally absurd. One instance, out of many, of this unfair mode of proceeding, we shall now lay before our readers.

"The Constitution contains no power," says he, "to make a king or to support kingly rule. With similar reason it may be said that it contains no power to make a slave, or to support a system of slavery. The absence of all such power is hardly more clear in one case than in the other. But, if there be no such power, all national legislation upholding slavery must be unconstitutional and void."

Thus covertly, and in company with the supposed power of Congress to make slaves or to institute slavery, Mr. Sumner denounces the power of Congress to enact a Fugitive Slave Law! He not only denounces it, but treats it as absurd in the extreme; just as absurd, indeed, as it would be to assert that Congress had power "to support kingly rule!" We can listen to the arguments of Mr. Sumner; but we cannot accept his mere opinion as authority that the power of Congress to enact such a law is so glaringly unconstitutional, is so monstrously absurd; for, however passionately that opinion may be declaimed, we cannot forget that a Fugitive Slave Law was passed by the Congress of 1793, received the signature of George Washington, and, finally, the judicial sanction of the Supreme Court of the United States. Mr. Sumner is but a man.

This advantage of mixing up with a glaring falsehood the idea he wishes to be rejected is not the only one which Mr. Sumner derives from his man of straw. By combating the position—"the popular belief," as he calls it—that "slavery is a national institution," he lays open a wide field for his peculiar powers of declamation. He calls up all the fathers—North and South—to bear witness against slavery, in order to show that it is not a national institution. He quotes colleges, and churches, and patriots, against slavery. Not content with this, he pours down furious invectives of his own, with a view to render slavery as odious as possible. But, since the simple question is, *What saith the Constitution*—why this fierce crusade against slavery? In deciding this very question, namely, the constitutionality of the Fugitive Slave Law of 1793, a high judicial authority has said that "the abstract proposition of the justice or injustice of slavery is wholly irrelevant here, and, I apprehend, ought not to have the slightest influence upon any member of this court."[211]

It ought not to have—and it did not have—the slightest influence on the highest judicial tribunal of New York, in which the above opinion was delivered. Much as the author of that opinion (Mr. Senator Bishop) abhorred slavery, he did not permit such an influence to reach his judgment. It would have contaminated his judicial integrity. But although before a judicial tribunal, about to decide on the constitutionality of a Fugitive Slave Law, the abstract proposition of the justice or injustice of slavery is out of place, yet at the bar of passion and prejudice it is well calculated, as Mr. Sumner must know, to exert a tremendous influence. Hence, if he can only get up the horror of his readers against slavery before he comes to the real question, namely, the constitutionality of the Fugitive Slave Law, he knows that his victory will be more than half gained. But we admonish him that passion and prejudice can only give a temporary éclat to his argument.

So much for the unfairness of Mr. Sumner. If we should notice all such instances of artful design in his speech, we should have no space for his logic. To this we would now invite the attention of the reader, in order to see if it be really "impregnable."

As we have already intimated, Mr. Sumner does not, like Mr. Seward, openly denounce the Constitution of his country. On the contrary, he professes the most profound respect for every part of that instrument, not even excepting the clause which demands the restoration of the fugitive from labor. But an examination of his argument, both *historical* and *logical*, will enable us, we trust, to estimate this profession at its real intrinsic worth.

We shall begin with his argument from history. In the examination of this argument, we beg to excuse ourselves from any further notice of all that vast array of historical proofs to show that "freedom is national and slavery sectional."[212] We shall consider those proofs alone which relate to the real point in controversy, namely, Has Congress the power to pass a Fugitive Slave Law?

Mr. Sumner argues, from the well-known sentiments of the framers of the Constitution with respect to slavery, that they intended to confer no such power on Congress. Thus, after quoting the sentiments of Gouverneur Morris, of Elbridge Gerry, of Roger Sherman, and James Madison, he adds: "In the face of these unequivocal statements, it is absurd to suppose that they consented *unanimously* to any provision by which the National Government, the work of their own hands, could be made the most offensive instrument of slavery." Such is the historical argument of Mr. Sumner. Let us see what it is worth.

Elbridge Gerry had said: "We ought to be careful NOT *to give any sanction to slavery;*"—language repeatedly quoted, and underscored as above, by Mr. Sumner. It is absurd, he concludes, to suppose that a man who could use such language had the least intention to confer a power on Congress to support slavery by the passage of a Fugitive Slave Law. This is one branch of his historical argument. It may appear perfectly conclusive to Mr. Sumner, and "entirely impregnable" to Mr. Chase; but, after all, it is not quite so invulnerable as they imagine. Mr. Sumner stopped his historical researches at a most convenient point for his argument. If he had only read a little further, he would have discovered that this same identical Elbridge Gerry was in the Congress of 1793, and VOTED FOR the Fugitive Slave Law then passed!

It fares no better with the historical argument to prove the opinion or intention of Roger Sherman. He had declared, it is true, that he was opposed to any clause in the Constitution "acknowledging men to be property." But we should not, with Mr. Sumner, infer from this that he never intended that Congress should possess a power to legislate in reference to slavery. For, unfortunately for such a conclusion, however confidently it may be drawn, or however dogmatically asserted, Roger Sherman himself was in the Senate of 1793, and was actually on the committee which reported the Fugitive Slave Law of that session! Thus, although the premiss of Mr. Sumner's argument is a historical fact, yet its conclusion comes directly into conflict with another historical fact!

We cannot, in the same way, refute the argument from the language of Gouverneur Morris, who said "that he never would concur in upholding domestic slavery," because he was not in the Congress of 1793. But Robert Morris was there, and, although he helped to frame the Constitution in 1787, he uttered not a syllable against the constitutionality of the Fugitive Slave Law. Indeed, this law passed the Senate by resolution simply, *the yeas and nays not having been called for!*

The words of Mr. Madison, who "thought it wrong to admit in the Constitution the idea that there could be property in man," are four or five times quoted in Mr. Sumner's speech. As we have already seen,[213] there cannot be, in the strict sense of the terms, "property in man;" for the soul is the man, and no one, except God, can own the soul. Hence Mr. Madison acted wisely, we think, in wishing to exclude such an expression from the Constitution, inasmuch as it would have been misunderstood by Northern men, and only shocked their feelings without answering any good purpose.

When we say that slaves are property, we merely mean that their masters have a right to their service or labor. This idea is recognized in the Constitution, and *this right is secured*. We ask no more. As Mr. Madison, and the whole South, had the *thing*, he did not care to wrangle about the *name*. We are told, again and again, that the word *slave* does not appear in the Constitution. Be it so. We care not, since our slaves are there recognized as "persons held to service" by those to whom "such service is due." It is repeated without end that the "Constitution acts on slaves as *persons*, and not as property." Granted; and if Northern men will, according to the mandate of the Constitution, only deliver up our fugitive servants, we care not whether they restore them as persons or as property. If we may only reclaim them as persons, and regain their service, we are perfectly satisfied. We utterly despise all such verbal quibbling.

Mr. Madison was above it. He acted wisely, we repeat, in refusing to shock the mind of any one, by insisting upon a mere word, and upon a word, too, which might not have conveyed a correct idea of his own views. But that Mr. Madison could, as he undersood the terms, regard slaves as property, we have the most incontestable evidence. For in the Convention of Virginia, called to ratify the Constitution of the United States, he said, "Another clause secures us that *property* which we now possess. At present, if any slave elopes to any of those States where slaves are free, he becomes emancipated by their laws, for the laws of the States are uncharitable to one another in this respect." He then quotes the provision from the Constitution relative to fugitives from labor, and adds: "This clause was expressly inserted to enable *owners* of slaves to reclaim them." So much for Mr. Sumner's main argument from the language of the members of the Convention of 1787.

Arguing from the sentiments of that convention with respect to slavery, he concludes that nothing could have been further from their intentions than to confer upon Congress the power to pass a uniform Fugitive Slave Law. He boldly asserts, that if a proposition to confer such a power upon Congress had "been distinctly made it would have been distinctly denied." "But no person in the convention," he says, "*not one of the reckless partisans of slavery, was so audacious as to make the proposition.*" Now we shall show that the above statement of his is diametrically opposed to the truth. We shall show that the members of the convention in question were perfectly willing to confer such a power upon Congress.

The reason why they were so is obvious to any one who has a real knowledge of the times about whose history Mr. Sumner so confidently declaims. This reason is well stated in the language of the Chancellor of New York whom we have already quoted. "The provision," says he, "as to persons escaping from servitude in one State into another, appears by their journal to have been adopted by a unanimous vote of the convention. At that time the existence of involuntary servitude, or the relation of master and servant, was known to and recognized by the laws of every State in the Union except Massachusetts, and *the legal right of recaption by the master existed in all*, AS A PART OF THE CUSTOMARY OR COMMON LAW OF THE WHOLE CONFEDERACY." Hence, instead of shocking the convention, a clause recognizing such right would have been merely declaratory of the "customary or common law," which then universally prevailed. The "history of the times" confirms this view, and furnishes no evidence against it.

Mr. Sumner tries to make a different impression. He lays great stress on the fact that it was not until late in the convention that the first clause relative to the surrender of fugitive slaves was introduced. But this fact agrees more perfectly with our view than with his. There was no haste about the introduction of such a provision, because it was well known that, whenever it should be introduced, it would pass in the affirmative without difficulty. And, in fact, when it was introduced, it "WAS UNANIMOUSLY ADOPTED." This single fact speaks volumes.

Let us now attend, for a moment, to Mr. Sumner's historical proofs. He quotes the following passage from the Madison Papers:—"Gen. (Charles Cotesworth) Pinckney was not satisfied with it. He seemed to wish some provision should be included in favor of property in slaves." "But," by way of comment, Mr. Sumner adds, "he made no proposition. Unwilling to shock the convention, and uncertain in his own mind, he only *seemed* to wish such a provision." Now, a bare abstract proposition to recognize property in men is one thing, and a clause to secure the return of fugitive slaves is quite another. The first, it is probable, would have been rejected by the convention; the last was actually and unanimously adopted by it.

Mr. Sumner's next proof is decidedly against him. Here it is "Mr. Butler and Mr. Charles Pinckney, both from South Carolina, now moved openly to require 'fugitive slaves and servants to be delivered up like criminals.' . . . . . . Mr. Wilson, of Pennsylvania, at once objected: 'This would oblige the executive of the State to do it at the public expense.' Mr. Sherman, of Connecticut, saw no more propriety in the public seizing and surrendering a slave or servant than a horse! Under the pressure of these objections the offensive proposition was quietly withdrawn."

Now mark the character of these objections. It is objected, not that it is wrong to deliver up fugitive slaves, but only that they should not be "delivered up like criminals;" that is, by a demand on the executive of the State to which they may have fled. And this objection is based on the ground that such a requisition would oblige the public to deliver them up at its own expense. Mr. Sherman insists, not that it is wrong to surrender fugitive slaves or fugitive horses, but only that the executive, or public, should not be called upon to surrender them. Surely, if these gentlemen had been so violently opposed to the restoration of fugitive slaves, here was a fair occasion for them to speak out; and as honest, outspoken men they would, no doubt, have made their sentiments known. But there is, in fact, not a syllable of such a sentiment uttered. There is not the slightest symptom of the existence of any such feeling in their minds. If any such existed, we must insist that Mr. Sumner has discovered it by instinct, and not by his researches in history.

The statement that "under the pressure of these objections the offensive propositon was *quietly withdrawn*" is not true. It was not quietly withdrawn; on the contrary, it was withdrawn with the assurance that it would be again introduced. "Mr. Butler withdrew his proposition," says Mr. Madison, "*in order that some particular provision might be made*, apart from this article."[214] Accordingly, the very next day he introduced a provision, which, as Mr. Madison declares, "was expressly inserted to enable owners of slaves to reclaim them."

These glosses of Mr. Sumner on the history of the times will appear important, if we view them in connection with his design. This design is to bring into doubt the idea that slaves are embraced in the clause of the Constitution which requires fugitives from service or labor to be delivered up. We should not suspect this design from the hints here thrown out, if it were not afterward more fully disclosed. "On the next day," says Mr. Sumner, "August 29th, profiting by the suggestions already made, Mr. Butler moved a proposition, substantially like that now found in the Constitution, *not directly for the surrender of 'fugitive slaves*,' as originally proposed, but as 'fugitives from service or labor,' which, without debate or opposition of any kind, was unanimously adopted." Was it then unanimously adopted because it was a clause for the surrender of "fugitives from service or labor" only, and not for the surrender of fugitive slaves?

Such appears to be the insinuation of Mr. Sumner. Be this as it may, it is certain that he has afterward said that it may be questioned whether "the language employed" in this clause "can be judicially regarded as justly applicable to fugitive slaves, *which is often and earnestly denied.*". . . . "*Still further,*" he says, in italics, "*to the courts of each State must belong the determination of the question, to which class of persons, according to just rules of interpretation, the phrase 'persons held to service or labor' is strictly applicable.*"

Mr. Sumner doubts, then, whether this provision, after all, refers to "fugitive slaves." Now, although he has said much in regard to "the effrontery of the Southern members of the convention" that formed the Constitution, we may safely defy him, or any other man, to point to any thing in their conduct which approximates to such audacity. What! the clause in question not designed to embrace fugitive slaves? Mr. Butler, even before he introduced the clause, declared, as we have seen, that such would be its design. It was so understood by every member of the convention; for there was not a man there who possessed the capacity to misunderstand so plain a matter; and it has been so understood by every man, of all parties and all factions, from that day down to the present. Not one of the hired advocates who have been employed, in different States, to argue against the constitutionality of the Fugitive Slave Law, has ever had the unblushing effrontery to contend that the clause in question is not applicable to fugitive slaves. Nay, more, until Mr. Sumner appeared, the frantic zeal of no abolitionist had ever so completely besotted his intellect as to permit him to take such ground. By Dr. Channing, by Mr. Seward, and by Mr. Chase, such application of the words in question is unhesitatingly admitted; and hence we dismiss Mr. Sumner's discovery with the contempt it deserves.

But to return. "The provision," says Mr. Sumner, "which showed itself thus tardily, and was so slightly noticed in the National Convention, was neglected in most of the contemporaneous discussions before the people." No wonder; for it was merely declaratory of the "customary or common law" of that day. "In the Conventions of South Carolina, North Carolina, and Virginia," he admits, "it was commended as securing important rights, though on this point there was a difference of opinion. In the Virginia Convention, an eminent character,—Mr. George Mason,—with others, expressly declared that there was 'no security of property coming within this section.'"

Now, we shall not stickle about the fact that Mr. Sumner has not given the very words of Mr. Mason, since he has given them in substance. But yet he has given them in such a way, and in such a connection, as to make a false impression. The words of Mr. Mason, taken in their proper connection, are as follows: "We have no security for the property of that kind (slaves) which we already have. There is no clause in this Constitution to secure it, *for they may lay such a tax as will amount to manumission.*" This shows his position, not as it is misrepresented by Mr. Sumner, but as it stands in his own words. If slave property may be rendered worthless by the taxation of Congress, how could it be secured by a clause which enables the owner to reclaim it? It would not be worth reclaiming. Such was the argument and true position of Mr. George Mason.

"Massachusetts," continues Mr. Sumner, "while exhibiting peculiar sensitiveness at any responsibility for slavery, seemed to view it with unconcern." If Massachusetts had only believed that the clause was intended to confer on Congress the power to pass a Fugitive Slave Law, into what flames of indignation would her sensitiveness have burst! So Mr. Sumner would have us to believe. But let us listen, for a moment, to the sober voice of history.

It was only about four years after the government went into operation that Congress actually exercised the power in question, and *passed a Fugitive Slave Law*. Where was Massachusetts then! Did she burst into flames of indignation? Her only voice, in reply, was as distinctly and as emphatically pronounced in favor of that law as was the voice of Virginia itself. With a single exception, her whole delegation in Congress,[215] with Fisher Ames at their head, voted for the Fugitive Slave Law of 1793! Not a whisper of disapprobation was heard from their constituents. As Mr. Sumner himself says, the passage of that act "drew little attention." Hence he would have us to believe that Massachusetts would have been stirred from her depths if the convention had conferred such a power upon Congress, and yet that she was not moved at all when Congress proceeded, as he maintains, to *usurp* and exercise that power!

This is not all. Every member from the free States, with the exception of five, recorded his vote in favor of the same law.[216] In the Senate, as we have already said, it was passed by resolution, and not by a recorded vote. No one, in either branch of Congress, uttered a syllable against the constitutionality of the law, though many of the most distinguished members of the very convention which framed the Constitution itself were there. Not to mention others, there were James Madison, and Roger Sherman, and Elbridge Gerry, and Rufus King, and Caleb Strong, and Robert Morris, and Oliver Elsworth; and yet from not one of these illustrious framers of the Constitution was a syllable uttered against the constitutionality of the law in question. Nay, the law was supported and enacted by themselves. What, then, in the face of these indubitable facts, becomes of all Mr. Sumner's far-fetched arguments from "the literature of the age" and from his multitudinous voices against slavery? It is absurd, says Mr. Sumner, to suppose that such men intended to confer any power upon Congress to pass a Fugitive Slave Law. It is a *fact*, we reply, that as members of Congress they proceeded, without hesitation or doubt, to exercise that very power. It "dishonors the memory of the fathers," says Mr. Sumner, to suppose they intended that Congress should possess such a power. How, then, will he vindicate the memory of the fathers against the imputation of his own doctrine that they, as members of Congress, must have knowingly usurped the power which, as members of the convention, they had intended not to confer?

One more of Mr. Sumner's historical arguments, and we are done with this branch of the subject. He deems it the most conclusive of all. It is founded on the arrangement of certain clauses of the Constitution, and is, we believe, perfectly original. We must refer the reader to the speech itself if he desire to see this very curious argument, since we cannot spare the room to give it a full and fair statement.

Nor is this at all necessary to our purpose, inasmuch as we intend to notice only one thing about this argument, namely, the wonderful effect it produces on the mind of its inventor. "The framers of the Constitution," says he, "were wise and careful men, who had a reason for what they did, and who understood the language which they employed." We can readily believe all this. Nor can we doubt that they "had a design in the peculiar arrangement" of the clauses adopted by them. That design, however, we feel quite sure, is different from the one attributed to them by Mr. Sumner. But let us suppose he is right, and then see what would follow.

The design attributed to them by Mr. Sumner was to make every one see, beyond the possibility of a mistake, that the Constitution confers no power on Congress to pass a Fugitive Slave Law. "They not only decline all addition of any such power to the compact," says he, "but, *to render misapprehension impossible,—to make assurance doubly sure,— to exclude any contrary conclusion*, they punctiliously arrange," etc. Now, if such were the case, then we ask if design of so easy accomplishment were ever followed by failure so wonderful?

They failed, in the first place, "to exclude a contrary conclusion" from the Supreme Courts of Massachusetts, of New York, and of Pennsylvania, all of which tribunals have decided that they *did* confer such a power upon Congress. In the second place, although those wise men labored to make "misapprehension impossible," yet, according to Mr. Sumner, the Supreme Court of the United States has entirely misapprehended them. So far from seeing that the power in question is not granted to Congress, this high tribunal decides that it is clearly and unquestionably granted. This is not all. The most marvellous failure is yet to come. For, after all their pains to make the whole world see their meaning, these wise men did not see it themselves, but went away, many of them, and, in the Congress of 1793, helped to pass a Fugitive Slave Law!

It is to be feared, indeed, that the failure would have been absolutely total but for the wonderful sagacity of a few abolitionists. For the design imputed to the framers of the Constitution, and which they took so much pains to disclose, had remained profoundly concealed from nearly all men, not excepting themselves, until it was detected by Messrs. Sumner, Chase, and company. But these have, at last, discovered it, and now see it as in a flood of light. Indeed, they see it with such transcendent clearness, with such marvellous perspicacity of vision, as to atone for the stupidity and blindness of the rest of mankind.

So much for Mr. Sumner's historical argument. His logical argument is, if possible, still more illogical than his historical. In regard to this, however, we shall be exceedingly brief, as we are sick of his sophisms, and long to be delivered from the pursuit of them.

He encounters, at the outset, "a difficulty" in the legislation of the Congress of 1793 and in the decision of the Supreme Court of the United States." But "on examination," says he, "this difficulty will disappear." Perhaps difficulty so great never vanished so suddenly from before any other man.

The authority of the Congress of 1793, though it contained so many of the most distinguished framers of the Constitution, is annihilated by a few bold strokes of Mr. Sumner's pen. One short paragraph, containing two ineffably weak arguments, does the business.

The first of these arguments is as follows: "The act of 1793 proceeded from a Congress that had already recognized the United States Bank, chartered by a previous Congress, which, though sanctioned by the Supreme Court, has been since in high quarters pronounced unconstitutional. If it erred as to the bank, it may have erred also as to fugitives from labor." We cannot conceive why such an argument should have been propounded, unless it were to excite a prejudice against the Congress of 1793 in the minds of those who may be opposed to a National Bank. For if we look at its conclusion we shall see that it merely aims to establish a point which no one would deny. It merely aims to prove that, as the Congress of 1793 was composed of fallible men, "so it may have erred!" We admit the conclusion, and therefore pass by the inherent weaknesses in the structure of the argument.

His second argument is this: "But the very act contains a capital error[217] on this very subject, so declared by the Supreme Court, in pretending to vest a portion of the judicial power of the nation in state officers. *This error takes from the act all authority as an interpretation of the Constitution.* I DISMISS IT." This passage, considered as an argument, is simply ridiculous. How many of the best laws ever enacted by man have, in the midst of much that is as clear as noonday, been found to contain an error! Should all, therefore, have been blindly rejected? As soon as the error has been detected, has any enlightened tribunal on earth ever said, "I dismiss" the whole?

By such a process we might have made as short work with Mr. Sumner's speech. If, after pointing out one error therein, we had dismissed the whole speech as worthless, we should have imitated his reasoning, and in our conclusion have come much nearer to the truth. If we should say, indeed, that because the sun has a spot on its surface it is therefore a great ball of darkness, our argument would be exactly like that of Mr. Sumner. But that great luminary would not refuse to shine in obedience to our contemptible logic. In like manner, the authority of the illustrious Congress of 1793, in which there were so many profound statesmen and pure patriots, will not be the less resplendent because Mr. Charles Sumner has, with Titanic audacity and Lilliputian weakness, assailed it with one of the most pitiful of all the pitiful sophisms that ever were invented by man.

In regard to the decision of the Supreme Court he says: "Whatever maybe the influence of this judgment as a rule to the judiciary, it can not arrest our duty as legislators. And here I adopt, with entire assent, the language of President Jackson, in his memorable veto, in 1832, of the Bank of the United States." He then quotes this language, in which he italicizes the following sentence: "*Each public officer, who takes an oath to support the Constitution, swears that he will support it as he understands it, and not as it is understood by others.*" With these authoritative words of Andrew Jackson," says he, "I dismiss this topic. The early legislation of Congress and the decisions of the Supreme Court can not stand in our way. I advance to the argument." We shall let him advance.

But we must say a few words in conclusion. Mr. Sumner swears to support the Constitution as he understands it; but how is it supported by him? Is it supported by him at all or in any way? Let us see. The clause respecting "persons held to service or labor," says he, imposes an obligation, not upon "the National Government, but upon the States." Is he then in favor of the States passing any law, or doing any act, by which fugitive slaves may be delivered up? "Never," he replies. Massachusetts will never do any such thing by his advice or consent. Surely, then, he will speak a kind word to the good people of Massachusetts, and advise them to do nothing in violation of this solemn compact of the Constitution. If he will do nothing to support the compact, surely he will do nothing to break it down. He will not permit us to indulge any such charitable hope. For it is his *avowed* object, by speech-making and by agitation, to create such a "public opinion" as "shall blast with contempt, indignation, and abhorrence, all who, *in whatever form*, or *under whatever name*, undertake to be agents"[218] in reclaiming fugitive slaves. Yea, upon the very officers of the law themselves, who, for this purpose, act under and by authority of the supreme laws of the land, he pours down scorn and derision. Even these, though in the discharge of an official duty, are—if it be in the power of Mr. Sumner—to be blasted with abhorrence, indignation, and contempt!

The Constitution declares that the fugitive slave "shall be delivered up." He shall NOT "be delivered up," says Mr. Sumner; and, in order to make his words good, he means to create a "public opinion," which no Southern master dare encounter. Nay, he rejoices to believe that such public opinion is, in some localities, already created and prepared for open resistance to the Constitution of the United States. "There are many," says he, "who will never shrink at any cost, and, notwithstanding all the atrocious penalties of this bill, from efforts to save a wandering fellow-man from bondage. They will offer him the shelter of their houses, and, IF NEED BE, WILL PROTECT HIS LIBERTY BY FORCE."[219] Horrible words! Words tending directly to a conflict in which the brightest hopes of humanity must perish, and the glory of the Republic be extinguished in oceans of blood.

In the face of such things, we are imperiously constrained to doubt Mr. Sumner's regard for the obligation of the oath which binds him to support the Constitution of his country. It is certain that he can rejoice in the breach of this obligation by others. A certain judge in Vermont, who, like every other State officer, had taken an oath to support the Constitution of the United States, just set Constitution, laws, evidence, all at defiance, and boldly declared that the fugitive should *not* be delivered up, *"unless the master could show a bill of sale from the Almighty."* This deed, which, in the language of Chancellor Walworth, is stamped with "the moral guilt of perjury," appears heroic to Mr. Sumner, by whom it is related with evident delight. It would seem, indeed, as if the moral sensibility of an abolitionist of his stamp is all drawn to a single point of his conscience, so that it can feel absolutely nothing except slavery. It seems dead to the obligation of an oath, to the moral guilt of perjury. Nay, it seems to rejoice in the very bravery of its perpetration, provided it only enables a fugitive slave to effect his escape.

Perhaps Mr. Sumner would seek to justify himself by declaring that the language *fugitive from services* does not include fugitive slaves. If so, we reply that the Vermont judge, whose infamous decision he approves, had no such fine pretext. It is Mr. Sumner, as we have seen, who first suggested this most excellent method of reconciling conscience with treachery to the Constitution. Though he professes the most profound respect for that instrument, he deliberately sets to work to undermine one of its most clear and unequivocal mandates. He does not, like Mr. Seward, openly smite the Constitution with his hand, or contemptuously kick it with his foot. *He betrays it with a kiss.*

Mr. Sumner admires the conduct of the Vermont judge; but he can heap the most frantic abuse on the acts of the best men America has produced. Though they be the deliberate public acts of a Clay, or a Calhoun, or a Webster, or a GEORGE WASHINGTON, his language is not the less violent, nor his raving vituperation the less malignant. In regard to the Fugitive Slave Law of 1850, he says: "And still further, as if to do a deed which should 'make heaven weep, all earth amazed,' this same Congress, in disregard of all the cherished safeguards of freedom, has passed a most cruel, unchristian, devilish act." The great difficulty under which Mr. Sumner labors, and which all the energy of his soul struggles to surmount, is to find language violent enough in which to denounce this "foul enactment," this "detestable and heaven-defying bill," this "monster act," which "sets at naught the best principles of the Constitution and the very laws of God!"

Now, this bill, let it be remembered, is liable to no objection which may not be urged against the Fugitive Slave Law of 1793. It will not be denied, indeed, that if the one of these laws be unconstitutional so also is the other, and that both must stand or fall together. Let it also be borne in mind that, as the one received the support of a Clay, and a

Calhoun, and a Webster, so the other received the sanction and the signature of George Washington. Yet, in the face of these facts, Mr. Sumner does not moderate his rage. They only seem to increase the intensity and the fury of his wrath. "The soul sickens," he cries, "in the contemplation of this legalized outrage. In the dreary annals of the past there are many acts of shame—there are many ordinances of monarchs, and laws which have become a byword and a hissing to the nations. But when we consider the country and the age, I ask fearlessly, what act of shame, what ordinance of monarch, what law, can compare in atrocity with this enactment of an American Congress?"

Not content with pouring floods of abuse on the law itself, Mr. Sumner proceeds to consign to infamy its authors and all who have given it their support. For, after furnishing examples of what he deems among the most atrocious transactions of the past, he adds: "I would not exaggerate. I wish to keep within bounds; but *I think no person can doubt* that the condemnation affixed to all these transactions and to their authors must be the lot hereafter of the Fugitive Slave Bill, and of every one, according to the measure of his influence, who gave it his support. Into the immortal catalogue of national crimes this law has now passed, drawing with it, by an inexorable necessity, its authors also, and chiefly him who, as President of the United States, set his name to the bill, and breathed into it that final breath without which it would have no life. Other Presidents may be forgotten, but the name signed to the Fugitive Slave Bill can never be forgotten. There are depths of infamy, as there are hights of fame. I regret to say what I must, but truth compels me. Better far for him had he never been born; better for his memory, and for the name of his children, had he never been President!"

If neither Mr. Fillmore nor George Washington swore to support the Constitution as Mr. Sumner understands it, we beg him to consider that *his opinion was not known* when they took the oath of office. Mr. Fillmore had, at that time, no better guide to go by than the decisions of the most enlightened judicial tribunals of his country, with the Supreme Court of the United States at their head. He was not so far raised above other men, nor possessed of so wonderful an insight into the Constitution, as Mr. Sumner; for he could understand it no better than its framers. Hence he was, no doubt, so conscious of his own fallibility that he could hardly look upon modesty as a crime, or upon a deference to the judicial tribunals of his country as infamous. We trust, therefore, that his good name will survive, and that his children will not blush to own it. It is certain that the American people will never believe, on the bare authority of Mr. Sumner, that, in his course regarding the Fugitive Slave Law, he planted his feet in the very "depths of infamy," when they can so clearly see that he merely trod in the footsteps of George Washington.

If what a man lacks in reason he could only make up in rage, then, after all, it would have to be concluded that Mr. Sumner is a very respectable Senator; for, surely, the violence of his denunciations is almost as remarkable as the weakness of his logic. Fortunately, however, it can hurt no one except himself or those whom he represents.

Certainly, the brightest names in the galaxy of American statesmen are not to be swept away by the filthy torrent of his invectives. The Clays, the Calhouns, the Websters, and the Washingtons of America, are, indeed, as far above the impotent rage of this Senator as the very stars of heaven are beyond his arm.[220]

§ III. *The right of Trial by Jury not impaired by the Fugitive Slave Law.*

It is alleged that the power to enact such a law does not reside in Congress, because no such power has been "expressly delegated," and because it is not "necessary and proper" to carry any expressly delegated authority into effect. We should have replied to this argument; but it has been urged before every tribunal in which the great question under consideration has been tried, and everywhere refuted. By Mr. Justice Nelson, in the Supreme Court of New York,[221] by Mr. Senator Bishop, in the Court of Errors in the same State,[222] and by Mr. Justice Story, in the Supreme Court of the United States, it has been so clearly, so powerfully, and so triumphantly demolished as to leave nothing more to be desired on the subject. And besides, it has been our object not so much to refute arguments against the law in question, or to establish that which has been so long established,[223] as to show on what slender grounds, and yet with what unbounded confidence, the greatest champions of abolitionism are accustomed to oppose the Constitution, the laws, the judicial decisions, and the uniform practice, of the whole government under which we live.

In pursuance of this design, there is another sophism of theirs, which it now devolves upon us to examine. We allude to the argument that the Fugitive Slave Law is unconstitutional, because it denies the right of trial by jury.

Is this still an open question? In the biography of Mr. Justice Story, published by his son, it is said: "The argument that the Act of 1793 was unconstitutional, because it did not provide for a trial by jury according to the requisitions of the sixth article in the amendment to the Constitution, having been suggested to my father on his return from Washington, he replied that this question was not argued by counsel nor considered by the court, and that he should still consider it an open one." Mr. Sumner adduces this "distinct statement that the necessity of trial by jury was not before the court;" and adds, "So that, in the estimation of the judge himself, it was still an open question."

In the case here referred to—Prigg v. The Commonwealth of Pennsylvania, reported in XVI. Peters—it is true that the question of trial by jury was not argued by counsel nor considered by the court. But if the greater includes the less, then this question was embraced in the decision; for, in that case, Prigg had seized the fugitive slave without process, and carried her away without any certificate from magistrate or judge in the State of Pennsylvania. The court declared that he had a right to do so under and by virtue of the Constitution of the United States. Most assuredly, if he had a constitutional right to such proceeding, then, in such cases, the Constitution dispenses with the necessity of trial by jury.

It was urged by counsel that such summary method of reclaiming fugitive slaves was unconstitutional; but the court decided otherwise. It was insisted by Mr. Hambly, just as it is now insisted by Mr. Sumner and others, that such arrest was unconstitutional, because it was made by the mere will of the party, and not, as the Constitution requires, "by due process of law." Thus the point was presented by the record, argued by the counsel, and overruled by the court.

In overruling this argument the court says: "The owner must, therefore, have the right to seize and repossess the slave which the local laws of his own State confer upon him as property; and we all know that this right of seizure and recaption is universally acknowledged in all the slaveholding States. Indeed, this is no more than a mere affirmance of the principles of the common law applicable to this very subject." Then, after a quotation from Blackstone, the court adds: "Upon this ground, we have not the slightest hesitation in holding that, under and in virtue of the Constitution, the owner of a slave is clothed with entire authority in every State in the Union to seize and recapture his slave whenever he can do it without any breach of the peace or any illegal violence."

In accordance with this opinion of the court—delivered by Mr. Justice Story—Mr. Chief Justice Taney says: the master "has a right, peaceably, to take possession of him, and carry him away, without any certificate or warrant from a judge of the District or Circuit Court of the United States, or from any magistrate of the State; and whosoever resists or obstructs him is a wrong-doer; and every State law which proposes, directly or indirectly, to authorize such resistance or obstruction, is null and void, and affords no justification to the individual or the officer of the State who acts under it. This right of the master being given by the Constitution of the United States, neither Congress nor a State Legislature can by any law or regulation impair it or restrict it.[224]

Hence it would have been well if Mr. Sumner and the son of Judge Story had looked into this decision again before they proclaimed the opinion that the right of trial by jury is, in such cases, still an open question. Mr. Justice Story himself must, on reflection, have seen that the off-hand expression attributed to him was erroneous. His more deliberate opinion is recorded, not only in the case of Prigg, but also in his "Commentaries on the Constitution of the United States." "It is obvious," says he, "that these provisions for the arrest and removal of fugitives of both classes contemplate summary ministerial proceedings, and not the ordinary courts of judicial investigations to ascertain whether the complaint be well-founded or the claim of ownership be established beyond all legal controversy. In cases of suspected crimes the guilt or innocence of the party is to be made out at his trial, and not upon the preliminary inquiry whether he shall be delivered up. All that would seem in such cases to be necessary is that there should be *primâ facie* evidence before the executive authority to satisfy its judgment that there is probable cause to believe the party guilty, such as, upon an ordinary warrant, would justify his commitment for trial. And in the cases of fugitive slaves there would seem to be the same necessity of requiring only *primâ facie* proofs of ownership, without putting the party to a formal assertion of his rights by a suit at the common law."[225]

But, since the abolitionists will discuss this point, then let it be considered an open question, and let them produce their arguments. The first we shall notice is from Mr. Sumner, who again reasons from the sentiments of the fathers. "At the close of the National Convention," says he, "Elbridge Gerry refused to sign the Constitution, because, among other things, it established 'a tribunal *without juries*, a Star Chamber as to civil cases.' Many united in his opposition, and, on the recommendation of the First Congress, this additional safeguard was adopted as an amendment." Thus, according to Mr. Sumner, Elbridge Gerry was the father of the clause in the Constitution which guarantees the right of trial by jury. Yet Elbridge Gerry never dreamed of applying this clause to the case of fugitive slaves; for, as we have already seen, he voted for the Fugitive Slave Law of 1793, in which such application of it is denied. Nor did any other member of that Congress propose the right of trial by jury in such cases.

No doubt there would have been opposition to the act of 1793 if any member of Congress had supposed, for a moment, that it denied the right of trial by jury to the fugitive slave. It does no such thing. It leaves that right unimpaired; and if any slave in the Union, whether fugitive or otherwise, desire such trial, it is secured to him by the Constitution and laws of the country. But he cannot have such trial where or in what State he chooses. If he lives in Richmond, he may have a trial by jury there; but he cannot escape to Boston, and there demand this as a right. The fugitive from labor, like the fugitive from justice, has a right to a trial by jury, but neither can claim to have this trial in any part of the world he pleases. The latter must be tried in "the vicinage" where the offense is alleged to have been committed, because there the witnesses are to be found. He has no right to flee from these and require them to follow him with their testimony. As he has a constitutional right to be tried in the vicinage of the alleged offense, so has the commonwealth a right to insist on his trial there. In like manner, and for a similar reason, if the colored man wishes to assert his freedom under the law, he may appeal to a jury of the country; but this must be done in the State under whose laws he is claimed as a slave and where the witnesses reside. He cannot fly to a distant State, and there demand a kind of trial which neither the Constitution, nor the laws, nor public expediency, secures to him. If he assert this right at all, he must assert it in conformity with the *undoubted right of the other party*, which is to be sued in this, as in all other personal actions, in the place where he resides.

In the face of these considerations, it is no wonder that the Congress of 1793 were so unanimous in regard to the Fugitive Slave Law. Though this law did not provide for a jury trial, yet its authors all knew that such trial was not denied to the fugitive slave, if he had a mind to claim it. Hence the law was passed by that Congress, without even an allusion to this modern abolition objection to its constitutionality. Among all the members of that body who had taken part in framing the Constitution of the United States,[226] not one was found to hint at such an objection. This objection is of more recent origin, if not of less respectable parentage.

An amendment to the law in question, allowing a trial by jury to the fugitive slave in a distant State, would indeed be a virtual denial of the constitutional right of the master. Either because the jury could not agree, or because distant testimony might be demanded, the trial would probably be continued, and put off, until the expense, the loss of time, and the worriment of vexatious proceedings, would be more than the slave is worth. The language of Mr. Chief Justice Taney, in relation to an action for damages by the master, is peculiarly applicable to such a trial by jury. The master "*would be compelled*," says he, "*to encounter the costs and expenses of a suit, prosecuted at a distance from his own home, and to sacrifice perhaps the value of his property in endeavoring* to obtain compensation." This is not the kind of remedy, says he, the Constitution "intended to give. The delivery of the property itself—its PROMPT AND IMMEDIATE DELIVERY—*is plainly required, and was intended to be secured.*" Such prompt and immediate delivery was a part of "the customary or common law" at the time the Constitution was adopted, and its framers, no doubt, intended that this practice should be enforced by the clause in question, as appears from the fact that so many of them concurred in the Act of 1793.

But if such right to a prompt and immediate delivery be guaranteed by the Constitution itself, then, with all due submission, we would ask, what power has Congress to limit or abridge this right? If under and by virtue of the Constitution this right to a prompt and immediate delivery be secured, then what power has Congress to say there shall *not* be a prompt or immediate delivery? "This right of the master," says Mr. Chief Justice Taney, "being given by the Constitution of the United States, NEITHER CONGRESS NOR A STATE LEGISLATURE CAN BY ANY LAW OR REGULATION IMPAIR IT OR RESTRICT IT." If this be sound doctrine,—and such we hold it to be,—then Congress has no constitutional power to impair or restrict the right in question, by giving the fugitive slave a trial by jury in the State to which he may have fled. This would not be to give a "prompt and immediate delivery," such as the Supreme Court declares the master is entitled to by the Constitution itself; it would be either to give no delivery at all, or else one attended with such delays, vexations, and costs, as would materially impair, if not wholly annihilate, the right in question.

It is right and proper, we think, that questions arising exclusively under our own laws should be tried in our own States and by our own tribunals. Hence we shall never consent, unless constrained by the judicial decision of the Supreme Court of the Union, to have such questions tried in States whose people and whose juries may, perhaps, be hostile to our interests and to our domestic institutions. For we are SOVEREIGN as well as they.

Only conceive such a trial by jury in a Northern State, with such an advocate for the fugitive slave as Mr. Chase, or Mr. Sumner, or some other flaming abolitionist! There sits the fugitive slave,—"one of the heroes of the age," as Mr. Sumner calls him, and the very embodiment of persecuted innocence. On the other hand is the master,—the vile "slave-hunter," as Mr. Sumner delights to represent him, and whom, if possible, he is determined "to blast with contempt, indignation, and abhorrence." The trial begins. The advocate appeals to the prejudices and the passions of the jury. He denounces slavery—about which neither he nor the jury know any thing—as the epitome of all earthly wrongs, as the sum and substance of all human woes. Now, suppose that on the jury there is *only one man*, who, like the Vermont judge, requires "a bill of sale from the Almighty" before he will deliver up a fugitive slave; or who, like Mr. Seward, sets his own private opinion above the Constitution of his country; or who, like Mr. Sumner, has merely sworn to support the supreme law as he understands it; and who, at the same time, possesses his capacity to understand it just exactly as he pleases: then what chance would the master have for a verdict? Just none at all. For that one man, however clear the master's evidence, would hang the jury, and the cause would have to be tried over again.

But suppose the whole twelve jurors should decide according to the law and the evidence, and give a verdict in favor of the claimant; would his rights then be secured? Very far from it. For there is the eager crowd, which never fails to flock to such trials, and which the inflammatory eloquence of the advocate has now wrought into a frenzy. Cannot such crowd, think you, furnish a mob to effect by force what every member of the jury had refused to accomplish by falsehood? If the master—if the abhorred "slave-hunter"—should escape from such a crowd with a sound body only, and without his property, he ought, we think, to deem himself exceedingly fortunate.

Mr. Winthrop, of Massachusetts, has advocated a trial by jury in such cases. He was, no doubt, perfectly sincere in the belief expressed by him, that under such a provision more fugitive slaves would be reclaimed than under the law as it now stands. But it is equally certain that neither Mr. Seward nor Mr. Chase was of this opinion when the one proposed, and the other voted for, a trial by jury in such cases. Neither of these Senators, we think we may confidently affirm, intended to aid the master in reclaiming his fugitive slaves.

"At any rate, sir," says Mr. Winthrop, "I shall vote for the amendment offered by the Senator from New Jersey, as right and just in itself, whatever may be its effects." That is to say, whatever may be the effect of a jury trial in such cases, he means to vote for it *as right and just in itself!* Whether this were a burst of passion merely, or the deliberate conviction of the author of it, we are not able to determine, but we shall trust it was the former. For surely such an opinion, if deliberately entertained, is creditable neither to a Senator nor to a jurist. Neither this, nor any other mode of trial, is "right in itself;" and when right at all, it is only so as a means to an end. It is only right when it subserves the great end of justice; and if it fail to answer this end it is then worse than worthless. Hence the statesman who declares that, "*whatever may be the effects*" of a particular mode of trial, he will nevertheless support it "as right and just in itself," thereby announces that he is prepared to sacrifice the end to the means,—a sentiment which, we venture to affirm, is more worthy of a fanatical declaimer than of the high-minded and accomplished Senator by whom it was uttered.

The great objection urged against the Fugitive Slave Law is that under it a freeman may be seized and reduced to slavery. This law, as well as every other, may, no doubt, be grossly abused, and made a cover for evil deeds. But is there no remedy for such evil deeds. Is there no protection for the free blacks of the North, except by a denial of the clear and unquestionable constitutional rights of the South? If not, then we should be willing to submit; but there is a remedy against such foul abuse of the law of Congress in question, and, as we conceive, a most ample remedy.

The master may recapture his fugitive slave. This is his constitutional right. But, in the language of the Supreme Court of New York, already quoted, if a villain, under cover of a pretended right, proceeds to carry off a freeman, he does so "*at his peril, and would be answerable like any other trespasser or kidnapper.*" He must be caught, however, before he can be punished. Let him be caught, let the crime be proved upon him, and we would most heartily concur in the law by which he should himself be doomed to slavery for life in the penitentiary.

The Fugitive Slave Law is not the only one liable to abuse. The innocent may be, and often have been, arrested for crime; but this is no reason why the law of arrest should be abolished, or even impaired in its operation. Nay, innocent persons have often been maliciously prosecuted; yet no one, on this account, ever dreamed of throwing obstacles in the way of prosecution for crime. The innocent have been made the victims of perjury; but who imagines that all swearing in courts of justice should therefore be abolished? Such evils and such crimes are sought to be remedied by separate legislation, and not by undermining the laws of which they are the abuses. In like manner, though we wish to see the free blacks of the North protected, and would most cheerfully lend a helping hand for that purpose, yet, at the same time, we would maintain our own constitutional rights inviolate. The villain who, under cover of the law made for the protection of our rights, should seek to invade the rights of Northern freemen, is as much abhorred by us as by any abolitionists on earth. Nor, on the other hand, have we any sympathy with those who, under cover of a law *to be made* for the protection of the free blacks of the North, seek to invade the rights of the South. We have no sympathy with either class of kidnappers.

Is it not wonderful that, while the abolitionists of the North create and keep up so great a clamor about the danger their free blacks are in, they do so little, and ask so little, either by legislation or otherwise, in order to protect them, except in such manner, or by such legislation, as shall aim a deadly blow at the rights and interests of the South? If they really wish to protect their free blacks, and if the laws are not already sufficient for that purpose, we are more than willing to assist in the passage of more efficient ones. But we are not willing to abandon the great right which the Constitution spreads, like an impenetrable shield, over Southern property to the amount of sixteen hundred millions of dollars.

The complaint in regard to the want of protection for the free blacks of the North is without just foundation. In the case of Jack *v.* Martin, decided in the Court of Errors of New York, we find the following language, which is here exactly in point:—"It was contended on the argument of this cause, with great zeal and earnestness, that, under the law of the United States, a freeman might be dragged from his family and home into captivity. This is supposing an extreme case, as I believe it is not pretended any such ever has occurred, or that any complaint of that character has ever been made; at all events, I cannot regard it as a very potent argument. The same position might as well be taken in the case of a fugitive from justice. It might be assumed that he was an innocent man, and entitled to be tried by a jury of the State where he was arrested, to ascertain whether he had violated the laws of the State from which he fled; whereas the fact is, the executive of this State would feel bound to deliver up the most exalted individual in this State, (however well satisfied he might be of his innocence,) if a requisition was made upon him by the executive of another State."

In the same case, when before the Supreme Court of New York, the court said: "In the case under review, the proceedings are before a magistrate of our own State, presumed to possess a sympathy with his fellow-citizens, and *where, upon the supposition that a freeman is arrested, he may readily procure the evidence of his freedom. If the magistrate should finally err in granting the certificate, the party can still resort to the protection of the national judiciary. The proceedings by which his rights have been invaded being under a law of Congress, the remedy for error or injustice belongs peculiarly to that high tribunal.* UNDER THEIR AMPLE SHIELD, THE APPREHENSION OF CAPTIVITY AND OPPRESSION CAN NOT BE ALARMING."

It is evident that when this opinion was pronounced by the Supreme Court of New York, it had not fathomed the depths of some men's capacity of being alarmed by apprehensions of captivity and oppression. The abolitionists will, whether or no, be most dreadfully alarmed. But the danger consists, not in the want of laws and courts to punish the kidnapper, but in the want of somebody to catch him. If he does all the mischief ascribed to him by the abolitionists, is it not wonderful that he is not caught by them? Rumor, with her thousand tongues, is clamorous about his evil deeds; and fanatical credulity, with her ten thousand ears, gives heed to the reports of rumor. But yet, somehow or other, the abolitionists, with all their fiery, restless zeal, never succeed in laying their hands on the offender himself. He must, indeed, be a most adroit, a most cunning, a most wonderful rogue. He boldly goes into a community in which so many are all eye, all ear, and all tongue, in regard to the black man's rights; he there steals a free negro, who himself has the power to tell when, where, and how, he became free; and yet, in open day, and amid ten thousand flaming guardians of freedom,[227] he escapes with perfect impunity! Is he not a most marvelous proper rogue? But perhaps the reason the abolitionists do not lay hands on him is that he is an imaginary being, who, though intangible and invisible, will yet serve just as well to create an alarm and keep up a great excitement as if he were a real personage.

§ IV. *The duty of the Citizen in regard to the Constitution of the United States.*

The Constitution, it is agreed on all sides, is "the supreme law of the land,"—of every State in the Union. The first duty of the citizen in regard to the Constitution is, then, to respect and obey each and every one of its provisions. If he repudiates or sets at naught this or that provision thereof, because it does not happen to agree with his own views or feelings, he does not respect the Constitution at all; he makes his own will and pleasure the supreme law. The true principle of loyalty resides not in his bosom. We may apply to him, and to the supreme law of the land, the language of an inspired apostle, that "whosoever shall keep the whole law, and yet offend in one point, he is guilty of all." He is guilty of all, because, by his willful disobedience in the one instance, he sets at naught the authority by which the whole was ordained and established.

In opposing the Fugitive Slave Law, it is forgotten by the abolitionists that, if no such law existed, the master would have, under the Constitution itself, the same right to reclaim his fugitive from labor, and to reclaim him in the same summary manner; for, as we have seen, the Supreme Court of the United States has decided that by virtue of the Constitution alone the master has a right to pursue and reclaim his fugitive slave, without even a writ or legal process. Hence, in opposing the Fugitive Slave Law because it allows a summary proceeding in such cases, the abolitionists really make war on the Constitution. The battery which they open against the Constitution is merely masked behind the Fugitive Slave Law; and thus the nature of their attack is concealed from the eyes of their non-legal followers.

But, says Mr. Chase, of Ohio, I do not agree with the Supreme Court of the United States. I oppose not the Constitution, but the decision of the Supreme Court. "A decision of the Supreme Court," says he, "cannot alter the Constitution." This is very true; but then, on the other hand, it is equally true that neither can his opinion alter the Constitution. But here the question arises, which is the rule of conduct for the true and loyal citizen,—the decision of the Supreme Court of the United States, or the opinion of Governor Chase? We decidedly prefer the former. "Sir," says Mr. Chase, "when gentlemen from the slave States ask us to support the Constitution, I fear they mean only their *construction* of the Constitution." We mean not so. We mean neither *our* nor *his* construction of the Constitution, but that construction only which has been given to it by the highest judicial tribunal in the land, by the supreme and final arbiter in all such conflicts of opinion.

But Mr. Chase opposes argument as well as opinion to the decision of the Supreme Court in regard to slavery. "What more natural," says he, "than that gentlemen from the slave States, in view of the questions likely to come before the Supreme Court, should desire that a majority of its members might have interests like those which they would desire to maintain! *Certain it is that some care has been taken to secure such a constitution of the court, and not without success.*" If Mr. Chase, or any other abolitionist, should insinuate that the decision in question is owing to such an unfair constitution of the Supreme Court, the answer is as easy and triumphant as the accusation would be infamous and vile; for, as is well known, the very decision which is so obnoxious to his sentiments was delivered by the great jurist of Massachusetts, Mr. Justice Story, and was concurred in by the other Northern members of the Court. This is not all. How did it happen that substantially the same decision has been rendered by the Supreme Courts of New York, Massachusetts, and Pennsylvania? Were these high tribunals also constituted with reference to the peculiar interests of the South?

The question is not whether the decision of the Supreme Court, or the opinion of Mr. Chase, the more perfectly reflects the Constitution. Even if he were infallible, as the Supreme Court certainly is not, we, the people of the United States, have not agreed that he shall decide such questions for us. And besides, it would be difficult, perhaps, to persuade the people that he is, for the determination of such questions, any more happily constituted than the Supreme Court itself, with all the manifold imperfections of its Southern members. But, however this may be, it is certain that until the people shall be so persuaded, and shall agree to abide by his opinions, it is the duty of the good citizen to follow the decisions of the great judicial tribunal provided by the Constitution of his country.

If you, good citizen of the North, have a right to set up your opinion in opposition to such decisions, then I have the same right, and so has every other member of the commonwealth. Thus, as many constructions of the Constitution would necessarily result as there are individual opinions in the land. Law and order would be at an end; a chaos of conflicting elements would prevail, and every man would do that which seemed right in his own eyes. The only escape from such anarchy is a just and loyal confidence in the judicial tribunals of the land—is a subjection of the intense egotism of the individual to the will of the nation, as expressed in the Constitution and expounded by the constitutional authorities. Hence, we mean to support the Constitution, not as *we* understand it nor as *you* understand it, but as it is understood by the Supreme Court of the United States. Such, it seems to us, is the only wise course—nay, is the imperative duty—of every citizen who does not intend to disorganize the fundamental law and revolutionize the government of his country.

It may be supposed, perhaps, by those who have reflected little on the subject, that the controversy respecting the Fugitive Slave Law is merely about the value of a few slaves. It is, in our opinion, far otherwise; it is a great constitutional question; and hence the deep interest which it has excited throughout the nation, as well as in the Senate of the United States. It is a question, as it appears to us, whether the Constitution or the abolitionists shall rule the country. The Fugitive Slave Law is, as we have seen, surrounded by the strongest possible evidences of its constitutionality; and hence, if this may be swept away as unconstitutional by the passions of a mad faction, then may every other legal defence be leveled before like storms, and all security annihilated. Hence, as the friends of law and order, we intend to take our stand right here, and defend this Act, which, although despised and abhorred by a faction, has received the sanction of the fathers, as well as of the great judicial tribunals, of the land.

We are asked to repeal this law—ay, by the most violent agitator of the North we are asked to repeal this law—for "*the sake of tranquillity and peace!*" But how can this bring peace? Suppose this law were repealed; would tranquillity be restored? We have not forgotten—nor can we be so easily made to forget—that this very agitator himself has declared, that slavery is "a wrong so transcendent" that no truce is to be allowed to it so long as it occupies a single foot of ground in the United States. Is it not, then, a delusive prospect of peace which is offered to us in exchange for the law in question?

Nor can we forget what other agitators have uttered respecting the abolition of slavery in the Southern States. "Slavery," said Mr. Seward, at a mass-meeting in Ohio, "can be limited to its present bounds; it can be ameliorated. It can be—and it *must* be—ABOLISHED, and you and I can and *must* do it." Does this look like peace, if the Fugitive Slave Law were only out of the way? Mr. Seward, from his place in the Senate of the United States, tells us how we must act among the people of the North, if, in reclaiming our fugitive slaves, we would not disturb their peace. But he had already exhorted the people of the North to "extend a cordial welcome" to our fugitive slaves, and to "defend them as they would their household gods." What, then, does he mean by peace?

This outcry, indeed, that the peace of the country is disturbed by the Fugitive Slave Law, is as great a delusion as ever was attempted to be palmed off on any people. If this law were repealed to-morrow, would agitation cease? Would the abolitionists of the North cease to proclaim that their doors are open, and their hospitality is ready, to receive the poor benighted blacks? (the blacks of the South, we mean; for we have never heard of their open doors, or cordial hospitality, for the poor free blacks of their own neighborhood.) But we have heard—from Dr. Channing himself—of "a convention at the North, of highly respected men, preparing and publishing an address to the slaves, in which they are exhorted to fly from bondage, and to *feel no scruple in seizing and using horse or boat which may facilitate their escape.*" Now, if the Fugitive Slave Law were repealed, would all such proceedings cease? Or if, under the Constitution as expounded by the Supreme Courts of the Union and of New York, and without any such law to back him, the master should seek to reclaim his property, would he be welcomed, or hooted and resisted, by the defenders of the fugitive from service? Let these things be considered, and it will be evident, we think, that the repeal of the law in question would only invite further aggressions, and from this prostrate outpost the real enemies of the peace of the country would march, if possible, over every other defense of the Constitution.

Hence, although we most ardently desire harmony and concord for the States of the Union, we shall never seek it by a surrender of the Constitution or the decisions of the Supreme Court. If it cannot be found under these, it cannot be found at all. Mr. Chase assures us, indeed, that just so long as the rule laid down by the Supreme Court in the case of Prigg prevails, we must "encounter difficulties, and serious difficulties."[228] If it must be so, then so be it. If the question be whether the decisions of the Supreme Court, or the dictation of demagogues, shall rule our destinies, then is our stand taken and our purpose immovably fixed.

We have a right to peace under the decisions of that august tribunal. It is neither right nor proper—it is contrary to every principle of natural justice—that either party to this great controversy should decide for itself. Hence, if the abolitionists will not submit to the decisions of the Supreme Court, we shall most assuredly refuse submission to their arrogant dictation. We can, from our inmost hearts, respect the feelings of those of our Northern brethren who may choose to remain passive in this matter, and leave us—by such aid as the law may afford—to reclaim our own fugitives from labor. For such we have only words of kindness and feelings of fraternal love. But as for those—and especially for those in high places—who counsel resistance to the laws and to the Constitution of the Republic, we hold them guilty of a high misdemeanor, and we shall ever treat them as disturbers of the public peace, nay, as enemies of the independence, the perpetuity, the greatness, and the glory of the Union under which, by the blessing of Almighty God, we have hitherto so wonderfully prospered.

THE BIBLE ARGUMENT:
OR, SLAVERY IN THE LIGHT OF DIVINE REVELATION.

BY

THORNTON STRINGFELLOW, D. D.,

OF RICHMOND, VIRGINIA.

THE BIBLE ARGUMENT:
OR,
SLAVERY IN THE LIGHT OF DIVINE REVELATION.

CIRCUMSTANCES exist among the inhabitants of these United States, which make it proper that the Scriptures should be carefully examined by Christians in reference to the institution of slavery, which exists in several of the States, with the approbation of those who profess unlimited subjection to God's revealed will.

It is branded by one portion of people, who take their rule of moral rectitude from the Scriptures, as a great sin; nay, the greatest of sins that exist in the nation. And they hold the obligation to exterminate it, to be paramount to all others.

If slavery be thus sinful, it behooves all Christians who are involved in the sin, to repent in dust and ashes, and wash their hands of it, without consulting with flesh and blood. Sin in the sight of God is something which God in his word makes known to be wrong, either by preceptive prohibition, by principles of moral fitness, or examples of inspired men, contained in the sacred volume. When these furnish no law to condemn human conduct, there is no transgression. Christians should produce a "thus saith the Lord," both for what they condemn as sinful, and for what they approve as lawful, in the sight of heaven.

It is to be hoped, that on a question of such vital importance as this to the peace and safety of our common country, as well as to the welfare of the church, we shall be seen cleaving to the Bible, and taking all our decisions about this matter, from its inspired pages. With men from the North, I have observed for many years a palpable ignorance of the Divine will, in reference to the institution of slavery. I have seen but a few who made the Bible their study, that had obtained a knowledge of what it did revea on this subject. Of late their denunciation of slavery as a sin, is loud and long.

I propose, therefore, to examine the sacred volume briefly, and if I am not greatly mistaken, I shall be able to make it appear that the institution of slavery has received, in the first place,

1st. The sanction of the Almighty in the Patriarchal age.

2d. That it was incorporated into the only National Constitution which ever emanated from God.

3d. That its legality was recognized, and its relative duties regulated, by Jesus Christ in his kingdom; and

4th. That it is full of mercy.

Before I proceed further, it is necessary that the terms used to designate the thing, be defined. It is not a name, but a thing, that is denounced as sinful; because it is supposed to be contrary to, and prohibited by the Scriptures.

Our translators have used the term servant, to designate a state in which persons were serving, leaving us to gather the *relation* between the party served, and the party rendering the service, from other terms. The term slave, signifies with us, a definite state, condition, or relation, which state, condition, or relation, is precisely that one which is denounced as sinful. This state, condition, or relation, is that in which one human being is held without his consent, by another, as property;[229] to be bought, sold, and transferred, together with increase, as property forever. Now, this precise thing, is denounced by a portion of the people of these United States, as the greatest individual and national sin that is among us, and is thought to be so hateful in the sight of God, as to subject the nation to ruinous judgments, if it be not removed. Now, I propose to show from the Scriptures, that this state, condition, or relation, did exist in the *patriarchal age*, and that the persons most extensively involved in the sin, if it be a sin, are the very persons who have been singled out by the Almighty, as the objects of his special regard—whose character and conduct he has caused to be held up as *models* for future generations. Before we conclude slavery to be a thing hateful to God, and a great sin in his sight, it is proper that we should search the records he has given us, with care, to see in what light he has looked upon it, and find the warrant for concluding, that we shall honor him by efforts to abolish it; which efforts, in their consequences, may involve the indiscriminate slaughter of the innocent and the guilty, the master and the servant. We all believe him to be a Being who is the same yesterday, to-day, and forever.

The first recorded language which was ever uttered in relation to slavery, is the inspired language of Noah. In God's stead he says, "Cursed be Canaan;" "a servant of servants shall he be to his brethren." "Blessed be the Lord God of Shem; and Canaan shall be his servant." "God shall enlarge Japheth, and he shall dwell in the tents of Shem; and Canaan shall be his servant."—Gen. ix: 25, 26, 27. Here, language is used, showing the *favor* which God would exercise to the posterity of Shem and Japheth, while they were holding the posterity of Ham in a state of *abject bondage*. May it not be said in truth, that God decreed this institution before it existed; and has he not connected its *existence* with prophetic tokens of special favor, to those who should be slave owners or masters? He is the same God now, that he was when he gave these views of his moral character to the world; and unless the posterity of Shem and Japheth, from whom have sprung the Jews, and all the nations of Europe and America, and a great part of Asia, (the African race that is in them excepted,)—I say, unless they are all dead, as well as the Canaanites or Africans, who descended from Ham, then it is quite possible that his favor may now be found with one class of men who are holding another class in bondage. Be this as it may, God *decreed slavery*—and shows in that decree, tokens of good-will to the master. The sacred records occupy but a short space from this inspired ray on this subject, until they bring to our notice, a man that is held up as a model, in all that adorns human nature, and as one that God delighted to honor. This man is Abraham, honored in the sacred records, with the appellation, "Father" of the "faithful." Abraham was a native of Ur, of the Chaldees. From thence the Lord called him to go to a country which he would show him; and he obeyed, not knowing whither he went. He stopped for a time at Haran, where his father died. From thence he "took Sarai his wife, and Lot his brother's son, and all their substance that they had gathered, and the souls they had gotten in Haran, and they went forth to go into the land of Canaan."—Gen. xii: 5.

All the ancient Jewish writers of note, and Christian commentators agree, that by the "souls they had gotten in Haran," as our translators render it, are meant their slaves, or those persons they had bought with their money in Haran. In a few years after their arrival in Canaan, Lot with all he had was taken captive. So soon as Abraham heard it, he armed three hundred and eighteen slaves that were born in his house, and retook him. How great must have been the entire slave family, to produce at this period of Abraham's life, such a number of young slaves able to bear arms.—Gen. xiv: 14.

Abraham is constantly held up in the sacred story, as the subject of great distinction among the princes and sovereigns of the countries in which he sojourned. This distinction was on account of his great wealth. When he proposed to buy a burying-ground at Sarah's death, of the children of Heth, he stood up and spoke with great humility of himself as "a stranger and sojourner among them," (Gen. xxiii: 4,) desirous to obtain a burying-ground. But in what light do they look upon him? "Hear us, my Lord, thou art a mighty prince among us."—Gen. xxiii: 6. Such is the light in which they viewed him. What gave a man such distinction among such a people? Not moral qualities, but great wealth, and its inseparable concomitant, power. When the famine drove Abraham to Egypt, he received the highest honors of the reigning sovereign. This honor at Pharaoh's court, was called forth by the visible tokens of immense wealth. In Genesis xii: 15, 16, we have the honor that was shown to him, mentioned, *with a list of his property*, which is given in these words, in the 16th verse: "He had sheep, and oxen, and he-asses, and men-servants, and maid-servants, and she-asses, and camels." The *amount* of his flocks may be inferred from the *number of slaves* employed in tending them. They were those he brought from Ur of the Chaldees, of whom the three hundred and eighteen were born; those gotten in Haran, where he dwelt for a short time, and those which he inherited from his father, who died in Haran. When Abraham *went up* from Egypt, it is stated in Genesis xiii: 2, that he was "*very rich*," not only in *flocks* and *slaves*, but in "*silver* and *gold*" also.

After the destruction of Sodom, we see him sojourning in the kingdom of Gerar. Here he received from the sovereign of the country, the honors of equality; and Abimelech, the king, (as Pharoah had done before him,) seeks Sarah for a wife, under the idea that she was Abraham's sister. When his mistake was discovered, he made Abraham a large present. Reason will tell us, that in selecting the items of this present, Abimelech was governed by the visible indications of Abraham's preference in the articles of wealth—and that above all, he would present him with nothing which Abraham's sense of moral obligation would not allow him to own. Abimelech's present is thus described in Genesis xx: 14, 16, "And Abimelech took sheep, and oxen, and men-servants, and women-servants, and a thousand pieces of silver, and gave them unto Abraham." This present discloses to us what constituted the most highly prized items of wealth, among these eastern sovereigns in Abraham's day.

God had promised Abraham's seed the land of Canaan, and that in his seed all the nations of the earth should be blessed. He reached the age of eighty-five, and his wife the age of seventy-five, while as yet, they had no child. At this period, Sarah's anxiety for the promised seed, in connection with her age, induced her to propose a female slave of the Egyptian stock, as a secondary wife, from which to obtain the promised seed. This alliance soon puffed the slave with pride, and she became insolent to her mistress—the mistress complained to Abraham, the master. Abraham ordered Sarah to exercise her authority. Sarah did so, and pushed it to severity, and the slave absconded. The divine oracles inform us, that the angel of God found this run-away bond-woman in the wilderness; and if God had commissioned this angel to improve this opportunity of teaching the world how much he abhorred slavery, he took a bad plan to acomplish it. For, instead of repeating a homily upon doing to others as we "would they should do unto us," and heaping reproach upon Sarah, as a hypocrite, and Abraham as a tyrant, and giving Hagar direction how she might get into Egypt, from whence (according to abolitionism) she had been unrighteously sold into bondage, the angel addressed her as "Hagar, Sarah's maid," Gen. xvi: 1, 9; (thereby recognizing the relation of master and slave,) and asks her, "whither wilt thou go?" and she said "I flee from the face of my mistress." Quite a wonder she honored Sarah so much as to call her mistress; but she knew nothing of abolition, and God by his angel did not become her teacher.

We have now arrived at what may be called an *abuse* of the institution, in which one person is the property of another, and under their control, and subject to their authority without their consent; and if the Bible be the book, which proposes to furnish the case which leaves it without doubt that God abhors the institution, here we are to look for it. What, therefore, is the doctrine in relation to slavery, in a case in which a rigid exercise of its arbitrary authority is called forth upon a helpless female; who might use a strong plea for protection, upon the ground of being the master's wife. In the face of this case, which is hedged around with aggravations as if God designed by it to awaken all the sympathy and all the abhorrence of that portion of mankind, who claim to have more mercy than God himself—but I say, in view of this strong case, what is the doctrine taught? Is it that God abhors the institution of slavery; that it is a reproach to good men; that the evils of the institution can no longer be winked at among saints; that Abraham's character must not be transmitted to posterity, with this stain upon it; that Sarah must no longer be allowed to live a stranger to the abhorrence God has for such conduct as she has been guilty of to this poor helpless female? I say, what is the doctrine taught? Is it so plain that it can be easily understood? and does God teach that she is a bond-woman or slave, and that she is to recognize Sarah as her mistress, and not her equal—that she must return and submit herself unreservedly to Sarah's authority? Judge for yourself, reader, by the angel's answer: "And the angel of the Lord said unto her, Return unto thy mistress, and submit thyself under her hands."—Gen. xvi: 9.

But, says the spirit of abolition, with which the Bible has to contend, you are building your house upon the sand, for these were nothing but hired servants; and their servitude designates no such state, condition, or relation, as that, in which one person is made the property of another, to be bought, sold, or transferred forever. To this, we have two an- swers in reference to the subject, *before giving the law*. In the first place, the term servant, in the schedules of property among the patriarchs, *does designate* the state, con- dition, or relation in which one person is the legal property of another, as in Gen. xxiv: 35, 36. Here Abraham's servant, who had been sent by his master to get a wife for his son Isaac, in order to prevail with the woman and her family, states, that the man for whom he sought a bride, was the son of a man whom God had greatly blessed with riches; which he goes on to enumerate thus, in the 35th verse: "He hath given him flocks, and herds, and silver, and gold, and men-servants, and maid-servants, and camels, and asses;" then in verse 36th, he states the disposition his master had made of his estate: "My mas- ter's wife bare a son to my master when she was old, and unto him he hath given all that he hath." Here, servants are enumerated with silver and gold as part of the patrimony. And, reader, bear it in mind; as if to rebuke the doctrine of abolition, servants are not on- ly inventoried as property, but as property which *God had given to Abraham*. After the death of Abraham, we have a view of Isaac at Gerar, when he had come into the posses- sion of this estate; and this is the description given of him: "And the man waxed great, and went forward, and grew until he became very great; for he had possession of flocks, and possession of herds, and *great store of servants*."—Gen. xxvi: 13, 14. This state in which servants are made chattels, he received as an inheritance from his father, and passed to his son Jacob.

Again, in Genesis xvii, we are informed of a covenant God entered into with Abra- ham; in which he stipulates to be a God to him and his *seed*, (not his servants,) and to give to his *seed* the land of Canaan for an everlasting possession. He expressly stipulates, that Abraham shall put the token of this covenant upon every servant born in his house, and upon every servant *bought with his money of any stranger*.—Gen. xvii: 12, 13. Here again servants are property. Again, more than four hundred years afterward, we find the *seed* of Abraham, on leaving Egypt, directed to celebrate the rite, that was ordained as a memorial of their deliverance, viz: the Passover, at which time the same institution which makes *property* of *men* and *women*, is recognized, and the *servant bought with money*, is given the privilege of partaking, upon the ground of his being circumcised *by his master*, while the hired servant, over whom the master had no such control, is excluded until he *voluntarily* submits to circumcision; showing clearly that the institution of involuntary slavery then carried with it a right, on the part of the master, *to choose* a religion *for the servant* who was his money, as Abraham did, by God's direction, when he imposed circumcision on those he had bought with his money,—when he was circumcised himself, with Ishmael his son, who was the only individual beside himself, on whom he had a right to impose it, except the bond-servants bought of the stranger with his money, and their children born in his house. The next notice we have of servants as property, is from God himself, when clothed with all the visible tokens of his presence and glory, on the top of Sinai, when he proclaimed his law to the millions that surrounded its base: "Thou shalt not covet thy neighbor's house, thou shalt not covet thy neighbor's wife, nor his man-servant, nor his maid-servant, nor his ox, nor his ass, nor any thing that is thy neighbor's."—Ex. xx: 17. Here is a patriarchal catalogue of property, having God for its author, the wife among the rest, who was then purchased, as Jacob purchased his two, by fourteen years' service. Here the term servant, as used by the Almighty, under the circumstances of the case could not be understood by these millions, as meaning any thing but property, because the night they left Egypt, a few weeks before, Moses, by Divine authority, recognized their servants as property, which they had bought with their money.

2d. In addition to the evidence from the context of these, and various other places, to prove the term servant to be identical in the import of its essential particulars with the term slave among us, there is unquestionable evidence, that *in the patriarchal age*, there are two distinct states of servitude alluded to, and which are indicated by two distinct terms, or by the same term, and an adjective to explain.

These two terms are first, servant or bond-servant; second, hireling or hired servant; the first indicating involuntary servitude; the second, voluntary servitude for stipulated wages, and a specified time. Although this admits of the clearest proof *under the law*, yet it admits of proof before the law given. On the night the Israelites left Egypt, which was before the law was given, Moses, in designating the qualifications necessary for the Passover, uses this language,—Exod. xii: 44, 45: "Every man's servant that is bought for money, when thou hast circumcised him, then shall he eat thereof. A foreigner and an hired servant shall not eat thereof." This language carries to the human mind, with irresistible force, the idea of *two distinct states*—one a state of *freedom*, the other a state of *bondage:* in one of which, a person is serving with his consent for wages; in the other of which a person is serving without his *consent*, according to his master's pleasure.

Again, in Job iii, Job expresses the strong desire he had been made by his afflictions to feel, that he had died in his infancy. "For now," says he, "should I have lain still and been quiet, I should have slept: then had I been at rest. There (meaning the grave) the wicked cease from troubling, and there the weary be at rest. There the prisoners rest together; they hear not the voice of the oppressor. The small and the great are there, and the servant is free from his master."—Job iii: 11, 13, 17, 18, 19. Now, I ask any common-sense man to account for the expression in this connection, "there the servant is free from his master." Afflictions are referred to, arising out of *states* or *conditions*, from which *ordinarily* nothing but *death* brings relief. *Death* puts an end to afflictions of body that are incurable, as he took his own to be, and therefore he desired it.

The troubles brought on good men by a wicked persecuting world, last for life; but in *death* the wicked cease from troubling,—*death* ends that *relation* or *state* out of which such troubles grow. The prisoners of the oppressors, in that age, stood in a *relation* to their *oppressor*, which led the oppressed to expect they would hear the voice of the *oppressor* until *death*. But *death* broke the *relation*, and was desired, because in the grave they would hear his voice no more.

All the distresses growing out of inequalities in human condition; as wealth and power on one side, and poverty and weakness on the other, were terminated by death; the grave brought both to a level: the small and the great are there, and there, (that is, in the grave,) he adds, the servant is free from his master; made so, evidently, by *death*. The *relation*, or *state* out of which his oppression had arisen, being destroyed by *death*, he would be freed from them, because he would, by *death*, be freed from his master who inflicted them. This view of the case, and this only, will account for the use of such language. But upon a supposition that a *state* or *relation* among men is referred to, that is *voluntary*, such as that between a *hired servant* and his *employer*, that can be *dissolved* at the pleasure of the *servant*, the language is without meaning, and perfectly unwarranted; while such a *relation* as that of *involuntary* and *hereditary* servitude, where the master had *unlimited power* over his servant, and in an age when cruelty was common, there is the greatest propriety in making the servant or slave, a *companion with himself, in affliction*, as well as the oppressed and afflicted, in every class where *death alone* dissolved the *state* or *condition*, out of which their afflictions grew. Beyond all doubt, this language refers to a state of *hereditary bondage*, from the afflictions of which, *ordinarily*, nothing in that day brought relief but *death*.

Again, in chapter 7th, he goes on to defend himself in his eager desire for death, in an address to God. He says, it is natural for a servant to desire the shadow, and a hireling his wages: "As the servant earnestly desireth the shadow, and as the hireling looketh for the reward of his work," so it is with me, should be supplied.—Job vii: 2. Now, with the previous light shed upon the use and meaning of these terms in the *patriarchal Scriptures*, can any man of candor bring himself to believe that two states or conditions are not here referred to, in one of which, the highest reward after toil is mere rest; in the other of which, the reward was wages? And how appropriate is the language in reference to these two states.

The *slave* is represented as earnestly desiring the *shadow*, because his condition allowed him no prospect of any thing more desirable; but the *hireling* as looking for the *reward of his work*, because *that* will be an equivalent for his fatigue.

So Job looked at *death*, as being to his *body* as the servant's *shade*, therefore he desired it; and like the *hireling's wages*, because *beyond the grave*, he hoped to reap the fruit of his doings. Again, Job (xxxi:) finding himself the subject of suspicion (see from verse 1 to 30) as to the rectitude of his past life, clears himself of various sins, in the most solemn manner, as unchastity, injustice in his dealings, adultery, contempt of his servants, unkindness to the poor, covetousness, the pride of wealth, etc. And in the 13th, 14th, and 15th verses he thus expresses himself: "If I did despise the cause of my manservant, or my maid-servant, when they contended with me, what then shall I do when God rises up? And when he visiteth, what shall I answer him? Did not he that made me in the womb, make him? And did not one fashion us in the womb?" Taking this language in connection with the language employed by Moses, in reference to the institution of involuntary servitude in *that age*, and especially in connection with the language which Moses employs *after the law was given*, and what else can be understood, than a reference to a class of duties that slave owners felt themselves above stooping to notice or perform, but which, nevertheless, it was the duty of the righteous man to discharge: for whatever proud and wicked men might think of a poor servant that stood in his estate, on an equality with brutes, yet, says Job, he that made me, made them, and if I despise their reasonable causes of complaint, for injuries which they are made to suffer, and for the redress of which I only can be appealed to, then what shall I do, and how shall I fare, when I carry my causes of complaint to him who is my master, and to whom only I can go for relief? When he visiteth me for despising *their cause*, what shall I answer him for *despising mine?* He means that he would feel self-condemned, and would be forced to admit the justice of the retaliation. But on the supposition that allusion is had to *hired servants*, who were *voluntarily* working for *wages* agreed upon, and who were the *subjects of rights* for the *protection of which*, their appeal would be to "the judges in the gate," as much as any other class of men, then there is no point in the statement. For *doing that* which can be *demanded as a legal right*, gives us no claim to the character of *merciful benefactors*. Job himself was a great slaveholder, and, like Abraham, Isaac, and Jacob, won no small portion of his claims to character with God and men from the manner in which he discharged his duty to his slaves. Once more: the conduct of Joseph in Egypt, *as Pharaoh's counsellor*, under all the circumstances, proves him a friend to absolute slavery, as a form of government better adapted to the state of the world at that time, than the one which existed in Egypt; for certain it is, that he peaceably effected a change in the fundamental law, by which a *state, condition, or relation*, between Pharaoh and the Egyptians was established, which answers to the one now denounced as sinful in the sight of God. Being warned of God, he gathered up all the surplus grain in the years of plenty, and sold it out in the years of famine, until he gathered up all the money; and when money failed, the Egyptians came and said, "Give us bread;" and Joseph said, "Give your cattle, and I will give for your cattle, if money fail." When that year was ended, they came unto him the second year, and said, "There is not aught left in sight of my Lord, but our bodies and our lands. Buy us and our lands for bread." And Joseph bought all the land of Egypt for Pharoah.

So the land became Pharoah's, and as for the people, he removed them to cities, from one end of the borders of Egypt, even to the other end thereof. Then Joseph said unto the people, "Behold! I have bought you this day, and your land for Pharoah; and they said, "we will be Pharoah's servants."—See Gen. xlvii: 14, 16, 19, 20, 21, 23, 25. Having thus changed the fundamental law, and created a state of entire *dependence* and *hereditary bondage*, he enacted in his sovereign pleasure, that they should give Pharoah one part, and take the other four parts of the productions of the earth to themselves. How far the hand of God was in this overthrow of liberty, I will not decide; but from the fact that he has singled out the greatest slaveholders of that age, as the objects of his special favor, it would seem that the institution was one furnishing great opportunities to exercise grace and glorify God, as it still does, where its duties are faithfully discharged.

I have been tedious on this first proposition, but I hope the importance of the subject to Christians as well as to statesmen will be my apology. I have written it, not for victory over an adversary, or to support error or falsehood, but to gather up God's will in reference to holding men and women in *bondage, in the patriarchal age.* And it is clear, in the first place, that God decreed this state before it existed. Second. It is clear that the highest manifestations of good-will which he ever gave to mortal man, was given to Abraham, in that covenant in which he required him to circumcise all his *male servants, which he had bought with his money*, and that were *born of them* in his house. Third. It is certain that he gave *these servants* as *property* to Isaac. Fourth. It is certain that, as the owner of *these slaves*, Isaac received similar tokens of God's favor. Fifth. It is certain that Jacob, who inherited from Isaac his father, received like tokens of divine favor. Sixth. It is certain, from a fair construction of language, that Job, who is held up by God himself as a model of human perfection, was a great slaveholder. Seventh. It is certain, when God showed honor, and came down to bless Jacob's posterity, in taking them by the hand to lead them out of Egypt, *they were the owners of slaves that were bought with money, and treated as property; which slaves* were allowed of God to unite in celebrating the divine goodness to their *masters*, while *hired servants* were excluded. Eighth. It is certain that God interposed to give Joseph the power in Egypt, which he used, to create a state, or condition, among the Egyptians, which *substantially agrees* with *patriarchal* and *modern slavery.* Ninth. It is certain, that in reference to this institution in Abraham's family, and the surrounding nations, for five hundred years, it is never censured in any communication made from God to men. Tenth. It is certain, when God put a *period* to *that dispensation*, he *recognised slaves as property on Mount Sinai*. If, therefore, it has become sinful since, it cannot be from the *nature of the thing*, but from the *sovereign pleasure of God in its prohibition*. We will therefore proceed to our second proposition, which is—

Second.—That it was incorporated in the only national constitution emanating from the Almighty. By common consent, that portion of time stretching from Noah, until the law was given to Abraham's posterity, at Mount Sinai, is called the patriarchal age; *this is the period we have reviewed*, in relation to this subject. From the giving of the law until the coming of Christ, is called the Mosaic or legal dispensation. From the coming of Christ to the end of time, is called the Gospel dispensation. The legal dispensation *is the period of time, we propose now to examine*, in reference to the institution of involuntary and hereditary slavery; in order to ascertain, whether, during this period, *it existed at all*, and *if it did exist*, whether with the *divine sanction*, or in *violation of the divine will*. This dispensation is called the legal dispensation, because it was the pleasure of God to take Abraham's posterity by miraculous power, then numbering near three millions of souls, and give them a written constitution of government, a country to dwell in, and a covenant of special protection and favor, for their obedience to his law until the coming of Christ. The laws which he gave them emanated from his sovereign pleasure, and were designed, in the first place, to make himself known in his essential perfections; second, in his moral character; third, in his relation to man; and fourth, to make known those principles of action by the exercise of which man attains his highest moral elevation, viz: supreme love to God, and love to others as to ourselves.

All the law is nothing but a preceptive exemplification of these two principles; consequently, the existence of a precept in the law, utterly irreconcilable with these principles, would destroy all claims upon us for an acknowledgment of its divine original. Jesus Christ himself has put his finger upon these two principles of human conduct, (Deut. vi: 5—Levit. xix: 18,) revealed in the law of Moses, and decided, that on them hang all the law and the prophets.

The Apostle Paul decides in reference to the relative duties of men, that whether written out in preceptive form in the law or not, they are all comprehended in this saying, viz: "thou shalt love thy neighbor as thyself." With these views to guide us, as to the acknowledged design of the law, viz: that of revealing the eternal principles of moral rectitude, by which human conduct is to be measured, so that sin may abound, or be made apparent, and righteousness be ascertained or known, we may safely conclude, that the institution of slavery, which legalizes the holding one person in bondage as property forever by another, if it be morally wrong, or at war with the principle which requires us to love God supremely, and our neighbor as ourself, will, if noticed at all in the law, be noticed, for the purpose of being condemned as sinful. And if the modern views of abilitionists be correct, we may expect to find the institution marked with such tokens of divine displeasure, as will throw all other sins into the shade, as comparatively small, when laid by the side of this monster. What, then, is true? Has God ingrafted hereditary slavery upon the constitution of government he condescended to give to his chosen people—that people, among whom he promised to dwell, and that he required to be holy? I answer, he has. It is clear and explicit. He enacts, first, that his chosen people may take their money, go into the slave markets of the surrounding nations, (the seven devoted nations excepted,) and purchase men-servants and women-servants, and give them, and their increase, to their children and their children's children, forever; and worse still for the refined humanity of our age—he guarantees to the foreign slaveholder perfect protection, while he comes in among the Israelites, for the purpose of dwelling, and raising and selling slaves, who should be acclimated and accustomed to the habits and institutions of the country. And worse still for the sublimated humanity of the present age, God passes with the right to buy and possess, the right to govern, by a severity which knows no bounds but the master's discretion. And if worse can be, for the morbid humanity we censure, he enacts that his own people may sell themselves and their families for limited periods, with the privilege of extending the time at the end of the sixth year to the fiftieth year or jubilee, if they prefer bondage to freedom. Such is the precise character of two institutions, found in the constitution of the Jewish commonwealth, emanating directly from Almighty God. For the fifteen hundred years, during which these laws were in force, God raised up a succession of prophets to reprove that people for the various sins into which they fell; yet there is not a reproof uttered against the institution of *involuntary slavery*, for any species of abuse that ever grew out of it. A severe judgment is pronounced by Jeremiah, (chapter xxxiv: see from the 8th to the 22d verse,) for an abuse or violation of the law, concerning the *voluntary* servitude of Hebrews; but the prophet pens it with caution, as if to show that it had no reference to any abuse that had taken place under the system of *involuntary slavery*, which existed by law among that people; the sin consisted in making hereditary bond-men and bond-women of Hebrews, which was positively forbidden by the law, and not for buying and holding one of another nation in hereditary bondage, which was as positively allowed by the law. And really, in view of what is passing in our country, and elsewhere, among men who profess to reverence the Bible, it would seem that these must be dreams of a distempered brain, and not the solemn truths of that sacred book.

Well, I will now proceed to make them good to the letter, see Levit. xxv: 44, 45, 46; "Thy bond-men and thy bond-maids which thou shalt have, shall be of the heathen that are round about you; of them shall ye buy bond-men and bond-maids. Moreover, of the children of the strangers that do sojourn among you, of them shall ye buy, and of their families that are with you, which they begat in your land. And they shall be your possession. And ye shall take them as an inheritance for your children after you, to inherit them for a possession they shall be your bond-men forever." I ask any candid man, if the words of this institution could be more explicit? It is from God himself; it authorizes that people, to whom he had become *king and law-giver*, to purchase men and women as property; to hold them and their posterity in bondage; and to will them to their children as a possession forever; and more, it allows *foreign slaveholders* to *settle* and *live among them; to breed slaves* and *sell them*. Now, it is important to a correct understanding of this subject, to connect with the right to *buy* and *possess*, as property, the amount of authority *to govern*, which is granted by the *law-giver;* this amount of authority is implied, in the first place, in the law which prohibits the exercise of rigid authority upon the Hebrews, who are allowed to sell themselves for limited times. "If thy brother be waxen poor, and be sold unto thee, thou shalt not *compel him* to serve as a *bond servant*, but as a *hired servant*, and as a *sojourner* he shall be with thee, and shall serve thee until the year of jubilee—*they shall not be sold as bond-men;* thou *shalt not rule over them with rigor*."—Levit. xxv: 39, 40, 41, 42, 43. It will be evident to all, that here are *two states* of servitude; in reference to *one* of which, *rigid* or *compulsory* authority, is *prohibited*, and that its *exercise is authorised in the other*.

Second.—In the criminal code, that conduct is punished with death, when done to a *freeman*, which is not punishable at all, when done *by a master to a slave*, for the express reason, that the slave is the *master's money*. "He that smiteth a man so that he die, shall surely be put to death."—Exod. xxi: 20, 21. "If a man smite his servant or his maid, with a rod, and he die under his hand, he shall be surely punished; notwithstanding, if he continue a day or two, he shall not be punished, for he is his money."—Exod. xxi: 20. Here is precisely the same crime: smiting a man so that he die; if it be a freeman, he shall surely be put to death, whether the man die under his hand, or live a day or two after; but if it be a servant, and the master continued the rod until the servant died under his hand, then it must be evident that such a chastisement could not be necessary for any purpose of wholesome or reasonable authority, and therefore he may by punished, but not with death. But if the death did not take place for a day or two, then it is to be *presumed*, that the master only aimed to use the rod, so far as was necessary to produce subordination, and for this, the law which allowed him to lay out his money in the slave, would protect him against all punishment. This is the common-sense principle which has been adopted substantially in civilized countries, where involuntary slavery has been instituted, from that day until this. Now, here are laws that authorize the holding of men and women in bondage, and chastising them with the rod, with a severity that terminates in death. And he who believes the Bible to be of divine authority, believes these laws were given by the Holy Ghost to Moses. I understand modern abolition sentiments to be sentiments of marked hatred against such laws; to be sentiments which would hold God himself in abhorrence, if he were to give such laws his sanction; but he has given them his sanction; therefore, they must be in harmony with his moral character. Again, the divine Lawgiver, in guarding the property right in slaves among his chosen people, sanctions principles which may work the separation of man and wife, father and children. Surely, my reader will conclude, if I make this good, I shall force a part of the saints of the present day to blaspheme the God of Israel. All I can say is, truth is mighty, and I hope it will bring us all to say, let God be true, in settling the true principles of humanity, and every man a liar who says slavery was inconsistent with it, in the days of the Mosaic law. Now for the proof: "If thou buy a Hebrew servant, six years shall he serve thee, and in the seventh he shall go out free for nothing; if he came in by himself, he shall go out by himself; if he were married, then his wife shall go out with him; if his master have given him a wife (one of his bond-maids) and she have borne him sons and daughters, the wife and her children shall be her master's and he shall go out by himself."—Exod. xxi: 2, 3, 4. Now, the God of Israel gives this man the option of being separated by the master, from his wife and children, or becoming himself a servant forever, with a mark of the fact, like our cattle, in the ear, that can be seen wherever he goes; for it is enacted, "If the servant shall plainly say, I love my master, my wife, and my children, I will not go out free, then his master shall bring him unto the judges, (in open court,) he shall also bring him unto the door, or unto the door post, (so that all in the court-house, and those in the yard may be witnesses, and his master shall bore his ear through with an awl; and he shall serve him forever." It is useless to spend more time in gathering up what is written in the Scriptures on this subject, from the giving of the law until the coming of Christ.

Here is the authority, from God himself, to hold men and women, and their increase, in slavery, and to transmit them as property forever; here is plenary power to govern them, whatever measure of severity it may require; provided only, that *to govern*, be the object in exercising it. Here is power given to the master, to separate man and wife, parent and child, by denying ingress to his premises, sooner than compel him to free or sell the mother, that the marriage relation might be honored. The *preference* is given of God to *enslaving the father* rather than *freeing the mother and children*.

Under every view we are allowed to take of the subject, the conviction is forced upon the mind, that from Abraham's day, until the coming of Christ, (a period of two thousand years,) this institution found favor with God. No marks of his displeasure are found resting upon it. It must, therefore, in its moral nature, be in harmony with those moral principles which he requires to be exercised by the law of Moses, and which are the principles that secure harmony and happiness to the universe, viz: supreme love to God, and the love of our neighbor as ourself.—Deut. vi: 5.—Levit. xix: 18. To suppose that God has laid down these fundamental principles of moral rectitude in his law, as the soul that must inhabit every preceptive requirement of that law, and yet to suppose he created relations among the Israelites, and prescribed relative duties growing out of these relations, that are hostile to the spirit of the law, is to suppose what will never bring great honor or glory to our Maker. But if I understand that spirit which is now warring against slavery, this is the position which the spirit of God forces it to occupy, viz: that God has ordained slavery, and yet slavery is the greatest of sins. Such was the state of the case when Jesus Christ made his appearance. We propose—

Third. To show that Jesus Christ recognized this institution as one that was lawful among men, and regulated its relative duties.

Having shown from the Scriptures, that slavery existed with Abraham and the patriarchs, with divine approbation, and having shown from the same source, that the Almighty incorporated it in the law, as an institution among Abraham's seed, until the coming of Christ, our precise object now is, to ascertain whether *Jesus Christ has abolished it*, or *recognized it* as a *lawful relation*, existing among men, and prescribed duties which belong to it, as he has other relative duties; such as those between husband and wife, parent and child, magistrate and subject.

And first, I may take it for granted, without proof, that he has not abolished it by commandment, for none pretend to this. This, by the way, is a singular circumstance, that Jesus Christ should put a system of measures into operation, which have for their object the subjugation of all men to him as a law-giver—kings, legislators, and private citizens in all nations; at a time, too, when hereditary slavery existed in all; and after it had been incorporated for fifteen hundred years into the Jewish constitution, immediately given by God himself. I say, it is passing strange, that under such circumstances, Jesus should fail to prohibit its further existence, if it was his intention to abolish it. Such an omission or oversight cannot be charged upon any other legislator the world has ever seen. But, says the abolitionist, he has introduced new moral principles, which will extinguish it as an unavoidable consequence, without a direct prohibitory command. What are they? "Do to others as you would they should do to you." Taking these words of Christ to be a body, inclosing a moral soul in them, what soul, I ask, is it?

The same embodied in these words of Moses, Levit. xix: 18; "thou shalt love thy neighbor as thyself;" or is it another? It cannot be another, but it must be the very same, because Jesus says, there are but two principles in being in God's moral government, *one* including all that is *due to God*, the *other* all that is *due to men*.

If, therefore, doing to others as we would they should do to us, means precisely what loving our neighbor as ourself means, then Jesus has added no new moral principle above those in the law of Moses, to prohibit slavery, for in his law is found this principle, and slavery also.

The very God that said to them, they should love him supremely, and their neighbors as themselves, said to them also, "of the heathen that are round about you, thou shalt buy bond-men and bond-women, and they shall be your possession, and ye shall take them as an inheritance for your children after you, to inherit them as a possession; they shall be your bond-men forever." Now, to suppose that Jesus Christ left his disciples to find out, without a revelation, that slavery must be abolished, as a natural consequence from the fact, that when God established the relation of master and servant under the law, he said to the master and servant, each of you must love the other as yourself, is, to say the least, making Jesus to presume largely upon the intensity of their intellect, that they would be able to spy out a discrepancy in the law of Moses, which God himself never saw. Again:

if "do to others as ye would they should do to you," is to abolish slavery, it will for the same reason, level all inequalities in human condition. It is not to be admitted, then, that Jesus Christ introduced any new moral principle that must, of necessity, abolish slavery. The principle relied on to prove it, stands boldly out to view in the code of Moses, as the *soul*, that must *regulate*, and *control*, the *relation* of *master and servant*, and therefore cannot abolish it.

Why a master cannot do to a servant, or a servant to a master, as he would have them do to him, as soon as a wife to a husband or a husband to a wife, I am utterly at a loss to know. The wife is "subject to her husband in all things" by divine precept. He is her "head," and God "suffers her not to usurp authority over him." Now, why in such a relation as this, we can do to others *as we* would they should do to us, any sooner than in a relation, securing to us what is just and equal as servants, and due respect and faithful service rendered with good will to us as masters, I am at a loss to conceive. I affirm then, first, (and no man denies,) that Jesus Christ has not abolished slavery by a prohibitory command: and second, I affirm, he has introduced no new moral principle which can work its destruction, under the gospel dispensation; and that the principle relied on for this purpose, is a fundamental principle of the Mosaic law, under which slavery was instituted by Jehovah himself: and third, with this absence of positive prohibition, and this absence of principle, to work its ruin, I affirm, that in all the Roman provinces, where churches were planted by the apostles, hereditary slavery existed, as it did among the Jews, and as it does now among us, (which admits of proof from history that no man will dispute who knows any thing of the matter,) and that in instructing such churches, the Holy Ghost by the apostles, has recognized the institution, as one *legally existing* among them, to be perpetuated in the church, and that its duties are prescribed.

Now for the proof: To the church planted at Ephesus the capital of the lesser Asia, Paul ordains by letter, subordination in the fear of God,—first between wife and husband; second, child and parent; third, servant and master; *all, as states, or conditions, existing among the members.*

The relative duties of each state are pointed out; those between the servant and master in these words: "Servants be obedient to them who are your masters, according to the flesh, with fear and trembling, in singleness of your heart as unto Christ; not with eye service as men pleasers, but as the servants of Christ, doing the will of God from the heart, with good-will, doing service, as to the Lord, and not to men, knowing that whatsoever good thing any man doeth, the same shall he receive of the Lord, whether he be bond or free. And ye masters do the same things to them, forbearing threatening, knowing that your master is also in heaven, neither is there respect of persons with him." Here, by the Roman law, the servant was property, and the control of the master unlimited, as we shall presently prove.

To the church at Colosse, a city of Phrygia, in the lesser Asia,—Paul in his letter to them, recognizes the three relations of wives and husbands, parents and children, servants and masters, as relations existing among the members; (here the Roman law was the same;) and to the servants and masters he thus writes: "Servants obey in all things your masters, according to the flesh: not with eye service, as men pleasers, but in singleness of heart, fearing God: and whatsoever you do, do it heartily, as to the Lord and not unto men; knowing that of the Lord ye shall receive the reward of the inheritance, for ye serve the Lord Christ. But he that doeth wrong shall receive for the wrong he has done; and there is no respect of persons with God. Masters give unto your servants that which is just and equal, knowing that you also have a master in heaven."

The same Apostle writes a letter to the church at Corinth;—a very important city, formerly called the eye of Greece, either from its location, or intelligence, or both, and consequently, an important point, for radiating light in all directions, in reference to subjects connected with the cause of Jesus Christ; and particularly, in the bearing of its practical precepts on civil society, and the political structure of nations. Under the direction of the Holy Ghost, he instructs the church, that, on this particular subject, *one general principle* was ordained of God, applicable alike in all countries and at all stages of the church's future history, and that it was this: "*as the Lord has called every one, so let him walk.*" "Let every man abide in the same calling wherein he is called." "Let every man wherein he is called, therein abide with God."—1 Cor. vii: 17, 20, 24. "*And so ordain I in all churches;*" vii: 17. The Apostle thus explains his meaning:

"Is any man called being circumcised? Let him not become uncircumcised."

"Is any man called in uncircumcision? Let him not be circumcised."

"Art thou called, being a servant? Care not for it, but if thou mayest be made free, use it rather;" vii: 18, 21. Here, by the Roman law, slaves were property,—yet Paul ordains, in this, and all other churches, that Christianity gave them no title to freedom, but on the contrary, required them not to care for being slaves, or in other words, to be contented with their *state*, or *relation*, unless they could be *made free*, in a lawful way.

Again, we have a letter by Peter, who is the Apostle of the circumcision—addressed especially to the Jews, who were scattered through various provinces of the Roman empire; comprising those provinces especially, which were the theater of their dispersion, under the Assyrians and Babylonians. Here, for the space of seven hundred and fifty years, they had resided, during which time those revolutions were in progress which terminated the Babylonian, Medo-Persian, and Macedonian empires, and transferred imperial power to Rome. These revolutionary scenes of violence left one half the human race (within the range of their influence,) in abject bondage to the other half. This was the state of things in these provinces addressed by Peter, when he wrote. The chances of war, we may reasonably conclude, had assigned a full share of bondage to this people, who were despised of all nations. In view of their enslaved condition to the Gentiles; knowing, as Peter did, their seditious character; foreseeing, from the prediction of the Saviour, the destined bondage of those who were then free in Israel, which was soon to take place, as it did, in the fall of Jerusalem, when all the males of seventeen, were sent to work in the mines of Egypt, as slaves to the State, and all the males under, amounting to upwards of ninety-seven thousand, were sold into domestic bondage;—I say, in view of these things, Peter was moved by the Holy Ghost to write to them, and his solicitude for such of them as were in slavery, is very conspicuous in his letter; (read carefully from 1 Peter, 2d chapter, from the 13th verse to the end;) but it is not the solicitude of an abolitionist. He thus addresses them: "Dearly beloved, I beseech you." He thus instructs them: "Submit yourselves to every ordinance of man for the Lord's sake." "For so is the will of God." "Servants, be subject to your masters with all fear, not only to the good and gentle, but also to the froward."—1 Peter ii: 11, 13, 15, 18. What an important document is this! enjoining political subjection to *governments of every form*, and Christian subjection on the part of servants to their masters, whether good or bad; for the purpose of showing forth to advantage, the *glory of the gospel*, and putting to silence the ignorance of foolish men, who might think it seditious.

By "every ordinance of man," as the context will show, is meant governmental regulations or laws, as was that of the Romans for enslaving their prisoners taken in war, instead of destroying their lives.

When such enslaved persons came into the church of Christ let them (says Peter) "be subject to their masters with all fear," whether such masters be good or bad. It is worthy of remark, that he says much to secure civil subordination to the State, and hearty and cheerful obedience to the masters, on the part of servants; yet he says nothing to masters in the whole letter. It would seem from this, that danger to the cause of Christ was on the side of *insubordination among the servants*, and a *want of humility with inferiors*, rather than *haughtiness among superiors* in the church.

Gibbon, in his Rome, vol. 1, pages 25, 26, 27, shows, from standard authorities, that Rome at this time swayed its scepter over one hundred and twenty millions of souls; that in every province, and in every family, *absolute slavery existed;* that it was at least fifty years later than the date of Peter's letters, before the absolute power of life and death over the slave was *taken from the master*, and *committed to the magistrate;* that about sixty millions of souls were held as property in this abject condition; that the price of a slave was four times that of an ox; that their punishments were very sanguinary; that in the second century, when their condition began to improve a little, emancipation was prohibited, except for great personal merit, or some public service rendered to the State; and that it was not until the third or fourth generation after freedom was obtained, that the descendants of a slave could share in the honors of the State. This is the *state, condition,* or *relation* among the *members of the apostolic churches*, whether among *Gentiles* or

Jews; which the Holy Ghost, by Paul for the Gentiles, and Peter for the Jews, recognizes as lawful; the mutual duties of which he prescribes in the language above. Now, I ask, can any man in his proper senses, from these premises, bring himself to conclude that slavery is *abolished by Jesus Christ*, or that obligations are imposed by him upon his disciples that are subversive of the institution? Knowing as we do from cotemporary historians, that the institution of slavery existed at the time and to the extent stated by Gibbon—what sort of a soul a man must have, who, with these facts before him, will conceal the truth on this subject, and hold Jesus Christ responsible for a scheme of treason that would, if carried out, have brought the life of every human being on earth at the time, into the most imminent peril, and that must have worked the destruction of half the human race?

At Rome, the authoritative centre of that vast theater upon which the glories of the cross were to be won, a church was planted. Paul wrote a long letter to them. On this subject it is full of instruction.

Abolition sentiments had not dared to show themselves so near the imperial sword. To warn the church against their treasonable tendency, was therefore unnecessary. Instead, therefore, of special precepts upon the subject of relative duties between master and servant, he lays down a system of practical morality, in the 12th chapter of his letter, which must commend itself equally to the king on his throne, and the slave in his hovel; for while its practical operation leaves the subject of earthly government to the discretion of man, it secures the exercise of sentiments and feelings that must exterminate every thing inconsistent with doing to others as we would they should do unto us: a system of principles that will give moral strength to governments; peace, security, and good-will to individuals; and glory to God in the highest. And in the 13th chapter, from the 1st to the end of the 7th verse, he recognizes human government as an ordinance of God, which the followers of Christ are to obey, honor, and support; not only from dread of punishment, but *for conscience sake;* which I believe abolitionism refuses most positively to do, to such governments as *from the force of circumstances* even *permit* slavery.

Again. But we are furnished with additional light, and if we are not greatly mistaken, with light which arose out of circumstances analogous to those which are threatening at the present moment to overthrow the peace of society, and deluge this nation with blood. To Titus whom Paul left in Crete, to set in order the things that were wanting, he writes a letter, in which he warns him of false teachers, that were to be dreaded on account of their doctrine. While they professed "to know God," that is, to know his will under the gospel dispensation, "in works they denied him;" that is, they did, and required others to do, what was contrary to his will under the gospel dispensation. "They were abominable," that is, to the Church and State, "and disobedient," that is, to the authority of the apostles, and the civil authority of the land. Titus, he then exhorts, "to speak the things that become sound doctrine;" that is, that the members of the church observe the law of the land,

and obey the civil magistrate; that "servants be obedient to their own masters, and please them well in all things," not "answering again, not purloining, but showing all good fidelity, that they may adorn the doctrine of God our Saviour in all things," *in that which subjects the ecclesiastical to the civil authority in particular*. "These things speak, and exhort and rebuke with all authority; let no man despise thee. Put them in mind to be subject to principalities and powers, to obey magistrates."—Titus i: 16, and ii: from 1 to 10, and iii: 1. The context shows that a doctrine was taught by these wicked men, which tended in its influence on servants, to bring the gospel of Christ into contempt in Church and State, because of its seditions and insubordinate character.

But at Ephesus, the capital of the lesser Asia, where Paul had labored with great success for three years—a point of great importance to the gospel cause—the Apostle left Timothy for the purpose of watching against the false teachers, and particularly against the abolitionists. In addition to a letter which he had addressed to this church previously, in which the mutual duty of master and servant is taught, and which has already been referred to, he further instructs Timothy by letter on the same subject: "Let as many servants as are under the yoke count their masters worthy of all honor, that the name of God and his doctrine be not blasphemed."—1 Tim. vi: 1. These were unbelieving masters, as the next verse will show. In this church at Ephesus, the circumstances existed, which are brought to light by Paul's letter to Timothy, that must silence every cavil, which men, who do not know God's will on this subject, may start until time ends. In an age filled with literary men, who are employed in transmitting historically, to future generations, the structure of society in the Roman Empire; that would put it in our power at this distant day, to know the state or condition of a slave in the Roman Empire, as well as if we had lived at the time, and to know beyond question, that his condition was precisely that one, which is now denounced as sinful: in such an age, and in such circumstances, Jesus Christ causes his will to be published to the world; and it is this, that if a Christian slave have an unbelieving master, who acknowledges no allegiance to Christ, this believing slave must count his master worthy of all honor, according to what the Apostle teaches the Romans, "Render, therefore, to all their dues, tribute to whom tribute is due, custom to whom custom is due, fear to whom fear, honor to whom honor."—Rom. xiii: 7. Now, honor is enjoined of God in the Scriptures, from children to parents—from husbands to wives—from subjects to magistrates and rulers, and here by Jesus Christ, from Christian slaves to unbelieving masters, who held them as property by law, with power over their very lives. And the command is remarkable. While we are commanded to honor father and mother, without adding to the precept "all honor," here a Christian servant is bound to render to his unbelieving master "all honor." Why is this? Because in the one case nature moves in the direction of the command; but in the other, against it. Nature being subjected to the law of grace, might be disposed to obey reluctantly; hence the amplitude of the command. But what purpose was to be answered by this devotion of the slave? The Apostle answers, "that the name of God and his doctrine (of subordination to the law-making power) be not blasphemed," as they certainly would by a contrary course on the part of the servant, for the most obvious reason in the world; while the sword would have been drawn against the gospel, and a war of extermination waged against its propagators, in every province of the Roman Empire, for there was slavery in all; and so it would be now.

But, says the caviler, these directions are given to Christian slaves whose masters did not acknowledge the authority of Christ to govern them; and are therefore defective as proof, that he approves of one Christian man holding another in bondage. Very well, we will see. In the next verse, (1 Timothy vi: 2,) he says, "and they that have believing masters, let them not despise them, because they are brethren, but rather do them service, because they are faithful and beloved, partakers of the benefit." Here is a great change; instead of a command to a believing slave to render to a believing master *all honor*, and thereby making that believing master in *honor* equal to an unbelieving master, here is rather an exhortation to the slave *not to despise him, because he is a believer*. Now, I ask, why the circumstance of a master becoming a believer in Christ, should become the cause of his believing slave despising him while that slave was supposed to acquiesce in the duty of rendering all honor to that master before he became a believer? I answer, *precisely*, and *only, because* there were *abolition teachers* among them, who *taught otherwise*, and consented not to wholesome words, *even the words of our Lord Jesus Christ.*—1 Timothy vii: 3; and "to the doctrine which is according to godliness," taught in the 8th verse, viz: having food and raiment, servants should therewith be content; for the pronoun us, in the 8th verse of this connection, means *especially* the *servants he was instructing*, as well as Christians in general. These men taught, that godliness abolished slavery, that it gave the title of freedom to the slave, and that so soon as a man professed to be subject to Christ, and refused to liberate his slaves, he was a hypocrite, and deserved not the countenance of any who bore the Christian name. Such men, the Apostle says, are "proud, (just as they are now,) knowing nothing," (that is, on this subject,) but "doating about questions, and strifes of words, whereof cometh envy, strife, railings, evil surmisings, perverse disputings of men of corrupt minds, and destitute of the truth, supposing that gain is godliness: from such withdraw thyself."—1 Tim. vi: 4, 5.

Such were the bitter fruits which abolition sentiments produced in the Apostolic day, and such precisely are the fruits they produce now.

Now, I say, here is the case made out, which certainly would call forth the command from Christ, to abolish slavery, if he ever intended to abolish it. Both the servant and the master were one in Christ Jesus. Both were members of the same church, both were under unlimited and voluntary obedience to the same divine law-giver.

No political objection existed at the time against their obedience to him on the subject of slavery; and what is the will, not of Paul, but of the Lord Jesus Christ, immediately in person, upon the case thus made out? Does he say to the master, having put yourself under my government, you must no longer hold your brother in bondage? Does he say to the slave, if your master does not release you, you must go and talk to him privately, about this trespass upon your rights under the law of my kingdom; and if he does not hear you, you must take two or three with you; and if he does not hear them then you must tell it to the church, and have him expelled from my flock, as a wolf in sheep's clothing? I say, what does the Lord Jesus say to this poor believing slave, concerning a master who held unlimited power over his person and life, under the Roman law? He tells him that the very circumstance of his master's being a brother, constitutes the reason why he should be more ready to do him service; for in addition to the circumstance of his being a brother who would be benefited by his service, he would as a brother give him what was just and equal in return, and "forbear threatening," much less abusing his authority over him, for that he (the master) also had a master in heaven, who was no respecter of persons. It is taken for granted, on all hands pretty generally, that Jesus Christ has at least been silent, or that he has not personally spoken on the subject of slavery. Once for all, I deny it. Paul, after stating that a slave was to honor an unbelieving master, in the 1st verse of the 6th chapter, says, in the 2d verse, that to a believing master, he is the rather to do service, because he who partakes of the benefit is his brother. He then says, if any man teach otherwise, (as all abolitionists then did, and now do,) and consent not to wholesome words, "even the words of our Lord Jesus Christ." Now, if our Lord Jesus Christ uttered such words, how dare we say he has been silent? If he has been silent, how dare the Apostle say these are the words of our Lord Jesus Christ, if the Lord Jesus Christ never spoke them? "Where, or when, or on what occasion he spoke them, we are not informed; but certain it is, that Paul has borne false witness, or that Jesus Christ has uttered the words that impose an obligation on servants, who are abject slaves, to render service with good-will from the heart, to believing masters, and to account their unbelieving masters as worthy of all honor, that the name of God and his doctrine be not blasphemed. Jesus Christ revealed to Paul the doctrine which Paul has settled throughout the Gentile world, (and by consequence, the Jewish world also,) on the subject of slavery, so far as it affects his kingdom. As we have seen, it is clear and full.

From the great importance of the subject, involving the personal liberty of half the human race at that time, and a large portion of them at all times since, it is not to be wondered at, that Paul would carry the question to the Saviour, and plead for a decisive expression of his will, that would forever do away the necessity of inferring any thing by reasoning from the premises laid down in the former dispensation; or in the patriarchal age; and at Ephesus, if not at Crete, the issue is fairly made, between Paul on the one side, and certain abolition teachers on the other, when, in addition to the official intelligence ordinarily given to the apostles by the Holy Ghost, to guide them into all truth, he affirms, that the doctrine of perfect civil subordination, on the part of hereditary slaves to their masters, whether believers or unbelievers, was one which he, Paul, taught in the words of the Lord Jesus Christ himself.

The Scriptures we have adduced from the New Testament, to prove the recognition of hereditary slavery by the Saviour, as a lawful relation in the sight of God, lose much of their force from the use of a word by the translators, which by time, has lost much of its original meaning; that is, the word *servant*. Dr. Johnson, in his Dictionary, says: "Servant is one of the few words, which by time has acquired a softer signification than its original, knave, degenerated into cheat. While *servant*, which signified originally, a person preserved from death by the conqueror, and reserved for slavery, signifies only an obedient attendant." Now, all history will prove that the servants of the New Testament addressed by the apostles, in their letters to the several churches throughout the Roman Empire, were such as were perserved from death by the conqueror, and taken into slavery. This was their condition, and it is a fact well known to all men acquainted with history. Had the word which designates their condition, in our translation, lost none of its original meaning, a common man could not have fallen into a mistake as to the condition indicated. But to waive this fact we are furnished with all the evidence that can be desired. The Saviour appeared in an age of learning—the enslaved condition of half the Roman Empire, at the time, is a fact embodied with all the historical records—the constitution God gave the Jews, was in harmony with the Roman regulations on the subject of slavery. In this state of things, Jesus ordered his gospel to be preached in all the world, and to every creature. It was done as he directed; and masters and servants, and persons in all conditions, were brought by the gospel to obey the Saviour. Churches were constituted. We have examined the letters written to the churches, composd of these materials. The result is, that each member is furnished with a law to regulate the duties of his civil station—from the highest to the lowest.

We will remark, in closing under this head, that we have shown from the text of the sacred volume, that when God entered into covenant with Abraham, it was with him as a slaveholder; that when he took his posterity by the hand in Egypt, five hundred years afterward to confirm the promise made to Abraham, it was done with them as slaveholders; that when he gave them a constitution of government, he gave them the right to perpetuate hereditary slavery; and that he did not for the fifteen hundred years of their national existence, express disapprobation toward the institution.

We have also shown from authentic history that the institution of slavery existed in every family, and in every province of the Roman Empire, at the time the gospel was published to them.

We have also shown from the New Testament, that all the churches are recognized as composed of masters and servants; and that they are instructed by Christ how to discharge their relative duties; and finally that in reference to the question which was then started, whether Christianity did not abolish the institution, or the right of one Christian to hold another Christian in bondage, we have shown, that "the words of our Lord Jesus Christ" are, that so far from this being the case, it adds to the obligation of the servant to render service with good-will to his master, and that gospel fellowship is not to be entertained with persons who will not consent to it!

I propose, in the fourth place, to show that the institution of slavery is full of mercy. I shall say but a few words on this subject. Authentic history warrants this conclusion, that for a long period of time, it was this institution alone which furnished a motive for sparing the prisoner's life. The chances of war, when the earth was filled with small tribes of men, who had a passion for it, brought to decision, almost daily, conflicts, where nothing but this institution interposed an inducement to save the vanquished. The same was true in the enlarged schemes of conquest, which brought the four great universal empires of the Scriptures to the zenith of their power.

The same is true in the history of Africa, as far back as we can trace it. It is only sober truth to say, that the institution of slavery has saved from the sword more lives, including their increase, than all the souls who now inhabit this globe.

The souls thus conquered and subjected to masters, who feared not God nor regarded men, in the days of Abraham, Job, and the patriarchs, were surely brought under great obligations to the mercy of God, in allowing such men as these to purchase them, and keep them in their families.

The institution when engrafted on the Jewish constitution, was designed principally, not to enlarge the number, but to ameliorate the condition of the slaves in the neighboring nations.

Under the gospel, it has brought within the range of gospel influence, millions of Ham's descendant's among ourselves, who but for this institution, would have sunk down to eternal ruin; knowing not God, and strangers to the gospel. In their bondage here on earth, they have been much better provided for, and great multitudes of them have been made the freemen of the Lord Jesus Christ, and left this world rejoicing in hope of the glory of God. The elements of an empire, which I hope will lead Ethiopia very soon to stretch out her hands to God, is the fruit of the institution here. An officious meddling with the institution, from feeling and sentiments unknown to the Bible, may lead to the extermination of the slave race among us, who, taken as a whole, are utterly unprepared for a higher civil state; but benefit them, it cannot. Their condition, *as a class*, is now better than that of any other equal number of laborers on earth, and is daily improving.

If the Bible is allowed to awaken the spirit, and control the philanthropy which works their good, the day is not far distant when the highest wishes of saints will be gratified, in having conferred on them all that the spirit of good-will can bestow. This spirit which was kindling into life, has received a great check among us of late, by that trait which the Apostle Peter reproves and shames in his officious countrymen, when he says: "But let none of you suffer as a murderer, or as a thief, or as an evil doer, or as a busy-body in other men's matters." Our citizens have been murdered—our property has been stolen, (if the receiver is as bad as the thief,)—our lives have been put in jeopardy—our characters traduced—and attempts made to force political slavery upon us in the place of domestic, by strangers who have no right to meddle with our matters. Instead of meditating generous things to our slaves, as a return for gospel subordination, we have to put on our armor to suppress a rebellious spirit, engendered by "false doctrine," propagated by men "of corrupt minds, and destitute of the truth," who teach them that the gain of freedom to the slave, is the only proof of godliness in the master. From such, Paul says we must withdraw ourselves; and if we fail to do it, and to rebuke them with all the authority which "the words of our Lord Jesus Christ" confer, we shall be wanting in duty to them, to ourselves, and to the world.

THORNTON STRINGFELLOW.

AN EXAMINATION OF ELDER GALUSHA'S REPLY TO DR. RICHARD FULLER OF SOUTH CAROLINA.

AFTER my essay on slavery was published in the *Herald*,[230] I sent a copy of it to a prominent abolition gentleman in New York, accompanied by a friendly letter.

This gentleman I selected as a correspondent, because of his high standing, intellectual attainments, and unquestioned piety. I frankly avowed to him my readiness to abandon slavery, so soon as I was convinced by the Bible that it was sinful, and requested him, "if the Bible contained precepts, and settled principles of conduct, in direct opposition to those portions of it upon which I relied, as furnishing the mind of the Almighty upon the subject of slavery, that he would furnish me with the knowledge of the fact." To this letter I received a friendly reply, accompanied by a printed communication containing the result of a prayerful effort which he had previously made, for the purpose of furnishing the very information to a friend at the South, which I sought to obtain at his hands.

It may be owing to my prejudices, or a want of intellect, that I fail to be convinced, by those portions of the Bible to which he refers, to prove that slavery is sinful. But as the support of truth is *my object*, and as I wish to have the answer of a good conscience toward God in this matter, I herewith publish, for the information of all into whose hands my first essay may have fallen, every passage in the Bible to which this distinguished brother refers me for "precepts and settled principles of conduct, in direct opposition to those portions of it upon which I relied, as furnishing the mind of the Almighty upon the subject of slavery."

1st. His reference to the sacred volume is this: "God hath made of one blood all nations of men." This is a Scripture truth which I believe; yet God decreed that Canaan should be a servant of servants to his brother—that is, an abject slave in his posterity. This God effected eight hundred years afterward, in the days of Joshua, when the Gibeonites were subjected to prepetual bondage, and made hewers of wood and drawers of water.—Joshua ix: 23.

Again, God ordained, as law-giver to Israel, that their captives taken in war should be enslaved.—Deut. xx: 10 to 15.

Again, God enacted that the Israelites should buy slaves of the heathen nations around them, and will them and their increase as property to their children forever.—Levit. xxv: 44, 45, 46. All these nations were *made of one blood*. Yet God ordained that some should be "chattel" slaves to others, and gave his special aid to effect it. In view of this incontrovertible fact, how can I believe this passage disproves the lawfulness of slavery in the sight of God? How can any sane man believe it, who believes the Bible?

2d. His second Scripture reference to disprove the lawfulness of slavery in the sight of God, is this: "God has said a man is better than a sheep." This is a Scripture truth which I fully believe—and I have no doubt, if we could ascertain what the Israelites had to pay for those slaves they bought with their money according to God's law, in Levit. xxv: 44, that we should find they had to pay more for them than they paid for sheep, for the reason assigned by the Saviour; that is, that a servant man is better than a sheep; for when he is done plowing, or feeding cattle, and comes in from the field, he will, at his master's bidding, prepare him his meal, and wait upon him till he eats it, while the master feels under no obligation even to thank him for it because he has done no more than his duty.—Luke xvii: 7, 8, 9. This, and other important duties, which the people of God bought their slaves to perform for them, by the permission of their Maker, were duties which sheep could not perform. But I cannot see what there is in it to blot out from the Bible a relation which God created, in which he made one man to be a slave to another.

3d. His third Scripture reference to prove the unlawfulness of slavery in the sight of God, is this: "God commands children to obey their parents, and wives to obey their husbands." This, I believe to be the will of Christ to Christian children and Christian wives—whether they are bond or free. But it is equally true that Christ ordains that Christianity shall not abolish slavery.—1 Cor. vii: 17, 21, and that he commands servants to obey their masters and to count them worthy of all honor.—1 Tim. vi: 1, 2. It is also true, that God allowed Jewish masters to use the rod to make them do it—and to use it with the severity requisite to accomplish the object.—Exod. xxi: 20,21. It is equally true, that Jesus Christ ordains that a Christian servant shall receive for the wrong he hath done.—Col. iii: 25. My correspondent admits, without qualification, that if they are property, it is right. But the Bible says, they were property.—Levit. xxv: 44, 45, 46.

The above reference, reader, *enjoins* the *duty* of two *relations*, which God ordained, but does not *abolish* a third *relation* which *God has ordained;* as the Scripture will prove, to which I have referred you, under the first reference made by my correspondent.

4th. His fourth Scripture reference is, to the *intention* of Abraham to give his estate to a servant, in order to prove that servant was not a slave. "What," he says, "property inherit property?" I answer, yes. Two years ago, in my county, William Hansbrough gave to his slaves his estate, worth forty or fifty thousand dollars. In the last five or six years, over two hundred slaves, within a few miles of me, belonging to various masters, have inherited portions of their masters' estates.

To render slaves valuable, the Romans qualified them for the learned professions, and all the various arts. They were teachers, doctors, authors, mechanics, etc. So with us, tradesmen of every kind are to be found among our slaves. Some of them are undertakers—

some farmers—some overseers, or stewards—some housekeepers—some merchants—some teamsters, and some money-lenders, who give their masters a portion of their income, and keep the balance. Nearly all of them have an income of their own—and was it not for the seditious spirit of the North, we would educate our slaves generally, and so fit them earlier for a more improved condition, and higher moral elevation.

But will all this, when duly certified, prove they are not slaves? No. Neither will Abraham's *intention* to give one of his servants his estate, prove that he was not a slave. Who had higher claims upon Abraham, before he had a child, than this faithful slave, born in his house, reared by his hand, devoted to his interest, and faithful in every trust?

5th. His fifth reference, my correspondent says, "forever sets the question at rest." It is this: "Thou shalt not deliver unto his master, the servant which is escaped from his master unto thee—he shall dwell with thee, even in that place which he shall choose, in one of thy gates, where it liketh him best; thou shalt not oppress him."

This my distinguished correspondent says, "forever puts the question at rest." My reader, I hope, will ask himself what question it puts to rest. He will please to remember, that it is brought to put this question to rest, "Is slavery sinful in the sight of God?" the Bible being judge—or "did God ever allow one man to hold property in another?"

My correspondent admits this to be the question at issue. He asks, "What is slavery?" And thus answers: "It is the principle involved in holding man as property." "This," he says: "is the point at issue." He says, "if it be right to hold man as property, it is right to treat him as property," etc. Now, conceding all in the argument, that can be demanded for this law about run-away slaves, yet it does not prove that slavery or holding property in man is sinful—because it is a part and parcel of the Mosaic law, given to Israel in the wilderness by the same God, who in the same wilderness enacted "that of the heathen that were round about them, they should buy bond-men and bond-women—also of the strangers that dwelt among them should they buy, and they should pass as an inheritance to their children after them, to possess them as bond-men forever."—Levit. xxv: 44.

How can I admit that a prohibition to deliver up a run-away slave, under the law of Moses, is proof that there was no slavery allowed under that law? Here is the law from God himself,—Levit. xxv: 44, authorizing the Israelites to buy slaves and transmit them and their increase as a possession to their posterity forever—and to make slaves of their captives taken in war.—Deut. xx: 10-15. Suppose, for argument's sake, I admit that God prohibited the delivery back of one of *these slaves*, when he fled from his master—would that prove that he was not a slave before he fled? Would that prove that he did not remain legally a slave in the sight of God, according to his own law, until he fled? The passage proves the very reverse of that which it is brought to prove. It proves that the slave is recognized by God himself as a slave, until he fled to the Israelites. My correspondent's exposition of this law seems based upon the idea that God, who had held fellowship with slavery among his people for five hundred years, and who had just given them a formal statute to legalize the purchase of slaves from the heathen, and to enslave their captives taken in war, was, nevertheless, desirous to abolish the institution. But, as if afraid to march directly up to his object, he was disposed to undermine what he was unwilling to attempt to overthrow.

Upon the principle that man is prone to think God is altogether such an one as himself, we may account for such an interpretation at the present time, by men north of Mason & Dixon's line. Our brethren there have held fellowship with this institution, by the constitutional oath they have taken to protect us in this property. Unable, constitutionally, to overthrow the institution, they see, or think they see, a sanction in the law of God to undermine it, by opening their gates and letting our run-away slaves "dwell among them where it liketh them best." If I could be astonished at any thing in this controversy, it would be to see sensible men engaged in the study of that part of the Bible which relates to the rights of property, as established by the Almighty himself, giving in to the idea that the Judge of the world, acting in the character of a national law-giver, would legalize a property right in slaves, *as he did*—give full power to the master to govern—secure the increase as an inheritance to posterity for all time to come—and then add a clause to legalize a fraud upon the unsuspecting purchaser. For what better is it, under this interpretation?

With respect to slaves purchased of the heathen, or enslaved by war, the law passed a clear title to them and their increase forever. With respect to the hired servants of the Hebrews, the law secured to the master a right to their service until the Sabbatic year or Jubilee—unless they were bought back by a near kinsman at a stated price in money when owned by a heathen master. But these legal rights, under these laws of heaven's King, by this interpretation, are all canceled—for the pecuniary loss, there is no redress—and for the insult no remedy, whenever a "liketh him best" man can induce the slave to run away. And worse still, the community of masters thus insulted and swindled, according to this interpretation, are bound to show respect and afford protection to the villains who practice it. Who can believe all this? I judge our Northern brethren will say, the Lord deliver us from such legislation as this. So say we. What, then, does this run-away law mean? It means that the God of Israel ordained his people to be an asylum for the slave who fled from heathen cruelty to them for protection; it is the law of nations—but surrendered under the Constitution by these States, who agreed to deliver them up. See, says God, ye oppress not the stranger. Thou shalt neither *vex* a stranger, nor *oppress* him.— Exod. xxii: 21.

His 6th reference to the Bible is this: "Do to others as ye would they should do to you." I have shown in the essay, that these words of our Saviour, embody the same moral principle, which is embodied by Moses in Levit. xix: 18, in these words, "Love thy neighbor as thyself." In this we can not be mistaken, because Jesus says there are but two such principles in God's moral government—*one* of supreme love of God—*another* of love to our neighbor as ourself. To the everlasting confusion of the argument from moral precepts, to overthrow the positive institution of slavery, this moral precept was given to regulate the mutual duties of this very relation, which God by law ordained for the Jewish commonwealth.

How can that which regulates the *duty*, overthrow the *relation* itself?

His 7th reference is, "They which are accounted to rule over the Gentiles, exercise lordship over them, but so it shall not be among you."

Turn to the passage, reader, in Mark x: 42; and try your ingenuity at expounding, and see if you can destroy one *relation* that has been created among men, because the *authority* given in another relation was *abused*. The Saviour refers to the *abuse* of State *authority*, as a warning to those who should be clothed with *authority* in his kingdom, not to *abuse* it, but to connect the use of it with humility. But how official humility in the kingdom of Christ, is to rob States of the right to make their own laws, dissolve the relation of slavery recognized by the Saviour as a lawful relation, and overthrow the right of property in slaves as settled by God himself, I know not. Paul, in drawing the character of those who oppose slavery, in his letter to Timothy, says, (vi: 4,) they are "proud, knowing nothing;" he means, that they were puffed with a conceit of their superior sanctity, while they were deplorably ignorant of the will of Christ on this subject. Is it not great pride that leads a man to think he is better than the Saviour? Jesus held fellowship with, and enjoined subjection to governments, which sanctioned slavery in its worst form—but abolitionists refuse fellowship for governments which have mitigated all its rigors.

God established the relation by law, and bestowed the highest manifestations of his favor upon slaveholders; and has caused it to be written as with a sunbeam in the Scriptures. Yet such saints would be refused the ordinary tokens of Christian fellowship among abolitionists. If Abraham were on earth, they could not let him, consistently, occupy their pulpits, to tell of the things God has prepared for them that love him. Job himself would be unfit for their communion. Joseph would be placed on a level with pirates. Not a single church planted by the apostles would make a fit home for our abolition brethren, (for they all had masters and slaves.) The apostles and their ministerial associates could not occupy their pulpits, for they fraternized with slavery, and upheld State authority upon the subject. Now, I ask, with due respect for all parties, can sentiments which lead to such results as these be held by any man, *in the absence of pride* of no ordinary character, whether he be sensible of it or not?

Again, whatever of intellect we may have—can that something which prompts to results like these be *Bible knowledge?*

Reference the 8th is favorable in *sound* if not in *sense*. It is in these words, "Neither be ye called *masters*, for one is your *master*, even Christ." I am free to confess, it is difficult to repress the spirit which the prophet felt when he witnessed the zeal of his deluded countrymen, at Mount Carmel. I think a sensible man ought to know better, than to refer me to such a passage, to prove slavery unlawful; yet my correspondent is a sensible man. However, I will balance it by an equal authority, for dissolving another relation. "Call no man *father* upon earth, for one is your *father* in heaven."

When the last abolishes the *relation* between *parent and child*, the first will abolish the *relation* between *master and servant*.

The 9th reference to prove slavery unlawful in the sight of God, is this: "He that stealeth a man, and selleth him, or if he be found in his hand, he shall surely be put to death." Wonderful!

I suppose that no State has ever established domestic slavery, which did not find such a law necessary. It is this institution which makes such a law needful. Unless slavery exists, there would be no motive to steal a man. And, the danger is greater in a slave State than a free one. Virginia has such a law, and so have all the States of North America.

Will these laws prove four thousand years hence that slavery did not exist in the United States? No—but why not! Because the statute will still exist, which authorizes us to buy bond-men and bond-women with our money, and give them and their increase as an inheritance to our children, forever. So the Mosaic statute still exists, which authorized the Jews to do the same thing, and God is its author.

Reference the 10th is: "Rob not the poor because he is poor. Let the oppressed go free; break every yoke; deliver him that is spoiled out of the hand of the oppressor. What doth the Lord require of thee but to do justly, love mercy, walk humbly with thy God. He that oppresseth the poor reproacheth his Maker." This *sounds* very well, reader, yet I propose to make every man who reads me, *confess*, that these Scriptures will not condemn slavery. Answer me this question: Are these, and such like passages, in the Old Testament, from whence they are all taken, intended to reprove and condemn that people, for doing what God, in his law gave them a right to do? I know you must answer, they were not; consequently, you confess they do not condemn slavery; because God gave them the right, by law, to purchase slaves of the heathen.—Levit. xxv: 44. And to make slaves of their captives taken in war.—Deut. xx: 14. The moral precepts of the Old or New Testament cannot make that wrong which God ordained to be his will, as he has slavery.

The 11th reference of my distinguished correspondent to the sacred volume, to prove that slavery is contrary to the will of Jesus Christ and sinful, is in these words: "Masters, give unto your servants that which is just and equal." The argument of my correspondent is this, that slavery is a relation, in which rights based upon *justice* cannot exist.

I answer, God ordained, after man sinned, that he, "should eat bread (that is, *have food and raiment*) in the sweat of his face."

He has since ordained, that some should be slaves to others, (as we have proved under the first reference.) *Therefore*, when food and raiment are withheld from him in slavery, it is *unjust*.

God has ordained food and raiment, as wages for the sweat of the face. Christ has ordained that with these, whether in slavery or freedom, his disciples shall be content.

The relation of master and slave, says Gibbon, existed in every province and in every family of the Roman Empire. Jesus ordains in the 13th chapter of Romans, from the 1st to the end of the 7th verse, and in 1 Peter, 2d chapter, 13th, 14th, and 15th verses, that the *legislative authority*, which created the relation, should be obeyed and honored by his disciples. But while he thus *legalises* the *relation* of master and slave as established by the civil law, he proceeds to prescribe the mutual duties which the parties, when they come into his kingdom, must perform to each other.

The reference of my correspondent to disprove the *relation*, is a part of what Jesus has prescribed on this subject to *regulate* the *duties* of the relation, and is itself proof that the relation existed—that its legality was recognized—and its duties prescribed by the Son of God through the Holy Ghost given to the apostles.

The 12th reference is, "Let as many servants as are under the yoke, count their masters worthy of all honor. And they that have believing masters, let them not despise them because they are brethren, but rather do them service, because they are faithful and beloved, partakers of the benefit." If my reader will turn to my remarks, in my first essay upon this Scripture, he will cease to wonder that it fails to convince me that slavery is sinful. I should think the wonder would be, that any man ever quoted it for such a purpose.

And lastly. My correspondent informs me that the Greek word "doulos," translated servant, means hired servant and not slave.

I reply, that the primary meaning of this Greek word, is in a singular state of preservation. God, as if foreseeing and providing for this controversy, has caused, in his providence, that its meaning in Greek dictionaries shall be thus given, "the opposite of free." Now, readers, what is the *opposite* of *free?* Is it a state somewhere *between* freedom and slavery? If freedom, as a condition, has an opposite, that opposite state is indicated by this very word "doulos." So says every Greek lexicographer. I ask, if this is not wonderful, that the Holy Ghost has used a term, so incapable of deceiving, and yet that that term should be brought forward for the purpose of deception. Another remarkable fact is this: the English word servant, originally meant precisely the same thing as the Greek word "doulos;" that is, says Dr. Johnson in his Dictionary, it meant formerly a captive taken in war, and reserved for slavery. These are two remarkable facts in the providence of God. But, reader, I will give you a Bible key, by which to decide for yourself, without foreign aid, whether *servant*, when it denotes a relation in society, where the other side of that relation is *master*, means *hired servant*. "Every man's servant that is bought for money shall eat thereof; but a hired servant shall not eat thereof."—Exod. xii; 44, 45. Here are two classes of servants alluded to—one was allowed to eat the Passover the night Israel left Egypt; the other not. What was the difference in these two classes? Were they both hired servants? If so, it should read, "Every hired servant that is bought for money shall eat thereof; but a hired servant that is bought for money, shall not eat thereof." My reader, why has the Holy Ghost, in presiding over the inspired pen, been thus particular? Is it too much to say, it was to provide against the delusion of the nineteenth century, which learned men would be practicing upon unlearned men, as well as themselves, on the subject of slavery? Who, with the Bible and their learning, would not be able to discover, that a servant bought with money was a slave; and that a hired servant was a free man? Again, Levit. xxv: 44, 45, and 46; "Thy bond-servants shall be of the heathen that are round about you, and of the children of the strangers that do sojourn among you, of them shall ye buy. And they shall be your possession, and ye shall take them as an inheritance, for your children after you, to inherit them for a possession, they shall be your bond-men forever."

Reader, were these hired servants? If so, they hired themselves for a long time. And what is very singular, they hired their posterity for all time to come. And what is still more singular, the wages were paid, not to the servant, but to a former owner or master. And what is still stranger, they hired themselves and their posterity to be an inheritance to their master and his posterity forever! Yet, reader, I am told by my distinguished correspondent, that servant in the Scriptures, when used to designate a relation, means only hired servant. Again, I ask, were the enslaved captives in Deut. xx: 10, 11, 12, 13, 14, 15, hired servants?

One of the greatest and best of men ever raised at the North, (I mean Luther Rice,) once told me when I quoted the law of God for the purchase of slaves from the heathen, (in order to silence his argument about "doulos," and hired servant,) I say he told me positively, there was no such law. When I opened the Bible and showed it to him, his shame was very visible. (And I hope he is not the only great and good man, that God will put to shame for being ignorant of his word.) But he never opened his mouth to me about slavery again while he lived.

If my reader does no *better* than he did, at least let him not fight against God for establishing the institution of "chattel" slavery in his kingdom, nor against me for believing he did do it. But, reader, if you have the hardihood to insist that these were hired servants, and not slaves after all, then, I answer, that ours are hired servants, too, and not slaves; and so the dispute ends favorably to the South, and it is lawful for us, according to abolition admissions, to hold them to servitude. For ours, we paid money to a former owner; so did the Jews for theirs. The increase of ours passes as an inheritance to our children, so did the increase of the Jewish servants pass as an inheritance to their children, to be an inheritance forever. And all this took place by the direction of God to his chosen people.

My correspondent thinks with Mr. Jefferson, that Jehovah has no attributes that will harmonize with slavery; and that all men are born free and equal. Now, I say let him throw away his Bible as Mr. Jefferson did his, and then they will be fit companions. But never disgrace the Bible by making Mr. Jefferson its expounder, nor Mr. Jefferson by deriving his sentiments from it. Mr. Jefferson did not bow to the authority of the Bible, and on this subject I do not bow to him. How can any man, who believes the Bible, admit for a moment that God intended to teach mankind by the Bible, that all are born free and equal?

Men who engage in this controversy ought to look into the Bible, and see what is in it about slavery. I do not know how to account for such men saying, as my correspondent does, that the slave of the Mosaic law, purchased of the heathen, was a hired servant; and that both he and the Hebrew hired servant of the same law, had a passport from God to run away from their masters with impunity, to prove which is the object of one of his quotations. Again, New Testament *servants* and *masters* are not the servants and masters of the Mosaic law, but the servants and masters of the Roman Empire. To go to the law of Moses to find out the statutes of the Roman Empire, is folly. Yet on this subject the difference is not great, and so far as humanity (in the abolition sense of it) is concerned, is in favor of the Roman law.

The laws of each made slaves to be property, and allowed them to be bought and sold. See Gibbon's Rome, vol. i: pp. 25, 26, and Levit. xxv: 44, 45, 46. The laws of each allowed prisoners taken in war to be enslaved. See Gibbon as above, and Deut. xx: 10-15. The difference was this: the Roman law allowed *men* taken in battle to be enslaved—the Jewish law required the *men* taken in battle to be put to death, and to enslave their wives and children. In the case of the Midianites, the mercy of enslaving some of the women was denied them because they had enticed the Israelites into sin, and subjected them to a heavy judgment under Balaam's counsel, and for a reason not assigned, the mercy of slavery was denied to the male children in this special case. See Numbers xxxi: 15, 16, 17.

The first letter to Timothy, while at Ephesus, if rightly understood, would do much to stay the hands of men, who have more zeal than knowledge on this subject. See again what I have written in my first essay on this letter. In addition to what I have there said, I would state, that the "*other doctrine*," 1 Tim. i: 3, which Paul says, must not be taught, I take to be a principle tantamount to this, that Jesus Christ proposed to subordinate the civil to ecclesiastical authority.

The doctrine which was "*according to godliness,*" 1 Tim, vi: 3, I take to be a principle which subordinated the church, or Christ in his members, to civil governments, or "the powers that be." One principle was seditious, and when consummated must end in the man of sin. The other principle was practically a quiet submission to government, as an ordinance of God in the hands of men.

The abolitionists, at Ephesus, in attempting to interfere with the relations of slavery, and to unsettle the rights of property, acted upon a principle, which statesmen must see, would in the end, subject the whole frame-work of government to the supervision of the church, and terminate in the man of sin, or a pretended successor of Christ, sitting in the temple of God, and claiming a right to reign over, and control the civil governments of the world. The Apostle, therefore, chapter ii: 1, to render the doctrine of subordination to the State a very prominent doctrine, and to cause the knowledge of it to spread among all who attended their worship, orders that the very first thing done by the church should be, that of making supplication, prayers, and intercessions, and giving God thanks for all men that were placed in authority, by the State, for the administration of civil government. He assigns the reason for this injunction, "that we may lead a quiet and peaceable life in all godliness and honesty."

My correspondent complains, that abolitionists at the North are not safe when they come among us. They are much safer than the saints of Ephesus would have been in the Apostolic day, if Paul would have allowed the seditious doctrine to be propagated which our Northern brethren think it such a merit to preach, when it subjects them to no risk. How can they expect, in the nature of things, to lead a quiet and peaceable life when they come among us? They are *organized* to overthrow our sovereignty—to put our lives in peril, and to trample upon Bible principles, by which the rights of property are to be settled.

Questions and strifes of words characterized the disputes of the abolitionists at Ephesus about slavery. It is amusing and painful to see the questions and strifes of words in the piece of my correspondent. Many of these questions are about our property right in slaves. The *substance of them* is this: that the present title is not good, because the original title grew out of violence and injustice. But, reader, our original title was obtained in the same way which God in his law authorized his people to obtain theirs. They obtained their slaves by purchase of those who made them captives in the hazards of war, or by conquest with their own sword. My correspondent speaks at one time as if ours were stolen in the first instance; but, as if forgetting that, in another place he says, that so great is the hazard attending the wars of Africa, that one life is lost for every two that are taken captive and sold into slavery. If this is stealing, it has at least the merit of being more manly than some that is practiced among us.

A case seems to have been preserved by the Holy Ghost, as if to rebuke this abolition doctrine about property rights. It is the case of the King of Ammon, a heathen, on the one side, and Jephtha, who "obtained a good report by faith," on the other. It is consoling to us that we occupy the ground Jephtha did—and we may well suspect the correctness of the other side, because it is the ground occupied by Ammon. The case is this: A heathen is seen menacing Israel. Jephtha is selected by his countrymen to conduct the controversy. He sends a message to his menacing neighbor, to know why he had come out against him. He returned for answer, that it was because Israel held property to which they had no right. Jephtha answered, they had had it in possession for three hundred years. Ammon replied, they had no right to it, because it was obtained in the first instance by violence. Jephtha replied, that it was held by the same sort of a title as that by which Ammon held his possessions—that is to say, whatever Ammon's god Chemosh enabled him to take in war, he considered to be his of right; and that Israel's God had assisted them to take this property, and they considered the title to be such an one as Ammon was bound to acknowledge.

Ammon stickled for the *eternal* principle of righteousness, and contended that it had been violated in the first instance. But, reader, in the appeal made to the sword, God vindicated Israel's title.—Judges xi: 12-32.

And if at the present time, we take ground with Ammon about the rights of property, I will not say how much work we may have to do, nor who will prove the rightful owner of my correspondent's domicil; but certain I am, that by his Ammonitish principle of settling the rights of property, he will be ousted.

Reader, in looking over the printed reply of my correspondent to his Southern friend, which occupies ten columns of a large newspaper, to see if I had overlooked any Scripture, I find I have omitted to notice one reference to the sacred volume, which was made by him, for the general purpose of showing that the Scriptures abound with moral principles, and call into exercise moral feelings inconsistent with slavery. It is this: "Inasmuch as you have done it unto one of the least of these my brethren, you have done it unto me." The design of the Saviour, in the parable from which these words are taken, in Matt. xxv, is, to impress strongly upon the human mind, that *character*, deficient in *correct moral feeling*, will prove fatal to human hopes in a coming day.

But, reader, will you stop and ask yourself, "What is correct moral feeling?" Is it abhorrence and hatred to the will and pleasure of God? Certainly not. Then it is not abhorrence and hatred of slavery, which seems to be a cardinal virtue at the North. It has been the will and pleasure of God to institute slavery by a law of his own, in that kingdom over which he immediately presided; and to give it his sanction when instituted by the laws of men. The most elevated morality is enjoined under both Testaments, upon the parties in this relation. There is nothing in the relation inconsistent with its exercise.

My reader will remember that the subject in dispute is, whether involuntary and hereditary slavery was ever lawful in the sight of God, the Bible being judge.

1. I have shown by the Bible, that God decreed this relation between the posterity of Canaan, and the posterity of Shem and Japheth.

2. I have shown that God executed this decree by aiding the posterity of Shem, (at a time when "they were holiness to the Lord,") to enslave the posterity of Canaan in the days of Joshua.

3. I have shown that when God ratified the covenant of promise with Abraham, he recognized Abraham as the owner of slaves he had bought with his money of the stranger, and recorded his approbation of the relation, by commanding Abraham to circumcise them.

4. I have shown that when he took Abraham's posterity by the hand in Egypt, five hundred years afterward, he publicly approbated the same relation, by permitting every slave they had bought with their money to eat the Passover, while he refused the same privilege to their *hired servants*.

5. I have shown that God, as their national law-giver, ordained by express statute, that they should buy slaves of the nations around them, (the seven devoted nations excepted,) and that these slaves and their increase should be a perpetual inheritance to their children.

6. I have shown that God ordained slavery by law for their captives taken in war, while he guaranteed a successful issue to their wars, so long as they obeyed him.

7. I have shown that when Jesus ordered his gospel to be published through the world, the relation of master and slave existed by law in every province and family of the Roman Empire, as it had done in the Jewish commonwealth for fifteen hundred years.

8. I have shown that Jesus ordained, that the legislative authority, which created this relation in that empire, should be obeyed and honored as an ordinance of God, as all government is declared to be.

9. I have shown that Jesus has prescribed the mutual duties of this relation in his kingdom.

10. And lastly, I have shown, that in an attempt by his professed followers to disturb this relation in the Apostolic churches, Jesus orders that fellowship shall be disclaimed with all such disciples, as seditious persons—whose conduct was not only dangerous to the State, but destructive to the true character of the gospel dispensation.

This being the case, as will appear by the recorded language of the Bible, to which we have referred you, reader, of what use is it to argue against it from moral requirements?

They regulate the duties of this and all other lawful relations among men—but they cannot abolish any relation, ordained or sanctioned of God, as is slavery.

I would be understood as referring for proof of this summary, to my first as well as my present essay.

When I first wrote, I did suppose the Scriptures had been examined by leading men in the opposition, and that prejudice had blinded their eyes. I am now of a different opinion. What will be the effect of this discussion, I will not venture to predict, knowing human nature as well as I do. But men who are capable of exercising candor must see, that it is not against an institution unknown to the Bible, or declared by its author to be sinful, that the North is waging war.

Their hostility must be transferred from us to God, who established slavery by law in that kingdom over which he condescended to preside; and to Jesus, who recognized it as a relation established in Israel by his Father, and in the Roman government by men, which he bound his followers to obey and honor.

In defending the institution as one which has the sanction of our Maker, I have done what I considered, under the peculiar circumstances of our common country, to be a Christian duty. I have set down naught in malice. I have used no sophistry. I have brought to the investigation of the subject, common sense. I have not relied on powers of argument, learning, or ingenuity. These would neither put the subject into the Bible nor take it out. It is a Bible question. I have met it fairly, and fully, according to the acknowledged principles of the abolitionists. I have placed before my reader what is in the Bible, to prove that slavery has the sanction of God, and is not sinful. I have placed before him what I suppose to be the quintessence of all that can be gleaned from the Bible to disprove it.

I have made a few plain reflections to aid the understanding of my reader. What I have written was designed for those who reverence the Bible as their counsellor—who take it for rules of conduct, and devotional sentiments.

I now commit it to God for his blessing, with a fervent desire, that if I have mistaken his will in any thing, he will not suffer my error to mislead another.

THORNTON STRINGFELLOW.

[The following letter, in substance, was written to a brother in Kentucky, who solicited a copy of my slavery pamphlet, as well as my opinion on the movement in that State, on the subject of emancipation.]

Dear Brother:——

I received your letter, and the slavery pamphlet which you requested me to send you, I herewith inclose.

When I published the first essay in that pamphlet, I intended to invite a discussion with Elder Galusha, of New York; and when I received Mr. Galusha's letter to Dr. Fuller, I still expected a discussion. But after manifesting, on his part, great pleasure in the out-set, for the opportunity tendered him by a Southern man, to discuss this subject, he ultimately declined it. This being the case, I did not at that time present as full a view of the subject as the Scriptures furnish. I have since thought of supplying this deficiency; and the condition of things in Kentucky furnishes a fit opportunity for saying to you, what I said to a brother in Pennsylvania, who, like yourself, requested me to send him a copy of my pamphlet.

I do not know that I could add any thing, beyond what I said to him, that would be useful to you. To this brother I said, among other things, that Dr. Wayland (in his discussion with Dr. Fuller,) relied principally upon *two arguments*, used by all the intelligent abolitionists, to overthrow the weight of Scriptural authority in support of slavery. The first of these arguments is designed to neutralize the sanction given to slavery by the law of Moses; and the second is designed to neutralize the sanction given to slavery by the New Testament.

The Dr. frankly admits, that the law of Moses did establish slavery in the Jewish commonwealth; and he admits with equal frankness, that it was incorporated as an ele-ment in the gospel church. For the purpose, however, of destroying the sanction thus given to the legality of the relation under the *law of Moses*, he assumes two things in rela-tion to it, which are expressly contradicted by the law. He assumes, in the first place, that the Almighty, under the law, gave a *special permission* to the Israelites to enslave the seven devoted nations, as a punishment for their sins. He then *assumes*, in the second place, that this *special permission* to enslave the seven nations, prohibited, by *implica-tion*, the enslaving of all other nations. The conclusion which the Dr. draws from the above assumptions is this—that a *special permission* under the law, to enslave a particu-lar people, as a punishment for their sins, is not a *general permission* under the gospel, to enslave all, or any other people. The premises here assumed, and from which this conclu-sion is drawn, are precisely the reverse of what is recorded in the Bible.

The Bible statement is this: that the Israelites under the law, so far from being permit-ted or required to enslave the seven nations, as a punishment for their sins, were expressly commanded to *destroy them utterly*. Here is the proof—Deut. vii: 1 and 2: "When the Lord thy God shall bring thee into the land whither thou goest to possess it, and hath cast out many nations before thee, the Hittities, and the Girgashites, and the Amorites, and the Canaanites, and the Perizzites, and the Hivites, and the Jebusites, seven nations greater and mightier than thou; and when the Lord thy God shall deliver them before thee, thou shalt smite them, *and utterly destroy them*, thou shalt make no covenant with then, nor show mercy unto them." And again, in Deut. xx: 16 and 17: "But the cities of these people, which the Lord thy God doth give thee for an inheritance, *thou shalt save alive nothing that breatheth.* But thou shalt *utterly destroy them*, namely, the Hittities, and the Amorites, the Canaanites, and the Perizzites, the Hivites, and the Jebusites, *as the Lord thy God hath commanded thee.*" This law was *delivered* by Moses, and was *executed* by Joshua some years afterward, to the letter.

Here is the proof of it, Josh. xi: 14 to 20 inclusive: "And all the spoil of these cities, and the cattle, the children of Israel took for a prey unto themselves; *but every man they smote with the edge of the sword until they had destroyed them, neither left they any to breathe.*"

"*As the Lord commanded Moses* his servant; so did Moses command Joshua, and *so did Joshua;* he left nothing undone of all that the Lord commanded Moses. So Joshua took all that land, the hills and all the south country, and all the land of Goshen, and the valley and the plain, and the mountain of Israel, and the valley of the same. Even from the mount Halak that goeth up to Sier, even unto Baalgad, in the valley of Lebanon, under mount Hermon, and all their kings he took, and smote them, and slew them. Joshua made war a long time with all these kings. There was not a city that made peace with the children of Israel, *save the Hivites, the inhabitants of Gibeon*, all others they took in battle. For it was of the Lord to harden their hearts, that they should come against Israel in the battle, *that he might destroy them utterly*, and that they might have no favor, but that he might destroy them, *as the Lord commanded Moses.*" In this account of their *destruction*, the Gibeonites, who deceived Joshua, are excepted, and the reason given is, that Joshua in their case, failed to ask counsel at the mouth of the Lord. Here is the proof: "And the men took of them victuals, and asked not counsel of the mouth of the Lord."— Josh. ix: 14. This counsel Joshua was expressly commanded to ask, when he was ordained some time before, to be the *executor* of God's *legislative will*, by Moses. Here is the proof—Numb. xxvii: 18-23: "And the Lord said unto Moses, Take thee Joshua, the son of Nun, a man in whom is the spirit, and lay thy hand upon him; and set him before Eleazar the priest, and before all the congregation; and give him a charge in their sight. And thou shalt put some of thine honor upon him, that all the congregation of the children of Israel may be obedient. *And he shall stand before Eleazar the priest, who shall ask counsel for him, after the judgment of Urim before the Lord: at his word shall they go out, and at his word shall they come in, both he and all the children of Israel with him, even all the congregation.* And Moses did as the Lord commanded him; and he took Joshua and set him before Eleazar the priest, and before all the congregation. And he laid his hands upon him, *and gave him a charge, as the Lord commanded by the hand of Moses.*" These scriptures furnish a palpable contradiction of the first assumption, that is—that the Lord gave a *special permission to enslave* the seven nations. The Lord ordered that they should be destroyed utterly.

As to the second assumption, so far from the Israelites being prohibited *by implication*, from enslaving the subjects of other nations, they were expressly authorized by the law *to make slaves by war, of any other nation*. Here is the proof—Deut. xx: 10 to 17 inclusive: "When thou comest nigh unto a city to fight against it, then proclaim peace unto it. And it shall be if it make thee answer of peace, and open unto thee, then it shall be, that all the people that is found therein, shall be tributaries unto thee, and they shall serve thee. And if it will make no peace with thee, but will make war against thee, then thou shalt besiege it. And when the Lord thy God hath delivered it into thy hands, then shalt thou smite every male thereof with the edge of the sword. *But the women and the little ones, and the cattle, and all that is in the city*, even all the spoils thereof, shalt thou take unto thyself; and thou shalt eat the spoil of thine enemies, which the Lord thy God hath given thee. *Thus shalt thou do unto all the cities which are very far off from thee which are not of the cities of these nations. But of the cities of these people, which the Lord thy God doth give thee for an inheritance, thou shalt save alive nothing that breatheth. But thou shalt utterly destroy them, namely, the Hittites, and the Amorites, the Canaanites, and the Perizzites, the Hivites, and the Jebusites, as the Lord thy God hath commanded thee.*" They were authorized also by the law, to purchase slaves with money of any nation except the seven. Here is the proof—Levit. xxv: 44, 45, and 46: "Both thy bond-men and thy bond-maids, which thou shalt have, shall be of the heathen that are round about you; (that is, round about the country given them of God, which was the country of the seven nations they were soon to occupy;) of them shall ye buy bond-men and bond-maids. Moreover, of the children of the strangers that do sojourn among you, (that is, the mixed multitude of strangers which come up with them from Egypt, mentioned in Exod. xii: 38,) of them shall ye buy, and of their families that are with you, which they begat in your land; and they shall be your possession. And ye shall take them as an inheritance for your children after you, to inherit them for a possession, they shall be your bond-men forever."

Now, let it be noted that this first law, of Deut. xx: above referred to, which authorized them to make slaves by war of any other nation, was executed *for the first time*, under the direction of Moses himself, when thirty-two thousand of the Midianites were enslaved. These slaves were not of the seven nations.

And it is worthy of further remark, that of each half, into which the Lord had these slaves divided, he claimed for his portion, one slave of every five hundred for the priests, and one slave of every fifty for the Levites. These slaves he gave to the priests and Levites, who were his representatives to be their property forever.—Numb. xxxi. These scriptures palpably contradict the Dr.'s second assumption—that is, that they were *prohibited by implication* from enslaving the subjects of any other nation. The Dr.'s assumptions being the antipodes of truth, they cannot furnish a conclusion that is warranted by the truth.

The conclusion authorized by the truth, is this: that the making of slaves by war, and the purchase of slaves with money, was legalized by the Almighty in the Jewish commonwealth, as regards the subject of *all nations except the seven.*

The second argument of the Dr.'s, as I remarked, is designed to neutralize the sanction given to slavery in the New Testament.

The Dr. frankly admits that slavery was sanctioned by the Apostles in the Apostolic churches. But to neutralize this sanction, he resorts to two more assumptions, not only without proof, but palpably contradicted by the Old and New Testament text. The first assumption is this—*that polygamy and divorce were both sins under the law of Moses, although sanctioned by the law.* And the second assumption is, that polygamy and divorce are *known to be sins under the gospel,* not by any gospel teaching or prohibition, but by the general principles of morality. From these premises the conclusion is drawn, that although slavery was sanctioned in the Apostolic church, yet it was a sin, because, like polygamy and divorce, it was contrary to the principles of the moral law. The premises from which this conclusion is drawn, are at issue with the word of God, and therefore the conclusion must be false. The first thing here assumed is, that polygamy and divorce, although sanctioned by the law of Moses, were both sins under that law. Now, so far from this being true, as to *polygamy,* it is a fact that polygamy was not only sanctioned, when men chose to practice it, but it was expressly enjoined by the law in certain cases, and a most humiliating penalty annexed to the breach of the command.—Deut. xxv: 5-9. As sin is defined by the Holy Ghost to be a transgression of the law, it is impossible that *polygamy* could have been a sin under the law, unless it was a sin to obey the law, and an act of righteousness to transgress it. That *polygamy* was a sin under the law, therefore, is palpably false.

As to *divorce,* the Almighty gave it the full and explicit sanction of his authority, in the law of Moses, for various causes.—Deut. xxiv: 1. For those causes, therefore, divorce could not have been a sin under the law, unless human conduct, in exact accordance with the law of God, was sinful. The first thing assumed by the Dr., therefore, that polygamy and divorce were both sins, under the law, is proved to be false. They were lawful, and therefore, could not be sinful.

The Dr.'s second assumption (with respect to polygamy and divorce,) is this, that they are *known* under the gospel to be sins, not by the prohibitory *precepts* of the gospel, but by the general *principles* of morality. This assumption is certainly a very astonishing one—for Jesus Christ in one breath has uttered language as perfectly subversive of all authority for polygamy and divorce in his kingdom, as light is subversive of darkness. The Pharisees, ever desirous of exposing him to the prejudices and passions of the

412

people, "asked him in the presence of great multitudes, who came with him from Galilee into the coasts of Judea beyond Jordan," whether he admitted, with Moses, the legality of divorce for every cause. Their object was to provoke him to the exercise of legislative authority; to whom he promptly replied, that God made man at the beginning, male and female, and ordained that the male and female by marriage, should be one flesh. And for satisfactory reasons, had sanctioned divorce among Abraham's seed; and then adds, as a law-giver, "But I say unto you, that whosoever shall put away his wife, (except for fornication,) and shall marry another, committeth adultery; and if a woman put away her husband, and marry again, she committeth adultery." Here polygamy and divorce die together. The law of Christ is, that *neither* party shall put the other away—that *either* party, taking another companion, while the first companion lives, is guilty of adultery—consequently, polygamy and divorce are prohibited forever, unless this law is violated—and that violation is declared to be adultery, which excludes from his kingdom.—1 Cor. vi: 9. After the church was organized, the Holy Ghost, by Paul, *commands*, let not the wife depart from her husband, but, and if she depart let her remain unmarried—and let not the husband put away his wife.—1 Cor. vii: 10. Here *divorce* is prohibited by *both parties;* a second marriage according to Christ, would be adultery, while the first companion lives; consequently, *polygamy* is prohibited also.

This second assumption, therefore, that polygamy and divorce are known to be sins by *moral principles* and *not by prohibitory precepts*, is swept away by the words of Christ, and the teaching of the Holy Ghost. These unauthorized and dangerous assumptions are the foundation, upon which the abolition structure is made to rest by the distinguished Dr. Wayland.

The facts with respect to polygamy and divorce, warrant precisely the opposite conclusion; that is, that if slavery under the gospel is sinful, then its sinfulness would have been made known by the gospel, as has been done with respect to polygamy and divorce. All three, polygamy, divorce and slavery, were *sanctioned* by the law of Moses. But under the gospel, slavery has been *sanctioned* in the church, while polygamy and divorce have been *excluded* from the church. It is manifest, therefore, that under the gospel, polygamy and divorce have been made sins, *by prohibition*, while slavery remains lawful because *sanctioned* and *continued*. The *lawfulness* of slavery under the gospel, rests upon the sovereign pleasure of Christ, in *permitting it;* and the *sinfulness* of polygamy and divorce, upon his sovereign pleasure in *prohibiting* their continuance. The law of Christ gives to the relation of slavery its full sanction. *That law* is to be found, first, in the *admission, by the apostles*, of slaveholders and their slaves into the gospel church; second, in the *positive injunction* by the Holy Ghost, of obedience on the part of Christian slaves in this relation, to their believing masters; third, in the *absence* of any injunction upon the believing master, under any circumstances, to dissolve this relation; fourth, in the *absence* of any instruction from Christ or the apostles, that the relation is sinful; and lastly, in the *injunction* of the Holy Ghost, delivered by Paul, *to withdraw* from all such as teach that this relation is sinful. Human conduct in exact accordance with the law of Christ thus proclaimed, and thus expounded by the Holy Ghost, in the conduct and teaching of the apostles, cannot be sinful.

There are other portions of God's word, in the light of which we may add to our stock of knowledge on this subject. For instance, the Almighty by Moses legalized marriage between female slaves and Abraham's male descendants. But under this law the wife remained a slave still. If she belonged to the husband, then this law gave freedom to her children; but if she belonged to another man, then her children, though born in lawful wedlock, were hereditary slaves.—Exod. xxi: 4. Again, if a man marries his own slave, then he lost the right to sell her—if he divorced her, then she gained her freedom.—Deut. xxi: 10 to 14, inclusive. Again, there was a law from God which granted rights to Abraham's sons under a matrimonial contract; for a violation of the rights conferred by this law, a *free woman, and her seducer*, forfeited their lives, Deut. xxii: 23 and 24; also 13 to 21, inclusive. But for the same offense, *a slave* only exposed herself to stripes, and her *seducer* to the penalty of a sheep.—Levit. xix: 20 to 22, inclusive. Again, there was a law which guarded his people, whether free or bond, from personal violence. If in vindictiveness, a man with an unlawful weapon, maimed his own slave by knocking out his eye, or his tooth, the slave was to be free for this wanton act of personal violence, as a penalty upon the master.—Exod. xxi: 26 to 27, inclusive. But for the same offense, committed against a free person, the offender had to pay an eye for an eye, and a tooth for a tooth, as the penalty.—Levit. xxiv: 19, 20, and Exod. xxi: 24 and 25, inclusive. Again, there was a law to guard the personal safety of the community against dangerous stock. If an ox, known to be dangerous, was suffered to run at large and kill a person, if the person so killed *was free*, then the owner forfeited his *life* for his neglect,—Exod. xxi: 29. But if the person so killed *was a slave*, then the offender was fined thirty shekels of silver.—Exod. xxi: 32. In some things, slaves among the Israelites, as among us, were invested with privileges above hired servants—they were privileged to eat the Passover, but hired servants were not, Exod. xii: 44, 45; and such as were owned by the priests and Levites were privileged to eat of the holy things of their masters, but hired servants dare not taste them.—Levit. xxii: 10, 11. These are statutes from the Creator of man. They are certainly predicated upon a view of things, in the Divine mind, that is *somewhat different* from that which makes an abolitionist; and, to say the least, they deserve consideration with all men who worship the God of the Bible, and not the God of their own imagination. They show very clearly, that our Creator is the *author* of social, moral, and political inequality among men. That so far from the Scriptures teaching, as abolitionists do, that all men have ever had a divine right to freedom and equality, they show, *in so many words*, that marriages were sanctioned of God as lawful, in which *he enacted*, that the children of free men should be born hereditary slaves. They show also, that he guarded the chastity of the free by the price of life, and the chastity of the slave by the rod. They show, that in the judgment of God, the life of a free man in the days of Moses, was too sacred for commutation, while a fine of thirty shekels of silver was sufficient to expiate for the death of a slave. As I said in my first essay, so I say now, this is a controversy between abolitionists and their Maker. I see not how, with their present views and in their present temper, they can stop short of blasphemy against that Being who enacted these laws.

Of late years, some obscure passages (which have no allusion whatever to the subject) have been brought forward to show, that God *hated slavery*, although the work of his own hands. Once for all, I challenge proof, that in the Old Testament or the New, *any reproof was ever uttered against involuntary slavery, or against any abuse of its authority*. Upon abolition principles, this is perfectly unaccountable, and of itself, is an unanswerable argument that the *relation* is not sinful.

The opinion has been announced also of late, that slavery among the Jews was felt to be an evil, and, by degrees, that they abolished it. To ascertain the correctness of this opinion, let the following consideration be weighed: After centuries of cruel *national bondage* practiced upon Abraham's seed in Egypt, they were brought in godly contrition to pour out "the effectual fervent prayer" of a righteous people, to the Almighty for mercy, and were answered by a covenant God, who sent Moses to deliver them from their bondage—but let it be remembered, that when this deliverance from bondage to the nation of Egypt was vouchsafed to them, they were extensive domestic slave owners. God had not by his providential dealings, nor in any other way, shown them the sin of domestic slavery—for they held on to their slaves, and brought them out as their property into the wilderness. And it is worthy of further remark, that the Lord, *before they left Egypt*, recognized these slaves *as property*, which they had bought with their money, and that he secured to these slaves privileges above hired servants, *simply because they were slaves.*—Exod. xii: 44, 45. And let it be noticed further, that the first law passed by the Almighty after proclaiming the ten commandments or moral constitution of the nation, was a law to regulate property rights in hereditary slaves, and to regulate property rights in Jewish hired servants for a term of years.—Exod. xxi: 1 to 6, inclusive. And let it be considered further, that when the Israelites were subjected to a cruel captivity in Babylon, more than eight hundred years after this, they were still extensive slave owners; that when humbled and brought to repentance for their sins, and the Lord restored them to their own land again, that he brought them back to their old homes as slave owners. Although greatly impoverished by a seventy years' captivity in a foreign land, yet the slaves which they brought up from Babylon bore a proportion of nearly one slave for every five free persons that returned, or about one slave for every family.—Ezra ii: 64, 65. Now, can we, in the face of these facts, believe they were tired of slavery when they came out of Egypt? It had then existed five hundred years. Or can we believe they were tired of it when they came up from Babylon? It had then existed among them fourteen hundred years. Or can we believe that God put them into these schools of affliction in Egypt and Babylon to teach them, (and all others through them,) the sinfulness of slavery, and yet, that he brought them out without giving them the first hint that involuntary slavery was a sin? And let it be further considered, that it was the business of the prophets which the Lord raised up, *to make known to them the sins for which his judgments were sent upon them*. The sins which he charged upon them in all his visitation are upon record. Let any man find involuntary slavery in any of God's indictments against them, and I will retract all I have ever written.

In my original essay, I said nothing of Paul's letter to Philemon, concerning Onesimus, a run-away slave, converted by Paul's preaching at Rome; and who was returned by the Apostle, with a most affectionate letter to his master, entreating the master to receive him again, and to forgive him. O, how immeasurably different Paul's conduct to this slave and his master, from the conduct of our abolition brethren! Which are we to think is guided by the Spirit of God? It is *impossible* that both can be guided by that Spirit, unless sweet water and bitter can come from the same fountain. This letter, itself, is sufficient to teach any man, capable of being taught in the ordinary way, that slavery is not, *in the sight of God, what it is in the sight of the abolitionists.*

I had prepared the argument furnished by this letter for my original essay; I afterward struck it out, because at that time, so little had the Bible been examined at the North in reference to slavery, that the abolitionists very generally thought that this was the only scripture which Southern slaveholders could find, giving any countenance to their views of slavery. To test the correctness of this opinion, therefore, I determined to make no allusion to it at that time.

Now, my dear sir, if from the evidence contained in the Bible to prove slavery a lawful relation among God's people under every dispensation, the assertion is still made, in the very face of this evidence, that slavery has *ever been* the greatest sin—*everywhere, and under all circumstances*—can you, or can any sane man bring himself to believe, that the mind capable of such a decision, is not capable of trampling the word of God under foot upon any subject?

If it were not known to be the fact, we could not admit that a Bible-reading man could bring himself to believe, with Dr. Wayland, that a thing made lawful by the God of heaven, was, notwithstanding, the greatest sin—and that Moses under the law, and Jesus Christ under the gospel, had sanctioned and regulated in practice, the greatest known sin on earth—and that Jesus had left his church to find out as best they might, that the law of God which established slavery under the Old Testament, and the precepts of the Holy Ghost which regulate the mutual duty of master and slave under the New Testament, were laws and precepts, to sanction and regulate among the people of God the greatest sin which was ever perpetrated.

It is by no means strange that it should have taken seventeen centuries to make such discoveries as the above, and it is worthy of note, that these discoveries were made at last by men who did not appear to know, at the time they made them, what was in the Bible on the subject of slavery, and who now appear unwilling that the teachings of the Bible should be spread before the people—this last I take to be the case, because I have been unable to get the Northern press to give it publicity.

Many anti-slavery men into whose hands my essays chanced to fall, have frankly confessed to me, that in their Bible reading, they had overlooked the plain teaching of the Holy Ghost, by taking what they read in the Bible about masters and servants, to have reference to hired servants and their employers.

You ask me for my opinion about the emancipation movement in the State of Kentucky. I hold that the emancipation of hereditary slaves by a State is not commanded, or in any way required by the Bible. The Old Testament and the New, sanction slavery, but under no circumstances enjoin its abolition, even among saints. Now, if religion, or the duty we owe our Creator, was inconsistent with slavery, then this could not be so. If pure religion, therefore, did not require its abolition under the law of Moses, nor in the church of Christ—we may safely infer, that our political, moral and social relations do not require it in a State; unless a State requires higher moral, social, and religious qualities in its subjects, than a gospel church.

Masters have been left by the Almighty, both under the patriarchal, legal, and gospel dispensations, to their individual discretion on the subject of emancipation.

The principle of justice inculcated by the Bible, refuses to sanction, it seems to me, such an outrage upon the rights of men, as would be perpetrated by any sovereign State, which, to-day, makes a thing to be property, and to-morrow, takes it from the lawful owners, *without political necessity or pecuniary compensation*. Now, if it be morally right for a majority of the people (and that majority possibly a meagre one, who may not own a slave) to take, without necessity or compensation, the property in slaves held by a minority, (and that minority a large one,) then it would be morally right for a majority, without property, to take any thing else that may be lawfully owned by the prudent and care-taking portion of the citizens.

As for intelligent philanthropy, it shudders at the infliction of certain ruin upon a whole race of helpless beings. If emancipation by law is philanthropic in Kentucky, it is, for the same reasons, philanthropic in every State in the Union. But nothing in the future is more certain, than that such emancipation would begin to work the degradation and final ruin of the slave race, from the day of its consummation.

Break the master's sympathy, which is inseparably connected with his property right in his slave, and that moment the slave race is placed upon a common level with all other competitors for the rewards of merit; but as the slaves are inferior in the qualities which give success among competitors in our country, extreme poverty would be their lot; and for the want of means to rear families, they would multiply slowly, and die out by inches, degraded by vice and crime, unpitied by honest and virtuous men, and heart-broken by sufferings without a parallel.

So long as States let masters alone on this subject, good men among them, both in the church and out of it, will struggle on, as experience may dictate and justify, for the benefit of the slave race. And should the time ever come, when emancipation in its consequences, will comport with the moral, social, and political obligations of Christianity, then Christian masters will invest their slaves with freedom, and then will the good-will of those follow the descendants of Ham, who, without any agency of their own, have been made in this land of liberty, their providential guardians.

Yours, with affection,
THORNTON STRINGFELLOW.

[It is or ought to be known to all men, that African slavery in the United States originated in, and is perpetuated by a social and political necessity, and that its continuance is demanded equally by the highest interests of both races. All writers on public law, from Drs. Channing and Wayland, among the abolitionists, up to the highest authorities on national law, admit the necessity and propriety of slavery in a social body, whenever men will not provide for their own wants, and yield obedience to the law which guards the rights of others. The guardianship and control of the black race, by the white, in this Union, is an indispensable Christian duty, to which we must as yet look, if we would secure the well-being of both races.]

STATISTICAL VIEW OF SLAVERY

To satisfy the conscientiousness of Christians, I published in the *Herald*, some years past, Bible evidence, to prove slavery a lawful relation among men. In a late communication you[231] refer to *this essay*, and express a wish that it should be republished. Many have expressed a similar wish.

Some who admit the *legality* of slavery in the sight of God, question the *expediency of its expansion*. It is believed by them to be an element that is hostile to the best interests of society, and therefore, great efforts have been, and are now being made, to exclude it from all the new States and Territories which may hereafter be organized upon our soil.

While the *expediency* of its *expansion* or *continuance*, are questions with which I have not heretofore meddled, yet I hold their *investigation* to be within the legitimate range of Christian duty.

If unquestionable *facts* and *experience* warrant the *conclusion*, that while slavery is lawful, yet its *continuance* or *expansion* among us is *inexpedient*, then let us act accordingly.

Being *prompted* by your request, I propose to examine *facts*, which are admitted the world over, as evidence of prosperity and happiness in a community, and to compare the evidence thus furnished in different sections of our country, where the experiment of freedom, and the experiment of slavery have been fully and fairly upon trial since the commencement of our colonial existence, that we may see, if possible, what is true on this subject. This seems to be the *unerring* method of coming at the truth. And if it shall appear, by such a comparison—fairly made—between States of equal age, where slavery and freedom have had a fair opportunity to produce their legitimate results, that in all the elements of prosperity, slaveholding States suffer nothing in the comparison—but that, in almost every particular, are decidedly in advance of the non-slaveholding States, why then we are bound to let the testimony of these facts control our judgment.

Every man and woman in the United States should not only be willing, but desirous to know, what is the matter-of-fact evidence on this all-absorbing question. It is but lately that any method existed, of coming at *undisputed* facts, which would throw light upon this subject. The Congress of the United States seeing this, thought proper to order that such facts as tend to demonstrate the relative prosperity of the different States of the Union, in religion—in morals—in the acquisition of wealth—in the increase of native population—in the prolongation of life—in the diminution of crime, etc., etc., should be ascertained, under oath, by competent and responsible agents, and that these facts should be published at the national expense for the benefit of the people: so that the people could, understandingly, apply the corrective for evils that might be found to exist in one locality, and profit by a knowledge of the greater prosperity that might be found to exist in another locality.

Up to that time, the non-slaveholding States affirmed, and the slaveholding States tacitly admitted, that by this test, the slaveholding States must suffer in the comparison, in some important items. The facts which belong to the subject, are now before the world, in the census of 1850.

It is my purpose to compare some of the most important of these facts, which have a bearing on this subject. I shall take for the most part, the six New England States, on one side, and the five old slave States, (extending from, and including Maryland and Georgia,) on the other side, for the comparison.

I select *these States*, not because they are the richest, (for they are not,) but because they all lie on the Atlantic side of the Union—because they were settled at or near the same time—because they have (within a fraction) an equal free population—and because it has been constantly affirmed, and almost universally admitted, that the advantages of freedom, and the disadvantages of slavery, have been more perfectly developed in these two sections, than they have been anywhere else in the United States. There have been no controlling circumstances at any time, since their first settlement, to neutralize the advantages of freedom on the one side, or to modify the evils of slavery on the other. Their mutual tendencies, without let or hindrance, have been in full and free operation for more than two centuries. This is surely a length of time quite sufficient to test the question now in controversy between the North and the South, as to the evils of slavery.

The first facts I shall examine are those which throw light on the progress made in each of these two localities in religion. Of all the evils ascribed to slavery by the free men of the North, none equals, in their estimation, its deleterious tendency upon *religion* and *morals*. Indeed, such is the *moral character*, ascribed by many at the North, who call themselves Christians, to a Southern slaveholder, that no degree of personal piety, of which he can be the subject, will bring them to admit that he is any thing but a God-abhorred miscreant, utterly unfit for the association of honorable men, much less Christian men.

In the outset of this examination, let me remark, that it is just and proper, in a comparative estimate of the tendency of freedom and slavery upon religion and morals, in these two sections of our country, that due allowance be made for the moral and religious character of the materials by which these two sections were originally settled. New England was settled by Puritans, who were remarkable for orthodox sentiments in religion—for high-toned religious conscientiousness, and a rigid personal piety; while these five slave

States were either settled, or received character from Cavaliers, who rather scoffed at pure religion, and were highly tinged with infidelity.

The stream does not, in its flow onward, carry with more certainty the characteristics of the fountain, than does progressive society, *generally*, the moral, social, and religious characteristics of its origin. The five slave States, in this comparison originated in a people of loose morals—strongly tinged with infidelity—and subjected, also, in their onward progress, to all the evil tendencies (if any there be) that are ascribed to slavery.

At the end of more than two centuries, we are comparing the progress which these five slave States have made in religion, with the progress made by six non-slaveholding States, whose subjects, when originally organized into communities, were in advance, in personal piety and religious conscientiousness, of any communities that had then been founded since the days of the apostles—and that have been, in their onward progress, from that time until this, free from all the supposed evils of slavery. If infidelity and slavery be antagonistic elements, almost, if not altogether, too strong for moral control in a community, it certainly ought not to seem strange, that with this original odds against them, these five old slave States should be found very far behind their more highly favoured Northern neighbors in religious attainments.

Religion being, at present, the subject of comparison, it may be appropriate to remark further, that the *Christian religion* is propagated by God's blessing upon the observance of his laws.

The fundamental law of God, *for its propagation* requires the gospel to be preached to every creature; because, in the divine plan, faith in the gospel was to make men Christians. The gospel was to be made the *power of God* unto salvation, to every one that *believeth. This faith* was to be originated by hearing the gospel, for "faith comes by hearing." All those efforts, therefore, in a community, which manifests the greatest solicitude on the part of the people, that the gospel should be *heard*, is credible evidence that the people who make these efforts, are the friends of Christ, and well-wishers to his cause. Now, all those *means* which are most likely to secure the ear of the people, are left by Christ to the *discretion* of his friends. They may use the market-place—the highways—the forests—or *any other place*, which in their judgment is most likely to get the ear of the people when the gospel is proclaimed. By common consent, however, within the limits of Christian civilization, they have agreed that suitable houses, in which the people can meet to hear the gospel, are the most suitable and proper means for securing the audience of the people, and as a consequence, the transforming power of the gospel upon the hearts and lives of those who hear.

With these views to guide us in estimating the value of the facts to be examined, we proceed to disclosures made by the census of 1850. We there learn that the free population of New England is two million seven hundred and twenty-eight thousand and sixteen; and that the free population of these five slave States is two million seven hundred and thirty thousand two hundred and fourteen; an excess of only two thousand one hundred and ninety-eight. This fraction we will drop out, and speak of them as equals. New England, then, with an equal population, has erected four thousand six hundred and seven churches; these five slave States have erected eight thousand and eighty-one churches. These New England churches will accommodate one million eight hundred and ninety-three thousand four hundred and fifty hearers; the churches of the five slave States will accommodate two million eight hundred and ninety-six thousand four hundred and seventy-two hearers. Thus we see that these slave States, with an equal free population, have erected nearly double the number of churches, and furnished accommodation for upwards of a million more persons, to hear the gospel, than can be accommodated in New England. In New England, nine hundred and thirty-four thousand, five hundred and sixty-six of its population (which is nearly one-third) are excluded from a seat in houses built for the purpose of enabling people to hear the gospel; while in these five Southern States, there is room enough for every hearer that could be crowded into the churches of New England, and then enough left to accommodate more than a million of slaves.

Including slaves, these five Southern States have a population of seven hundred and twenty thousand four hundred and ten more than New England; yet while there are seven hundred and twenty thousand four hundred and ten persons less in New England to provide for, there are two hundred thousand more persons in New England who can't find a seat in the house of God to hear the gospel, than there are in these five slave States.

The next fact set forth in the census, which I will examine, is equally *suggestive*. These four thousand six hundred and seven churches in New England are valued at nineteen million three hundred and sixty-two thousand six hundred and thirty-four dollars. These eight thousand and eighty-one churches in the five slave States are valued at eleven million one hundred and forty-nine thousand one hundred and eighteen dollars. Here is an immense expenditure in New England to erect churches; yet we see that those New England churches, when erected, will seat one million three thousand and twenty-two persons less than those erected by the slave States, at a cost of eight million one hundred and thirteen thousand five hundred and sixteen dollars less money. What prompted to such an expenditure as this? Was it worldly pride? or was it godly humility? Does it exhibit the evidence of humility, and a desire to glorify God, by a provision that shall enable *all the people* to hear the gospel? or does it exhibit the evidence of pride, that seeks to glorify the wealthy contributors, who occupy these costly temples to the exclusion of the humble poor? We must all draw our own conclusions. A mite, given to God from a right spirit, was declared by the Saviour to be more than all the costly gifts of wealthy pride, which were cast into the offerings of God. The Saviour informed the messenger of John the Baptist, that *one of the signs* by which to decide the *presence* of the Messiah, was to be found in the fact that the poor had the gospel preached to them. When we exclude the poor, we may safely conclude we exclude Christ.

It is legitimate to conclude, therefore, that all the arrangements found among a people, which palpably defeat the preaching of the gospel to the poor, are arrangements which throw a shade of deep suspicion upon the character of those who make them. *Costly palaces* were never built for the poor; they are neither suitable nor proper to secure the preaching of the gospel to every creature.

There is still another fact revealed in the census, that furnishes material for reflection when the effects of slavery upon religion are being tried. The six New England States were originally settled by *orthodox* Christians—by men who manifested a very high regard for the interests of pure religion; the five slave States, by men who scoffed at religion, and who were subjected, also, to the so-called curse of slavery; yet, at the end of over two hundred years, we have to deduct from the four thousand six hundred and seven churches built up by New England orthodoxy and freedom, the *astonishing number* of two hundred and two Unitarian, and two hundred and eighty-five Universalist churches—while from the five slave States, we have to deduct from the eight thousand and eighty-one churches which they have built, only one Unitarian, and seven Universalist churches. New England regards these four hundred and eighty-seven churches, which she has built, to be the product of *blind guides*, that are *leaders of the blind*. Is it not strange (she herself being judge) that New England orthodoxy and personal freedom should beget this vast amount of infidelity; while slaveholders and slavery have begotten so little of it in the same length of time? Is there nothing in all this to render the correctness of Northern views questionable, as to the deleterious tendency of slavery? The facts, however, are given to the world in the census of 1850. All are left to draw from these facts their own conclusions. One of these conclusions must be, that there is something else in the world to corrupt religion and morals, besides slaveholders and slavery.

It is not improper to refer to some historical facts in this connection, which are not in the census, but which, nevertheless, we all know to exist. There are *isms* at the North whose name is Legion. According to the universal standard of *orthodoxy*, we are compelled to exclude the *subjects* of these isms from the pale of Christianity. What the relative proportion is, North and South, of such of these isms as have been nurtured into *organized* existence, we have no certain means of knowing—and I do not wish to do injustice, or to be offensive, in statements which are not susceptible of proof by facts and figures—yet, I suppose that in the five slave States, a man might wear himself out in travel, and never find one of these isms with an *organized* existence. To find a single individual, would be doing more than most men have done, with whom I am acquainted. But how is it in New England? The soil seems to suit them—they grow up like Jonah's gourd. Some are warring with great zeal against the social, and some against the religious institutions of society. Why is this? The institution of slavery has not produced, at the North, the moral obliquity, out of which they grow—a reverence for the Bible has not produced it. How is their existence, then, to be accounted for at the North, under institutions, whose tendency is supposed to be so favorable to moral and religious prosperity?

And how is their utter absence to be accounted for at the South, where the institution of slavery is supposed to be so fatal to morality, religion and virtue? I will leave it for others to explain this fact. It is a mysterious fact, according to the modes of reasoning at the North. It is assumed by the North, that slavery tends to produce social, moral, and religious evils. This assumption is flatly contradicted by the facts of the census. These facts can never be explained by the *New England theory*. There was an *ancient theory*, held by men who were righteous in their own eyes, that no good thing could come out of Nazareth. By that theory Christ himself was condemned. It is not wonderful, therefore, that his friends should share the same fate.

The next disclosure of the census, which we will compare, are those which relate to the social prosperity of a people. Are they wealthy? are they healthy? are they in conditions to raise families, etc.?

These questions indicate the *elements* which belong to the item now to be examined. States are made up of families. Wealth is a blessing in those States which have it so distributed, as to give the greatest number of homes to the families which compose them. Wealth, so distributed in States, as to diminish the number of homes, is a curse to the families which compose them. Home is the nursery and shield of virtue. No right-minded man or woman, who had the means, could ever consent to have a family without a home; and no State should make wealth her boast, whose families are extensively without homes.

New England has five hundred and eighteen thousand five hundred and thirty-two families, and four hundred and forty-seven thousand seven hundred and eighty-nine dwellings. The five slave States have five hundred and six thousand nine hundred and sixty-eight families, and four hundred and ninety-six thousand three hundred and sixty-nine dwellings. Here we see the astonishing fact, that with an equal population, New England has eleven thousand five hundred and sixty-four more families than these five slave States, and that these five slave States have forty-eight thousand five hundred and eighty more dwellings than New England—so that New England actually has seventy thousand seven hundred and forty-three families without a home. In New England one family in every *seven* is without a home, while in these five old slave States only one family in every *fifty-two* is without a home.

According to the average number of persons composing a family, New England has three hundred and seventy-three thousand seven hundred of her people thrown upon the world without a place to call home.

It is truly painful to think of the effects upon morals and virtue, which must flow from this state of things; and it is a pleasure to a philanthropic heart to think of the superior condition of the slaveholding people, who so generally have homes, where parents can throw the shield of protection around their offspring, and guard them against the dangers and demoralizing tendencies of an unprotected condition.

There is another class of facts, equally astonishing, disclosed by the census, and which belong to the comparison we are now making, between States which were organized originally by Puritan orthodoxy and New England freedom on one side, and by infidel slaveholders and slavery on the other. They are facts which relate to natural increase in a State. One of the boasts of Northern freemen is the *increase* of their population. With such a climate as New England, it was to be expected that the people would increase faster, and live longer, than in the climate of these five slave States. It is well known that a large portion of the population of these five Southern States have a fatal climate to contend with, and that everywhere else on the globe, under similar circumstances, a diminished increase of births, and an increased amount of deaths has been the result. But the census, as if disregarding climate, and slavery, and the universal experience of all ages, testifies that there is twenty-seven per cent. more of births, and thirty-three per cent. less of deaths in the five old slave States, than there is in the six New England States.

New England, with an equal population, and eleven thousand five hundred and sixty-four more families, has sixteen thousand five hundred and thirty-four less annual births, and ten thousand one hundred and fifty-two more annual deaths, than these five sickly old Southern slave States. The annual births in New England are sixty-one thousand one hundred and forty-eight; and in the five slave States seventy-seven thousand six hundred and eighty-three. In New England the annual deaths are forty-two thousand three hundred and sixty-eight; in the five slave States thirty-two thousand two hundred and sixteen.

In New England the ratio of births is one to forty-four; in the five slave States one to thirty-five. In New England the ratio of deaths is one to sixty-four; in the five slave States it is one to eighty-five.

The slaves are not in this estimate of births and deaths; they are in the census, however, and that shows that they multiply considerably faster, and are less liable to die than the freemen of New England.

Here are facts which contradict all history and all experience. In a sickly Southern climate, among slaveholders, people actually multiply faster, and die slower, than they do among freemen without slavery, in one of the purest and healthiest Northern climates in the world. How is this to be accounted for? Why do people multiply rapidly? Is it because they live in a healthy climate? Why do they die rapidly? Is it because they live in a sickly climate? Our census contradicts both suppositions. Where, then, does the cause lie? Will excluding slavery from a community cause them to multiply more rapidly and die slower? The census says, No!

The census testifies that the proportion of births is twenty-seven per cent. greater, and the proportion of deaths thirty-three per cent. less, among slaveholders, in a community where slavery has existed for more than two hundred years, under all the disadvantages of a sickly climate, than among free men in the pure climate of New England. A man, in his right mind, will demand an explanation of these astonishing facts. They are easily explained. The census discloses a degree of *poverty* in New England, which scatters seventy thousand families to the four winds of heaven, and *feeds* (as we shall presently see) the *poor-house*, with one hundred and thirty-five per cent. more of paupers than is found in these slave States. This is no condition of things to increase births, or diminish deaths, unless brothels give *increase*, and squalid poverty the requisite sympathy and aid, to recover the sick and dying, from the period of infancy to that of old age.

We proceed to compare other facts, which have a bearing upon the relative merits of different institutions in securing social prosperity.

In every country there is a class to be found in such utter destitution, that they must either be supported by charity, or perish of want. This destitution arises, generally, from oppressive exactions or excessive vice, and is evidence of the tendency of social institutions, and the superiority of one over another, in securing the greatest amount of individual prosperity and comfort.

With these views to aid us, we will compare some facts belonging to New England and these five old slave States. With an equal population, New England has thirty-three thousand four hundred and thirty-one paupers; these five slave States have fourteen thousand two hundred and twenty-one. Here is an excess of paupers in New England, notwithstanding her boasted prosperity, of one hundred and thirty-five per cent. over these five slave States. And if to these *continual paupers* we were to add the number (as given in State returns) that are partially aided in New England, the addition would be awful. But I suppose New England will strive to wipe off this stain of regular pauperism, by throwing the blame of it upon the *foreigners* among them. It should be remembered, however, as an offset to this, that these foreigners are all from non-slaveholding countries. From their infancy they have shared the blessings of freedom and free institutions; therefore they ought to be admitted, as homogeneous materials, in the social organizations of New England, which we are now comparing with Southern slaveholding communities.

But as foreign paupers are distinguished in the census from native born citizens, we will now (in the comparison) exclude them in both sections. The number of paupers will then be, for New England, eighteen thousand nine hundred and sixty-six; for the five slave States, eleven thousand seven hundred and twenty-eight—leaving to New England, which is considered the model section of the world in all that is lovely in religious and social prosperity, seven thousand two hundred and thirty-eight more of her native sons in the poor-house, (or nearly seventy per cent.,) than are to be found in this condition in an equal population in these five Southern States.

The ratio of New England's *native sons* in the poor-house is one to one hundred and forty-three; of these five slave States one to two hundred and thirty-four. The ratio of New England's *entire population* in the poor-house is one to eighty-one; the ratio of the entire population of these five slave States is one to one hundred and seventy-one.

The Saviour asks if a good tree can bring forth evil fruit, or an evil tree good fruit. Here is an exhibition of the *fruit* borne by *New England freedom* and *Southern slavery*. The Saviour gives every man a right to judge the tree by the fruit, and declares such to be righteous judgment.

There is another item in the census which throws much light on the comparative comfort and happiness of the people in these two localities. It is neither physical destitution, criminal degradation, nor mental suffering; but it is an effect which is known to flow from one, or the other, or all three of these *conditions* as causes; therefore it is an important item in determining the amount of destitution, degradation, and suffering, which exist in a community.

When we see effects which are known to flow from certain causes—the causes may be concealed—yet we know that they exist by the effects we see. With these remarks I proceed to state a fact disclosed in the census, as it exists in New England, and as it exists in these five old slave States.

In New England, with an equal population, we find that three thousand eight hundred and twenty-nine of her white children have been crushed by sufferings *of some sort*, to the condition of insanity, while in these five old slave States there are only two thousand three hundred and twenty-six of her white children who have been called to suffer, in their earthly pilgrimage, a degree of anguish beyond mental endurance. Here is a difference of more than sixty per cent. in favor of these five States, as to conditions of suffering that are beyond endurance among men. Very poor evidence this, of the superior happiness and comfort of New England.

But while her white children are called to suffer over sixty per cent. more of these crushing sorrows than those of these five States, how is it with her black children in freedom, compared with the family here in slavery, from which the most of them have fled, that they might enjoy the blessings of liberty? It is exceedingly interesting to see the benefits and blessings which New England freedom and Puritan sympathy have conferred upon them.

Here are the facts of the census upon this subject:

Among the free negroes of New England, one is deaf or dumb for every three thousand and five; while among the slaves of these States there is only one for every six thousand five hundred and fifty-two. In New England one free negro is blind for every eight hundred and seventy; while in these States there is only one blind slave for every two thousand six hundred and forty-five. In New England there is one free negro insane or an idiot for every nine hundred and eighty; while in these States there is but one slave for every three thousand and eighty.

Can any man bring himself to believe, with these facts before him, that freedom in New England has proved a blessing to this race of people, or that slavery is to them a curse in the Southern States? In non-slaveholding States, *money* will be the *master of poverty*. These facts enumerated show the fruits of such a relation the world over. The slave of money, while nominally free, has none to care for him at those periods, and in those conditions of his life, when he is not able to render service or labor. Childhood, old age, and sickness, are conditions which make sympathy indispensable. Nominal freedom, combined with poverty, can not secure it in those conditions, because it can not render service or labor. The slave of the South enjoys this sympathy in all conditions from birth till death. There is a spontaneous heart-felt flow of it, to soothe his sorrows, to supply his wants, and smooth his passage to the grave. Interest, honor, humanity, public opinion, and the law, all *combine* to awaken it, and to promote its activity.

Many facts of the character here examined have been disclosed in State statistics, and others in the Federal census; some of which I shall hereafter notice, that show with the most unquestionable certainty, that freedom to this race, in our country, is a curse.

The facts which we have now examined, if they prove any thing, prove that religion has prospered more among slaveholders at the South, than it has among free men in New England. Slaveholders have made a much more extensive and suitable provision for the people of all classes to hear the gospel, than has been made by the freemen of New England. Slaveholders have almost entirely frowned down the attempts of blind-guides to corrupt the gospel, or mislead the people. Among them organized bodies to overthrow the moral, social, and religious institutions of society, are unknown.

If the facts already examined prove any thing, they prove that wealth, among slaveholders, is much more equally distributed—so that very few, compared with New England, are without homes.

The facts examined prove also, beyond question, that the unbearable miseries which have their source in the heartless exactions of excessive wealth, or extreme poverty, are more than sixty per cent. greater in New England than in these States, and that one hundred and thirty-five per cent. more of New England's toiling millions have to bear the degradation of the poor-house, or die of want, than are to be found in this condition in these five slave States.

The facts we have examined, prove also, that under all the disadvantages of climate, the natural increase of the slave States is sixty per cent. greater than it is in New England—twenty-seven per cent. of it by increased annual births, and thirty-three per cent. of it by diminished annual deaths. These are the most astonishing facts ever presented to the world. They speak a language that ought to be read and studied by all men. In the present state of our country, they ought to be prayerfully pondered and not disregarded.

But notwithstanding all this, the aggregate wealth of New England is a source of exultation and pride among her sons. They believe, with a blind and stubborn tenacity, that slavery tends to poverty, and freedom to wealth.

It cannot be denied that the aggregate earnings of the toiling millions—when *hoarded* by a *few*—may grow faster than it will when these millions are allowed to take from it a daily supply, equal to their reasonable wants. And it cannot be denied that New England has great aggregate wealth.

The facts of the census show, however, that it is very unequally divided among her people. The question now to be tried is, whether the *few* in New England have *hoarded* this wealth, and can now *show it*, or whether they have squandered it upon their lusts, and are unable to *show it*.

This last and prominent boast of increased aggregate wealth in New England, over that accumulated by slaveholders, we will now test by the census of 1850. This is the standard adopted by our National Legislature for its decision.

Before we examine the facts, however, let a few reflections which belong to the subject be weighed.

The people of these five slave States are now, and ever have been, an agricultural people. The people of the New England States are a commercial and manufacturing people. New England has, in proportion to numbers, the richest and most extensive commerce in the world. In manufacturing skill and enterprise, they have no superiors on the globe. They have ever reproached the South for investing their income in slavelabor, in preference to commerce and manufactures. It has been the settled conviction among nations, that investments in commerce and manufactures give the greatest, and those in agriculture the smallest profits. It is the settled conviction of the non-slaveholding States that investments in slave labor, for agricultural purposes, is the worst of all investments, and tends greatly to lessen its profits. This has been proclaimed to the South so long by our Northern neighbors, that many here have been brought to believe it, and to regret the existence of slavery among us on that account, if on no other. With these observations we turn to the census.

The census of 1850 tells us that New England, with a population now numbering two million seven hundred, and twenty-eight thousand and sixteen, with all the advantages of a commercial and manufacturing investment, and with the most energetic and enterprising free men on earth, to give that investment its greatest productiveness, has accumulated wealth, in something over two hundred years, to the amount of one billion three million four hundred and sixty-six thousand one hundred and eighty-one dollars; while these five slave States, with an equal population, have, in the same time, accumulated wealth to the amount of one billion four hundred and twenty million nine hundred and eighty-nine thousand five hundred and seventy-three dollars.

Here we see the indisputable fact that these five agricultural States, with slavery, have accumulated an excess of aggregate wealth over the amount accumulated in New England in the same time, of four hundred and seventeen million five hundred and twenty-three thousand three hundred and two dollars—so that the property belonging to New England, if equally divided, would give to each citizen but three hundred and sixty-seven dollars, while that belonging to the five slave States, if equally divided, would give to each citizen the sum of five hundred and twenty dollars—a difference in favor of each citizen in these five slave States of one hundred and fifty-three dollars.

I am aware, however, of an opinion that some other non-slaveholding States, have been much more successful in the accumulation of wealth, than the six New England States, and that New York, Pennsylvania, and Ohio, are of this favored number. Lest a design to deceive, by concealing this supposed fact, should be attributed to the writer, we will see what the census says as to these three more favored States. By the census of 1850 we learn that New York, instead of being able to divide three hundred and sixty-seven dollars with her citizens, as New England could with hers, is only able to divide two hundred and thirty-one dollars; Pennsylvania two hundred and fourteen, and Ohio two hundred and nineteen. These several averages among freemen at the North, and in New England, stand against the average of five hundred and twenty dollars, which these five old impoverished Southern slave States could divide with their citizens.

These facts must astonish our Northern neighbors, so long accustomed to believe that slavery was the fruitful source of poverty, with all its imagined evils; and these facts will astonish many at the South, so long accustomed to hear it affirmed that slavery had produced these evils, and while they were without the means of knowing, of course they feared that it was so.

That every thing may appear, however, which will throw additional light on the subject, I will state that Massachusetts, which is the *richest* non-slaveholding State, could divide with each of her citizens five hundred and forty-eight dollars. But on the other hand, South Carolina could divide one thousand and one dollars, Louisiana eight hundred and six dollars, Mississippi seven hundred and two dollars, and Georgia six hundred and thirty-eight dollars, with their citizens.

Rhode Island, which is the next *richest* non-slaveholding State to that of Massachusetts, could divide with her citizens five hundred and twenty-six dollars; one other non-slaveholding State (Connecticut) could divide with her citizens three hundred and twenty-one dollars. After this, the next *highest* non-slaveholding State could divide two hundred and eighty; the next highest two hundred and thirty-one; the next highest two hundred and twenty-eight; the next highest two hundred and nineteen; the next highest two hundred and fourteen dollars. After this, the division ranges, among the non-slaveholding States, from one hundred and sixty-six down to one hundred and thirty-four dollars—which last sum is the amount that the so-called rich and prosperous Illinois could divide with her population.

In the slaveholding States that are *less wealthy* than South Carolina, Louisiana, Mississippi, and Georgia, already noticed; Alabama could divide with her citizens five hundred and eleven dollars; Maryland four hundred and twenty-three; Virginia four hundred and three; Kentucky three hundred and seventy-seven; and North Carolina three hundred and sixty-seven. All these States are much *richer* than the *third richest* non-slaveholding State of the Union, viz: Connecticut. After this, Tennessee could divide two hundred and forty-eight dollars, and Missouri, which is the poorest of all the slave States, one hundred and sixty-six dollars.

We will now give the *general average* of the *non-slaveholding States*, (California excepted, which in 1850 had not had time to exhibit any fixed character,) and then the *general average* of the *slaveholding States* of the *whole Union*.

The population of all the free States is thirteen million two hundred and fourteen thousand three hundred and eighty; the free population of all the slave States is six million three hundred and twelve thousand eight hundred and ninety-nine. These thirteen million two hundred and fourteen thousand three hundred and eighty of freemen have accumulated an aggregate of property estimated at three billion one hundred and eighty-six million six hundred and eighty-three thousand eight hundred and twenty four dollars; while these six million three hundred and twelve thousand eight hundred and ninety-nine of slaveholders have accumulated an aggregate of two billion seven hundred and seventy-five million one hundred and twenty-one thousand, six hundred and forty-four dollars' worth of property.

Here we see that a population of Northern freemen, one hundred and nine *per cent.* greater than the number of Southern freemen in the slave States, have accumulated but sixteen *per cent. more* of property.

In a division of the property accumulated by all the non-slaveholding States, it will give to each citizen two hundred and thirty-three dollars; while all accumulated by the various slave States, will give to each citizen four hundred and thirty-nine dollars—nearly double. Were we to give the slaves an equal share with the whites, in an average division of aggregate wealth, the slaveholding States, with their slaves included, would then be able to give each person two hundred and ninety-one dollars instead of two hundred and thirty-three dollars, which is all the free States have to divide with their people.

Is it possible, with these facts before us, to believe that slavery tends to poverty. Such is the testimony of the census on the relative wealth of these two sections of our country. It proves that slavery, as an agricultural investment, is more profitable than an investment in commerce and manufactures. The facts which have been reviewed prove with equal clearness, that where slavery exists, the white race, and the black, have prospered more in their religious, social and moral condition, than either race has prospered, where slavery has been excluded. We see that an increased amount of poverty and wretchedness has to be borne in New England by both races. Ecclesiastical statistics will show an increased amount of prosperity in religion that is overwhelming.

Such is the prostration of moral restraint at the North, that, in their cities, standing armies are necessary to guard the persons and property of unoffending citizens, and to execute the laws upon reckless offenders. This state of things is unknown in the slave States.

The census shows that slavery has been a blessing to the white race in these slave States. They have prospered more in religion, they have more homes, are wealthier, multiply faster, and live longer than in New England, and they are exempt from the curse of organized infidelity and lawless violence.

A comparison of the slave's condition at the South, with that of his own race in freedom at the South, shows with equal clearness, that slavery, in these States, has been, and now is, a blessing to this race of people in all the essentials of human happiness and comfort. Our slaves all have homes, are bountifully provided for in health, cared for and kindly nursed in childhood, sickness, and old age; multiply faster, live longer, are free from all the corroding ills of poverty and anxious care, labor moderately, enjoy the blessings of the gospel, and let alone by wicked men, are contented and happy.

Ex-Governor Smith, a few years past, in his message to the Legislature of this State, showed, if I remember correctly, that seven-tenths more of crime was chargeable to free negroes than to the whites and slaves. By the census of 1850, the ratio of whites in the Penitentiary of Virginia, for ten years, was one to twenty-three thousand and three, while the ratio for the free negroes was one to three thousand and one. For the same length of time, in the Penitentiary of Massachusetts, the average of whites was one to seven thousand five hundred and eighty-seven, instead of one to twenty-three thousand and three, as in Virginia; and in Massachusetts the average of free negroes in the Penitentiary, for this length of time, was one to two hundred and fifty, instead of one to three thousand and one, as in Virginia. Here we see that for an average of ten years, two hundred and fifty free negroes at the North, commit annually as much crime as twenty-three thousand and three white persons at the South; and that two hundred and fifty free negroes, in a non-slaveholding State, commit annually as much crime as three thousand and one free negroes in a slaveholding State. We see, also, that seven thousand five hundred and eighty-seven white persons at the North, commit annually as much crime as twenty-three thousand and three white persons commit at the South. In the cities, criminal degradation at the North is from three to five times greater with the whites than at the South, and from ten to ninety-three times greater with the free negroes at the North, than with the whites at the South, and about twelve times greater than with the free negroes at the South.

The Federal census, and the State records, show not very far from this proportion of criminal degradation, chargeable to this race of people when invested with *the freedom of New England*. Can we, with these facts before us, think that freedom to this race, in our country, is a blessing to them?

In Africa, the condition of the aborigines in freedom is now, and ever has been, as much below that of their enslaved sons in these States, as the condition of a brute, is beneath that of a man. Slavery is becoming, to this people, so manifestly a blessing in our country, that fugitives from labor are constantly returning to their masters again, after tasting the blessings, or rather the awful curse to them, of freedom in non-slaveholding States; and while I write, those who are lawfully free in this State, are praying our Legislature for a law that will allow them to become slaves.

But before I dismiss the subject of wealth entirely, let me remark, that while the census testifies that an agricultural people, with African slave labor, increases wealth faster than free labor, employed in agriculture, manufactures and commerce, yet reason demands that it should be satisfactorily accounted for. It is well known that laboring freemen at the North are more skillful, work longer in a day, labor harder while at it, live on cheaper food, and less of it, than laborers at the South.

How, then, is it to be accounted for that the aggregate increase of wealth is less with them than it is with Southern slaveholders? Among many reasons that might be assigned, I will mention three. The first is, that half the people at the North (this is ascertained to be about the amount) live in villages, towns and cities. The second reason is, that the cost of living in cities (as has been ascertained) is about double what it is in the country—to this *cost* we must *add*, for the *imprudent* indulgences of *pride* and *fashion;* and to *this* we must *add*, for a thousand *indulgences*, in violation of *moral propriety*, all of which are almost unknown in country life. The third reason is to be found in the great amount of pauperism and crime produced by city life. In the city of New York, for instance, according to the American Almanac, there were received in 1847, at the principal alms-houses of the city, twenty-eight thousand six hundred and ninety-two persons, and *out-door relief* was given *from the public funds* to thirty-four thousand five hundred and seventy-two more—making in all seventy-three thousand two hundred and sixty-four persons, or one out of every five, in the city of New York, dependent, more or less, on *public charity*. The total cost of this, to the city, was three hundred and nineteen thousand two hundred and ninety-three dollars and eighty-eight cents. In 1849, in the Mayor's message, the estimate for the same thing is four hundred thousand dollars. In Massachusetts, according to the report of the Secretary of State in 1848, the number of constant and occasional paupers, in the *whole State*, was one to every twenty of the whole population. The proportion in the cities, I suppose, would equal New York, which, as we have seen, is one to five. To this *public burden* in cities, we must add an immense *unknown amount* of *private charity*, which is not needed in country life.

Crime in Northern cities keeps pace with *pauperism*. In *Boston*, according to official State reports a few years past, one person out of every fourteen males, and one out of every twenty-eight females, was arraigned for criminal offenses. According to the census of 1850, there were in the *State* of Massachusetts, in a population of nine hundred and ninety-four thousand five hundred and fourteen, the number of seven thousand two hundred and fifty convictions for crime. In Virginia, the same year, in a population of one million four hundred and twenty-one thousand six hundred and sixty-one, there were one hundred and seven convictions for crime.

In the *State* of New York the proportion of crime is about the same as in Massachusetts. In the *city* of New York, in 1848 or 1849, there were sentenced to the *State Prison* one hundred and nineteen men and seventeen women; to the *Penitentiary* seven hundred men and one hundred and seventy women; to the *City Prison* one hundred and sixty-two men and sixty-seven women—making a total of one thousand two hundred and thirty-five criminals. Here is an amount of crime in a single city, that equals all in the fifteen slave States together. In the *State* of New York, according to the census of 1850, there was, in a population of three million and ninety-seven thousand three hundred and four, the number of ten thousand two hundred and seventy-nine convictions for crime; while in South Carolina, in a population of six hundred and sixty-eight thousand five hundred and seven, (which is considerably over one-fifth) there were only forty-six convictions for crime.

To live in cities filled with such an amount of poverty and criminal degradation, as the census discloses, at the North, standing armies of policemen, firemen, etc., are absolutely necessary to secure the people against lawless violence. Now subtract from the products of labor the *cost* of city life—the cost of vain and criminal indulgences, the *support* of *paupers*, and the *machinery* to guard innocence and punish crime—and the wonder ceases that wealth accumulates slowly—the wonder is that it accumulates at all. What is accumulated, must be principally from commerce and manufactures. The system of abandoning the country and congregating in cities, tends directly to concentrate wealth into the hands of a few, and to diffuse poverty and crime among the masses of the people.

These facts of poverty and crime at the North, which are exhibited by the census, will help to explain the seeming mystery that the South multiplies by natural increase faster than the North. In 1845, according to her statistical report, Massachusetts had seven-eighths of her marriageable young women working in factories under male overseers. The census of 1840 shows that, with fewer adults, Virginia had one hundred thousand more children than Massachusetts. In the census of 1850 the proportion in favor of Virginia is still greater.

Pauperism, in Massachusetts and New York, according to the State census, increased between 1836 and 1848 ten times faster than wealth or population.

In the slaveholding States there is less than a tenth of the people in cities—pauperism is almost unknown—the people are on farms—the style of living is less costly by half, but greatly superior in quality and comfort—according to the census, there is but little crime—almost all have homes—the amount of agricultural labor does not fluctuate—the farms are not cultivated by the spade and hoe, but are large enough to justify a system of enlarged agricultural operations by the aid of horse power. The result is that more is saved, and the proceeds more equally distributed between capital and labor, or the rich and the poor.

The South did not seek or desire the responsibility, and the onerous burden, of civilizing and christianizing these degraded savages; but God, in his mysterious providence, brought it about. He allowed England, and her Puritan sons at the North, from the love of gain, to become the willing instruments, to force African slaves upon the Cavaliers of the South. These Cavaliers were a noble race of men. They remonstrated against this outrage to the last. They preferred indented labor from the mother country, which they were securing as they needed it. A descendant of theirs, in drafting the Declaration of Independence, made this outrage one of the prominent causes for dissolving all political connection with the mother country. But God intended (as we now see) to bless these savages, by forcing us against our wills, to become their masters and guardians; and he has abundantly blessed us, also, (as we now see) for allowing his word to be our counselor in this relation. We were forced by his word to admit the relation to be lawful, and he enabled us to admit and feel the great responsibility devolved upon us as their divinely appointed protectors.

The North, after pocketing the price of these savages, refused to bear any part of the burden of training and elevating them; and finally, with France and England, turned them loose by emancipation, and ignored the word of God in justification of the deed, by declaring that to hold them in slavery was sinful. The result is, that the portion they held of this degraded race, is immersed in poverty, wretchedness and crime, without a parallel in civilized communities, and are less in number now, than the original importations from Africa, (so says the Superintendent of the census;) while the portion held by us is in high comfort, regularly improving in morals and intellect, and multiplying more rapidly than the white race at the North. It does seem, from the facts of the census, that this (so-called) philanthropy has been a curse to *both races, at the North, and in the West Indies*, and that it is displeasing in the sight of God. The census exhibits unmistakable evidence that, without a change, the emancipated portion of the race, *in these localities*, will ultimately perish, and that this catastrophe is to be hastened by poverty and criminal degradation. The census shows that those who are *responsible* for this deed are subjected *in our country*, by annual *births* and *deaths*, to a *decrease* of sixty per cent., and to a much *heavier per cent.* than this, *of poverty and crime*.

But while these are the results to both races at the North, prosperity, unequaled in the annals of the world, has attended us (as the census shows) in almost every thing we have put our hands to, both for this life and that which is to come. The *satisfaction* is ours, also, of *knowing* that these degraded outcasts, which were thrown upon our hands, have not only been *cared for*, but *elevated in the scale of being*, and brought to share largely in the blessings of intellectual, social, and religious culture.

But for their *enslaved condition* here, they would have remained until this hour in their *original degradation.*

In view of all the facts compared, I would ask all who feel interested in the great question now agitating our country, to let these facts be their guide and counselor in deciding the issue. Are the people of the North warranted from these facts, in believing they would honor God and benefit men by overthrowing the institution of slavery, if they could.

These facts testify plainly, that where African slavery has existed in our country for more than two hundred years, the social and religious condition of men has improved more rapidly than it has under the best arrangements of exclusive freedom.

These facts show that, with the advantages of the best location and climate upon the globe, and a high degree of moral, religious, and social intelligence to commence with, those communities at the North who excluded this element from their organizations, are actually behind slaveholding communities, in religion, in wealth, in the increase of their race, and in the comforts of their condition. If this be so, (and the census testifies that it is,) what will justify the North in efforts to involve both sections of our country in civil war and disunion, because slavery exists in one section of it? And if the institution of African slavery has certainly improved the condition of both races in our country, (and the census testifies that it has,) why should they hazard all the blessings vouchsafed to the North and the South sooner than suffer its expansion over new territory?

The expansion of African slavery (according to the test by which we are now trying it) has never yet done injury in this Union. In Texas slaveholders were called to organize a State, (not in this Union at the time,) which in 1850 had a population of two hundred and twelve thousand five hundred and ninety-two. The individuals composing it originally, were the most lawless set of adventurers that ever lived. Did slavery disqualify slave-holders from organizing a social body, even out of these materials, that could secure the highest results in human progress? What is now the social, moral, and religious complexion of Texas? In the essentials of prosperity it is ahead, under equal circumstances, of any portion of the Union. Slaveholders, in the providence of God, had to organize States on the Gulf of Mexico, and on the banks of the Mississippi, after the acquisition of Louisiana from France, and Florida from Spain. The original materials (numbering upwards of seventy thousand) of which these States were composed, had been trained under the most pernicious system of morals that ever existed among a civilized people. The result in this case, also, will testify that slavery does not paralyze communities in the accumulation of wealth, or in the correction of moral, social, and religious evils. The census shows that in all these items these new slave States which have been added to our Union, have greatly outstripped their non-slaveholding equals in age. The temples of the Lord are now seen studding these slaveholding localities over, and are vocal with his praise—the moral majesty of the law is a paramount power. The amount of paupers and criminals, in some of them, is less than one-seventieth part that is chargeable to some of their twin sisters of equal age, (who are free[232]) nurseries of literature and science are multiplying rapidly, and promising the highest results—prosperity, in these slaveholding communities, in crowning the efforts of good men to arrest vice, to promote virtue, to diminish want, to create plenty, and to arrange the elements of progress for the highest social, moral, and religious results.

There is another historical fact which deserves to be weighed, in making up a judgment on the expansion of slavery. Within the present century, the colonies of Mexico and South America, in imitation of our example, threw off the colonial yoke, and established independent governments. All of these States, except one, preferred the non-slaveholding model, and *excluded* the element of *slavery:* that one, which is Brazil, preferred the model adopted by the Southern States of this Union, and *retained* African *slavery*.

All of those States, which *excluded slavery*, have been visited, in rapid succession, with *insurrection, revolution, and fearful anarchy;* while Brazil has enjoyed tranquillity, from the commencement of her independent political existence until the present hour. This remarkable fact has occurred, too, in a State where the slaves are two to one of the other race. The slaves in the United States are one to two of the other race. Is not this fact, like all those examined, *God's providential voice?* and does He not, in these facts, speak a language that we can *read and understand?*

Now, shall we, in view of these facts, rebel against the teachings of His providence, as it is now made known to us in the census, and claim for ourselves more wisdom than he has displayed, in *allowing such results* to be the product of *slaveholding communities?*

We cannot put an end to African slavery, if we would—and we ought not, if we could—until God opens a door to *make its termination a blessing, and not a curse*. When He does that, slavery in this Union will end.

With Christian affection, yours,
THORNTON STRINGFELLOW.

SLAVERY IN THE LIGHT OF SOCIAL ETHICS.

BY

CHANCELLOR HARPER,

OF SOUTH CAROLINA.

INFLUENCE OF SLAVERY ON SOCIAL LIFE.

Necessity of Investigation—Vindicators of Slavery—Slavery a means of Civilization—Prejudices of Abolitionism—Discussion of the Declaration of Independence—Rights of Society—Self-Preservation—The greatest good to the greatest number—Ambiguity in moral Investigation—Influence of Slavery on Civilization—The Slavery of England's Civilization—How Slavery retards the evils of Civilization—Servitude Inevitable—Abuses of Slavery and of Free Labor—Social ties, master and slave—Intellectual advancement—Morals of Slavery, and of Free Labor—Marriage relation and licentiousness—Virtues of Slavery—Security from Evils—Insecurity of Free Labor—Menial occupations necessary—Utopianism—Slavery and the servitude of Civilization contrasted—The African an inferior variety of the human race—Elevating influence of Slavery on the slave, on the master, on statesmen—Duties of master—Elevation of female character—Necessity of Slavery in tropical climates—Examples from history—Southern States—Insurrections impossible—Military strength of Slavery—Advantageous consequences of the increase of slaves—Destructive consequences of Emancipation to our country, and to the world—Kakistocracy—White emigration—Amalgamation—Deplorable results of Fanaticism.

THE institution of domestic slavery exists over far the greater portion of the inhabited earth. Until within a very few centuries, it may be said to have existed over the whole earth—at least in all those portions of it which had made any advances toward civilization. We might safely conclude then, that it is deeply founded in the nature of man and the exigencies of human society. Yet, in the few countries in which it has been abolished—claiming, perhaps justly, to be furthest advanced in civilization and intelligence, but which have had the smallest opportunity of observing its true character and effects—it is denounced as the most intolerable of social and political evils. Its existence, and every hour of its continuance, is regarded as the crime of the communities in which it is found. Even by those in the countries alluded to, who regard it with the most indulgence or the least abhorrence—who attribute no criminality to the present generation—who found it in existence, and have not yet been able to devise the means of abolishing it,—it is pronounced a misfortune and a curse injurious and dangerous always, and which must be finally fatal to the societies which admit it. This is no longer regarded as a subject of argument and investigation. The opinions referred to are assumed as settled, or the truth of them as self-evident. If any voice is raised among ourselves to extenuate or to vindicate, it is unheard. The judgment is made up. We can have no hearing before the tribunal of the civilized world. Yet, on this very account, it is more important that we, the inhabitants of the slaveholding States of America, insulated as we are, by this institution, and cut off, in some degree, from the communion and sympathies of the world by which we are surrounded, or with which we have intercourse, and exposed continually to their animadversions and attacks, should thoroughly understand this subject, and our strength and weakness in relation to it. If it be thus criminal, dangerous, and fatal; and if it be possible to devise means of freeing ourselves from it, we ought at once to set about the employing of those means. It would be the most wretched and imbecile fatuity, to shut our eyes to the impending dangers and horrors, and "drive darkling down the current of our fate," till we are overwhelmed in the final destruction. If we are tyrants, cruel, unjust, oppressive, let us humble ourselves and repent in the sight of heaven, that the foul stain may be cleansed, and we enabled to stand erect as having common claims to humanity with our fellow-men.

But if we are nothing of all this; if we commit no injustice or cruelty; if the maintenance of our institutions be essential to our prosperity, our character, our safety, and the safety of all that is dear to us, let us enlighten our minds and fortify our hearts to defend them.

It is a somewhat singular evidence of the indisposition of the rest of the world to hear any thing more on this subject, that perhaps the most profound, original, and truly philosophical treatise, which has appeared within the time of my recollection,[233] seems not to have attracted the slightest attention out of the limits of the slaveholding States themselves. If truth, reason, and conclusive argument, propounded with admirable temper and perfect candor, might be supposed to have an effect on the minds of men, we should think this work would have put an end to agitation on the subject. The author has rendered inappreciable service to the South in enlightening them on the subject of their own institutions, and turning back that monstrous tide of folly and madness which, if it had rolled on, would have involved his own great State along with the rest of the slaveholding States in a common ruin. But beyond these, he seems to have produced no effect whatever. The denouncers of slavery, with whose production the press groans, seems to be unaware of his existence—unaware that there is a reason to be encountered or argument to be answered. They assume that the truth is known and settled, and only requires to be enforced by denunciation.

Another vindicator of the South has appeared in an individual who is among those that have done honor to American literature.[234] With conclusive argument, and great force of expression, he has defended slavery from the charge of injustice or immorality, and shown clearly the unspeakable cruelty and mischief which must result from any scheme of abolition. He does not live among slaveholders, and it can not be said of him, as of others, that his mind is warped by interest, or his moral sense blunted by habit and familiarity with abuse. These circumstances, it might be supposed, would have secured him hearing and consideration. He seems to be equally unheeded, and the work of denunciation, disdaining argument, still goes on.

President Dew has shown that the institution of slavery is a principal cause of civilization. Perhaps nothing can be more evident than that it is the sole cause. If any thing can be predicated as universally true of uncultivated man, it is that he will not labor beyond what is absolutely necessary to maintain his existence. Labor is pain to those who are unaccustomed to it, and the nature of man is averse to pain. Even with all the training, the helps, and motives of civilization, we find that this aversion can not be overcome in many individuals of the most cultivated societies. The coercion of slavery alone is adequate to form man to habits of labor. Without it, there can be no accumulation of property, no providence for the future, no tastes for comfort or elegancies, which are the characteristics and essentials of civilization. He who has obtained the command of another's labor, first begins to accumulate and provide for the future, and the foundations of civilization are laid. We find confirmed by experience that which is so evident in theory. Since the existence of man upon the earth, with no exception whatever, either of ancient or modern times, every society which has attained civilization, has advanced to it through this process.

Will those who regard slavery as immoral, or crime in itself, tell us that man was not intended for civilization, but to roam the earth as a biped brute? That he was not to raise his eyes to Heaven, or be conformed in his nobler faculties to the image of his Maker? Or will they say that the Judge of all the earth has done wrong in ordaining the means by which alone that end can be obtained? It is true that the Creator can make the wickedness as well as the wrath of man to praise him, and bring forth the most benevolent results from the most atrocious actions. But in such cases, it is the motive of the actor alone which condemns the action. The act itself is good, if it promotes the good purposes of God, and would be approved by him, if that result only were intended. Do they not blaspheme the providence of God who denounce as wickedness and outrage, that which is rendered indispensable to his purposes in the government of the world? Or at what stage of the progress of society will they say that slavery ceases to be necessary, and its very existence becomes sin and crime? I am aware that such argument would have little effect on those with whom it would be degrading to contend—who pervert the inspired writings—which in some parts expressly sanction slavery, and throughout indicate most clearly that it is a civil institution, with which religion has no concern—with a shallowness and presumption not less flagrant and shameless than his, who would justify murder from the text, "and Phineas arose and executed judgment."

There seems to be something in this subject which blunts the preceptions, and darkens and confuses the understandings and moral feelings of men. Tell them that, of necessity, in every civilized society, there must be an infinite variety of conditions and employments, from the most eminent and intellectual, to the most servile and laborious; that the negro race, from their temperament and capacity, are peculiarly suited to the situation which they occupy, and not less happy in it than any corresponding class to be found in the world; prove incontestably that no scheme of emancipation could be carried into effect without the most intolerable mischiefs and calamities to both master and slave, or without probably throwing a large and fertile portion of the earth's surface out of the pale of civilization—and you have done nothing. They reply, that whatever may be the consequence, you are bound to do *right;* that man has a right to himself, and man cannot have property in man; that if the negro race be naturally inferior in mind and character, they are not less entitled to the rights of humanity; that if they are happy in their condition, it affords but the stronger evidence of their degradation, and renders them still more objects of commiseration. They repeat, as the fundamental maxim of our civil policy, that all men are born free and equal, and quote from our Declaration of Independence, "that men are endowed by their Creator with certain inalienable *rights*, among which are life, liberty, and the pursuit of happiness."

It is not the first time that I have had occasion to observe that men may repeat with the utmost confidence, some maxim or sentimental phrase, as self-evident or admitted truth, which is either palpably false, or to which, upon examination, it will be found that they attach no definite idea. Notwithstanding our respect for the important document which declared our independence, yet if any thing be found in it, and especially in what may be regarded rather as its ornament than its substance—false, sophistical or unmeaning, that respect should not screen it from the freest examination.

All men are born free and equal. Is it not palpably nearer the truth to say that no man was ever born free, and that no two men were ever born equal? Man is born in a state of the most helpless dependence on others. He continues subject to the absolute control of others, and remains without many of the civil and all of the political privileges of his society, until the period which the laws have fixed as that at which he is supposed to have attained the maturity of his faculties. Then inequality is further developed, and becomes infinite in every society, and under whatever form of government. Wealth and poverty, fame or obscurity, strength or weakness, knowledge or ignorance, ease or labor, power or subjection, mark the endless diversity in the condition of men.

But we have not arrived at the profundity of the maxim. This inequality is, in a great measure, the result of abuses in the institutions of society. They do not speak of what exists, but of what ought to exist. Every one should be left at liberty to obtain all the advantages of society which he can compass, by the free exertion of his faculties, unimpeded by civil restraints. It may be said that this would not remedy the evils of society which are complained of. The inequalities to which I have referred, with the misery resulting from them, would exist in fact under the freest and most popular form of government that man could devise. But what is the foundation of the bold dogma so confidently announced? Females are human and rational beings. They may be found of better faculties, and better qualified to exercise political privileges, and to attain the distinctions of society, than many men; yet who complains of the order of society by which they are excluded from them? For I do not speak of the few who would desecrate them; do violence to the nature which their Creator has impressed upon them; drag them from the position which they necessarily occupy for the existence of civilized society, and in which they constitute its blessing and ornament—the only position which they have ever occupied in any human society—to place them in a situation in which they would be alike miserable and degraded. Low as we descend in combating the theories of presumptuous dogmatists, it cannot be necessary to stoop to this. A youth of eighteen may have powers which cast into the shade those of any of his more advanced cotemporaries. He may be capable of serving or saving his country, and if not permitted to do so now, the occasion may have been lost forever. But he can exercise no political privilege, or aspire to any political distinction. It is said that, of necessity, society must exclude from some civil and political privileges those who are unfitted to exercise them, by infirmity, unsuitableness of character, or defect of discretion; that of necessity there must be some general rule on the subject, and that any rule which can be devised will operate with hardship and injustice on individuals. This is all that can be said, and all that need be said. It is saying, in other words, that the privileges in question are no matter of natural right, but to be settled by convention, as the good and safety of society may require. If society should disfranchise individuals convicted of infamous crimes, would this be an invasion of natural right? Yet this would not be justified on the score of their moral guilt, but that the good of society required or would be promoted by it. We admit the existence of a moral law, binding on societies as on individuals. Society must act in good faith. No man, or body of men, has a right to inflict pain or privation on others, unless with a view, after full and impartial deliberation, to prevent a greater evil. If this deliberation be had, and the decision made in good faith, there can be no imputation of moral guilt. Has any politician contended that the very existence of governments in which there are orders privileged by law, constitutes a violation of morality; that their continuance is a crime, which men are bound to put an end to, without any consideration of the good or evil to result from the change? Yet this is the natural inference from the dogma of the natural equality of men as applied to our institution of slavery—an equality not to be invaded without injustice and wrong, and requiring to be restored instantly, unqualifiedly, and without reference to consequences.

This is sufficiently common-place, but we are sometimes driven to common-place. It is no less a false and shallow, than a presumptuous philosophy, which theorizes on the affairs of men as a problem to be solved by some unerring rule of human reason, without reference to the designs of a superior intelligence, so far as he has been placed to indicate them, in their creation and destiny. Man is born to subjection. Not only during infancy is he dependent, and under the control of others; at all ages, it is the very bias of his nature, that the strong and the wise should control the weak and the ignorant. So it has been since the days of Nimrod. The existence of some form of slavery in all ages and countries, is proof enough of this. He is born to subjection as he is born in sin and ignorance. To make any considerable progress in knowledge, the continued efforts of successive generations, and the diligent training and unwearied exertions of the individual, are requisite. To make progress in moral virtue, not less time and effort, aided by superior help, are necessary; and it is only by the matured exercise of his knowledge and his virtue, that he can attain to civil freedom. Of all things, the existence of civil liberty is most the result of artificial institution. The proclivity of the natural man is to domineer or to be subservient. A noble result, indeed, but in the attaining of which, as in the instances of knowledge and virtue, the Creator, for his own purposes, has set a limit beyond which we cannot go.

But he who is most advanced in knowledge, is most sensible of his own ignorance, and how much must forever be unknown to man in his present condition. As I have heard it expressed, the further you extend the circle of light, the wider is the horizon of darkness. He who has made the greatest progress in moral purity, is most sensible of the depravity, not only of the world around him, but of his own heart, and the imperfection of his best motives; and this he knows that men must feel and lament so long as they continue men. So when the greatest progress in civil liberty has been made, the enlightened lover of liberty will know that there must remain much inequality, much injustice, much *slavery*, which no human wisdom or virtue will ever be able wholly to prevent or redress. As I have before had the honor to say to this Society, the condition of our whole existence is but to struggle with evils—to compare them—to choose between them, and, so far as we can, to mitigate them. To say that there is evil in any institution, is only to say that it is human.

And can we doubt but that this long discipline and laborious process, by which men are required to work out the elevation and improvement of their individual nature and their social condition, is imposed for a great and benevolent end? Our faculties are not adequate to the solution of the mystery, why it should be so; but the truth is clear, that the world was not intended for the seat of universal knowledge, or goodness, or happiness, or freedom.

Man has been endowed by his Creator with certain inalienable rights, among which are life, liberty, and the pursuit of happiness. What is meant by the *inalienable* right of liberty? Has any one who has used the words ever asked himself this question? Does it mean that a man has no right to alienate his own liberty—to sell himself and his posterity for slaves? This would seem to be the more obvious meaning. When the word *right* is used, it has reference to some law which sanctions it, and would be violated by its invasion. It must refer either to the general law of morality, or the law of the country—the law of God or the law of man. If the law of any country permitted it, it would of course be absurd to say that the law of that country was violated by such alienation. If it have any meaning in this respect, it must mean that though the law of the country permitted it, the man would be guilty of an immoral act who should thus alienate his liberty. A fit question for schoolmen to discuss, and the consequences resulting from its decision as important as from any of theirs. Yet who will say that the man pressed by famine, and in prospect of death, would be criminal for such an act? Self-preservation, as is truly said, is the first law of nature. High and peculiar characters, by elaborate cultivation, may be taught to prefer death to slavery, but it would be folly to prescribe this as a duty to the mass of mankind.

If any rational meaning can be attributed to the sentence I have quoted, it is this:— That the society, or the individuals who exercise the powers of government, are guilty of a violation of the law of God or of morality, when, by any law or public act, they deprive men of life or liberty, or restrain them in the pursuit of happiness. Yet every government does, and of necessity must, deprive men of life and liberty for offenses against society. Restrain them in the pursuit of happiness! Why all the laws of society are intended for nothing else but to restrain men from the pursuit of happiness, according to their own ideas of happiness or advantage—which the phrase must mean if it means any thing. And by what right does society punish by the loss of life or liberty? Not on account of the moral guilt of the criminal—not by impiously and arrogantly assuming the prerogative of the Almighty, to dispense justice or suffering, according to moral desert. It is for its own protection—it is the right of self-defense. If there existed the blackest moral turpitude, which by its example or consequences, could be of no evil to society, government would have nothing to do with that. If an action, the most harmless in its moral character, could be dangerous to the security of society, society would have the perfect right to punish it. If the possession of a black skin would be otherwise dangerous to society, society has the same right to protect itself by disfranchising the possessor of civil privilege, and to continue the disability to his posterity, if the same danger would be incurred by its removal. Society inflicts these forfeitures for the security of the lives of its members; it inflicts them for the security of their property, the great essential of civilization; it inflicts them also for the protection of its political institutions, the forcible attempt to overturn which, has always been justly regarded as the greatest crime; and who has questioned its right so to inflict? "Man can not have property in man"—a phrase as full of meaning as, "who slays fat oxen should himself be fat." Certainly he may, if the laws of society allow it, and if it be on sufficient grounds, neither he nor society do wrong.

And is it by this—as we must call it, however recommended to our higher feelings by its associations—well-sounding, but unmeaning verbiage of natural equality and inalienable rights, that our lives are to be put in jeopardy, our property destroyed, and our political institutions overturned or endangered? If a people had on its borders a tribe of barbarians, whom no treaties or faith could bind, and by whose attacks they were constantly endangered, against whom they could devise no security, but that they should be exterminated or enslaved; would they not have the right to enslave them, and keep them in slavery so long as the same danger would be incurred by their manumission? If a civilized man and a savage were by chance placed together on a desolate island, and the former, by the superior power of civilization, would reduce the latter to subjection, would he not have the same right? Would this not be the strictest self-defense? I do not now consider, how far we can make out a similar case to justify our enslaving of the negroes. I speak to those who contend for inalienable rights, and that the existence of slavery always, and under all circumstances, involves injustice and crime.

As I have said, we acknowledge the existence of a moral law. It is not necessary for us to resort to the theory which resolves all right into force. The existence of such a law is imprinted on the hearts of all human beings. But though its existence be acknowledged, the mind of man has hitherto been tasked in vain to discover an unerring standard of morality. It is a common and undoubted maxim of morality, that you shall not do evil that good may come. You shall not do injustice or commit an invasion of the rights of others, for the sake of a greater ulterior good. But what is injustice, and what are the rights of others? And why are we not to commit the one or invade the other? It is because it inflicts pain or suffering, present or prospective, or cuts them off from enjoyment which they might otherwise attain. The Creator has sufficiently revealed to us that *happiness* is the great end of existence, the sole object of all animated and sentient beings. To this he has directed their aspirations and efforts, and we feel that we thwart his benevolent purposes when we destroy or impede that happiness. This is the only *natural* right of man. All other rights result from the conventions of society, and these, to be sure, we are not to invade, whatever good may appear to us likely to follow. Yet are we in no instance to inflict pain or suffering, or disturb enjoyment, for the sake of producing a greater good? Is the madman not to be restrained who would bring destruction on himself or others? Is pain not to be inflicted on the child, when it is the only means by which he can be effectually instructed to provide for his own future happiness? Is the surgeon guilty of wrong who amputates a limb to preserve life? Is not the object of all penal legislation, to inflict suffering for the sake of greater good to be secured to society?

By what right is it that man exercises dominion over the beasts of the field; subdues them to painful labor, or deprives them of life for his sustenance or enjoyment? They are not rational beings. No, but they are the creatures of God, sentient beings, capable of suffering and enjoyment, and entitled to enjoy according to the measure of their capacities. Does not the voice of nature inform every one, that he is guilty of wrong when he inflicts on them pain without necessity or object? If their existence be limited to the present life, it affords the stronger argument for affording them the brief enjoyment of which it is capable. It is because the greater good is effected; not only to man but to the inferior animals themselves. The care of man gives the boon of existence to myriads who would never otherwise have enjoyed it, and the enjoyment of their existence is better provided for while it lasts. It belongs to the being of superior faculties to judge of the relations which shall subsist between himself and inferior animals, and the use he shall make of them; and he may justly consider himself, who has the greater capacity of enjoyment, in the first instance. Yet he must do this conscientiously, and no doubt, moral guilt has been incurred by the infliction of pain on these animals, with no adequate benefit to be expected. I do no disparagement to the dignity of human nature, even in its humblest form, when I say that on the very same foundation, with the difference only of circumstance and degree, rests the right of the civilized and cultivated man, over the savage and ignorant. It is the order of nature and of God, that the being of superior faculties and know-knowledge, and therefore of superior power, should control and dispose of those who are inferior. It is as much in the order of nature, that men should enslave each other, as that other animals should prey upon each other. I admit that he does this under the highest moral responsibility, and is most guilty if he wantonly inflicts misery or privation on beings more capable of enjoyment or suffering than brutes, without necessity or any view to the greater good which is to result. If we conceive of society existing without government, and that one man by his superior strength, courage or wisdom, could obtain the mastery of his fellows, he would have a perfect right to do so. He would be morally responsible for the use of his power, and guilty if he failed to direct them so as to promote their happiness as well as his own. Moralists have denounced the injustice and cruelty which have been practiced towards our aboriginal Indians, by which they have been driven from their native seats and exterminated, and no doubt with much justice. No doubt, much fraud and injustice has been practiced in the circumstances and the manner of their removal. Yet who has contended that civilized man had no moral right to possess himself of the country? That he was bound to leave this wide and fertile continent, which is capable of sustaining uncounted myriads of a civilized race, to a few roving and ignorant barbarians? Yet if any thing is certain, it is certain that there were no means by which he could possess the country, without exterminating or enslaving them. Savage and civilized man cannot live together, and the savage can be tamed only by being enslaved or by having slaves. By enslaving alone could he have preserved them.[235] And who shall take upon himself to decide that the more benevolent course, and more pleasing to God, was pursued towards them, or that it would not have been better that they had been enslaved generally, as they were in particular instances? It is a refined philosophy, and utterly false in its application to general nature, or the mass of human kind, which teaches that existence is not the greatest of all boons, and worthy of being preserved even under the most adverse circumstances. The strongest instinct of all animated beings sufficiently proclaims this. When the last red man shall have vanished from our forests, the sole remaining traces of his blood will be found among our enslaved population.[236] The African slave trade has given, and will give, the boon of existence to millions and millions in our country, who would otherwise never have enjoyed it, and the enjoyment of their existence is better provided for while it lasts. Or if, for the rights of man over inferior animals, we are referred to revelation, which pronounces—"ye shall have dominion over the beasts of the field, and over the fowls of the air," we refer to the same, which declares not the less explicitly—

"Both the bond-men and bond-maids which thou shalt have, shall be of the heathen that are among you. Of them shall you buy bond-men and bond-maids."

"Moreover of the children of strangers that do sojourn among you, of them shall ye buy, and of their families that are with you, which they begot in your land, and they shall be your possession. And ye shall take them as an inheritance for your children after you, to inherit them by possession. They shall be your bond-men forever."

In moral investigations, ambiguity is often occasioned by confounding the intrinsic nature of an action, as determined by its consequence, with the motives of the actor, involving moral guilt or innocence. If poison be given with a view to destroy another, and it cures him of disease, the poisoner is guilty, but the act is beneficent in its results. If medicine be given with a view to heal, and it happens to kill, he who administered it is innocent, but the act is a noxious one. If they who begun and prosecuted the slave trade, practiced horrible cruelties and inflicted much suffering—as no doubt they did, though these have been much exaggerated—for merely selfish purposes, and with no view to future good, they were morally most guilty. So far as unnecessary cruelty was practiced, the motive and the act were alike bad. But if we could be sure that the entire effect of the trade has been to produce more happiness than would otherwise have existed, we must pronounce it good, and that it has happened in the ordering of God's providence, to whom evil cannot be imputed. Moral guilt has not been imputed to Las Casas, and if the importation of African slaves into America, had the effect of preventing more suffering than it inflicted, it was good, both in the motive and the result. I freely admit that, it is hardly possible to justify morally, those who begun and carried on the slave trade. No speculation of future good to be brought about, could compensate the enormous amount of evil it occasioned.

If we should refer to the common moral sense of mankind, as determined by their conduct in all ages and countries, for a standard of morality, it would seem to be in favor of slavery. The will of God, as determined by utility, would be an infallible standard, if we had an unerring measure of utility. The utilitarian philosophy, as it is commonly understood, referring only to the animal wants and employments, and physical condition of man, is utterly false and degrading. If a sufficiently extended definition be given to utility, so as to include every thing that may be a source of enjoyment or suffering, it is for the most part useless. How can you compare the pleasures resulting from the exercise of the understanding, the taste and the imagination, with the animal enjoyments of the senses—the gratification derived from a fine poem with that from a rich banquet? How are we to weigh the pains and enjoyments of one man highly cultivated and of great sensibility, against those of many men of blunter capacity for enjoyment or suffering? And if we could determine with certainty in what utility consists, we are so short-sighted with respect to consequences—the remote results of our best considered actions are so often wide of our anticipations, or contrary to them, that we should still be very much in the dark. But though we cannot arrive at absolute certainty with respect to the utility of actions, it is always fairly matter of argument. Though an imperfect standard, it is the best we have, and perhaps the Creator did not intend that we should arrive at perfect certainty with regard to the morality of many actions. If, after the most careful examination of consequences that we are able to make, with due distrust of ourselves, we impartially, and in good faith, decide for that which appears likely to produce the greatest good, we are free from moral guilt. And I would impress most earnestly, that with our imperfect and limited faculties, and short-sighted as we are to the future, we can rarely, very rarely indeed, be justified in producing considerable present evil or suffering, in the expectation of remote future good—if indeed this can ever be justified.

In considering this subject, I shall not regard it in the first instance in reference to the present position of the slaveholding States, or the difficulties which lie in the way of their emancipating their slaves, but as a naked, abstract question—whether it is better that the institution of praedial and domestic slavery should, or should not, exist in civilized society. And though some of my remarks may seem to have such a tendency, let me not be understood as taking upon myself to determine that it is better that it should exist. God forbid that the responsibility of deciding such a question should ever be thrown on me or my countrymen. But this I will say, and not without confidence, that it is in the power of no human intellect to establish the contrary proposition—that it is better it should not exist. This is probably known but to one being, and concealed from human sagacity.

There have existed in various ages, and we now see existing in the world, people in every stage of civilization, from the most barbarous to the most refined. Man, as I have said, is not born to civilization. He is born rude and ignorant. But it will be, I suppose, admitted that it is the design of his Creator that he should attain to civilization: that religion should be known, that the comforts and elegancies of life should be enjoyed, that letters and arts should be cultivated; in short, that there should be the greatest possible development of moral and intellectual excellence. It can hardly be necessary to say any thing of those who have extolled the superior virtues and enjoyments of savage life—a life of physical wants and sufferings, of continual insecurity, of furious passions and depraved vices. Those who have praised savage life, are those who have known nothing of it, or who have become savages themselves. But as I have said, so far as reason or universal experience instruct us, the institution of slavery is an essential process in emerging from savage life. It must then produce good, and promote the designs of the Creator.

I add further, *that slavery anticipates the benefits of civilization, and retards the evils of civilization*. The former part of this proposition has been so fully established by a writer of great power of thought—though I fear his practical conclusions will be found of little value—that it is hardly necessary to urge it.[237] Property—the accumulation of capital, as it is commonly called—is the first element of civilization. But to accumulate, or to use capital to any considerable extent, the combination of labor is necessary. In early stages of society, when people are thinly scattered over an extensive territory, the labor necessary to extensive works cannot be commanded. Men are independent of each other. Having the command of abundance of land, no one will submit to be employed in the service of his neighbor. No one, therefore, can employ more capital than he can use with his own hands, or those of his family, nor have an income much beyond the necessaries of life. There can, therefore, be little leisure for intellectual pursuits, or means of acquiring the comforts or elegancies of life. It is hardly necessary to say, however, that if a man has the command of slaves, he may combine labor, and use capital to any required extent, and therefore accumulate wealth. He shows that no colonies have been successfully planted without some sort of slavery. So we find the fact to be. It is only in the slaveholding States of our Confederacy, that wealth can be acquired by agriculture—which is the general employment of our whole country. Among us, we know that there is no one, however humble his beginning, who, with persevering industry, intelligence, and orderly and virtuous habits, may not attain to considerable opulence. So far as wealth has been accumulated in the States which do not possess slaves, it has been in cities by the pursuits of commerce, or lately, by manufactures. But the products of slave labor furnish more than two-thirds of the materials of our foreign commerce, which the industry of those States is employed in transporting and exchanging; and among the slaveholding States is to be found the great market for all the productions of their industry, of whatever kind. The prosperity of those States, therefore, and the civilization of their cities, have been for the most part created by the existence of slavery. Even in the cities, but for a class of population, which our institutions have marked as servile, it would be scarcely possible to preserve the ordinary habitudes of civilized life, by commanding the necessary menial and domestic service.

Every stage of human society, from the most barbarous to the most refined, has its own peculiar evils to mark it as the condition of mortality; and perhaps there is none but omnipotence who can say in which the scale of good or evil most preponderates. We need say nothing of the evils of savage life. There is a state of society elevated somewhat above it, which is to be found in some of the more thinly peopled portions of our own country—the rudest agricultural state—which is thus characterized by the author to whom I have referred: "The American of the back woods has often been described to the English as grossly ignorant, dirty, unsocial, delighting in rum and tobacco, attached to nothing but his rifle, adventurous, restless, more than half savage. Deprived of social enjoyments or excitements, he has recourse to those of savage life, and becomes (for in this respect the Americans degenerate) unfit for society." This is no very inviting picture, which, though exaggerated, we know not to be without likeness. The evils of such a state, I suppose, will hardly be thought compensated by unbounded freedom, perfect equality, and ample means of subsistence.

But let us take another stage in the progress—which to many will appear to offer all that is desirable in existence, and realize another Utopia. Let us suppose a state of society in which all shall have property, and there shall be no great inequality of property—in which society shall be so much condensed as to afford the means of social intercourse, without being crowded, so as to create difficulty in obtaining the means of subsistence—

in which every family that chooses may have as much land as will employ its own hands, while others may employ their industry in forming such products as it may be desirable to exchange with them. Schools are generally established, and the rudiments of education universally diffused. Religion is taught, and every village has its church, neat, though humble, lifting its spire to heaven. Here is a situation apparently the most favorable to happiness. I say *apparently*, for the greatest source of human misery is not in external circumstances, but in men themselves—in their depraved inclinations, their wayward passions and perverse wills. Here is room for all the petty competition, the envy, hatred, malice and dissimulation that torture the heart in what may be supposed the most sophisticated states of society; and though less marked and offensive, there may be much of the licentiousness.

But apart from this, in such a condition of society, if there is little suffering, there is little high enjoyment. The even flow of life forbids the high excitement which is necessary for it. If there is little vice, there is little place for the eminent virtues, which employ themselves in controlling the disorders and remedying the evils of society, which, like war and revolution, call forth the highest powers of man, whether for good or for evil. If there is little misery, there is little room for benevolence. Useful public institutions we may suppose to be created, but not such as are merely ornamental. Elegant arts can be little cultivated, for there are no means to reward the artists; nor the higher literature, for no one will have leisure or means to cultivate it for its own sake. Those who acquire what may be called liberal education, will do so in order to employ it as the means of their own subsistence or advancement in a profession, and literature itself will partake of the sordidness of trade. In short, it is plain that in such a state of society, the moral and intellectual faculties cannot be cultivated to their highest perfection.

But whether that which I have described be the most desirable state of society or no, it is certain that it can not continue. Mutation and progress is the condition of human affairs. Though retarded for a time by extraneous or accidental circumstances, the wheel must roll on. The tendency of population is to become crowded, increasing the difficulty of obtaining subsistence. There will be some without any property except the capacity for labor. This they must sell to those who have the means of employing them, thereby swelling the amount of their capital, and increasing inequality. The process still goes on. The number of laborers increases until there is a difficulty in obtaining employment. Then competition is established. The remuneration of the laborer becomes gradually less and less; a larger and larger proportion of the product of his labor goes to swell the fortune of the capitalist; inequality becomes still greater and more invidious, until the process ends in the establishment of just such a state of things, as the same author describes as now existing in England. After a most imposing picture of her greatness and resources; of her superabounding capital, and all pervading industry and enterprise; of her public institutions for purposes of art, learning and benevolence; her public improvements, by which intercourse is facilitated, and the convenience of man subserved; the conveniences and luxuries of life enjoyed by those who are in possession of fortune, or have profitable employments; of all, in short, that places her at the head of modern civilization, he proceeds to give the reverse of the picture. And here I shall use his own words: "The laboring class compose the bulk of the people; the great body of the people; the vast majority of the people—these are the terms by which English writers and speakers usually describe those whose only property is their labor."

"Of comprehensive words, the two most frequently used in English politics, are distress and pauperism. After these, of expressions applied to the state of the poor, the most common are vice and misery, wretchedness, sufferings, ignorance, degradation, discontent, depravity, drunkenness, and the increase of crime; with many more of the like nature."

He goes on to give the details of this inequality and wretchedness, in terms calculated to sicken and appal one to whom the picture is new. That he has painted strongly we may suppose; but there is ample corroborating testimony, if such were needed, that the representation is substantially just. Where so much misery exists, there must of course be much discontent, and many have been disposed to trace the sources of the former in vicious legislation, or the structure of government; and the author gives the various schemes, sometimes contradictory, sometimes ludicrous, which projectors have devised as a remedy for all this evil to which flesh is heir. That ill-judged legislation may have sometimes aggravated the general suffering, or that its extremity may be mitigated by the well-directed efforts of the wise and virtuous, there can be no doubt. One purpose for which it has been permitted to exist is, that it may call forth such efforts, and awaken powers and virtues which would otherwise have slumbered for want of object. But remedy there is none, unless it be to abandon their civilization. This inequality, this vice, this misery, this *slavery*, is the price of England's civilization. They suffer the lot of humanity. But perhaps we may be permitted humbly to hope, that great, intense and widely spread as this misery undoubtedly is in reality, it may yet be less so than in appearance. We can estimate but very, very imperfectly the good and evil of individual condition, as of different states of society. Some unexpected solace arises to alleviate the severest calamity. Wonderful is the power of custom, in making the hardest condition tolerable; the most generally wretched life has circumstances of mitigation, and moments of vivid enjoyment, of which the more seemingly happy can scarcely conceive; though the lives of individuals be shortened, the aggregate of existence is increased; even the various forms of death accelerated by want, familiarized to the contemplation, like death to the soldier on the field of battle, may become scarcely more formidable than what we are accustomed to regard as nature's ordinary outlets of existence. If we could perfectly analyze the enjoyments and sufferings of the most happy, and the most miserable man, we should perhaps be startled to find the difference so much less than our previous impressions had led us to conceive. But it is not for us to assume the province of omniscience. The particular theory of the author quoted, seems to be founded on an assumption of this sort—that there is a certain stage in the progress, when there is a certain balance between the demand for labor, and the supply of it, which is more desirable than any other—when the territory is so thickly peopled that all can not own land and cultivate the soil for themselves, but a portion will be compelled to sell their labor to others; still leaving, however, the wages of labor high, and the laborer independent. It is plain, however, that this would in like manner partake of the good and the evil of other states of society. There would be less of equality and less rudeness, than in the early stages; less civilization, and less suffering, than in the latter.

It is the competition for employment, which is the source of this misery of society, that gives rise to all excellence in art and knowledge. When the demand for labor exceeds the supply, the services of the most ordinarily qualified laborer will be eagerly retained. When the supply begins to exceed, and competition is established, higher and higher qualifications will be required, until at length when it becomes very intense, none but the most consummately skillful can be sure to be employed. Nothing but necessity can drive men to the exertions which are necessary so to qualify themselves. But it is not in arts, merely mechanical alone, that this superior excellence will be required. It will be extended to every intellectual employment; and though this may not be the effect in the instance of every individual, yet it will fix the habits and character of the society, and prescribe everywhere, and in every department, the highest possible standard of attainment.

But how is it that the existence of slavery, as with us, will retard the evils of civilization? Very obviously. It is the intense competition of civilized life, that gives rise to the excessive cheapness of labor, and the excessive cheapness of labor is the cause of the evils in question. Slave labor can never be so cheap as what is called free labor. Political economists have established as the natural standard of wages in a fully peopled country, the value of the laborer's existence. I shall not stop to inquire into the precise truth of this proposition. It certainly approximates the truth. Where competition is intense, men will labor for a bare subsistence, and less than a competent subsistence. The employer of free laborers obtains their services during the time of their health and vigor, without the charge of rearing them from infancy, or supporting them in sickness or old age. This charge is imposed on the employer of slave labor, who, therefore, pays higher wages, and cuts off the principal source of misery—the wants and sufferings of infancy, sickness, and old age. Laborers too will be less skillful, and perform less work—enhancing the price of that sort of labor. The poor laws of England are an attempt—but an awkward and empirical attempt—to supply the place of that which we should suppose the feelings of every human heart would declare to be a natural obligation—that he who has received the benefit of the laborer's services during his health and vigor, should maintain him when he becomes unable to provide for his own support. They answer their purpose, however, very imperfectly, and are unjustly and unequally imposed. There is no attempt to apportion the burden according to the benefit received—and perhaps there could be none. This is one of the evils of their condition.

In periods of commercial revulsion and distress, like the present, the distress, in countries of free labor, falls principally on the laborers. In those of slave labor, it falls almost exclusively on the employer. In the former, when a business becomes unprofitable, the employer dismisses his laborers or lowers their wages. But with us, it is the very period at which we are least able to dismiss our laborers; and if we would not suffer a further loss, we can not reduce their wages. To receive the benefit of the services of which they are capable, we must provide for maintaining their health and vigor. In point of fact, we know that this is accounted among the necessary expenses of management. If the income of every planter of the Southern States were permanently reduced one-half, or even much more than that, it would not take one jot from the support and comforts of the slaves. And this can never be materially altered, until they shall become so unprofitable that slavery must be of necessity abandoned. It is probable that the accumulation of individual wealth will never be carried to quite so great an extent in a slaveholding country, as in one of free labor; but a consequence will be, that there will be less inequality and less suffering.

Servitude is the condition of civilization. It was decreed, when the command was given, "be fruitful, and multiply and replenish the earth, and subdue it," and when it was added, "in the sweat of thy face shalt thou eat bread." And what human being shall arrogate to himself the authority to pronounce that our form of it is worse in itself, or more displeasing to God, than that which exists elsewhere? Shall it be said that the servitude of other countries grows out of the exigency of their circumstances, and therefore society is not responsible for it? But if we know that in the progress of things it is to come, would it not seem the part of wisdom and foresight, to make provision for it, and thereby, if we can, mitigate the severity of its evils? But the fact is not so. Let any one who doubts, read the book to which I have several times referred, and he may be satisfied that it was forced upon us by the extremest exigency of circumstances, in a struggle for very existence. Without it, it is doubtful whether a white man would be now existing on this continent— certain, that if there were, they would be in a state of the utmost destitution, weakness, and misery. It was forced on us by necessity, and further fastened upon us by the superior authority of the mother country. I, for one, neither deprecate nor resent the gift. Nor did we institute slavery. The Africans brought to us had been, speaking in the general, slaves in their own country, and only underwent a change of masters. In the countries of Europe, and the States of our Confederacy, in which slavery has ceased to exist, it was abolished by positive legislation. If the order of nature has been departed from, and a forced and artificial state of things introduced, it has been, as the experience of all the world declares, by them and not by us.

That there are great evils in a society where slavery exists, and that the institution is liable to great abuse, I have already said. To say otherwise, would be to say that they were not human. But the whole of human life is a system of evils and compensations. We have no reason to believe that the compensations with us are fewer, or smaller in proportion to the evils, than those of any other condition of society. Tell me of an evil or abuse; of an instance of cruelty, oppression, licentiousness, crime or suffering, and I will point out, and often in five fold degree, an equivalent evil or abuse in countries where slavery does not exist.

Let us examine without blenching, the actual and alleged evils of slavery, and the array of horrors which many suppose to be its universal concomitants. It is said that the slave is out of the protection of the law; that if the law purports to protect him in life and limb, it is but imperfectly executed; that he is still subject to excessive labor, degrading blows, or any other sort of torture, which a master pampered and brutalized by the exercise of arbitrary power, may think proper to inflict; he is cut off from the opportunity of intellectual, moral, or religious improvement, and even positive enactments are directed against his acquiring the rudiments of knowledge; he is cut off forever from the hope of raising his condition in society, whatever may be his merit, talents, or virtues, and therefore deprived of the strongest incentive to useful and praiseworthy exertion; his physical degradation begets a corresponding moral degradation: he is without moral principle, and addicted to the lowest vices, particularly theft and falsehood; if marriage be not disallowed, it is little better than a state of concubinage, from which results general licentiousness, and the want of chastity among females—this indeed is not protected by law, but is subject to the outrages of brutal lust; both sexes are liable to have their dearest affections violated; to be sold like brutes; husbands to be torn from wives, children from parents;—this is the picture commonly presented by the denouncers of slavery.

It is a somewhat singular fact that when there existed in our State no law for punishing the murder of a slave, other than a pecuniary fine, there were, I will venture to say, at least ten murders of freemen, for one murder of a slave. Yet it is supposed they are all less protected, or less secure than their masters. Why they are protected by their very situation in society, and therefore less need the protection of law. With any other person than their master, it is hardly possible for them to come into such sort of collision as usually gives rise to furious and revengeful passions; they offer no temptation to the murderer for gain; against the master himself, they have the security of his own interest, and by his superintendence and authority, they are protected from the revengeful passions of each other. I am by no means sure that the cause of humanity has been served by the change in jurisprudence, which has placed their murder on the same footing with that of a freeman. The change was made in subserviency to the opinions and clamor of others who were utterly incompetent to form an opinion on the subject; and a wise act is seldom the result of legislation in this spirit. From the fact which I have stated, it is plain that they less need protection. Juries are, therefore, less willing to convict, and it may sometimes happen that the guilty will escape all punishment. *Security* is one of the compensations of their humble position. We challenge the comparison, that with us there have been fewer murders of slaves, than of parents, children, apprentices, and other murders, cruel and unnatural, in society where slavery does not exist.

But short of life or limb, various cruelties may be practiced as the passions of the master may dictate. To this the same reply has been often given—that they are secured by the master's interest. If the state of slavey is to exist at all, the master must have, and ought to have, such power of punishment as will compel them to perform the duties of their station. And is not this for their advantage as well as his? No human being can be contented, who does not perform the duties of his station. Has the master any temptation to go beyond this? If he inflicts on him such punishment as will permanently impair his strength, he inflicts a loss on himself, and so if he requires of him excessive labor. Compare the labor required of the slave, with those of the free agricultural or manufacturing laborer in Europe, or even in the more thickly peopled portions of the non-slaveholding States of our Confederacy—though these last are no fair subjects of comparison—they enjoying, as I have said, in a great degree, the advantages of slavery along with those of an early and simple state of society. Read the English Parliamentary reports, on the condition of the manufacturing operatives, and the children employed in factories. And such is the impotence of man to remedy the evils which the condition of his existence has imposed on him, that it is much to be doubted whether the attempts by legislation to improve their situation, will not aggravate its evils. They resort to this excessive labor as a choice of evils. If so, the amount of their compensation will be lessened also with the diminished labor; for this is a matter which legislation can not regulate. Is it the part of benevolence then to cut them off even from this miserable liberty of choice? Yet would these evils exist in the same degree, if the laborers were the *property* of the master— having a direct interest in preserving their lives, their health and strength? Who but a driveling fanatic has thought of the necessity of protecting domestic animals from the cruelty of their owners? And yet are not great and wanton cruelties practiced on these animals? Compare the whole of the cruelties inflicted on slaves throughout our Southern country, with those elsewhere, inflicted by ignorant and depraved portions of the community, on those whom the relations of society put into their power—of brutal husbands on their wives; of brutal parents—subdued against the strongest instincts of nature to that brutality by the extremity of their misery—on their children; of brutal masters on apprentices. And if it should be asked, are not similar cruelties inflicted, and miseries endured, in your society? I answer, in no comparable degree. The class in question are placed under the control of others, who are interested to restrain their excesses of cruelty or rage. Wives are protected from their husbands, and children from their parents. And this is no inconsiderable compensation of the evils of our system; and would so appear, if we could form any conception of the immense amount of misery which is elsewhere thus inflicted. The other class of society, more elevated in their position, are also (speaking of course in the general) more elevated in character, and more responsible to public opinion.

But besides the interest of their master, there is another security against cruelty. The relation of master and slave, when there is no mischievous interference between them, is, as the experience of all the world declares, naturally one of kindness. As to the fact, we should be held interested witnesses, but we appeal to universal nature. Is it not natural that a man should be attached to that which is *his own*, and which has contributed to his convenience, his enjoyment, or his vanity? This is felt even toward animals and inanimate objects. How much more toward a being of superior intelligence and usefulness, who can appreciate our feelings towards him, and return them? Is it not natural that we should be interested in that which is dependent on us for protection and support? Do not men everywhere contract kind feelings toward their dependents? Is it not natural that men should be more attached to those whom they have long known,—whom, perhaps, they have reared or been associated with from infancy—than to one with whom their connection has been casual and temporary? What is there in our atmosphere or institutions, to produce a perversion of the general feelings of nature? To be sure, in this as in all other relations, there is frequent cause of offense or excitement—on one side, for some omission of duty, on the other, on account of reproof or punishment inflicted. But this is common to the relation of parent and child; and I will venture to say, that if punishment be justly inflicted—and there is no temptation to inflict it unjustly—it is as little likely to occasion permanent estrangement or resentment as in that case. Slaves are perpetual children. It is not the common nature of man, unless it be depraved by his own misery, to delight in witnessing pain. It is more grateful to behold contented and cheerful beings, than sullen and wretched ones. That men are sometimes wayward, depraved and brutal, we know. That atrocious and brutal cruelties have been perpetrated on slaves, and on those who were not slaves, by such wretches, we also know. But that the institution of slavery has a natural tendency to form such a character, that such crimes are more common, or more aggravated than in other states of society, or produce among us less surprise and horror, we utterly deny, and challenge the comparison. Indeed, I have little hesitation in saying, that if full evidence could be obtained, the comparison would result in our favor, and that the tendency of slavery is rather to humanize than to brutalize.

The accounts of travelers in oriental countries, give a very favorable representation of the kindly relations which exist between the master and slave; the latter being often the friend, and sometimes the heir of the former. Generally, however, especially if they be English travelers—if they say any thing which may seem to give a favorable complexion to slavery, they think it necessary to enter their protest, that they shall not be taken to give any sanction to slavery as it exists in America. Yet human nature is the same in all countries. There are very obvious reasons why in those countries there should be a nearer approach to equality in their manners. The master and slave are often of cognate races, and therefore tend more to assimilate. There is, in fact, less inequality in mind and character, where the master is but imperfectly civilized. Less labor is exacted, because the master has fewer motives to accumulate. But is it an injury to a human being, that regular, if not excessive labor, should be required of him? The primeval curse, with the usual benignity of providential contrivance, has been turned into the solace of an existence that would be much more intolerable without it. If they labor less, they are much more subject to the outrages of capricious passions. If it were put to the choice of any human being, would he prefer to be the slave of a civilized man, or of a barbarian or semi-barbarian? But if the general tendency of the institution in those countries is to create kindly relations, can it be imagined why it should operate differently in this? It is true, as suggested by President Dew—with the exception of the ties of close consanguinity, it forms one of the most intimate relations of society. And it will be more and more so, the longer it continues to exist. The harshest features of slavery were created by those who were strangers to slavery—who supposed that it consisted in keeping savages in subjection by violence and terror. The severest laws to be found on our statute book, were enacted by such, and such are still found to be the severest masters. As society becomes settled, and the wandering habits of our countrymen altered, there will be a larger and larger proportion of those who were reared by the owner, or derived to him from his ancestors, and who therefore will be more and more intimately regarded, as forming a portion of his family.

It is true that the slave is driven to labor by stripes; and if the object of punishment be to produce obedience or reformation, with the least permanent injury, it is the best method of punishment. But is it not intolerable, that a being formed in the image of his Maker, should be degraded by *blows?* This is one of the perversions of mind and feeling, to which I shall have occasion again to refer. Such punishment would be degrading to a freeman, who had the thoughts and aspirations of a freeman. In general, it is not degrading to a slave, nor is it felt to be so. The evil is the bodily pain. Is it degrading to a child? Or if in any particular instance it would be so felt, it is sure not to be inflicted—unless in those rare cases which constitute the startling and eccentric evils, from which no society is exempt, and against which no institution of society can provide.

The slave is cut off from the means of intellectual, moral, and religious improvement, and in consequence his moral character becomes depraved, and he addicted to degrading vices. The slave receives such instruction as qualifies him to discharge the duties of his particular station. The Creator did not intend that every individual human being should be highly cultivated, morally and intellectually, for, as we have seen, he has imposed conditions on society which would render this impossible. There must be general mediocrity, or the highest cultivation must exist along with ignorance, vice, and degradation. But is there in the aggregate of society, less opportunity for intellectual and moral cultivation, on account of the existence of slavery? We must estimate institutions from their aggregate of good or evil. I refer to the views which I have before expressed to this society. It is by the existence of slavery, exempting so large a portion of our citizens from the necessity of bodily labor, that we have a greater proportion than any other people, who have leisure for intellectual pursuits, and the means of attaining a liberal education. If we throw away this opportunity, we shall be morally responsible for the neglect or abuse of our advantages, and shall most unquestionably pay the penalty. But the blame will rest on ourselves, and not on the character of our institutions.

I add further, notwithstanding that *equality* seems to be the passion of the day, if, as Providence has evidently decreed, there can be but a certain portion of intellectual excellence in any community, it is better that it should be *unequally* divided. It is better that a part should be fully and highly cultivated, and the rest utterly ignorant. To constitute a society, a variety of offices must be discharged, from those requiring but the lowest degree of intellectual power, to those requiring the very highest, and it should seem that the endowments ought to be apportioned according to the exigencies of the situation. In the course of human affairs, there arise difficulties which can only be comprehended or surmounted by the strongest native power of intellect, strengthened by the most assiduous exercise, and enriched with the most extended knowledge—and even these are sometimes found inadequate to the exigency. The first want of society is—leaders. Who shall estimate the value to Athens, of Solon, Aristides, Themistocles, Cymon, or Pericles? If society have not leaders qualified, as I have said, they will have those who will lead them blindly to their loss and ruin. Men of no great native power of intellect, and of imperfect and superficial knowledge, are the most mischievous of all—none are so busy, meddling, confident, presumptuous, and intolerant. The whole of society receives the benefit of the exertions of a mind of extraordinary endowments. Of all communities, one of the least desirable, would be that in which imperfect, superficial, half-education should be universal. The first care of a State which regards its own safety, prosperity, and honor, should be, that when minds of extraordinary power appear, to whatever department of knowledge, art or science, their exertions may be directed, the means should be provided for their most consummate cultivation. Next to this, that education should be as widely extended as possible.

Odium has been cast upon our legislation, on account of its forbidding the elements of education to be communicated to slaves. But, in truth, what injury is done to them by this? He who works during the day with his hands, does not read in intervals of leisure for his amusement, or the improvement of his mind—or the exceptions are so very rare, as scarcely to need the being provided for. Of the many slaves whom I have known capable of reading, I have never known one to read any thing but the Bible, and this task they impose on themselves as matter of duty. Of all methods of religious instruction, however, this, of reading for themselves, would be the most inefficient—their comprehension is defective, and the employment is to them an unusual and laborious one. There are but very few who do not enjoy other means more effectual for religious instruction. There is no place of worship opened for the white population, from which they are excluded. I believe it a mistake, to say that the instructions there given are not adapted to their comprehension, or calculated to improve them. If they are given as they ought to be—practically, and without pretension, and are such as are generally intelligible to the free part of the audience, comprehending all grades of intellectual capacity,—they will not be unintelligible to slaves. I doubt whether this be not better than instruction, addressed specially to themselves—which they might look upon as a devise of the master's, to make them more obedient and profitable to himself. Their minds, generally, show a strong religious tendency, and they are fond of assuming the office of religious instructors to each other; and perhaps their religious notions are not much more extravagant than those of a large portion of the free population of our country. I am not sure that there is a much smaller proportion of them, than of the free population, who make some sort of religious profession. It is certainly the master's *interest* that they should have proper religious sentiments, and if he fails in his duty toward them, we may be sure that the consequences will be visited not upon them, but upon him.

If there were any chance of their elevating their rank and condition in society, it might be matter of hardship, that they should be debarred those rudiments of knowledge which open the way to further attainments. But this they know can not be, and that further attainments would be useless to them. Of the evil of this, I shall speak hereafter. A knowledge of reading, writing, and the elements of arithmetic, is convenient and important to the free laborer, who is the transactor of his own affairs, and the guardian of his own interests—but of what use would they be to the slave? These alone do not elevate the mind or character, if such elevation were desirable.

If we estimate their morals according to that which should be the standard of a free man's morality, then I grant they are degraded in morals—though by no means to the extent which those who are unacquainted with the institution seem to suppose. We justly suppose, that the Creator will require of man the performance of the duties of the station in which his providence has placed him, and the cultivation of the virtues which are adapted to their performance; that he will make allowance for all imperfection of knowledge, and the absence of the usual helps and motives which lead to self-correction and improvement. The degradation of morals relate principally to loose notions of honesty, leading to petty thefts; to falsehood and to licentious intercourse between the sexes. Though with respect even to these, I protest against the opinion which seems to be elsewhere entertained, that they are universal, or that slaves, in respect to them, might not well bear a comparison with the lowest laborious class of other countries. But certainly there is much dishonesty leading to petty thefts. It leads, however, to nothing else. They have no contracts or dealings which might be a temptation to fraud, nor do I know that their characters have any tendency that way. They are restrained by the constant, vigilant, and interested superintendence which is exercised over them, from the commission of offenses of greater magnitude—even if they were disposed to them—which I am satisfied they are not. Nothing is so rarely heard of, as an atrocious crime committed by a slave; especially since they have worn off the savage character which their progenitors brought with them from Africa. Their offenses are confined to petty depredations, principally for the gratification of their appetites, and these for reasons already given, are chiefly confined to the property of their owner, which is most exposed to them. They could make no use of a considerable booty, if they should obtain it. It is plain that this is a less evil to society in its consequences and example, than if committed by a freeman, who is master of his own time and actions. With reference to society then, the offense is less in itself—and may we not hope that it is less in the sight of God? A slave has no hope that by a course of integrity, he can materially elevate his condition in society, nor can his offense materially depress it, or affect his means of support, or that of his family. Compared to the freeman, he has no character to establish or to lose. He has not been exercised to self-government, and being without intellectual resources, can less resist the solicitations of appetite. Theft in a freeman is a crime; in a slave, it is a vice. I recollect to have heard it said, in reference to some question of a slave's theft which was agitated in a Court, "Courts of Justice have no more to do with a slave's stealing, than with his lying—that is a matter for the domestic forum." It was truly said—the theft of a slave is no offense against society. Compare all the evils resulting from this, with the enormous amount of vice, crime, and depravity, which in an European, or one of our Northern cities, disgusts the moral feelings, and render life and property insecure. So with respect to his false-hood. I have never heard or observed, that slaves have any peculiar proclivity to falsehood, unless it be in denying or concealing their own offenses, or those of their fel-lows. I have never heard of falsehood told by a slave for a malicious purpose. Lies of vanity are sometimes told, as among the weak and ignorant of other conditions. False-hood is not attributed to an individual charged with an offense before a Court of Justice, who pleads *not guilty*—and certainly the strong temptation to escape punishment, in the highest degree extenuates, if it does not excuse, falsehood told by a *slave*. If the object be to screen a a fellow slave, the act bears some semblance of fidelity, and perhaps truth could not be told without breach of confidence. I know not how to characterize the false-hood of a slave.

It has often been said by the denouncers of slavery, that marriage does not exist among slaves. It is difficult to understand this, unless willful falsehood were intended. We know that marriages are contracted; may be, and often are, solemnized with the forms usual among other classes of society, and often faithfully adhered to during life. The law has not provided for making those marriages indissoluble, nor could it do so. If a man abandons his wife, being without property, and being both property themselves, he cannot be required to maintain her. If he abandons his wife, and lives in a state of concu-binage with another, the law cannot punish him for bigamy. It may perhaps be meant that the chastity of wives is not protected by law from the outrages of violence. I answer, as with respect to their lives, that they are protected by manners, and their position. Who ever heard of such outrages being offered? At least as seldom, I will venture to say, as in other communities of different forms of polity. One reason doubtless may be, that often there is no disposition to resist. Another reason also may be, that there is little temptation to such violence, as there is so large a proportion of this class of females who set little value on chastity, and afford easy gratification to the hot passions of men. It might be supposed, from the representations of some writers, that a slaveholding country was one wide stew for the indulgence of unbridled lust. Particular instances of intemperate and shameless debauchery are related, which may perhaps be true, and it is left to be inferred that this is the universal state of manners. Brutes and shameless debauchees there are in every country; we know that if such things are related as general or characteristic, the representation is false. Who would argue from the existence of a Col. Chartres in England, or of some individuals who might, perhaps, be named in other portions of this country, of the horrid dissoluteness of manners occasioned by the want of the institution of slavery? Yet the argument might be urged quite as fairly, and really it seems to me with a little more justice—for there such depravity is attended with much more pernicious consequences. Yet let us not deny or extenuate the truth. It is true that in this respect the morals of this class are very loose, (by no means so universally so as is often supposed,) and that the passions of men of the superior caste, tempt and find gratification in the easy chastity of the females. This is evil, and to be remedied, if we can do so, without the introduction of greater evil. But evil is incident to every condition of society, and as I have said, we have only to consider in which institution it most predominates.

Compare these prostitutes of our country, (if it is not injustice to call them so,) and their condition with those of other countries—the seventy thousand prostitutes of London, or of Paris, or the ten thousand of New York, or our other Northern cities. Take the picture given of the first from the author whom I have before quoted. "The laws and customs of England conspire to sink this class of English women into a state of vice and misery below that which necessarily belongs to their condition. Hence their extreme degradation, their troopers' oaths, their love of gin, their desperate recklessness, and the shortness of their miserable lives.

"English women of this class, or rather girls, for few of them live to be women, die like sheep with the rot; so fast that soon there would be none left, if a fresh supply were not obtained equal to the number of deaths. But a fresh supply is always obtained without the least trouble; seduction easily keeps pace with prostitution or mortality. Those that die are, like factory children that die, instantly succeeded by new competitors for misery and death." There is no hour of a summer's or a winter's night, in which there may not be found in the streets a ghastly wretch, expiring under the double tortures of disease and famine. Though less aggravated in its features, the picture of prostitution in New York or Philadelphia would be of like character.

In such communities, the unmarried woman who becomes a mother, is an outcast from society—and though sentimentalists lament the hardship of the case, it is justly and necessarily so. She is cut off from the hope of useful and profitable employment, and driven by necessity to further vice. Her misery, and the hopelessness of retrieving, render her desperate, until she sinks into every depth of depravity, and is prepared for every crime that can contaminate and infest society. She has given birth to a human being, who, if it be so unfortunate as to survive its miserable infancy, is commonly educated to a like course of vice, depravity, and crime.

Compare with this the female slave under similar circumstances. She is not a less useful member of society than before. If shame be attached to her conduct, it is such shame as would be elsewhere felt for a venial impropriety. She has not impaired her means of support, nor materially impaired her character, or lowered her station in society; she has done no great injury to herself, or any other human being. Her offspring is not a burden but an acquisition to her owner; his support is provided for, and he is brought up to usefulness; if the fruit of intercourse with a freeman, his condition is, perhaps, raised somewhat above that of his mother. Under these circumstances, with imperfect knowledge, tempted by the strongest of human passions—unrestrained by the motives which operate to restrain, but are so often found insufficient to restrain the conduct of females elsewhere, can it be matter of surprise that she should so often yield to the temptation? Is not the evil less in itself, and in reference to society—much less in the sight of God and man? As was said of theft—the want of chastity, which among females of other countries is sometimes vice, sometimes crime—among the free of our own, much more aggravated; among slaves, hardly deserves a harsher term than that of weakness. I have heard of complaint made by a free prostitute, of the greater countenance and indulgence shown by society toward colored persons of her profession, (always regarded as of an inferior and servile class, though individually free,) than to those of her own complexion. The former readily obtain employment; are even admitted into families, and treated with some degree of kindness and familiarity, while any approach to intercourse with the latter is shunned as contamination. The distinction is habitually made, and it is founded on the unerring instinct of nature. The colored prostitute is, in fact, a far less contaminated and depraved being. Still many, in spite of temptation, do preserve a perfectly virtuous conduct, and I imagine it hardly ever entered into the mind of one of these, that she was likely to be forced from it by authority or violence.

It may be asked, if we have no prostitutes from the free class of society among ourselves. I answer, in no assignable proportion. With general truth, it might be said, that there are none. When such a case occurs, it is among the rare evils of society. And apart from other and better reasons, which we believe to exist, it is plain that it must be so, from the comparative absence of temptation. Our brothels, comparatively very few—and these should not be permitted to exist at all—are filled, for the most part, by importations from the cities of our confederate States, where slavery does not exist. In return for the benefits which they receive from our slavery, along with tariffs, libels, opinions, moral, religious, or political—they furnish us also with a supply of thieves and prostitutes. Never, but in a single instance, have I heard of an imputation on the general purity of manners, among the free females of the slaveholding States. Such an imputation, however, and made in coarse terms, we have never heard here—*here* where divorce was never known—where no court was ever polluted by an action for criminal conversation with a wife—where it is related rather as matter of tradition, not unmingled with wonder, that a Carolinian woman of education and family, proved false to her conjugal faith—an imputation deserving only of such reply as self-respect would forbid us to give, if respect for the author of it did not. And can it be doubted, that this purity is caused by, and is a compensation for the evils resulting from the existence of an enslaved class of more relaxed morals?

It is mostly the warm passions of youth, which give rise to licentious intercourse. But I do not hesitate to say, that the intercourse which takes place with enslaved females, is less depraving in its effects, than when it is carried on with females of their own caste. In the first place, as like attracts like, that which is unlike repels; and though the strength of passion be sufficient to overcome the repulsion, still the attraction is less. He feels that he is connecting himself with one of an inferior and servile caste, and that there is something of degradation in the act. The intercourse is generally casual; he does not make her habitually an associate, and is less likely to receive any taint from her habits and manners. He is less liable to those extraordinary fascinations, with which worthless women sometimes entangle their victims, to the utter destruction of all principle, worth and vigor of character. The female of his own race offers greater allurements. The haunts of vice often present a show of elegance, and various luxury tempts the senses. They are made an habitual resort, and their inmates associates, till the general character receives a taint from the corrupted atmosphere. Not only the practice is licentious, but the understanding is sophisticated; the moral feelings are bewildered, and the boundaries of virtue and vice are confused. Where such licentiousness very extensively prevails, society is rotten to the heart.

But is it a small compensation for the evils attending the relation of the sexes among the enslaved class, that they have universally the opportunity of indulging in the first instinct of nature, by forming matrimonial connections? What painful restraint—what constant effort to struggle against the strongest impulses are habitually practiced elsewhere, and by other classes? And they must be practiced, unless greater evils would be encountered. On the one side, all the evils of vice, with the miseries to which it leads—on the other, a marriage cursed and made hateful by want—the sufferings of children, and agonizing apprehensions concerning their future fate. Is it a small good that the slave is free from all this? He knows that his own subsistance is secure, and that his children will be in as good a condition as himself. To a refined and intellectual nature, it may not be difficult to practice the restraint of which I have spoken. But the reasoning from such to the great mass of mankind, is most fallacious. To these, the supply of their natural and physical wants, and the indulgence of the natural domestic affections, must, for the most part, afford the greatest good of which they are capable. To the evils which sometimes attend their matrimonial connections, arising from their looser morality, slaves, for obvious reasons, are comparatively insensible. I am no apologist of vice, nor would I extenuate the conduct of the profligate and unfeeling, who would violate the sanctity of even these engagements, and occasion the pain which such violations no doubt do often inflict. Yet such is the truth, and we can not make it otherwise. We know that a woman's having been before a mother, is very seldom indeed an objection to her being made a wife. I know perfectly well how this will be regarded by a class of reasoners or declaimers, as imposing a character of deeper horror on the whole system; but still, I will say, that if they are to be exposed to the evil, it is mercy that the sensibility to it should be blunted. Is it no compensation also for the vices incident to slavery, that they are, to a great degree, secured against the temptation to greater crimes, and more atrocious vices, and the miseries which attend them; against their own disposition to indolence, and the profligacy which is its common result?

But if they are subject to the vices, they have also the virtues of slaves. Fidelity—often proof against all temptation—even death itself—an eminently cheerful and social temper—what the Bible imposes as a duty, but which might seem an equivocal virtue in the code of modern morality—submission to constituted authority, and a disposition to be attached to, as well as to respect those, whom they are taught to regard as superiors. They may have all the knowledge which will make them useful in the station in which God has been pleased to place them, and may cultivate the virtues which will render them acceptable to him. But what has the slave of any country to do with heroic virtues, liberal knowledge, or elegant accomplishments? It is for the master; arising out of his situation—imposed on him as duty—dangerous and disgraceful if neglected—to compensate for this, by his own more assiduous cultivation, of the more generous virtues, and liberal attainments.

It has been supposed one of the great evils of slavery, that it affords the slave no opportunity of raising himself to a higher rank in society, and that he has, therefore, no inducement to meritorious exertion, or the cultivation of his faculties. The indolence and carelessnes of the slave, and the less productive quality of his neighbor, are traced to the want of such excitement. The first compensation for this disadvantage, is his security. If he can rise no higher, he is just in the same degree secured against the chances of falling lower. It has been sometimes made a question whether it were better for man to be freed from the perturbations of hope and fear, or to be exposed to their vicissitudes. But I suppose there could be little question with respect to a situation, in which the fears must greatly predominate over the hopes. And such, I apprehend, to be the condition of the laboring poor in countries where slavery does not exist. If not exposed to present suffering, there is continual apprehension for the future—for themselves—for their children—of sickness and want, if not of actual starvation. They expect to improve their circumstances! Would any person of ordinary candor, say that there is one in a hundred of them, who does not well know, that with all the exertion he can make, it is out of his power materially to improve his circumstances? I speak not so much of menial servants, who are generally of a superior class, as of agricultural and manufacturing laborers. They labor with no such view. It is the instinctive struggle to preserve existence, and when the superior efficiency of their labor over that of our slaves is pointed out, as being animated by a free man's hopes, might it not well be replied—it is because they labor under a sterner compulsion. The laws interpose no obstacles to their raising their condition in society. 'Tis a great boon—but as to the great mass, they know that they never will be able to raise it—and it should seem not very important in effect, whether it be the interdict of law, or imposed by the circumstances of the society. One in a thousand is successful. But does his success compensate for the sufferings of the many who are tantalized, baffled, and tortured in vain attempts to attain a like result? If the individual be conscious of intellectual power, the suffering is greater. Even where success is apparently attained, he sometimes gains it but to die—or with all capacity to enjoy it exhausted—worn out in the struggle with fortune. If it be true that the African is an inferior variety of the human race, of less elevated character, and more limited intellect, is it not desirable that the inferior laboring class should be made up of such, who will conform to their condition without painful aspirations and vain struggles?

The slave is certainly liable to be sold. But, perhaps, it may be questioned, whether this is a greater evil than the liability of the laborer, in fully peopled countries, to be dismissed by his employer, with the uncertainty of being able to obtain employment, or the means of subsistence elsewhere. With us, the employer can not dismiss his laborer without providing him with another employer. His means of subsistence are secure, and this is a compensation for much. He is also liable to be separated from wife and child—though not more frequently, that I am aware of, than the exigency of their condition compels the separation of families among the labering poor elsewhere—but from native character and temperament, the separation is much less severely felt. And it is one of the compensations, that he may sustain these relations, without suffering a still severer penalty for the indulgence.

The love of liberty is a noble passion—to have the free, uncontrolled disposition of ourselves, our words and actions. But alas! it is one in which we know that a large portion of the human race can never be gratified. It is mockery, to say that the laborer any where has such disposition of himself—though there may be an approach to it in some peculiar, and those, perhaps, not the most desirable, states of society. But unless he be properly disciplined and prepared for its enjoyment, it is the most fatal boon that could be conferred—fatal to himself and others. If slaves have less freedom of action than other laborers, which I by no means admit, they are saved in a great degree from the responsibility of self-government, and the evils springing from their own perverse wills. Those who have looked most closely into life, and know how great a portion of human misery is derived from these sources—the undecided and wavering purpose—producing ineffectual exertion, or indolence with its thousand attendant evils—the wayward conduct—intemperance or profligacy—will most appreciate this benefit. The line of a slave's duty is marked out with precision, and he has no choice but to follow it. He is saved the double difficulty, first of determining the proper course for himself, and then of summoning up the energy which will sustain him in pursuing it.

If some superior power should impose on the laborious poor of any other country—this as their unalterable condition—you shall be saved from the torturing anxiety concerning your own future support, and that of your children, which now pursues you through life, and haunts you in death—you shall be under the necessity of regular and healthful, though not excessive labor—in return, you shall have the ample supply of your natural wants—you may follow the instinct of nature in becoming parents, without apprehending that this supply will fail yourselves or your children—you shall be supported and relieved in sickness, and in old age, wear out the remains of existence among familiar scenes and accustomed associates, without being driven to beg, or to resort to the hard and miserable charity of a work-house—you shall of necessity be temperate, and shall have neither the temptation nor opportunity to commit great crimes, or practice the more destructive vices—how inappreciable would the boon be thought! And is not this a very near approach to the condition of our slaves? The evils of their situation they but lightly feel, and would hardly feel at all, if they were not seduously instructed into sensibility. Certain it is, that if their fate were at the absolute disposal of a council of the most enlightened philanthropists in Christendom, with unlimited resources, they could place them in no situation so favorable to themselves, as that which they at present occupy. But whatever good there may be, or whatever mitigation of evil, it is worse than valueless, because it is the result of *slavery*.

I am aware, that however often answered, it is likely to be repeated again and again—how can that institution be tolerable, by which a large class of society is cut off from the hope of improvement in knowledge; to whom blows are not degrading; theft no more than a fault; falsehood and the want of chastity almost venial, and in which a husband or parent looks with comparative indifference, on that which, to a freeman, would be the dishonor of a wife or child?

But why not, if it produces the greatest aggregate of good? Sin and ignorance are only evils, because they lead to misery. It is not our institution, but the institution of nature, that in the progress of society a portion of it should be exposed to want, and the misery which it brings, and therefore involved in ignorance, vice, and depravity. In anticipating some of the good, we also anticipate a portion of the evil of civilization. But we have it in a mitigated form. The want and the misery are unknown; the ignorance is less a misfortune, because the being is not the guardian of himself, and partly on account of that involuntary ignorance, the vice is less vice—less hurtful to man, and less displeasing to God.

There is something in this word *slavery* which seems to partake of the qualities of the insane root, and distempers the minds of men. That which would be true in relation to one predicament, they misapply to another, to which it has no application at all. Some of the virtues of a freeman would be the vices of slaves. To submit to a blow, would be degrading to a freeman, because he is the protector of himself. It is not degrading to a slave—neither is it to a priest or woman. And is it a misfortune that it should be so? The freeman of other countries is compelled to submit to indignities hardly more endurable than blows—indignities to make the sensitive feelings shrink, and the proud heart swell; and this very name of freeman gives them double rancor. If when a man is born in Europe, it were certainly foreseen that he was destined to a life of painful labor—to obscurity, contempt, and privation—would it not be mercy that he should be reared in ignorance and apathy, and trained to the endurance of the evils he must encounter? It is not certainly foreseen as to any individual, but it is foreseen as to the great mass of those born of the laboring poor; and it is for the mass, not for the exception, that the institutions of society are to provide. Is it not better that the character and intellect of the individual should be suited to the station which he is to occupy? Would you do a benefit to the horse or the ox, by giving him a cultivated understanding or fine feelings? So far as the mere laborer has the pride, the knowledge, or the aspirations of a freeman, he is unfitted for his situation, and must doubly feel its infelicity. If there are sordid, servile, and laborious offices to be performed, is it not better that there should be sordid, servile, and laborious beings to perform them? If there were infallible marks by which individuals of inferior intellect, and inferior character, could be selected at their birth—would not the interests of society be served, and would not some sort of fitness seem to require, that they should be selected for the inferior and servile offices? And if this race be generally marked by such inferiority, is it not fit that they should fill them?

I am well aware that those whose aspirations are after a state of society from which evil shall be banished, and who look in life for that which life will never afford, contemplate that all the offices of life may be performed without contempt or degradation—all be regarded as equally liberal, or equally respected.[238] But theorists cannot control nature and bend her to their views, and the inequality of which I have before spoken is deeply founded in nature. The offices which employ knowledge and intellect, will always be regarded as more liberal than those which require the labor of the hands. When there is competition for employment, he who gives it bestows a favor, and it will be so received. He will assume superiority from the power of dismissing his laborers, and from fear of this, the latter will practice deference, often amounting to servility. Such in time will become the established relation between the employer and the employed, the rich and the poor. If want be accompanied with sordidness and squalor, though it be pitied, the pity will be mixed with some degree of contempt. If it lead to misery, and misery to vice, there will be disgust and aversion.

What is the essential character of *slavery*, and in what does it differ from the *servitude* of other countries? If I should venture on a definition, I should say that where a man is compelled to labor at the will of another, and to give him much the greater portion of the product of his labor, there *slavery* exists; and it is immaterial by what sort of compulsion the will of the laborer is subdued. It is what no human being would do without some sort of compulsion. He can not be compelled to labor by blows.[239] No—but what difference does it make, if you can inflict any other sort of torture which will be equally effectual in subduing the will? if you can starve him, or alarm him for the subsistence of himself or his family?[240] And is it not under this compulsion that the *freeman* labors? I do not mean in every particular case, but in the general. Will any one be hardy enough to say that he is at his own disposal, or has the government of himself? True, he may change his employer if he is dissatisfied with his conduct toward him; but this is a privilege he would in the majority of cases gladly abandon, and render the connection between them indissoluble. There is far less of the interest and attachment in his relation to his employer, which so often exists between the master and the slave, and mitigates the condition of the latter. An intelligent English traveler has characterized as the most miserable and degraded of all beings, "a masterless slave." And is not the condition of the laboring poor of other countries too often that of masterless slaves! Take the following description of a *free* laborer, no doubt highly colored, quoted by the author to whom I have before referred.

"What is that defective being, with calfless legs and stooping shoulders, weak in body and mind, inert, pusillanimous and stupid, whose premature wrinkles and furtive glance, tell of misery and degradation? That is an English peasant or pauper, for the words are synonymous. His sire was a pauper, and his mother's milk wanted nourishment. From infancy his food has been bad, as well as insufficient; and he now feels the pains of unsatisfied hunger nearly whenever he is awake. But half clothed, and never supplied with more warmth than suffices to cook his scanty meals, cold and wet come to him, and stay by him with the weather. He is married, of course; for to this he would have been driven by the poor laws, even if he had been, as he never was, sufficiently comfortable and prudent to dread the burden of a family. But though instinct and the overseer have given him a wife, he has not tasted the highest joys of husband and father. His partner and his little ones being like himself, often hungry, seldom warm, sometimes sick without aid, and always sorrowful without hope, are greedy, selfish, and vexing; so, to use his own expression, he hates the sight of them, and resorts to his hovel, only because a hedge affords less shelter from the wind and rain. Compelled by parish law to support his family, which means to join them in consuming an allowance from the parish, he frequently conspires with his wife to get that allowance increased, or prevent its being diminished. This brings beggary, trickery, and quarrelling, and ends in settled craft. Though he have the inclination, he wants the courage to become, like more energetic men of his class, a poacher or smuggler on a large scale, but he pilfers occasionally, and teaches his children to lie and steal. His subdued and slavish manner toward his great neighbors, shows that they treat him with suspicion and harshness. Consequently, he at once dreads and hates them; but he will never harm them by violent means. Too degraded to be desperate, he is only thoroughly depraved. His miserable career will be short; rheumatism and asthma are conducting him to the work-house; where he will breathe his last without one pleasant recollection, and so make room for another wretch, who may live and die in the same way." And this description, or some other not much less revolting, is applied to "the bulk of the people, the great body of the people." Take the following description of the condition of childhood, which has justly been called eloquent.[241]

"The children of the very poor have no young times; it makes the very heart bleed, to overhear the casual street talk between a poor woman and her little girl, a woman of the better sort of poor, in a condition rather above the squalid beings we have been contemplating. It is not of toys, of nursery books, of summer holidays, (fitting that age,) of the promised sight or play; of praised sufficiency at school. It is of mangling and clear starching; of price of coals, or of potatoes. The questions of the child, that should be the very outpourings of curiosity in idleness, are marked with forecast and melancholy providence. It has come to be a woman, before it was a child. It has learnt to go to market; it chaffers, it haggles, it envies, it murmurs; it is knowing, acute, sharpened; it never prattles." Imagine such a description applied to the children of negro slaves, the most vacant of human beings, whose life is a holiday.

And this people, to whom these horrors are familiar, are those who fill the world with clamor, concerning the injustice and cruelty of slavery. I speak in no invidious spirit. Neither the laws nor the government of England are to be reproached with the evils which are inseparable from the state of their society—as little, undoubtedly, are we to be reproached with the existence of our slavery. Including the whole of the United States—and for reasons already given, the whole ought to be included, as receiving in no unequal degree the benefit—may we not say justly that we have less slavery, and more mitigated slavery, than any other country in the civilized world?

That they are called free, undoubtedly aggravates the sufferings of the slaves of other regions. They see the enormous inequality which exists, and feel their own misery, and can hardly conceive otherwise, than that there is some injustice in the institutions of society to occasion these. They regard the apparently more fortunate class as oppressors, and it adds bitterness that they should be of the same name and race. They feel indignity more acutely, and more of discontent and evil passion is excited; they feel that it is mockery that calls them free. Men do not so much hate and envy those who are separated from them by a wide distance, and some apparently impassable barrier, as those who approach nearer to their own condition, and with whom they habitually bring themselves into comparison. The slave with us is not tantalized with the name of freedom, to which his whole condition gives the lie, and would do so if he were emancipated to-morrow. The African slave sees that nature herself has marked him as a separate—and if left to himself, I have no doubt he would feel it to be an inferior—race, and interposed a barrier almost insuperable to his becoming a member of the same society, standing on the same footing of right and privilege with his master.

That the African negro is an inferior variety of the human race, is, I think, now generally admitted, and his distinguishing characteristics are such as peculiarly mark him out for the situation which he occupies among us. And these are no less marked in their original country, than as we have daily occasion to observe them. The most remarkable is their indifference to personal liberty. In this they have followed their instincts since we have any knowledge of their continent, by enslaving each other; but contrary to the experience of every race, the possession of slaves has no material effect in raising the character, and promoting the civilization of the master. Another trait is the want of domestic affections, and insensibility to the ties of kindred. In the travels of the Landers, after speaking of a single exception, in the person of a woman who betrayed some transient emotion in passing by the country from which she had been torn as a slave, the authors add: "that Africans, generally speaking, betray the most perfect indifference on losing their liberty, and being deprived of their relatives, while love of country is equally a stranger to their breasts, as social tenderness or domestic affection." "Marriage is celebrated by the natives as unconcernedly as possible; a man thinks as little of taking a wife, as of cutting an ear of corn—affection is altogether out of the question." They are, however, very submissive to authority, and seem to entertain great reverence for chiefs, priests, and masters. No greater indignity can be offered an individual, than to throw opprobrium on his parents. On this point of their character I think I have remarked, that, contrary to the instinct of nature in other races, they entertain less regard for children than for parents, to whose authority they have been accustomed to submit. Their character is thus summed up by the travellers quoted: "The few opportunities we have had of studying their characters, induce us to believe that they are a simple, honest, inoffensive, but weak, timid, and cowardly race. They seem to have no social tenderness, very few of those amiable private virtues which could win our affections, and none of those public qualities that claim respect or command admiration. The love of country is not strong enough in their bosoms to incite them to defend it against a despicable foe; and of the active energy, noble sentiments, and contempt of danger which distinguishes the North American tribes and other savages, no traces are to be found among this slothful people. Regardless of the past, as reckless of the future, the present alone influences their actions. In this respect, they approach nearer to the nature of the brute creation, than perhaps any other people on the face of the globe." Let me ask if this people do not furnish the very material out of which slaves ought to be made, and whether it be not an improving of their condition to make them the slaves of civilized masters? There is a variety in the character of the tribes. Some are brutally and savagely ferocious and bloody, whom it would be mercy to enslave. From the travelers' account, it seems not unlikely that the negro race is tending to extermination, being daily encroached on and overrun by the superior Arab race. It may be, that when they shall have been lost from their native seats, they may be found numerous, and in no unhappy condition, on the continent to which they have been transplanted.

The opinion which connects form and features with character and intellectual power, is one so deeply impressed on the human mind, that perhaps there is scarcely any man who does not almost daily act upon it, and in some measure verify its truth. Yet in spite of this intimation of nature, and though the anatomist and physiologist may tell them that the races differ in every bone and muscle, and in the proportion of brain and nerves, yet there are some who, with a most bigoted and fanatical determination to free themselves from what they have prejudged to be prejudice, will still maintain that this physiognomy, evidently tending to that of the brute, when compared to that of the Caucasian race, may be enlightened by as much thought, and animated by as lofty sentiment. We who have the best opportunity of judging, are pronounced to be incompetent to do so, and to be blinded by our interest and prejudices—often by those who have no opportunity at all—and we are to be taught to distrust or disbelieve that which we daily observe, and familiarly know, on such authority. Our prejudices are spoken of. But the truth is, that, until very lately, since circumstances have compelled us to think for ourselves, we took our opinions on this subject, as on every other, ready formed from the country of our origin. And so deeply rooted were they, that we adhered to them, as most men will do to deeply rooted opinions, even against the evidence of our own observation, and our own senses. If the inferiority exists, it is attributed to the apathy and degradation produced by slavery. Though of the hundreds of thousand scattered over other countries, where the laws impose no disability upon them, none has given evidence of an approach to even mediocrity of intellectual excellence; this, too, is attributed to the slavery of a portion of their race. They are regarded as a servile caste, and degraded by opinion, and thus every generous effort is repressed. Yet though this should be the general effect, this very estimation is calculated to produce the contrary effect in particular instances. It is observed by Bacon, with respect to deformed persons and eunuchs, that though in general there is something of perversity in the character, the disadvantage often leads to extraordinary displays of virtue and excellence. "Whoever hath any thing fixed in his person that doth induce contempt, hath also a perpetual spur in himself, to rescue and deliver himself from scorn." So it would be with them, if they were capable of European aspirations—genius, if they possessed it, would be doubly fired with noble rage to rescue itself from this scorn. Of course, I do not mean to say that there may not be found among them some of superior capacity to many white persons; but that great intellectual powers are, perhaps, never found among them, and that in general their capacity is very limited, and their feelings animal and coarse—fitting them peculiarly to discharge the lower, and merely mechanical offices of society.

And why should it not be so? We have among domestic animals infinite varieties, distinguished by various degrees of sagacity, courage, strength, swiftness, and other qualities. And it may be observed, that this is no objection to their being derived from a common origin, which we suppose them to have had. Yet these accidental qualities, as they may be termed, however acquired in the first instance, we know that they transmit unimpaired to their posterity for an indefinite succession of generations. It is most important that these varieties should be preserved, and that each should be applied to the purposes for which it is best adapted. No philo-zoost, I believe, has suggested it as desirable that these varieties should be melted down into one equal, undistinguished race of curs or road horses.

Slavery, as it is said in an eloquent article published in a Southern periodical work,[242] to which I am indebted for other ideas, "has done more to elevate a degraded race in the scale of humanity; to tame the savage; to civilize the barbarous; to soften the ferocious; to enlighten the ignorant, and to spread the blessings of Christianity among the heathen, than all the missionaries that philanthropy and religion have ever sent forth."[243] Yet unquestionable as this is, and though human ingenuity and thought may be tasked in vain to devise any other means by which these blessings could have been conferred, yet a sort of sensibility which would be only mawkish and contemptible, if it were not mischievous, affects still to weep over the wrongs of "injured Africa." Can there be a doubt of the immense benefit which has been conferred on the race, by transplanting them from their native, dark, and barbarous regions, to the American continent and islands? There, threefourths of the race are in a state of the most deplorable personal slavery. And those who are not, are in a scarcely less deplorable condition of political slavery, to barbarous chiefs—who value neither life nor any other human right, or enthralled by priests to the most abject and atrocious superstitions. Take the following testimony of one of the few disinterested observers, who has had an opportunity of observing them in both situations.[244] "The wild savage is the child of passion, unaided by one ray of religion or morality to direct his course, in consequence of which his existence is stained with every crime that can debase human nature to a level with the brute creation. Who can say that the slaves in our colonies are such? Are they not, by comparison with their still savage brethren, enlightened beings? Is not the West Indian negro, therefore, greatly indebted to his master for making him what he is—for having raised him from the state of debasement in which he was born, and placed him in a scale of civilized society? How can he repay him? He is possessed of nothing—the only return in his power is his servitude. The man who has seen the wild African, roaming in his native woods, and the well fed, happy looking negro of the West Indies, may, perhaps, be able to judge of their comparative happiness; the former, I strongly suspect, would be glad to change his state of boasted freedom, starvation, and disease, to become the slave of sinners, and the commiseration of saints."[245] It was a useful and beneficent work, approaching the heroic, to tame the wild horse, and subdue him to the use of man; how much more to tame the nobler animal that is capable of reason, and subdue him to usefulness?

We believe that the tendency of slavery is to elevate the character of the master. No doubt the character—especially of youth—has sometimes received a taint and premature knowledge of vice, from the contact and association with ignorant and servile beings of gross manners and morals. Yet still we believe that the entire tendency is to inspire disgust and aversion toward their peculiar vices. It was not without a knowledge of nature, that the Spartans exhibited the vices of slaves by way of negative example to their children. We flatter ourselves that the view of this degradation, mitigated as it is, has the effect of making probity more strict, the pride of character more high, the sense of honor more strong, than is commonly found where this institution does not exist. Whatever may be the prevailing faults or vices of the masters of slaves, they have not commonly been understood to be those of dishonesty, cowardice, meanness, or falsehood. And so most unquestionably it ought to be. Our institutions would indeed be intolerable in the sight of God and man, if, condemning one portion of society to hopeless ignorance and comparative degradation, they should make no atonement by elevating the other class by higher virtues, and more liberal attainments—if, besides degraded slaves, there should be ignorant, ignoble, and degraded freemen. There is a broad and well marked line, beyond which no slavish vice should be regarded with the least toleration or allowance. One class is cut off from all interest in the State—that abstraction so potent to the feelings of a generous nature. The other must make compensation by increased assiduity and devotion to its honor and welfare. The love of wealth—so laudable when kept within proper limits, so base and mischievous when it exceeds them—so infectious in its example—an infection to which I fear we have been too much exposed—should be pursued by no arts in any degree equivocal, or at any risk of injustice to others. So surely as there is a just and wise governor of the universe, who punishes the sins of nations and communities, as well as of individuals, so surely shall we suffer punishment, if we are indifferent to that moral and intellectual cultivation of which the means are furnished to us, and to which we are called and incited by our situation.

I would to heaven I could express, as I feel, the conviction how necessary this cultivation is, not only to our prosperity and consideration, but to our safety and very existence. We, the slaveholding States, are in a hopeless minority in our own confederated Republic—to say nothing of the great confederacy of civilized States. It is admitted, I believe, not only by slaveholders, but by others, that we have sent to our common councils more than our due share of talent, high character and eloquence.[246] Yet in spite of all these most strenuously exerted, measures have been sometimes adopted which we believed to be dangerous and injurious to us, and threatening to be fatal. What would be our situation, if, instead of these, we were only represented by ignorant and groveling men, incapable of raising their views beyond a job or petty office, and incapable of commanding bearing or consideration? May I be permitted to advert—by no means invidiously— to the late contest carried on by South Carolina against Federal authority, and so happily terminated by the moderation which prevailed in our public counsels. I have often reflected, what one circumstance, more than any other, contributed to the successful issue of a contest, apparently so hopeless, in which one weak and divided State was arrayed against the whole force of the confederacy—unsustained, and uncountenanced, even by those who had a common interest with her. It seemed to me to be, that we had for leaders an unusual number of men of great intellectual power, co-operating cordially and in good faith, and commanding respect and confidence at home and abroad, by elevated and honorable character. It was from these that we—the followers at home—caught hope and confidence in the gloomiest aspect of our affairs. These, by their eloquence and the largeness of their views, at least shook the faith of the dominant majority in the wisdom and justice of their measures—or the practicability of carrying them into successful effect; and by their bearing and well known character, satisfied them that South Carolina would do all that she had pledged herself to do. Without these, how different might have been the result? And who shall say what at this day would have been the aspect of the now flourishing fields and cities of South Carolina? Or rather, without these, it is probable the contest would never have been begun; but that, without even the animation of a struggle, we should have sunk silently into a hopeless and degrading subjection. While I have memory—in the extremity of age—in sickness—under all the reverses and calamities of life—I shall have one source of pride and consolation—that of having been associated—according to my humbler position—with the noble spirits who stood prepared to devote themselves for Liberty—the Constitution—the Union. May such character and such talent never be wanting to South Carolina.

I am sure that it is unnecessary to say to an assembly like this, that the conduct of the master to his slave should be distinguished by the utmost humanity. That we should indeed regard them as wards and dependents on our kindness, for whose well-being in every way we are deeply responsible. This is no less the dictate of wisdom and just policy, than of right feeling. It is wise with respect to the services to be expected from them. I have never heard of an owner whose conduct in their management was distinguished by undue severity, whose slaves were not in a great degree worthless to him. A cheerful and kindly demeanor, with the expression of interest in themselves and their affairs, is, perhaps, calculated to have a better effect on them, than what might be esteemed more substantial favors and indulgences. Throughout nature, attachment is the reward of attachment. It is wise, too, in relation to the civilized world around us, to avoid giving occasion to the odium which is so industriously excited against ourselves and our institutions. For this reason, public opinion should, if possible, bear even more strongly and indignantly than it does at present, on masters who practice any wanton cruelty on their slaves. The miscreant who is guilty of this, not only violates the law of God and of humanity, but as far as in him lies, by bringing odium upon, endangers the institutions of his country, and the safety of his countrymen. He casts a shade upon the character of every individual of his fellow-citizens, and does every one of them a personal injury. So of him who indulges in any odious excess of intemperate or licentious passion. It is detached instances of this sort, of which the existence is, perhaps, hardly known among ourselves, that, collected with pertinacious and malevolent industry, affords the most formidable weapons to the mischievous zealots, who array them as being characteristic of our general manners and state of society.

I would by no means be understood to intimate, that a vigorous, as well as just government, should not be exercised over slaves. This is part of our duty toward them, no less obligatory than any other duty, and no less necessary toward their well-being than to ours. I believe that at least as much injury has been done and suffering inflicted by weak and injudicious indulgence, as by inordinate severity. He whose business is to labor, should be made to labor, and that with due diligence, and should be vigorously restrained from excess or vice. This is no less necessary to his happiness than to his usefulness. The master who neglects this, not only makes his slaves unprofitable to himself, but discontented and wretched—a nuisance to his neighbors and to society.

I have said that the tendency of our institution is to elevate the female character, as well as that of the other sex, and for similar reasons. In other states of society, there is no well-defined limit to separate virtue and vice. There are degrees of vice, from the most flagrant and odious, to that which scarcely incurs the censure of society. Many individuals occupy an unequivocal position and as society becomes accustomed to this, there will be a less peremptory requirement of purity in female manners and conduct, and often the whole of the society will be in a tainted and uncertain condition with respect to female virtue. Here, there is that certain and marked line, above which there is no toleration or allowance for any approach to license of manners or conduct, and she who falls below it, will fall far below even the slave. How many will incur this penalty?

And permit me to say, that this elevation of the female character is no less important and essential to us, than the moral and intellectual cultivation of the other sex. It would indeed be intolerable, if, when one class of the society is necessarily degraded in this respect, no compensation were made by the superior elevation and purity of the other. Not only essential purity of conduct, but the utmost purity of manners, and I will add, though it may incur the formidable charge of affectation or prudery,—a greater severity of decorum than is required elsewhere, is necessary among us. Always should be strenuously resisted the attempts which have been sometimes made to introduce among us the freedom of foreign European, and especially of continental manners. This freedom, the remotest in the world from that which sometimes springs from simplicity of manners, is calculated and commonly intended to confound the outward distinctions of virtue and vice. It is to prepare the way for licentiousness—to produce this effect—that if those who are clothed with the outward color and garb of vice, may be well received by society, those who are actually guilty may hope to be so too. It may be said, that there is often perfect purity where there is very great freedom of manners. And, I have no doubt, this may be true in particular instances, but it is never true of any *society* in which this is the general state of manners. What guards can there be to purity, when every thing that *may possibly* be done innocently, is habitually practiced; when there can be no impropriety which is not vice. And what must be the depth of the depravity when there is a departure from that which they admit as principle. Besides, things which may perhaps be practiced innocently where they are familiar, produce a moral dilaceration in the course of their being introduced where they are new. Let us say, we will not have the manners of South Carolina changed.

I have before said that free labor is cheaper than the labor of slaves, and so far as it is so the condition of the free laborer is worse. But I think President Dew has sufficiently shown that this is only true of Northern countries. It is matter of familiar remark that the tendency of warm climates is to relax the human constitution and indispose to labor. The earth yields abundantly—in some regions almost spontaneously—under the influence of the sun, and the means of supporting life are obtained with but slight exertion; and men will use no greater exertion than is necessary to the purpose. This very luxuriance of vegetation, where no other cause concurs, renders the air less salubrious, and even when positive malady does not exist, the health is habitually impaired. Indolence renders the constitution more liable to these effects of the atmosphere, and these again aggravate the indolence. Nothing but the coercion of slavery can overcome the repugnance to labor under these circumstances, and by subduing the soil, improve and render wholesome the climate.

It is worthy of remark, that there does not now exist on the face of the earth, a people in a tropical climate, or one approaching to it, where slavery does not exist, that is in a state of high civilization, or exhibits the energies which mark the progress toward it. Mexico and the South American Republics,[247] starting on their new career of independence, and having gone through a farce of abolishing slavery, are rapidly degenerating, even from semi-barbarism. The only portion of the South American continent which seems to be making any favorable progress, in spite of a weak and arbitrary civil government, is Brazil, in which slavery has been retained. Cuba, of the same race with the continental republics, is daily and rapidly advancing in industry and civilization; and this is owing exclusively to her slaves. St. Domingo is struck out of the map of civilized existence, and the British West Indies will shortly be so. On the other continent, Spain and Portugal are degenerate, and their rapid progress is downward. Their southern coast is infested by disease, arising from causes which industry might readily overcome, but that industry they will never exert. Greece is still barbarous, and scantily peopled. The work of an English physician, distinguished by strong sense and power of observation,[248] gives a most affecting picture of the condition of Italy,—especially south of the Appenines. With the decay of industry, the climate has degenerated toward the condition from which it was first rescued by the labor of slaves. There is poison in every man's veins, affecting the very springs of life, dulling or extinguishing, with the energies of the body, all energy of mind, and often exhibiting itself in the most appalling forms of disease. From year to year the pestilential atmosphere creeps forward, narrowing the circles within which it is possible to sustain human life. With disease and misery, industry still more rapidly decays, and if the process goes on, it seems that Italy too will soon be ready for another experiment in colonization.

Yet once it was not so, when Italy was possessed by the masters of slaves; when Rome contained her millions, and Italy was a garden; when their iron energies of body corresponded with the energies of mind which made them conquerors in every climate and on every soil; rolled the tide of conquest, not as in later times, from the South to the North; extended their laws and their civilization, and created them lords of the earth.

"What conflux issuing forth or entering in;
Prætors, pro-consuls to their provinces,
Hasting, or on return in robes of state.
Lictors and rods, the ensigns of their power,
Legions and cohorts, turms of horse and wings:
Or embassies from regions far remote,
In various habits, on the Appian road,
Or on th' Emilian; some from furthest South,
Syene, and where the shadow both way falls,
Meroe, Nilotic isle, and more to West,
The realms of Bocchus to the Blackmoor sea;
From th' Asian kings, and Parthian among these;
From India and the golden Chersonese,
And utmost India's isle, Taprobona,
Dusk faces, with white silken turbans wreathed;
From Gallia, Gades, and the British West;
Germans, and Scythians, and Sarmatians, North
Beyond Danubius to the Tauric Pool!
All nations now to Rome obedience pay."

Such was, and such is, the picture of Italy. Greece presents a contrast not less striking. What is the cause of the great change? Many causes, no doubt, have occurred; but though

"War, famine, pestilence, and flood and fire,
Have dealt upon the seven-hilled city's pride,"
I will venture to say that nothing has dealt upon it more heavily than the loss of domestic slavery. Is not this evident? If they had slaves, with an energetic civil government, would the deadly miasma be permitted to overspread the Campagna, and invade Rome herself? Would not the soil be cultivated, and the wastes reclaimed? A late traveller[249] mentions a canal, cut for miles through rock and mountain, for the purpose of carrying off the waters of the lake of Celano, on which thirty thousand Roman slaves were employed for eleven years, and which remains almost perfect to the present day. This, the government of Naples was ten years in repairing with an hundred workmen. The imperishable works of Rome which remain to the present day were, for the most part, executed by slaves. How different would be the condition of Naples, if for her wretched lazzaroni were substituted

negro slaves, employed in rendering productive the plains whose fertility now serves only to infect the air!

To us, on whom this institution is fastened, and who could not shake it off, even if we desired to do so, the great republics of antiquity offer instruction of inestimable value. They teach us that slavery is compatible with the freedom, stability, and long duration of civil government, with denseness of population, great power, and the highest civilization. And in what respect does this modern Europe, which claims to give opinions to the world, so far excel them—notwithstanding the immense advantages of the Christian religion and the discovery of the art of printing? They are not more free, nor have performed more glorious actions, nor displayed more exalted virtue. In the higher departments of intellect—in all that relates to taste and imagination—they will hardly venture to claim equality. Where they have gone beyond them in the results of mechanical philosophy, or discoveries which contribute to the wants and enjoyments of physical life, they have done so by the help of means with which they were furnished by the Grecian mind—the mother of civilization—and only pursued a little further the tract which that had always pointed out. In the development of intellectual power, they will hardly bear comparison. Those noble republics in the pride of their strength and greatness, may have anticipated for themselves—as some of their poets did for them—an everlasting duration and predominance. But they could not have anticipated, that when they had fallen under barbarous arms, that when arts and civilization were lost, and the whole earth in darkness—the first light should break from their tombs—that in a renewed world, unconnected with them by ties of locality, language or descent, they should still be held the models of all that is profound in science, or elegant in literature, or all that is great in character, or elevated in imagination. And perhaps when England herself, who now leads the war with which we are on all sides threatened, shall have fulfilled her mission, and like the other glorious things of the earth, shall have passed away; when she shall have diffused her noble race and noble language, her laws, her literature, and her civilization, over all quarters of the earth, and shall perhaps be overrun by some Northern horde—sunk into an ignoble and anarchical democracy,[250] or subdued to the dominion of some Cæsar,—demagogue and despot,—then, in Southern regions, there may be found many republics, triumphing in Grecian arts and civilization, and worthy of British descent and Roman institutions.

If, after a time, when the mind and almost the memory of the republic were lost, Romans degenerated, they furnish conclusive evidence that this was owing not to their domestic, but to their political slavery. The same thing is observed over all the Eastern monarchies; and so it must be, wherever property is insecure, and it is dangerous for a man to rise himself to such eminence by intellectual or moral excellence, as would give him influence over his society. So it is in Egypt; and the other regions bordering the Mediterranean, which once comprehended the civilization of the world, where Carthage,

Tyre, and Phœnicia flourished. In short, the uncontradicted experience of the world is, that in the Southern States where good government and predial and domestic slavery are found, there are prosperity and greatness; where either of these conditions is wanting, degeneracy and barbarism. The former, however, is equally essential in all climates and under all institutions. And can we suppose it to be the design of the Creator, that these regions, constituting half of the earth's surface, and the more fertile half, and more capable of sustaining life, should be abandoned forever to depopulation and barbarism? Certain it is that they will never be reclaimed by the labor of freemen. In our own country, look at the lower valley of the Mississippi, which is capable of being made a far greater Egypt. In our own State, there are extensive tracts of the most fertile soil, which are capable of being made to swarm with life. These are at present pestilential swamps, and valueless, because there is abundance of other fertile soil in more favorable situations, which demand all and more than all the labor which our country can supply. Are these regions of fertility to be abandoned at once and forever to the alligator and tortoise—with here and there perhaps a miserable, shivering, crouching *free* black savage? Does not the finger of heaven itself seem to point to a race of men—not to be enslaved by us, but already enslaved, and who will be in every way benefited by the change of masters—to whom such climate is not uncongenial, who, though disposed to indolence, are yet patient and capable of labor, on whose whole features, mind and character, nature has indelibly written—slave;—and indicate that we should avail ourselves of these in fulfilling the first great command to subdue and replenish the earth.

It is true that this labor will be dearer than that of Northern countries, where, under the name of freedom, they obtain cheaper and perhaps better slaves. Yet it is the best we can have, and this too has its compensation. We see it compensated at present by the superior value of our agricultural products. And this superior value they must probably always have. The Southern climate admits of a greater variety of productions. Whatever is produced in Northern climates, the same thing, or something equivalent, may be produced in the Southern. But the Northern have no equivalent for the products of Southern climates. The consequence will be, that the products of Southern regions will be demanded all over the civilized world. The agricultural products of Northern regions are chiefly for their own consumption. They must therefore apply themselves to the manufacturing of articles of luxury, elegance, convenience, or necessity,—which requires cheap labor—for the purpose of exchanging them with their Southern neighbors. Thus nature herself indicates that agriculture should be the predominating employment in Southern countries, and manufactures in Northern. Commerce is necessary to both—but less indispensable to the Southern, which produce within themselves a greater variety of things desirable to life. They will therefore have somewhat less of the commercial spirit. We must avail ourselves of such labor as we can command. The slave must labor, and is inured to it; while the necessity of energy in his government, of watchfulness, and of preparation and power to suppress insurrection, added to the moral force derived from the habit of command, may help to prevent the degeneracy of the master.

The task of keeping down insurrection is commonly supposed by those who are strangers to our institutions, to be a very formidable one. Even among ourselves, accustomed as we have been to take our opinions on this as on every other subject, ready formed from those whom we regarded as instructors, in the teeth of our own observation and experience, fears have been entertained which are absolutely ludicrous. We have been supposed to be nightly reposing over a mine, which may at any instant explode to our destruction. The first thought of a foreigner sojourning in one of our cities, who is awaked by any nightly alarm, is of servile insurrection and massacre. Yet if any thing is certain in human affairs, it is certain and from the most obvious considerations, that we are more secure in this respect than any civilved and fully peopled society upon the face of the earth. In every such society, there is a much larger proportion than with us, of persons who have more to gain than to lose by the overthrow of government, and the embroiling of social order. It is in such a state of things that those who were before at the bottom of society, rise to the surface. From causes already considered, they are peculiarly apt to consider their sufferings the result of injustice and misgovernment, and to be rancorous and embittered accordingly. They have every excitement, therefore, of resentful passion, and every temptation which the hope of increased opulence, or power or consideration can hold out, to urge them to innovation and revolt. Supposing the same disposition to exist in equal degree among our slaves, what are their comparative means or prospect of gratifying it? The poor of other countries are called free. They have, at least, no one interested to exercise a daily and nightly superintendence and control over their conduct and actions. Emissaries of their class may traverse, unchecked, every portion of the country, for the purpose of organizing insurrection. From their greater intelligence, they have greater means of communicating with each other. They may procure and secrete arms. It is not alone the ignorant, or those who are commonly called the poor, that will be tempted to revolution. There will be many disappointed men, and men of desperate fortune—men perhaps of talent and daring—to combine them and direct their energies. Even those in the higher ranks of society who contemplate no such result, will contribute to it, by declaiming on their hardships and rights.

With us, it is almost physically impossible that there should be any very extensive combination among the slaves. It is absolutely impossible that they should procure and conceal efficient arms. Their emissaries traversing the country, would carry their commissions on their foreheads. If we suppose among them an individual of sufficient talent and energy to qualify him for a revolutionary leader, he could not be so extensively known as to command the confidence, which would be necessary to enable him to combine and direct them. Of the class of freemen, there would be no individual so poor or degraded (with the exception perhaps of here and there a reckless and desperate outlaw and felon) who would not have much to lose by the success of such an attempt; every one, therefore, would be vigilant and active to detect and suppress it. Of all impossible things, one of the most impossible would be a successful insurrecction of our slaves, originating with themselves.

Attempts at insurrection have indeed been made—excited, as we believe, by the agitation of the abolitionists and declaimers on slavery; but these have been in every instance promptly suppressed. We fear not to compare the riots, disorder, revolt and bloodshed, which have been committed in our own, with those of any other civilized communities, during the same lapse of time. And let it be observed under what extraordinary circumstances our peace has been preserved. For the last half century, one half of our population has been admonished in terms the most calculated to madden and excite, that they are the victims of the most grinding and cruel injustice and oppression. We know that these exhortations continually reach them, through a thousand channels which we cannot detect, as if carried by the birds of the air—and what human being, especially when unfavorably distinguished by outward circumstances, is not ready to give credit when he is told that he is the victim of injustice and oppression? In effect, if not in terms, they have been continually exhorted to insurrection. The master has been painted as a criminal, tyrant and robber, justly obnoxious to the vengeance of God and man, and they have been assured of the countenance and sympathy, if not of the active assistance, of all the rest of the world. We ourselves have in some measure pleaded guilty to the impeachment. It is not long since a great majority of our free population, servile to the opinions of those whose opinions they had been accustomed to follow, would have admitted slavery to be a great evil, unjust and indefensible in principle, and only to be vindicated by the stern necessity which was imposed upon us. Thus stimulated by every motive and passion which ordinarily actuate human beings—not as to a criminal enterprise, but as to something generous and heroic—what has been the result? A few imbecile and uncombined plots—in every instance detected before they broke out into action, and which perhaps if undetected would never have broken into action. One or two sudden, unpremeditated attempts, frantic in their character, if not prompted by actual insanity, and these instantly crushed. As it is, we are not less assured of safety, order, and internal peace, than any other people; and but for the pertinacious and fanatical agitations of the subject, would be much more so.

This experience of security, however, should admonish us of the folly and wickedness of those who have sometimes taken upon themselves to supersede the regular course of law, and by rash and violent acts to punish supposed disturbers of the peace of society. This can admit of no justification or palliation whatever. Burke, I think, somewhere remarked something to this effect,—that when society is in the last stage of depravity— when all parties are alike corrupt, and alike wicked and unjustifiable in their measures and objects, a good man may content himself with standing neuter, a sad and disheartened spectator of the conflict between the rival vices. But are we in this wretched condition? It is fearful to see with what avidity the worst and most dangerous characters of society seize on the occasion of obtaining the countenance of better men, for the purpose of throwing off the restraints of law. It is always these who are most zealous and forward in constituting themselves the protectors of the public peace. To such men—men without reputation, or principle, or stake in society—disorder is the natural element. In that, desperate fortunes and the want of all moral principle and moral feeling constitute power. They are eager to avenge themselves upon society. Anarchy is not so much the absence of government, as the government of the worst—not aristocracy, but kakistocracy—a state of things, which to the honor of our nature, has seldom obtained among men, and which perhaps was only fully exemplified during the worst times of the French Revolution, when that horrid hell burnt with its most lurid flame. In such a state of things, to be accused is to be condemned—to protect the innocent is to be guilty; and what perhaps is the worst effect, even men of better nature, to whom their own deeds are abhorrent, are goaded by terror to be forward and emulous in deeds of guilt and violence. The scenes of lawless violence which have been acted in some portions of our country, rare and restricted as they have been, have done more to tarnish its reputation than a thousand libels. They have done more to discredit, and if any thing could, to endanger, not only our domestic, but our republican institutions, than the abolitionists themselves. Men can never be permanently and effectually disgraced but by themselves, and rarely endangered but by their own injudicious conduct, giving advantage to the enemy. Better, far better, would it be to encounter the dangers with which we are supposed to be threatened, than to employ such means for averting them. But the truth is, that in relation to this matter, so far as respects actual insurrection, when alarm is once excited, danger is absolutely at an end. Society can then employ legitimate and more effectual measures for its own protection. The very commission of such deeds is proof that they are unnecessary. Let those who attempt them, then, or make any demonstration toward them, understand that they will meet only the discountenance and abhorrence of all good men, and the just punishment of the laws they have dared to outrage.

It has commonly been supposed, that this institution will prove a source of weakness in relation to military defense against a foreign country. I will venture to say that in a slaveholding community, a larger military force may be maintained permanently in the field, than in any State where there are not slaves. It is plain that almost the whole of the able bodied free male population, making half of the entire able bodied male population, may be maintained in the field, and this without taking in any material degree from the labor and resources of the country. In general, the labor of our country is performed by slaves. In other countries, it is their laborers that form the material of their armies. What proportion of these can be taken away without fatally crippling their industry and resources? In the war of the Revolution, though the strength of our State was wasted and paralyzed by the unfortunate divisions which existed among ourselves, yet it may be said with general truth, that every citizen was in the field, and acquired much of the qualities of the soldier.

It is true that this advantage will be attended with its compensating evils and disadvantages; to which we must learn to submit, if we are determined on the maintenance of our institutions. We are, as yet, hardly at all aware how little the maxims and practices of modern civilized governments will apply to us. Standing armies, as they are elsewhere constituted, we cannot have; for we have not, and for generations cannot have, the materials out of which they are to be formed. If we should be involved in serious wars, I have no doubt but that some sort of conscription, requiring the service of all citizens for a considerable term, will be necessary. Like the people of Athens, it will be necessary that every citizen should be a soldier, and qualified to discharge efficiently the duties of a soldier. It may seem a melancholy consideration, that an army so made up should be opposed to the disciplined mercenaries of foreign nations. But we must learn to know our true situation. But may we not hope, that made up of superior materials, of men having home and country to defend; inspired by higher pride of character, of greater intelligence, and trained by an effective, though honorable discipline, such an army will be more than a match for mercenaries. The efficiency of an army is determined by the qualities of its officers, and may we not expect to have a greater proportion of men better qualified for officers, and possessing the true spirit of military command. And let it be recollected that if there were otherwise reason to apprehend danger from insurrection, there will be the greatest security when there is the largest force on foot within the country. Then it is that any such attempt would be most instantly and effectually crushed.

And, perhaps, a wise foresight should induce our State to provide, that it should have within itself such military knowledge and skill as may be sufficient to organize, discipline, and command armies, by establishing a military academy or school of discipline. The school of the militia will not do for this. From the general opinion of our weakness, if our country should at any time come into hostile collision, we shall be selected for the point of attack; making us, according to Mr. Adam's anticipation, the Flanders of the United States. Come from what quarter it may, the storm will fall upon us. It is known that lately, when there was apprehension of hostility with France, the scheme was instantly devised of invading the Southern States and organizing insurrection. In a popular English periodical work, I have seen the plan suggested by an officer of high rank and reputation in the British army, of invading the Southern States at various points and operating by the same means. He is said to be a gallant officer, and certainly had no conception that he was devising atrocious crime, as alien to the true spirit of civilized warfare, as the poisoning of streams and fountains. But the folly of such schemes is no less evident than their wickedness. Apart from the consideration of that which experience has most fully proved to be true—that in general their attachment and fidelity to their masters is not to be shaken, and that from sympathy with the feelings of those by whom they are surrounded, and from whom they derive their impressions, they contract no less terror and aversion toward an invading enemy; it is manifest that this recourse would be an hundred fold more available to us than to such an enemy. They are already in our possession, and we might at will arm and organize them in any number that we might think proper. The Helots were a regular constituent part of the Spartan armies. Thoroughly acquainted with their characters, and accustomed to command them, we might use any strictness of discipline which would be necessary to render them effective, and from their habits of subordination already formed, this would be a task of less difficulty. Though morally most timid, they are by no means wanting in physical strength of nerve. They are excitable by praise; and directed by those in whom they have confidence, would rush fearlessly and unquestioning upon any sort of danger. With white officers and accompanied by a strong white cavalry, there are no troops in the world from whom there would be so little reason to apprehend insubordination or mutiny.

This, I admit, might be a dangerous resource, and one not to be resorted to but in great extremity. But I am supposing the case of our being driven to extremity. It might be dangerous to disband such an army, and reduce them with the habits of soldiers, to their former condition of laborers. It might be found necessary, when once embodied, to keep them so, and subject to military discipline—a permanent standing army. This in time of peace would be expensive, if not dangerous. Or if at any time we should be engaged in hostilities with our neighbors, and it were thought advisable to send such an army abroad to conquer settlements for themselves, the invaded regions might have occasion to think that the scourge of God was again let loose to afflict the earth.

President Dew has very fully shown how utterly vain are the fears of those, who, though there may be no danger for the present, yet apprehend great danger for the future, when the number of slaves shall be greatly increased. He has shown that the larger and more condensed society becomes, the easier it will be to maintain subordination, supposing the relative number of the different classes to remain the same—or even if there should be a very disproportionate increase of the enslaved class. Of all vain things, the vainest and that in which man most shows his impotence and folly, is the taking upon himself to provide for a very distant future—at all events by any material sacrifice of the present. Though experience has shown that revolutions and political movements—unless when they have been conducted with the most guarded caution and moderation—have generally terminated in results just the opposite of what was expected from them, the angry ape will still play his fantastic tricks, and put in motion machinery, the action of which he no more comprehends or foresees than he comprehends the mysteries of infinity. The insect that is borne upon the current will fancy that he directs its course. Besides the fear of insurrection and servile war, there is also alarm lest, when their numbers shall be greatly increased, their labor will become utterly unprofitable, so that it will be equally difficult for the master to retain and support them, or to get rid of them. But at what age of the world is this likely to happen? At present, it may be said that almost the whole of the Southern portion of this continent is to be subdued to cultivation; and in the order of Providence, this is the task allotted to them. For this purpose, more labor will be required for generations to come than they will be able to supply. When that task is accomplished, there will be many objects to which their labor may be directed.

At present they are employed in accumulating individual wealth, and this in one way, to wit, as agricultural laborers—and this is, perhaps, the most useful purpose to which their labor can be applied. The effect of slavery has not been to counteract the tendency to dispersion, which seems epidemical among our countrymen, invited by the unbounded extent of fertile and unexhausted soil, though it counteracts many of the evils of dispersion. All the customary trades, professions and employments, except the agricultural, require a condensed population for their profitable exercise. The agriculturist who can command no labor but that of his own hands, or that of his family, must remain comparatively poor and rude. He who acquires wealth by the labor of slaves, has the means of improvement for himself and his children. He may have a more extended intercourse, and consequently means of information and refinement, and may seek education for his children where it may be found. I say, what is obviously true, that he has the *means* of obtaining those advantages; but I say nothing to palliate or excuse the conduct of him who, having such means, neglects to avail himself of them.

I believe it to be true, that in consequence of our dispersion, though individual wealth is acquired, the face of the country is less adorned and improved by useful and ornamental public works, than in other societies of more condensed population, where there is less wealth. But this is an effect of that which constitutes perhaps our most conspicuous advantage. Where population is condensed, they must have the evils of condensed population, and among these is the difficulty of finding profitable employment for capital. He who has accumulated even an inconsiderable sum, is often puzzled to know what use to make of it. Ingenuity is therefore tasked to cast about for every enterprise which may afford a chance of profitable investment. Works useful and ornamental to the country, are thus undertaken and accomplished, and though the proprietors may fail of profit, the community no less receives the benefit. Among us, there is no such difficulty. A safe and profitable method of investment is offered to every one who has capital to dispose of, which is further recommended to his feelings by the sense of independence and the comparative leisure which the employment affords to the proprietor engaged in it. It is for this reason that few of our citizens engage in the pursuits of commerce. Though these may be more profitable, they are also more hazardous and more laborious.

When the demand for agricultural labor shall be fully supplied, then of course the labor of slaves will be directed to other employment and enterprises. Already it begins to be found, that in some instances it may be used as profitably in works of public improvement. As it becomes cheaper and cheaper, it will be applied to more various purposes and combined in larger masses. It may be commanded and combined with more facility than any other sort of labor; and the laborer, kept in stricter subordination, will be less dangerous to the security of society than in any other country, which is crowded and overstocked with a class of what are called free laborers. Let it be remembered that all the great and enduring monuments of human art and industry—the wonders of Egypt—the everlasting works of Rome—were created by the labor of slaves. There will come a stage in our progress when we shall have facilities for executing works as great as any of these—more useful than the pyramids—not less magnificent than the sea of Moeris. What the end of all is to be; what mutations lie hid in the womb of the distant future; to what convulsions our societies may be exposed—whether the master, finding it impossible to live with his slaves, may not be compelled to abandon the country to them—of all this it were presumptuous and vain to speculate.

I have hitherto, as I proposed, considered it as a naked, abstract question of the comparative good and evil of the institution of slavery. Very far different indeed is the practical question presented to us, when it is proposed to get rid of an institution which has interwoven itself with every fibre of the body politic; which has formed the habits of our society, and is consecrated by the usage of generations. If this be not a vicious prescription, which the laws of God forbid to ripen into right, it has a just claim to be respected by all tribunals of man. If the negroes were now free, and it were proposed to enslave them, then it would be incumbent on those who proposed the measure to show clearly that their liberty was incompatible with the public security. When it is proposed to innovate on the established state of things, the burden is on those who propose the innovation, to show that advantage will be gained from it. There is no reform, however necessary, wholesome or moderate, which will not be accompanied with some degree of inconvenience, risk or suffering. Those who acquiesce in the state of things which they found existing, can hardly be thought criminal. But most deeply criminal are they who give rise to the enormous evil with which great revolutions in society are always attended, without the fullest assurance of the greater good to be ultimately obtained. But if it can be made to appear, even probably, that no good will be obtained, but that the results will be evil and calamitous as the process, what can justify such innovations? No human being can be so mischievous—if acting consciously, none can be so wicked as those who, finding evil in existing institutions, run blindly upon change, unforeseeing and reckless of consequences, and leaving it to chance or fate to determine whether the end shall be improvement, or greater and more intolerable evil. Certainly the instincts of nature prompt to resist intolerable oppression. For this resistance no rule can be prescribed, but it must be left to the instincts of nature. To justify it, however, the insurrectionists should at least have a reasonable probability of success, and be assured that their condition will be improved by success. But most extraordinary is it, when those who complain and clamor are not those who are supposed to feel the oppression, but persons at a distance from them, and who can hardly at all appreciate the good or the evil of their situation. It is the unalterable condition of humanity, that men must achieve civil liberty for themselves. The assistance of allies has sometimes enabled nations to repel the attacks of foreign power, never to conquer liberty against their own internal government.

In one thing I concur with the abolitionsts; that if emancipation is to be brought about, it is better that it should be immediate and total. But let us suppose it to be brought about in any manner, and then inquire what would be the effects.

The first and most obvious effect, would be to put an end to the cultivation of our great Southern staple. And this would be equally the result, if we suppose the emancipated negroes to be in no way distinguished from the free laborers of other countries, and that their labor would be equally effective. In that case, they would soon cease to be laborers for hire, but would scatter themselves over our unbounded territory, to become independent land owners themselves. The cultivation of the soil on an extensive scale, can only be carried on where there are slaves, or in countries superabounding with free labor. No such operations are carried on in any portions of our own country where there are not slaves. Such are carried on in England, where there is an overflowing population and intense competition for employment. And our institutions seem suited to the exigencies of our respective situations. There, a much greater number of laborers is required at one season of the year than at another, and the farmer may enlarge or diminish the quantity of labor he employs, as circumstances may require. Here, about the same quantity of labor is required at every season, and the planter suffers no inconvenience from retaining his laborers throughout the year. Imagine an extensive rice or cotton plantation cultivated by free laborers, who might perhaps *strike* for an increase of wages, at a season when the neglect of a few days would insure the destruction of the whole crop. Even if it were possible to procure laborers at all, what planter would venture to carry on his operations under such circumstances? I need hardly say that these staples can not be produced to any extent where the proprietor of the soil cultivates it with his own hands. He can do little more than produce the necessary food for himself and his family.

And what would be the effect of putting an end to the cultivation of these staples, and thus annihilating, at a blow, two-thirds or three-fourths of our foreign commerce? Can any sane mind contemplate such a result without terror? I speak not of the utter poverty and misery to which we ourselves would be reduced, and the desolation which would overspread our own portion of the country. Our slavery has not only given existence to millions of slaves within our own territories, it has given the means of subsistence, and therefore existence, to millions of freemen in our confederate States; enabling them to send forth their swarms to overspread the plains and forests of the West, and appear as the harbingers of civilization. The products of the industry of those States are in general similar to those of the civilized world, and are little demanded in their markets. By exchanging them for ours, which are everywhere sought for, the people of these States are enabled to acquire all the products of art and industry, all that contributes to convenience or luxury, or gratifies the taste or the intellect, which the rest of the world can supply. Not only on our own continent, but on the other, it has given existence to hundreds of thousands, and the means of comfortable subsistence to millions. A distinguished citizen of our own State, than whom none can be better qualified to form an opinion, has lately stated that our great staple, cotton, has contributed more than any thing else of later times to the progress of civilization. By enabling the poor to obtain cheap and becoming clothing, it has inspired a taste for comfort, the first stimulus to civilization. Does not *self-defense*, then, demand of us steadily to resist the abrogation of that which is productive of so much good? It is more than self-defense. It is to defend millions of human beings, who are far removed from us, from the intensest suffering, if not from being struck out of existence. It is the defense of human civilization.

But this is but a small part of the evil which would be occasioned. After President Dew, it is unnecessary to say a single word on the practicability of colonizing our slaves. The two races, so widely separated from each other by the impress of nature, must remain together in the same country. Whether it be accounted the result of prejudice or reason, it is certain that the two races will not be blended together so as to form a homogenous population. To one who knows any thing of the nature of man and human society, it would be unnecessary to argue that this state of things can not continue; but that one race must be driven out by the other, or exterminated, or again enslaved. I have argued on the supposition that the emancipated negroes would be as efficient as other free laborers. But whatever theorists, who know nothing of the matter, may think proper to assume, we well know that this would not be so. We know that nothing but the coercion of slavery can overcome their propensity to indolence, and that not one in ten would be an efficient laborer. Even if this disposition were not grounded in their nature, it would be a result of their position. I have somewhere seen it observed, that to be degraded by opinion, is a thousand fold worse, so far as the feelings of the individuals are concerned, than to be degraded by the laws. *They* would be thus degraded, and this feeling is incompatible with habits of order and industry. Half our population would at once be paupers. Let an inhabitant of New-York or Philadelphia conceive of the situation of their respective States, if one-half of their population consisted of free negroes. The tie which now connects them, being broken, the different races would be estranged from each other, and hostility would grow up between them. Having the command of their own time and actions, they could more effectually combine insurrection, and provide the means of rendering it formidable. Released from the vigilant superintendence which now restrains them, they would infallibly be led from petty to greater crimes, until all life and property would be rendered insecure. Aggression would beget retaliation, until open war—and that a war of extermination—were established. From the still remaining superiority of the white race, it is probable that they would be the victors, and if they did not exterminate, they must again reduce the others to slavery—when they could be no longer fit to be either slaves or freemen. It is not only in self-defense, in defense of our country and of all that is dear to us, but in defense of the slaves themselves, that we refuse to emancipate them.

If we suppose them to have political privileges, and to be admitted to the elective franchise, still worse results may be expected.[251] It is hardly necessary to add any thing to what has been said by Mr. Paulding on this subject who has treated it fully. It is already known, that if there be a class unfavorably distinguished by any peculiarity from the rest of society, this distinction forms a tie which binds them to act in concert, and they exercise more than their due share of political power and influence—and still more, as they are of inferior character and looser moral principle. Such a class form the very material for demogogues to work with. Other parties court them, and concede to them. So it would be with the free blacks in the case supposed. They would be used by unprincipled politicians, of irregular ambition, for the advancement of their schemes, until they should give them political power and importance beyond even their own intentions. They would be courted by excited parties in their contests with each other. At some time, they may perhaps attain political ascendancy, and this is more probable, as we may suppose that there will have been a great emigration of whites from the country. Imagine the government of such legislators. Imagine then the sort of laws that will be passed, to confound the invidious distinction which has been so long assumed over them, and, if possible, to obliterate the very memory of it. These will be resisted. The blacks will be tempted to avenge themselves by oppression and proscription of the white race, for their long superiority. Thus matters will go on, until universal anarchy, or kakistocracy, the government of the worst, is fully established. I am persuaded that if the spirit of evil should devise to send abroad upon the earth all possible misery, discord, horror, and atrocity, he could contrive no scheme so effectual as the emancipation of negro slaves within our country.

The most feasible scheme of emancipation, and that which I verily believe would involve the least danger and sacrifice, would be that the *entire* white population should emigrate, and abandon the country to their slaves. Here would be triumph to philanthropy. This wide and fertile region would be again restored to ancient barbarism—to the worst of all barbarism—barbarism corrupted and depraved by intercourse with civilization. And this is the consummation to be wished, upon a *speculation*, that in some distant future age, they may become so enlightened and improved, as to be capable of sustaining a position among the civilized races of the earth. But I believe moralists allow men to defend their homes and their country, even at the expense of the lives and liberties of others.

Will any philanthropist say that the evils, of which I have spoken, would be brought about only by the obduracy, prejudices, and overweening self-estimation of the whites in refusing to blend the races by marriage, and so create a homogenous population?[252] But what, if it be not prejudice, but truth, and nature, and right reason, and just moral feeling? As I have before said, throughout the whole of nature, like attracts like, and that which is unlike repels. What is it that makes so unspeakably loathsome, crimes not to be named, and hardly alluded to? Even among the nations of Europe, so nearly homogenous, there are some peculiarities of form and feature, mind and character, which may be generally distinguished by those accustomed to observe them. Though the exceptions are numerous, I will venture to say that not in one instance in a hundred, is the man of sound and unsophisticated tastes and propensities so likely to be attracted by the female of a foreign stock, as by one of his own, who is more nearly conformed to himself. Shakspeare spoke the language of nature, when he made the senate and people of Venice attribute to the effect of witchcraft, Desdemona's passion for Othello—though, as Coleridge has said, we are to conceive of him not as a negro, but as a high bred Moorish chief.

If the negro race, as I have contended, be inferior to our own in mind and character, marked by inferiority of form and features, then ours would suffer deterioration from such intermixture. What would be thought of the moral conduct of the parent who should voluntarily transmit disease, or fatuity, or deformity to his offspring? If man be the most perfect work of the Creator, and the civilized European man the most perfect variety of the human race, is he not criminal who would desecrate and deface God's fairest work; estranging it further from the image of himself, and conforming it more nearly to that of the brute? I have heard it said, as if it afforded an argument, that the African is as well satisfied of the superiority of his own complexion, form, and features, as we can be of ours. If this were true, as it is not, would any one be so recreant to his own civilization, as to say that his opinion ought to weigh against ours—that there is no universal standard of truth, and grace, and beauty—that the Hottentot Venus may perchance possess as great perfection of form as the Medicean? It is true, the licentious passions of men overcome the natural repugnance, and find transient gratification in intercourse with females of the other race. But this is a very different thing from making her the associate of life, the companion of the bosom and the hearth. Him who would contemplate such an alliance for himself, or regard it with patience, when proposed for a son, or daughter, or sister, we should esteem a degraded wretch—with justice, certainly, if he were found among ourselves—and the estimate would not be very different if he were found in Europe. It is not only in defense of ourselves, of our country, and of our own generation, that we refuse to emancipate our slaves, but to defend our posterity and race from degeneracy and degradation.

Are we not justified then in regarding as criminals, the fanatical agitators whose efforts are intended to bring about the evils I have described? It is sometimes said that their zeal is generous and disinterested, and that their motives may be praised, though their conduct be condemned. But I have little faith in the good motives of those who pursue bad ends. It is not for us to scrutinize the hearts of men, and we can only judge of them by the tendency of their actions. There is much truth in what was said by Coleridge. "I have never known a trader in philanthropy who was not wrong in heart somehow or other. Individuals so distinguished, are usually unhappy in their family relations—men not benevolent or beneficent to individuals, but almost hostile to them, yet lavishing money and labor and time on the race—the abstract notion." The prurient love of notoriety actuates some. There is much luxury in sentiment, especially if it can be indulged at the expense of others, and if there be added some share of envy or malignity, the temptation to indulgence is almost irresistible. But certainly they may be justly regarded as criminal, who obstinately shut their eyes and close their ears to all instruction with respect to the true nature of their actions.

It must be manifest to every man of sane mind that it is impossible for them to achieve ultimate success; even if every individual in our country, out of the limits of the slave-holding States, were united in their purposes. They can not have even the miserable triumph of St. Domingo—of advancing through scenes of atrocity, blood and massacre, to the restoration of barbarism. They may agitate and perplex the world for a time. They may excite to desperate attempts and particular acts of cruelty and horror, but these will always be suppressed or avenged at the expense of the objects of their truculent philanthropy. But short of this, they can hardly be aware of the extent of the mischief they perpetrate. As I have said, their opinions, by means to us inscrutable, do very generally reach our slave population. What human being, if unfavorably distinguished by outward circumstances, is not ready to believe when he is told that he is the victim of injustice? Is it not cruelty to make men restless and dissatisfied in their condition, when no effort of theirs can alter it? The greatest injury is done to their characters, as well as to their happiness. Even if no such feelings or designs should be entertained or conceived by the slave, they will be attributed to him by the master, and all his conduct scanned with a severe and jealous scrutiny. Thus distrust and aversion are established, where, but for mischievous interference, there would be confidence and good-will, and a sterner control is exercised over the slave who thus becomes the victim of his cruel advocates.[253]

An effect is sometimes produced on the minds of slaveholders, by the publications of the self-styled philanthropists, and their judgments staggered and consciences alarmed. It is natural that the oppressed should hate the oppressor. It is still more natural that the oppressor should hate his victim. Convince the master that he is doing injustice to his slave, and he at once begins to regard him with distrust and malignity. It is a part of the constitution of the human mind, that when circumstances of necessity or temptation induce men to continue in the practice of what they believe to be wrong, they become desperate and reckless of the degree of wrong. I have formerly heard of a master who accounted for his practicing much severity upon his slaves, and exacting from them an unusual degree of labor, by saying that the thing (slavery) was altogether wrong, and therefore it was well to make the greatest possible advantage out of it. This agitation occasions some slaveholders to hang more loosely on their country. Regarding the institution as of questionable character, condemned by the general opinion of the world, and one which must shortly come to an end, they hold themselves in readiness to make their escape from the evil which they anticipate. Some sell their slaves to new masters (always a misfortune to the slave) and remove themselves to other societies, of manners and habits uncongenial to their own. And though we may suppose that it is only the weak and the timid who are liable to be thus affected, still it is no less an injury and public misfortune. Society is kept in an unquiet and restless state, and every sort of improvement is retarded.

Some projectors suggest the education of slaves, with a view to prepare them for freedom—as if there were any method of a man's being educated to freedom, but by himself. The truth is, however, that supposing that they are shortly to be emancipated, and that they have the capacities of any other race, they are undergoing the very best education which it is possible to give. They are in the course of being taught habits of regular and patient industry, and this is the first lesson which is required. I suppose that their most zealous advocates would not desire that they should be placed in the high places of society immediately upon their emancipation, but that they should begin their course of freedom as laborers, and raise themselves afterward as their capacities and characters might enable them. But how little would what are commonly called the rudiments of education, add to their qualifications as laborers? But for the agitation which exists, however, their education would be carried further than this. There is a constant tendency in our society to extend the sphere of their employments, and consequently to give them the information which is necessary to the discharge of those employments. And this, for the most obvious reason, it promotes the master's interest. How much would it add to the value of a slave, that he should be capable of being employed as a clerk, or be able to make calculations as a mechanic? In consequence, however, of the fanatical spirit which has been excited, it has been thought necessary to repress this tendency by legislation, and to prevent their acquiring the knowledge of which they might make a dangerous use. If this spirit were put down, and we restored to the consciousness of security, this would be no longer necessary, and the process of which I have spoken would be accelerated. Whenever indications of superior capacity appeared in a slave, it would be cultivated; gradual improvement would take place, until they might be engaged in as various employments as they were among the ancients—perhaps even liberal ones. Thus, if in the adorable providence of God, at a time and in a manner which we can neither foresee nor conjecture, they are to be rendered capable of freedom and to enjoy it, they would be prepared for it in the best and most effectual, because in the most natural and gradual manner. But fanaticism hurries to its effect at once. I have heard it said, God does good, but it is by imperceptible degrees; the devil is permitted to do evil, and he does it in a hurry. The beneficent processes of nature are not apparent to the senses. You cannot see the plant grow, or the flower expand. The volcano, the earthquake, and the hurricane, do their work of desolation in a moment. Such would be the desolation, if the schemes of fanatics were permitted to have effect. They do all that in them lies to thwart the beneficent purposes of providence. The whole tendency of their efforts is to aggravate present suffering, and to cut off the chance of future improvement, and in all their bearings and results, have produced, and are likely to produce, nothing but "pure, unmixed, dephlegmated, defecated evil."

If Wilberforce or Clarkson were living, and it were inquired of them "can you be sure that you have promoted the happiness of a single human being?" I imagine that, if they considered conscientiously, they would find it difficult to answer in the affirmative. If it were asked "can you be sure that you have not been the cause of suffering, misery and death to thousands,"—when we recollect that they probably stimulated the exertions of the *amis des noirs* in France, and that through the efforts of these the horrors of St. Domingo were perpetrated—I think they must hesitate long to return a decided negative. It might seem cruel, if we could, to convince a man who has devoted his life to what he esteemed a good and generous purpose, that he has been doing only evil—that he has been worshiping a horrid fiend, in the place of the true God. But fanaticism is in no danger of being convinced.[254] It is one of the mysteries of our nature, and of the divine government, how utterly disproportioned to each other are the powers of doing evil and of doing good. The poorest and most abject instrument, that is utterly imbecile for any purpose of good, seems sometimes endowed with almost the powers of omnipotence for mischief. A mole may inundate a province—a spark from a forge may conflagrate a city—a whisper may separate friends—a rumor may convulse an empire—but when we would do benefit to our race or country, the purest and most chastened motives, the most patient thought and labor, with the humblest self-distrust, are hardly sufficient to assure us that the results may not disappoint our expectations, and that we may not do evil instead of good. But are we therefore to refrain from efforts to benefit our race and country? By no means: but these motives, this labor and self-distrust are the only conditions upon which we are permitted to hope for success. Very different indeed is the course of those whose precipitate and ignorant zeal would overturn the fundamental institutions of society, uproar its peace and endanger its security, in pursuit of a distant and shadowy good, of which they themselves have formed no definite conception—whose atrocious philosophy would sacrifice a generation—and more than one generation—for any hypothesis.

SLAVERY IN THE LIGHT OF POLITICAL SCIENCE.

BY

J. H. HAMMOND,

OF SOUTH CAROLINA.

J. H. Agnew

LETTER I

Statement of the Question—Slave Trade increased by the efforts made to suppress it—Title to Slaves, to Lands—Abstract Ideas—Is Slavery Sin?—Argument from the Old Testament—Argument from the New Testament—The "Higher Law"—Political Influence of Slavery—Free Labor Police—In war, Slavery is Strength—Code of Honor—Mercantile Credit—Religion and Education—Licentiousness and Purity—Economy of Slave Labor, and of Free Labor—Responsibility of Power—Kindness and Cruelty—Curtailment of Privileges—Punishment of Slaves, children and soldiers—Police of Slavery—Condition of Slaves—Condition of Free Laborers in England—Slavery a necessary condition of human Society—Moral Suasion of the Abolitionists—Coolie Labor—Results of Emancipation in the West Indies—Revival of the Slave Trade by Emancipationists—Results of Emancipation in the United States—Radicalism of the present Age.

SILVER BLUFF, (SO. CA.,) JANUARY 28, 1845.

SIR: I received, a short time ago, a letter from the Rev. Willoughby M. Dickinson, dated at your residence, "Playford Hall, near Ipswich, 26th November, 1844," in which was inclosed a copy of your Circular Letter, addressed to professing Christians in our Northern States, having no concern with slavery, and to others there. I presume that Mr. Dickinson's letter was written with your knowledge, and the document inclosed with your consent and approbation. I therefore feel that there is no impropriety in my addressing my reply directly to yourself, especially as there is nothing in Mr. Dickinson's communication requiring serious notice. Having abundant leisure, it will be a recreation to devote a portion of it to an examination and free discussion of the question of slavery as it exists in our Southern States: and since you have thrown down the gauntlet to me, I do not hesitate to take it up.

Familiar as you have been with the discussions of this subject in all its aspects, and under all the excitements it has occasioned for sixty years past, I may not be able to present much that will be new to you. Nor ought I to indulge the hope of materially affecting the opinions you have so long cherished, and so zealously promulgated. Still, time and experience have developed facts, constantly furnishing fresh tests to opinions formed sixty years since, and continually placing this great question in points of view, which could scarcely occur to the most consummate intellect even a quarter of a century ago: and which may not have occurred yet to those whose previous convictions, prejudices, and habits of thought, have thoroughly and permanently biased them to one fixed way of looking at the matter: while there are peculiarities in the operation of every social system, and special local as well as moral causes materially affecting it, which no one, placed at the distance you are from us, can fully comprehend or properly appreciate. Besides, it may be possibly, a novelty to you to encounter one who conscientiously believes the domestic slavery of these States to be not only an inexorable necessity for the present, but a moral and humane institution, productive of the greatest political and social advantages, and who is disposed, as I am, to defend it on these grounds.

I do not propose, however, to defend the African slave trade. That is no longer a question. Doubtless great evils arise from it as it has been, and is now conducted: unnecessary wars and cruel kidnapping in Africa: the most shocking barbarities in the middle passage: and perhaps a less humane system of slavery in countries continually supplied with fresh laborers at a cheap rate. The evils of it, however, it may be fairly presumed, are greatly exaggerated. And if I might judge of the truth of transactions stated as occurring in this trade, by that of those reported as transpiring among us, I should not hesitate to say, that a large proportion of the stories in circulation are unfounded, and most of the remainder highly colored.

On the passage of the Act of Parliament prohibiting this trade to British subjects rests, what you esteem, the glory of your life. It required twenty years of arduous agitation, and the intervening extraordinary political events, to convince your countrymen, and among the rest your pious king, of the expediency of the measure: and it is but just to say, that no one individual rendered more esessential service to the cause than you did. In reflecting on the subject, you can not but often ask yourself: What, after all, has been accomplished; how much human suffering has been averted; how many human beings have been rescued from transatlantic slavery? And on the answers you can give these questions, must in a great measure, I presume, depend the happiness of your life. In framing them, how frequently must you be reminded of the remark of Mr. Grosvenor, in one of the early debates upon the subject, which I believe you have yourself recorded, "that he had twenty objections to the abolition of the slave trade: the first was, *that it was impossible*—the rest he need not give." Can you say to yourself, or to the world, that this *first* objection of Mr. Grosvenor has been yet confuted? It was estimated at the commencement of your agitation in 1787, that forty-five thousand Africans were annually transported to America and the West Indies. And the mortality of the middle passage, computed by some at five, is now admitted not to have exceeded nine per cent. Notwithstanding your Act of Parliament, the previous abolition by the United States, and that all the powers in the world have subsequently prohibited this trade—some of the greatest of them declaring it piracy, and covering the African seas with armed vessels to prevent it—Sir Thomas Fowel Buxton, a coadjutor of yours, declared in 1840, that the number of Africans now annually sold into slavery beyond the sea, amounts, at the very least, to one hundred and fifty thousand souls; while the mortality of the middle passage has increased, in consequence of the measures taken to suppress the trade, to twenty-five or thirty per cent. And of the one hundred and fifty thousand slaves who have been captured and liberated by British men-of-war, since the passage of your Act, Judge Jay, an American abolitionist, asserts that one hundred thousand, or two-thirds, have perished between their capture and liberation. Does it not really seem that Mr. Grosvenor was a prophet? That though nearly all the "impossibilities" of 1787 have vanished, and become as familiar *facts* as our household customs, under the magic influence of steam, cotton, and universal peace, yet this wonderful prophecy still stands, defying time and the energy and genius of mankind. Thousands of valuable lives, and fifty millions of pounds sterling, have been thrown away by your government in fruitless attempts to overturn it. I hope you have not lived too long for your own happiness, though you have been spared to see that in spite of all your toils and those of your fellow laborers, and the accomplishment of all that human agency could do, the African slave trade has increased three-fold under your own eyes—more rapidly, perhaps, than any other ancient branch of commerce—and that your efforts to suppress it, have affected *nothing more* than a three-fold increase of its horrors. There is a God who rules this world—all-powerful—far-seeing: He does not permit his creatures to foil his designs. It is he who, for his all-wise, though to us often inscrutable purposes, throws "impossibilities" in the way of our fondest hopes and most strenuous exertions. Can you doubt this?

Experience having settled the point, that this trade *can not be abolished by the use of force*, and that blockading squadrons serve only to make it more profitable and more cruel, I am surprised that the attempt is persisted in, unless it serves as a cloak to other purposes. It would be far better than it now is, for the African, if the trade was free from all restrictions, and left to the mitigation and decay which time and competition would surely bring about. If kidnapping, both secretly, and by war made for the purpose, could be by any means prevented in Africa, the next greatest blessing you could bestow upon that country would be to transport its actual slaves in comfortable vessels across the Atlantic. Though they might be perpetual bondsmen, still they would emerge from darkness into light—from barbarism into civilization—from idolatry to Christianity—in short from death to life.

But let us leave the African slave trade, which has so signally defeated the *philanthropy* of the world, and turn to American slavery, to which you have now directed your attention, and against which a crusade has been preached as enthusiastic and ferocious as that of Peter the Hermit—destined, I believe, to be about as successful. And here let me say, there is a vast difference between the two, though you may not acknowledge it. The wisdom of ages has concurred in the justice and expediency of establishing rights by prescriptive use, however tortuous in their origin they may have been. You would deem a man insane, whose keen sense of equity would lead him to denounce your right to the lands you hold, and which perhaps you inherited from a long line of ancestry, because your title was derived from a Saxon or Norman conqueror, and your lands were originally wrested by violence from the vanquished Britons. And so would the New England abolitionists regard any one who would insist that he should restore his farm to the descendants of the slaughtered red men, to whom God had as clearly given it as he gave life and freedom to the kidnapped African. That time does not consecrate wrong, is a fallacy which all history exposes; and which the best and wisest men of all ages and professions of religious faith have practically denied. The means, therefore, whatever they may have been, by which the African race now in this country have been reduced to slavery, cannot affect us, since they are our property, as your land is yours, by inheritance or purchase and prescriptive right. You will say that man cannot hold *property in man*. The answer is, that he can and *actually does* hold property in his fellow all the world over, in a variety of forms, and *has always done so*. I will show presently his authority for doing it.

If you were to ask me whether I am an advocate of slavery in the abstract, I should probably answer, that I am not, according to my understanding of the question. I do not like to deal in abstractions. It seldom leads to any useful ends. There are few universal truths. I do not now remember any single moral truth universally acknowledged. We have no assurance that it is given to our finite understanding to comprehend abstract moral truth. Apart from revelation and the inspired writings, what ideas should we have even of God, salvation, and immortality? Let the heathen answer. Justice itself is impalpable as an abstraction, and abstract liberty the merest phantasy that ever amused the imagination. This world was made for man, and man for the world as it is. We ourselves, our relations with one another and with all matter, are real, not ideal. I might say that I am no more in favor of slavery in the abstract, than I am of poverty, disease, deformity, idiocy, or any other inequality in the condition of the human family; that I love perfection, and think I should enjoy a millennium such as God has promised. But what would it amount to? A pledge that I would join you to set about eradicating those apparently inevitable evils of our nature, in equalizing the condition of all mankind, consummating the perfection of our race, and introducing the millennium? By no means. To effect these things, belongs exclusively to a higher power. And it would be well for us to leave the Almighty to perfect his own works and fulfill his own covenants. Especially, as the history of the past shows how entirely futile all human efforts have proved, when made for the purpose of aiding him in carrying out even his revealed designs, and how invariably he has accomplished them by unconscious instruments, and in the face of human expectation. Nay more, that every attempt which has been made by fallible man to extort from the world obedience to his "abstract" notions of right and wrong, has been invariably attended with calamities dire, and extended just in proportion to the breadth and vigor of the movement. On slavery in the abstract, then, it would not be amiss to have as little as possible to say. Let us contemplate it as it is. And thus contemplating it, the first question we have to ask ourselves is, whether it is contrary to the will of God, as revealed to us in his Holy Scriptures—the only certain means given us to ascertain his will. If it is, then slavery is a sin. And I admit at once that every man is bound to set his face against it, and to emancipate his slaves, should he hold any.

Let us open these Holy Scriptures. In the twentieth chapter of Exodus, seventeenth verse, I find the following words: "Thou shalt not covet thy neighbor's house, thou shalt not covet thy neighbor's wife, nor his man-servant, nor his maid-servant, nor his ox, nor his ass, nor any thing that is thy neighbor's"—which is the tenth of those commandments that declare the essential principles of the great moral law delivered to Moses by God himself. Now, discarding all technical and verbal quibbling as wholly unworthy to be used in interpreting the word of God, what is the plain meaning, undoubted intent, and true spirit of this commandment? Does it not emphatically and explicitly forbid you to disturb your neighbor in the enjoyment of his property; and more especially of that which is here specifically mentioned as being lawfully, and by this commandment made sacredly his? Prominent in the catalogue stands his "man-servant and his maid-servant," who are thus distinctly *consecrated as his property*, and guaranteed to him for his exclusive benefit, in the most solemn manner. You attempt to avert the otherwise irresistible conclusion, that slavery was thus ordained by God, by declaring that the word "slave" is not used here, and is not to be found in the Bible, And I have seen many learned dissertations on this point from abolition pens. It is well known that both the Hebrew and Greek words translated "servant" in the Scriptures, means also, and most usually, "slave." The use of the one word, instead of the other, was a mere matter of taste with the translators of the Bible, as it has been with all the commentators and religions writers, the latter of whom have, I believe, for the most part, adopted the term "slave," or used both terms indiscriminately. If, then, these Hebrew and Greek words include the idea of both systems of servitude, the conditional and unconditional, they should, as the major includes the minor proposition, be always translated "slaves," unless the sense of the whole text forbids it. The real question, then is, what idea is intended to be conveyed by the words used in the commandment quoted? And it is clear to my mind, that as no limitation is affixed to them, and the express intention was to secure to mankind the peaceful enjoyment of every species of property, that the terms "men-servants and maid-servants" include all classes of servants, and establish a lawful, exclusive, and indefeasible interest equally in the "Hebrew brother who shall go out in the seventh year," and "the yearly hired servant," and "those purchased from the heathen round about," who were to be "bond-men forever," *as the property of their fellow-man*.

You cannot deny that there were among the Hebrews "bond-men forever." You cannot deny that God especially authorized his chosen people to purchase "bond-men forever" from the heathen, as recorded in the twenty-fifth chapter of Leviticus, and that they are there designated by the very Hebrew word used in the tenth commandment. Nor can you deny that a "BOND-MAN FOREVER" is a "SLAVE;" yet you endeavor to hang an argument of immortal consequence upon the wretched subterfuge, that the precise word "slave" is not to be found in the *translation* of the Bible. As if the translators were canonical expounders of the Holy Scriptures, and *their words*, not *God's meaning*, must be regarded as his revelation.

It is vain to look to Christ or any of his apostles to justify such blasphemous perversions of the word of God. Although slavery in its most revolting form was everywhere visible around them, no visionary notions of piety or philanthropy ever tempted them to gainsay the LAW, even to mitigate the cruel severity of the existing system. On the contrary, regarding slavery as an *established*, as well as *inevitable condition of human society*, they never hinted at such a thing as its termination on earth, any more than that "the poor may cease out of the land," which God affirms to Moses shall never be: and they exhort "all servants under the yoke" to "count their masters as worthy of all honor:" "to obey them in all things according to the flesh; not with eye-service as men-pleasers, but in singleness of heart, fearing God;" "not only the good and gentle, but also the froward:" "for what glory is it if when ye are buffeted for your faults ye shall take it patiently? but if when ye do well and suffer for it ye take it patiently, this is acceptable to God." St. Paul actually apprehended a run-away slave, and sent him to his master! Instead of deriving from the gospel any sanction for the work you have undertaken, it would be difficult to imagine sentiments and conduct more strikingly in contrast, than those of the apostles and the abolitionists.

It is impossible, therefore, to suppose that slavery is contrary to the will of God. It is equally absurd to say that American slavery differs in form or principle from that of the chosen people. *We accept the Bible terms as the definition of our slavery, and its precepts as the guide of our conduct.* We desire nothing more. Even the right to "buffet," which is esteemed so shocking, finds its express license in the gospel. 1 Peter ii. 20. Nay, what is more, God directs the Hebrews to "bore holes in the ears of their brothers" to *mark* them, when under certain circumstances they become *perpetual slaves.* Exodus xxi. 6.

I think, then, I may safely conclude, and I firmly believe, that American slavery is not only not a sin, but especially commanded by God through Moses, and approved by Christ through his apostles. And here I might close its defense; for what God ordains, and Christ sanctifies, should surely command the respect and toleration of man. But I fear there has grown up in our time a transcendental religion, which is throwing even transcendental philosophy into the shade—a religion too pure and elevated for the Bible; which seeks to erect among men a higher standard of morals than the Almighty has revealed, or our Saviour preached; and which is probably destined to do more to impede the extension of God's kingdom on earth than all the infidels who have ever lived. Error is error. It is as dangerous to deviate to the right hand as to the left. And when men, professing to be holy men, and who are by numbers so regarded, declare those things to be sinful which our Creator has expressly authorized and instituted, they do more to destroy his authority among mankind than the most wicked can effect, by proclaiming that to be innocent which he has forbidden. To this self-righteous and self-exalted class belong all the abolitionists whose writings I have read. With them it is no end of the argument to prove your propositions by the text of the Bible, interpreted according to its plain and palpable meaning, and as understood by all mankind for three thousand years before their time. They are more ingenious at construing and interpolating to accommodate it to their new-fangled and ethereal code of morals, than ever were Voltaire and Hume in picking it to pieces, to free the world from what they considered a delusion. When the abolitionists proclaim "man-stealing" to be a sin, and show me that it is so written down by God, I admit them to be right, and shudder at the idea of such a crime. But when I show them that to hold "bond-men forever" is ordained by God, *they deny the Bible, and set up in its place a law of their own making.* I must then cease to reason with them on this branch of the question. Our religion differs as widely as our manners. The great Judge in our day of final account must decide between us.

Turning from the consideration of slaveholding in its relations to man as an accountable being, let us examine it in its influence on his political and social state. Though, being foreigners to us, you are in no wise entitled to interfere with the civil institutions of this country, it has become quite common for your countrymen to decry slavery as an enormous political evil to us, and even to declare that our Northern States ought to withdraw from the Confedracy rather than continue to be contaminated by it. The American abolitionists appear to concur fully in these sentiments, and a portion, at least, of them are incessantly threatening to dissolve the Union. Nor should I be at all surprised if they succeed. It would not be difficult, in my opinion, to conjecture which region, the North or South, would suffer most by such an event. For one, I should not object, by any means, to cast my lot in a confederacy of States whose citizens might all be slaveholders.

I indorse without reserve the much abused sentiment of Governor M'Duffie, that "slavery is the corner-stone of our republican edifice;" while I repudiate, as ridiculously absurd, that much lauded but nowhere accredited dogma of Mr. Jefferson, that "all men are born equal."[255] No society has ever yet existed, and I have already incidentally quoted the highest authority to show that none ever will exist, without a natural variety of classes. The most marked of these must, in a country like ours, be the rich and the poor, the educated and the ignorant. It will scarcely be disputed that the very poor have less leisure to prepare themselves for the proper discharge of public duties than the rich; and that the ignorant are wholly unfit for them at all. In all countries save ours, these two classes, or the poor rather, who are presumed to be necessarily ignorant, are by law expressly excluded from all participation in the management of public affairs. In a Republican Government this can not be done. Universal suffrage, though not essential in theory, seems to be in fact a necessary appendage to a republican system. Where universal suffrage obtains, it is obvious that the government is in the hands of a numerical majority; and it is hardly necessary to say that in every part of the world more than half the people are ignorant and poor. Though no one can look upon poverty as a crime, and we do not here generally regard it as any objection to a man in his individual capacity, still it must be admitted that it is a wretched and insecure government which is administered by its most ignorant citizens, and those who have the least at stake under it. Though intelligence and wealth have great influence here, as everywhere, in keeping in check reckless and unenlightened numbers, yet it is evident to close observers, if not to all, that these are rapidly usurping all power in the non-slaveholding States, and threaten a fearful crisis in republican institutions there at no remote period. In the slaveholding States, however, nearly one-half of the whole population, and those the poorest and most ignorant, have no political influence whatever, because they are slaves. Of the other half, a large proportion are both educated and independent in their circumstances, while those who unfortunately are not so, being still elevated far above the mass, are higher toned and more deeply interested in preserving a stable and well-ordered government, than the same class in any other country. Hence, slavery is truly the "corner-stone" and foundation of every well-designed and durable "republican edifice."

With us every citizen is concerned in the maintenance of order, and in promoting honesty and industry among those of the lowest class who are our slaves; and our habitual vigilance renders standing armies, whether of soldiers or policemen, entirely unnecessary. Small guards in our cities, and occasional patrols in the country, insure us a repose and security known no where else. You can not be ignorant that, excepting the United States, there is no country in the world whose existing government would not be overturned in a month, but for its standing armies, maintained at an enormous and destructive cost to those whom they are destined to overawe—so rampant and combative is the spirit of discontent wherever nominal free labor prevails, with its extensive privileges and its dismal servitude. Nor will it be long before the "*free States*" of this Union will be compelled to introduce the same expensive machinery, to preserve order among their "free and equal" citizens. Already has Philadelphia organized a permanent battalion for this purpose; New York, Boston and Cincinnati will soon follow her example; and then the smaller towns and densely populated counties. The intervention of their militia to repress violations of the peace is becoming a daily affair. A strong government, after some of the old fashions—though probably with a new name—sustained by the force of armed mercenaries, is the ultimate destiny of the non-slaveholding section of this confederacy, and one which may not be very distant.

It is a great mistake to suppose, as is generally done abroad, that in case of war slavery would be a source of weakness. It did not weaken Rome, nor Athens, nor Sparta, though their slaves were comparatively far more numerous than ours, of the same color for the most part with themselves, and large numbers of them familiar with the use of arms. I have no apprehension that our slaves would seize such an opportunity to revolt. The present generation of them, born among us, would never think of such a thing at any time, unless instigated to it by others. Against such instigations we are always on our guard. In time of war we should be more watchful and better prepared to put down insurrections than at any other periods. Should any foreign nation be so lost to every sentiment of civilized humanity, as to attempt to erect among us the standard of revolt, or to invade us with black troops, for the base and barbarous purpose of stirring up servile war, their efforts would be signally rebuked. Our slaves could not be easily seduced, nor would any thing delight them more than to assist in stripping Cuffee of his regimentals to put him in the cotton-field, which would be the fate of most black invaders, without any very prolix form of "apprenticeship." If, as I am satisfied would be the case, our slaves remained peaceful on our plantations, and cultivated them in time of war under the superintendence of a limited number of our citizens, it is obvious that we could put forth more strength in such an emergency, at less sacrifice, than any other people of the same numbers. And thus we should in every point of view, "out of this nettle danger, pluck the flower safety."

How far slavery may be an advantage or disadvantage to those not owning slaves, yet united with us in political association, is a question for their sole consideration. It is true that our representation in Congress is increased by it. But so are our taxes; and the non-slaveholding States, being the majority, divide among themselves far the greater portion of the amount levied by the Federal Government. And I doubt not that, when it comes to a close calculation, they will not be slow in finding out that the balance of profit arising from the connection is vastly in their favor.

In a social point of view the abolitionists pronounce slavery to be a monstrous evil. If it was so, it would be our own peculiar concern, and superfluous benevolence in them to lament over it. Seeing their bitter hostility to us, they might leave us to cope with our own calamities. But they make war upon us out of excess of charity, and attempt to purify by covering us with calumny. You have read and assisted to circulate a great deal about affrays, duels and murders, occurring here, and all attributed to the terrible demoralization of slavery. Not a single event of this sort takes place among us, but it is caught up by the abolitionists, and paraded over the world, with endless comments, variations and exaggerations. You should not take what reaches you as a mere sample, and infer that there is a vast deal more you never hear. You hear all, and more than all, the truth.

It is true that the point of honor is recognized throughout the slave region, and that disputes of certain classes are frequently referred for adjustment, to the "trial by combat." It would not be appropriate for me to enter, in this letter, into a defense of the practice of duelling, nor to maintain at length, that it does not tarnish the character of a people to acknowledge a standard of honor. Whatever evils may arise from it, however, they can not be attributed to slavery, since the same custom prevails both in France and England. Few of your Prime Ministers, of the last half century even, have escaped the contagion, I believe. The affrays, of which so much is said, and in which rifles, bowie-knives and pistols are so prominent, occur mostly in the frontier States of the South-West. They are naturally incidental to the condition of society, as it exists in many sections of these recently settled countries, and will as naturally cease in due time. Adventurers from the older States, and from Europe, as desperate in character as they are in fortune, congregate in these wild regions, jostling one another and often forcing the peaceable and honest into rencontres in self-defense. Slavery has nothing to do with these things. Stability and peace are the first desires of every slaveholder, and the true tendency of the system. It could not possibly exist amid the eternal anarchy and civil broils of the ancient Spanish dominions in America. And for this very reason, domestic slavery has ceased there. So far from encouraging strife, such scenes of riot and bloodshed, as have within the last few years disgraced our Northern cities, and as you have lately witnessed in Birmingham and Bristol and Wales, not only never have occurred, but I will venture to say, never will occur in our slaveholding States. The only thing that can create a mob (as you might call it) here, is the appearance of an abolitionist, whom the people assemble to chastise. And this is no more of a mob, than a rally of shepherds to chase a wolf out of their pastures would be one.

But we are swindlers and repudiators? Pennsylvania is not a slave State. A majority of the States which have failed to meet their obligations punctually are non-slaveholding; and two-thirds of the debt said to be repudiated is owed by these States. Many of the States of this Union are heavily encumbered with debt—none so hopelessly as England. Pennsylvania owes $22 for each inhabitant—England $222, counting her paupers in. Nor has there been any repudiation definite and final, of a lawful debt, that I am aware of. A few States have failed to pay some installments of interest. The extraordinary financial difficulties which occurred a few years ago will account for it. Time will set all things right again. Every dollar of both principal and interest, owed by any State, North or South, will be ultimately paid, *unless the abolition of slavery overwhelms us all in one common ruin.* But have no other nations failed to pay? When were the French Assignats redeemed? How much interest did your National Bank pay on its immense circulation, from 1797 to 1821, during which period that circulation was inconvertible, and for the time *repudiated?* How much of your national debt has been incurred for money borrowed to meet the interest on it, thus avoiding delinquency in detail, by insuring inevitable bankruptcy and repudiation in the end? And what sort of operation was that by which your present Ministry recently expunged a handsome amount of that debt, by substituting, through a process just not compulsory, one species of security for another? I am well aware that the faults of others do not excuse our own, but when failings are charged to slavery, which are shown to occur to equal extent where it does not exist, surely slavery must be acquitted of the accusation.

It is roundly asserted, that we are not so well educated nor so religious here as elsewhere. I will not go into tedious statistical statements on these subjects. Nor have I, to tell the truth, much confidence in the details of what are commonly set forth as statistics. As to education, you will probably admit that slaveholders should have more leisure for mental culture than most people. And I believe it is charged against them, that they are peculiarly fond of power, and ambitious of honors. If this be so, as all the power and honors of this country are won mainly by intellectual superiority, it might be fairly presumed, that slaveholders would not be neglectful of education. In proof of the accuracy of this presumption, I point you to the facts, that our Presidential chair has been occupied for forty-four out of fifty-six years, by slaveholders; that another has been recently elected to fill it for four more, over an opponent who was a slaveholder also; and that in the Federal Offices and both Houses of Congress, considerably more than a due proportion of those acknowledged to stand in the first rank are from the South. In this arena, the intellects of the free and slave States meet in full and fair competition. Nature must have been unusually bountiful to us, or we have been at least reasonably assiduous in the cultivation of such gifts as she has bestowed—unless indeed you refer our superiority to moral qualities, which I am sure *you* will not. More wealthy we are not; nor would mere wealth avail in such rivalry.

The piety of the South is inobtrusive. We think it proves but little, though it is a confident thing for a man to claim that he stands higher in the estimation of his Creator, and is less a sinner than his neighbor. If vociferation is to carry the question of religion, the North, and probably the Scotch, have it. Our sects are few, harmonious, pretty much united among themselves, and pursue their avocations in humble peace. In fact, our professors of religion seem to think—whether correctly or not—that it is their duty "to do good in secret," and to carry their holy comforts to the heart of each individual, without reference to class *or color*, for his special enjoyment, and not with a view to exhibit their zeal before the world. So far as numbers are concerned, I believe our clergymen, when called on to make a showing, have never had occasion to blush, if comparisons were drawn between the free and slave States. And although our presses do not teem with controversial pamphlets, nor our pulpits shake with excommunicating thunders, the daily walk of our religious communicants furnishes, apparently, as little food for gossip as is to be found in most other regions. It may be regarded as a mark of our want of excitability—though that is a quality accredited to us in an eminent degree—that few of the remarkable religious *Isms* of the present day have taken root among us. We have been so irreverent as to laugh at Mormonism and Millerism, which have created such commotions further North; and modern prophets have no honor in our country. Shakers, Rappists, Dunkers, Socialists, Fourrierists, and the like, keep themselves afar off. Even Puseyism has not yet moved us. You may attribute this to our domestic slavery if you choose. I believe you would do so justly. There is no material here for such characters to operate upon.

But your grand charge is, that licentiousness in intercourse between the sexes, is a prominent trait of our social system, and that it necessarily arises from slavery. This is a favorite theme with the abolitionists, male and female. Folios have been written on it. It is a common observation, that there is no subject on which ladies of eminent virtue so much delight to dwell, and on which in especial learned old maids, like Miss Martineau, linger with such an insatiable relish. They expose it in the slave States with the most minute observance and endless iteration. Miss Martineau, with peculiar gusto, relates a series of scandalous stories, which would have made Boccacio jealous of her pen, but which are so ridiculously false as to leave no doubt, that some wicked wag, knowing she would write a book, has furnished her materials—a game too often played on tourists in this country. The constant recurrence of the female abolitionists to this topic, and their bitterness in regard to it, cannot fail to suggest to even the most charitable mind, that

"Such rage without betrays the fires within."

Nor are their immaculate coadjutors of the other sex, though perhaps less specific in their charges, less violent in their denunciations. But recently in your island, a clergyman has, at a public meeting, stigmatized the whole slave region as a "brothel." Do these people thus cast stones, being "without sin?" Or do they only

"Compound for sins they are inclined to
By damning those they have no mind to."

Alas that David and Solomon should be allowed to repose in peace—that Leo should be almost canonized, and Luther more than sainted—that in our own day courtezans should be formally licensed in Paris, and tenements in London rented for years to women of the town for the benefit of the church, with the knowledge of the bishop—and the poor slave States of America alone pounced upon, and offered up as a holocaust on the altar of immaculateness, to atone for the abuse of natural instinct by all mankind; and if not actually consumed, at least exposed, anathematized and held up to scorn, by those who

"Write,
Or with a rival's or an eunuch's spite."

But I do not intend to admit that this charge is just or true. Without meaning to profess uncommon modesty, I will say that I wish the topic could be avoided. I am of opinion, and I doubt not every right-minded man will concur, that the public exposure and discussion of this vice, even to rebuke, invariably does more harm than good; and that if it cannot be checked by instilling pure and virtuous sentiments, it is far worse than useless to attempt to do it, by exhibiting its deformities. I may not, however, pass it over; nor ought I to feel any delicacy in examining a question, to which the slaveholder is invited and challenged by clergymen and virgins. So far from allowing, then, that licentiousness pervades this region, I broadly assert, and I refer to the records of our courts, to the public press, and to the knowledge of all who have ever lived here, that among our white population there are fewer cases of divorce, separation, crim. con., seduction, rape and bastardy, than among any other five millions of people on the civilized earth. And this fact I believe will be conceded by the abolitionists of this country themselves. I am almost willing to refer it to them and submit to their decision on it. I would not hesitate to do so, if I thought them capable of an impartial judgment on any matter where slavery is in question. But it is said, that the licentiousness consists in the constant intercourse between white males and colored females. One of your heavy charges against us has been, that we regard and treat those people as brutes; you now charge us with habitually taking them to our bosoms. I will not comment on the inconsistency of these accusations. I will not deny that some intercourse of the sort does take place. Its character and extent, however, are grossly and atrociously exaggerated. No authority, divine or human, has yet been found sufficient to arrest all such irregularities among men. But it is a known fact, that they are perpetrated here, for the most part, in the cities. Very few mulattoes are reared on our plantations. In the cities, a large proportion of the inhabitants do not own slaves. A still larger proportion are natives of the North, or foreigners. They should share, and justly, too, an equal part in this sin with the slaveholders. Facts cannot be ascertained, or I doubt not, it would appear that they are the chief offenders. If the truth be otherwise, then persons from abroad have stronger prejudices against the African race than we have. Be this as it may, it is well known, that this intercourse is regarded in our society as highly disreputable. If carried on habitually, it seriously affects a man's standing, so far as it is known; and he who takes a colored mistress—with rare and extraordinary exceptions—loses caste at once. You will say that *one* exception should damn our whole country. How much less criminal is it to take a white mistress? In your eyes it should be at least an equal offense. Yet look around you at home, from the cottage to the throne, and count how many mistresses are kept in unblushing notoriety, without loss of caste. Such cases are nearly unknown here, and down even to the lowest walks of life, it is almost invariably fatal to a man's position and prospects to keep a mistress openly, whether white or black. What Miss Martineau relates of a young man's purchasing a colored concubine from a lady, and avowing his designs, is too absurd even for contradiction. No person would dare to allude to such a subject, in such a manner, to any decent female in this country.

After all, however, the number of the mixed breed, in proportion to that of the black, is infinitely small, and out of the towns next to nothing. And when it is considered that the African race has been among us for two hundred years, and that those of the mixed breed continually intermarry—often rearing large families—it is a decided proof of our continence, that so few comparatively are to be found. Our misfortunes are two-fold. From the prolific propagation of these mongrels among themselves, we are liable to be charged by tourists with delinquencies where none have been committed, while, where one has been, it cannot be concealed. Color marks indelibly the offense, and reveals it to every eye. Conceive that, even in your virtuous and polished country, if every bastard, through all the circles of your social system, was thus branded by nature and known to all, what shocking developments might there not be! How little indignation might your saints have to spare for the licentiousness of the slave region. But I have done with this disgusting topic. And I think I may justly conclude, after all the scandalous charges which tea-table gossip, and long-gowned hypocrisy have brought against the slaveholders, that a people whose men are proverbially brave, intellectual and hospitable, and whose women are unaffectedly chaste, devoted to domestic life, and happy in it, can neither be degraded nor demoralized, whatever their institutions may be. My decided opinion is, that our system of slavery contributes largely to the development and culture of those high and noble qualities.

In an economical point of view—which I will not omit—slavery presents some difficulties. As a general rule, I agree it must be admitted, that free labor is cheaper than slave labor. It is a fallacy to suppose that ours is *unpaid labor*. The slave himself must be paid for, and thus his labor is all purchased at once, and for no trifling sum. His price was, in the first place, paid mostly to your countrymen, and assisted in building up some of those colossal English fortunes, since illustrated by patents of nobility, and splendid piles of architecture, stained and cemented, if you like the expression, with the blood of kidnapped innocents; but loaded with no heavier curses than abolition and its begotten fanaticisms have brought upon your land—some of them fulfilled, some yet to be. But besides the first cost of the slave, he must be fed and clothed, well fed and well clothed, if not for humanity's sake, that he may do good work, retain health and life, and rear a family to supply his place. When old or sick, he is a clear expense, and so is the helpless portion of his family. No poor law provides for him when unable to work, or brings up his children for our service when we need them. These are all heavy charges on slave labor. Hence, in all countries where the denseness of the population has reduced it to a matter of perfect certainty, that labor can be obtained, whenever wanted, and the laborer be forced, by sheer necessity, to hire for the smallest pittance that will keep soul and body together, and rags upon his back while in actual employment—dependent at all other times on alms or poor rates—in all such countries it is found cheaper to pay this pittance, than to clothe, feed, nurse, support through childhood, and pension in old age, a race of slaves. Indeed, the advantage is so great as speedily to compensate for the loss of the value of the slave. And I have no hesitation in saying, that if I could cultivate my lands on these terms, I would, without a word, resign my slaves, provided they could be properly disposed of. But the question is, whether free or slave labor is cheapest to us in this country, at this time, situated as we are. And it is decided at once by the fact that we can not avail ourselves of any other than slave labor. We neither have, nor can we procure, other labor to any extent, or on any thing like the terms mentioned. We must, therefore, content ourselves with our dear labor, under the consoling reflection that what is lost to us, is gained to humanity; and that, inasmuch as our slave costs us more than your free men costs you, by so much is he better off. You will promptly say, emancipate your slaves, and then you will have free labor on suitable terms. That might be if there were five hundred where there now is one, and the continent, from the Atlantic to the Pacific, was as densely populated as your Island. But until that comes to pass, no labor can be procured in America on the terms you have it.

While I thus freely admit that to the individual proprietor slave labor is dearer than free, I do not mean to admit as equally clear that it is dearer to the community and to the State. Though it is certain that the slave is a far greater consumer than your laborer, the year round, yet your pauper system is costly and wasteful. Supported by your community at large, it is not administered by your hired agents with that interested care and economy—not to speak of humanity—which mark the management of ours, by each proprietor, for his own non-effectives; and is both more expensive to those who pay, and less beneficial to those who receive its bounties. Besides this, slavery is rapidly filling up our country with a hardy and healthy race, peculiarly adapted to our climate and productions, and conferring signal political and social advantages on us as a people, to which I have already referred.

I have yet to reply to the main ground on which you and your coadjutors rely for the overthrow of our system of slavery. Failing in all your attempts to prove that it is sinful in its nature, immoral in its effects, a political evil, and profitless to those who maintain it, you appeal to the sympathies of mankind, and attempt to arouse the world against us by the most shocking charges of tyranny and cruelty. You begin by a vehement denunciation of "the irresponsible power of one man over his fellow men." The question of the responsibility of power is a vast one. It is the great political question of modern times. Whole nations divide off upon it and establish different fundamental systems of government. That "responsibility," which to one set of millions seems amply sufficient to check the government, to the support of which they devote their lives and fortunes, appears to another set of millions a mere mockery of restraint. And accordingly as the opinions of these millions differ, they honor each other with the epithets of "serfs" or "anarchists." It is ridiculous to introduce such an idea as this into the discussion of a mere domestic institution; but since you have introduced it, I deny that the power of the slaveholder in America is "irresponsible." He is responsible to God. He is responsible to the world—a responsibility which abolitionists do not intend to allow him to evade—and in acknowledgment of which, I write you this letter. He is responsible to the community in which he lives, and to the laws under which he enjoys his civil rights. Those laws do not permit him to kill, to maim, or to punish beyond certain limits, or to overtask, or to refuse to feed and clothe his slave. In short, they forbid him to be tyrannical or cruel. If any of these laws have grown obsolete, it is because they are so seldom violated, that they are forgotten. You have disinterred one of them, from a compilation by some Judge Stroud of Philadelphia, to stigmatize its inadequate penalties for killing, maiming, etc. Your object appears to be—you can have no other—to produce the impression, that it must be often violated on account of its insufficiency. You say as much, and that it marks our estimate of the slave. You forget to state that this law was enacted by *Englishmen*, and only indicates *their* opinion of the reparation due for these offenses. Ours is proved by the fact, though perhaps unknown to Judge Stroud or yourself, that we have essentially altered this law; and the murder of a slave has for many years been punishable with death in this State. And so it is, I believe, in most or all of the slave States. You seem well aware, however, that laws have been recently passed in all these States, making it penal to teach slaves to read. Do you know what occasioned their passage, and renders their stringent enforcement necessary? I can tell you. It was the abolition agitation. If the slave is not allowed to read his Bible, the sin rests upon the abolitionists; for they stand prepared to furnish him with a key to it, which would make it, not a book of hope, and love, and peace, but of despair, hatred and blood; which would convert the reader, not into a Christian, but a demon. To preserve him from such a horrid destiny, it is a sacred duty which we owe to our slaves, not less than to ourselves, to interpose the most decisive means. If the Catholics deem it wrong to trust the Bible to the hands of ignorance, shall we be excommunicated because we will not give it, and with it the corrupt and fatal commentaries of the abolitionists, to our slaves? Allow our slaves to read your writings, stimulating them to cut our throats! Can you believe us to be such unspeakable fools?

I do not know that I can subscribe in full to the sentiment so often quoted by the abolitionists, and by Mr. Dickinson in his letter to me: "*Homo sum humani nihil a me alienum puto*," as translated and practically illustrated by them. Such a doctrine would give wide authority to every one for the most dangerous intermeddling with the affairs of others. It will do in poetry—perhaps in some sorts of philosophy—but the attempt to make it a household maxim, and introduce it into the daily walks of life, has caused many a "homo" a broken crown; and probably will continue to do it. Still, though a slaveholder, I freely acknowledge my obligations as a man; and that I am bound to treat humanely the fellow-creatures whom God has intrusted to my charge. I feel, therefore, somewhat sensitive under the accusation of cruelty, and disposed to defend myself and fellow-slaveholders against it. It is certainly the interest of all, and I am convinced that it is also the desire of every one of us, to treat our slaves with proper kindness. It is necessary to our deriving the greatest amount of profit from them. Of this we are all satisfied. And you snatch from us the only consolation we Americans could derive from the opprobrious imputation of being wholly devoted to making money, which your disinterested and gold-despising countrymen delight to cast upon us, when you nevertheless declare that we are ready to sacrifice it for the pleasure of being inhuman. You remember that Mr. Pitt could not get over the idea that self-interest would insure kind treatment to slaves, until you told him your woful stories of the middle passage. Mr. Pitt was right in the first instance, and erred, under your tuition, in not perceiving the difference between a temporary and permanent ownership of them. Slaveholders are no more perfect than other men. They have passions. Some of them, as you may suppose, do not at all times restrain them. Neither do husbands, parents and friends. And in each of these relations, as serious suffering as frequently arises from uncontrolled passions, as ever does in that of master and slave, and with as little chance of indemnity. Yet you would not on that account break them up. I have no hesitation in saying that our slaveholders are kind masters, as men usually are kind husbands, parents and friends—as a general rule, kinder. A bad master—he who overworks his slaves, provides ill for them, or treats them with undue severity—loses the esteem and respect of his fellow-citizens to as great an extent as he would for the violation of any of his social and most of his moral obligations. What the most perfect plan of management would be, is a problem hard to solve. From the commencement of slavery in this country, this subject has occupied the minds of all slaveholders, as much as the improvement of the general condition of mankind has those of the most ardent philanthropists; and the greatest progressive amelioration of the system has been effected. You yourself acknowledge that in the early part of your career you were exceedingly anxious for the *immediate* abolition of the slave trade, lest those engaged in it should so mitigate its evils as to destroy the force of your arguments and facts. The improvement you then *dreaded* has gone on steadily here, and would doubtless have taken place in the slave trade, but for the measures adopted to suppress it.

Of late years we have not only been annoyed, but greatly embarrassed in this matter, by the abolitionists. We have been compelled to curtail some privileges; we have been debarred from granting new ones. In the face of discussions which aim at loosening all ties between master and slave, we have in some measure to abandon our efforts to attach them to us, and control them through their affections and pride. We have to rely more and more on the power of fear. We must, in all our intercourse with them, assert and maintain strict mastery, and impress it on them that they are slaves. This is painful to us, and certainly no present advantage to them. But it is the direct consequence of the abolition agitation. We are determined to continue masters, and to do so we have to draw the rein tighter and tighter day by day to be assured that we hold them in complete check. How far this process will go on, depends wholly and solely on the abolitionists. When they desist, we can relax. We may not before. I do not mean by all this to say that we are in a state of actual alarm and fear of our slaves; but under existing circumstances we should be ineffably stupid not to increase our vigilance and strengthen our hands. You see some of the fruits of your labors. I speak freely and candidly—not as a colonist, who, though a slaveholder, has a master; but as a free white man, holding, under God, and resolved to hold, my fate in my own hands; and I assure you that my sentiments, and feelings, and determinations, are those of every slaveholder in this country.

The research and ingenuity of the abolitionists, aided by the invention of run-away slaves—in which faculty, so far as improvizing falsehood goes, the African race is without a rival—have succeeded in shocking the world with a small number of pretended instances of our barbarity. The only wonder is, that considering the extent of our country, the variety of our population, its fluctuating character, and the publicity of all our transactions, the number of cases is so small. It speaks well for us. Yet of these, many are false, all highly colored, some occurring half a century, most of them many years ago; and no doubt a large proportion of them perpetrated by foreigners. With a few rare exceptions, the emigrant Scotch and English are the worst masters among us, and next to them our Northern fellow-citizens. Slaveholders born and bred here are always more humane to slaves, and those who have grown up to a large inheritance of them, the most so of any— showing clearly that the effect of the system is to foster kindly feelings. I do not mean so much to impute innate inhumanity to foreigners, as to show that they come here with false notions of the treatment usual and necessary for slaves, and that newly acquired power here, as everywhere else, is apt to be abused. I cannot enter into a detailed examination of the cases stated by the abolitionists. It would be disgusting, and of little avail. I know nothing of them. I have seen nothing like them, though born and bred here, and have rarely heard of any thing at all to be compared to them. Permit me to say that I think most of *your* facts must have been drawn from the West Indies, where undoubtedly slaves were treated much more harshly than with us. This was owing to a variety of causes, which might, if necessary, be stated. One was, that they had at first to deal more extensively with barbarians fresh from the wilds of Africa; another, and a leading one, the absenteeism of proprietors. Agents are always more unfeeling than owners, whether placed over West Indian or American slaves, or Irish tenantry. We feel this evil greatly even here. You describe the use of *thumb screws*, as one mode of punishment among us. I doubt if a thumb screw can be found in America. I never saw or heard of one in this country. Stocks are rarely used by private individuals, and confinement still more seldom, though both are common punishments for whites, all the world over. I think they should be more frequently resorted to with slaves, as substitutes for flogging, which I consider the most injurious and least efficacious mode of punishing them for serious offenses. It is not degrading, and unless excessive, occasions little pain. You may be a little astonished, after all the flourishes that have been made about "cart whips," etc., when I say flogging is not the most degrading punishment in the world. It may be so to a white man in most countries, but how is it to the white boy? That necessary coadjutor of the schoolmaster, the "birch," is never thought to have rendered infamous the unfortunate victim of pedagogue ire; nor did Solomon in his wisdom dream that he was counseling parents to debase their offspring, when he exhorted them not to spoil the child by sparing the rod. Pardon me for recurring to the now exploded ethics of the Bible. Custom, which, you will perhaps agree, makes most things in this world good or evil, has removed all infamy from the punishment of the lash to the slave. Your blood boils at the recital of stripes inflicted on a man; and you think you should be frenzied to see your own child flogged. Yet see how completely this is ideal, arising from the fashions of society. You doubtless submitted to the rod yourself, in other years, when the smart was perhaps as severe as it would be now; and you have never been guilty of the folly of revenging yourself on the Preceptor, who, in the plenitude of his "irresponsible power," thought proper to chastise your son. So it is with the negro, and the negro father.

As to chains and irons, they are rarely used; never, I believe, except in cases of running away. You will admit that if we pretend to own slaves, they must not be permitted to abscond whenever they see fit; and that if nothing else will prevent it, these means must be resorted to. See the inhumanity necessarily arising from slavery, you will exclaim. Are such restraints imposed on no other class of people, giving no more offense? Look to your army and navy. If your seamen, impressed from their peaceful occupations, and your soldiers, recruited at the gin-shops—both of them as much kidnapped as the most unsuspecting victim of the slave trade, and doomed to a far more wretched fate—if these men manifest a propensity to desert, the heaviest manacles are their mildest punishment. It is most commonly death, after summary trial. But armies and navies, you say, are indispensable, and must be kept up at every sacrifice. I answer, that they are no more indispensable than slavery is to us—and to *you;* for you have enough of it in your country, though the form and name differ from ours.

Depend upon it that many things, and in regard to our slaves, most things which appear revolting at a distance, and to slight reflection, would, on a nearer view and impartial comparison with the customs and conduct of the rest of mankind, strike you in a very different light. Remember that on our estates we dispense with the whole machinery of public police and public courts of justice. Thus we try, decide, and execute the sentences, in thousands of cases, which in other countries would go into the courts. Hence, most of the acts of our alleged cruelty, which have any foundation in truth. Whether our patriarchal mode of administering justice is less humane than the Assizes, can only be determined by careful inquiry and comparison. But this is never done by the abolitionists. All our punishments are the outrages of "irresponsible power." If a man steals a pig in England, he is transported—torn from wife, children, parents, and sent to the antipodes, infamous, and an outcast forever, though probably he took from the superabundance of his neighbor to save the lives of his famishing little ones. If one of our well fed negroes, merely for the sake of fresh meat, steals a pig, he gets perhaps forty stripes. If one of your cottagers breaks into another's house, he is hung for burglary. If a slave does the same here, a few lashes, or it may be, a few hours in the stocks, settles the matter. Are our courts or yours the most humane? If slavery were not in question, you would doubtless say ours is mistaken lenity. Perhaps it often is; and slaves too lightly dealt with sometimes grow daring. Occasionally, though rarely, and almost always in consequence of excessive indulgence, an individual rebels. This is the highest crime he can commit. It is treason. It strikes at the root of our whole system. His life is justly forfeited, though it is never intentionally taken, unless after trial in our public courts. Sometimes, however, in capturing, or in self-defense, he is unfortunately killed. A legal investigation always follows. But, terminate as it may, the abolitionists raise a hue and cry, and another "shocking case" is held up to the indignation of the world by tender-hearted male and female philanthropists, who would have thought all right had the master's throat been cut, and would have triumphed in it.

I cannot go into a detailed comparison between the penalties inflicted on a slave in our patriarchal courts, and those of the Courts of Sessions, to which freemen are sentenced in all civilized nations; but I know well that if there is any fault in our criminal code, it is that of excessive mildness.

Perhaps a few general facts will best illustrate the treatment this race receives at our hands. It is acknowledged that it increases at least as rapidly as the white. I believe it is an established law, that population thrives in proportion to its comforts. But when it is considered that these people are not recruited by immigration from abroad, as the whites are, and that they are usually settled on our richest and least healthy lands, the fact of their equal comparative increase and greater longevity, outweighs a thousand abolition falsehoods, in favor of the leniency and providence of our management of them. It is also admitted that there are incomparably fewer cases of insanity and suicide among them than among the whites. The fact is, that among the slaves of the African race these things are almost wholly unknown. However frequent suicide may have been among those brought from Africa, I can say that in my time I cannot remember to have known or heard of a single instance of deliberate self-destruction, and but of one of suicide at all. As to insanity, I have seen but one permanent case of it, and that twenty years ago. It cannot be doubted that among three millions of people there must be some insane and some suicides; but I will venture to say that more cases of both occur annually among every hundred thousand of the population of Great Britain, than among all our slaves. Can it be possible, then, that they exist in that state of abject misery, goaded by constant injuries, outraged in their affections, and worn down with hardships, which the abolitionists depict, and so many ignorant and thoughtless persons religiously believe?

With regard to the separation of husbands and wives, parents and children, nothing can be more untrue than the inferences drawn from what is so constantly harped on by abolitionists. Some painful instances perhaps may occur. Very few that can be prevented. It is, and it always has been, an object of prime consideration with our slaveholders, to keep families together. Negroes are themselves both perverse and comparatively indifferent about this matter. It is a singular trait, that they almost invariably prefer forming connections with slaves belonging to other masters, and at some distance. It is, therefore, impossible to prevent separations sometimes, by the removal of one owner, his death, or failure, and dispersion of his property. In all such cases, however, every reasonable effort is made to keep the parties together, if they desire it. And the negroes forming these connections, knowing the chances of their premature dissolution, rarely complain more than we all do of the inevitable strokes of fate. Sometimes it happens that a negro prefers to give up his family rather than separate from his master. I have known such instances. As to willfully selling off a husband, or wife, or child, I believe it is rarely, very rarely done, except when some offense has been committed demanding "transportation." At sales of estates, and even at sheriff's sales, they are always, if possible, sold in families. On the whole, notwithstanding the migratory character of our population, I believe there are more families among our slaves, who have lived and died together without losing a single member from their circle, except by the process of nature, and in the enjoyment of constant, uninterrupted communion, than have flourished in the same space of time, and among the same number of civilized people in modern times. And to sum up all, if pleasure is correctly defined to be the absence of pain—which, so far as the great body of mankind is concerned, is undoubtedly its true definition—I believe our slaves are the happiest three millions of human beings on whom the sun shines. Into their Eden is coming Satan in the guise of an abolitionist.

As regards their religious condition, it is well known that a majority of the communicants of the Methodist and Baptist churches of the South are colored. Almost everywhere they have precisely the same opportunities of attending worship that the whites have, and, beside special occasions for themselves exclusively, which they prefer. In many places not so accessible to clergymen in ordinary, missionaries are sent, and mainly supported by their masters, for the particular benefit of the slaves. There are none I imagine who may not, if they like, hear the gospel preached at least once a month—most of them twice a month, and very many every week. In our thinly settled country the whites fare no better. But in addition to this, on plantations of any size, the slaves who have joined the church are formed into a class, at the head of which is placed one of their number, acting as deacon or leader, who is also sometimes a licensed preacher. This class assembles for religious exercises weekly, semi-weekly, or oftener, if the members choose. In some parts, also, Sunday schools for blacks are established, and Bible classes are orally instructed by discreet and pious persons. Now where will you find a laboring population possessed of greater religious advantages than these? Not in London, I am sure, where it is known that your churches, chapels, and religions meeting-houses, of all sorts, can not contain one-half of the inhabitants.

I have admitted, without hesitation, what it would be untrue and profitless to deny, that slaveholders are responsible to the world for the humane treatment of the fellow-beings whom God has placed in their hands. I think it would be only fair for you to admit, what is equally undeniable, that every man in independent circumstances, all the world over, and every government, is to the same extent responsible to the whole human family, for the condition of the poor and laboring classes in their own country, and around them, wherever they may be placed, to whom God has denied the advantages he has given themselves. If so, it would naturally seem the duty of true humanity and rational philanthropy to devote their time and labor, their thoughts, writings and charity, first to the objects placed as it were under their own immediate charge. And it must be regarded as a clear evasion and skillful neglect of this cardinal duty, to pass from those whose destitute situation they can plainly see, minutely examine, and efficiently relieve, to inquire after the condition of others in no way intrusted to their care, to exaggerate evils of which they can not be cognizant, to expend all their sympathies and exhaust all their energies on these remote objects of their unnatural, not to say dangerous, benevolence; and finally, to calumniate, denounce, and endeavor to excite the indignation of the world against their unoffending fellow-creatures for not hastening, under their dictation, to redress wrongs which are stoutly and truthfully denied, while they themselves go but little further in alleviating those chargeable on them than openly and unblushingly to acknowledge them. There may be indeed a sort of merit in doing so much as to make such an acknowledgment, but it must be very modest if it expects appreciation.

Now I affirm, that in Great Britain the poor and laboring classes of your own race and color, not only your fellow-beings, but your *fellow-citizens*, are more miserable and degraded, morally and physically, than our slaves; to be elevated to the actual condition of whom, would be to these, *your fellow-citizens*, a most glorious act of *emancipation*. And I also affirm, that the poor and laboring classes of our older free States would not be in a much more enviable condition, but for our slavery. One of their own Senators has declared in the United States Senate, "that the repeal of the Tariff would reduce New England to a howling wilderness." And the American Tariff is neither more or less than a system by which the slave States are plundered for the benefit of those States which do not tolerate slavery.

To prove what I say of Great Britain to be true, I make the following extracts from the Reports of Commissioners appointed by Parliament, and published by order of the House of Commons. I can make but few and short ones. But similar quotations might be made to any extent, and I defy you to deny that these specimens exhibit the real condition of your operatives in every branch of your industry. There is of course a variety in their sufferings. But the same incredible amount of toil, frightful destitution, and utter want of morals, characterize the lot of every class of them.

Collieries—"I wish to call the attention of the Board to the pits about Brampton. The seams are so thin that several of them have only two feet headway to all the working. They are worked altogether by boys from eight to twelve years of age, on all-fours, with a dog belt and chain. The passages being neither ironed nor wooded, and often an inch or two thick with mud. In Mr. Barnes' pit these poor boys have to drag the barrows with one hundred weight of coal or slack sixty times a day sixty yards, and the empty barrows back, without once straightening their backs, unless they chose to stand under the shaft, and run the risk of having their heads broken by a falling coal."—Report on Mines, 1842, p. 71. "In Shropshire the seams are no more than eighteen or twenty inches."—Ibid, p. 67. "At the Booth pit," says Mr. Scriven, "I walked, rode, and crept eighteen hundred yards to one of the nearest faces."—Ibid. "Chokedamp, firedamp, wild fire, sulphur and water, at all times menace instant death to the laborers in these mines." "Robert North, aged 16: Went into the pit at seven years of age, to fill up skips. I drew about twelve months. When I drew by the girdle and chain my skin was broken, and the blood ran down. I durst not say any thing. If we said any thing, the butty, and the reeve, who works under him, would take a stick and beat us."—Ibid. "The usual punishment for theft is to place the culprit's head between the legs of one of the biggest boys, and each boy in the pit—sometimes there are twenty—inflicts twelve lashes on the back and rump with a cat."—Ibid. "Instances occur in which children are taken into these mines to work as early as four years of age, sometimes at five, not unfrequently at six and seven, while from eight to nine is the ordinary age at which these employments commence."—Ibid. "The wages paid at these mines is from two dollar fifty cents to seven dollars fifty cents per month for laborers, according to age and ability, and out of this they must support themselves. They work twelve hours a day."—Ibid.

In Calico Printing.—"It is by no means uncommon in all the districts for children five or six years old to be kept at work fourteen to sixteen hours consecutively."—Report on Children, 1842, p. 59.

I could furnish extracts similar to these in regard to every branch of your manufactures, but I will not multiply them. Every body knows that your operatives habitually labor from twelve to sixteen hours, men, women, and children, and the men occasionally twenty hours per day. In lace-making, says the last quoted report, children sometimes commence work at two years of age.

Destitution.—It is stated by your Commissioners that forty thousand persons in Liverpool, and fifteen thousand in Manchester, live in cellars; while twenty-two thousand in England pass the night in barns, tents, or the open air. "There have been found such occurrences as seven, eight, and ten persons in one cottage, I cannot say for one day, but for whole days, without a morsel of food. They have remained on their beds of straw for two successive days, under the impression that in a recumbent posture the pangs of hunger were less felt."—Lord Brougham's Speech, 11th July, 1842. A volume of frightful scenes might be quoted to corroborate the inferences to be necessarily drawn from the facts here stated. I will not add more, but pass on to the important inquiry as to

Morals and Education.—"Elizabeth Barrett, aged 14: I always work without stockings, shoes, or trowsers. I wear nothing but a shift. I have to go up to the headings with the men. *They are all naked there.* I am got used to that."—Report on Mines. "As to illicit sexual intercourse it seems to prevail universally, and from an early period of life." "The evidence might have been doubled, which attest the early commencement of sexual and promiscuous intercourse among boys and girls." "A lower condition of morals, in the fullest sense of the term, could not, I think, be found. I do not mean by this that there are many more prominent vices among them, but that moral feelings and sentiments do not exist. *They have no morals.*" "Their appearance, manners, and moral natures—so far as the word *moral* can be applied to them—are in accordance with their half-civilized condition."—Report on Children. "More than half a dozen instances occurred in Manchester, where a man, his wife, and his wife's grown-up-sister, habitually occupied the same bed."—Report on Sanitary Condition. "Robert Crucilow, aged 16: I don't know any thing of Moses—never heard of France. I don't know what America is. Never heard of Scotland or Ireland. Can't tell how many weeks there are in a year. There are twelve pence in a shilling, and twenty shillings in a pound. There are eight pints in a gallon of ale."—Report on Mines. "Ann Eggly, aged 18: I walk about and get fresh air on Sundays. I never go to church or chapel. I never heard of Christ at all."—Ibid. Others: "The Lord sent Adam and Eve on earth to save sinners." "I don't know who made the world; I never heard about God." "I don't know Jesus Christ—I never saw him—but I have seen Foster who prays about him." "Employer: You have expressed surprise at Thomas Mitchel's not hearing of God. I judge there are few colliers here about that have."—Ibid. I will quote no more. It is shocking beyond endurance to turn over your records, in which the condition of your laboring classes is but too faithfully depicted. Could our slaves but see it, they would join us in lynching the abolitionists, which, by the by, they would not now be loth to do. We never think of imposing on them such labor, either in amount or kind. We never put them to *any work*, under ten, more generally at twelve years of age, and then the very lightest. Destitution is absolutely unknown—never did a slave starve in America; while in moral sentiments and feelings, in religious information, and even in general intelligence, they are infinitely the superiors of your operatives. When you look around you, how dare you talk to us before the world of slavery? For the condition of your wretched laborers, you, and every Briton who is not one of them, are responsible before God and man. If you are really humane, philanthropic, and charitable, here are objects for you. Relieve them. Emancipate them. Raise them from the condition of brutes, to the level of human beings—of American slaves, at least. Do not for an instant suppose that the *name* of being freemen is the slightest comfort to them, situated as they are, or that the bombastic boast that "whoever touches British soil stands redeemed, regenerated, and disenthralled," can meet with any thing but the ridicule and contempt of mankind, while that soil swarms, both on and under its surface, with the most abject and degraded wretches that ever bowed beneath the oppressor's yoke.

I have said that slavery is an established and inevitable condition to human society. I do not speak of the *name*, but the *fact*. The Marquis of Normanby has lately declared your operatives to be "*in effect slaves*." Can it be denied? Probably, for such philanthropists as your abolitionists care nothing for facts. They deal in terms and fictions. It is the *word* "slavery" which shocks their tender sensibilities; and their imaginations associate it with "hydras and chimeras dire." The thing itself, in its most hideous reality, passes daily under their view unheeded—a familiar face, touching no chord of shame, sympathy or indignation. Yet so brutalizing is your iron bondage that the English operative is a by-word through the world. When favoring fortune enables him to escape his prison-house, both in Europe and America he is shunned. "With all the skill which fourteen hours of daily labor from the tenderest age has ground into him, his discontent, which habit has made second nature, and his depraved propensities, running riot when freed from his wonted fetters, prevent his employment whenever it is not a matter of necessity. If we derived no other benefit from African slavery in the Southern States than that it deterred your *freedmen* from coming hither, I should regard it an inestimable blessing.

And how unaccountable is that philanthropy, which closes its eyes upon such a state of things as you have at home, and turns its blurred vision to our affairs beyond the Atlantic, meddling with matters which no way concern them—presiding, as you have lately done, at meetings to denounce the "iniquity of our laws" and "the atrocity of our practices," and to sympathize with infamous wretches imprisoned here for violating decrees promulgated both by God and man? Is this doing the work of "your Father which is in heaven," or is it seeking only "that you may have glory of man?" Do you remember the denunciation of our Saviour, "Woe unto you, Scribes and Pharisees; hypocrites! for ye make clean the outside of the cup and platter, but within they are full of extortion and excess."

But after all, supposing that every thing you say of slavery be true, and its abolition a matter of the last necessity, how do you expect to effect emancipation, and what do you calculate will be the result of its accomplishment? As to the means to be used, the abolitionists, I believe, affect to differ, a large proportion of them pretending that their sole purpose is to apply "moral suasion" to the slaveholders themselves. As a matter of curiosity, I should like to know what their idea of this "moral suasion" is. Their discourses—yours is no exception—are all tirades, the exordium, argument and peroration, turning on the epithets "tyrants," "thieves," "murderers," addressed to us. They revile us as "atrocious monsters," "violators of the laws of nature, God and man," our homes the abode of every iniquity, our land a "brothel." We retort, that they are "incendiaries" and "assassins." Delightful argument! Sweet, potent "moral suasion!" What slave has it freed—what proselyte can it ever make? But if your course was wholly different—if you distilled nectar from your lips, and discoursed sweetest music, could you reasonably indulge the hope of accomplishing your object by such means? Nay, supposing that we were all convinced, and thought of slavery precisely as you do, at what era of "moral suasion" do you imagine you could prevail on us to give up a thousand millions of dollars in the value of our slaves, and a thousand millions of dollars more in the depreciation of our lands, in consequence of the want of laborers to cultivate them? Consider: were ever any people, civilized or savage, persuaded by any argument, human or divine, to surrender voluntarily two thousand millions of dollars? Would you think of asking five millions of Englishmen to contribute, either at once or gradually, four hundred and fifty millions of pounds sterling to the cause of philanthropy, even if the purpose to be accomplished was not of doubtful goodness? If you are prepared to undertake such a scheme, try it at home. Collect your fund—return us the money for our slaves, and do with them as you like. Be all the glory yours, fairly and honestly won. But you see the absurdity of such an idea. Away, then, with your pretended "moral suasion." You know it is mere nonsense. The abolitionists have no faith in it themselves. Those who expect to accomplish any thing count on means altogether different. They aim, first, to alarm us: that failing, to compel us by force to emancipate our slaves, at our own risk and cost. To these purposes they obviously direct all their energies. Our Northern liberty-men endeavored to disseminate their destructive doctrine among our slaves, and excite them to insurrection. But we have put an end to that, and stricken terror into them. They dare not show their faces here. Then they declared they would dissolve the Union. Let them do it. The North would repent it far more than the South. We are not alarmed at the idea. We are well content to give up the Union sooner than sacrifice two thousand millions of dollars, and with them all the rights we prize. You may take it for granted that it is impossible to persuade or alarm us into emancipation, or to making the first step toward it. Nothing, then, is left to try, but sheer force. If the abolitionists are prepared to expend their own treasure and shed their own blood as freely as they ask us to do ours, let them come. We do not court the conflict; but we will not and we cannot shrink from it. If they are not ready to go so far; if, as I expect, their philanthropy recoils from it; if they are looking only for *cheap* glory, let them turn their thoughts elsewhere, and leave us in peace. Be the sin, the danger and the evils of slavery all our own. We compel, we ask none to share them with us.

I am well aware that a notable scheme has been set on foot to achieve abolition by making what is by courtesy called "free" labor so much cheaper than slave labor as to force the abandonment of the latter. Though we are beginning to *manufacture with slaves*, I do not think you will attempt to pinch your operatives closer in Great Britain. You cannot curtail the rags with which they vainly attempt to cover their nakedness, nor reduce the porridge which barely, and not always, keeps those who have employment from perishing of famine. When you can do this, we will consider whether our slaves may not dispense with a pound or two of bacon per week, or a few garments annually. Your aim, however, is to cheapen labor in the tropics. The idea of doing this by exporting your "bold yeomanry" is, I presume, given up. Cromwell tried it when he *sold* the captured followers of Charles into *West Indian slavery*, where they speedily found graves. Nor have your recent experiments on British and even Dutch constitutions succeeded better. Have you still faith in carrying thither your coolies from Hindostan? Doubtless that once wild robber race, whose highest eulogium was that they did not murder merely for the love of blood, have been tamed down, and are perhaps "keen for immigration," for since your civilization has reached it, plunder has grown scarce in Guzerat. But what is the result of the experiment thus far? Have the coolies, ceasing to handle arms, learned to handle spades, and proved hardy and profitable laborers? On the contrary, broken in spirit and stricken with disease at home, the wretched victims whom you have hitherto kidnapped for a bounty, confined in depots, put under hatches and carried across the ocean—forced into "voluntary immigration," have done little but lie down and die on the *pseudo* soil of freedom. At the end of five years two-thirds, in some colonies a larger proportion, are no more! Humane and pious contrivance! To alleviate the fancied sufferings of the accursed posterity of Ham, you sacrifice by a cruel death two-thirds of the children of the blessed Shem—and demand the applause of Christians—the blessing of heaven! If this "experiment" is to go on, in God's name try your hand upon the Thugs. That other species of "immigration" to which you are resorting I will consider presently.

But what do you calculate will be the result of emancipation, by whatever means accomplished? You will probably point me, by way of answer, to the West Indies—doubtless to Antigua, the great boast of abolition. Admitting that it has succeeded there—which I will do for the sake of the argument—do you know the reason of it? The true and only causes of whatever success has attended it in Antigua are, that the population was before crowded, and all or nearly all the arable land in cultivation. The emancipated negroes could not, many of them, get away if they desired; and knew not where to go, in case they did. They had, practically, no alternative but to remain on the spot; and remaining, they must work on the terms of the proprietors, or perish—the strong arm of the mother country forbidding all hope of seizing the land for themselves. The proprietors, well knowing that they could thus command labor for the merest necessities of life, which was much cheaper than maintaining the non-effective as well as effective slaves in a style which decency and interest, if not humanity, required, willingly accepted half their value, and at once realized far more than the interest on the other half in the diminution of their expenses, and the reduced comforts of the *freemen*. One of your most illustrious judges, who was also a profound and philosophical historian, has said "that villeinage was not abolished, but went into decay in England." This was the process. This has been the process wherever (the name of) villeinage or slavery has been successfully abandoned. Slavery, in fact, "went into decay" in Antigua. I have admitted that, under similar circumstances, it might profitably cease here—that is, profitably to the individual proprietors. Give me half the value of my slaves, and compel them to remain and labor on my plantation, at ten to eleven cents a day, as they do in Antigua, supporting themselves and families, and you shall have them to-morrow, and if you like dub them "free." Not to stickle, I would surrender them without price. No—I recall my words: My humanity revolts at the idea. I am attached to my slaves, and would not have act or part in reducing them to such a condition. I deny, however, that Antigua, as a community, is, or ever will be, as *prosperous* under present circumstances, as she was before abolition, though fully ripe for it. The fact is well known. The reason is that the African, if not a distinct, is an inferior race, and never will effect, as it never has effected, as much in any other condition as in that of slavery.

I know of no *slaveholder* who has visited the West Indies since slavery was abolished, and published *his* views of it. All our facts and opinions come through the friends of the experiment, or at least those not opposed to it. Taking these, even without allowance, to be true as stated, I do not see where the abolitionists find cause for exultation. The tables of exports, which are the best evidences of the condition of a people, exhibit a woful falling off—excused, it is true, by unprecedented droughts and hurricanes, to which their free labor seems unaccountably more subject than slave labor used to be. I will not go into detail. It is well known that a large proportion of British legislation and expenditure, and that proportion still constantly increasing, is most anxiously devoted to repairing the monstrous error of emancipation. You are actually galvanizing your expiring colonies. The truth, deduced from all the facts, was thus pithily stated by the *London Quarterly Review*, as long ago as 1840: "None of the benefits anticipated by mistaken good intentions have been realized, while every evil wished for by knaves and foreseen by the wise has been painfully verified. The wild rashness of fanaticism has made the emancipation of the slaves equivalent to the loss of one-half of the West Indies, and yet put back the chance of negro civilization."—Art. Ld. Dudley's Letters. Such are the *real fruits* of your never-to-be-too-much-glorified abolition, and the valuable dividend of your twenty millions of pounds sterling invested therein.

If any further proof was wanted of the utter and well-known, though not yet openly avowed, failure of West Indian emancipation, it would be furnished by the startling fact, that THE AFRICAN SLAVE TRADE HAS BEEN ACTUALLY REVIVED UNDER THE AUSPICES AND PROTECTION OF THE BRITISH GOVERNMENT. Under the specious guise of "immigration," they are replenishing those Islands with slaves from the coast of Africa. Your colony of Sierra Leone, founded on that coast to prevent the slave trade, and peopled, by the bye, in the first instance, by negroes stolen from these States during the Revolutionary War, is the depot to which captives taken from slavers by your armed vessels are transported. I might say returned, since nearly half the Africans carried across the Atlantic are understood to be embarked in this vicinity. The wretched survivors, who are there set at liberty, are immediately seduced to "immigrate" to the West Indies. The business is systematically carried on by black "delegates," sent expressly from the West Indies, where, on arrival, the "immigrants" are *sold into slavery* for twenty-one years, under conditions ridiculously trivial and wickedly void, since few or none will ever be able to derive any advantage from them. The whole prime of life thus passed in bondage, it is contemplated, and doubtless it will be carried into effect, to turn them out in their old age to shift for themselves, and to supply their places with fresh and vigorous "immigrants." Was ever a system of slavery so barbarous devised before? Can you think of comparing it with ours? Even your own religious missionaries at Sierra Leone denounce it "as worse than the slave state in Africa." And your black delegates, fearful of the influence of these missionaries, as well as on account of the inadequate supply of captives, are now preparing to procure the able-bodied and comparatively industrious Kroomen of the interior, by *purchasing from their headmen* the privilege of inveigling them to the West India market! So ends the magnificent farce—perhaps I should say tragedy, of West India abolition! I will not harrow your feelings by asking you to review the labors of your life and tell me what you and your brother enthusiasts have accomplished for "injured Africa," but while agreeing with Lord Stowell, that "villeinage decayed," and admitting that slavery might do so also, I think I am fully justified by passed and passing events in saying, as Mr. Grosvenor said of the slave trade, that its *abolition* is "impossible."

Yon are greatly mistaken, however, if you think that the consequences of emancipation here would be similar and no more injurious than those which followed from it in your little sea-girt West India Islands, where nearly all were blacks. The system of slavery is not in "decay" with us. It flourishes in full and growing vigor. Our country is boundless in extent. Dotted here and there with villages and fields, it is, for the most part, covered with immense forests and swamps of almost unknown size. In such a country, with a people so restless as ours, communicating of course some of that spirit to their domestics, can you conceive that any thing short of the power of the master over the slave, could confine the African race, notoriously idle and improvident, to labor on our plantations? Break this bond, but for a day, and these plantations will be solitudes. The negro loves change, novelty, and sensual excitements of all kinds, *when awake*. "Reason and order," of which Mr. Wilberforce said "liberty was the child," do not characterize him. Released from his present obligations, his first impulse would be to go somewhere. And here no natural boundaries would restrain him. At first they would all seek the towns, and rapidly accumulate in squalid groups upon their outskirts. Driven thence by the "armed police," which would immediately spring into existence, they would scatter in all directions. Some bodies of them might wander toward the "free" States, or to the Western wilderness, marking their tracks by their depredations and their corpses. Many would roam wild in our "big woods." Many more would seek the recesses of our swamps for secure covert. Few, very few of them, could be prevailed on to do a stroke of work, none to labor continuously, while a head of cattle, sheep or swine could be found in our ranges, or an ear of corn nodded in our abandoned fields. These exhausted, our folds and poultry yards, barns and store-houses, would become their prey. Finally, our scattered dwellings would be plundered, perhaps fired, and the inmates murdered. How long do you suppose that we could bear these things? How long would it be before we should sleep with rifles at our bedsides, and never move without one in our hands? This work once begun, let the story of our British ancestors and the aborigines of this country tell the sequel. Far more rapid, however, would be the catastrophe. "Ere many moons went by," the African race would be exterminated, or reduced again to slavery, their ranks recruited, after your example, by fresh "emigrants" from their fatherland.

Is timely preparation and gradual emancipation suggested to avert these horrible consequences? I thought your experience in the West Indies had, at least, done so much as to explode that idea. If it failed there, much more would it fail here, where the two races, approximating to equality in numbers, are daily and hourly in the closest contact. Give room for but a single spark of real jealousy to be kindled between them, and the explosion would be instantaneous and universal. It is the most fatal of all fallacies, to suppose that these two races can exist together, after any length of time, or any process of preparation, on terms at all approaching to equality. Of this, both of them are finally and fixedly convinced. They differ essentially, in all the leading traits which characterize the varieties of the human species, and color draws an indelible and insuperable line of separation between them. Every scheme founded upon the idea that they can remain together on the same soil, beyond the briefest period, in any other relation than precisely that which now subsists between them, is not only preposterous, but fraught with deepest danger. If there was no alternative but to try the "experiment" here, reason and humility dictate that the sufferings of "gradualism" should be saved, and the catastrophe of "immediate abolition" enacted as rapidly as possible. Are you impatient for the performance to commence? Do you long to gloat over the scenes I have suggested, but could not hold the pen to portray? In your long life many such have passed under your review. You know that *they* are not "*impossible.*" Can they be to your taste? Do you believe that in laboring to bring them about, the abolitionists are doing the will of God? No! God is not there. It is the work of Satan. The arch-fiend, under specious guises, has found his way into their souls, and with false appeals to philanthropy, and foul insinuations to ambition, instigates them to rush headlong to the accomplishment of his diabolical designs.

We live in a wonderful age. The events of the last three quarters of a century appear to have revolutionized the human mind. Enterprise and ambition are only limited in their purposes by the horizon of the imagination. It is the transcendental era. In philosophy, religion, government, science, arts, commerce, nothing that has been is to be allowed to be. Conservatism, in any form, is scoffed at. The slightest taint of it is fatal. Where will all this end? If you can tolerate one ancient maxim, let it be that the best criterion of the future is the past. That, if any thing, will give a clue. And, looking back only through your time, what was the earliest feat of this same transcendentalism? The rays of the new moral Drummond Light were first concentrated to a focus at Paris, to illuminate the universe. In a twinkling it consumed the political, religious and social systems of France. It could not be extinguished there until literally drowned in blood. And then, from its ashes arose that supernatural man, who, for twenty years, kept affrighted Europe in convulsions. Since that time, its scattered beams, refracted by broader surfaces, have, nevertheless, continued to scathe wherever they have fallen. What political structure, what religious creed, but has felt the galvanic shock, and even now trembles to its foundations? Mankind, still horror-stricken by the catastrophe of France, have shrunk from rash experiments upon social systems. But they have been practicing in the East, around the Mediterranean, and through the West India Islands. And growing confident, a portion of them seem desperately bent on kindling the all-devouring flame in the bosom of our land. Let it once again blaze up to heaven, and another cycle of blood and devastation will dawn upon the world. For our own sake, and for the sake of those infatuated men who are madly driving on the conflagration; for the sake of human nature, we are called on to strain every nerve to arrest it. And be assured our efforts will be bounded only with our being. Nor do I doubt that five millions of people, brave, intelligent, united, and prepared to hazard every thing, will, in such a cause, with the blessing of God, sustain themselves. At all events, come what may, it is ours to meet it.

We are well aware of the light estimation in which the abolitionists, and those who are taught by them, profess to hold us. We have seen the attempt of a portion of the Free Church of Scotland to reject our alms on the ground that we are "slave-drivers," after sending missionaries to solicit them. And we have seen Mr. O'Connell, the "irresponsible master" of millions of ragged serfs, from whom, poverty stricken as they are, he contrives to wring a splendid privy purse, throw back with contumely, the "tribute" of his own countrymen from this land of "miscreants." These people may exhaust their slang, and make blackguards of themselves, but they cannot defile us. And as for the suggestion to exclude slaveholders from your London clubs, we scout it. Many of us, indeed, do go to London, and we have seen your breed of gawky lords, both there and here, but it never entered into our conceptions to look on them as better than ourselves. The American slaveholders, collectively or individually, ask no favors of any man or race who tread the earth. In none of the attributes of men, mental or physical, do they acknowledge or fear superiority elsewhere. They stand in the broadest light of the knowledge, civilization and improvement of the age, as much favored of heaven as any of the sons of Adam. Exacting nothing undue, they yield nothing but justice and courtesy, even to royal blood. They cannot be flattered, duped, nor bullied out of their rights or their propriety. They smile with contempt at scurrility and vaporing beyond the seas, and they turn their backs upon it where it is "irresponsible;" but insolence that ventures to look them in the face, will never fail to be chastised.

I think I may trust you will not regard this letter as intrusive. I should never have entertained an idea of writing it, had you not opened the correspondence. If you think any thing in it harsh, review your own—which I regret that I lost soon after it was received—and you will probably find that you have taken your revenge beforehand. If you have not, transfer an equitable share of what you deem severe, to the account of the abolitionists at large. They have accumulated against the slaveholders a balance of invective, which, with all our efforts, we shall not be able to liquidate much short of the era in which your national debt will be paid. At all events, I have no desire to offend you personally, and, with the best wishes for your continued health, I have the honor to be,

Your obedient servant,
J. H. HAMMOND.

Thos. Clarkson, Esq.

LETTER II

Ignorance of Abolitionists—Arguments of Abolitionists refuted—Abolitionism leads to Infidelity—Law of Force a law of Love—Wages of Slaves and of hired labor—Results of emancipation to the world—Falsehoods of Abolitionists—English estimate of our Northern citizens—British interference in the politics of our country—Sensitiveness of the Southern People—Rise and progress of Fanaticism.

SILVER BLUFF, S. C., March 24, 1845.

SIR—In my letter to you of the 28th January—which I trust you have received ere this—I mentioned that I had lost your circular letter soon after it had come to hand. It was, I am glad to say, only mislaid, and has within a few days been recovered. A second perusal of it induces me to resume my pen. Unwilling to trust my recollections from a single reading, I did not, in my last communication, attempt to follow the course of your argument, and meet directly the points made and the terms used. I thought it better to take a general view of the subject, which could not fail to traverse your most material charges. I am well aware, however, that for fear of being tedious, I omitted many interesting topics altogether, and abstained from a complete discussion of some of those introduced. I do not propose now to *exhaust* the subject; which it would require volumes to do; but without waiting to learn—which I may never do—your opinion of what I have already said, I sit down to supply some of the deficiencies of my letter of January, and, with your circular before me, to reply to such parts of it as have not been fully answered.

It is, I perceive, addressed, among others, to "such as have never visited the Southern States" of this confederacy, and professes to enlighten their ignorance of the actual "condition of the poor slave in their own country." I can not help thinking you would have displayed prudence in confining the circulation of your letter altogether to such persons. You might then have indulged with impunity in giving, as you have done, a picture of slavery, drawn from your own excited imagination, or from those impure fountains, the Martineaus, Marryatts, Trollopes, and Dickenses, who have profited by catering, at our expense, to the jealous sensibilities and debauched tastes of your countrymen. Admitting that you are familiar with the history of slavery, and the past discussions of it, as I did, I now think rather broadly, in my former letter, what can *you know* of the true *condition* of the "poor slave" here? I am not aware that you have ever visited this country, or even the West Indies. Can you suppose, that because you have devoted your life to the investigation of the subject—commencing it under the influence of an enthusiasm, so melancholy at first, and so volcanic afterwards, as to be nothing short of hallucination—pursuing it as men of *one idea* do every thing, with the single purpose of establishing your own view of it—gathering your information from discharged seamen, disappointed speculators, factious politicians, visionary reformers and scurrilous tourists—opening your ears to every species of complaint, exaggeration and falsehood, that interested ingenuity could invent, and never for a moment questioning the truth of any thing that could make for your cause—can you suppose that all this has qualified you, living the while in England, to form or approximate toward the formation of a correct opinion of the condition of slaves among us? I know the power of self-delusion. I have not the least doubt, that you think yourself the very best informed man alive on this subject, and that many think so likewise. So far as facts go, even after deducting from your list a great deal that is not fact, I will not deny that, probably, your collection is the most extensive in existence. But as to the *truth* in regard to slavery, there is not an adult in this region but knows more of it than you do. *Truth* and *fact* are, you are aware, by no means synonymous terms. Ninety-nine facts may constitute a falsehood: the hundredth, added or alone, gives the truth. With all your knowledge of facts, I undertake to say that you are entirely and grossly ignorant of the real condition of our slaves. And from all that I can see, you are equally ignorant of the essential principles of human association revealed in history, both sacred and profane, on which slavery rests, and which will perpetuate it forever in some form or other. However you may declaim against it; however powerfully you may array atrocious incidents; whatever appeals you may make to the heated imaginations and tender sensibilities of mankind, believe me, your total blindness to the *whole truth*, which alone constitutes *the truth*, incapacitates you from ever making an impression on the sober reason and sound common sense of the world. You may seduce thousands—you can convince no one. Whenever and wherever you or the advocates of your cause can arouse the passions of the weak-minded and the ignorant, and bringing to bear with them the interests of the vicious and unprincipled, overwhelm common sense and reason—as God sometimes permits to be done—you may triumph. Such a triumph we have witnessed in Great Britain. But I trust it is far distant here; nor can it, from its nature, be extensive or enduring. Other classes of reformers, animated by the same spirit as the abolitionists, attack the institution of marriage, and even the established relations of parent and child. And they collect instances of barbarous cruelty and shocking degradation, which rival, if they do not throw into the shade, your slavery statistics. But the rights of marriage and parental authority rests upon truths as obvious as they are unchangeable—coming home to every human being,—self-impressed forever on the individual mind, and can not be shaken until the whole man is corrupted, nor subverted until civilized society becomes a putrid mass. Domestic slavery is not so universally understood, nor can it make such a direct appeal to individuals or society beyond its pale. Here, prejudice and passion have room to sport at the expense of others. They may be excited and urged to dangerous action, remote from the victims they mark out. They may, as they have done, effect great mischief, but they can not be made to maintain, in the long run, dominion over reason and common sense, nor ultimately put down what God has ordained.

You deny, however, that slavery is sanctioned by God, and your chief argument is, that when he gave to Adam dominion over the fruits of the earth and the animal creation, he stopped there. "He never gave him any further right over his fellow-men." You restrict the descendants of Adam to a very short list of rights and powers, duties and responsibities, if you limit them solely to those conferred and enjoined in the first chapter of Genesis. It is very obvious that in this narrative of the Creation, Moses did not have it in view to record any part of the law intended for the government of man in his social or political state. Eve was not yet created; the expulsion had not yet taken place; Cain was unborn; and no allusion whatever is made to the manifold decrees of God to which these events gave rise. The only serious answer this argument deserves, is to say, what is so manifestly true, that God's not expressly giving to Adam "any right over his fellow-men" by no means excluded him from conferring that right on his descendants; which he in fact did. We know that Abraham, the chosen one of God, exercised it and held property in his fellow-man, even anterior to the period when property in land was acknowledged. We might infer that God had authorized it. But we are not reduced to inference or conjecture. At the hazard of fatiguing you by repetition, I will again refer you to the ordinances of the Scriptures. Innumerable instances might be quoted where God has given and commanded men to assume dominion over their fellow-men. But one will suffice. In the twenty-fifth chapter of Leviticus, you will find *domestic slavery—precisely such as is maintained at this day in these States—ordained and established by God, in language which I defy you to pervert so as to leave a doubt on any honest mind that this institution was founded by him, and decreed to be perpetual.* I quote the words:

Leviticus xxv. 44-46: "Both thy bond-men and thy bond-maids which thou shalt have, shall be of the heathen [Africans] that are round about you: of *them ye shall buy bond-men and bond-maids.*

"Moreover, of the children of the strangers that do sojourn among you, of them shall ye buy, *and of their families that are with you which they begat in your land* [descendants of Africans?] and they shall be your possession.

"*And ye shall take them as an inheritance for your children after you, to inherit them for a possession.* THEY SHALL BE YOUR BOND-MEN FOREVER."

What human legislature could make a decree more full and explicit than this? What court of law or chancery could defeat a title to a slave couched in terms so clear and complete as these? And this is the *law of God*, whom you pretend to worship, while you denounce and traduce us for respecting it.

It seems scarcely credible, but the fact is so, that you deny this law so plainly written, and in the face of it have the hardihood to declare that "though slavery is not *specifically,* yet it is *virtually, forbidden* in the Scriptures, because all the crimes which necessarily arises out of slavery, and which can arise from no other source, are reprobated there and threatened with divine vengeance." Such an unworthy subterfuge is scarcely entitled to consideration. But its gross absurdity may be exposed in few words. I do not know what crimes you particularly allude to as arising from slavery. But you will perhaps admit—not because they are denounced in the decalogue, which the abolitionists respect only so far as they choose, but because it is the *immediate interest* of most men to admit—that disobedience to parents, adultery, and stealing, are crimes. Yet these crimes "necessarily arise from" the relations of parent and child, marriage, and the possession of private property; at least they "can arise from no other sources." Then, according to your argument, it is "virtually forbidden" to marry, to beget children, and to hold private property! Nay, it is forbidden to live, since murder can only be perpetrated on living subjects. You add that "in the same way the gladiatorial shows of old, and other barbarous customs, were not specifically forbidden in the New Testament, and yet Christianity was the sole means of their suppression." This is very true. But these shows and barbarous customs thus suppressed were not *authorised by God.* They were not ordained and commanded by God for the benefit of his chosen people and mankind, as the purchase and holding of bond-men and bond-maids were. Had they been they would never have been "suppressed by Christianity" any more than slavery can be by your party. Although Christ came "not to destroy but fulfill the law," he nevertheless did formally abrogate some of the ordinances promulgated by Moses, and all such as were at war with his mission of "peace and good-will on earth." He "specifically" annuls, for instance, one "barbarous custom" sanctioned by those ordinances, where he says, "ye have heard that it hath been said, an eye for an eye, and a tooth for a tooth; but I say unto you that ye resist not evil, but whosoever shall smite thee on the right cheek, turn to him the other also." Now, in the time of Christ, it was usual for masters to put their slaves to death on the slightest provocation. They even killed and cut them up to feed their fishes. He was undoubtedly aware of these things, as well as of the law and commandment I have quoted. He could only have been restrained from denouncing them, as he did the "*lex talionis,*" because he knew that in despite of these barbarities the institution of slavery was at the bottom a sound and wholesome, as well as lawful one. Certain it is, that in his wisdom and purity he did not see proper to interfere with it. In your wisdom, however, you make the sacrilegious attempt to overthrow it.

You quote the denunciation of Tyre and Sidon, and say that "the chief reason given by the prophet Joel for their destruction, was, that they were notorious beyond all others for carrying on the slave trade." I am afraid you think we have no Bibles in the slave States, or that we are unable to read them. I can not otherwise account for your making this reference, unless indeed your own reading is confined to an expurgated edition, prepared for the use of abolitionists, in which every thing relating to slavery that militates against their view of it is left out. The prophet Joel denounces the Tyrians and Sidonians, because "the children also of Judah and the children of Jerusalem have ye sold unto the Grecians." And what is the divine vengeance for this "notorious slave trading?" Hear it. "And I will sell your sons and daughters into the hands of the children of Judah, and they shall sell them to the Sabeans, to a people far off; for the Lord hath spoken it." Do you call this a condemnation of slave trading? The prophet makes God himself a participator in the crime, if that be one. "The Lord hath spoken it," he says, that the Tyrians and Sidonians shall be *sold into slavery to strangers*. Their real offense was, in enslaving the chosen people; and their sentence was a repetition of the old command, to make slaves of the heathen round about.

I have dwelt upon your scriptural argument, because you profess to believe the Bible; because a large proportion of the abolitionists profess to do the same, and to act under its sanction; because your circular is addressed in part to "professing Christians;" and because it is from that class mainly that you expect to seduce converts to your anti-christian, I may say, infidel doctrines. It would be wholly unnecessary to answer you, to any one who reads the Scriptures for himself, and construes them according to any other formula than that which the abolitionists are wickedly endeavoring to impose upon the world. The scriptural sanction of slavery is in fact so palpable, and so strong, that both wings of your party are beginning to acknowledge it. The more sensible and moderate admit, as the organ of the Free Church of Scotland, the *North British Review*, has lately done, that they "*are precluded by the statements and conduct of the Apostles from regarding mere slaveholding as essentially sinful*," while the desperate and reckless, who are bent on keeping up the agitation at every hazard, declare, as has been done in the *Anti-Slavery Record*, "If our inquiry turns out in favor of slavery, IT IS THE BIBLE THAT MUST FALL, AND NOT THE RIGHTS OF HUMAN NATURE." You can not, I am satisfied, much longer maintain before the world the Christian platform from which to wage war upon our institutions. Driven from it, you must abandon the contest, or, repudiating REVELATION, rush into the horrors of NATURAL RELIGION.

You next complain that our slaves are kept in bondage by the "law of force." In what country or condition of mankind do you see human affairs regulated merely by the law of love? Unless I am greatly mistaken, you will, if you look over the world, find nearly all certain and permanent rights, civil, social, and I may even add religious, resting on and ultimately secured by the "law of force." The power of majorities—of aristocracies—of kings—nay of priests, for the most part, and of property, resolves itself at last into "force," and could not otherwise be long maintained. Thus, in every turn of your argument against our system of slavery, you advance, whether conscious of it or not, radical and revolutionary doctrines calculated to change the whole face of the world, to overthrow all government, disorganize society, and reduce man to a state of nature—red with blood, and shrouded once more in barbaric ignorance. But you greatly err, if you suppose, because we rely on force in the last resort to maintain our supremacy over our slaves, that ours is a stern and unfeeling domination, at all to be compared in hard-hearted severity to that exercised, not over the mere laborer only, but by the higher over each lower order, wherever the British sway is acknowledged. You say, that if those you address were "to spend one day in the South, they would return home with impressions against slavery never to be erased." But the fact is universally the reverse. I have known numerous instances, and I never knew a single one, where there was no other cause of offense, and no object to promote by falsehood, that individuals from the non-slaveholding States did not, after residing among us long enough to understand the subject, "return home" *to defend our slavery*. It is matter of regret that you have never tried the experiment yourself. I do not doubt you would have been converted, for I give you credit for an honest though perverted mind. You would have seen how weak and futile is all abstract reasoning about this matter, and that, as a building may not be less elegant in its proportions, or tasteful in its ornaments, or virtuous in its uses, for being based upon granite, so a system of human government, though founded on force, may develope and cultivate the tenderest and purest sentiments of the human heart. And our patriarchal scheme of domestic servitude is indeed well calculated to awaken the higher and finer feelings of our nature. It is not wanting in its enthusiasm and its poetry. The relations of the most beloved and honored chief, and the most faithful and admiring subjects, which, from the time of Homer, have been the theme of song, are frigid and unfelt compared with those existing between the master and his slaves—who served his father, and rocked his cradle, or have been born in his household, and look forward to serve his children—who have been through life the props of his fortune, and the objects of his care—who have partaken of his griefs, and looked to him for comfort in their own—whose sickness he has so frequently watched over and relieved—whose holidays he has so often made joyous by his bounties and his presence; for whose welfare, when absent, his anxious solicitude never ceases, and whose hearty and affectionate greetings never fail to welcome him home. In this cold, calculating, ambitious world of ours, there are few ties more heartfelt, or of more benignant influence, than those which mutually bind the master and the slave, under our ancient system, handed down from the father of Israel. The unholy purpose of the abolitionists is, to destroy by defiling it; to infuse into it the gall and bitterness which rankle in their own envenomed bosoms; to poison the minds of the master and the servant; turn love to hatred, array *"force" against force*, and hurl all

"With hideous rain and combustion, down
To bottomless perdition."

You think it a great "crime" that we do not pay our slaves "wages," and on this account pronounce us "robbers." In my former letter, I showed that the labor of our slaves was not without great cost to us, and that in fact they themselves receive more in return for it than your hirelings do for theirs. For what purpose do men labor, but to support themselves and their families in what comfort they are able? The efforts of mere physical labor seldom suffice to provide more than a livelihood. And it is a well known and shocking fact, that while few operatives in Great Britain succeed in securing a comfortable living, the greater part drag out a miserable existence, and sink at last under absolute want. Of what avail is it that you go through the form of paying them a pittance of what you call "wages," when you do not, in return for their services, allow them what alone they ask—and have a just right to demand—enough to feed, clothe and lodge them, in health and sickness, with reasonable comfort. Though we do not give "wages" *in money*, we do this for *our slaves*, and they are therefore better rewarded than *yours*. It is the prevailing vice and error of the age, and one from which the abolitionists, with all their saintly pretensions, are far from being free, to bring every thing to the standard of money. You make gold and silver the great test of happiness. The American slave must be wretched indeed, because he is not compensated for his services *in cash*. It is altogether praiseworthy to pay the laborer a shilling a day, and let him starve on it. To supply all his wants abundantly, and at all times, yet withhold from him *money*, is among "the most reprobated crimes." The fact can not be denied, that the mere laborer is now, and always has been, everywhere that barbarism has ceased, enslaved. Among the innovations of modern times, following "the decay of villeinage," has been the creation of a new system of slavery. The primitive and patriarchal, which may also be called the sacred and natural system, in which the laborer is under the personal control of a fellow-being endowed with the sentiments and sympathies of humanity, exists among us. It has been almost everywhere else superseded by the modern *artificial money power system*, in which man—his thews and sinews, his hopes and affections, his very being, are all subjected to the dominion of *capital*—a monster without a heart—cold, stern, arithmetical—sticking to the bond—taking ever "the pound of flesh"—working up human life with engines, and retailing it out by weight and measure. His name of old was "Mammon, the least erected spirit that fell from heaven." And it is to extend his empire that you and your deluded coadjutors dedicate your lives. You are stirring up mankind to overthrow our heaven-ordained system of servitude, surrounded by innumerable checks, designed and planted deep in the human heart by God and nature, to substitute the absolute rule of this "spirit reprobate," whose proper place was hell.

You charge us with looking on our slaves "as chattels or brutes," and enter into a somewhat elaborate argument to prove that they have "human forms," "talk," and even "think." Now the fact is, that however you may indulge in this strain for effect, it is the abolitionists, and not the slaveholders, who, practically, and in the most important point of view, regard our slaves as "chattels or brutes." In your calculations of the consequences of emancipation, you pass over entirely those which must prove most serious, and which arise from the fact of their being *persons*.

You appear to think that we might abstain from the use of them as readily as if they were machines to be laid aside, or cattle that might be turned out to find pasturage for themselves. I have heretofore glanced at some of the results that would follow from breaking the bonds of so many *human beings*, now peacefully and happily linked into our social system. The tragic horrors, the decay and ruin that would for years, perhaps for ages, brood over our land, if it could be accomplished, I will not attempt to portray. But do you fancy the blight would, in such an event, come to us alone? The diminution of the sugar crop of the West Indies affected Great Britain only, and there chiefly the poor. It was a matter of no moment to capital, that labor should have one comfort less. Yet it has forced a reduction of the British duty on sugar. Who can estimate the consequences that must follow the annihilation of the cotton crop of the slaveholding States? I do not undervalue the importance of other articles of commerce, but no calamity could befall the world at all comparable to the sudden loss of two millions of bales of cotton annually. From the deserts of Africa to the Siberian wilds—from Greenland to the Chinese wall,—there is not a spot of earth but would feel the sensation. The factories of Europe would fall with a concussion that would shake down castles, palaces, and even thrones; while the "purse-proud, elbowing insolence" of our Northern monopolist would soon disappear forever under the smooth speech of the pedlar, scourging our frontiers for a livelihood, or the bluff vulgarity of the South Sea whaler, following the harpoon amid storms and shoals. Doubtless the abolitionists think we could grow cotton without slaves, or that at worst the reduction of the crop would be moderate and temporary. Such gross delusions show how profoundly ignorant they are of our condition here.

You declare that "the character of the people of the South has long been that of *hardened infidels*, who fear not God, and have no regard for religion." I will not repeat what I said in my former letter on this point. I only notice it to ask you how you could possibly reconcile it to your profession of a Christian spirit, to make such a malicious charge—to defile your soul with such a calumny against an unoffending people?

"You are old;
Nature in you stands on the very verge
Of her confine. You should be ruled and led
By some discretion."
May God forgive you.

Akin to this, is the wanton and furious assault made on us by Mr. Macaulay, in his late speech on the sugar duties, in the House of Commons, which has just reached me. His denunciations are wholly without measure, and, among other things, he asserts "that slavery in the United States wears its worst form; that, boasting of our civilization and freedom, and frequenting Christian churches, we breed up slaves, nay, beget children for slaves, and sell them at so much a-head." Mr. Macaulay is a reviewer, and he knows that he is "nothing if not critical." The practice of his trade has given him the command of all the slashing and vituperative phrases of our language, and the turn of his mind leads him to the habitual use of them. He is an author, and as no copy-right law secures for him from this country a consideration for his writings, he is not only independent of us, but naturally hates every thing American. He is the representative of Edinburgh; it is his cue to decry our slavery, and in doing so he may safely indulge the malignity of his temper, his indignation against us, and his capacity for railing. He has suffered once, for being in advance of his time in favor of abolition, and he does not intend that it shall be forgotten, or his claim passed over, to any crumb which may now be thrown to the vociferators in the cause. If he does not know that the statements he has made respecting the slaveholders of this country are vile and atrocious falsehoods, it is because he does not think it worth his while to be sure he speaks the truth, so that he speaks to his own purpose.

"Hic niger est, hunc tu, Romane caveto."

Such exhibitions as he has made, may draw the applause of a British House of Commons, but among the sound and high-minded thinkers of the world they can only excite contempt and disgust.

But you are not content with depriving us of all religious feelings. You assert that our slavery has also "demoralized the Northern States," and charge upon it not only every common violation of good order there, but the "Mormon murders," the "Philadelphia riots," and all "the exterminating wars against the Indians." I wonder that you did not increase the list by adding that it had caused the recent inundation of the Mississippi, and the hurricane in the West Indies—perhaps the insurrection of Rebecca, and the war in Scinde. You refer to the law prohibiting the transmission of abolition publications through the mail, as proof of general corruption! You could not do so, however, without noticing the late detected espionage over the British post office by a minister of state. It is true, as you say, it "occasioned a general outburst of national feeling"—from the opposition; and a "Parliamentary inquiry was instituted"—that is, moved, but treated quite cavalierly. At all events, though the fact was admitted, Sir James Graham yet retains the Home Department. For one, I do not undertake to condemn him. Such things are not against the laws and usages of your country. I do not know fully what reasons of state may have influenced him and justified his conduct. But I do know that there is a vast difference in point of "national morality" between the discretionary power residing in your government to open any letter in the public post office, and a well-defined and limited law to prevent the circulation of certain specified incendiary writings by means of the United States mail.

Having now referred to every thing like argument on the subject of slavery, that is worthy of notice in your letter, permit me to remark on its tone and style, and very extraordinary bearing upon other institutions of this country. You commence by addressing certain classes of our people, as belonging to "a nation whose character is *now so low* in the estimation of the civilized world;" and throughout you maintain this tone. Did the Americans who were "under your roof last summer" inform you that such language would be gratifying to their fellow-citizens "having no practical concern with slaveholding?" Or do the infamous libels on America, which you read in our abolition papers, induce you to believe that all that class of people are, like the abolitionists themselves, totally destitute of patriotism or pride of country? Let me tell you that you are grossly deceived. And although your stock-brokers and other speculators, who have been bitten in American ventures, may have raised a stunning "cry" against us in England, there is a vast body of people here besides slaveholders, who justly

"Deem their own land of every land the pride,
Beloved by heaven o'er all the world beside,"
and who *know* that at this moment we rank among the first powers of the world—a position which we not only claim, but are always ready and able to maintain.

The style you assume in addressing your Northern friends, is in perfect keeping with your apparent estimation of them. Though I should be the last, perhaps, to criticise mere style, I could not but be struck with the extremely simple manner of your letter. You seem to have thought you were writing a tract for benighted heathen, and telling wonders never before suggested to their imagination, and so far above their untutored comprehension as to require to be related in the primitive language of "the child's own book." This is sufficiently amusing; and would be more so, but for the coarse and bitter epithets you continually apply to the poor slaveholders—epithets which appear to be stereotyped for the use of abolitionists, and which form a large and material part of all their arguments.

But, perhaps, the most extraordinary part of your letter is your bold denunciation of "*the shameful compromises*" of our Constitution, and your earnest recommendation to those you address to overthrow or revolutionize it. In so many words you say to them, "*you must either separate yourselves* from all political connection with the South, and make your own laws; or if you do not choose such a separation, you must break up *the political ascendency which the Southern have had for so long a time over the Northern States*. The italics in this, as in all other quotations, are your own. It is well for those who circulate your letter here, that the Constitution you denounce requires an overt act to constitute treason. It may be tolerated for an American by birth, to use on his own soil the freedom of speaking and writing which is guaranteed him, and abuse our Constitution, our Union, and our people. But that a foreigner should use such seditious language, in a circular letter addressed to a portion of the American people, is a presumption well calculated to excite the indignation of all. The party known in this country as the abolition party has long since avowed the sentiments you express, and adopted the policy you enjoin. At the recent presidential election, they gave over 62,000 votes for their own candidate, and held the balance of power in two of the largest States—wanting but little of doing it in several others. In the last four years their vote has quadrupled. Should the infatuation continue, and their vote increase in the same ratio for the next four years, it will be as large as the vote of the *actual slaveholders* of the Union. Such a prospect is, doubtless, extremely gratifying to you. It gives hope of a contest on such terms as may insure the downfall of slavery or our Constitution. The South venerates the Constitution, and is prepared to stand by it forever, *such as it came from the hands of our fathers;* to risk every thing to defend and maintain it *in its integrity*. But the South is under no such delusion as to believe that it derives any *peculiar* protection from the Union. On the contrary, it is well known we incur *peculiar danger*, and that we bear far more than our por-portion of the burdens. The apprehension is also fast fading away that any of the dreadful consequences commonly predicted will necessarily result from a separation of the States. And *come what may*, we are firmly resolved that OUR SYSTEM OF DOMESTIC SLAVERY SHALL STAND. The fate of the Union, then—but, thank God, not of republican govern-ment—rests mainly in the hands of the people to whom your letter is addressed—the "professing Christians of the Northern States having no concern with slaveholding," and whom with incendiary zeal you are endeavoring to stir up to strife—without which fana-ticism can neither live, move, nor have any being.

We have often been taunted for our sensitiveness in regard to the discussion of sla-very. Do not suppose it is because we have any doubts of our rights, or scruples about asserting them. There was a time when such doubts and scruples were entertained. Our ancestors opposed the introduction of slaves into this country, and a feeling adverse to it was handed down from them. The enthusiastic love of liberty fostered by our Revolution strengthened this feeling. And before the commencement of the abolition agitation here, it was the common sentiment that it was desirable to get rid of slavery. Many thought it our duty to do so. When that agitation arose, we were driven to a close examination of the subject in all its bearings, and the result has been an *universal conviction* that in hold-ing slaves we violate no law of God,—inflict no injustice on any of his creatures—while the terrible consequences of emancipation to all parties and the world at large, clearly revealed to us, make us shudder at the bare thought of it. The slaveholders are, therefore, indebted to the abolitionists for perfect ease of conscience, and the satisfaction of a set-tled and unanimous determination in reference to this matter. And could their agitation cease now, I believe, after all, the good would preponderate over the evil of it in this country. On the contrary, however, it is urged on with frantic violence, and the abolition-ists, reasoning in the abstract, as if it were a mere moral or metaphysical speculation, or a minor question in politics, profess to be surprised at our exasperation. In their ignorance and recklessness, they seem to be unable to comprehend our feelings or position. The subversion of our rights, the destruction of our property, the disturbance of our peace and the peace of the world, are matters which do not appear to arrest their consideration. When revolutionary France proclaimed "hatred to kings and unity to the republic," and inscribed on her banners "France risen against tyrants," she professed to be only worship-ing "abstract rights." And if there can be such things, perhaps she was. Yet all Europe *rose* to put her sublime theories down. They declared her an enemy to the common peace; that her doctrines alone violated the "law of neighborhood," and, as Mr. Burke said, justly entitled them to anticipate the "damnum nondum factum" of the civil law. Danton, Barrere, and the rest were apparently astonished that umbrage should be taken. The parallel between them and the abolitionists holds good in all respects.

The rise and progress of this fanaticism is one of the phenomena of the age in which we live. I do not intend to repeat what I have already said, or to trace its career more minutely at present. But the legislation of Great Britain will make it historical, and doubt-less you must feel some curiosity to know how it will figure on the page of the annalist. I think I can tell you. Though I have accorded and do accord to you and your party, great influence in bringing about the parliamentary action of your country, you must not expect to go down to posterity as the only cause of it. Though *you* trace the progenitors of aboli-tion from 1516, through a long stream with divers branches, down to the period of its triumph in your country, it has not escaped contemporaries, and will not escape posterity, that England, without much effort, sustained the storm of its scoffs and threats, until the moment arrived when she thought her colonies fully supplied with Africans; and declared against the slave trade, only when she deemed it unnecessary to her, and when her colo-nies, full of slaves, would have great advantages over others not so well provided. Nor did she agree to West India emancipation, until, discovering the error of her previous cal-culation, it became an object to have slaves free throughout the Western world, and, on the ruins of the sugar and cotton-growers of America and the Islands, to build up her great slave empire in the East; while her indefatigable exertions, still continued, to en-graft the right of search upon the law of nations, on the plea of putting an end to the forever increasing slave trade, are well understood to have chiefly in view the complete establishment of her supremacy at sea.[256] Nor must you flatter yourself that your party will derive historic dignity from the names of the illustrious British statesmen who have acted with it. Their country's ends were theirs. They have stooped to use you, as the most illustrious men will sometimes use the vilest instruments, to accomplish their own pur-poses. A few philanthropic common places and rhetorical flourishes, "in the abstract," have secured them your "sweet voices," and your influence over the tribe of mawkish sentimentalists. Wilberforce may have been yours, but what was he besides, but a weal-thy county member? You must, therefore, expect to stand on your own merits alone before posterity, or rather that portion of it that may be curious to trace the history of the delusions which, from time to time, pass over the surface of human affairs, and who may trouble themselves to look through the ramifications of transcendentalism, in this era of extravagances. And how do you expect to appear in their eyes? As Christians, piously endeavoring to enforce the will of God, and carry out the principles of Christianity? Cer-tainly not, since you deny or pervert the Scriptures in the doctrines you advance; and in your conduct, furnish a glaring contrast to the examples of Christ and the apostles. As philanthropists, devoting yourselves to the cause of humanity, relieving the needy, com-forting the afflicted, creating peace and gladness and plenty round about you? Certainly not, since you turn from the needy, the afflicted; from strife, sorrow and starvation which surround you; close your eyes and hands upon them; shut out from your thoughts and feelings the human misery which is real, tangible, and within your reach, to indulge your morbid imagination in conjuring up woes and wants among a strange people in distant lands, and offering them succor in the shape of costless denunciations of their best friends, or by scattering among them "firebrands, arrows and death." Such folly and madness, such wild mockery and base imposture, can never win for you, in the sober judgment of future times, the name of philanthropists. Will you even be regarded as worthy citizens? Scarcely, when the purposes you have in view, can only be achieved by revolutionizing governments and overturning social systems, and when you do not hesitate, zealously and earnestly, to recommend such measures. Be assured, then, that posterity will not regard the abolitionists as Christians, philanthropists, or virtuous citizens. It will, I have no doubt, look upon the mass of the party as silly enthusiasts, led away by designing characters, as is the case with all parties that break from the great, acknowledged ties which bind civilized man in fellowship. The leaders themselves will be regarded as *mere ambitious men;* not taking rank with those whose ambition is "eagle-winged and sky-aspiring," but belonging to that mean and selfish class, who are instigated by "rival-hating envy," and whose base thirst is for *notoriety;* who cloak their designs under vile and impious hypocrisies, and, unable to shine in higher spheres, devote themselves to fanaticism, as a trade. And it will be perceived that, even in that, they shunned the highest walk. Religious fanaticism was an old established vocation, in which something brilliant was required to attract attention. They could not be George Foxes, nor Joanna Southcotes, nor even Joe Smiths. But the dullest pretender could discourse a jumble of pious bigotry, natural rights, and driveling philanthropy. And, addressing himself to aged folly and youthful vanity, to ancient women, to ill-gotten wealth, to the reckless of all classes, who love excitement and change, offer each the cheapest and the safest glory in the market. Hence, their numbers; and, from number and clamor, what impression they have made on the world.

Such, I am persuaded, is the light in which the abolitionists will be viewed by the posterity their history may reach. Unless, indeed—which God forbid—circumstances should so favor as to enable them to produce a convulsion which may elevate them higher on the "bad eminence" where they have placed themselves.

I have the honor to be
Your obedient servant,
J. H. HAMMOND.

THOMAS CLARKSON, Esq.

NOTE.—The foregoing Letters were not originally intended for publication. In preparing them for the press, they have been revised. The alterations and corrections made, however, have been mostly verbal. Had the writer felt at liberty to condense the two letters into one, and bring up the history of abolition to the period of publication, he might have presented a more concise and perfect argument, and illustrated his views more forcibly, by reference to facts recently developed. For example, since writing the first, the letter of Mr. Clarkson, as President of the British Anti-Slavery Society, to Sir Robert Peel, denouncing the whole scheme of "Immigration," has reached him; and after he had forwarded the last, he saw it stated, that Mr. Clarkson had, as late as the first part of

April, addressed the Earl of Aberdeen, and declared, that all efforts to suppress the African slave trade had fully failed. It may be confidently expected, that it will be ere long announced from the same quarter, that the "experiment" of West India emancipation has also proved a complete abortion.

Should the terms which have been applied to the abolitionists appear to any as unduly severe, let it be remembered, that the direct aim of these people is to destroy us by the most shocking of all processes; and that, having a large portion of the civilized world for their audience, they daily and systematically heap upon us the vilest calumnies and most unmitigated abuse. Clergymen lay aside their Bibles, and females unsex themselves, to carry on this horrid warfare against slave holders.

SLAVERY IN THE LIGHT OF ETHNOLOGY.

BY

S. A. CARTWRIGHT, M.D.

OF LOUISIANA.

SLAVERY
IN
THE LIGHT OF ETHNOLOGY.

PHILOSOPHY OF THE NEGRO CONSTITUTION, ELICITED BY QUESTIONS PROPOUNDED BY DR. C. R. HALL, OF TORQUAY, ENGLAND, THROUGH PROF. JACKSON, OF MASSACHUSETTS MEDICAL COLLEGE, BOSTON, TO SAML. A. CARTWRIGHT, M.D., NEW ORLEANS.

[Reprinted from the New Orleans Medical and Surgical Journal.]
To PROF. JACKSON, Boston:—

Dear Sir:—The paper of mine, alluded to by your London correspondent, Dr. Hall, which he saw in the medical work you mention, is not, as he supposes, "*The Report on the diseases and physical peculiarities of the Negro race,*" the physicians of Louisiana, in convention assembled, appointed me to make; but only some additional observations intended for students and those persons whose want of knowledge of Comparative Anatomy prevented them from understanding the Report. The Appendix, intended for students, was published in the *Charleston* (South Carolina) *Medical Journal,* and also in the work you mention, under the caption of the original Report to the Medical Convention, and *the Report itself was omitted* by the editors of those works under the erroneous impression, that the Appendix for students contained the substance of that paper; whereas it does so only in the sense that the four first rules contain the substance of the arithmetic. No wonder your intelligent correspondent should not find, in the Appendix of the Report, the information he was seeking, and hence the questions he asks you to refer to me for solution. I herewith beg leave to send you a copy of the "*Report on the diseases and physical peculiarities of the Negro race,*" which the Louisiana physicians appointed me to make to the State Medical Society. In that paper your correspondent will find most of the questions he asks already answered.

I thank you for the opportunity thus afforded me of supplying an omission in the Southern works above alluded to, of a paper, very imperfect and defective, it is true, yet embodying in a small space the results of the experience and observation of a Southern practitioner, extending through a period of active service of a third of a century's duration, and which had the honor to meet with the approbation of the physicians generally of the South. To the few questions not answered therein I propose to reply, and at the same time to extend my remarks on that branch of the subject more directly connected with the particular object of your correspondent's investigations.

To the question, "Is not Phthisis very common among the slaves of the slave States and unknown among the native Africans at home?" I reply in the negative, that Phthisis, so far from being common among the slaves of the slave States, is very seldom met with. As to the native Africans at home, little or nothing is known of their diseases. They have no science or literature among them, and never had. The word Consumption, is applied to two very different diseases among negroes. The Cachexia Africana, Dirt-eating of the English, and Mal d'Estomac of the French, commonly called Negro Consumption, is a very different malady from Phthisis Pulmonalis, properly so called. The Cachexia Africana, like other spanœmic states of the system, may run into Phthisis, or become complicated with it. Dr. Hall asks, in what does the peculiarity of Negro Consumption consist? It consists in being an anœmatosis and not a tuberculosis. Not having seen my Report, he may have inferred that it was a tubercular disease—whereas it is an erythism of mind connected with spanœmia. Negroes, however, are sometimes, though rarely, afflicted with tubercula pulmonum, or Phthisis, properly so called, which has some peculiarities. With them it is more palpably a secondary disease than it appears to be among white people. European physicians are just beginning to see and acknowledge the truth taught by our Rush in the last century, that what is called Phthisis Pulmonalis is not a primary, but a secondary disease; the tubercles of the lungs not being a cause, but an effect of the primary or original vice of blood origin, or as he called it, general debility. For half a century the attention of the medical profession has been directed to the special and ultimate results of Phthisis, instead of the primary condition of the system causing the formation of tubercles. The new knowledge, derived from the stethoscope, by detecting those abnormal deposits of abortive nutrition, called tubercles, has been received for more than its worth, and has greatly served to keep up the delusion of treating effects instead of causes. The tubercular deposits, revealed by auscultation, are not only the effects of abortive nutrition, but the latter is itself the effect of some derangement in the digestive and respiratory functions, vitiating the nutritive fluids, and producing what Rush called general debility. The defect in the respiratory organs arises from the fact, long overlooked, that in a great many persons, particularly the Anglo-Saxons, the lungs are inadequate to the task of depurating the superabundant blood, which is thrown upon them at the age of maturity, unless aided by an occasional blood-letting, active and abundant exercise of the muscles in the open air, and a nutritious diet, as advised by the American Hippocrates, Benjamin Rush. White children sometimes have Phthisis, but here, as everywhere, it is a rare complaint before maturity (twenty-one in the male and eighteen in the female.) The lymphatic and nervous temperament predominating until then, secures them against this fell destroyer of the master race of men. Phthisis is, par excellence, a disease of the sanguineous temperament, fair complexion, red or flaxen hair, blue eyes, large blood vessels, and a bony encasement too small to admit the full and free expansion of the lungs, enlarged by the superabundant blood, which is determined to those organs during that first half-score of years immediately succeeding puberty. Well-formed chests offer no impediment to its inroads, if the volume of blood be out of proportion to the expansibility and capacity of the pulmonary organs. Hence it is most apt to occur precisely at, and immediately following, that period of life known as matureness, when the sanguineous system becomes fully developed and gains the mastery, so to speak, over the lymphatic and nervous systems. With negroes, the sanguineous never gains the mastery over the lymphatic and nervous systems. Their digestive powers, like children, are strong, and their secretions and excretions copious, excepting the urine, which is rather scant. At the age of maturity they do not become dyspeptic and feeble with softening and attenuation of the muscles, as among those white people suffering the ills of a defective system of physical education, and a want of a wholesome, nutritious diet.

Your correspondent asks, "*Do the slaves consume much sugar, or take rum in intoxicating quantities?*"

They do not consume much sugar, but are occasionally supplied with molasses. Their diet consists principally of pickled pork and corn bread, rice, hominy, beans, peas, potatoes, yams, pumpkins and turnips. Soups, tea, coffee and slops, are seldom used by those in health, and they object to all such articles of diet, as making them weak. They prefer the fattest pork to the lean. In the Atlantic States salted fish is substituted for or alternated with pork—the shad, mackerel and herring, principally the latter. In Cuba pickled beef is used, but they prefer pork. Their diet is of the most nutritious kind, and they will not labor with much effect on any other than a strong, rich diet. With very few exceptions, they do not take rum or other intoxicating drinks, except as a medicine, or in holiday times. Something equivalent to the "*Maine Liquor Law*," (which you can explain to your correspondent,) has long been in practical operation on all well regulated Southern plantations. The experience of two centuries testifies to the advantages of restraining the black population, *by arbitrary power*, from the free use of intoxicating poisons. Man has no better natural right to poison himself or his neighbor, than to maim, wound or kill himself or his neighbor. In regard to intoxicating drinks, the negroes of the South are under wiser laws than any other people in the Union—those of Maine excepted. But these wise unwritten laws do not so well protect those negroes who reside in or near towns and villages, and are not under proper discipline. The Melanic race have a much stronger propensity to indulge in the intemperate use of ardent spirits than white people. They appear to have a natural fondness for alcoholic drinks and tobacco. They need no schooling, as the fair skin races do, to acquire a fondness for either. Nearly all chew tobacco or smoke, and are not sickened and disgusted with the taste of that weed as white men always are when they first begin to use it. As an instance of their natural love for ardent spirits, I was called to a number of negro children, who found a bottle of whisky under a bed, and drank it all without dilution, although it was the first they had ever tasted. It contained arsenic, and had been placed where they found it by the father of some of the children, with a view of poisoning a supposed enemy. But with that want of forethought, so characteristic of the negro race, he did not think of the greater probability of his own children finding and drinking the poison than the enemy he intended it for.

I am asked, "*If I have determined by my own observation the facts in regard to the darker color of the secretions, the flesh, the membranes and the blood of the negro than the white man—or is the statement made on the authority of others?*"

The statement is made on the authority of some of the most distinguished anatomists and physiologists of the last century, confirmed by my own repeated observations. The authorities to which I particularly refer are Malpighi, Stubner, Meckel, Pechlin, Albinus, Sœmmering, Virey and Ebel. Almost every year of my professional life, except a few years when abroad, I have made post mortem examinations of negroes, who have died of various diseases, and I have invariably found the darker color pervading the flesh and the membranes to be very evident in all those who died of acute diseases. Chronic ailments have a tendency to destroy the coloring matter, and generally cause the mucous surfaces to be paler and whiter than in the white race.

I now come to the main and important question—the last of the series, and the most important of all, viz: "*How is it ascertained that negroes consume less oxygen than white people?*"

I answer, by the spirometer. I have delayed my reply to make some further experiments on this branch of the subject. The result is, that the expansibility of the lungs is considerably less in the black than the white race of similar size, age and habit. A white boy expelled from his lungs a larger volume of air than a negro half a head taller and three inches larger around the chest. The deficiency in the negro may be safely estimated at 20 per cent, according to a number of observations I have made at different times. Thus, 174 being the mean bulk of air receivable by the lungs of a white person of five feet in height, 140 cubic inches are given out by a negro of the same stature. It must be remembered, however, that great variations occur in the bulk of air which can be expelled from the chest, depending much upon the age, size, health and habits of each individual. But, as a general rule, it may be safely stated, that a white man, of the same age and size, who has been bred to labor, is, in comparison to the negro, extra capacious. To judge the negro by spirometrical observations made on the white man, would indicate, in the former a morbid condition when none existed. But I am free to confess that this is a subject open to further observations. My estimate may be under or over the exact difference of the capacity of the two races for the consumption of oxygen.

The question is also answered *anatomically*, by the comparatively larger size of the liver, and the smaller size of the lungs; and *physiologically*, by the *roule* the liver performs in the negro's economy being greater, and that of the lungs and kidneys less, than in the white man. But I have not the honor to be the first to call attention to the difference in the pulmonary apparatus of the negro and the white man, and to the fact of the deficiency in the renal secretion. The honor is due to Thomas Jefferson, the third President of the United States. In his Notes on Virginia, Mr. Jefferson suggested that there was a difference in the pulmonary apparatus of negroes, and that they do not extricate as much caloric from the air by respiration, and consesequently consume less oxygen. He also called attention to the fact of the defective action of the kidneys. He remarks, "To our reproach be it said, that although the negro race has been under our eye for a century and a half, it has not been considered as a subject of natural history." Another half century has passed away, and nothing has yet been done to acquire a knowledge of the diseases and physical peculiarities of a people, constituting nearly a moiety of the population of fifteen States of the American confederacy, and whose labor, in cultivating a single plant, which no other operatives but themselves can cultivate without sacrificing ease, comfort, health and life, affords a cheap material, in sufficient abundance, to clothe the naked of the whole world. Even the little scientific knowledge heretofore acquired concerning them, has been so far forgotten, that when I enumerated a few of their anatomical and physical peculiarities, well known to the medical men of the seventeenth and eighteenth centuries, I was supposed by some of my cotemporaries in the South to be broaching no-velties and advancing speculations wild and crude. But I would not be understood as underrating the editors of the *Charleston Medical Journal* and some other Southern writ-ers, for mistaking anatomical facts for wild speculations, and condemning them as such in their editorial apologies for not publishing the same. The fault lies not with them, but in that system of education which seems intended to keep physicians, divines, and all other classes of men in Egyptian darkness of every thing pertaining to the philosophy of the negro constitution. It is only the country and village practitioners of the Southern States (among professional men,) who appear to know any thing at all about the peculiar nature of negroes—having derived their knowledge, not from books or schools, but in the field of experience. It is the latter class of medical men, by far the most numerous in the South, who have with great unanimity sustained my feeble efforts to make the negro's peculiar nature known, and the important fact that he consumes less oxygen than the white man. Until his defective hæmatosis be made an element in calculating the best means for improving the negro's condition, our Northern people ought not to wonder at finding their colored population, born to freedom by the side of the church and school-house door, in a lower species of degradation, after trying for half a century or more to elevate them, than an equal number of slaves any where to be found in the South. "Will not a lover of natural history," says Mr. Jefferson, "one who views the gradations in all the races of animals with the eye of philosophy, excuse an effort to keep those of the de-partment of man as distinct as nature formed them?" But no effort has since been made to draw the distinctions between the black and the white races by the knife of the anatomist, but much false logic has been introduced into our books and schools, to argue down the distinctions which nature has made. It is to anatomy and physiology we should look, when vindicating the liberty of human nature, to see that its dignity and best interest be preserved. "Among the Romans," says Mr. Jefferson, "emancipation required but one ef-fort, but with us a second is necessary, unknown to history." This second belongs properly to natural history; the difference in the last not being artificial, as among the

Romans, or the present Britons, requiring only an act of legislation or a revolution to efface forever, but natural, which no human laws or governmental changes can ever obliterate. The framers of our Constitution were aware of these facts, and built the Constitution upon the basis of natural distinctions or physical differences in the two races composing the American population. A very important difference between the two will be found in the fact of the greater amount of oxygen consumed by the one than the other. If the Constitution be worth defending, surely the great truths of natural history, on which it rests as a basis, are worth being made known and regarded by our statesmen. That negroes consume less oxygen than the white race, is proved by their motions being proverbially much slower, and their want of muscular and mental activity. But to comprehend fully the weight of this proof of their defective hæmatosis, it is necessary to bear in mind one of the great leading truths disclosed by comparative anatomy. Cuvier was the first to demonstrate beyond a doubt that muscular energy and activity are in direct proportion to the development and activity of the pulmonary organs. In his 29th lesson, vol. vii, p. 17, D'Anatomie Comparée, he says, "*Dans les animaux vertebrés cette quantité de respiration fait connaître presque par un calcul mathématique la nature particulière de chaque class.*" In the preceding page he says,—"That the relations observed in the different animals, between the quantity of their respiration and the energy of their motive force, is one of the finest demonstrations that comparative anatomy can furnish to physiology, and at the same time one of the best applications of comparative anatomy to natural history." The slower motions of the owl prove to the natural historian that it consumes less oxygen than the eagle. By the same physiological principle he can tell that the herring is the most active among fish, and the flounder the slowest, by merely seeing the gills of each: those of the herring being very large, prove that it consumes much oxygen and is very active; while the flounder, with its small gills, consumes but little, and is very slow in its motions as a necessary consequence. Hence the habitual slower motions of the negro than the white man, is a positive proof that he consumes less oxygen. The slow gait of the negro is an important element to be taken into consideration in studying his nature. I have the authority of one of the very best observers of mankind, that this element in the negro's economy is particularly worthy of being studied. It is no less an authority than the father of his country, the first President of the United States, the illustrious Washington. Washington knew better, perhaps, than any other man what the white man could do; his power of endurance and strength of wind under a given speed of motion. Yet he found that all his observations on the white race were inapplicable to negroes. To know what they could do, and to ascertain their power of endurance and strength of wind, new observations had to be made, and he made them accordingly. He made them on his own negroes. He saw they did not move like the soldiers he had been accustomed to command. Their motions were much slower, and they performed their tasks in a more dilatory manner; the amount of labor they could perform in a given time, with ease and comfort to themselves, could not be told by his knowledge of what white men could do. He therefore noted the gait or movements natural to negroes, and made observations himself of how much they could effect in a given time, under the slow motions or gait natural to them. He did this to enable him to judge of what would be a reasonable service to expect from them, and to know when they loitered and when they performed their duty. Those persons unacquainted with the important truth that negroes are naturally slower in their motions than white people, judging the former by the latter, often attempt to drive them into the same brisk motions. But a day's experience ought to be enough to teach them that every attempt to drive negroes to the performance of tasks equal to what the white laborer would voluntarily impose upon himself, is an actual loss to the master; who, instead of getting more service out of them, actually gets less, and soon none, if such a course be persisted in; because they become disabled in body and indisposed in mind to perform any service at all. Every master or overseer, although he may know nothing of the law above mentioned, discovered by Cuvier, may soon learn from experience the important fact, that there is no other alternative than to let their negroes assume, *by their own instincts*, the natural gait or movement peculiar to them, and then, like Washington, observe what can be effected in a given time by that given gait or movement, and to ask for nor expect more. In vol. ii, pages 511 to 512, (Washington's Writings, published by Jared Sparks) are recorded a few of the observations made by the father of his country on his own slaves, as an illustration of the preceding remarks. It is to be regretted that Mr. Sparks, out of deference to a modern species of idolatry (all fanaticism is idolatry,) which has taken deep root in Great Britain and despotic Europe, and has from thence been transplanted into our republic, particularly in the Northern portion of it, should have suppressed so much of the valuable observations of Washington on the negro race, as only to publish a small fragment of the extensive knowledge his comprehensive mind had stored up on this important subject, well known to his neighbors. The fragment informs us, that on a certain day he visited his plantations, and found that certain negro slaves there mentioned, by the names of George, Tom and Mike, had only hewed a certain number of feet—whereupon Washington sat down and observed their motions, letting them proceed their own way," and ascertained how many feet each hewed in one hour and a quarter. He also made observations on his sawyers at the same time and in the same manner. From the data thus acquired he ascertained, in the short space of an hour and a quarter, how many feet would be a day's work for hewing, and how many for sawing, under their usual slow gait or movement. This hewing and sawing were of poplar. "What may be the difference, therefore," says Washington, "between the working of this wood and other, some future observations must make known." But Mr. Sparks, out of deference to the new school of idolatry, having its head quarters in Exeter Hall, omitted, almost entirely, the publication of any more observations on the subject. It is no less idolatry to set up an anti-scriptural dogma and to make it a rule of action, than to worship a block or a graven image in the place of the true God. The true God has said in the Pentateuch, the most authentic books of the Bible, "*And of the heathen shall ye buy bond-men and bond-maids* [slaves] *and your children shall inherit them after you, and they shall be your bondmen* [slaves] *forever.*" Leviticus, chap. xxv, verses 44, 45, 46. But the Dogma or Negro god of Exeter Hall says that "*negro slavery is sin*," and that it is contrary to the moral sense or conscience. Medicine was anciently called the divine art; to be entitled to hold that appellation, ought it not to lend its aid to arrest in this happy republic the progress of idolatry, which is only another name for fanaticism? And will your learned correspondent help to arrest it in England? Or will he, like Prichard, Todd, and others, make science bow to the policy of his government?—To build up India at the expense of our Union? The subject of his investigations, tubercular disease, if properly studied, leads directly to that species of knowledge, enabling him to determine on physiological principles, which is the best system of ethics, that taught in the Bible, *to enslave the Canaanite*, or that taught in Exeter Hall, *to set him free?* It will lead him to the discovery, that the negro, or Canaanitish race, consume less oxygen than the white, and that as a necessary consequence of the deficient aeration of the blood in the lungs, a hebetude of mind and body is the inevitable physiological effect; thus making it a mercy and a blessing to negroes to have persons in authority set over them, to provide for and take care of them. Under the dogma or new commandment to free the Canaanite, practically exercised in Van Dieman's Land and at the Cape of Good Hope, the poor negro race have become nearly annihilated. Whereas under that system of ethics taught in the Bible and made a rule of action in the Southern States, the descendants of Canaan are more rapidly increasing in numbers, and have more of the comforts and pleasures of life, and more morality and Christianity among them than any others of the same race on any other portion of the globe. They are daily bought and sold, and inherited as property, as the Scriptures said they should be. Whereas in all those countries and places in which they are set free, in obedience to the dogma that "slavery is sin," they rapidly degenerate into barbarism, as they are doing in the West Indies, or become extinct as in Van Dieman's Land. The physiological fact that negroes consume less oxygen indicates the superior wisdom of the precepts taught in the Bible regarding those people, to any promulgated from Exeter Hall. Experience also proves the former to be the best. You hear of the poor negroes, or colored people, as you call them, being beaten with many stripes by their masters and overseers. But owing to the fact that they consume less oxygen than white people, and the other physical differences founded on difference of structure, they beat one another, when free from the white man's authority, with ten stripes where they would get one from him. They are as much in slavery in Boston as in New Orleans. They suffer more from corporeal or other punishments in the cellars and dark lanes and alleys of Boston, New York and Philadelphia, by the cruel tyranny practiced by the strong over the weak and helpless, than an equal number in Southern slavery. In slavery the stripes fall upon the evil disposed, vicious, buck negro fellows. But when removed from the white man's authority, the latter make them fall on helpless women and children, the weak and the infirm. Good conduct, so far from being a protection, invites aggression.

But what connection have these observations, you may say, with the subject of Dr. Hall's inquiries, and what light do they throw on tubercular disease? They show that there exists an intimate connection between the amount of oxygen consumed in the lungs and the phenomena of body and mind. They point to a people whose respiratory apparatus is so defective, that they have not sufficient industry and mental energy to provide for themselves, or resolution sufficiently strong to prevent them, when in freedom, from being subjected to the arbitrary, capricious will of the drunken and vicious of their own color, who may happen to have greater physical strength and more cunning; they show that Phthisis is a disease of the master race, and not of the slave race—that it is the bane of that master race of men, known by an active hæmatosis; by the brain receiving a larger quantity of aerated blood than it is entitled to; by the strong development of the circulating system; by the energy of intellect; by the strength and activity of the muscular system; the vivid imagination; the irritable, mobile, ardent and inflammatory temperament, and the indomitable will and love of freedom. Whereas the negro constitution, being the opposite of all this, is not subject to Phthisis, although it partakes of what is called the scrofulous diathesis. In the negro constitution, as the Frenchman would say, "*l'arbre arteriel cede sa prominance à l'arbre veineuse,*" spreading coldness, languor and want of energy over the entire system. The white fluids, or lymphatic temperament, predominating, they are not so liable as the fair race, to inflammatory diseases of the lungs, or any other organ; but from the superabundant viscidities and mucosities of their mucous surfaces, they are more liable to engorgements and pulmonary congestions than any other race of men. In proof of which I beg leave to refer your correspondent to a standard work entitled "Observations sur les Maladies des Negres, par M. Dazille. Paris, 1776."

Pneumonia, without subjective symptoms, is very common among them. Diphtheretic affections, so common among white children, are very rare among negroes. Intercurrent Pneumonia is more common among them than any other class of people. It is met with in Typhoid fevers, Rheumatism and hepatic derangements, to which they are very liable in the cold season. The local malady requires a different treatment, to correspond with the general disorder. Bad, vicious, ungovernable negroes are subject, to what might properly be termed, Scorbutic Pneumonia—a blood disease, requiring anti-scorbutics. Scorbutic negroes are always vicious or worthless. A course of anti-scorbutics will reform their morals, and make good negroes out of worthless ones. They are liable to suffocative orthopnœa after measles, and die unless bled and purged. But purgatives are injurious in almost all their other affections involving the respiratory organs, except such as act especially on the liver. They check expectoration, says Dazille, and lay the foundations of those effusions and depots of matter so often mistaken for genuine Phthisis. Auscultation cannot well be made available with them. The nose pleads to the eye and touch to form the diagnosis, without calling into requisition the ear. A single examination by auscultation, in persons abounding with so much phlegm, is not sufficient to arrive at a correct diagnosis. Repeated examinations in various postures are too tedious in execution, and too offensive to the auscultator, to come into general use in diagnosing the diseases of the Melanic race. This valuable mode of exploration, so useful in many cases, as practiced by experts, has of late years been carried to a ridiculous extreme, in being made to deceive and delude more practitioners than it enlightens, from the haste and inexperience of those who practice it. With negroes it is unnecessary, except in some rare instances. Their diseases, like their passions, have each its peculiar expression stamped in the countenance. They are like young children in this respect. They cannot disguise their countenance like white people. An intelligent and observant observer can tell from their countenance when they are plotting mischief, or have committed some crime; when they are satisfied or dissatisfied; when in pleasure or in pain; when troubled or disturbed in mind; or when telling a falsehood instead of the truth. An observant physician has only to bring the old science of prosoposcopia, so much used by Hippocrates in forming his diagnosis, to bear upon negroes, to be able, by a little experience, to ascertain the most of them at a glance by the expression of their countenance.

They are very subject to fevers, attended with an obstructed circulation of air and blood in the pulmonary organs. Their abundant mucosities often prevent the ingress of air into the air cells, bloating their lips and cheeks, which are coated with a tenacious saliva. A cessation of digestion from too full a meal, or some hepatic or other derangement, is soon attended with such a copious exudation of mucosities, filling the air cells and tracheal passages, as to cause apoplexy, which with them is only another name for asphyxia. The head has nothing to do with it. So abundant are the mucosities in negroes, that those in the best health have a whitish, pasty mucus, of considerable thickness on the tongue, leading a physician not acquainted with them to suppose that they were dyspeptic, or otherwise indisposed. The lungs of the white man are the main outlets for the elimination of carbonic acid formed in the tissues. Negroes, however, by an instinctive habit of covering their mouth, nose, head and face with a blanket, or some other covering, when they sleep, throw upon the liver an additional duty to perform, in the excretion of carbonic acid. Any cause, obstructing the action of the liver, quickly produces with them a grave malady, the retention of carbonic acid in the blood soon poisoning them.

Hence with white people a moderate degree of hepatic obstruction, by a residence in swampy districts, is often found beneficial in diminishing the exalted sensibility and irritability of phthisical patients. Viscous engorgements of the lungs destroy more negroes than all other diseases combined. They are distinguished from inflammatory affections by the pyrexial symptoms not being strongly marked, or marked at all—by the puffy or bloated appearance of the face and lips—by the slavering mouth—the highly charged tongue—and by the torpor of mind and body. In a word, all the symptoms point to a deficient aeration of the blood, or a kind of half way asphyxia. A torpid state of the system, listlessness and inactivity almost approaching to asphyxia from the diminished quantity of oxygen consumed by the lungs of the negro, form a striking contrast with the energetic, active, restless, persevering Anglo-Saxon, with a tendency to phlogosis and phthisis pulmonalis, from the surplus quantity of oxygen consumed by his lungs. Blistering the nape of the neck, so irritating in nearly all of the diseases of the Saxon race, is almost a sovereign remedy or specific for a large proportion of the complaints that negroes are subject to; because most of them arise from defective respiratory action. Hence whipping the lungs to increased action by the application of blisters over the origin of the respiratory nerves, a remedy so inexpedient and so often contra-indicated in most of the maladies of the white man, has a magic charm about it in the treatment of those of the negro. The magic effect of a blister to that part of the Ethiopian's body, in a large class of his ailments, although well known to most of the planters and overseers of the Southern States, is scarcely known at all to the medical profession beyond those boundaries. Even here, where that portion of the profession who have had much experience in the treatment of their diseases, and are aware of the simple fact itself, do not profit by it in many cases where it is indicated; because they do not perceive the indication clearly, so long as the rationale of the remedy remains unexplained.

Your asking for the proofs of my assertion, "that the negro consumes less oxygen than the white man," has led me into a new, extensive and unexplored field of science, where the rationale of that and many other important facts may be found springing up spontaneously. We have medical schools in abundance teaching the art of curing the ailments, and even the most insignificant sores, incident to the half-starved, oppressed pauper population of Europe—a population we have not got, never had and never can have, so long as we have negro slaves to work in the cane, cotton and rice fields, where the white man, from the physiological laws governing his economy, *can not labor and live:* but where the negro thrives, luxuriates and enjoys existence more than any laboring peasantry to be found on the continent of Europe; yet we have no schools or any chair in our numerous institutions of medical learning to teach the art of curing and preventing the diseases peculiar to our immense population of negro slaves, or to make them more efficient and valuable, docile and manageable; comfortable, happy and contented by still further improving their condition, which can only be done by studying their nature, and not by the North and South bandying epithets—not by the quackery which prescribes the same remedy, the liberty elixir, for all constitutions. The two races, the Anglo-Saxon and the negro, have antipodal constitutions. The former abounds with red blood, even penetrating the capillaries and the veins, flushing the face and illuminating the countenance; the skin white; lips thin; nose high; hair auburn, flaxen, red or black; beard thick and heavy; eyes brilliant; will strong and unconquerable; mind and muscles full of energy and activity. The latter, with molasses blood sluggishly circulating and scarcely penetrating the capillaries; skin ebony, and the mucous membranes and muscles partaking of the darker hue pervading the blood and the cutis; lips thick and protuberant; nose broad and flat; scalp covered with a coarse, crispy wool in thick naps; beard wanting or consisting of a few scattering woolly naps, in the "*bucks*," provincially so called; mind and body dull and slothful; will weak, wanting or subdued. The study of such opposite organizations, the one prone to Phthisis and the other not, can not fail to throw some light on tubercular disease, the subject of your correspondent, Dr. Hall's present investigation. In contrasting the typical white man, having an excess of red blood and a liability to inflammatory and tuberculous complaints and disorders of the digestive system, with the typical negro, deficient aerated blood, and abounding in mucosites, having an active liver and a strong digestion, and a proclivity strongly marked to fall into congestions, or cold humid engorgements approaching asphyxia, I hope he will be able to find in this unpolished communication something useful.

I have the honor to be, with great respect,
SAML. A. CARTWRIGHT, M.D.

New Orleans, July 19th, 1852.

APPENDIX.
NATURAL HISTORY OF THE PROGNATHOUS SPECIES OF MANKIND.

It is not intended by the use of the term Prognathous to call in question the black man's humanity or the unity of the human races as a *genus*, but to prove that the species of the genus homo are not a unity, but a plurality, each essentially different from the others—one of them being so unlike the other two—the oval-headed Caucasian and the pyramidal-headed Mongolian—as to be actually prognathous, like the brute creation; not that the negro is a brute, or half man and half brute, but a genuine human being, anatomically constructed, about the head and face, more like the monkey tribes and the lower order of animals than any other species of the genus man. Prognathous is a technical term derived from *pro*, before, and *gnathos*, the jaws, indicating that the muzzle or mouth is anterior to the brain. The lower animals, according to Cuvier, are distinguished from the European and Mongol man by the mouth and face projecting further forward in the profile than the brain. He expresses the rule thus: *face anterior, cranium posterior*. The typical negroes of adult age, when tried by this rule, are proved to belong to a different species from the man of Europe or Asia, because the head and face are anatomically constructed more after the fashion of the simiadiæ and the brute creation than the Caucasian and Mongolian species of mankind, their mouth and jaws projecting beyond the forehead containing the anterior lobes of the brain. Moreover, their faces are proportionally larger than their crania, instead of smaller, as in the other two species of the genus man. Young monkeys and young negroes, however, are not prognathous like their parents, but become so as they grow older. The head of the infant ourang outang is like that of a well formed Caucasian child in the projection and hight of the forehead and the convexity of the vertea. The brain appears to be larger than it really is, because the face, at birth, has not attained its proportional size. The face of the Caucasian infant is a little under its proportional size when compared with the cranium. In the infant negro and ourang outang it is greatly so. Although so much smaller in infancy than the cranium, the face of the young monkey ultimately outgrows the cranium; so, also, does the face of the young negro, whereas in the Caucasian, the face always continues to be smaller than the cranium. The superfices of the face at puberty exceeds that of the hairy scalp both in the negro and the monkey, while it is always less in the white man. Young monkeys and young negroes are superior to white children of the same age in memory and other intellectual faculties. The white infant comes into the world with its brain inclosed by fifteen disunited bony plates—the occipital bone being divided into four parts, the sphenoid into three, the frontal into two, each of the two temporals into two, which, with the two parietals, make fifteen plates in all—the vomer and ethmoid not being ossified at birth. The bones of the head are not only disunited, but are more or less overlapped at birth, in consequence of the largeness of the Caucasian child's head and the smallness of its mother's pelvis, giving the head an elongated form, and an irregular, knotty feel to the touch. The negro infant, however, is born with a small, hard, smooth, round head like a gourd. Instead of the frontal and temporal bones being divided into six plates, as in the white child, they form but one bone in the negro infant. The head is not only smaller than that of the white child, but the pelvis of the negress is wider than that of the white woman—its greater obliquity also favors parturition and prevents miscarriage.

Negro children and white children are alike at birth in one remarkable particular— they are both born *white*, and so much alike, as far as color is concerned, as scarcely to be distinguished from each other. In a very short time, however, the skin of the negro infant begins to darken and continues to grow darker until it becomes of a shining black color, provided the child be healthy. The skin will become black whether exposed to the air and light or not. The blackness is not of as deep a shade during the first years of life, as afterward. The black color is not so deep in the female as in the male, nor in the feeble, sickly negro as in the robust and healthy. Blackness is a characteristic of the prognathous species of the genus homo, but all the varieties of all the prognathous species are not equally black. Nor are the individuals of the same family or variety equally so. The lighter shades of color, when not derived from admixture with Mongolian or Caucasian blood, indicate degeneration in the prognathous species. The Hottentots, Bushmen and aborigines of Australia are inferior in mind and body to the typical African of Guinea and the Niger.

The typical negroes themselves are more or less superior or inferior to one another precisely as they approximate to or recede from the typical standard in color and form, due allowance being made for age and sex. The standard is an oily, shining black, and as far as the conformation of the head and face is concerned and the relative proportion of nervous matter outside of the cranium to the quantity of cerebral matter within it, is found between the simiadiæ[257] and the Caucasian. Thus, in the typical negro, a perpendicular line, let fall from the forehead, cuts off a large portion of the face, throwing the mouth, the thick lips, and the projecting teeth anterior to the cranium, but not the entire face, as in the lower animals and monkey tribes. When all, or a greater part of the face is thrown anterior to the line, the negro approximates the monkey anatomically more than he does the true Caucasian; and when little or none of the face is anterior to the line, he approximates that mythical being of Dr. Van Evrie, a *black white man*, and almost ceases to be a negro. The black man occasionally seen in Africa, called the *Bature Dutu*, with high nose, thin lips, and long straight hair, is not a negro at all, but a Moor tanned by the climate—because his children, not exposed to the sun, do not become black like himself. The typical negro's nervous system is modeled a little different from the Caucasian and somewhat like the ourang outang. The medullary spinal cord is larger and more developed than in the white man, but less so than in the monkey tribes. The occipital foramen, giving exit to the spinal cord, is a third longer, says Cuvier, in proportion to its breadth, than in the Caucasian, and is so oblique as to form an angle of 30° with the horizon, yet not so oblique as in the simiadæ, but sufficiently so to throw the head somewhat backward and the face upward in the erect position. Hence, from the obliquity of the head and the pelvis, the negro walks steadier with a weight on his head, as a pail of water for instance, than without it; whereas, the white man, with a weight on his head, has great difficulty in maintaining his centre of gravity, owing to the occipital foramen forming no angle with the cranium, the pelvis, the spine, or the thighs—all forming a straight line from the crown of the head to the sole of the foot without any of the obliquities seen in the negro's knees, thighs, pelvis and head—and still more evident in the ourang outang.

The nerves of organic life are larger in the prognathous species of mankind than in the Caucasian species, but not so well developed as in the simiadiæ. The brain is about a tenth smaller in the prognathous man than in the Frenchman, as proved by actual measurement of skulls by the French savans, Palisot and Virey. Hence, from the small brain and the larger nerves, the digestion of the prognathous species is better than that of the Caucasian, and its animal appetites stronger, approaching the simiadiæ but stopping short of their beastiality. The nostrils of the prognathous species of mankind open higher up than they do in the white or olive species, but not so high up as in the monkey tribes. In the gibbon, for instance, they open between the orbits. Although the typical negro's nostrils open high up, yet owing to the nasal bones being short and flat, there is no projection or prominence formed between his orbits by the bones of the nose, as in the Caucasian species. The nostrils, however, are much wider, about as wide from wing to wing, as the white man's mouth from corner to corner, and the internal bones, called the turbinated, on which the olfactory nerves are spread, are larger and project nearer to the opening of the nostrils than in the white man. Hence the negro approximates the lower animals in his sense of smell, and can detect snakes by that sense alone. All the senses are more acute, but less delicate and discriminating, than the white man's. He has a good ear for melody but not for harmony, a keen taste and relish for food but less discriminating between the different kinds of esculent substances than the Caucasian. His lips are immensely thicker than any of the white race, his nose broader and flatter, his chin smaller and more retreating, his foot flatter, broader, larger, and the heel longer, while he has scarcely any calves at all to his legs when compared to an equally healthy and muscular white man. He does not walk flat on his feet but on the outer sides, in consequence of the sole of the foot having a direction inwards, from the legs and thighs being arched outwards and the knees bent. The verb, from which his Hebrew name is derived, points out this flexed position of the knees, and also clearly expresses the servile type of his mind. Ham, the father of Canaan, when translated into plain English, reads that a black man was the father of the slave or knee-bending species of mankind.

The blackness of the prognathous race, known in the world's history as Canaanites, Cushites, Ethiopians, black men or negroes, is not confined to the skin, but pervades, in a greater or less degree, the whole inward man down to the bones themselves, giving the flesh and the blood, the membranes and every organ and part of the body, except the bones, a darker hue than in the white race. Who knows but what Canaan's mother may have been a genuine Cushite, as black inside as out, and that Cush, which means blackness, was the mark put upon Cain? Whatever may have been the mark set upon Cain, the negro, in all ages of the world, has carried with him a mark equally efficient in preventing him from being slain—the mark of blackness. The wild Arabs and hostile American Indians invariably catch the black wanderer and make a slave of him instead of killing him, as they do the white man.

Nich. Pechlin, in a work written last century entitled "De cute Athiopum," Albinus, in another work, entitled "De sede et causa coloris Athiop," as also the great German anatomists, Meiners, Ebel, and Sœmmering, all bear witness to the fact that the muscles, blood, membranes, and all the internal organs of the body, (the bones alone excepted,) are of a darker hue in the negro than in the white man. They estimate the difference in color to be equal to that which exists between the hare and the rabbit. Who ever doubts the fact, or has none of those old and impartial authorities at hand—impartial because they were written before England adopted the policy of pressing religion and science in her service to place white American republican freemen and Guinea negroes upon the same platform—has only to look into the mouth of the first healthy typical negro he meets to be convinced of the truth, that the entire membraneous lining of the inside of the cheeks, lips and gums is of a much darker color than in the white man.

The negro, however, must be healthy and in good condition—sickness, hard usage and chronic ailments, particularly that cachexia, improperly called consumption, speedily extracts the coloring matter out of the mucous membranes, leaving them paler and whiter than in the Caucasian. The bleaching process of bad health or degeneration begins in the blood, membranes and muscles, and finally extracts so much of the coloring pigment out of the skin, as to give it a dull ashy appearance, sometimes extracting the whole of it, converting the negro into the albino. Albinoism or cucosis does not necessarily imply hybridism. It occurs among the pure Africans from any cause producing a degeneration of the species. Hybridism, however, is the most prolific source of that degeneration. Sometimes the degeneration shows itself by white spots, like the petals of flowers, covering different parts of the skin. The Mexicans are subject to a similar degeneration, only that the spots and stripes are black instead of white. It is called the pinto with them. Even the pigment of the iris and the coloring matter of the albino's hair is absorbed, giving it a silvery white appearance, and converting him into a clairvoyant at night. According to Professors Brown, Seidy and Gibbs, the negro's hair is not tubular, like the white man's, but it is eccentrically elliptical, with flattened edges, the coloring matter residing in the epidermis, and not in tubes. In the place of a tube, the shaft of each hair is surrounded with a scaly covering like sheep's wool, and, like wool, is capable of being felted. True hair does not possess that property. The degeneration called albinoism has a remarkable influence upon the hair, destroying its coarse, nappy, wooly appearance, and converting it into fine, long, soft, silky, curly threads. Often, the whole external skin, so remarkably void of hair in the healthy negro, becomes covered with a very fine, silky down, scarcely perceptible to the naked eye, when transformed into the albino.

Mr. Bowen, the celebrated Baptist missionary, [see his work entitled Central Africa and Missionary Labors from 1849 to 1856, by T. J. Bowen, Charleston, Southern Baptist Publication Society, 1857,] met with a great many cases of leucosis in Soudan or Negroland, back of Liberia, and erroneously concluded that these people had very little, if any negro blood in them, and would be better subjects for missionary labors than the blacks of the same country. They are, however, nothing but *white* black men, a degeneration of the negro proper, and are even less capable of perpetuating themselves than the hybrids or mulattoes. Mr. Bowen is at a loss to account for the depopulation, which he verifies has been going on in Soudan the last fifty years, threatening to leave the country, at no distant time, bare of inhabitants, unless roads be constructed by the Christians of the Southern States for commercial intercourse, and double exertions made to civilize and Christianize the waning population of Central Africa before it entirely disappears. The good missionary, though sent out from Georgia, was evidently taught in that British school which assumes that there is only a single species in the genus homo, in opposition to the Bible, that clearly designates three. That school quotes the references in the sacred volume, implying unity in the genus—a unity which no one denies—to disprove the existence of distinct species, and upon this fallacy builds the theory that negro, Indian and white men are beings exactly alike, because they are human beings. *Ergo*, the liberty so beneficial to the white man, would be equally so to the negro—disregarding as a fable those words of the Bible expressly declaring that the latter *shall be servant of servants* to the former—words which would not have been there if that kind of subordination called slavery was not the normal condition of the race of Ham. To expect to civilize or Christianize the negro without the intervention of slavery is to expect an impossibility.

Mr. Bowen's experience and natural good sense occasionally got the better of his theoretical views. Thus, at page 90, we find him confessing that "the native African negroes ought to have masters in obedience to the demands of natural justice." At page 149 he lets us into the secret of the depopulating process which has been going on in Central Africa the last fifty years. While standing among some negroes in Ikata, a town in Central Africa, a capricious mulatto chief sent some officers among the company, who singled out a poor fellow who had offended the chief by saying that as he let a white man into town, he might let in a Dahomey man also, and presented him with an empty bag with the message: "*The king says you must send me your head.*" The Rev. missionary, who was present at the beheading, made no comment further than to state the fact. But he might have added that the blood of that negro, and millions of others, will be required at the hands of Victoria Regina and the United States for having officiously destroyed the value of negro property in Africa by breaking up the only trade that ever protected the native Africans against the butcheries, cruelties and oppressions of their mulatto, Moorish and Mahommedan tyrants. It is these butcheries and cruelties, and the little care taken of the black man in Africa, the last fifty years, since he became valueless through British and American philanthropy, that lie at the root of the depopulating process which is going on in the dark land of the Niger. Empty bags are now filled with heads instead of cowries. Mr. Bowen was surprised to see so few black men in Soudan, where, half a century ago, he says they were so numerous. But he rather regards it as a fortunate circumstance, as he has no hope of Christianizing the typical negro, except through slavery to Christian masters—and that idea is abhorrent to the school in which he was taught; but he has more hope from the mixed races, and these, he confesses, can not be effectually Christianized until civilized. He deplores the bad example of the black race, among them, their polygamy, etc., as greatly in the way of civilizing the mulattoes. But he has overlooked the important fact, as many do, that the existence of the hybrids themselves depends upon the existence of the typical Africans. The extinction of the latter must, of necessity, be soon followed by the extinction of the former, as they can not, for any length of time, propagate among themselves.

Mr. Bowen inferred that the negroes of Central Africa, although diminishing in numbers, are rising higher in the scale of humanity, from the very small circumstance that they do not emit from their bodies so strong and so offensive an odor as the negro slaves of Georgia and the Carolinas do, nor are their skins of so deep a black. This is a good illustration of the important truth, that all the danger of the slavery question lies in the ignorance of Scripture and the natural history of the negro. A little acquaintance with the negro's natural history would prove to Mr. Bowen that the strong odor emitted by the negro, like the deep pigment of the skin, is an indication of high health, happiness, and good treatment, while its deficiency is a sure sign of unhappiness, disease, bad treatment, or degeneration. The skin of a happy, healthy negro is not only blacker and more oily than an unhappy, unhealthy one, but emits the strongest odor when the body is warmed by exercise and the soul is filled with the most pleasurable emotions. In the dance called *patting juber*, the odor emitted from the men, intoxicated with pleasure, is often so powerful as to throw the negro women into paroxysms of unconsciousness, vulgo hysterics. On another point of much importance there is no practical difference between the Rev. missionary and that clear-headed, bold, and eccentric old Methodist, Dr. McFarlane. Both believe that the Bible can do ignorant, sensual savages no good; both believe that nothing but compulsatory power can restrain uncivilized barbarians from polygamy, inebriety, and other sinful practices.

The good missionary, however, believes in the possibility of civilizing the inferior races by the money and means of the Christian nations lavishly bestowed, after which he thinks it will be no difficult matter to convert them to Christianity. Whereas the venerable Methodist believes in the impossibility of civilizing them, and therefore concludes that the Written Word was not intended for those inferior races who can not read it. When the philosophy of the prognathous species of mankind is better understood, it will be seen how they, the lowest of the human species, can be made partakers, equally with the highest, in the blessings and benefits of the Written Word of God. The plantation laws against polygamy, intoxicating drinks, and other besetting sins of the negro race in the savage state, are gradually and silently converting the African barbarian into a moral, rational, and civilized being, thereby rendering the heart a fit tabernacle for the reception of Gospel truths. The prejudices of many, perhaps the majority of the Southern people, against educating the negroes they hold in subjection, arise from some vague and indefinite fears of its consequences, suggested by the abolition and British theories built on the false assumption that the negro is a white man with a black skin. If such an assumption had the smallest degree of truth in it, the more profound the ignorance and the deeper sunk in barbarism the slaves were kept, the better it would be for them and their masters. But experience proves that masters and overseers have nothing at all to fear from civilized and intelligent negroes, and no trouble whatever in managing them—that all the trouble, insubordination and danger arise from the uncivilized, immoral, rude, and grossly ignorant portion of the servile race. It is not the ignorant semi-barbarian that the master or overseer intrusts with his keys, his money, his horse or his gun, but the most intelligent of the plantation—one whose intellect and morals have undergone the best training. An educated negro, one whose intellect and morals have been cultivated, is worth double the price of the wild, uncultivated, black barbarian of Cuba and will do twice as much work, do it better and with less trouble.

The prejudice against educating the negroes may also be traced to the neglect of American divines in making themselves acquainted with Hebrew literature. What little the most of them know of the meaning of the untranslated terms occurring in the Bible, and the signification of the verbs from which they are derived, is mostly gathered from British commentators and glossary-makers, who have blinked the facts that disprove the Exeter Hall dogma, that negro slavery is sin against God. Hence, even in the South, the important Biblical truth, that the white man derives his authority to govern the negro from the Great Jehovah, is seldom proclaimed from the pulpit. If it were proclaimed, the master race would see deeper into their responsibilities, and look closer into the duties they owe to the people whom God has given them as an inheritance, and their children after them, so long as time shall last. That man has no faith in the Scriptures who believes that education could defeat God's purposes, in subjecting the black man to the government of the white. On the contrary, experience proves its advantages, to both parties. Aside and apart from Scripture authority, natural history reveals most of the same facts, in regard to the negro that the Bible does. It proves the existence of at least three distinct species of the genus man, differing in their instincts, form, habits and color. The white species having qualities denied to the black—one with a free and the other with a servile mind—one a thinking and reflective being, the other a creature of feeling and imitation, almost void of reflective faculties, and consequently unable to provide for and take care of himself. The relation of master and slave would naturally spring up between two such different species of men, even if there was no Scripture authority to support it. The relation thus established, being natural, would be drawn closer together, instead of severed, by the inferior imitating the superior in all his ways, or in other words, acquiring an education.

ON THE CAUCASIANS AND THE AFRICANS.

SEVERAL years ago we published some original and ingenious views of Dr. Cartwright, of New Orleans, upon the subject of negroes and their characteristics. The matter is more elaborately treated by him in the following paper:—*De Bows Review.*

THE Nilotic monuments furnish numerous portraits of the negro races, represented as slaves, sixteen hundred years before the Christian era. Although repeatedly drawn from their native barbarism and carried among civilized nations, they soon forget what they learn and relapse into barbarism. If the inherent potency of the prognathous type of mankind had been greater than it actually is, sufficiently great to give it the independence of character that the American Indian possesses, the world would have been in a great measure deprived of cotton and sugar. The red man is unavailable as a laborer in the cane or cotton field, or any where else, owing to the unalterable ethnical laws of his character. The white man can not endure toil under the burning sun of the cane and cotton field, and live to enjoy the fruits of his labor. The African will starve rather than engage in a regular system of agricultural labor, unless impelled by the stronger will of the white man. When thus impelled, experience proves that he is much happier, during the hours of labor in the sunny fields, than when dozing in his native woods and jungles. He is also eminently qualified for a number of employments, which the instincts of the white man regard as degrading. If the white man be forced by necessity into employments abhorrent to his instincts, it tends to weaken or destroy that sentiment or principle of honor or duty, which is the mainspring of heroic actions, from the beginning of historical times to the present, and is the basis of every thing great and noble in all grades of white society.

The importance of having these particular employments, regarded as servile and degrading by the white man, attended to by the black race, whose instincts are not repugnant to them, will be at once apparent to all those who deem the sentiment of honor or duty as worth cultivating in the human breast. It is utterly unknown to the prognathous race of mankind, and has no place in their language. When the language is given to them they can not comprehend its meaning, or form a conception of what is meant by it. Every white man, who has not been degraded, had rather be engaged in the most laborious employments, than to serve as a lacquey or body servant to another white man or being like himself. Whereas, there is no office which the negro or mulatto covets more than that of being a body servant to a real gentleman. There is no office which gives him such a high opinion of himself, and it is utterly impossible for him to attach the idea of degradation to it. Those identical offices which the white man instinctively abhors, are the most greedily sought for by negroes and mulattoes, whether slave or free, in preference to all other employments. North or South, free or slave, they are ever at the elbow, behind the table, in hotels and steamboats; ever ready, with brush in hand, to brush the coat or black the shoes, or to perform any menial service which may be required, and to hold out the open palm for the dime. The innate love to act as body servant or lacquey is too strongly developed in the negro race to be concealed. It admirably qualifies them for waiters and house servants, as their strong muscles, hardy frames, and the positive pleasure that labor in a hot sun confers on them, abundantly qualify them for agricultural employment in a hot climate.

Hence, the primordial cell germ of the Nigritians has no more potency than what is sufficient to form a being with physical power, when its dynamism becomes exhausted, dropping the creature in the wilderness with the mental organization too imperfect to enable him to extricate himself from barbarism. If Nature had intended the prognathous race for barbarism as the end and object of their creation, they would have been like lions and tigers, fierce and untamable. So far from being like ferocious beasts, they are endowed with a will so weak, passions so easily subdued, and dispositions so gentle and affectionate, as readily to fall under subjection to the wild Arab, or any other race of men. Hence they are led about in gangs of an hundred or more by a single individual, even by an old man, or a cripple, if he be of the white race and possessed of a strong will. The Nigritian has such little command over his own muscles, from the weakness of his will, as almost to starve, when a little exertion and forethought would procure him an abundance. Although he has exaggerated appetites and exaggerated senses, calling loudly for their gratification, his will is too weak to command his muscles to engage in such kinds of labor as would readily procure the fruits to gratify them. Like an animal in a state of hibernation, waiting for the external aid of spring to warm it into life and power, so does the negro continue to doze out a vegeto-animal existence in the wilderness, unable to extricate himself therefrom—his own will being too feeble to call forth the requisite muscular exertion. His muscles not being exercised, the respiration is imperfect, and the blood is imperfectly vitalized. Torpidity of body and hebetude of mind are the effects thereof, which disappear under bodily labor, because that expands the lungs, vitalizes the blood, and wakes him up to a sense of pleasure and happiness unknown to him in the vegeto-animal or hibernating state. Nothing but will is wanting to transform the torpid, unhappy tenant of the wilderness into a rational and happy thing—the happiest being on earth, as far as sensual pleasures are concerned.

The white man has an exaggerated will, more than he has use for; because it frequently drives his own muscles beyond their physical capacity of endurance. The will is not a faculty confined within the periphery of the body. It can not, like the imagination, travel to immeasurable distances from the body, and in an instant of time go and return from Aldabran, or beyond the boundaries of the solar system. Its flight is confined to the world and to limits more or less restricted—the less restricted in some than in others. The will has two powers—direct and indirect. It is the direct motive power of the muscular system. It indirectly exerts a dynamic force upon surrounding objects when associated with knowledge. It gives to knowledge its power. Every thing that is made was made by the Infinite Will associated with infinite knowledge. The will of man is but a spark of the Infinite Will, and its power is only circumscribed by his knowledge. A man possessing a knowledge of the negro character can govern an hundred, a thousand, or ten thousand of the prognathous race by his will alone, easier than one ignorant of that character can govern a single individual of that race by the whip or a club. However disinclined to labor the negroes may be, they can not help themselves; they are obliged to move and to exercise their muscles when the white man, acquainted with their character, *wills* that they should do so. They can not resist that will, so far as labor of body is concerned. If they resist, it is from some other cause than that connected with their daily labor. They have an instinctive feeling of obedience to the stronger will of the white man, requiring nothing more than moderate labor. So far, their instincts compel obedience to will as one of his rights. Beyond that, they will resist his will and be refractory, if he encroaches on what they regard as their rights, viz: the right to hold property in him as he does in them, and to disburse that property to them in the shape of meat, bread and vegetables, clothing, fuel and house-room, and attention to their comforts when sick, old, infirm, and unable to labor; to hold property in him as a conservator of the peace among themselves, and a protector against trespassers from abroad, whether black or white; to hold property in him as impartial judge and an honest jury to try them for offenses, and a merciful executioner to punish them for violations of the usages of the plantation or locality.

With those rights acceded to them, no other compulsion is necessary to make them perform their daily tasks than *his will be done*. It is not the whip, as many suppose, which calls forth those muscular exertions, the result of which is sugar, cotton, breadstuffs, rice, and tobacco. These are products of the white man's will, acting through the muscles of the prognathous race in our Southern States. If that will were withdrawn, and the plantations handed over as a gracious gift to the laborers, agricultural labor would cease for the want of that spiritual power called the will, to move those machines—the muscles. They would cease to move here, as they have in Hayti. If the prognathous race were expelled the land, and their place supplied with double their number of white men, agricultural labor in the South would also cease, as far as sugar and cotton are concerned, for the want of muscles that could endure exercise in the smothering heat of a cane or cotton field. Half the white laborers of Illinois are prostrated with fevers from a few days' work in stripping blades in a Northern corn field, owing to the confinement of the air by the close proximity of the plants. Cane and cotton plants form a denser foliage than corn—a thick jungle, where the white man pants for breath, and is overpowered by the heat of the sun at one time of day, and chilled by the dews and moisture of the plants at another. Negroes glory in a close, hot atmosphere; they instinctively cover their head and faces with a blanket at night, and prefer laying with their heads to the fire, instead of their feet. This ethnical peculiarity is in harmony with their efficiency as laborers in hot, damp, close, suffocating atmosphere—where instead of suffering and dying, as the white man would, they are healthier, happier, and more prolific than in their native Africa—producing, under the white man's will, a great variety of agricultural products, besides upward of three millions of bales of cotton, and three hundred thousand hogsheads of sugar. Thus proving that subjection to his will is normal to them, because, under the influence of his will, they enjoy life more than in any other condition, rapidly increase in numbers, and steadily rise in the scale of humanity.

The power of a stronger will over a weaker, or the power of one living creature to act on and influence another, is an ordinance of nature, which has its parallel in the inorganic kingdom, where ponderous bodies, widely separated in space, influence one another so much as to keep up a constant interplay of action and reaction throughout nature's vast realms. The same ordinance which keeps the spheres in their orbits and holds the satellites in subordination to the planets, is the ordinance that subjects the negro race to the empire of the white man's will. From that ordinance the snake derives its power to charm the bird, and the magician his power to amuse the curious, to astonish the vulgar, and to confound the wisdom of the wise. Under that ordinance, our four millions of negroes are as unalterably bound to obey the white man's will, as the four satellites of Jupiter the superior magnetism of that planet. If individual masters, by releasing individual negroes from the power of their will, can not make them free or release them from subordination to the instinctive public sentiment or will of the aggregate white population, which as rigidly excludes them, in the so-called free States, from the drawing room and parlor as it does pots and kettles and other kinds of kitchen furniture. The subjugation of equals by artifice or force is tyranny or slavery; but there is no such thing in the United States, because equals are on a perfect equality here. The subordination of the Nigritian to the Caucasian would never have been imagined to be a condition similar to European slavery, if any regard had been paid to ethnology. Subordination of the inferior race to the superior is a normal, and not a forced condition. Chains and standing armies are the implements used to force the obedience of equals to equals—of one white man to another. Whereas, the obedience of the Nigritian to the Caucasian is *spontaneous* because it is normal for the weaker will to yield obedience to the stronger. The ordinance which subjects the negro to the empire of the white man's will, was plainly written on the heavens during our Revolutionary war. It was then that the power of the united will of the American people rose to its highest degree of intensity.

Every colony was a slaveholding colony excepting one; yet the people, particularly that portion of them residing in districts where the black population was greatest, hastened to meet in the battle-field the powerful British armies in front of them, and the interminable hosts of Indian warriors in the wilderness behind them, leaving their wives and children, their old men and cripples, for seven long years, *to their negroes to take care of*. Did the slaves, many of whom were savages recently imported from Africa, butcher them, as white or Indian slaves surely would have done, and fly to the enemy's standard for the liberty, land, money, rum, savage luxuries and ample protection so abundantly promised and secured to all who would desert their master's families? History answers that not one in a thousand joined their masters' enemies; but, on the contrary, they continued quietly their daily labors, even in those districts where they outnumbered the white population ten to one. They not only produced sufficient breadstuffs to supply the families of their masters, but a surplus of flour, pork, and beef was sent up from the slaveholding districts of Virginia to Washington's starving army in Pennsylvania. [See Botta's History.] These agricultural products were created by savages, naturally so indolent in their native Africa, as to prefer to live on ant eggs and caterpillars rather than labor for a subsistence; but for years in succession they continued to labor in the midst of their masters' enemies—dropping their hoes when they saw the red coats, running to tell their mistress, and to conduct her and the children through by-paths to avoid the British troopers, and when the enemy were out of sight returning to their work again. The sole cause of their industry and fidelity is due to the spiritual influence of the white race over the black.

The empire of the white man's will over the prognathous race is not absolute, however. It can not force exercise beyond a certain speed; neither the will nor physical force can drive negroes, for a number of days in succession, beyond a very moderate daily labor—about one-third less than the white man voluntarily imposes on himself. If force be used to make them do more, they invariably do less and less, until they fall into a state of impassivity, in which they are more plague than profit—worthless as laborers, insensible and indifferent to punishment, or even to life; or, in other words, they fall into the disease which I have named Dysesthæsia Ethiopica, characterized by hebetude of mind and insensibility of body, caused by over working and bad treatment. Some knowledge of the ethnology of the prognathous race is absolutely necessary for the prevention and cure of this malady in all its various forms and stages. Dirt eating, or Cachexia Africana, is another disease, like Dysesthæsia Ethiopica, growing out of ethnical elements peculiar to the prognathous race. The ethnical elements assimilating the negro to the mule, although giving rise to the last named disease, are of vast importance to the prognathous race, because they guarantee to that race an ample protection against the abuses of arbitrary power. A white man, like a blooded horse, can be worked to death. Not so the negro, whose ethnical elements, like the mule, restricts the limits of arbitrary power over him.

Among the four millions of the prognathous race in the United States, it will be difficult, if not impossible, to find a single individual negro, whom the white man, armed with arbitrary power, has ever been able to make hurt himself at work. It is beyond the power of the white man to drive the negro into this long continued and excessive muscular exertions such as the white laborers of Europe often impose upon themselves to satisfy a greedy boss, under fear of losing their places, and thereby starving themselves and families. Throughout England, nothing is more common than decrepitude, premature old age, and a frightful list of diseases, caused by long continued and excessive muscular exertion. Whereas, all America can scarcely furnish an example of the kind among the prognathous race. The white men of America have performed many prodigies, but they have never yet been able to make a negro overwork himself.

There are other elements peculiar to the Nigritian, on which the disease, called negro consumption, or Cachexia Africana, depends. But these belong to that class which subject the negro to the white man's spiritual empire over him. When that spiritual empire is not maintained in all its entirety, or in other words, when the negro is badly governed, he is apt to fall under the spiritual influence of the artful and designing of his own color, and Cachexia Africana, or consumption, is the consequence. Better throw medicine to the dogs, than give it to a negro patient impressed with the belief that he has walked over poison specially laid for him, or been in some other way tricked or conjured. He will surely die, unless treated in accordance with his ethnological peculiarities, and the hallucination expelled.

There never has been an insurrection of the prognathous race against their masters; and from the nature of the ethnical elements of that race, there never can be. Hayti is no exception, it will be seen, when the true history of the so-called insurrection of that island is written. There have been neighborhood disturbances and bloodshed, caused by fanaticism, and by mischievous white men getting among them and infusing their will into them, or mesmerizing them. But, fortunately, there is an ethnological law of their nature which estops the evil influence of such characters by limiting their influence strictly to personal acquaintances. The prognathous tribes in every place and country are jealous and suspicious of all strangers, black or white, and have ever been so.

Prior to the emancipation act in the British West Indies, the famous Exeter Hall Junto sent out a number of emissaries of the East India Company to Jamaica, in the garb of missionaries. After remaining a year or two in the assumed character of Christian ministers, they began to preach insurrectionary doctrines, and caused a number of so-called insurrections to break out simultaneously in different parts of the island. The insurgents in every neighborhood were confined to the personal acquaintances of the Exeter Hall miscreants, who succeeded in infusing their will only into those who had listened to their incendiary harangues. This was proved upon them by the genuine missionaries, who had long been on the island, and had gathered into their various churches a vast number of converts. For, in no instance, did a single convert, or any other negro, join in the numerous insurrectionary movements who had not been personally addressed by the wolves in sheep's clothing. The Christian missionaries, particularly the Methodists, Baptist, Moravians, and Catholics, were very exact in collecting the evidence of this most important ethnological truth, in consequence of some of the planters, at the first outbreak, having confounded them with the Exeter Hall incendiaries.

The planters finally left the Christian missionaries and their flocks undisturbed, but proceeded to expel the false missionaries, to hang their converts, and to burn down their chapels. The event proved that they were wrong in not hanging the white incendiaries; because they went home to England, preached a crusade—traveling all over the United Kingdom—proclaiming, as they went, that they had left God's houses in flames throughout Jamaica, and God's people hanging like dogs from the trees in that sinful island. This so inflamed public sentiment in Great Britain against the planters, as to unite all parties in loud calls for the immediate passage of the emancipation act. There is good reason to believe that the English ministry, in view of the probable effect of that measure on the United States, and the encouragement it would afford to the culture of sugar and other tropical products in the East Indies and Mauritius, had previously determined to make negro freedom a leading measure in British policy, well knowing that its effect would be to Africanize the sugar and cotton growing regions of America. The ethnology of the prognathous race does not stop at proving that subordination to the white race is its normal condition. It goes further, and proves that social and political equality is abnormal to it, whether educated or not. Neither negroes nor mulattoes know how to use power when given to them. They always use it capriciously and tyrannically. Tschudi, a Swiss naturalist, [see Tschudi's Travels in Peru, London, 1848,] says, "that in Lima and Peru generally, the free negroes are a plague to society. Dishonesty seems to be a part of their very nature. Free born negroes, admitted into the houses of wealthy families, and have received, in early life, a good education, and treated with kindness and liberality, do not differ from their uneducated brother."

Tschudi is mistaken in supposing that dishonesty is too deeply rooted in the negro character to be removed. They are dishonest when in the abnormal condition without a master. They are also dishonest when in a state of subordination, called slavery, badly provided for and not properly disciplined and governed. But when properly disciplined, instructed, and governed, and their animal wants provided for, it would be difficult to find a more honest, faithful, and trustworthy people than they are. When made contented and happy, as they always should be, they reflect their master in their thoughts, morals, and religion, or at least they are desirous of being like him. They imitate him in every thing, as far as their imitative faculties, which are very strong, will carry them. They take a pride in his wealth, or in any thing which distinguishes him, as if they formed a part of himself, as they really do, being under the influence of his will, and in some measure assimilated, in their spiritual nature, to him—loving him with all the warm and devoted affection which children manifest to their parents. He is sure of their love and friendship, although all the world may forsake him. But to create and maintain this happy relation, he must govern them with strict reference to their ethnological peculiarities. He must treat them as inferiors, not as equals, as they are not satisfied with equality, and will despise a master who attempts to raise any one or more of them to an equality with himself; because they become jealous and suspicious that their master's favorites will exercise a sinister influence over him against them.

Impartiality of treatment in every particular, down to a hat or pair of shoes, is what they all regard as one of their dearest rights. Hence, any special favors or gifts to one, is an offense to all the rest. They also regard as a right, when punished, not to be punished in anger, but with cool deliberation. They will run from an angry or enraged master or overseer, armed with a gun or a pistol. They regard all overseers who come into the field armed with deadly weapons as cowards, and all cowards have great difficulty in governing them. It is not physical force which keeps them in subjection, but the spiritual force of the white man's will. One unarmed brave man can manage a thousand by the moral force of his will alone, much better than an hundred cowards with guns in their hands. They also require as a right when punished, to be punished with a switch or a whip, and not with a stick or the fist. In this particular the ethnical law of their nature is different from all other races of men. It is exactly the reverse of that of the American Indian. The Indian will murder any man who strikes him with a switch, a cowhide, or a whip, twenty years afterward, if he gets an opportunity; but readily forgets blows, however severe, inflicted on him with the fist, a cudgel, or a tomahawk. A remarkable ethnological peculiarity of the prognathous race is, that any deserved punishment, inflicted on them with a switch, cowhide, or whip, puts them into good humor with themselves and the executioner of the punishment, provided he manifest satisfaction by regarding the offense as atoned for.

The negro requires government in every thing, the most minute. The Indian, on the contrary, submits to government in nothing whatever. Mr. Jefferson was the first to notice this ethnical law of the red man. [See his letter to Gilmer, June 7, 1816, vol. iv, page 279, Jefferson's Correspondence.] "Every man with them," (the Indians,) says Mr. Jefferson, "is perfectly free to follow his own inclinations; but if, in doing this, he violates the rights of another, he is punished by the disesteem of society or tomahawked. Their leaders conduct them by the influence of their characters only; and they follow or not, as they please, him of whose character, for wisdom or war, they have the highest opinion, but, of all things, they least think of subjecting themselves to the will of one man." Whereas the black man requires government even in his meat and drink, his clothing, and hours of repose. Unless under the government of one man to prescribe rules of conduct to guide him, he will eat too much meat and not enough of bread and vegetables; he will not dress to suit the season, or kind of labor he is engaged in, nor retire to rest in due time to get sufficient sleep, but sit up and doze by the fire nearly all night. Nor will the women undress the children and put them regularly to bed. Nature is no law unto them. They let their children suffer and die, or unmercifully abuse them, unless the white man or woman prescribe rules in the nursery for them to go by. Whenever the white woman superintends the nursery, whether the climate be cold or hot, they increase faster than any other people on the globe; but on large plantations, remote from her influence, the negro population invariably diminishes, unless the overseer take upon himself those duties in the lying-in and nursery department, which on small estates are attended to by the mistress. She often sits up at night with sick children and administers to their wants, when their own mothers are nodding by them, and would be sound asleep if it were not for her presence. The care that white women bestow on the nursery, is one of the principal causes why three hundred thousand Africans, originally imported into the territory of the United States have increased to four millions, while in the British West Indies the number imported, exceeded, by several millions, the actual population. It is also the cause why the small proprietors of negro property in Maryland, Virginia, Kentucky, and Missouri are able to supply the loss on the large Southern plantations, which are cut off from the happy influence of the presiding genius over civilization, morality, and population—the white woman.

The prognathous race require government also in their religious exercises, or they degenerate into fanatical saturnalia. A discreet white man or woman should always be present to regulate their religious meetings.

Here the investigation into the ethnology of the prognathous race must close, at least, for the present, leaving the most interesting part, Fetichism, the indigenous religion of the African tribes, untouched. It is the key to the negro character, which is difficult to learn from mere experience. Those who are not accustomed to them have great trouble and difficulty in managing negroes; and in consequence thereof treat them badly. If their ethnology was better and more generally understood, their value would be greatly increased, and their condition, as a laboring class, would be more enviable, compared to the European peasants, than it already is.

572

SLAVERY IN THE LIGHT OF INTERNATIONAL LAW.

BY

E. N. ELLIOTT, L.L.D.,

OF MISSISSIPPI.

SLAVERY
IN THE
LIGHT OF INTERNATIONAL LAW.

THERE are some who deny the unity of the human race; with such we have no controversy, but it is a part of our religious belief, that "God made of one blood all nations that dwell on the face of the earth;" and on this we would base one of our arguments for the subordination of a part of the human family. It is not necessary to the vindication of our cause, or of truth, to deny the authority, or to fritter away the evident meaning of any part of the word of God, as is done by most of the abolitionists. It is sufficient for our purpose that we have shown that the negro is an inferior variety of the human race; that he is inferior in his physical structure, and in his mental and moral organization. This orgnization incapacitates him for emerging, by his own will and power, from barbarism, and achieving civilization and refinement. History teaches the same lesson. We find Africa to-day, just as it was three thousand years ago. When God created man he said to him, "Be fruitful and multiply and replenish the earth, and subdue it, and have dominion over the fish of the sea, and over the fowl of the air, and over every living thing that moveth on the face of the earth." And again, upon the re-creation after the flood, he repeated the command, in almost the same words, to Noah and his sons. This command shows that God had a purpose with regard to the physical world, in placing man upon it, and that man has a mission to fulfill in subduing it, and acquiring a control, not only over animate but also over inanimate nature. Indeed, the one is essential to the other. Man can not control and subdue the inferior animals, until he has acquired some control over the powers of nature. Place him in the forest naked and unarmed, and many of the animals are his superiors; but endow his mind with a knowledge of nature's laws, and thus enable him to make them subservient to his purposes, and he becomes irresistible; a god on earth. In fulfilling this command, man elevates his nature as he increases his knowledge, and thereby extends his powers. God requires that every part of the human family shall fulfill this great command, and contribute their part in rendering subservient to human use, all the faculties of nature. Nay, even where the one talent is misimproved, he takes it away and gives it to him, who has ten talents. It is on this principle that it is right and in accordance with the ordinance of God, to dispossess of their lands, mines, waterpowers, harbors, etc., a savage nation, possessing, but not improving them, and convert them to the uses of the world of mankind. This is the warrant for the conflict of civilization with barbarism. Not to go back to former times, it is this precept which has converted the former howling wilderness of this Western World, into an earthly paradise, affording an ample subsistence to happy millions of the most enlightened of the human family. It is this that causes effete dynasties and nations to disappear from the face of the world, and their places to be supplied by those full of life and energy. It is this that is rolling back and blotting out the mongrel races of the New World, to make room for the onward march of a higher civilization.

The manifest destiny men are not so far wrong after all; but instead of destiny, it is the purpose and ordinance of God. Upon this principle has England acted in reference to India, Australia, China, and in almost every region of the globe. It is upon this principle that Europe is now controlling the destinies of the Old World, as the United States, if they are true to themselves, will control the destinies of the New. This has governed us in requiring that Japan should open her ports to the commerce, and her coal mines to the navies of the world; that she should enrol herself in the brotherhood of nations, and perform her part in the great drama of life. It is upon this principle that England, France, and the United States, are requiring the same thing of China; and it is upon this principle that the vagrant is arrested in your streets and sent to the work-house.

These principles are clearly enunciated, and ably defended by J. Q. Adams in his celebrated speech on the Chinese question, delivered in 1841. It is true, that he applies them to the rights of commerce only; but by legitimate deduction, they are as applicable to the rights of labor, as to the rights of commerce. Although nations and races have always acted on these principles, yet at the time of the delivery of this speech, so startling were the positions assumed by Mr. Adams, that but few could be found who were prepared to defend them, yet none were able to controvert them. Their general adoption at the present day only shows what history has so long taught, that master minds are generally in advance of their age.

In the "Memoir of J. Q. Adams," by Josiah Quincy, we have a report of this speech. Speaking of the Chinese war, Mr. Adams says, "that by the law of nations is to be understood, not one code of laws, binding alike on all nations of the earth, but a system of rules, varying according to the condition and character of the nations concerned. There is a law of nations among Christian communities, which is the law recognized by the Constitution of the United States, as obligatory upon them in their intercourse with European States and colonies. But we have a different law of nations regulating our intercourse with the Indian tribes on this continent; another between us and the woolly-headed nations of Africa; another with the Barbary powers; another with the flowery land, or Celestial empire." Then, reasoning on the rights of property, established by labor, by occupation, by compact, he maintains "that the right of exchange, barter—in other words, of commerce—necessarily follows; that a state of nature among men is a state of peace; the pursuit of happiness, man's natural right; that is the duty of all men to contribute, as much as is in their power, to one another's happiness, and that there is no other way by which they can so well contribute to the comfort and well-being of one another, as by commerce, or the mutual exchange of equivalents." These views and principles he thus illustrates:

"The duty of commercial intercourse between nations, is laid down in terms sufficiently positive by Vattel, but he afterwards qualifies it by a restriction, which, unless itself restricted, annuls it altogether. He says that, although the general duty of commercial intercourse is incumbent upon nations, yet every nation may exclude any particular branch or article of trade, which it may deem injurious to its interests. This can not be denied. But then a nation may multiply these particular exclusions, until they become general, and equivalent to a total interdict of commerce; and this, time out of mind, has been the inflexible policy of the Chinese empire. So says Vattel, without affixing any note of censure upon it. Yet it is manifestly incompatible with the position which he had previously laid down, that commercial intercourse between nations is a moral obligation upon them all."

The same doctrine, with regard to the duties of *individuals* in a community, that is here advanced by Mr. Adams with regard to *races* and *nations*, is thus set forth in Blackstone's Commentaries, book iv, chap. xxxiii: "*There is not a more necessary, or more certain maxim, in the frame and constitution of society, than that every individual must contribute his share, in order to the well-being of the community.*"

The first principle laid down by Mr. Adams is, that the same code of international law does not apply to all nations alike, but that it varies with the condition and character of the people; that one code of laws applies to the enlightened and Christian nations of Europe, but an entirely different one to the pagan, woolly-headed, barbarians of Africa. What would be just and right with regard to the African, would be eminently unjust towards the European. Though it would be a great wrong to reduce the European to a condition of servitude, it does not follow that it would be equally wrong to enslave the African. If all the human races were alike, one code of international laws would apply to the whole, but so long as the African continues to be an inferior race, they must be treated as such.

But again, Mr. Adams clearly lays down the principle that no nation or race can be permitted, in any way, to isolate itself from the community of nations, but is morally bound to contribute all in its power to the well-being of the whole race, at the same time that it secures its own. If it possesses territory which it occupies, but does not improve, it must yield it to the claims of civiilization. If it has productions valuable to the world, it is morally bound to exchange them. If it has ports, harbors, coal mines, or other facilities for commerce and manufactures, it must allow other nations to participate in its advantages. If it has a superabundant supply of labor, it must be rendered available. If, then, it is right that civilization and progress should appropriate the hunting grounds of the Indian race; if it is right that China and Japan should be required to open their ports to the commerce of the world, it must be equally right that the great store house of labor in Africa should be opened for the benefit of the human race. In the Western World, a vast continent of fertile land and propitious climate, was possessed, not improved, by a sparse hunter race; but the law of God and of nations required that the earth should be subdued and replenished, and now God has enlarged Japheth, and he dwells in these tents of Shem. China, Japan, and other regions of Asia, are inhabited by teeming millions, rich in the productions of art, yet scarcely able to obtain a meagre sustenance, and rigidly excluding all intercourse with the outer world, but at the demands of commerce the barriers are broken down, and they, in common with other nations, are benefited by the change. Africa has long possessed a superabundant population of indolent, degraded, pagan savages, useless to the world and to themselves. Numberless efforts have been made to elevate them in the scale of existence, in their own country, but all in vain. Even when partially civilized, under the control of the white man, they soon relapse into barbarism, if emancipated from this control. But a colony of them, some two hundred years since, were imported into the Western World, and placed subordinate to the white race; and now, if we are to believe the abolitionists, they have improved so rapidly as to have become equal, if not superior, to the white race. Certainly they are far superior to their ancestors, or their brethren in Africa. At the same time, they have conferred an equal benefit on the world. They supply a demand for labor which can not otherwise be met, and their products not only clothe the civilized world, but also are the life-blood of its commerce.

It is not necessary to the discussion of this topic, that we should show *what* are the laws of nations, applicable to the different races enumerated by Mr. Adams; though it is manifest to the most casual observer, that the laws applicable to them are radically different. What would be thought of a minister at the court of St. James, who should propose to carry out with Great Britain, the same course of policy we pursue towards the Indian tribes; or of the English minister at our capital, who would exact from us the concessions required of the rajahs of India, or the chiefs of Australia? The radical difference is this: among civilized and Christian nations, the law recognizes a perfect equality, and requires an entire reciprocity; but between an elevated and a degraded or inferior race, this inequality is recognized, and an influence and a superiority is accorded to the one, which is denied to the other. This is well illustrated by our present intercourse with Mexico, and should we establish a protectorate over that unhappy country, for their good and our own, it would be in strict accordance with these principles. With some nations we have diplomatic intercourse, on terms of perfect equality and reciprocity; others we treat as inferiors, and assume over them some degree of control, while we nevertheless recognize them as legitimate governments. But there are other nations or races, with whom we form no diplomatic relations, and whose governments we do not recognize. In this latter class are included most of the inhabitants of Africa, and of Hayti; or in other words, the *negro race*. The reason is, that those nations performing their duties to the human race, according to the ordinance of God, are to be recognized as not needing our assistance, or requiring our guardianship; those fulfilling only in part, should be considered in a state of tutelage, but those that fulfill none, or but few of these duties, require to be made subservient to the superior races, in order that they may fulfill the great ends of their existence. This subordination has existed in all times, among all nations, and with all races. But as soon as any race became so developed as no longer to require it, it ceased to exist. In this way, and in this alone,—except by the deportation of the slaves—has slavery ever ceased to exist, in any community; nor can it be otherwise in the future. Emancipation in name, is not always freedom in reality. The free blacks of our Northern States and the West Indies, are, as a mass, more abject slaves than any on our Southern plantations. Nor is it possible for them to acquire a more elevated position, until they shall have acquired the requisite qualifications for that position.

At the present time, with the exception of serfdom, peonage, and political slavery, this subordination is confined to the negro race. Why is this so? Manifestly because they have shown themselves incapable, in their own land, of emerging from barbarism, achieving civilization and refinement, performing their duties to the human race, and becoming entitled to a position as equals among the nations of the earth. Until such improvement takes place as shall entitle them to this exalted position, their own happiness and well-being, their duties to the human race, the claims of civilization, the progress of society, the law of nations, and the ordinance of God, require that they should be placed in a subordinate position to a superior race. Experience also shows us that this is their normal and natural position. In their native land they still are what they have always been, a pagan, savage, servile race, fulfilling their duties neither to themselves, to God, nor to the human race; but under the tutelage of a superior race, they are elevated in the scale of existence, improved mentally, morally, and physically, and are thus enabled to do their part in contributing to the well-being of the human race. But so far as our experience goes, this development is not permanent, but is liable to retrogression as soon as the influence of the superior race is removed. Like the electro-magnet, whose power is lost the moment it is insulated from the vivifying power of electricity, so the servile race loses its power when removed from the control of a superior intellect. The example of our own free blacks, those emancipated in the West Indies, Sierra Leone, and even Liberia, are conclusive on this point.

It becomes us not to speculate too curiously concerning God's plan in governing the world, much less to strive to thwart his purposes with our puny arms; he will work out his purposes of good to the human race, in his own good time and way, whether it meets our views or not. But from the revelation of his purpose concerning the descendants of the three progenitors of the human race after the flood, it is manifest that the children of Ham were to be a servile race; as their final disinthrallment is nowhere spoken of, it is exceedingly improbable that slavery will cease to exist till the end of time. It is true that Ethiopia shall stretch forth her hands to God; but this is being fulfilled on a grander scale than ever before has been witnessed, even in our midst, in this Western World, where God has enlarged Japheth, where he dwells in the tents of Shem, and where Cainan is his servant.

PORT GIBSON, MISSISSIPPI, *February 22, 1860.*

DRED SCOTT DECISION.
SUPREME COURT OF THE UNITED STATES,
DECEMBER TERM, 1856.
DRED SCOTT
versus
JOHN F. A. SANDFORD.

DRED SCOTT, PLAINTIFF IN ERROR, *v.* JOHN F. A. SANDFORD.

THIS case was brought up, by writ of error, from the Circuit Court of the United States for the district of Missouri.

It was an action of trespass *vi et armis* instituted in the Circuit Court by Scott against Sandford.

Prior to the institution of the present suit, an action was brought by Scott for his freedom in the Circuit Court of St. Louis county, (State court,) where there was a verdict and judgment in his favor. On a writ of error to the Supreme Court of the State, the judgment below was reversed, and the case remanded to the Circuit Court, where it was continued to await the decision of the case now in question.

The declaration of Scott contained three counts: one, that Sandford had assaulted the plaintiff; one, that he had assaulted Harriet Scott, his wife; and one, that he had assaulted Eliza Scott and Lizzie Scott, his children.

Sandford appeared, and filed the following plea:

> DRED SCOTT
>   *v.*   } *Plea to the Jurisdiction of the Court.*
> JOHN F. A. SANDFORD.

APRIL TERM, 1854.

And the said John F. A. Sandford, in his own proper person, comes and says that this court ought not to have or take further cognizance of the action aforesaid, because he says that said cause of action, and each and every of them, (if any such have accrued to the said Dred Scott,) accrued to the said Dred Scott out of the jurisdiction of this court, and exclusively within the jurisdiction of the courts of the State of Missouri, for that, to wit: the said plaintiff, Dred Scott, is not a citizen of the State of Missouri, as alleged in his declaration, because he is a negro of African descent; his ancestors were of pure African blood, and were brought into this country and sold as negro slaves, and this the said Sandford is ready to verify. Wherefore, he prays judgment whether this court can or will take further cognizance of the action aforesaid.

JOHN F. A. SANDFORD.

To this plea there was a demurrer in the usual form, which was argued in April, 1854, when the court gave judgment that the demurrer should be sustained.

In May, 1854, the defendant, in pursuance of an agreement between counsel, and with the leave of the court, pleaded in bar of the action:

1. Not guilty.

2. That the plaintiff was a negro slave, the lawful property of the defendant, and, as such, the defendant gently laid his hands upon him, and thereby had only restrained him, as the defendant had a right to do.

3. That with respect to the wife and daughters of the plaintiff, in the second and third counts of the declaration mentioned, the defendant had, as to them, only acted in the same manner, and in virtue of the same legal right.

In the first of these pleas, the plaintiff joined issue; and to the second and third, filed replications alleging that the defendant, of his own wrong and without the cause in his second and third pleas alleged, committed the trespasses, etc.

The counsel then filed the following agreed statement of facts, viz:

In the year 1834, the plaintiff was a negro slave belonging to Dr. Emerson, who was a surgeon in the army of the United States. In that year, 1834, said Dr. Emerson took the plaintiff from the State of Missouri to the military post at Rock Island, in the State of Illinois, and held him there as a slave until the month of April or May, 1836. At the time last mentioned, said Dr. Emerson removed the plaintiff from said military post at Rock Island to the military post at Fort Snelling, situate on the west bank of the Mississippi river, in the Territory known as Upper Louisiana, acquired by the United States of France, and situate north of the latitude of thirty-six degrees thirty minutes north, and north of the State of Missouri. Said Dr. Emerson held the plaintiff in slavery at said Fort Snelling, from said last-mentioned date until the year 1838.

In the year 1835, Harriet, who is named in the second count of the plaintiff's declaration, was the negro slave of Major Taliaferro, who belonged to the army of the United

States. In that year, 1835, said Major Taliaferro took said Harriet to said Fort Snelling, a military post, situated as hereinbefore stated, and kept her there as a slave until the year 1836, and then sold and delivered her as a slave at said Fort Snelling unto the said Dr. Emerson hereinbefore named. Said Dr. Emerson held said Harriet in slavery at said Fort Snelling until the year 1838.

In the year 1836, the plaintiff and said Harriet at said Fort Snelling, with the consent of said Dr. Emerson, who then claimed to be their master and owner, intermarried, and took each other for husband and wife. Eliza and Lizzie, named in the third count of the plaintiff's declaration, are the fruit of that marriage. Eliza is about fourteen years old, and was born on board the steamboat Gipsey, north of the north line of the State of Missouri, and upon the river Mississippi. Lizzie is about seven years old, and was born in the State of Missouri, at the military post called Jefferson Barracks.

In the year 1838, said Dr. Emerson removed the plaintiff and said Harriet and their said daughter Eliza, from said Fort Snelling to the State of Missouri, where they have ever since resided.

Before the commencement of this suit, said Dr. Emerson sold and conveyed the plaintiff, said Harriet, Eliza, and Lizzie, to the defendant, as slaves, and the defendant has ever since claimed to hold them and each of them as slaves.

At the times mentioned in the plaintiff's declaration, the defendant, claiming to be owner as aforesaid, laid his hands upon said plaintiff, Harriet, Eliza, and Lizzie, and imprisoned them, doing in this respect, however, no more than what he might lawfully do if they were of right his slaves at such times.

Further proof may be given on the trial for either party.

It is agreed that Dred Scott brought suit for his freedom in the Circuit Court of St. Louis county; that there was a verdict and judgment in his favor; that on a writ of error to the Supreme Court, the judgment below was reversed, and the same remanded to the Circuit Court, where it has been continued to await the decision of this case.

In May, 1854, the cause went before a jury, who found the following verdict, viz: "As to the first issue joined in this case, we of the jury find the defendant not guilty; and as to the issue secondly above joined, we of the jury find that before and at the time when, etc., in the first count mentioned, the said Dred Scott was a negro slave, the lawful property of the defendant; and as to the issue thirdly above joined, we, the jury, find that before and at the time when, etc., in the second and third counts mentioned, the said Harriet, wife of said Dred Scott, and Eliza and Lizzie, the daughters of the said Dred Scott, were negro slaves, the lawful property of the defendant."

Whereupon, the court gave judgment for the defendant.

After an ineffectual motion for a new trial, the plaintiff filed the following bill of exceptions.

On the trial of this cause by the jury, the plaintiff, to maintain the issues on his part, read to the jury the following agreed statement of facts, (see agreement above.) No further testimony was given to the jury by either party. Thereupon the plaintiff moved the court to give to the jury the following instruction, viz:

"That, upon the facts agreed to by the parties, they ought to find for the plaintiff. The court refused to give such instruction to the jury, and the plaintiff, to such refusal, then and there duly excepted."

The court then gave the following instruction to the jury, on motion of the defendant:

"The jury are instructed, that upon the facts in this case, the law is with the defendant." The plaintiff excepted to this instruction.

Upon these exceptions, the case came up to this court.

It was argued at December term, 1855, and ordered to be reargued at the present term.

It was now argued by Mr. Blair and Mr. G. F. Curtis for the plaintiff in error, and by Mr. Geyer and Mr. Johnson for the defendant in error.

Mr. Chief Justice Taney delivered the opinion of the court.

This case has been twice argued. After the argument of the last term, differences of opinion were found to exist among the members of the court; and as the questions in controversy are of the highest importance, and the court was at that time much pressed by the ordinary business of the term, it was deemed advisable to continue the case, and direct a reargument on some of the points, in order that we might have an opportunity of giving to the whole subject a more deliberate consideration. It has accordingly been again argued by counsel, and considered by the court; and I now proceed to deliver its opinion.

There are two leading questions presented by the record:

1. Had the Circuit Court of the United States jurisdiction to hear and determine the case between these parties? And

2. If it had jurisdiction, is the judgment it has given erroneous or not?

The plaintiff in error, who was also the plaintiff in the court below, was, with his wife and children, held as slaves by the defendant, in the State of Missouri; and he brought this action in the Circuit Court of the United States for that district, to assert the title of himself and his family to freedom.

The declaration is in the form usually adopted in that State to try questions of this description, and contains the averment necessary to give the court jurisdiction; that he and the defendant are citizens of different States; that is, that he is a citizen of Missouri, and the defendant a citizen of New York.

The defendant pleaded in abatement to the jurisdiction of the court, that the plaintiff was not a citizen of the State of Missouri, as alleged in his declaration, being a negro of African descent, whose ancestors were of pure African blood, and who were brought into this country and sold as slaves.

To this plea the plaintiff demurred, and the defendant joined in demurrer. The court overruled the plea, and gave judgment that the defendant should answer over. And he therefore put in sundry pleas in bar, upon which issues were joined; and at the trial the verdict and judgment were in his favor. Whereupon the plaintiff brought this writ of error.

Before we speak of the pleas in bar, it will be proper to dispose of the questions which have arisen on the plea in abatement.

That plea denies the right of the plaintiff to sue in a court of the United States, for the reasons therein stated.

If the question raised by it is legally before us, and the court should be of opinion that the facts stated in it disqualify the plaintiff from becoming a citizen, in the sense in which that word is used in the Constitution of the United States, then the judgment of the Circuit Court is erroneous and must be reversed.

It is suggested, however, that this plea is not before us; and that as the judgment in the court below on this plea was in favor of the plaintiff, he does not seek to reverse it, or bring it before the court for revision by his writ of error; and also that the defendant waived this defense by pleading over, and thereby admitted the jurisdiction of the court.

But in making this objection, we think the peculiar and limited jurisdiction of courts of the United States has not been adverted to. This peculiar and limited jurisdiction, has made it necessary, in these courts, to adopt different rules and principles of pleading, so far as jurisdiction is concerned, from those which regulate courts of common law in England, and in the different States of the Union which have adopted the common-law rules.

In these last-mentioned courts, where their character and rank are analogous to that of a Circuit Court of the United States; in other words, where they are what the law terms courts of general jurisdiction; they are presumed to have jurisdiction, unless the contrary appears. No averment in the pleadings of the plaintiff is necessary, in order to give jurisdiction. If the defendant objects to it, he must plead it specially, and unless the fact on which he relies is found to be true by a jury, or admitted to be true by the plaintiff, the jurisdiction can not be disputed in an appellate court.

Now, it is not necessary to inquire whether in courts of that description a party who pleads over in bar, when a plea to the jurisdiction has been ruled against him, does or does not waive his plea; nor whether upon a judgment in his favor on the pleas in bar, and a writ of error brought by the plaintiff, the question upon the plea in abatement would be open for revision in the appellate court. Cases that may have been decided in such courts, or rules that may have been laid down by common-law pleaders, can have no influence in the decision in this court. Because, under the Constitution and laws of the United States, the rules which govern the pleadings in its courts, in questions of jurisdiction, stand on different principles and are regulated by different laws.

This difference arises, as we have said, from the peculiar character of the Government of the United States. For although it is sovereign and supreme in its appropriate sphere of action, yet it does not possess all the powers which usually belong to the sovereignty of a nation. Certain specified powers, enumerated in the Constitution, have been conferred upon it; and neither the legislative, executive, nor judicial departments of the Government can lawfully exercise any authority beyond the limits marked out by the Constitution. And in regulating the judicial department, the cases in which the courts of the United States shall have jurisdiction are particularly and specifically enumerated and defined; and they are not authorized to take cognizance of any case which does not come within the description therein specified. Hence, when a plaintiff sues in a court of the United States, it is necessary that he should show, in his pleadings, that the suit he brings is within the jurisdiction of the court, and that he is entitled to sue there. And if he omits to do this, and should, by any oversight of the Circuit Court, obtain a judgment in his favor, the judgment would be reversed in the appellate court for want of jurisdiction in the court below. The jurisdiction would not be presumed, as in the case of a common-law English or State court, unless the contrary appeared. But the record, when it comes before the appellate court, must show, affirmatively, that the inferior court had authority, under the Constitution, to hear and determine the case. And if the plaintiff claims a right to sue in a Circuit Court of the United States, under that provision of the Constitution which gives jurisdiction in controversies between citizens of different States, he must distinctly aver in his pleadings that they are citizens of different States; and he can not maintain his suit without showing that fact in the pleadings.

This point was decided in the case of Bingham *v.* Cabot, (in 3 Dall., 382,) and ever since adhered to by the court. And in Jackson *v.* Ashton (8 Pet., 148,) it was held that the objection to which it was open could not be waived by the opposite party, because consent of parties could not give jurisdiction.

It is needless to accumulate cases on this subject. Those already referred to, and the cases of Capron *v.* Van Noorden, (in 2 Cr. 126.,) and Montalet *v.* Murray, (4 Cr., 46,) are sufficient to show the rule of which we have spoken. The case of Capron *v.* Van Noorden strikingly illustrates the difference between a common-law court and a court of the United States.

If, however, the fact of citizenship is avered in the declaration, and the defendant does not deny it, and put it in issue by plea in abatement, he can not offer evidence at the trial to disprove it, and consequently can not avail himself of the objection in the appellate court, unless the defect should be apparent in some other part of the record. For if there is no plea in abatement, and the want of jurisdiction does not appear in any other part of the transcript brought up by the writ of error, the undisputed averment of citizenship in the declaration must be taken in this court to be true. In this case, the citizenship is averred, but it is denied by the defendant in the manner required by the rules of pleading, and the fact upon which the denial is based is admitted by the demurrer. And, if the plea and demurrer, and judgment of the court below upon it, are before us upon this record, the question to be decided is, whether the facts stated in the plea are sufficient to show that the plaintiff is not entitled to sue as a citizen in a court of the United States.

We think they are before us. The plea in abatement and the judgment of the court upon it, are a part of the judicial proceedings in the Circuit Court, and are there recorded as such; and a writ of error always brings up to the superior court the whole record of the proceedings in the court below. And in the case of the United States *v.* Smith, (11 Wheat., 172,) this court said, that the case being brought up by writ of error, the whole record was under the consideration of this court. And this being the case in the present instance, the plea in abatement is necessarily under consideration; and it becomes, therefore, our duty to decide whether the facts stated in the plea are or are not sufficient to show that the plaintiff is not entitled to sue as a citizen in a court of the United States.

This is certainly a very serious question, and one that now for the first time has been brought for decision before this court. But it is brought here by those who have a right to bring it, and it is our duty to meet it and decide it.

The question is simply this: Can a negro whose ancestors were imported into this country, and sold as slaves, become a member of the political community formed and brought into existence by the Constitution of the United States, and as such become entitled to all the rights and privileges and immunities guaranteed to the citizen? One of which rights is the privilege of suing in a court of the United States in the cases specified in the Constitution.

It will be observed, that the plea applies to that class of persons only whose ancestors were negroes of the African race, and imported into this country, and sold and held as slaves. The only matter in issue before the court, therefore, is, whether the descendants of such slaves, when they shall be emancipated, or who are born of parents who had become free before their birth, are citizens of a State, in the sense in which the word citizen is used in the Constitution of the United States. And this being the only matter in dispute on the pleadings, the court must be understood as speaking in this opinion of that class only, that is, of those persons who are the descendants of Africans who were imported into this country, and sold as slaves.

The situation of this population was altogether unlike that of the Indian race. The latter, it is true, formed no part of the colonial communities, and never amalgamated with them in social connections or in government. But although they were uncivilized, they were yet a free and independent people, associated together in nations or tribes, and governed by their own laws. Many of these political communities were situated in territories to which the white race claimed the ultimate right of dominion. But that claim was acknowledged to be subject to the right of the Indians to occupy it as long as they thought proper, and neither the English nor colonial Governments claimed or exercised any dominion over the tribe or nation by whom it was occupied, nor claimed the right to the possession of the territory, until the tribe or nation consented to cede it. These Indian Governments were regarded and treated as foreign Governments, as much so as if an ocean had separated the red man from the white; and their freedom has constantly been acknowledged, from the time of the first emigration to the English colonies to the present day, by the different Governments which succeeded each other. Treaties have been negotiated with them, and their alliance sought for in war; and the people who compose these Indian political communities have always been treated as foreigners not living under our Government. It is true that the course of events has brought the Indian tribes within the limits of the United States under subjection to the white race; and it has been found necessary, for their sake as well as our own, to regard them as in a state of pupilage, and to legislate to a certain extent over them and the territory they occupy. But they may, without doubt, like the subjects of any other foreign Government, be naturalized by the authority of Congress, and become citizens of a State, and of the United States; and if an individual should leave his nation or tribe, and take up his abode among the white population, he would be entitled to all the rights and privileges which would belong to an emigrant from any other foreign people.

We proceed to examine the case as presented by the pleadings.

The words "people of the United States" and "citizens" are synonymous terms, and mean the same thing. They both describe the political body who, according to our republican institutions, form the sovereignty, and who hold the power and conduct the Government through their representatives. They are what we familiarly call the "sovereign people," and every citizen is one of this people, and a constituent member of this sovereignty. The question before us is, whether the class of persons described in the plea in abatement compose a portion of this people, and are constituent members of this sovereignty? We think they are not, and that they are not included, and were not intended to be included, under the word "citizens" in the Constitution, and can therefore claim none of the rights and privileges which that instrument provides for and secures to citizens of the United States. On the contrary, they were at that time considered as a subordinate and inferior class of beings, who had been subjugated by the dominant race, and, whether emancipated or not, yet remained subject to their authority, and had no rights or privileges but such as those who held the power and the government might choose to grant them.

It is not the province of the court to decide upon the justice or injustice, the policy or impolicy, of these laws. The decision of that question belonged to the political or law-making power; to those who formed the sovereignty and framed the Constitution. The duty of the court is, to interpret the instrument they have framed, with the best lights we can obtain on the subject, and to administer it as we find it, according to its true intent and meaning when it was adopted.

In discussing this question, we must not confound the rights of citizenship which a State may confer within its own limits, and the rights of citizenship as a member of the Union. It does not by any means follow, because he has all the rights and privileges of a citizen of a State, that he must be a citizen of the United States. He may have all the rights and privileges of the citizen of a State, and yet not be entitled to the rights and privileges of a citizen in any other State. For, previous to the adoption of the Constitution of the United States, every State had the undoubted right to confer on whomsoever it pleased the character of citizen, and to endow him with all its rights. But this character of course was confined to the boundaries of the State, and gave him no rights or privileges in other States beyond those secured to him by the laws of nations and the comity of States. Nor have the several States surrendered the power of conferring these rights and privileges by adopting the Constitution of the United States. Each State may still confer them upon an alien, or any one it thinks proper, or upon any class or description of persons; yet he would not be a citizen in the sense in which that word is used in the Constitution of the United States, nor entitled to sue as such in one of its courts, nor to the privileges and immunities of a citizen in the other States. The rights which he would acquire would be restricted to the State which gave them. The Constitution has conferred on Congress the right to establish an uniform rule of naturalization, and this right is evidently exclusive, and has always been held by this court to be so. Consequently, no State, since the adoption of the Constitution, can by naturalizing an alien invest him with the rights and privileges secured to a citizen of a State under the Federal Government, although, so far as the State alone was concerned, he would undoubtedly be entitled to the rights of a citizen, and clothed with all the rights and immunities which the Constitution and laws of the State attached to that character.

It is very clear, therefore, that no State can, by any act or law of its own, passed since the adoption of the Constitution, introduce a new member into the political community created by the Constitution of the United States. It cannot make him a member of this community by making him a member of its own. And for the same reason it cannot introduce any person or description of persons, who were not intended to be embraced in this new political family, which the Constitution brought into existence, but were intended to be excluded from it.

The question then arises, whether the provisions of the Constitution, in relation to the personal rights and privileges to which the citizen of a State should be entitled, embraced the negro African race, at that time in this country, or who might afterward be imported, who had then or should afterward be made free in any State; and to put it in the power of a single State to make him a citizen of the United States, and endue him with the full rights of citizenship in every other State without their consent? Does the Constitution of the United States act upon him whenever he shall be made free under the laws of a State, and raised there to the rank of a citizen, and immediately clothe him with all the privileges of a citizen in every other State, and in its own courts?

The court think the affirmative of these propositions cannot be maintained. And if it cannot, the plaintiff in error could not be a citizen of the State of Missouri, within the meaning of the Constitution of the United States, and, consequently, was not entitled to sue in its courts.

It is true, every person, and every class and description of persons, who were at the time of the adoption of the Constitution recognized as citizens in the several States, became also citizens of this new political body; but none other; it was formed by them, and for them and their posterity, but for no one else. And the personal rights and privileges guaranteed to citizens of this new sovereignty were intended to embrace those only who were then members of the several State communities, or who should afterward by birthright or otherwise become members, according to the provisions of the Constitution and the principles on which it was founded. It was the union of those who were at that time members of distinct and separate political communities into one political family, whose power, for certain specified purposes, was to extend over the whole territory of the United States. And it gave to each citizen rights and privileges outside of his State which he did not before possess, and placed him in every other State upon a perfect equality with its own citizens as to rights of person and rights of property; it made him a citizen of the United States.

It becomes necessary, therefore, to determine who were citizens of the several States when the Constitution was adopted. And in order to do this, we must recur to the governments and institutions of the thirteen colonies, when they separated from Great Britain and formed new sovereignities, and took their places in the family of independent nations. We must inquire who, at that time, were recognized as the people or citizens of a State, whose rights and liberties had been outraged by the English Government; and who declared their independence, and assumed the powers of Government to defend their rights by force of arms.

In the opinion of the court, the legislation and histories of the times, and the language used in the Declaration of Independence, show, that neither the class of persons who had been imported as slaves, nor their descendants, whether they had become free or not, were then acknowledged as a part of the people, nor intended to be included in the general words used in that memorable instrument.

It is difficult at this day to realize the state of public opinion in relation to that unfortunate race, which prevailed in the civilized and enlightened portions of the world at the time of the Declaration of Independence, and when the Constitution of the United States was framed and adopted. But the public history of every European nation displays it in a manner too plain to be mistaken.

They had for more than a century before been regarded as beings of an inferior order, and altogether unfit to associate with the white race, either in social or political relations; and so far inferior, that they had no rights which the white man was bound to respect; and that the negro might justly and lawfully be reduced to slavery for his benefit. He was bought and sold, and treated as an ordinary article of merchandise and traffic, whenever a profit could be made by it. This opinion was at that time fixed and universal in the civilized portion of the white race. It was regarded as an axiom in morals as well as in politics, which no one thought of disputing, or supposed to be open to dispute; and men in every grade and position in society daily and habitually acted upon it in their private pursuits, as well as in matters of public concern, without doubting for a moment the correctness of this opinion.

And in no nation was this opinion more firmly fixed or more uniformly acted upon than by the English Government and English people. They not only seized them on the coast of Africa, and sold them or held them in slavery for their own use; but they took them as ordinary articles of merchandise to every country where they could make a profit on them, and were far more extensively engaged in this commerce, than any other nation in the world.

The opinion thus entertained and acted upon in England was naturally impressed upon the colonies they founded on this side of the Atlantic. And, accordingly, a negro of the African race was regarded by them as an article of property, and held, and bought and sold as such, in every one of the thirteen colonies which united in the Declaration of Independence, and afterward formed the Constitution of the United States. The slaves were more or less numerous in the different colonies, as slave labor was found more or less profitable. But no one seems to have doubted the correctness of the prevailing opinion of the time.

The legislation of the different colonies furnishes positive and indisputable proof of this fact.

It would be tedious, in this opinion, to enumerate the various laws they passed upon this subject. It will be sufficient, as a sample of the legislation which then generally prevailed throughout the British colonies, to give the laws of two of them; one being still a large slaveholding State, and the other the first State in which slavery ceased to exist.

The province of Maryland, in 1717, (chap, xiii, s. 5,) passed a law declaring "that if any free negro or mulatto intermarry with any white woman, or if any white man shall intermarry with any negro or mulatto woman, such negro or mulatto shall become a slave during life, excepting mulattoes born of white women, who, for such intermarriage, shall only become servants for seven years, to be disposed of as the justices of the county court, where such marriage so happens, shall think fit; to be applied by them toward the support of a public school within the said county. And any white man or white woman who shall intermarry as aforesaid, with any negro or mulatto, such white man or white woman shall become servants during the term of seven years, and shall be disposed of by the justices as aforesaid, and be applied to the uses aforesaid."

The other colonial law to which we refer was passed by Massachusetts in 1705, (chap, vi.) It is entitled "An act for the better preventing of a spurious and mixed issue," etc.; and it provides, that "if any negro or mulatto shall presume to smite or strike any person of the English or other Christian nation, such negro or mulatto shall be severely whipped, at the discretion of the justices before whom the offender shall be convicted."

And "that none of her Majesty's English or Scottish subjects, nor of any other Christian nation, within this province, shall contract matrimony with any negro or mulatto; nor shall any person, duly authorized to solemnize marriage, presume to join any such in marriage, on pain of forfeiting the sum of fifty pounds; one moiety thereof to her Majesty, for and toward the support of the Government within this province, and the other moiety to him or them that shall inform and sue for the same in any of her Majesty's courts of record within the province, by bill, plaint, or information."

We give both of these laws in the words used by the respective legislative bodies, because the language in which they are framed, as well as the provisions contained in them, show, too plainly to be misunderstood, the degraded condition of this unhappy race. They were still in force when the Revolution began, and are a faithful index to the state of feel-

591

ing toward the class of persons of whom they speak, and of the position they occupied throughout the thirteen colonies, in the eyes and thoughts of the men who framed the Declaration of Independence and established the State Constitutions and Governments. They show that a perpetual and impassable barrier was intended to be erected between the white race and the one which they had reduced to slavery, and governed as subjects with absolute and despotic power, and which they then looked upon as so far below them in the scale of created beings, that intermarriages between white persons and negroes or mulattoes were regarded as unnatural and immoral, and punished as crimes, not only in the parties, but in the person who joined them in marriage. And no distinction in this respect was made between the free negro or mulatto and the slave, but this stigma, of the deepest degradation, was fixed upon the whole race.

We refer to these historical facts for the purpose of showing the fixed opinions concerning that race, upon which the statesmen of that day spoke and acted. It is necessary to do this, in order to determine whether the general terms used in the Constitution of the United States, as to the rights of man and the rights of the people, was intended to include them, or to give to them or their posterity the benefit of any of its provisions.

The language of the Declaration of Independence is equally conclusive:

It begins by declaring "that when in the course of human events it becomes necessary for one people to dissolve the political bands which have connected them with another, and to assume among the powers of the earth the separate and equal station to which the laws of nature and nature's God entitle them, a decent respect for the opinions of mankind requires that they should declare the causes which impel them to the separation."

It then proceeds to say: "We hold these truths to be self-evident: that all men are created equal; that they are endowed by their Creator with certain unalienable rights; that among them is life, liberty, and the pursuit of happiness; that to secure these rights, Governments are instituted, deriving their just powers from the consent of the governed."

The general words above quoted would seem to embrace the whole human family, and if they were used in a similar instrument at this day would be so understood. But it is too clear for dispute, that the enslaved African race were not intended to be included, and formed no part of the people who framed and adopted this declaration; for if the language, as understood in that day, would embrace them, the conduct of the distinguished men who framed the Declaration of Independence would have been utterly and flagrantly inconsistent with the principles they asserted; and instead of the sympathy of mankind, to which they so confidently appealed, they would have deserved and received universal rebuke and reprobation.

Yet the men who framed this declaration were great men—high in literary acquirements—high in their sense of honor, and incapable of asserting principles inconsistent with those on which they were acting. They perfectly understood the meaning of the language they used, and how it would be understood by others; and they knew that it would not in any part of the civilized world be supposed to embrace the negro race, which by common consent, had been excluded from civilized Governments and the family of nations, and doomed to slavery. They spoke and acted according to the then established doctrines and principles, and in the ordinary language of the day, and no one misunderstood them. The unhappy black race were separated from the white by indelible marks, and laws long before established, and were never thought of or spoken of except as property, and when the claims of the owner or the profit of the trader were supposed to need protection.

This state of public opinion had undergone no change when the Constitution was adopted, as is equally evident from its provisions and language.

The brief preamble sets forth by whom it was formed, for what purposes, and for whose benefit and protection. It declares that it is formed by the *people* of the United States; that is to say, by those who were members of the different political communities in the several States; and its great object is declared to be to secure the blessings of liberty to themselves and their posterity. It speaks in general terms of the *people* of the United States, and of *citizens* of the several States, when it is providing for the exercise of the powers granted or the privileges secured to the citizen. It does not define what description of persons are intended to be included under these terms, or who shall be regarded as a citizen and one of the people. It uses them as terms so well understood, that no further description or definition was necessary.

But there are two clauses in the Constitution which point directly and specifically to the negro race as a separate class of persons, and show clearly that they were not regarded as a portion of the people or citizens of the Government then formed.

One of these clauses reserves to each of the thirteen States the right to import slaves until the year 1808, if it thinks proper. And the importation which it thus sanctions was unquestionably of persons of the race of which we are speaking, as the traffic in slaves in the United States had always been confined to them. And by the other provision the States pledge themselves to each other to maintain the right of property of the master, by delivering up to him any slave who may have escaped from his service, and be found within their respective territories. By the first above-mentioned clause, therefore, the right to purchase and hold this property is directly sanctioned and authorized for twenty years by the people who framed the Constitution. And by the second, they pledge themselves to maintain and uphold the right of the master in the manner specified, as long as the Government they then formed should endure. And these two provisions show, conclusively, that neither the description of persons therein referred to, nor their descendants, were embraced in any of the other provisions of the Constitution; for certainly these two clauses were not intended to confer on them or their posterity the blessings of liberty, or any of the personal rights so carefully provided for the citizen.

No one of that race had ever migrated to the United States voluntarily; all of them had been brought here as articles of merchandise. The number that had been emancipated at that time were but few in comparison with those held in slavery; and they were identified in the public mind with the race to which they belonged, and regarded as a part of the slave population rather than the free. It is obvious that they were not even in the minds of the framers of the Constitution when they were conferring special rights and privileges upon the citizens of a State in every other part of the Union.

Indeed, when we look to the condition of this race in the several States at the time, it is impossible to believe that these rights and privileges were intended to be extended to them.

It is very true, that in that portion of the Union where the labor of the negro race was found to be unsuited to the climate and unprofitable to the master, but few slaves were held at the time of the Declaration of Independence; and when the Constitution was adopted, it had entirely worn out in one of them, and measures had been taken for its gradual abolition in several others. But this change had not been produced by any change of opinion in relation to this race; but because it was discovered, from experience, that slave labor was unsuited to the climate and productions of these States: for some of the States, where it had ceased or nearly ceased to exist, were actively engaged in the slave trade, procuring cargoes on the coast of Africa, and transporting them for sale to those parts of the Union where their labor was found to be profitable, and suited to the climate and productions. And this traffic was openly carried on, and fortunes accumulated by it, without reproach from the people of the States where they resided. And it can hardly be supposed that, in the States where it was then countenanced in its worst form—that is, in the seizure and transportation—the people could have regarded those who were emancipated as entitled to equal rights with themselves.

And we may here again refer, in support of this proposition, to the plain and unequivocal language of the laws of the several States, some passed after the Declaration of Independence and before the Constitution was adopted, and some since the Government went into operation.

We need not refer, on this point, particularly to the laws of the present slaveholding States. Their statute books are full of provisions in relation to this class, in the same spirit with the Maryland law which we have before quoted. They have continued to treat them as an inferior class, and to subject them to strict police regulations, drawing a broad line of distinction between the citizen and the slave races, and legislating in relation to them upon the same principle which prevailed at the time of the Declaration of Independence. As relates to these States, it is too plain for argument, that they have never been regarded

594

as a part of the people or citizens of the State, nor supposed to possess any political rights which the dominant race might not withhold or grant at their pleasure. And as long ago as 1822, the Court of Appeals of Kentucky decided that free negroes and mulattoes were not citizens within the meaning of the Constitution of the United States; and the correctness of this decision is recognized, and the same doctrine affirmed, in 1 Meig's Tenn. Reports, 331.

And if we turn to the legislation of the States where slavery had worn out, or measures taken for its speedy abolition, we shall find the same opinions and principles equally fixed and equally acted upon.

Thus, Massachusetts, in 1786, passed a law similar to the colonial one of which we have spoken. The law of 1786, like the law of 1705, forbids the marriage of any white person with any negro, Indian, or mulatto, and inflicts a penalty of fifty pounds upon any one who shall join them in marriage; and declares all such marriages absolutely null and void, and degrades thus the unhappy issue of the marriage by fixing upon it the stain of bastardy. And this mark of degradation was renewed and again impressed upon the race, in the careful and deliberate preparation of their revised code, published in 1836. This code forbids any person from joining in marriage any white person with any Indian, negro, or mulatto, and subjects the party who shall offend in this respect, to imprisonment, not exceeding six months in the common jail, or to hard labor, and to a fine of not less than fifty nor more than two hundred dollars; and like the law of 1786, it declares the marriage to be absolutely null and void. It will be seen that the punishment is increased by the code upon the person who shall marry them, by adding imprisonment to a pecuniary penalty.

So, too, in Connecticut. We refer more particularly to the legislation of this State, because it was not only among the first to put an end to slavery within its own territory, but was the first to fix a mark of reprobation upon the African slave trade. The law last mentioned was passed in October, 1788, about nine months after the State had ratified and adopted the present Constitution of the Unitied States; and by that law it prohibited its own citizens, under severe penalties, from engaging in the trade, and declared all policies of insurance on the vessel or cargo made in the State to be null and void. But up to the time of the adoption of the Constitution, there is nothing in the legislation of the State indicating any change of opinion as to the relative rights and position of the white and black races in this country, or indicating that it meant to place the latter, when free, upon a level with its citizens. And certainly nothing which would have led the slaveholding States to suppose that Connecticut designed to claim for them, under the new Constitution, the equal rights and privileges and rank of citizens in every other State.

The first step taken by Connecticut upon this subject was as early as 1774, when it passed an act forbidding the further importation of slaves into the State. But the section containing the prohibition is introduced by the following preamble:

"And whereas the increase of slaves in this State is injurious to the poor, and inconvenient."

This recital would appear to have been carefully introduced, in order to prevent any misunderstanding of the motive which induced the Legislature to pass the law, and places it distinctly upon the interest and convenience of the white population—excluding the inference that it might have been intended in any degree for the benefit of the other.

And in the act of 1784, by which the issue of slaves, born after the time therein mentioned, were to be free at a certain age, the section is again introduced by a preamble assigning a similar motive for the act. It is in these words:

"Whereas sound policy requires that the abolition of slavery should be effected as soon as may be consistent with the rights of individuals, and the public safety and welfare"—showing that the right of property in the master was to be protected, and that the measure was one of policy, and to prevent the injury and inconvenience, to the whites, of a slave population in the State.

And still further pursuing its legislation, we find that in the same statute passed in 1774, which prohibited the further importation of slaves into the State, there is also a provision by which any negro, Indian, or mulatto servant, who was found wandering out of the town or place to which he belonged, without a written pass such as is therein described, was made liable to be seized by any one, and taken before the next authority to be examined and delivered up to his master—who was required to pay the charge which had accrued thereby. And a subsequent section of the same law provides, that if any free negro shall travel without such pass, and shall be stopped, seized, or taken up, he shall pay all charges arising thereby. And this law was in full operation when the Constitution of the United States was adopted, and was not repealed till 1797. So that up to that time free negroes and mulattoes were associated with servants and slaves in the police regulations established by the laws of the State.

And again, in 1833, Connecticut passed another law, which made it penal to set up or establish any school in that State for the instruction of persons of the African race not inhabitants of the State, or to instruct or teach in any such school or institution, or board or harbor for that purpose, any such person, without the previous consent in writing of the civil authority of the town in which such school or institution might be.

And it appears by the case of Crandall *v.* the State, reported in 10 Conn. Rep., 340, that upon an information filed against Prudence Crandall for a violation of this law, one of the points raised in the defense was, that the law was a violation of the Constitution of the United States; and that the persons instructed, although of the African race, were citizens of other States, and therefore entitled to the rights and privileges of citizens in the State of Connecticut. But Chief Justice Dagget, before whom the case was tried, held, that persons of that description were not citizens of a State, within the meaning of the word citizen in the Constitution of the United States, and were not therefore entitled to the privileges and immunities of citizens in other States.

The case was carried up to the Supreme Court of Errors of the State, and the question fully argued there. But the case went off upon another point, and no opinion was expressed on this question.

We have made this particular examination into the legislative and judicial action of Connecticut, because, from the early hostility it displayed to the slave trade on the coast of Africa, we may expect to find the laws of that State as lenient and favorable to the subject race as those of any other State in the Union; and if we find that at the time the Constitution was adopted, they were not even there raised to the rank of citizens, but were still held and treated as property, and the laws relating to them passed with reference altogether to the interest and convenience of the white race, we shall hardly find them elevated to a higher rank any where else.

A brief notice of the laws of two other States, and we shall pass on to other considerations.

By the laws of New Hampshire, collected and finally passed in 1815, no one was permitted to be enrolled in the militia of the State but free white citizens; and the same provision is found in a subsequent collection of the laws, made in 1855. Nothing could more strongly mark the entire repudiation of the African race. The alien is excluded, because, being born in a foreign country, he can not be a member of the community until he is naturalized. But why are the African race, born in the State, not permitted to share in one of the highest duties of a citizen? The answer is obvious; he is not, by the institutions and laws of the State, numbered among its people. He forms no part of the sovereignty of the State, and is not therefore called on to uphold and defend it.

Again, in 1822, Rhode Island, in its revised code, passed a law forbidding persons who were authorized to join persons in marriage, from joining in marriage any white person with any negro, Indian, or mulatto, under the penalty of two hundred dollars, and declaring all such marriages absolutely null and void; and the same law was again re-enacted in its revised code of 1844. So that, down to the last-mentioned period, the strongest mark of inferiority and degradation was fastened upon the African race in that State.

It would be impossible to enumerate and compress in the space usually allotted to an opinion of a court, the various laws, marking the condition of this race, which were passed from time to time after the Revolution, and before and since the adoption of the Constitution of the United States. In addition to those already referred to, it is sufficient to say, that Chancellor Kent, whose accuracy and research no one will question, states in the sixth edition of his Commentaries (published in 1846, 2 vols., 258, note *b*,) that in no part of the country except Maine, did the African race, in point of fact, participate equally with the whites in the exercise of civil and political rights.

The legislation of the States therefore shows, in a manner not to be mistaken, the inferior and subject condition of that race at the time the Constitution was adopted, and long afterward, throughout the thirteen States by which that instrument was framed; and it is hardly consistent with the respect due to these States, to suppose that they regarded at that time, as fellow citizens and members of the sovereignty, a class of beings whom they had thus stigmatized; whom, as we are bound, out of respect to the State sovereignties, to assume they had deemed it just and necessary thus to stigmatize, and upon whom they had impressed such deep and enduring marks of inferiority and degradation; or that when they met in convention to form the Constitution, they looked upon them as a portion of their constituents, or designed to include them in the provisions so carefully inserted for the security and protection of the liberties and rights of their citizens. It cannot be supposed that they intended to secure to them rights, and privileges, and rank, in the new political body throughout the Union, which every one of them denied within the limits of its own dominion. More especially, it can not be believed that the large slaveholding States regarded them as included in the word citizens, or would have consented to a Constitution which might compel them to receive them in that character from another State. For if they were so received, and entitled to the privileges and immunities to citizens, it would exempt them from the operation of the special laws and from the police regulations which they considered to be necessary for their own safety. It would give to persons of the negro race, who were recognized as citizens in any one State of the Union, the right to enter every other State whenever they pleased, singly or in companies, without pass or passport, and without obstruction, to sojourn there as long as they pleased, to go where they pleased at every hour of the day or night without molestation, unless they committed some violation of law for which a white man would be punished; and it would give them the full liberty of speech in public and in private upon all subjects upon which its own citizens might speak; to hold public meetings upon political affairs, and to keep and carry arms wherever they went. And all of this would be done in the face of the subject race of the same color, both free and slaves, and inevitably producing discontent and insubordination among them, and endangering the peace and safety of the State.

It is impossible, it would seem, to believe that the great men of the slaveholding States, who took so large a share in framing the Constitution of the United States, and exercised so much influence in procuring its adoption, could have been so forgetful or regardless of their own safety and the safety of those who trusted and confided in them.

Besides, this want of foresight and care would have been utterly inconsistent with the caution displayed in providing for the admission of new members into this political family. For, when they gave to the citizens of each State the privileges and immunities of citizens in the several States, they at the same time took from the several States the power of naturalization, and confined that power exclusively to the Federal Government. No State was willing to permit another State to determine who should or should not be admitted as one of its citizens, and entitled to demand equal rights and privileges with their own people, within their own territories. The right of naturalization was therefore, with one accord, surrendered by the States, and confided to the Federal Government. And this power granted to Congress to establish an uniform rule of *naturalization* is, by the well understood meaning of the word, confined to persons born in a foreign country, under a foreign Government. It is not a power to raise to the rank of a citizen any one born in the United States, who, from birth or parentage, by the laws of the country, belongs to an inferior and subordinate class. And when we find the States guarding themselves from the indiscreet or improper admission by other States of emigrants from other countries, by giving the power exclusively to Congress, we can not fail to see that they could never have left with the States a much more important power—that is, the power of transforming into citizens a numerous class of persons, who in that character would be much more dangerous to the peace and safety of a large portion of the Union, than the few foreigners one of the States might improperly naturalize

The Constitution upon its adoption obviously took from the States all power by any subsequent legislation to introduce as a citizen into the political family of the United States any one, no matter where he was born, or what might be his character or condition; and it gave to Congress the power to confer this character upon those only who were born outside of the dominions of the United States. And no law of a State, therefore, passed since the Constitution was adopted, can give any right of citizenship outside of its own territory.

A clause similar to the one in the Constitution, in relation to the rights and immunities of citizens of one State in the other States, was contained in the articles of Confederation. But there is a difference of language, which is worthy of note. The provision in the Articles of Confederation was "that the *free inhabitants* of each of the States, paupers, vagabonds, and fugitives from justice, excepted, should be entitled to all the privileges and immunities of free citizens in the several States."

It will be observed, that under this Confederation, each State had the right to decide for itself, and in its own tribunals, whom it would acknowledge as a free inhabitant of another State. The term *free inhabitant*, in the generality of its terms, would certainly include one of the African race who had been manumitted. But no example, we think, can be found of his admission to all the privileges of citizenship in any State of the Union after these articles were formed, and while they continued in force. And, notwithstanding the generality of the words "free inhabitants," it is very clear that, according to their accepted meaning in that day, they did not include the African race, whether free or not: for the fifth section of the ninth article provides that Congress should have the power "to agree upon the number of land forces to be raised, and to make requisitions from each State for its quota in proportion to the number of *white* inhabitants in such State, which requisition should be binding."

Words could hardly have been used which more strongly mark the line of distinction between the citizen and the subject; the free and the subjugated races. The latter were not even counted when the inhabitants of a State were to be embodied in proportion to its numbers for the general defense. And it can not for a moment be supposed, that a class of persons thus separated and rejected from those who formed the sovereignty of the States, were yet intended to be included under the words "free inhabitants," in the preceding article, to whom privileges and immunities were so carefully secured in every State.

But although this clause of the articles of Confederation is the same in principle with that inserted in the Constitution, yet the comprehensive word *inhabitant*, which might be construed to include an emancipated slave, is omitted; and the privilege is confined to *citizens* of the State. And this alteration in words would hardly have been made, unless a different meaning was intended to be conveyed, or a possible doubt removed. The just and fair inference is, that as this privilege was about to be placed under the protection of the General Government, and the words expounded by its tribunals, and all power in relation to it taken from the State and its courts, it was deemed prudent to describe with precision and caution the persons to whom this high privilege was given—and the word *citizen* was on that account substituted for the words *free inhabitant*. The word citizen excluded, and no doubt intended to exclude, foreigners who had not become citizens of some one of the States when the Constitution was adopted; and also every description of persons who were not fully recognized as citizens in the several States. This, upon any fair construction of the instruments to which we have referred, was evidently the object and purpose of this change of words.

To all this mass of proof we have still to add, that Congress has repeatedly legislated upon the same construction of the Constitution that we have given. Three laws, two of which were passed almost immediately after the Government went into operation, will be abundantly sufficient to show this. The two first are particularly worthy of notice, because many of the men who assisted in framing the Constitution, and took an active part in procuring its adoption, were then in the halls of legislation, and certainly understood what they meant when they used the words "people of the United States" and "citizen" in that well-considered instrument.

The first of these acts is the naturalization law, which was passed at the second session of the first Congress, March 26, 1790, and confines the right of becoming citizens "*to aliens being free white persons.*"

Now, the Constitution does not limit the power of Congress in this respect to white persons. And they may, if they think proper, authorize the naturalization of any one of any color, who was born under allegiance to another Government. But the language of the law above quoted, shows that citizenship at that time was perfectly understood to be confined to the white race; and that they alone constituted the sovereignty in the Government.

Congress might, as we before said, have authorized the naturalization of Indians, because they were aliens and foreigners. But, in their then untutored and savage state, no one would have thought of admitting them as citizens in a civilized community. And, moreover, the atrocities they had but recently committed, when they were the allies of Great Britain in the Revolutionary war, were yet fresh in the recollection of the people of the United States, and they were even then guarding themselves against the threatened renewal of Indian hostilities. No one supposed then that any Indian would ask for, or was capable of enjoying the privileges of an American citizen, and the word white was not used with any particular reference to them.

Neither was it used with any reference to the African race imported into or born in this country; because Congress had no power to naturalize them, and therefore there was no necessity for using particular words to exclude them.

It would seem to have been used merely because it followed out the line of division which the Constitution has drawn between the citizen race, who formed and held the Government, and the African race, which they held in subjection and slavery, and governed at their own pleasure.

Another of the early laws of which we have spoken, is the first militia law, which was passed in 1792, at the first session of the second Congress. The language of this law is equally plain and significant with the one just mentioned. It directs that every "free able-bodied white male citizen" shall be enrolled in the militia. The word *white* is evidently used to exclude the African race, and the word "citizen" to exclude unnaturalized foreigners; the latter forming no part of the sovereignty, owing it no allegiance, and therefore under no obligation to defend it. The African race, however, born in the country, did owe allegiance to the Government, whether they were slaves or free; but it is repudiated, and rejected from the duties and obligations of citizenship in marked language.

The third act to which we have alluded is even still more decisive; it was passed as late as 1813, (2 Stat., 809,) and it provides: "that from and after the termination of the war in which the United States are now engaged with Great Britain, it shall not be lawful to employ, on board of any public or private vessels of the United States, any person or persons except citizens of the United States, *or* persons of color, natives of the United States."

Here the line of distinction is drawn in express words. Persons of color, in the judgment of Congress, were not included in the word citizens, and they are described as another and different class of persons, and authorized to be employed, if born in the United States.

And even as late as 1820, (chap. civ, sec. 8,) in the charter to the city of Washington, the corporation is authorized "to restrain and prohibit the nightly and other disorderly meetings of slaves, free negroes, and mulattoes," thus associating them together in its legislation; and after prescribing the punishment that may be inflicted on the slaves, proceeds in the following words: "And to punish such free negroes and mulattoes by penalties not exceeding twenty dollars for any one offense; and in case of the inability of any such free negro or mulatto to pay any such penalty and cost thereon, to cause him or her to be confined to labor for any time not exceeding six calendar months." And in a subsequent part of the same section, the act authorizes the corporation "to prescribe the terms and conditions upon which free negroes and mulattoes may reside in the city."

This law, like the laws of the States, shows that this class of persons were governed by special legislation directed expressly to them, and always connected with provisions for the government of slaves, and not with those for the government of free white citizens. And after such an uniform course of legislation as we have stated; by the colonies, by the States, and by Congress, running through a period of more than a century, it would seem that to call persons thus marked and stigmatized, "citizens" of the United States, "fellow-citizens," a constituent part of the sovereignty, would be an abuse of terms, and not calculated to exalt the character of an American citizen in the eyes of other nations.

The conduct of the Executive Department of the Government has been in perfect harmony upon this subject with this course of legislation. The question was brought officially before the late William Wirt, when he was Attorney General of the United States, in 1821, and he decided that the words "citizens of the United States" were used in the acts of Congress in the same sense as in the Constitution; and that free persons of color were not citizens, within the meaning of the Constitution and laws; and this opinion has been confirmed by that of the late Attorney General, Caleb Cushing, in a recent case, and acted upon by the Secretary of State, who refused to grant passports to them as "citizens of the United States."

But it is said that a person may be a citizen, and entitled to that character, although he does not possess all the rights which may belong to other citizens; as, for example, the right to vote, or to hold particular offices; and that yet, when he goes into another State, he is entitled to be recognized there as a citizen, although the State may measure his rights by the rights which it allows to persons of a like character or class resident in the State, and refuse to him the full rights of citizenship.

This argument overlooks the language of the provision in the Constitution of which we are speaking.

Undoubtedly, a person may be a citizen, that is, a member of the community who form the sovereignty, although he exercises no share of the political power, and is incapacitated from holding particular office. Women and minors, who form a part of the political family, can not vote; and when a property qualification is required to vote or hold a particular office, those who have not the necessary qualification can not vote or hold the office, yet they are citizens.

So, too, a person may be entitled to vote by the law of the State, who is not a citizen even of the State itself. And in some of the States of the Union foreigners not naturalized are allowed to vote. And the State may give the right to free negroes and mulattoes, but that does not make them citizens of the State, and still less of the United States. And the provision in the Constitution giving privileges and immunities in other States, does not apply to them.

Neither does it apply to a person who, being the citizen of a State, migrates to another State. For then he becomes subject to the laws of the State in which he lives, and he is no longer a citizen of the State from which he removed. And the State in which he resides may then, unquestionably, determine his *status* or condition, and place him among the class of persons who are not recognized as citizens, but belong to an inferior and subject race; and may deny him the privileges and immunities enjoyed by its citizens.

But so far as mere rights of persons are concerned, the provision in question is confined to citizens of a State who are temporarily in another State without taking up their residence there. It gives them no political rights in the State, as to voting or holding office, or in any other respect. For a citizen of one State has no right to participate in the government of another. But if he ranks as a citizen in the State to which he belongs, within the meaning of the Constitution of the United States, then, whenever he goes into another State, the Constitution clothes him, as to the rights of person, with all the privileges and immunities which belong to citizens of the State. And if persons of the African race are citizens of a State, and of the United States, they would be entitled to all these privileges and immunities in every State, and the State could not restrict them; for they would hold these privileges and immunities under the paramount authority of the Federal Government, and its courts would be bound to maintain and enforce them, the Constitution and laws of the State to the contrary notwithstanding. And if the States could limit or restrict them, or place the party in an inferior grade, this clause of the Constitution would be unmeaning, and could have no operation; and would give no rights to the citizen when in another State. He would have none but what the State itself chose to allow him. This is evidently not the construction or meaning of the clause in question. It guaranties rights, to the citizen, and the State can not withhold them. And these rights are of a character and would lead to consequences which make it absolutely certain that the African race were not included under the name of citizens of a State, and were not in the contemplation of the framers of the Constitution when these privileges and immunities were provided for the protection of the citizen in other States.

The case of Legrand *v.* Darnall (2 Peters, 664) has been referred to for the purpose of showing that this court has decided that the descendant of a slave may sue as a citizen in a court of the United States; but the case itself shows that the question did not arise and could not have arisen in the case.

It appears from the report, that Darnell was born in Maryland, and was the son of a white man by one of his slaves, and his father executed certain instruments to manumit him, and devised to him some landed property in the State. This property Darnall afterward sold to Legrand, the appellant, who gave his notes for the purchase-money. But becoming afterward apprehensive that the appellee had not been emancipated according to the laws of Maryland, he refused to pay the notes until he could be better satisfied as to Darnell's right to convey. Darnall, in the mean time, had taken up his residence in Pennsylvania, and brought suit on the notes, and recovered judgment in the Circuit Court for the district of Maryland.

The whole proceeding, as appears by the report, was an amicable one; Legrand being perfectly willing to pay the money, if he could obtain a title, and Darnall not wishing him to pay unless he could make him a good one. In point of fact, the whole proceeding was under the direction of the counsel who argued the case for the appellee, who was the mutual friend of the parties, and confided in by both of them, and whose only object was to have the rights of both parties established by judicial decision in the most speedy and least expensive manner.

Legrand, therefore, raised no objection to the jurisdiction of the court in the suit at law, because he was himself anxious to obtain the judgment of the court upon his title. Consequently, there was nothing in the record before the court to show that Darnall was of African descent, and the usual judgment and award of execution was entered. And Legrand thereupon filed his bill on the equity side of the Circuit Court, stating that Darnall was born a slave, and had not been legally emancipated, and could not therefore take the land devised to him, nor make Legrand a good title; and praying an injunction to restrain Darnall from proceeding to execution on the judgment, which was granted. Darnall answered, averring in his answer that he was a free man, and capable of conveying a good title. Testimony was taken on this point, and at the hearing the Circuit Court was of opinion that Darnall was a free man and his title good, and dissolved the injunction and dismissed the bill; and that decree was affirmed here, upon the appeal of Legrand.

Now, it is difficult to imagine how any question about the citizenship of Darnall, or his right to sue in that character, can be supposed to have risen or been decided in that case. The fact that he was of African descent was first brought before the court upon the bill in equity. The suit at law had then passed into judgment and award of execution, and the Circuit Court, as a court of law, had no longer any authority over it. It was a valid and legal judgment, which the court that rendered it had not the power to reverse or set aside. And unless it had jurisdiction as a court of equity to restrain him from using its process as a court of law, Darnall, if he thought proper, would have been at liberty to proceed on his judgment, and compel the payment of the money, although the allegations in the bill were true, and he was incapable of making a title. No other court could have enjoined him, for certainly no State equity court could interfere in that way with the judgment of a Circuit Court of the United States.

But the Circuit Court as a court of equity certainly had equity jurisdiction over its own judgment as a court of law, without regard to the character of the parties; and had not only the right, but it was its duty—no matter who were the parties in the judgment—to prevent them from proceeding to enforce it by execution, if the court was satisfied that the money was not justly and equitably due. The ability of Darnall to convey did not depend upon his citizenship, but upon his title to freedon. And if he was free, he could hold and convey property, by the laws of Maryland, although he was not a citizen. But if he was by law still a slave, he could not. It was therefore the duty of the court, sitting as a court of equity in the latter case, to prevent him from using its process, as a court of common law, to compel the payment of the purchase-money, when it was evident that the purchaser must lose the land. But if he was free and could make a title, it was equally the duty of the court not to suffer Legrand to keep the land, and refuse the payment of the money, upon the ground that Darnall was incapable of suing or being sued as a citizen in a court of the United States. The character or citizenship of the parties had no connection with the question of jurisdiction, and the matter in dispute had no relation to the citizenship of Darnall. Nor is such a question alluded to in the opinion of the Court.

Beside, we are by no means prepared to say that there are not many cases, civil as well as criminal, in which a Circuit Court of the United States may exercise jurisdiction, although one of the African race is a party; that broad question is not before the court. The question with which we are now dealing is, whether a person of the African race can be a citizen of the United States, and become thereby entitled to a special privilege, by virtue of his title to that character, and which, under the Constitution, no one but a citizen can claim. It is manifest that the case of Legrand and Darnall has no bearing on that question, and can have no application to the case now before the court.

This case, however, strikingly illustrates the consequences that would follow the construction of the Constitution which would give the power contended for to a State. It would in effect give it also to an individual. For if the father of young Darnall had manumitted him in his lifetime, and sent him to reside in a State which recognized him as a citizen, he might have visited and sojourned in Maryland when he pleased, and as long as he pleased, as a citizen of the United States; and the State officers and tribunals would be compelled, by the paramount authority of the Constitution, to receive him and treat him as one of its citizens, exempt from the laws and police of the State in relation to a person of that description, and allow him to enjoy all the rights and privileges of citizenship without respect to the laws of Maryland, although such laws were deemed by it absolutely essential to its own safety.

The only two provisions which point to them and include them, treat them as property, and make it the duty of the Government to protect it; no other power, in relation to this race, is to be found in the Constitution; and as it is a Government of special, delegated, powers, no authority beyond these two provisions can be constitutionally exercised. The Government of the United States had no right to interfere for any other purpose but that of protecting the rights of the owner, leaving it altogether with the several States to deal with this race, whether emancipated or not, as each State may think justice, humanity, and the interests and safety of society, require. The States evidently intended to reserve this power exclusively to themselves.

No one, we presume, supposes that any change in public opinion or feeling, in relation to this unfortunate race, in the civilized nations of Europe or in this country, should induce the court to give to the words of the Constitution a more liberal construction in their favor than they were intended to bear when the instrument was framed and adopted. Such an argument would be altogether inadmissible in any tribunal called on to interpret it. If any of its provisions are deemed unjust, there is a mode prescribed in the instrument itself, by which it may be amended; but while it remains unaltered, it must be construed now as it was understood at the time of its adoption. It is not only the same in words, but the same in meaning, and delegates the same powers to the Government, and reserves and secures the same rights and privileges to citizens; and as long as it continues to exist in its present form, it speaks not only in the same words, but with the same meaning and intent with which it spoke when it came from the hands of its framers, and was voted on and adopted by the people of the United States. Any other rule of construction would abrogate the judicial character of this court, and make it the mere reflex of the popular opinion or passion of the day. This court was not created by the Constitution for such purposes. Higher and graver trusts have been confided to it, and it must not falter in the path of duty.

What the construction was at that time, we think can hardly admit of doubt. We have the language of the Declaration of Independence and of the Articles of Confederation, in addition to the plain words of the Constitution itself; we have the legislation of the different States, before, about the time, and since, the Constitution was adopted; we have the legislation of Congress, from the time of its adoption to a recent period; and we have the constant and uniform action of the Executive Department, all concurring together, and leading to the same result. And if any thing in relation to the construction of the Constitution can be regarded as settled, it is that which we now give to the word "citizen" and the word "people."

And upon a full and careful consideration of the subject, the court is of opinion, that, upon the facts stated in the plea in abatement, Dred Scott was not a citizen of Missouri within the meaning of the Constitution of the United States, and not entitled as such to sue in its courts; and, consequently, that the Circuit Court had no jurisdiction of the case, and that the judgment on the plea in abatement is erroneous.

We are aware that doubts are entertained by some of the members of the court, whether the plea in abatement is legally before the court upon this writ of error: but if that plea is regarded as waived, or out of the case upon any other ground, yet the question as to the jurisdiction of the Circuit Court is presented on the face of the bill of exception itself, taken by the plaintiff at the trial; for he admits that he and his wife were born slaves, but endeavors to make out his title to freedom and citizenship by showing that they were taken by their owner to certain places, hereinafter mentioned, where slavery could not by law exist, and that they thereby became free, and upon their return to Missouri became citizens of that State.

Now, if the removal, of which he speaks, did not give them their freedom, then by his own admission he is still a slave, and whatever opinions may be entertained in favor of the citizenship of a free person of the African race, no one supposes that a slave is a citizen of the State or of the United States. If, therefore, the acts done by his owner did not make them free persons, he is still a slave, and certainly incapable of suing in the character of a citizen.

The principle of law is too well settled to be disputed, that a court can give no judgment for either party, where it has no jurisdiction; and if, upon the showing of Scott himself, it appeared that he was still a slave, the case ought to have been dismissed, and the judgment against him and in favor of the defendant for costs, is, like that on the plea in abatement, erroneous, and the suit ought to have been dismissed by the Circuit Court for want of jurisdiction in that court.

But, before we proceed to examine this part of the case, it may be proper to notice an objection taken to the judicial authority of this court to decide it; and it has been said, that as this court has decided against the jurisdiction of the Circuit Court on the plea in abatement, it has no right to examine any question presented by the exception; and that any thing that it may say upon that part of the case will be extra judicial, and mere orbita dicta.

This is a manifest mistake; there can be no doubt as to the jurisdiction of this court to revise the judgment of a Circuit Court, and to reverse it for any error apparent on the record, whether it be the error of giving judgment in a case over which it had no jurisdiction, or any other material error; and this, too, whether there is a plea in abatement or not.

The objection appears to have arisen from confounding writs of error to a State court, with writs of error to a Circuit Court of the United States. Undoubtedly, upon a writ of error to a State court, unless the record shows a case that gives jurisdiction, the case must be dismissed for want of jurisdiction in *this court*. And if it is dismissed on that ground, we have no right to examine and decide upon any question presented by the bill of exceptions, or any other part of the record. But writs of error to a State Court, and to a Circuit Court of the United States, are regulated by different laws, and stand upon entirely different principles. And in a writ of error to a Circuit Court of the United States, the whole record is before this court for examination and decision; and if the sum in controversy is large enough to give jurisdiction, it is not only the right, but it is the judicial duty of the court, to examine the whole case as presented by the record; and if it appears upon its face that any material error or errors have been committed by the court below, it is the duty of this court to reverse the judgment, and remand the case. And certainly an error in passing a judgment upon the merits in favor of either party, in a case which it was not authorized to try, and over which it had no jurisdiction, is as grave an error as a court can commit.

The plea in abatement is not a plea to the jurisdiction of this court, but to the jurisdiction of the Circuit Court. And it appears by the record before us, that the Circuit Court committed an error, in deciding that it had jurisdiction, upon the facts in the case, admitted by the pleadings. It is the duty of the appellate tribunal to correct this error; but that could not be done by dismissing the case for want of jurisdiction here—for that would leave the erroneous judgment in full force, and the injured party without remedy. And the appellate court therefore exercises the power for which alone appellate courts are constituted, by reversing the judgment of the court below for this error. It exercises its proper and appropriate jurisdiction over the judgment and proceedings of the Circuit Court, as they appear upon the record brought up by the writ of error.

The correction of one error in the court below does not deprive the appellate court of the power of examining further into the record, and correcting any other material errors which may have been committed by the inferior court. There is certainly no rule of law—nor any practice—nor any decision of a court—which even questions this power in the appellate tribunal. On the contrary, it is the daily practice of this court, and of all appellate courts where they reverse the judgment of an inferior court for error, to correct by its opinions whatever errors may appear on the record material to the case; and they have always held it to be their duty to do so where the silence of the court might lead to misconstruction or future controversy, and the point has been relied on by either side, and argued before the court.

In the case before us, we have already decided that the Circuit Court erred in deciding that it had jurisdiction upon the facts admitted by the pleadings. And it appears that, in the further progress of the case, it acted upon the erroneous principle it had decided on the pleadings, and gave judgment for the defendant, where, upon the facts admitted in the exception, it had no jurisdiction.

We are at a loss to understand upon what principle of law, applicable to appellate jurisdiction, it can be supposed that this court has not judicial authority to correct the last-mentioned error, because they had before corrected the former; or by what process of reasoning it can be made out, that the error of an inferior court in actually pronouncing judgment for one of the parties, in a case in which it had no jurisdiction, cannot be looked into or corrected by this court, because we have decided a similar question presented in the pleadings. The last point is distinctly presented by the facts contained in the plaintiff's own bill of exceptions, which he himself brings here by this writ of error. It was the point which chiefly occupied the attention of the counsel on both sides in the argument—and the judgment which this court must render upon both errors is precisely the same. It must, in each of them, exercise jurisdiction over the judgment, and reverse it for the errors committed by the court below; and issue a mandate to the Circuit Court to conform its judgment to the opinion pronounced by this court, by dismissing the case for want of jurisdiction in the Circuit Court. This is the constant and invariable practice of this court, where it reverses a judgment for want of jurisdiction in the Circuit Court.

It can scarcely be necessary to pursue such a question further. The want of jurisdiction in the court below may appear on the record without any plea in abatement. This is familiarly the case where a court of chancery has exercised jurisdiction in a case where the plaintiff had a plain and adequate remedy at law, and it so appears by the transcript when brought here by appeal. So also where it appears that a court of admiralty has exercised jurisdiction in a case belonging exclusively to a court of common law. In these cases there is no plea in abatement. And for the same reason, and upon the same principles, where the defect of jurisdiction is patent on the record, this court is bound to reverse the judgment, although the defendant has not pleaded in abatement to the jurisdiction of the inferior court.

The cases of Jackson *v.* Ashton and of Capron *v.* Van Noorden, to which we have referred in a previous part of this opinion, are directly in point. In the last-mentioned case, Capron brought an action against Van Noorden in a Circuit Court of the United States, without showing, by the usual averments of citizenship, that the court had jurisdiction.

There was no plea in abatement put in, and the parties went to trial upon the merits. The court gave judgment in favor of the defendant with costs. The plaintiff thereupon brought his writ of error, and this court reversed the judgment given in favor of the defendant, and remanded the case with directions to dismiss it, because it did not appear by the transcript that the Circuit Court had jurisdiction.

The case before us still more strongly imposes upon this court the duty of examining whether the court below has not committed an error, in taking jurisdiction and giving a judgment for costs in favor of the defendant; for in Capron *v.* Van Noorden the judgment was reversed, because it did *not appear* that the parties were citizens of different States. They might or might not be. But in this case it *does appear* that the plaintiff was born a slave; and if the facts upon which he relies have not made him free, then it appears affirmatively on the record that he is not a citizen, and consequently his suit against Sandford was not a suit between citizens of different States, and the court had no authority to pass any judgment between the parties. The suit ought, in this view of it, to have been dismissed by the Circuit Court, and its judgment in favor of Sandford is erroneous, and must be reversed.

It is true that the result either way, by dismissal or by a judgment for the defendant, makes very little, if any, difference in a pecuniary or personal point of view to either party. But the fact that the result would be very nearly the same to the parties in either form of judgment, would not justify this court in sanctioning an error in the judgment which is patent on the record, and which, if sanctioned, might be drawn into precedent, and lead to serious mischief and injustice in some future suit.

We proceed, therefore, to inquire whether the facts relied on by the plaintiff entitled him to his freedom.

The case, as he himself states it, on the record brought here by his writ of error, is this:

The plaintiff was a negro slave, belonging to Dr. Emerson, who was a surgeon in the army of the United States. In the year 1834, he took the plaintiff from the State of Missouri to the military post at Rock Island, in the State of Illinois, and held him there as a slave until the month of April or May, 1836. At the time last-mentioned, said Dr. Emerson removed the plaintiff from said miltary post at Rock Island to the military post at Fort Snelling, situate on the west bank of the Mississippi river, in the territory known as Upper Louisiana, acquired by the United States of France, and situate north of the latitude of thirty-six degrees thirty minutes north, and north of the State of Missouri. Said Dr. Emerson held the plaintiff in slavery at said Fort Sneling, from said last-mentioned date until the year 1838.

In the year 1835, Harriet, who is named in the second count of the plaintiff's declaration, was the negro slave of Major Taliaferro, who belonged to the army of the United

States. In that year, 1835, said Major Taliaferro took said Harriet to said Fort Snelling, a military post, situated as hereinbefore stated, and kept her there as a slave until the year 1836, and then sold and delivered her as a slave, at said Fort Snelling, unto the said Dr. Emerson hereinbefore named. Said Dr. Emerson held said Harriet in slavery at said Fort Snelling until the year 1838.

In the year 1836, the plaintiff and Harriet intermarried, at Fort Snelling, with the consent of Dr. Emerson, who then claimed to be their master and owner. Eliza and Lizzie, named in the third count of the plaintiff's declaration, are the fruit of that marriage. Eliza is about fourteen years old, and was born on board the steamboat Gipsey, north of the north line of the State of Missouri, and upon the river Mississippi. Lizzie is about seven years old, and was born in the State of Missouri, at the military post called Jefferson Barracks.

In the year 1838, said Dr. Emerson removed the plaintiff and said Harriet, and their said daughter Eliza, from said Fort Snelling to the State of Missouri, where they have ever since resided.

Before the commencement of this suit, said Dr. Emerson sold and conveyed the plaintiff, and Harriet, Eliza, and Lizzie, to the defendant, as slaves, and the defendant has ever since claimed to hold them, and each of them, as slaves.

In considering this part of the controversy, two questions arise: 1. Was he, together with his family, free in Missouri by reason of the stay in the territory of the United States hereinbefore mentioned? And, 2. If they were not, is Scott himself free by reason of his removal to Rock Island, in the State of Illinois, as stated in the above admissions?

We proceed to examine the first question.

The act of Congress, upon which the plaintiff relies, declares that slavery and involuntary servitude, except as a punishment for crime, shall be forever prohibited in all that part of the territory ceded by France, under the name of Louisiana, which lies north of thirty-six degrees thirty minutes north latitude, and not included within the limits of Missouri. And the difficulty which meets us at the threshold of this part of the inquiry is, whether Congress was authorized to pass this law under any of the powers granted to it by the Constitution; for if the authority is not given by that instrument, it is the duty of this court to declare it void and inoperative, and incapable of conferring freedom upon any one who is held as a slave under the laws of any one of the States.

The counsel for the plaintiff has laid much stress upon that article in the Constitution which confers on Congress the power "to dispose of and make all needful rules and regulations respecting the territory or other property belonging to the United States;" but, in the judgment of the court, that provision has no bearing on the present controversy, and the power there given, whatever it may be, is confined, and was intended to be confined, to the territory which at that time belonged to, or was claimed by, the United States, and was within their boundaries as settled by the treaty with Great Britain, and can have no influence upon a territory afterward acquired from a foreign Government. It was a special provision for a known and particular territory, and to meet a present emergency, and nothing more.

A brief summary of the history of the times, as well as the careful and measured terms in which the article is framed, will show the correctness of this proposition.

It will be remembered that, from the commencement of the Revolutionary war, serious difficulties existed between the States, in relation to the disposition of large and unsettled territories which were included in the chartered limits of some of the States. And some of the other States, and more especially Maryland, which had no unsettled lands, insisted that as the unoccupied lands, if wrested from Great Britain, would owe their preservation to the common purse and the common sword, the money arising from them ought to be applied in just proportion among the several States to pay the expenses of the war, and ought not to be appropriated to the use of the State in whose chartered limits they might happen to lie, to the exclusion of the other States, by whose combined efforts and common expense the territory was defended and preserved against the claim of the British Government.

These difficulties caused much uneasiness during the war, while the issue was in some degree doubtful, and the future boundaries of the United States yet to be defined by treaty, if we achieved our independence.

The majority of the Congress of the Confederation obviously concurred in opinion with the State of Maryland, and desired to obtain from the States which claimed it a cession of this territory, in order that Congress might raise money on this security to carry on the war. This appears by the resolution passed on the 6th of September, 1780, strongly urging the States to cede these lands to the United States, both for the sake of peace and union among themselves, and to maintain the public credit; and this was followed by the resolution of October 10th, 1780, by which Congress pledged itself, that if the lands were ceded, as recommended by the resolution above mentioned, they should be disposed of for the common benefit of the United States, and be settled and formed into distinct republican States, which should become members of the Federal Union, and have the same rights of sovereignty, and freedom, and independence, as other States.

But these difficulties became much more serious after peace took place, and the boundaries of the United States were established. Every State, at that time, felt severely the pressure of its war debt; but in Virginia, and some other States, there were large territories of unsettled lands, the sale of which would enable them to discharge their obligations without much inconvenience while other States, which had no such resource, saw before them many years of heavy and burdensome taxation; and the latter insisted, for the reasons before stated, that these unsettled lands should be treated as the common property of the States, and the proceeds applied to their common benefit.

The letters from the statesmen of that day will show how much this controversy occupied their thoughts, and the dangers that were apprehended from it. It was the disturbing element of the time, and fears were entertained that it might dissolve the Confederation by which the States were then united.

These fears and dangers were, however, at once removed, when the State of Virginia, in 1784, voluntarily ceded to the United States the immense tract of country lying northwest of the river Ohio, and which was within the acknowledged limits of the State. The only object of the State, in making this cession, was to put an end to the threatening and exciting controversy, and to enable the Congress of that time to dispose of the lands, and appropriate the proceeds as a common fund for the common benefit of the States. It was not ceded because it was inconvenient to the State to hold and govern it, nor from any expectation that it could be better or more conveniently governed by the United States.

The example of Virginia was soon afterward followed by other States, and, at the time of the adoption of the Constitution, all of the States similarly situated, had ceded their unappropriated lands, except North Carolina and Georgia. The main object for which the cessions were desired and made, was on account of their money value, and to put an end to a dangerous controversy, as to who was justly entitled to the proceeds when the land should be sold. It is necessary to bring this part of the history of these cessions thus distinctly into view, because it will enable us the better to comprehend the phraseology of the article in the Constitution, so often referred to in the argument.

Undoubtedly the powers of sovereignty and the eminent domain were ceded with the land. This was essential, in order to make it effectual, and to accomplish its objects. But it must be remembered that, at that time, there was no Government of the United States in existence with enumerated and limited powers; what was then called the United States, were thirteen separate, sovereign, independent States, which had entered into a league or confederation for their mutual protection and advantage, and the Congress of the United States was composed of the representatives of these separate sovereignties, meeting together, as equals, to discuss and decide on certain measures which the States, by the Articles of Confederation, had agreed to submit to their decision. But this Confederation had none of the attributes of sovereignty in legislative, executive, or judicial power. It was little more than a congress of ambassadors, authorized to represent separate nations, in matters in which they had a common concern.

It was this congress that accepted the cession from Virginia. They had no power to accept it under the Articles of Confederation. But they had an undoubted right, as independent sovereignties, to accept any cession of territory for their common benefit, which all of them assented to; and it is equally clear, that as their common property, and having no superior to control them, they had the right to exercise absolute dominion over it, subject only to the restrictions which Virginia had imposed in her act of cession. There was, at we have said, no Government of the United States then in existence with special enumerated and limited powers. The territory belonged to sovereignties, who, subject to the limitations above mentioned, had a right to establish any form of Government they pleased, by compact or treaty among themselves, and to regulate rights of person and rights of property in the territory, as they might deem proper. It was by a Congress, representing the authority of these several and separate sovereignties, and acting under their authority and command (but not from any authority derived from the Articles of Confederation,) that the instrument usually called the ordinance of 1787 was adopted; regulating in much detail the principles and the laws by which this territory should be governed; and among other provisions, slavery is prohibited in it. We do not question the power of the States, by agreement among themselves, to pass this ordinance, nor its obligatory force in the territory, while the confederation or league of the States in their separate sovereign character continued to exist.

This was the state of things when the Constitution of the United States was formed. The territory ceded by Virginia, belonged to the several confederated States as common property, and they had united in establishing in it a system of government and jurisprudence, in order to prepare it for admission as States, according to the terms of cession. They were about to dissolve this federative Union, and to surrender a portion of their independent sovereignty to a new Government, which, for certain purposes, would make the people of the several States one people, and which was to be supreme and controlling, within its sphere of action throughout the United States; but this Government was to be carefully limited in its powers, and to exercise no authority beyond those expressly granted by the Constitution, or necessarily to be implied from the language of the instrument, and the objects it was intended to accomplish; and as this league of States would, upon the adoption of the new Government, cease to have any power over the territory, and the ordinance they had agreed upon be incapable of execution and a mere nullity, it was obvious that some provision was necessary to give the new Government sufficient power to enable it to carry into effect the objects for which it was ceded, and the compacts and agreements which the States had made with each other in the exercise of their powers of sovereignty. It was necessary that the lands should be sold to pay the war debt; that a Government and system of jurisprudence should be maintained in it, to protect the citizens of the United States who should migrate to the territory, in their rights of person and of property. It was also necessary that the new Government, about to be adopted, should be authorized to maintain the claim of the United States to the unappropriated lands of North Carolina and Georgia, which had not then been ceded, but the cession of which was confidently anticipated upon some terms that would be arranged between the General Government and these two States. And, moreover, there were many articles of value besides this property in land, such as arms, military stores, munitions, and ships of war, which were the common property of the States, when acting in their independent characters as confederates, which neither the new Government nor any one else would have a right to take possession of, or control, without authority from them; and it was to place these things under the guardianship and protection of the new Government, and to clothe it with the necessary powers, that the clause was inserted in the Constitution which gives Congress the power "to dispose of and make all needful rules and regulations respecting the territory or other property belonging to the United States." It was intended for a specific purpose, to provide for the things we have mentioned. It was to transfer to the new Government the property then held in common by the States, and to give to that Government power to apply it to the objects for which it had been destined by mutual agreement among the States before their league was dissolved. It applied only to the property which the States held in common at that time, and has no reference whatever to any territory or other property which the new sovereignty might afterward itself acquire.

The language used in the clause, the arrangement and combination of the powers, and the somewhat unusual phraseology it uses, when it speaks of the political power to be exercised in the government of the territory, all indicate the design and meaning of the clause to be such as we have mentioned. It does not speak of *any* territory, nor of *Territories*, but uses language which, according to its legitimate meaning, points to a particular thing. The power is given in relation only to *the* territory of the United States—that is, to a territory then in existence, and then known or claimed as the territory of the United States. It begins its enumeration of powers by that of disposing, in other words, making sale of the lands, or raising money from them, which, as we have already said, was the main object of the cession, and which is accordingly the first thing provided for in the article. It then gives the power which was necessarily associated with the disposition and sale of the lands—that is, the power of making needful rules and regulations respecting the territory. And whatever construction may now be given to these words, every one, we think, must admit that they are not the words usually employed by statesmen in giving supreme power of legislation. They are certainly very unlike the words used in the power granted to legislate over territory which the new Government might afterwards itself obtain by cession from a State, either for its seat of Government, or for forts, magazines, arsenals, dock yards, and other needful buildings. And the same power of making needful rules respecting the territory is, in precisely the same language, applied to the *other* property belonging to the United States—associating the power over the territory in this respect with the power over movable or personal property—that is, the ships, arms, and munitions of war, which then belonged in common to the State sovereignties. And it will hardly be said, that this power, in relation to the last-mentioned objects, was deemed necessary to be thus specially given to the new Government, in order to authorize it to make needful rules and regulations respecting the ships it might itself build, or arms and munitions of war it might itself manufacture or provide for the public service.

No one, it is believed, would think a moment of deriving the power of Congress to make needful rules and regulations in relation to property of this kind from this clause of the Constitution. Nor can it, upon any fair construction, be applied to any property, but that which the new Government was about to receive from the confederated States. And if this be true as to this property, it must be equally true and limited as to the territory, which is so carefully and precisely coupled with it—and like it referred to as property in the power granted. The concluding words of the clause appear to render this construction irresistible; for, after the provisions we have mentioned, it proceeds to say, "that nothing in the Constitution shall be so construed as to prejudice any claims of the United States, or of any particular State."

Now, as we have before said, all of the States, except North Carolina and Georgia, had made the cession before the Constitution was adopted, according to the resolution of Congress of October 10, 1780. The claims of other States, that the unappropriated lands in these two States should be applied to the common benefit, in like manner, was still insisted on, but refused by the States. And this member of the clause in question evidently applies to them, and can apply to nothing else. It was to exclude the conclusion that either party, by adopting the Constitution, would surrender what they deem their rights. And when the latter provision relates so obviously to the unappropriated lands not yet ceded by the States, and the first clause makes provision for those then actually ceded, it is impossible, by any just rule of construction, to make the first provision general, and extend to all territories, which the Federal Goverenment might in any way afterwards acquire, when the latter is plainly and unequivocally confined to a particular territory; which was a part of the same controversy, and involved in the same dispute, and depended upon the same principles. The union of the two provisions in the same clause shows that they were kindred subjects; and that the whole clause is local, and relates only to lands, within the limits of the United States, which had been or then were claimed by a State; and that no other territory was in the mind of the framers of the Constitution, or intended to be embraced in it. Upon any other construction it would be impossible to account for the insertion of the last provision in the place where it is found, or to comprehend why, or for what object, it was associated with the previous provision.

This view of the subject is confirmed by the manner in which the present Government of the United States dealt with the subject as soon as it came into existence. It must be borne in mind that the same States that formed the Confederation also formed and adopted the new Government, to which so large a portion of their former sovereign powers were surrendered. It must also be borne in mind that all of these same States which had then ratified the new Constitution were represented in the Congress which passed the first law for the government of this territory; and many of the members of that legislative body had been deputies from the States under the confederation—had united in adopting the ordinance of 1787, and assisted in forming the new Government under which they were then acting, and whose powers they were then exercising. And it is obvious from the law they passed to carry into effect the principles and provisions of the ordinance, that they regarded it as the act of the States done in the exercise of their legitimate powers at the time. The new Government took the territory as it found it, and in the condition in which it was transferred, and did not attempt to undo any thing that that had been done. And, among the earliest laws passed under the new Government, is one reviving the ordinance of 1787, which had become inoperative and a nullity upon the adoption of the Constitution. This law introduces no new form or principles for its government, but recites, in the preamble, that it is passed in order that this ordinance may continue to have full effect, and proceeds to make only those rules and regulations which were needful to adapt it to the new Government, into whose hands the power had fallen. It appears, therefore, that this Congress regarded the purposes to which the land in this Territory was to be applied, and the form of government and principles of jurisprudence which were to prevail there, while it remained in the territorial state, as already determined on by the States when they had full power and right to make the decision; and that the new Government, having received it in this condition, ought to carry substantially into effect the plans and principles which had been previously adopted by the States, and which, no doubt, the States anticipated when they surrendered their power to the new Government. And if we regard this clause of the Constitution as pointing to this Territory, with a Territorial Government already established in it, which had been ceded to the States for the purposes hereinbefore mentioned—every word in it is perfectly appropriate and easily understood, and the provisions it contains are in perfect harmony with the objects for which it was ceded, and with the condition of its government as a Territory at the time. We can, then, easily account for the manner in which the first Congress legislated on the subject—and can also understand why this power over the Territory was associated in the same clause with the other property of the United States, and subjected to the like power of making needful rules and regulations. But if the clause is construed in the expanded sense contended for, so as to embrace any territory acquired from a foreign nation by the present Government, and to give it in such territory a despotic and unlimited power over persons and property, such as the confederated States might exercise in their common property, it would be difficult to account for the phraseology used, when compared with other grants of power—and also for its association with the other provisions in the same clause.

The Constitution has always been remarkable for the felicity of its arrangement of different subjects, and the perspicuity and appropriateness of the language it uses. But if this clause is construed to extend to territory acquired by the present Government from a foreign nation, outside of the limits of any charter from the British Government to a colony, it would be difficult to say, why it was deemed necessary to give the Government the power to sell any vacant lands belonging to the sovereignty which might be found within it; and if this was necessary, why the grant of this power should precede the power to legislate over it and establish a Government there; and still more difficult to say, why it was deemed necessary so specially and particularly to grant the power to make needful rules and regulations in relation to any personal or movable property it might acquire there. For the words, *other property*, necessarily, by every known rule of interpretation, must mean property of a different description from territory or land. And the difficulty would perhaps be insurmountable in endeavoring to account for the last member of the sentence, which provides that "nothing in this Constitution shall be so construed as to prejudice any claims of the United States or any particular State," or to say how any particular State could have claims in or to a territory ceded by a foreign Government, or to account for associating this provision with the preceding provisions of the clause, with which it would appear to have no connection.

The words "needful rules and regulations" would seem, also, to have been cautiously used for some definite object. They are not the words usually employed by statesmen, when they mean to give the powers of sovereignty, or to establish a Government, or to authorize its establishment. Thus, in the law to renew and keep alive the ordinance of 1787, and to re-establish the Government, the title of the law is: "An act to provide for the government of the territory northwest of the river Ohio." And in the Constitution, when granting the power to legislate over the territory that may be selected for the seat of Government independently of a State, it does not say Congress shall have power "to make all needful rules and regulations respecting the territory;" but it declares that "Congress shall have power to exercise exclusive legislation in all cases whatsoever over such District (not exceeding ten miles square) as may, by cession of particular States and the acceptance of Congress, become the seat of the Government of the United States.

The words "rules and regulations" are usually employed in the Constitution in speaking of some particular specified power which it means to confer on the Government, and not, as we have seen, when granting general powers of legislation. As, for example, in the peculiar power to Congress "to make rules for the government and regulation of the land and naval forces, or the particular and specific power to regulate commerce;" "to establish an uniform *rule* of naturalization;" "to coin money and *regulate* the value thereof." And to construe the words of which we are speaking as a general and unlimited grant of sovereignty over territories which the Government might afterward acquire, is to use them in a sense and for a purpose for which they were not used in any other part of the instrument. But if confined to a particular Territory, in which a Government and laws had already been established, but which would require some alterations to adapt it to the new Government, the words are peculiarly applicable and appropriate for that purpose.

The necessity of this special provision in relation to property and the rights or property held in common by the confederated States, is illustrated by the first clause of the sixth article. This clause provides that "all debts, contracts, and engagements entered into before the adoption of this Constitution, shall be as valid against the United States under this Government as under the Confederation." This provision, like the one under consideration, was indispensable if the new Constitution was adopted. The new Government was not a mere change in a dynasty, or in a form of government, leaving the nation or sovereignty the same, and clothed with all the rights, and bound by all the obligations of the preceding one. But when the present United States came into existence under the new Government, it was a new political body, and a new nation, then for the first time taking its place in the family of nations. It took nothing by succession from the Confederation. It had no right, as its successor, to any property or rights of property which it had acquired, and was not liable for any of its obligations. It was evidently viewed in this light by the framers of the Constitution. And as the several States would cease to exist in their former confederated character upon the adoption of the Constitution, and could not, in that character, again assemble together, special provisions were indispensable to transfer to the new Government the property and rights which at that time they held in common; and at the same time to authorize it to lay taxes and appropriate money to pay the common debt which they had contracted; and this power could only be given to it by special provisions in the Constitution. The clause in relation to the territory and other property of the United States provided for the first, and the clause last quoted provides for the other. They have no connection with the general powers and rights of sovereignty delegated to the new Government, and can neither enlarge nor diminish them. They were inserted to meet a present emergency, and not to regulate its powers as a Government.

Indeed, a similar provision was deemed necessary, in relation to treaties made by the Confederation; and when in the clause next succeeding the one of which we have last spoken, it is declared that treaties shall be the supreme law of the land, care is taken to include, by express words, the treaties made by the confederated States. The language is: "and all treaties made, or which shall be made, under the authority of the United States, shall be the supreme law of the land."

Whether, therefore, we take the particular clause in question, by itself, or in connection with the other provisions of the Constitution, we think it clear, that it applies only to the particular territory of which we have spoken, and cannot, by any just rule of interpretation, be extended to territory which the new Government might afterward obtain from a foreign nation. Consequently, the power which Congress may have lawfully exercised in this Territory, while it remained under a Territorial Government, and which may have been sanctioned by judicial decision, can furnish no justification and no argument to support a similar exercise of power over territory afterward acquired by the Federal Government. We put aside, therefore, any argument, drawn from precedents, showing the extent of the power which the General Government exercised over slavery in this Territory, as altogether inapplicable to the case before us.

But the case of the American and Ocean Insurance Companies *v.* Canter (1 Pet., 511) has been quoted as establishing a different construction of this clause of the Constitution. There is, however, not the slightest conflict between the opinion now given and the one referred to; and it is only by taking a single sentence out of the latter and separating it from the context, that even an appearance of conflict can be shown. We need not comment on such a mode of expounding an opinion of the court. Indeed it most commonly misrepresents instead of expounding it. And this is fully exemplified in the case referred to, where, if one sentence is taken by itself, the opinion would appear to be in direct conflict with that now given; but the words which immediately follow that sentence show that the court did not mean to decide the point, but merely affirmed the power of Congress to establish a Government in the Territory, leaving it an open question, whether that power was derived from this clause in the Constitution, or was to be necessarily inferred from a power to acquire territory by cession from a foreign Government. The opinion on this part of the case is short, and we give the whole of it to show how well the selection of a single sentence is calculated to mislead.

The passage referred to is in page 542, in which the court, in speaking of the power of Congress to establish a Territorial Government in Florida until it should become a State, uses the following language:

"In the mean time Florida continues to be a Territory of the United States, governed by that clause of the Constitution which empowers Congress to make all needful rules and regulations respecting the territory or other property of the United States. Perhaps the power of governing a Territory belonging to the United States, which has not, by becoming a State, acquired the means of self-government, may result, necessarily, from the facts that it is not within the jurisdiction of any particular State, and is within the power and jurisdiction of the United States. The right to govern may be the inevitable consequence of the right to acquire territory. *Whichever may be the source from which the power is derived, the possession of it is unquestionable.*"

It is thus clear, from the whole opinion on this point, that the court did not mean to decide whether the power was derived from the clause in the Constitution, or was the necessary consequence of the right to acquire. They do decide that the power in Congress is unquestionable, and in this we entirely concur, and nothing will be found in this opinion to the contrary. The power stands firmly on the latter alternative put by the court—that is, as "*the inevitable consequence of the right to acquire territory.*"

And what still more clearly demonstrates that the court did not mean to decide the question, but leave it open for future consideration, is the fact that the case was decided in the Circuit Court by Mr. Justice Johnson, and his decision was affirmed by the Supreme Court. His opinion at the circuit is given in full in a note to the case, and in that opinion he states, in explicit terms, that the clause of the Constitution applies only to the territory then within the limits of the United States, and not to Florida, which had been acquired by cession from Spain. This part of his opinion will be found in the note in page 517 of the report. But he does not dissent from the opinion of the Supreme Court; thereby showing that, in his judgment, as well as that of the court, the case before them did not call for a decision on that particular point, and the court abstained from deciding it. And in a part of its opinion subsequent to the passage we have quoted, where the court speak of the legislative power of Congress in Florida, they still speak with the same reserve. And in page 546, speaking of the power of Congress to authorize the Territorial Legislature to establish courts there, the court say: "They are legislative courts, created in virtue of the general right of sovereignty which exists in the Government, or in virtue of that clause which enables Congress to make all needful rules and regulations respecting the territory belonging to the United States."

It has been said that the construction given to this clause is new, and now for the first time brought forward. The case of which we are speaking, and which has been so much discussed, shows that the fact is otherwise. It shows that precisely the same question came before Mr. Justice Johnson, at his circuit, thirty years ago—was fully considered by him, and the same construction given to the clause in the Constitution which is now given by this court. And that upon an appeal from his decision the same question was brought before this court, but was not decided because a decision upon it was not required by the case before the court.

There is another sentence in the opinion which has been commented on, which even in a still more striking manner shows how one may mislead or be misled by taking out a single sentence from the opinion of a court, and leaving out of view what precedes and follows. It is in page 546, near the close of the opinion, in which the court say: "In legislating for them," (the territories of the United States,) "Congress exercises the combined powers of the General and of a State Government." And it is said, that as a State may unquestionably prohibit slavery within its territory, this sentence decides in effect that Congress may do the same in a territory of the United States, exercising there the powers of a State, as well as the power of the General Government.

The examination of this passage in the case referred to, would be more appropriate when we come to consider in another part of this opinion what power Congress can constitutionally exercise in a Territory, over the rights of person or rights of property of a citizen. But, as it is in the same case with the passage we have before commented on, we dispose of it now, as it will save the court from the necessity of referring again to the case. And it will be seen upon reading the page in which this sentence is found, that it has no reference whatever to the power of Congress over rights of person or rights of property—but relates altogether to the power of establishing judicial tribunals to administer the laws constitutionally passed, and defining the jurisdiction they may exercise.

The law of Congress establishing a Territorial Government in Florida, provided that the Legislature of the Territory should have legislative powers over "all rightful objects of legislation; but no law should be valid which was inconsistent with the laws and Constitution of the United States."

Under the power thus conferred, the Legislature of Florida passed an act, erecting a tribunal at Key West to decide cases of salvage. And in the case of which we are speaking, the question arose whether the Territorial Legislature could be authorized by Congress to establish such a tribunal, with such powers; and one of the parties among other objections, insisted that Congress could not under the Constitution authorize the Legislature of the Territory to establish such a tribunal with such powers, but that it must be established by Congress itself; and that a sale of cargo made under its order, to pay salvors, was void, as made without legal authority, and passed no property to the purchaser.

It is in disposing of this objection that the sentence relied on occurs, and the court begin that part of the opinion by stating with great precision the point which they are about to decide.

They say: "It has been contended that by the Constitution of the United States, the judicial power of the United States extends to all cases of admiralty and maritime jurisdiction; and that the whole of the judicial power must be vested 'in one Supreme Court, and in such inferior courts as Congress shall from time to time ordain and establish.' Hence it has been argued that Congress can not vest admiralty jurisdiction in courts created by the Territorial Legislature."

And after thus clearly stating the point before them, and which they were about to decide, they proceed to show that these Territorial tribunals were not constitutional courts, but merely legislative, and that Congress might, therefore, delegate the power to the Territorial Government to establish the court in question; and they conclude that part of the opinion in the following words: "Although admiralty jurisdiction can be exercised in the States in those courts only which are established in pursuance of the third article of the Constitution, the same limitation does not extend to the Territories. In legislating for them, Congress exercises the combined powers of the General and State Governments."

Thus it will be seen by these quotations from the opinion, that the court, after stating the question it was about to decide in a manner too plain to be misunderstood, proceeded to decide it, and announced, as the opinion of the tribunal, that in organizing the judicial department of the Government in a Territory of the United States, Congress does not act under, and is not restricted by, the third article in the Constitution, and is not bound, in a Territory, to ordain and establish courts in which the judges hold their offices during good behaviour, but may exercise the discretionary power which a State exercises in establishing its judicial department, and regulating the jurisdiction of its courts, and may authorize the Territorial Government to establish, or may itself establish, courts in which the judges hold their offices for a term of years only; and may vest in them judicial power upon subjects confided to the judiciary of the United States. And in doing this, Congress undoubtedly exercises the combined power of the General and a State Government. It exercises the discretionary power of a State Government in authorizing the establishment of a court in which the judges hold their appointments for a term of years only, and not during good behaviour; and it exercises the power of the General Government in investing that court with admiralty jurisdiction, over which the General Government had exclusive jurisdiction in the Territory.

No one, we presume, will question the correctness of that opinion; nor is there any thing in conflict with it in the opinion now given. The point decided in the case cited has no relation to the question now before the court. That depended on the construction of the third article of the Constitution, in relation to the judiciary of the United States, and the power which Congress might exercise in a Territory in organizing the judicial department of the Government. The case before us depends upon other and different provisions of the Constitution, altogether separate and apart from the one above mentioned. The question as to what courts Congress may ordain or establish in a Territory to administer laws which the Constitution authorizes it to pass, and what laws it is or is not authorized by the Constitution to pass, are widely different—are regulated by different and separate articles of the Constitution, and stand upon different principles. And we are satisfied that no one who reads attentively the page in Peters' Reports to which we have referred, can suppose that the attention of the court was drawn for a moment to the question now before this court, or that it meant in that case to say that Congress had a right to prohibit a citizen of the United States from taking any property which he lawfully held into a Territory of the United States.

This brings us to examine by what provision of the Constitution the present Federal Government, under its delegated and restricted powers, is authorized to acquire territory outside of the original limits of the United States, and what powers it may exercise therein over the person or property of a citizen of the United States, while it remains a Territory, and until it shall be admitted as one of the States of the Union.

There is certainly no power given by the Constitution to the Federal Government to establish or maintain colonies bordering on the United States or at a distance, to be ruled and governed at its own pleasure; nor to enlarge its territorial limits in any way, except by the admission of new States. That power is plainly given; and if a new State is admitted, it needs no further legislation from Congress, because the Constitution itself defines the relative rights and powers, and duties of the State, and the citizens of the State, and the Federal Government. But no power is given to acquire a Territory to be held and governed permanently in that character.

And indeed the power exercised by Congress to acquire territory and establish a Government there, according to its own unlimited discretion, was viewed with great jealousy by the leading statesmen of the day. And in the Federalist, (No. 38,) written by Mr. Madison, he speaks of the acquisition of the Northwestern Territory by the confederated States, by the cession from Virginia, and the establishment of a Government there, as an exercise of power not warranted by the Articles of Confederation, and dangerous to the liberties of the people. And he urges the adoption of the Constitution as a security and safeguard against such an exercise of power.

We do not mean, however, to question the power of Congress in this respect. The power to expand the territory of the United States by the admission of new States is plainly given; and in the construction of this power by all the departments of the Government, it has been held to authorize the acquisition of territory, not fit for admission at the time, but to be admitted as soon as its population and situation would entitle it to admission. It is acquired to become a State, and not to be held as a colony and governed by Congress with absolute authority; and as the propriety of admitting a new State is committed to the sound discretion of Congress, the power to acquire territory for that purpose, to be held by the United States until it is in a suitable condition to become a State upon an equal footing with the other States, must rest upon the same discretion. It is a question for the political department of the Government, and not the judicial; and whatever the political department of the Government shall recognize as within the limits of the United States, the judicial department is also bound to recognize, and to administer in it the laws of the United States, so far as they apply, and to maintain in the Territory the authority and rights of the Government, and also the personal rights and rights of property of individual citizens, as secured by the Constitution. All we mean to say on this point is, that, as there is no express regulation in the Constitution defining the power which the General Government may exercise over the person or property of a citizen in a Territory thus acquired, the court must necessarily look to the provisions and principles of the Constitution, and its distribution of powers, for the rules and principles by which its decision must be governed.

Taking this rule to guide us, it may be safely assumed that citizens of the United States who migrate to a Territory belonging to the people of the United States, cannot be ruled as mere colonists, dependent upon the will of the General Government, and to be governed by any laws it may think proper to impose. The principle upon which our Government rests, and upon which alone they continue to exist, is the union of States, sovereign and independent within their own limits in their internal and domestic concerns, and bound together as one people by a General Government, possessing certain enumerated and restricted powers, delegated to it by the people of the several States, and exercising supreme authority within the scope of the powers granted to it, throughout the dominion of the United States. A power, therefore, in the General Government to obtain and hold colonies and dependent territories, over which they might legislate without restriction, would be inconsistent with its own existence in its present form. Whatever it acquires, it acquires for the benefit of the people of the several States who created it. It is their trustee acting for them, and charged with the duty of promoting the interests of the whole people of the whole Union in the exercise of the powers specifically granted.

At the time when the Territory in question was obtained by cession from France, it contained no population fit to be associated together and admitted as a State; and it therefore was absolutely necessary to hold possession of it, as a Territory belonging to the United States, until it was settled and inhabited by a civilized community capable of self-government, and in a condition to be admitted on equal terms with the other States as a member of the Union. But, as we have before said, it was acquired by the General Government, as the representative and trustee of the people of the United States, and it must therefore be held in that character for their common and equal benefit; for it was the people of the several States, acting through their agent and representative, the Federal Government, who in fact acquired the Territory in question, and the Government holds it for their common use until it shall be associated with the other States as a member of the Union.

But until that time arrives, it is undoubtedly necessary that some Government should be established in order to organize society, and to protect the inhabitants in their persons and property; and as the people of the United States could act in this matter only through the Government which represented them, and through which they spoke and acted when the Territory was obtained, it was not only within the scope of its powers, but it was its duty to pass such laws and establish such a Government as would enable those by whose authority they acted to reap the advantages anticipated from its acquisition, and to gather there a population which would enable it to assume the position to which it was destined among the States of the Union. The power to acquire necessarily carries with it the power to preserve and apply to the purposes for which it was acquired. The form of government to be established necessarily rested in the discretion of Congress. It was their duty to establish the one that would be best suited for the protection and security of the citizens of the United States, and other inhabitants who might be authorized to take up their abode there, and that must always depend upon the existing condition of the Territory, as to the number and character of its inhabitants, and their situation in the Territory. In some cases a Government, consisting of persons appointed by the Federal Government, would best subserve the interests of the Territory, when the inhabitants were few and scattered, and new to one another. In other instances, it would be more advisable to commit the powers of self-government to the people who had settled in the Territory, as being the most competent to determine what was best for their own interests. But some form of civil authority would be absolutely necessary to organize and preserve civilized society, and prepare it to become a State; and what is the best form must always depend on the condition of the territory at the time, and the choice of the mode must depend upon the exercise of a discretionary power by Congress, acting within the scope of its constitutional authority, and not infringing upon the rights of person or rights of property of the citizen who might go there to reside, or for any other lawful purpose. It was acquired by the exercise of this discretion, and it must be held and governed in like manner, until it is fitted to be a State.

But the power of Congress over the person or property of a citizen can never be a mere discretionary power under our Constitution and form of Government. The powers of the Government and the rights and privileges of the citizen are regulated and plainly defined by the Constitution itself. And when the Territory becomes a part of the United States, the Federal Government enters into possession in the character impressed upon it by those who created it. It enters upon it with its powers over the citizen strictly defined, and limited by the Constitution, from which it derives its own existence, and by virtue of which alone it continues to exist and act as a Government and sovereignty. It has no power of any kind beyond it; and it cannot, when it enters a Territory of the United States, put off its character, and assume discretionary or despotic powers which the Constitution has denied to it. It cannot create for itself a new character separated from the citizens of the United States, and the duties it owes them under the provisions of the Constitution. The Territory being a part of the United States, the Government and the citizen both enter it under the authority of the Constiution, with their respective rights defined and marked out; and the Federal Government can exercise no power over his person or property, beyond what that instrument confers, nor lawfully deny any right which it has reserved.

A reference to a few of the provisions of the Constitution will illustrate this proposition.

For example, no one, we presume, will contend that Congress can make any law in a Territory respecting the establishment of religion, or the free exercise thereof, or abridging the freedom of speech or of the press, or the right of the people of the Territory peacably to assemble, and to petition the Government for the redress of grievances.

Nor can Congress deny to the people the right to keep and bear arms, nor the right to trial by jury, nor compel any one to be a witness against himself in a criminal proceeding.

These powers, and others, in relation to rights of person, which it is not necessary here to enumerate, are, in express and positive terms, denied to the General Government; and the rights of private property have been guarded with equal care. Thus the rights of property are united with the rights of person, and placed on the same ground by the fifth amendment to the Constitution, which provides that no person shall be deprived of life, liberty, and property, without due process of law. And an act of Congress which deprives a citizen of the United States of his liberty or property, merely because he came himself or brought his property into a particular Territory of the United States, and who had committed no offense against the laws, could hardly be dignified with the name of due process of law.

So, too, it will hardly be contended that Congress could by law quarter a soldier in a house in a Territory without the consent of the owner, in time of peace; nor in time of war, but in a manner prescribed by law. Nor could they by law forfeit the property of a citizen in a Territory who was convicted of treason, for a longer period than the life of the person convicted; nor take private property for public use without just compensation.

The powers over person and property of which we speak are not only not granted to Congress, but are in express terms denied, and they are forbidden to exercise them. And this prohibition is not confined to the States, but the words are general, and extend to the whole territory over which the Constitution gives it power to legislate, including those portions of it remaining under Territorial Government, as well as that covered by States. It is a total absence of power everywhere within the dominion of the United States, and places the citizens of a Territory, so far as these rights are concerned, on the same footing with citizens of the States, and guards them as firmly and plainly against any inroads which the General Government might attempt, under the plea of implied or incidental powers. And if Congress itself cannot do this—if it is beyond the powers conferred on the Federal Government—it will be admitted, we presume, that it could not authorize a Territorial Government to exercise them. It could confer no power on any local Government, established by its authority, to violate the provisions of the Constitution.

It seems, however, to be supposed, that there is a difference between property in a slave and other property, and that different rules may be applied to it in expounding the Constitution of the United States. And the laws and usages of nations, and the writings of eminent jurists upon the relation of master and slave and their mutual rights and duties, and the powers which Governments may exercise over it, have been dwelt upon in the argument.

But in considering the question before us, it must be borne in mind that there is no law of nations standing between the people of the United States and their Government, and interfering with their relation to each other. The powers of the Government, and the rights of the citizen under it, are positive and practical regulations plainly written down. The people of the United States have delegated to it certain enumerated powers, and forbidden it to exercise others. It has no power over the person or property of a citizen but what the citizens of the United States have granted. And no laws or usages of other nations, or reasoning of statesmen or jurists upon the relations of master and slave, can enlarge the powers of the Government, or take from the citizens the rights they have reserved. And if the Constitution recognizes the right of property of the master in a slave, and makes no distinction between that description of property and other property owned by a citizen, no tribunal, acting under the authority of the United States, whether it be legislative, executive, or judicial, has a right to draw such a distinction, or deny to it the benefit of the provisions and guarantees which have been provided for the protection of private property against the encroachments of the Government.

Now, as we have already said in an earlier part of this opinion, upon a different point, the right of property in a slave is distinctly and expressly affirmed in the Constitution. The right to traffic in it, like an ordinary article of merchandise and property, was guaranteed to the citizens of the United States, in every State that might desire it, for twenty years. And the Government in express terms is pledged to protect it in all future time, if the slave escapes from his owner. This is done in plain words—too plain to be misunderstood. And no word can be found in the Constitution which gives Congress a greater power over slave-property, or which entitles property of that kind to less protection than property of any other description. The only power conferred is the power coupled with the duty of guarding and protecting the owner in his rights.

Upon these considerations, it is the opinion of the court that the act of Congress which prohibited a citizen from holding and owning property of this kind in the territory of the United States north of the line therein mentioned, is not warranted by the Constitution, and is therefore void; and that neither Dred Scott himself, nor any of his family, were made free by being carried into this territory; even if they had been carried there by the owner, with the intention of becoming a permanent resident.

We have so far examined the case, as it stands under the Constitution of the United States, and the powers thereby delegated to the Federal Government.

But there is another point in the case which depends on State power and State law. And it is contended, on the part of the plaintiff, that he is made free by being taken to Rock Island, in the State of Illinois, independently of his residence in the territory of the United States; and being so made free, he was not again reduced to a state of slavery by being brought back to Missouri.

Our notice of this part of the case will be very brief; for the principle on which it depends was decided in this court, upon much consideration in the case of Strader et al. *v.* Graham, reported in 10th Howard, 82. In that case, the slaves had been taken from Kentucky to Ohio, with the consent of the owner, and afterward brought back to Kentucky. And this court held that their *status* or condition, as free or slave, depended upon the laws of Kentucky, when they were brought back into that State, and not of Ohio; and that this court had no jurisdiction to revise the judgment of a State court upon its own laws. This was the point directly before the court, and the decision that this court had not jurisdiction turned upon it, as will be seen by the report of the case.

So in this case. As Scott was a slave when taken into the State of Illinois by his owner, and was there held as such, and brought back in that character, his *status*, as free or slave, depended on the laws of Missouri, and not of Illinois.

It has, however, been urged in the argument, that by the laws of Missouri he was free on his return, and that this case, therefore, can not be governed by the case of Strader et al. *v.* Graham, where it appeared, by the laws of Kentucky, that the plaintiffs continued to be slaves on their return from Ohio. But whatever doubts or opinions may, at one time, have been entertained upon this subject, we are satisfied, upon a careful examination of all the cases decided in the State courts of Missouri referred to, that it is now firmly settled by the decisions of the highest court in the State, that Scott and his family upon their return were not free, but were, by the laws of Missouri, the property of the defendant; and that the Circuit Court of the United States had no jurisdiction, when, by the laws of the State, the plaintiff was a slave, and not a citizen.

Moreover, the plaintiff, it appears, brought a similar action against the defendant in the State Court of Missouri, claiming the freedom of himself and his family upon the same grounds and the same evidence upon which he relies in the case before the court. The case was carried before the Supreme Court of the State; was fully argued there; and that court decided that neither the plaintiff nor his family were entitled to freedom, and were still the slaves of the defendant; and reversed the judgment of the inferior State court, which had given a different decision. If the plaintiff supposed that this judgment of the Supreme Court of the State was erroneous, and that this court had jurisdiction to revise and reverse it, the only mode by which he could legally bring it before this court was by writ of error directed to the Supreme Court of the State, requiring it to transmit the record to this court. If this had been done, it is too plain for argument that the writ must have been dismissed for want of jurisdiction in this court. The case of Strader and others *v.* Graham is directly in point; and, indeed, independent of any decision, the language of the 25th section of the act of 1789 is too clear and precise to admit of controversy.

But the plaintiff did not pursue the mode prescribed by law for bringing the judgment of a State court before this court for revision, but suffered the case to be remanded to the inferior State court, where it is still continued, and is, by agreement of parties, to await the judgment of this court on the point. All of this appears on the record before us, and by the printed report of the case.

And while the case is yet open and pending in the inferior State court, the plaintiff goes into the Circuit Court of the United States, upon the same case and the same evidence, and against the same party, and proceeds to judgment, and then brings here the same case from the Circuit Court, which the law would not have permitted him to bring directly from the State court. And if this court takes jurisdiction in this form, the result, so far as the rights of the respective parties are concerned, is in every respect substantially the same as if it had in open violation of law entertained jurisdiction over the judgment of the State court upon a writ of error, and revised and reversed its judgment upon the ground that its opinion upon the question of law was erroneous. It would ill become this court to sanction such an attempt to evade the law, or to exercise an appellate power in this circuitous way, which it is forbidden to exercise in the direct and regular and invariable forms of judicial proceedings.

Upon the whole, therefore, it is the judgment of this court, that it appears by the record before us that the plaintiff in error is not a citizen of Missouri, in the sense in which that word is used in the Constitution; and that the Circuit Court of the United States, for that reason, had no jurisdiction in the case; and could give no judgment in it. Its judgment for the defendant must, consequently, be reversed, and a mandate issued, directing the suit to be dismissed for want of jurisdiction

POINTS DECIDED.

I.

1. Upon a writ of error to a Circuit Court of the United States, the transcript of the record of all the proceedings in the case is brought before this court, and is open to its inspection and revision.

2. When a plea to the jurisdiction, in abatement, is overruled by the court upon demurrer, and the defendant pleads in bar, and upon these pleas the final judgment of the court is in his favor—if the plaintiff brings a writ of error, the judgment of the court upon the plea in abatement is before this court, although it was in favor of the plaintiff—and if the court erred in overruling it, the judgment must be reversed, and a mandate issued to the Circuit Court to dismiss the case for want of jurisdiction.

3. In the Circuit Courts of the United States, the record must show that the case is one in which by the Constitution and laws of the United States, the court had jurisdiction—and if this does not appear, and the court gives judgment either for plaintiff or defendant, it is error, and the judgment must be reversed by this court—and the parties cannot by consent waive the objection to the jurisdiction of the Circuit Court.

4. A free negro of the African race, whose ancestors were brought to this country and sold as slaves, is not a "citizen" within the meaning of the Constitution of the United States.

5. When the Constitution was adopted, they were not regarded in any of the States as members of the community which constituted the State, and were not numbered among its "people or citizens." Consequently, the special rights and immunities guaranteed to citizens do not apply to them. And not being "citizens" within the meaning of the Constitution, they are not entitled to sue in that character in a court of the United States, and the Circuit Court has not jurisdiction in such a suit.

6. The only two clauses in the Constitution which point to this race, treat them as persons whom it was morally lawful to deal in as articles of property and to hold as slaves.

7. Since the adoption of the Constitution of the United States, no State can by any subsequent law make a foreigner or any other description of persons citizens of the United States, nor entitle them to the rights and privileges secured to citizens by that instrument.

8. A State, by its laws passed since the adoption of the Constitution, may put a foreigner or any other description of persons upon a footing with its own citizens, as to all the rights and privileges enjoyed by them within its dominion, and by its laws. But that

will not make him a citizen of the United States, nor entitle him to sue in its courts, nor to any of the privileges and immunities of a citizen in another State.

9. The change in public opinion and feeling in relation to the African race, which has taken place since the adoption of the Constitution, cannot change its construction and meaning, and it must be construed and administered now according to its true meaning and intention when it was formed and adopted.

10. The plaintiff having admitted, by his demurrer to the plea in abatement, that his ancestors were imported from Africa and sold as slaves, he is not a citizen of the State of Missouri according to the Constitution of the United States, and was not entitled to sue in that character in the Circuit Court.

11. This being the case, the judgment of the court below, in favor of the plaintiff on the plea in abatement, was erroneous.

II.

1. But if the plea in abatement is not brought up by this writ of error, the objection to the citizenship of the plaintiff is still apparent on the record, as he himself, in making out his case, states that he is of African descent, was born a slave, and claims that he and his family became entitled to freedom by being taken by their owner to reside in a territory where slavery is prohibited by act of Congress—and that, in addition to this claim, he himself became entitled to freedom by being taken to Rock Island, in the State of Illinois—and being free when he was brought back to Missouri, he was by the laws of that State a citizen.

2. If, therefore, the facts he states do not give him or his family a right to freedom, the plaintiff is still a slave, and not entitled to sue as a "citizen," and the judgment of the Circuit Court was erroneous on that ground also, without any reference to the plea in abatement.

3. The Circuit Court can give no judgment for plaintiff or defendant in a case where it has not jurisdiction, no matter whether there be a plea in abatement or not. And unless it appears upon the face of the record, when brought here by writ of error, that the Circuit Court had jurisdiction, the judgment must be reversed.

The case of Capron v. Van Noorden (2 Cranch, 126) examined, and the principles thereby decided, reaffirmed.

4. When the record, as brought here by writ of error, does not show that the Circuit Court had jurisdiction, this court has jurisdiction to revise and correct the error, like any other error in the court below. It does not and cannot dismiss the case for want of jurisdiction here; for that would leave the erroneous judgment of the court below in full force,

and the party injured without remedy. But it must reverse the judgment, and, as in any other case of reversal, send a mandate to the Circuit Court to conform its judgment to the opinion of this court.

5. The difference of the jurisdiction in this court in the cases of writs of error to State courts and to Circuit Courts of the United States, pointed out; and the mistakes made as to the jurisdiction of this court in the latter case, by confounding it with its limited jurisdiction in the former.

6. If the court reverses a judgment upon the ground that it appears by a particular part of the record that the Circuit Court had not jurisdiction, it does not take away the jurisdiction of this court to examine into and correct, by a reversal of the judgment, any other errors, either as to the jurisdiction or any other matter, where it appears from other parts of the record that the Circuit Court had fallen into error. On the contrary, it is the daily and familiar practice of this court to reverse on several grounds, where more than one error appears to have been committed. And the error of a Circuit Court in its jurisdiction stands on the same ground, and is to be treated in the same manner as any other error upon which its judgment is founded.

7. The decision, therefore, that the judgment of the Circuit Court upon the plea in abatement is erroneous, is no reason why the alleged error apparent in the exception should not also be examined, and the judgment reversed on that ground also, if it discloses a want of jurisdiction in the Circuit Court.

It is often the duty of this court, after having decided that a particular decision of the Circuit Court was erroneous, to examine into other alleged errors, and to correct them if they are found to exist. And this has been uniformly done by this court, when the questions are in any degree connected with the controversy, and the silence of the court might create doubts which would lead to further and useless litigation.

III.

1. The facts upon which the plaintiff relies did not give him his freedom, and make him a citizen of Missouri.

2. The clause in the Constitution authorizing Congress to make all needful rules and regulations for the government of the territory and other property of the United States, applies only to territory within the chartered limits of some one of the States when they were colonies of Great Britain, and which was surrendered by the British Government to the old Confederation of the States, in the treaty of peace. It does not apply to territory acquired by the present Federal Government, by treaty or conquest, from a foreign nation.

The case of the American and Ocean Insurance Companies *v.* Canter (1 Peters, 511) referred to and examined, showing that the decision in this case is not in conflict with that opinion, and that the court did not, in the case referred to, decide upon the construction of the clause of the Constitution above mentioned, because the case before them did not make it necessary to decide the question.

3. The United States, under the present Constitution, cannot acquire territory to be held as a colony, to be governed at its will and pleasure. But it may acquire territory which, at the time, has not a population that fits it to become a State, and may govern it as a Territory until it has a population which, in the judgment of Congress, entitles it to be admitted as a State of the Union.

4. During the time it remains a Territory, Congress may legislate over it within the scope of its constitutional powers in relation to citizens of the United States—and may establish a Territorial Government—and the form of this local Government must be regulated by the discretion of Congress, but with powers not exceeding those which Congress itself, by the Constitution, is authorized to exercise over citizens of the United States, in respect to their rights of persons or rights of property.

IV.

1. The territory thus acquired, is acquired by the people of the United States for their common and equal benefit, through their agent and trustee, the Federal Government. Congress can exercise no power over the rights of person or property of a citizen in the Territory which is prohibited by the Constitution. The Government and the citizen, whenever the Territory is open to settlement, both enter it with their respective rights defined and limited by the Constitution.

2. Congress has no right to prohibit the citizens of any particular State or States from taking up their home there, while it permits citizens of other States to do so. Nor has it a right to give privileges to one class of citizens which it refuses to another. The territory is acquired for their equal and common benefit—and if open to any, it must be open to all upon equal and the same terms.

3. Every citizen has a right to take with him into the Territory any article of property which the Constitution of the United States recognizes as property.

4. The Constitution of the United States recognizes slaves as property, and pledges the Federal Government to protect it. And Congress cannot exercise any more authority over property of that description than it may constitutionally exercise over property of any other kind.

5. The act of Congress, therefore, prohibiting a citizen of the United States from taking with him his slaves when he removes to the Territory in question to reside, is an

exercise of authority over private property which is not warranted by the Constitution—and the removal of the plaintiff, by his owner, to that Territory, gave him no title to freedom.

V.

1. The plaintiff himself acquired no title to freedom by being taken, by his owner, to Rock Island, in Illinois, and brought back to Missouri. This court has heretofore decided that the *status* or condition of a person of African descent depended on the laws of the State in which he resided.

2. It has been settled by the decisions of the highest court in Missouri, that by the laws of that State, a slave does not become entitled to his freedom, where the owner takes him to reside in a State where slavery is not permitted, and afterwards brings him back to Missouri.

Conclusion. It follows that it is apparent upon the record that the court below erred in its judgment on the plea in abatement, and also erred in giving judgment for the defendant, when the exception shows that the plaintiff was not a citizen of the United States. And as the Circuit Court had no jurisdiction, either in the case stated in the plea in abatement, or in the one stated in the exception, its judgment in favor of the defendant is erroneous, and must be reversed.

THE
FUGITIVE SLAVE LAW.
BY
REV. CHARLES HODGE, D.D.
OF NEW JERSEY.

THE FUGITIVE SLAVE LAW.

NOTE.—We have affixed, by way of comment to "the decision of the Supreme Court in the Dred Scott case," the following able paper from the pen of Prof. Hodge. It lucidly explains the source and sanction of Civil Government, and deduces therefrom the duties and responsibilities of the governed.—ED.

Alleged Immorality of the Law answered—Duty of Obedience—Government a Divine Institution—The Warrant of Government is not the consent of the governed—Infidel Doctrines—Deductions from this Doctrine—Decision of the Supreme Court—Objections answered—Conscience and the Law—Duty of Executive Officers—Duty of Private Citizens—Objections answered—Right of Revolution—Summary application of these principles to the Fugitive Slave Law—Conclusion.

THERE is no more obvious duty, at the present time, resting on American Christians, ministers and people, than to endeavor to promote kind feelings between the South and the North. All fierce addresses to the passions, on either side, are fratricidal. It is an offense against the gospel, against our common country, and against God. Every one should endeavor to diffuse right principles, and thus secure right feeling and action, under the blessing of God in every part of the land. If the South has no such grounds of complaint as would justify them before God and the human race, whose trustees in one important sense they are, in dissolving the Union, how is it with the North? Are they justifiable in the violent resistance to the fugitive slave bill, which has been threatened or attempted? This opposition in a great measure has been confined to the abolitionists as a party, and as such they are a small minority of the people. They have never included in their ranks either the controlling intellect or moral feeling at the North. Their fundamental principle is anti-scriptural and therefore irreligious. They assume that slaveholding is sinful. This doctrine is the life of the sect. It has no power over those who reject that principle, and therefore it has not gained ascendency over those whose faith is governed by the word of God.

We have ever maintained that the proper method of opposing this party, and of counteracting its pernicious influence, was to exhibit clearly the falsehood of its one idea, viz: that slaveholding is a sin against God. The discussion has now taken a new turn. It is assumed that the fugitiue slave law of the last Congress, (1850) is unconstitutional, or if not contrary to the Constitution, contrary to the law of God. Under this impression many who have never been regarded as abolitionists, have entered their protest against the law, and some in their haste have inferred from its supposed unconstitutionality or immorality that it ought to be openly resisted. It is obvious that the proper method of dealing with the subject in this new aspect, is to demonstrate that the law in question is according to the Constitution of the land; that it is not inconsistent with the divine law; or, admitting its unconstitutionality or immorality, that the resistance recommended is none the less a sin against God. We do not propose to discuss either of the two former of these propositions. The constitutionality of the law may safely be left in the hands of the constituted authorities. It is enough for us that there is no flagrant and manifest inconsistency between the law and the constitution; that the first legal authorities in the land pronounce them perfectly consistent; and that there is no difference in principle between the present law and that of 1793 on the same subject, in which the whole country has acquiesced for more than half a century. We would also say that after having read some of the most labored disquisitions designed to prove that the fugitive slave bill subverts the fundamental principles of our federal compact, we have been unable to discover the least force in the arguments adduced.

As to the immorality of the law, so far as we can discover, the whole stress of the argument in the affirmative rests on two assumptions. First, that the law of God in Deuteronomy, expressly forbids the restoration of a fugitive slave to his owner; and secondly, that slavery itself being sinful, it must be wrong to enforce the claims of the master to the service of the slave. As to the former of these assumptions, we would simply remark, that the venerable Prof. Stuart in his recent work, "Conscience and the Constitution," has clearly proved that the law in Deuteronomy has no application to the present case. The thing there forbidden is the restoration of a slave who had fled from a heathen master and taken refuge among the worshipers of the true God. Such a man was not to be forced back into heathenism. This is the obvious meaning and spirit of the command. That it has no reference to slaves who had escaped from Hebrew masters, and fled from one tribe or city to another, is plain from the simple fact that the Hebrew laws recognized slavery. It would be a perfect contradiction if the law authorized the purchase and holding of slaves, and yet forbid the enforcing the right of possession. There could be no such thing as slavery, in such a land as Palestine, if the slave could recover his liberty by simply moving from one tribe to another over an imaginary line, or even from the house of his master to that of his next neighbor. Besides, how inconsistent is it in the abolitionists in one breath to maintain that the laws of Moses did not recognize slavery, and in the next, that the laws about the restoration of slaves referred to the slaves of Hebrew masters. According to their doctrine, there could be among the Israelites no slaves to restore. They must admit either that the law of God allowed the Hebrews to hold slaves, and then there is an end to their arguments against the sinfulness of slaveholding; or acknowledge that the law representing the restoration of slaves referred only to fugitives from the heathen, and then there is an end to their argument from this enactment against the law under consideration.

The way in which abolitionists treat the Scriptures makes it evident that the command in Deuteronomy is urged not so much out of regard to the authority of the word of God, as an argumentum ad hominem. Wherever the Scriptures either in the Old or New Testament recognize the lawfulness of holding slaves, they are tortured without mercy to force from them a different response; and where, as in this case, they appear to favor the other side of the question, abolitionists quote them rather to silence those who make them the rule of their faith, than as the ground of their own convictions. Were there no such law as that in Deuteronomy in existence, or were there a plain injunction to restore a fugitive from service to his Hebrew master, it is plain from their principles that they would none the less fiercely condemn the law under consideration. Their opposition is not founded on the scriptural command. It rests on the assumption that the master's claim is iniquitous and ought not to be enforced.[258] Their objections are not to the mode of delivery, but to the delivery itself. Why else quote the law in Deuteronomy, which apparently forbids such surrender of the fugitive to his master? It is clear that no effective enactment could be framed on this subject which would not meet with the same opposition. We are convinced, by reading the discussions on this subject, that the immorality attributed to the fugitive slave law resolves itself into the assumed immorality of slaveholding. No man would object to restoring an apprentice to his master; and no one would quote Scripture or search for arguments to prove it sinful to restore a fugitive slave, if he believed slaveholding to be lawful in the sight of God. This being the case, we feel satisfied that the mass of people at the North, whose conscience and action are ultimately determined by the teachings of the Bible, will soon settle down into the conviction that the law in question is not in conflict with the law of God.

But suppose the reverse to be the fact; suppose it clearly made out that the law passed by Congress in reference to fugitive slaves is contrary to the Constitution or to the law of God, what is to be done? What is the duty of the people under such circumstances? The answers given to this question are very different, and some of them so portentous that the public mind has been aroused and directed to the consideration of the nature of civil government and of the grounds and limits of the obedience due to the laws of the land. As this is a subject not merely of general interest at this time, but of permanent importance, we purpose to devote to its discussion the few following pages.

Our design is to state in few words in what sense government is a divine institution, and to draw from that doctrine the principles which must determine the nature and limits of the obedience which is due the laws of the land.

That the Bible, when it asserts that all power is of God, or the powers that be are ordained of God, does not teach that any one form of civil government has been divinely appointed as universally obligatory, is plain because the Scriptures contain no such prescription. There are no directions given as to the form which civil governments shall assume. All the divine commands on this subject, are as applicable under one form as another. The direction is general; obey the powers that be. The propsition is unlimited; all power is of God; i. e., government, whatever its form, is of God. He has ordained it. The most pointed scriptural injunctions on this subject were given during the usurped or tyrannical reign of military despots. It is plain that the sacred writers did not, in such passages, mean to teach that a military despotism was the form of government which God had ordained as of perpetual and universal obligation. As the Bible enjoins no one form, so the people of God in all ages, under the guidance of his Spirit, have lived with a good conscience, under all the diversities of organization of which human government is susceptible.

Again, as no one form of government is prescribed, so neither has God determined preceptively who are to exercise civil power. He has not said that such power must be hereditary, and descend on the principle of primogeniture. He has not determined whether it shall be confined to males to the exclusion of females; or whether all offices shall be elective. These are not matters of divine appointment, and are not included in the proposition that all power is of God. Neither is it included in this proposition that government is in such a sense ordained of God that the people have no control in the matter. The doctrine of the Bible is not inconsistent with the right of the people, as we shall endeavor to show in the sequel, to determine their own form of government and to select their own rulers.

When it is said government is of God, we understand the Scriptures to mean, first, that it is a divine institution and not a mere social compact. It does not belong to the category of voluntary associations such as men form for literary, benevolent, or commercial purposes. It is not optional with men whether government shall exist. It is a divine appointment, in the same sense as marriage and the church are divine institutions. The former of these is not a mere civil contract, nor is the church as a visible spiritual community a mere voluntary society. Men are under obligation to recognize its existence, to join its ranks and submit to its laws. In like manner it is the will of God that civil government should exist. Men are bound by his authority to have civil rulers for the punishment of evil doers, and for the praise of them that do well. This is the scriptural doctrine, as opposed to the deistical theory of a social compact as the ultimate ground of all human governments.

It follows from this view of the subject that obedience to the laws of the land is a religious duty, and that disobedience is of the specific nature of sin; this is a principle of vast importance. It is true that the law of God is so broad that it binds a man to every thing that is right, and forbids every thing that is wrong; and consequently that every violation even of a voluntary engagement is of the nature of an offense against God. Still there is a wide difference between disobedience to an obligation voluntarily assumed, and which has no other sanction than our own engagement, and disregard of an obligation directly imposed of God. St. Peter recognizes this distinction when he said to Annanias, Thou hast not lied unto men but unto God. All lying is sinful, but lying to God is a higher crime than lying to men. There is greater irreverence and contempt of the divine presence and authority, and a violation of an obligation of a higher order. Every man feels that the marriage vows have a sacred character which could not belong to them, if marriage was merely a civil contract. In like manner the divine institution of government elevates it into the sphere of religion, and adds a new and higher sanction to the obligations which it imposes. There is a specific difference, more easily felt than described, between what is religious and what is merely moral; between disobedience to man and resistance to an ordinance of God.

A third point included in the scriptural doctrine on this subject is, that the actual existence of any government creates the obligation of obedience. That is, the obligation does not rest either on the origin or the nature of the government, or on the mode in which it is administered. It may be legitimate or revolutionary, despotic or constitutional, just or unjust, so long as it exists it is to be recognized and obeyed within its proper sphere. The powers that be are ordained of God in such sense that the possession of power is to be referred to his providence. It is not by chance, nor through the uncontrolled agency of men, but by divine ordination that any government exists. The declaration of the apostle just quoted was uttered under the reign of Nero. It is as true of his authority as of that of the Queen of England, or that of our own President, that it was of God. He made Nero Emperor. He required all within the limits of the Roman empire to recognize and obey him so long as he was allowed to occupy the throne. It was not necessary for the early Christians to sit in judgment on the title of every new emperor, whenever the pretorian guards chose to put down one and put up another; neither are God's people now in various parts of the world called upon to discuss the titles and adjudicate the claims of their rulers. The possession of civil power is a providential fact, and is to be regarded as such. This does not imply that God approves of every government which he allows to exist. He permits oppressive rulers to bear sway, just as he permits famine or pestilence to execute his vengeance. A good government is a blessing, a bad government is a judgment; but the one as much as the other is ordained of God, and is to be obeyed not only for fear but also for conscience sake.

A fourth principle involved in the proposition that all power is of God is, that the magistrate is invested with a divine right. He represents God. His authority is derived from Him. There is a sense in which he represents the people and derives from them his power; but in a far higher sense he is the minister of God. To resist him is to resist God, and "they that resist shall receive unto themselves damnation." Thus saith the Scriptures. It need hardly be remarked that this principle relates to the nature, and not to the extent, of the power of the magistrate. It is as true of the lowest as of the highest; of a justice of the peace as of the President of the United States; of a constitutional monarch as of an absolute sovereign. The principle is that the authority of rulers is divine, and not human, in its origin. They exercise the power which belongs to them of divine right. The reader, we trust, will not confound this doctrine with the old doctrine of "the divine right of kings." The two things are as different as day and night. We are not for reviving a defunct theory of civil government; a theory which perished, at least among Anglo-Saxons, at the expulsion of James II. from the throne of England. That monarch took it with him into exile, and it lies entombed with the last of the Stuarts. According to that theory God had established the monarchical form of government as universally obligatory. There could not consistently with his law be any other. The people had no more right to renounce that form of government than the children of a family have to resolve themselves into a democracy. In the second place, it assumed that God had determined the law of succession as well as the form of government. The people could not change the one any more than the other; or any more than children could change their father, or a wife her husband. And thirdly, as a necessary consequence of these principles, it inculcated in all cases the duty of passive obedience. The king holding his office immediately from God, held it entirely independent of the will of the people, and his responsibility was to God alone. He could not forfeit his throne by any injustice however flagrant. The people, if in any case they could not obey, were obliged to submit; resistance or revolution was treason against God. We have already remarked that the scriptural doctrine is opposed to every one of these principles. The Bible does not prescribe any one form of government; it does not determine who shall be depositories of civil power; and it clearly recognizes the right of revolution. In asserting, therefore, the divine right of rulers, we are not asserting any doctrine repudiated by our forefathers, or inconsistent with civil liberty in its widest rational extent.

Such, as we understand it, is the true nature of civil government. It is a divine institution and not a mere voluntary compact. Obedience to the magistrate and laws is a religious duty; and disobedience is a sin against God. This is true of all forms of government. Men living under the Turkish Sultan are bound to recognize his authority, as much as the subjects of a constitutional monarch, or the fellow-citizens of an elective president, are bound to recognize their respective rulers. All power is of God, and the powers that be are ordained of God, in such sense that all magistrates are to be regarded as his ministers, acting in his name and with his authority, each within his legitimate sphere; beyond which he ceases to be a magistrate.

That this is the doctrine of the Scriptures on this subject can hardly be doubted. The Bible never refers to the consent of the governed, the superiority of the rulers, or to the general principles of expediency, as the ground of our obligation to the higher powers. The obedience which slaves owe their masters, children their parents, wives their husbands, people their rulers, is always made to rest on the divine will as its ultimate foundation. It is part of the service which we owe to God. We are required to act, in all these relations, not as men-pleasers, but as the servants of God. All such obedience terminates on our Master who is in heaven. This gives the sublimity of spiritual freedom even to the service of a slave. It is not in the power of man to reduce to bondage those who serve God, in all the service they render their fellow-men. The will of God, therefore, is the foundation of our obligation to obey the laws of the land. His will, however, is not an arbitrary determination; it is the expression of infinite intelligence and love. There is the most perfect agreement between all the precepts of the Bible and the highest dictates of reason. There is no command in the word of God of permanent and universal obligation, which may not be shown to be in accordance with the laws of our own higher nature. This is one of the strongest collateral arguments in favor of the divine origin of the Scriptures. In appealing therefore to the Bible in support of the doctrine here advanced, we are not, on the one hand appealing to an arbitrary standard, a mere statute book, a collection of laws which create the obligations they enforce; nor, on the other hand, to "the reason and nature of things" in the abstract, which after all is only our own reason; but we are appealing to the infinite intelligence of a personal God, whose will, because of his infinite excellence, is necessarily the ultimate ground and rule of all moral obligation. This, however, being the case, whatever the Bible declares to be right is found to be in accordance with the constitution of nature and our own reason. All that the Scriptures, for example, teach of the subordination of children to their parents, of wives to their husbands, has not its foundation, but its confirmation, in the very nature of the relation of the parties. Any violation of the precepts of the Bible, on these points, is found to be a violation of the laws of nature, and certainly destructive. In like manner it is clear from the social nature of man, from the dependence of men upon each other, from the impossibility of attaining the end of our being in this world, otherwise than in society and under an ordered government, that it is the will of God that such society should exist. The design of God in this matter is as plain as in the constitution of the universe. We might as well maintain that the laws of nature are the result of chance, or that marriage and parental authority have no other foundation than human law, as to assert that civil government has no firmer foundation than the will of man or the quicksands of expediency. By creating men social beings, and making it necessary for them to live in society, God has made his will as thus revealed the foundation of all civil government.

This doctrine is but one aspect of the comprehensive doctrine of Theism, a doctrine which teaches the existence of a personal God, a Spirit infinite, eternal, and unchangeable, in his being, wisdom, power, justice, holiness, goodness, and truth; a God who is everywhere present upholding and governing all his creatures and all their actions. The universe is not a machine left to go of itself. God did not at first create matter and impress upon it certain laws and then leave it to their blind operation. He is everywhere present in the material world, not superseding secondary causes, but so upholding and guiding their operations, that the intelligence evinced is the omnipresent intelligence of God, and the power exercised is the *potestas ordinata* of the Great First Cause. He is no less supreme in his control of intelligent agents. They indeed are free, but not independent. They are governed in a manner consistent with their nature; yet God turns them as the rivers of waters are turned. All events depending on human agency are under his control. God is in history. Neither chance nor blind necessity determine the concatenation or issues of things. Nor is the world in the hands of its inhabitants. God has not launched our globe on the ocean of space and left its multitudinous crew to direct its course without his interference. He is at the helm. His breath fills the sails. His wisdom and power are pledged for the prosperity of the voyage. Nothing happens, even to the falling of a sparrow, which is not ordered by him. He works all things after the counsel of his will. It is by him that kings reign and princes decree justice. He puts down one, and raises up another. As he leads out the stars by night, marshaling them as a host, calling each one by its name, so does he order all human events. He raises up nations and appoints the bounds of their habitation. He founds the empires of the earth and determines their form and their duration. This doctrine of God's universal providence is the foundation of all religion. If this doctrine be not true, we are without God in the world. But if it is true, it involves a vast deal. God is everywhere in nature and in history. Every thing is a revelation of his presence and power. We are always in contact with him. Every thing has a voice, which speaks of his goodness or his wrath; fruitful seasons proclaim his goodness, famine and pestilence declare his displeasure. Nothing is by chance. The existence of any particular form of government is as much his work, as the rising of the sun or falling of the rain. It is something he has ordained for some wise purpose, and it is to be regarded as his work. If all events are under God's control, if it is by him that kings reign, then the actual possession of power is as much a revelation of his will that it should be obeyed, as the possession of wisdom or goodness is a manifestation of his will that those endowed with those gifts, should be reverenced and loved. It follows, therefore, from the universal providence of God, that "the powers that be are ordained of God." We have no more right to refuse obedience to an actually existing government because it is not to our taste, or because we do not approve of its measures, than a child has the right to refuse to recognize a wayward parent; or a wife a capricious husband.

The religious character of our civil duties flows also from the comprehensive doctrine that the will of God is the ground of all moral obligation. To seek that ground either in "the reason and nature of things," or in expediency, is to banish God from the moral world, as effectually as the mechanical theory of the universe banishes him from the physical universe and from history. Our allegiance on that hypothesis is not to God but to reason or to society. This theory of morals therefore, changes the nature of religion and of moral obligation. It modifies and degrades all religious sentiment and exercises; it changes the very nature of sin, of repentance and obedience, and gives us, what is a perfect solecism, a religion without God. According to the Bible, our obligation to obey the laws of the land is not founded on the fact that the good of society requires such obedience, or that it is a dictate of reason, but on the authority of God. It is part of the service which we owe to him. This must be so if the doctrine is true that God is our moral governor, to whom we are responsible for all our acts, and whose will is both the ground and the rule of all our obligations.

We need not, however, dwell longer on this subject. Although it has long been common to look upon civil government as a human institution, and to represent the consent of the governed as the only ground of the obligation of obedience, yet this doctrine is so notoriously of infidel origin, and so obviously in conflict with the teachings of the Bible, that it can have no hold on the convictions of a Christian people. It is no more true of the state than it is of the family, or of the church. All are of divine institution. All have their foundation in his will. The duties belonging to each are enjoined by him and are enforced by his authority. Marriage is indeed a voluntary covenant. The parties select each other, and the state may make laws regulating the mode in which the contract shall be ratified; and determining its civil effects. It is, however, none the less an ordinance of God. The vows it includes are made to God; its sanction is found in his law; and its violation is not a mere breach of contract or disobedience to the civil law, but a sin against God. So with regard to the church, it is in one sense a voluntary society. No man can be forced by other men to join its communion. If done at all it must be done with his own consent, yet every man is under the strongest moral obligation to enter its fold. And when enrolled in the number of its members his obligation to obedience does not rest on his consent; it does not cease should that consent be withdrawn. It rests on the authority of the church as a divine institution. This is an authority no man can throw off. It presses him everywhere and at all times with the weight of a moral obligation. In a sense analogous to this the state is a divine institution. Men are bound to organize themselves into a civil government. Their obligation to obey its laws does not rest upon their compact in this case, any more than in the others above referred to. It is enjoined by God. It is a religious duty, and disobedience is a direct offense against him. The people have indeed the right to determine the form of the government under which they are to live, and to modify it from time to time to suit their changing condition. So, though to a less extent, or within narrower limits, they have a right to modify the form of their ecclesiastical governments, a right which every church has exercised, but the ground and nature of the obligation to obedience remains unchanged. This is not a matter of mere theory. It is of primary practical importance and has an all-pervading influence on national character. Every thing indeed connected with this subject depends on the answer to the question, Why are we obliged to obey the laws? If we answer because we made them; or because we assent to them, or framed the government which enacts them; or because the good of society enjoins obedience, or reason dictates it, then the state is a human institution; it has no religious sanction; it is founded on the sand; it ceases to have a hold on the conscience and to commend itself as a revelation of God to be reverenced and obeyed as a manifestation of his presence and will. But, on the other hand, if we place the state in the same category with the family and the church, and regard it as an institution of God, then we elevate it into a higher sphere; we invest it with religious sanctions and it become pervaded by a divine presence and authority, which immeasurably strengthens, while it elevates its power. Obedience for conscience' sake is as different from obedience from fear, or from voluntary consent, or regard to human authority, as the divine from the human.

Such being, as we conceive, the true doctrine concerning the nature of the state, it is well to inquire into the necessary deductions from this doctrine. If government be a divine institution, and obedience to the laws a matter resting on the authority of God, it might seem to follow that in no case could human laws be disregarded with a good conscience. This, as we have seen, is in fact the conclusion drawn from these premises by the advocates of the doctrine "of passive obedience." The command, however, to be subject to the higher powers is not more unlimited in its statement than the command, "children obey your parents in all things." From this latter command no one draws the conclusion that unlimited obedience is due from children to their parents. The true inference doubtless is, in both cases, that obedience is the rule, and disobedience the exception. If in any instance a child refuse compliance with the requisition of the parent, or a citizen with the law of the land, he must be prepared to justify such disobedience at the bar of God. Even divine laws may in some cases be dispensed with. Those which indeed are founded on the nature of God, such as the command to love Him and our neighbor, are necessarily immutable. But those which are founded on the present constitution of things, though permanent as general rules of action, may on adequate grounds, be violated without sin. The commands, Thou shalt not kill, Thou shalt not steal, Remember the sabbath day to keep it holy, are all of permanent authority; and yet there may be justifiable homicide, and men may profane the sabbath and be blameless. In like manner the command to obey the laws, is a divine injunction, and yet there are cases in which disobedience is a duty. It becomes then of importance to determine what these cases are; or to ascertain the principles which limit the obedience which we owe to the state. It follows from the divine institution of government that its power is limited by the design of God in its institution, and by the moral law. The family, the church and the state are all divine institutions, designed for specific purposes. Each has its own sphere, and the authority belonging to each is necessarily confined within its own province. The father appears in his household as its divinely appointed head. By the command of God all the members of that household are required to yield him reverence and obedience. But he can not carry his parental authority into the church or the state; nor can he appear in his family as a magistrate or church officer. The obedience due to him is that which belongs to a father, and not to a civil or ecclesiastical officer, and his children are not required to obey him in either of those capacities. In like manner the officers of the church have within their sphere a divine right to rule, but they can not claim civil authority on the ground of the general command to the people to obey those who have the care of souls. Heb. xiii: 17. As the church officer loses his power when he enters the forum; so does the civil magistrate when he enters the church. His right to rule is a right which belongs to him as representing God in the state—he has no commission to represent God either in the family or the church; and therefore, he is entitled to no obedience if he claims an authority which does not belong to him. This is a very obvious principle, and is of wide application. It not only limits the authority of civil officers to civil affairs, but limits the extent due to the obedience to be rendered even in civil matters to the officers of the state. A justice of the peace has no claim to the obedience due to a governor of a state; nor a governor of a state to that which belongs to the President of the Union; nor the President of the Union to that which may be rightfully claimed by an absolute sovereign. A military commander has no authority over the community as a civil magistrate, nor can he exercise such authority even over his subordinates. This principle applies in all its force to the law-making power. The legislature can not exercise any power which does not belong to them. They can not act as judges or magistrates unless such authority has been actually committed to them. They are to be obeyed as legislators; and in any other capacity their decisions or commands do not bind the conscience. And still further, their legislative enactments have authority only when made in the exercise of their legitimate powers. In other words, an unconstitutional law is no law. If our Congress, for example, were to pass a bill creating an order of nobility, or an established church, or to change the religion of the land, or to enforce a sumptuary code, it would have no more virtue and be entitled to no more deference than a similar enactment intended to bind the whole country passed by a town council. This we presume will not be denied. God has committed unlimited power to no man and to no set of men, and the limitation which he has assigned to the power conferred, is to be found in the design for which it was given. That design is determined in the case of the family, the church and the state, by the nature of these institutions, by the general precepts of the Bible, or by the providence of God determining the peculiar constitution under which these organizations are called to act. The power of a parent was greater under the old dispensation than it is now; the legitimate authority of the church is greater under some modes of organization than under others; and the power of the state as represented in its constituted authorities is far more extensive in some countries than in others. The theory of the British government is that the parliament is the whole state in convention, and therefore it exercises powers which do not belong to our Congress, which represents the state only for certain specified purposes. These diversities, however, do not alter the general principle, which is, that rulers are to be obeyed in the exercise of their legitimate authority; that their commmands or requirements beyond their appropriate spheres are void of all binding force. This is a principle which no one can dispute.

A second principle is no less plain. No human authority can make it obligatory on us to commit sin. If all power is of God it can not be legitimately used against God. This is a dictate of natural conscience, and is authenticated by the clearest teachings of the word of God. The apostles when commanded to abstain from preaching Christ refused to obey, and said: "Whether it be right in the sight of God to hearken unto you more than unto God, judge ye." No human law could make it binding on the ministers of the gospel, in our day, to withhold the message of salvation from their fellow-men. It requires no argument to prove that men can not make it right to worship idols, to blaspheme God, to deny Christ. It is sheer fanaticism thus to exalt the power of the government above the authority of God. This would be to bring back upon us some of the worst doctrines of the middle ages as to the power of the pope and of earthly sovereigns. Good men in all ages of the world have always acted on the principle that human laws can not bind the conscience when they are in conflict with the law of God. Daniel openly, in the sight of his enemies, prayed to the God of heaven in despite of the prohibition of his sovereign. Shadrach, Meshech and Abednego refused to bow down, at the command of the king, to the golden image. The early Christians disregarded all those laws of Pagan Rome requiring them to do homage to false gods. Protestants with equal unanimity refused to submit to the laws of their papal sovereigns enjoining the profession of Romish errors. That these men were right no man, with an enlightened conscience, can deny; but they were right only on the principle that the power of the state and of the magistrate is limited by the law of God. It follows then from the divine institution of government, that its power to bind the conscience to obedience is limited by the design of its appointment and the moral law. All its power being from God, it must be subordinate to him. This is a doctrine which, however, for a time and in words, it may be denied, is too plain and too important not to be generally recognized. It is a principle too which should at all times be publicly avowed. The very sanctity of human laws requires it. Their real power and authority lie in their having a divine sanction. To claim for them binding force when destitute of such sanction, is to set up a mere semblance for a reality, a suit of armor with no living man within. The stability of human government and the authority of civil laws require that they should be kept within the sphere where they repose on God, and are pervaded by his presence and power. Without him nothing human can stand. All power is of God; and if of God, divine; and if divine, in accordance with his holy law.

But who are the judges of the application of these principles? Who is to determine whether a particular law is unconstitutional or immoral? So far as the mere constitutionality of a law is concerned, it may be remarked, that there is in most states, as in our own, for example, a regular judicial tribunal to which every legislative enactment can be submitted, and the question of its conformity to the constitution authoritatively decided. In all ordinary cases, that is, in all cases not involving some great principle or some question of conscience, such decisions must be held to be final, and to bind all concerned not only to submission but obedience. A law thus sanctioned becomes instinct with all the power of the state, and further opposition brings the recusants into conflict with the government; a conflict in which no man for light reasons can with a good conscience engage. Still it can not be denied, and ought not to be concealed, that the ultimate decision must be referred to his own judgment. This is a necessary deduction from the doctrine that obedience to law is a religious duty. It is a primary principle that the right of private judgment extends over all questions of faith and morals. No human power can come between God and the conscience. Every man must answer for his own sins, and therefore every man must have the right to determine for himself what is sin. As he can not transfer his responsibility, he can not transfer his right of judgment. This principle has received the sanction of good men in every age of the world. Daniel judged for himself of the binding force of the command not to worship the true God. So did the apostles when they continued to preach Christ, in opposition to all the constituted authorities. The laws passed by Pagan Rome requiring the worship of idols had the sanction of all the authorities of the empire, yet on the ground of their private judgment the Christians refused to obey them. Protestants in like manner refused to obey the laws of Papal Rome, though sustained by all the authority both of the church and state. In all these cases the right of private judgment can not be disputed. Even where no question of religion or morality is directly concerned, this right is undeniable. Does any one now condemn Hampden for refusing to pay "ship-money?" Does any American condemn our ancestors for resisting the stamp-act, though the authorities of St. Stephen's and Westminster united in pronouncing the imposition constitutional? However this principle may be regarded when stated in the abstract, every individual instinctively acts upon it in his own case. Whenever a command is issued by one in authority over us, we immediately and almost unconsciously determine for ourselves, first, whether he had a right to give the order; and secondly, whether it can with a good conscience be obeyed. If this decision is clearly in the negative, we at once determine to refuse obedience on our own responsibility. Let any man test this point by an appeal to his own consciousness. Let him suppose the President of the United States to order him to turn Romanist or Pagan; or Congress to pass a bill requiring him to blaspheme God; or a military superior to command him to commit treason or murder—does not his conscience tell him he would on the instant refuse? Would he, or could he wait until the constitutionality of such requisitions had been submitted to the courts? or if the courts should decide against him, would that at all alter the case? Men must be strangely oblivious of the relation of the soul to God, the instinctive sense which we possess of our allegiance to him, and of the self-evidencing power with which his voice reaches the reason and the conscience, to question the necessity which every man is under to decide all questions touching his duty to God for himself.

It may indeed be thought that this doctrine is subversive of the authority of government. A moment's reflection is sufficient to dispel this apprehension. The power of laws rests on two foundations, fear and conscience. Both are left by this doctrine in their integrity. The former, because the man refuses obedience at his peril. His private conviction that the law is unconstitutional or immoral does not abrogate it, or impede its operation. If arraigned for its violation, he may plead in his justification his objections to the authority of the law. If these objections are found valid by the competent authorities, he is acquitted; if otherwise, he suffers the penalty. What more can the state ask? All the power the state, as such, can give its laws, lies in their penalty. A single decision by the ultimate authority in favor of a law, is a revelation to the whole body of the people that it can not be violated with impunity. The sword of justice hangs over every transgressor. The motive of fear in securing obedience, is therefore, as operative under this view of the subject, as it can be under any other. What, however, is of far more consequence, the power of conscience is left in full force. Obedience to the law is a religious duty, enjoined by the word of God and enforced by conscience. If, in any case, it be withheld, it is under a sense of responsibility to God; and under the conviction that if this conscientious objection be feigned, it aggravates the guilt of disobedience as a sin against God an hundred fold; and if it be mistaken, it affords no palliation of the offense. Paul was guilty in persecuting the church, though he thought he was doing God service. And the man, who by a perverted conscience, is led to refuse obedience to a righteous law, stands without excuse at the bar of God. The moral sanction of civil laws, which gives them their chief power, and without which they must ultimately become inoperative, cannot possibly extend further than this. For what is that moral sanction? It is a conviction that our duty to God requires our obedience; but how can we feel that duty to God requires us to do what God forbids? In other words, a law which we regard as immoral, can not present itself to the conscience as having divine authority. Conscience, therefore, is on the side of the law wherever and whenever this is possible from the nature of the case. It is a contradiction to say that conscience enforces what conscience condemns. This then is all the support which the laws of the land can possibly derive from our moral convictions. The allegiance of conscience is to God. It enforces obedience to all human laws consistent with that allegiance; further than this it can not by possibility go. And as the decisions of conscience are, by the constitution of our nature, determined by our own apprehensions of the moral law, and not by authority, it follows of necessity that every man must judge for himself, and on his own responsibility, whether any given law of man conflicts with the law of God or not.

We would further remark on this point that the lives and property of men have no greater protection than that which, on this theory, is secured for the laws of the state. The law of God says: Thou shalt not kill. Yet every man does, and must judge when and how far this law binds his conscience. It is admitted, on all hands, that there are cases in which its obligation ceases. What those cases are each man determines for himself, but under his two fold responsibility to his country and to God. If, through passion or any other cause, he errs as to what constitutes justifiable homicide, he must bear the penalty attached to murder, by the law of God and man. It is precisely so in the case before us. God has commanded us to obey the magistrate as his minister and representative. If we err in our judgment as to the cases in which the command ceases to be binding, we fall into the hands of justice, both human and divine. Can more than this be necessary? Can any thing be gained by trying to make God require us to break his own commands? Can conscience be made to sanction the violation of the moral law? Is not this the way to destroy all moral distinctions, and to prostrate the authority of conscience, and with it the very foundation of civil government? Is not all history full of the dreadful consequences of the doctrine that human laws can make sin obligatory, and that those in authority can judge for the people what is sin? What more than this is needed to justify all the persecutions for righteousness' sake since the world began? What hope could there be, on this ground, for the preservation of religion or virtue, in any nation on the earth? If the principle be once established, that the people are bound to obey all human laws, or that they are not to judge for themselves when their duty to God requires them to refuse such obedience, then there is not only an end of all civil and religious liberty, but the very nature of civil government, as a divine institution, is destroyed. It becomes first atheistical, and then diabolical. Then the massacre of St. Bartholomew's, the decrees of the French National Assembly, and the laws of Pagan Rome against Christians, and of its Papal successor against Protestants, were entitled to reverent obedience. Then, too, may any infidel party which gains the ascendency in a state, as has happened of late in Switzerland, render it morally obligatory upon all ministers to close their churches, and on the people to renounce the gospel. This is not an age or state of the world in which to advance such doctrines. There are too many evidences of the gathering powers of evil, to render it expedient to exalt the authority of man above that of God, or emancipate men from subjection to their Master in heaven, that they may become more obedient to their masters on earth. We are advocating the cause of civil government, of the stability and authority of human laws, when we make every thing rest on the authority of God, and when we limit every human power by subordinating it to him. We hold, therefore, that it is not only one of the plainest principles of morals, that no immoral law can bind the conscience, and that every man must judge of its character for himself, and on his own responsibility; but that this doctrine is essential to all religious liberty, and to the religious sanction of civil government. If you deny this principle, you thereby deny that government is a divine institution, and denying that, you deprive it of its vital energy, and send it tottering to a dishonored grave.

But here the great practical question arises, What is to be done when the law of the land comes into conflict with the law of God—or, which is to us the same thing, with our convictions of what that law demands? In answer to this question we would remark, in the first place, that in most cases, the majority of the people have nothing to do, except peaceably to use their influence to have the law repealed. The mass of the people have nothing actively to do with the laws. Very few enactments of the government touch one in a thousand in the population. We may think a protective tariff not only inexpedient, but unequal and therefore unjust. But we have nothing to do with it. We are not responsible for it, and are not called upon to enforce it. The remark applies even to laws of a higher character, such, *e. g.* as a law proclaiming an unjust war; forbidding the introduction of the Bible into public schools; requiring homage or sanction to be given to idolatrous services by public officers, etc., etc. Such laws do not touch the mass of the people. They do not require them either to do or abstain from doing, any thing which conscience forbids or enjoins; and therefore their duty in the premises may be limited to the use of legitimate means to have laws of which they disapprove repealed.

In the second place, those executive officers who are called upon to carry into effect a law which requires them to do what their conscience condemns, must resign their office, if they would do their duty to God. Some years since, General Maitland (if we remember the name correctly) of the Madras Presidency, in India, resigned a lucrative and honorable post, because he could not conscientiously give the sanction to the Hindoo idolatry required by the British authorities. And within the last few months, we have seen hundreds of Hessian officers throw up their commissions rather than trample on the constitution of their country. On the same principles the non-conformists in the time of Charles II. and the ministers of the Free Church of Scotland, in our day, gave up their stipends and their positions, because they could not with a good conscience carry into effect the law of the land. It is not intended that an executive officer should, in all cases, resign his post rather than execute a law which in his private judgment he may regard as unconstitutional or unjust. The responsibility attaches to those who make, and not to those who execute the laws. It is only when the act, which the officer is called upon to perform, involves personal criminality, that he is called upon to decline its execution. Thus in the case of war; a military officer is not the proper judge of its justice. That is not a question between him and the enemy, but between his government and the hostile nation. On the supposition that war itself is not sinful, the act which the military officer is called upon to perform is not criminal, and he may with a good conscience carry out the commands of his government, whatever may be his private opinion of the justice of the war. All such cases no doubt are more or less complicated, and must be decided each on its own merits. The general principle, however, appears plain, that it is only when the act required of an executive officer involves personal criminality, that he is called upon to resign. This is a case that often occurs. In Romish countries, as Malta, for example, British officers have been required to do homage to the host, and on their refusal have been cashiered. An instance of this kind occurred a few years ago, and produced a profound sensation in England. This was clearly a case of great injustice. The command was an unrighteous one. The duty of the officer was to resign rather than obey. Had the military authorities taken a fair view of the question, they must have decided that the command to bow to the host, was not obligatory, because *ultra vires*. But if such an order was insisted upon, the conscientious Protestant must resign his commission.

The next question is, What is the duty of private citizens in the case supposed, *i. e.*, when the civil law either forbids them to do what God commands, or commands them to do what God forbids? We answer, their duty is not obedience, but submission. These are different things. A law consists of two parts, the precept and the penalty. We obey the one, and submit to the other. When we are required by the law to do what our conscience pronounces to be sinful, we can not obey the precept, but we are bound to submit without resistance to the penalty. We are not authorized to abrogate the law, nor forcibly to resist its execution, no matter how great its injustice or cruelty. On this principle holy men have acted in all ages. The apostles did not obey the precept of the Jewish laws forbidding them to preach Christ, but neither did they resist the execution of the penalty attached to the violation of those laws. Thus it was with all the martyrs; they would not offer incense to idols, but refused not to be led to the stake. Had Cranmer, on the ground of the iniquity of the law condemning him to death, killed the officers who came to carry it into effect, he would have been guilty of murder. Here is the great difference which is often over-looked. The right of self-defense is appealed to as justifying resistance even to death, against all attempts to deprive us of our liberty. We have this right in reference to unauthorized individuals, but not in reference to the officers of the law. Had men without authority entered Cranmer's house, and attempted to take his life, his resistance, even if attended with the loss of life, would have been justifiable. But no man has the right to resist the execution of the law. What could be more iniquitous than the laws condemning men to death for the worship of God. Yet to these laws Christians and Protestants yielded unresisting submission. This is an obvious duty, flowing from the divine institution of government. There is no power but of God, and the powers that be are ordained of God. Whosoever, therefore, resisteth the power resisteth the ordinance of God; and they that resist shall receive to themselves damnation. Thus Paul reasoned. If the power is of God, it can not be rightfully resisted; it must be obeyed or submitted to. Are wicked, tyrannical, Pagan powers of God? Certainly they are. Does not he order all things? Does any man become a king without God's permission granted in mercy or in judgment? Was not Nero to be recognized as emperor? Would it not be a sin to refuse submission to Nicholas of Russia, or to the Sultan of Turkey? Are rulers to be obeyed only for their goodness? Is it only kind and reasonable masters, parents, or husbands, who are to be recognized as such? It is no doubt true, that in no case is unlimited authority granted to men; and that obedience to the precepts of our superiors is limited by the nature of their office, and by the moral law; but this leaves their authority untouched, and the obligation to submission where we can not obey, unimpaired.

Have we then got back to the old doctrine of "passive obedience" by another route? Not at all. The scriptural rule above recited relates to individuals. It prescribes the duty of submission even to unjust and wicked laws, on the part of men in their separate capacity;

but it does not deny the right of revolution as existing in the community. What the Scriptures forbid, is that any man should undertake to resist the law. They do not forbid either change in the laws or change in the government. There is an obvious difference between these two things, viz: the right of resistance on the part of individuals, and the right of revolution on the part of the people. This latter right we argue from the divine institution of government itself. God has revealed his will that government should exist, but he has not prescribed the form which it shall assume. In other words, he has commanded men to organize such government, but has left the form to be determined by themselves. This is a necessary inference. It follows from the mere silence of Scripture and nature on this subject, that it is left free to the determination of those to whom the general command is given. In the next place, this right is to be inferred from the design of civil government. That design is the welfare of the people. It is the promotion of their physical and moral improvement; the security of life and property; the punishment of evil doers, and the praise of those who do well. If such is the end which God designs government to answer, it must be his will that it should be made to accomplish that purpose, and consequently that it may be changed from time to time, so as to secure that end. No one form of government is adapted to all states of society, any more than one suit of clothes is proper to all stages of life. The end for which clothing is designed, supposes the right to adapt it to that end. In like manner the end government is intended to answer, supposes the right to modify it whenever such modification is necessary. If God commands men to accomplish certain ends, and does not prescribe the means, he does thereby leave the choice of the means to their discretion. And any institution which fails to accomplish the end intended by it, if it has not a divine sanction as to its form, may lawfully be so changed as to suit the purpose for which it was appointed. We hold, therefore, that the people have, by divine right, the authority to change, not only their rulers, but their form of government, whenever the one or the other, instead of promoting the well-being of the community, is unjust or injurious. This is a right which, like all other prerogatives, may be exercised unwisely, capriciously, or even unjustly, but still it is not to be denied. It has been recognized and exercised in all ages of the world, and with the sanction of the best of men. It is as unavoidable and healthful as the changes in the body to adapt it to the increasing vigor of the mind, in its progress from infancy to age. The progress of society depends on the exercise of this right. It is impossible that its powers should be developed, if it were to be forever wrapt up in its swaddling clothes, or coffined as a mummy. The early Christians submitted quietly to the unjust laws of their Pagan oppressors, until the mass of the community became Christians, and then they revolutionized the government. Protestants acted in the same way with their papal rulers. So did our forefathers, and so may any people whose form of government no longer answers the end for which God has commanded civil government to be instituted. The Quakers are now a minority in all the countries in which they exist, and furnish an edifying example of submission to the laws which they can not conscientiously obey. But should they come, in any political society, to be the controlling power, it is plain they would have the right to conduct it on their own principles.

The right of revolution therefore is really embedded in the right to serve God. A government which interferes with that service, which commands what God forbids, or forbids what he commands, we are bound by our duty to him to change as soon as we have the power. If this is not so, then God has subjected his people to the necessity of always submitting to punishment for obeying his commands, and has cut them off from the only means which can insure their peaceful and secure enjoyment of the liberty to do his will. No one, however, in our land, or of the race to which we belong, will be disposed to question the right of the people to change their form of government. Our history forbids all diversity of sentiment on this subject. We are only concerned to show that the scriptural doctrine of civil government is perfectly consistent with that right; or rather that the right is one of the logical deductions from that doctrine.

We have thus endeavored to prove that government is a divine institution; that obedience to the laws is a religious duty; that such obedience is due in all cases in which it can be rendered with a good conscience; that when obedience can not be yielded without sinning against God, then our duty as individuals is quietly to submit to the infliction of the penalty attached to disobedience; and that the right of resistance or of revolution rests only in the body of people for whose benefit government is instituted.

The application of these principles to the case of the fugitive slave law is so obvious, as hardly to justify remark. The great body of the people regard that law as consistent with the constitution of the country and the law of God. Their duty, therefore, in the premises, whether they think it wise or unwise, is perfectly plain. Those who take the opposite view of the law, having in the great majority of cases, nothing to do with enforcing it, are in no measure responsible for it. Their duty is limited to the use of peaceable and constitutional means to get it repealed. A large part of the people of this country thought the acquisition of Louisiana; the admission of Texas into the Union by a simple resolution; the late Mexican war; were either unjust or unconstitutional, but there was no resistance to these measures. None was made, and none would have been justifiable. So in the present case, as the people generally are not called upon either to do, or to forbear from doing, any thing their conscience forbids, all resistance to the operation of this law on their part must be without excuse. With regard to the executive officers, whose province it is to carry the law into effect, though some of them may disapprove of it as unwise, harsh, or oppressive, still they are bound to execute it, unless they believe the specific act which they are called upon to perform involves personal criminality, and then their duty is the resignation of their office, and not resistance to the law. There is the most obvious difference between an officer being called upon, for example, to execute a decision of a court, which in his private opinion he thinks unjust, and his being called upon to blaspheme, or commit murder. The latter involves personal guilt, the former does not. He is not the judge of the equity or propriety of the decision which he is required to carry into effect. It is evident that the wheels of society would be stopped, if every officer of the government, and every minister of justice should feel that he is authorized to sit in judgment on the wisdom or righteousness of any law he was called upon to execute. He is responsible for his own acts, and not for the judgments of others, and therefore when the execution of a law or of a command of a superior does not require him to sin, he is free to obey.

Again, in those cases in which we, as private individuals, may be called upon to assist in carrying the fugitive slave law into effect, if we can not obey, we must do as the Quakers have long done with regard to our military laws, i. e. quietly submit. We have no right to resist, or in any way to impede the operation of the law. Whatever sin there is in it, does not rest on us, any more than the sin of our military system rests on the Quakers.[259]

And finally as regards the fugitives themselves, their obvious duty is submission. To them the law must appear just as the laws of the Pagans against Christians, or of Romanists against Protestants, appeared to those who suffered from them. And the duty in both cases is the same. Had the martyrs put to death the officers of the law, they would in the sight of God and man have been guilty of murder. And any one who teaches fugitive slaves to resort to violence even to the sacrifice of life, in resisting the law in question, it seems to us, is guilty of exciting men to murder. As before remarked, the principle of self-defense does not apply in this case. Is there no difference between a man who kills an assassin who attempts his life on the highway, and the man who, though knowing himself to be innocent of the crime for which he has been condemned to die, should kill the officers of justice? The former is a case of justifiable homicide, the other is a case of murder. The officers of justice are not the offenders. They are not the persons responsible for the law or the decision. That responsibility rests on the government. Private vengeance can not reach the state. And if it could, such vengeance is not the remedy ordained by God for such evils. They are to be submitted to, until the government can be changed. How did our Lord act when he was condemned by an oppressive judgment, and with wicked hands crucified and slain? Did he kill the Roman soldiers? Has not he left us an example that we should follow his steps: who did no sin, neither was guile found in his mouth; who, when he was reviled, reviled not again; when he suffered, he threatened not; but committed himself unto him that judgeth righteously. On this principle did all his holy martyrs act; and on this principle are we bound to act in submitting to the laws of the land, even when we deem them oppressive or unjust.

The principles advocated in this paper appear to us so elementary, that we feel disposed to apologize for presenting them in such a formal manner. But every generation has to learn the alphabet for itself. And the mass of men are so occupied with other matters, that they do not give themselves time to discriminate. Their judgments are dictated, in many cases, by their feelings, or their circumstances. One man simply looks to the hardship of forcing a slave back to bondage, and he impulsively counsels resistance unto blood. Another looks to the evils which follow from resistance to law, and he asserts that human laws are in all cases to be obeyed. Both are obviously wrong. Both would overthrow all government. The one by justifying every man's taking the law into his own hands; and the other by destroying the authority of God, which is the only foundation on which human government can rest. It is only by acting on the direction of the Divine Wisdom incarnate: "Render unto Cæsar the things that are Cæsar's, and unto God the things that are God's," that these destructive extremes are to be avoided. Government is a divine institution; obedience to the laws is commanded by God; and yet like all other divine commands of the same class, there are cases in which it ceases to be obligation. Of these cases every one must judge for himself on his own responsibility to God and man; but when he cannot obey, his duty is to submit. The divinely appointed remedy for unjust or oppressive legislation is not private or tumultuous opposition, but the repeal of unrighteous enactments, or the reorganization of the government.

What, however, we have had most at heart in the preparation of this article, is the exhibition of the great principle that all authority reposes on God; that all our obligations terminate on him; that government is not a mere voluntary compact, and obedience to law an obligation which rests on the consent of the governed. We regard this as a matter of primary importance. The character of men and of communities depends, to a great extent on their faith. The theory of morals which they adopt determines their moral charactcter. If they assume that expediency is the rule of duty, that a thing is right because it produces happiness, or wrong because it produces misery, that this tendency is not merely the test between right and wrong, but the ground of the distinction, then, the specific idea of moral excellence and obligation is lost. All questions of duty are merged into a calculation of profit and loss. There is no sense of God; reason or society takes his place, and an irreligious, calculating cast of character is the inevitable result. This is counteracted, in individuals and the community by various causes, for neither the character of a man nor that of a society is determined by any one opinion; but its injurious influence may nevertheless be most manifest and deplorable. No man can fail to see the deteriorating influence of this theory of morals on public character both in this country and in England. If we would make men religious and moral, instead of merely cute, let us place God before them; let us teach them that his will is the ground of their obligations; that they are responsible to him for all their acts; that their allegiance as moral agents is not to reason or to society, but to the heart-searching God; that the obligation to obey the laws of the land does not rest on their consent to them, but to the fact government is of God; that those who resist the magistrate, resist the ordinance of God, and that they who resist, shall receive unto themselves damnation. This is the only doctrine which can give stablity either to morals or to government. Man's allegiance is not to reason in the abstract, nor to society, but to a personal God, who has power to destroy both soul and body in hell. This is a law revealed in the constitution of our nature, as well as by the lips of Christ. And to no other sovereign can the soul yield rational obedience. We might as well attempt to substitute some mechanical contrivance of our own, for the law of gravitation, as a means of keeping the planets in their orbits, as to expect to govern men by any thing else than the fear of an Infinite God.

THE BIBLE ARGUMENT ON SLAVERY.

BY CHARLES HODGE, D.D.,
OF PRINCETON, N. J.

NOTE.—This Essay of Dr. Hodge, was designed by the Editor, to follow that of Dr. Stringfellow, but the copy was not received until the stereotyping had progressed nearly to the close of the volume.

Infatuation of the Abolitionists—Necessity of Correct Opinions—Statement of the Question—Slavery as Treated by Christ and his Apostles—Slaveholding not Sinful—Answer to this Argument—Dr. Channing's Answer—Admissions—Reply to the Abolition Argument—Mr. Birney's Admissions—Argument from the Old Testament—Polygamy and Divorce—Inalienable Rights.

EVERY one must be sensible that a very great change has, within a few years, been produced in the feelings, if not in the opinions of the public in relation to slavery. It is now the most exciting topic of discussion. Nor is the excitement in society confined to discussion alone. Designs and plans, of the most reprehensible character, are boldly avowed and defended. What has produced this lamentable state of things? No doubt many circumstances have combined in its production. We think, however, that all impartial observers must acknowledge, that by far the most prominent cause is the conduct of the abolitionists. . . . . Nor is it by argument that the abolitionists have produced the present unhappy excitement. Argument has not been the characteristic of their publications. Denunciations of slaveholding, as manstealing, robbery, piracy, and worse than murder; consequent vituperation of slaveholders as knowingly guilty of the worst of crimes; passionate appeals to the feelings of the inhabitants of the Northern States; gross exaggerations of the moral and physical condition of the slaves, have formed the staple of their addresses to the public.[260] We do not mean to say that there has been no calm and Christian discussion of the subject. We mean merely to state what has, to the best of our knowledge, been the predominent character of the anti-slavery publications. There is one circumstance which renders the error and guilt of this course of conduct chargeable, in a great measure, on the abolitionists as a body, and even upon those of their number who have pursued a different course. We refer to the fact that they have upheld the most extreme publications, and made common cause with the most reckless declaimers. The wildest ravings of the *Liberator* have been constantly lauded; agents have been commissioned whose great distinction was a talent for eloquent vituperation; coincidence of opinion as to the single point of immediate emancipation has been sufficient to unite men of the most discordant character. There is in this conduct such a strange want of adaptation between the means and the end which they profess to have in view, as to stagger the faith of most persons in the sincerity of their professions, who do not consider the extremes to which even good men may be carried, when they allow one subject to take exexclusive possession of their minds. We do not doubt their sincerity, but we marvel at their delusion. They seem to have been led by the mere impulse of feeling, and a blind imitation of their predecessors in England, to a course of measures, which, though rational under one set of circumstances, is the hight of infatuation under another. The English abolitionists addressed themselves to a community, which, though it owned no slaves, had the power to abolish slavery, and was therefore responsible for its continuance. Their object was to rouse that community to immediate action. For this purpose they addressed themselves to the feelings of the people; they portrayed in the strongest colors the misery of the slaves; they dilated on the gratuitous crime of which England was guilty in perpetuating slavery, and did all they could to excite the passions of the public. This was the course most likely to succeed, and it did succeed. Suppose, however, that the British parliament had no power over the subject; that it rested entirely with the colonial Assemblies to decide whether slavery should be abolished or not. Does any man believe the abolitionists would have gained their object? Did they in fact make converts of the planters? Did they even pretend that such was their design? Every one knows that their conduct produced a state of almost frantic excitement in the West India Islands; that so far from the public feeling in England producing a moral impression upon the planters favorable to the condition of the slaves, its effect was directly the reverse. It excited them to drive away the missionaries, to tear down the chapels, to manifest a determination to rivet still more firmly the chains on their helpless captives, and to resist to the utmost all attempts for their emancipation or even improvement. All this was natural, though it was all, under the circumstances, of no avail, except to rouse the spirit of the mother country, and to endanger the result of the experiment of emancipation, by exasperating the feelings of the slaves. Precisely similar has been the result of the efforts of the American abolitionists as regards the slaveholders of America. They have produced a state of alarming exasperation at the South, injurious to the slave and dangerous to the country, while they have failed to enlist the feelings of the North. This failure has resulted, not so much from diversity of opinion on the abstract question of slavery; or from want of sympathy among Northern men in the cause of human rights, as from the fact, that the common sense of the public has been shocked by the incongruity and folly of hoping to effect the abolition of slavery in one country, by addressing the people of another. We do not expect to abolish despotism in Russia, by getting up indignation meetings in New York. Yet for all the purposes of legislation on this subject, Russia is not more a foreign country to us than South Carolina. The idea of inducing the Southern slaveholder to emancipate his slaves by denunciation, is about as rational as to expect the sovereigns of Europe to grant free institutions, by calling them tyrants and robbers. Could we send our denunciations of despotism among the subjects of those monarchs, and rouse the people to a sense of their wrongs and a determination to redress them, there would be some prospect of success. But our Northern abolitionists disclaim, with great earnestness, all intention of allowing their appeals to reach the ears of the slaves. It is, therefore, not to be wondered at, that the course pursued by the anti-slavery societies, should produce exasperation at the South, without conciliating sympathy at the North. The impolicy of their conduct is so obvious, that men who agree with them as to all their leading principles, not only stand aloof from their measures, but unhesitatingly condemn their conduct. This is the case with Dr. Channing. Although his book was written rather to repress the feeling of opposition to these societies, than to encourage it, yet he fully admits the justice of the principal charges brought against them. We extract a few passages on the subject. "The abolitionists have done wrong, I believe; nor is their wrong to be winked at, because done fanatically, or with good intentions; for how much mischief may be wrought with good designs! They have fallen into the common error of enthusiasts, that of exaggerating their object, of feeling as if no evil existed but that which they opposed, and as if no guilt could be compared with that of countenancing and upholding it. The tone of their newspapers, as far as I have seen them, has often been fierce, bitter, and abusive." p. 133. "Another objection to their movements is, that they have sought to accomplish their object by a system of agitation; that is, by a system of affiliated societies gathered, and held together, and extended, by passionate eloquence." "The abolitionists might have formed an association; but it should have been an elective one. Men of strong principles, judiciousness, sobriety, should have been carefully sought as members. Much good might have been accomplished by the co-operation of such philanthropists. Instead of this, the abolitionists sent forth their orators, some of them transported with fiery zeal, to sound the alarm against slavery through the land, to gather together young and old, pupils from schools, females hardly arrived at years of discretion, the ignorant, the excitable, the impetuous, and to organize these into associations for the battle against oppression. Very unhappily they preached their doctrine to the colored people, and collected these into societies.[261] To this mixed and excitable multitude, minute, heartrending descriptions of slavery were given in the piercing tones of passion; and slaveholders were held up as monsters of cruelty and crime." p. 136. "The abolitionists often speak of Luther's vehemence as a model to future reformers. But who, that has read history, does not know that Luther's reformation was accompanied by tremendous miseries and crimes, and that its progress was soon arrested? and is there not reason to fear, that the fierce, bitter, persecuting spirit, which he breathed into the work, not only tarnished its glory, but limited its power? One great principle which we should lay down as immovably true, is, that if a good work can not be carried on by the calm, self-controlled, benevolent spirit of Christianity, then the time for doing it has not come. God asks not the aid of our vices. He can overrule them for good, but they are not to be chosen instruments of human happiness."

p. 138. "The adoption of the common system of agitation by the abolitionists has proved signally unsuccessful. From the beginning it created alarm in the considerate, and strengthened the sympathies of the free States with the slaveholder. It made converts of a few individuals, but alienated multitudes. Its influence at the South has been evil without mixture.[262] It has stirred up bitter passions and a fierce fanaticism, which have shut every ear and every heart against its arguments and persuasions. These effects are the more to be deplored, because the hope of freedom to the slaves lies chiefly in the dispositions of his master. The abolitionist indeed proposed to convert the slaveholders; and for this end he approached them with vituperation, and exhausted on them the vocabulary of abuse! And he has reaped as he sowed." p. 142.

Unmixed good or evil, however, in such a world as ours, is a very rare thing. Though the course pursued by the abolitionists has produced a great preponderance of mischief, it may incidentally occasion no little good. It has rendered it incumbent on every man to endeavor to obtain, and, as far as he can, to communicate definite opinions and correct principles on the whole subject. The community are very apt to sink down into indifference to a state of things of long continuance, and to content themselves with vague impressions as to right and wrong on important points, when there is no call for immediate action. From this state the abolitionists have effectually roused the public mind. The subject of slavery is no longer one on which men are allowed to be of no mind at all. The question is brought up before all of our public bodies, civil and religious. Almost every ecclesiastical society has in some way been called to express an opinion on the subject; and these calls are constantly repeated. Under these circumstances, it is the duty of all in their appropriate sphere, to seek for truth, and to utter it in love.

"The first question," says Dr. Channing, "to be proposed by a rational being, is not what is profitable, but what is right. Duty must be primary, prominent, most conspicuous, among the objects of human thought and pursuit. If we cast it down from its supremacy, if we inquire first for our interests and then for our duties we shall certainly err. We can never see the right clearly and fully, but by making it our first concern. . . . Right is the supreme good, and includes all other goods. In seeking and adhering to it, we secure our true and only happiness. All prosperity, not founded on it, is built on sand. If human affairs are controlled, as we believe, by almighty rectitude and impartial goodness, then to hope for happiness from wrong doing is as insane as to seek health and prosperity by rebelling against the laws of nature, by sowing our seed on the ocean, or making poison our common food. There is but one unfailing good; and that is, fidelity to the everlasting law written on the heart, and re-written and re-published in God's word.

"Whoever places this faith in the everlasting law of rectitude must, of course, regard the question of slavery, first, and chiefly, as a moral question. All other considerations will weigh little with him compared with its moral character and moral influences. The following remarks, therefore, are designed to aid the reader in forming a just moral judgment of slavery. Great truths, inalienable rights, everlasting duties, these will form the chief subjects of this discussion. There are times when the assertion of great principles is the best service a man can render society. The present is a moment of bewildering excitement, when men's minds are stormed and darkened by strong passions and fierce conflicts; and also a moment of absorbing worldliness, when the moral law is made to bow to expediency, and its high and strict requirements are decried or dismissed as metaphysical abstractions, or impracticable theories. At such a season to utter great principles without passion, and in the spirit of unfeigned and universal good will, and to engrave them deeply and durably on men's minds, is to do more for the world, than to open mines of wealth, or to frame the most successful schemes of policy."

No man can refuse assent to these principles. The great question, therefore, in relation to slavery is, what is right? What are the moral principles which should control our opinions and conduct in regard to it? Before attempting an answer to this question, it is proper to remark, that we recognize no authoritative rule of truth and duty but the word of God. Plausible as may be the arguments deduced from general principles to prove a thing to be true or false, right and wrong, there is almost always room for doubt and honest diversity of opinion. Clear as we may think the arguments against despotism, there ever have been thousands of enlightened and good men, who honestly believe it to be of all forms of government the best and most acceptable to God. Unless we can approach the consciences of men, clothed with some more imposing authority than that of our own opinions and arguments, we shall gain little permanent influence. Men are too nearly upon a par as to their powers of reasoning, and ability to discover truth, to make the conclusions of one mind an authoritative rule for others. It is our object, therefore, not to discuss the subject of slavery upon abstract principles, but to ascertain the scriptural rule of judgment and conduct in relation to it. We do not intend to enter upon any minute or extended examination of scriptural passages, because all that we wish to assume, as to the meaning of the word of God, is so generally admitted as to render the labored proof of it unnecessary.

It is on all hands acknowledged that, at the time of the advent of Jesus Christ, slavery in its worst forms prevailed over the whole world. The Saviour found it around him in Judea; the apostles met with it in Asia, Greece and Italy. How did they treat it? Not by the denunciation of slaveholding as necessarily and universally sinful. Not by declaring that all slaveholders were men-stealers and robbers, and consequently to be excluded from the church and the kingdom of heaven. Not by insisting on immediate emancipation. Not by appeals to the passions of men on the evils of slavery, or by the adoption of a system of universal agitation. On the contrary, it was by teaching the true nature, dignity, equality and destiny of men; by inculcating the principles of justice and love; and by leaving these principles to produce their legitimate effects in ameliorating the condition of all classes of society. We need not stop to prove that such was the course pursued by our Saviour and his apostles, because the fact is in general acknowledged, and various reasons are assigned, by the abolitionists and others, to account for it. The subject is hardly alluded to by Christ in any of his personal instructions. The apostles refer to it, not to pronounce upon it as a question of morals, put to prescribe the relative duties of masters and slaves. They caution those slaves who have believing or Christian masters, not to despise them because they were on a perfect religious equality with them, but to consider the fact that their masters were their brethren, as an additional reason for obedience. It is remarkable that there is not even an exhortation to masters to liberate their slaves, much less is it urged as an imperative and immediate duty. They are commanded to be kind, merciful and just; and to remember that they have a Master in heaven. Paul represents this relation as of comparatively little account: "Let every man abide in the same calling wherein he was called. Art thou called being a servant (or slave), care not for it; though, should the opportunity of freedom be presented, embrace it. These external relations, however, are of little importance, for every Christian is a freeman in the highest and best sense of the word, and at the same time is under the strongest bonds to Christ," 1 Cor. vii: 20-22. It is not worth while to shut our eyes to these facts. They will remain, whether we refuse to see them and be instructed by them or not. If we are wiser, better, more courageous than Christ and his apostles, let us say so; but it will do no good, under a paroxysm of benevolence, to attempt to tear the Bible to pieces, or to exhort, by violent exegesis, a meaning foreign to its obvious sense. Whatever inferences may be fairly deducible from the fact, the fact itself can not be denied that Christ and his inspired followers did treat the subject of slavery in the manner stated above. This being the case, we ought carefully to consider their conduct in this respect, and inquire what lessons that conduct should teach us.

We think no one will deny that the plan adopted by the Saviour and his immediate followers must be the correct plan, and therefore obligatory upon us, unless it can be shown that their circumstances were so different from ours, as to make the rule of duty different in the two cases. The obligation to point out and establish this difference, rests of course upon those who have adopted a course diametrically the reverse of that which Christ pursued. They have not acquitted themselves of this obligation. They do not seem to have felt it necessary to reconcile their conduct with his; nor does it appear to have occurred to them, that their violent denunciations of slaveholding and of slaveholders is an indirect reflection on his wisdom, virtue, or courage. If the present course of the abolitionists is right, then the course of Christ and the apostles were wrong. For the circumstances of the two cases are, as far as we can see, in all essential particulars, the same. They appeared as teachers of morality and religion, not as politicians. The same is the fact with our abolitionists. They found slavery authorized by the laws of the land. So do we. They were called upon to receive into the communion of the Christian Church, both slave owners and slaves. So are we. They instructed these different classes of persons as to their respective duties. So do we. Where then is the difference between the two cases? If we are right in insisting that slaveholding is one of the greatest of all sins; that it should be immediately and universally abandoned as a condition of church communion, or admission into heaven, how comes it that Christ and his apostles did not pursue the same course? We see no way of escape from the conclusion that the conduct of the modern abolitionists, being directly opposed to that of the authors of our religion, must be wrong and ought to be modified or abandoned.

An equally obvious deduction from the fact above referred to, is, that slaveholding is not necessarily sinful. The assumption of the contrary is the great reason why the modern abolitionists have adopted their peculiar course. They argue thus: slaveholding is under all circumstances sinful, it must, therefore, under all circumstances, and at all hazards, be immediately abandoned. This reasoning is perfectly conclusive. If there is error any where, it is in the premises, and not in the deduction. It requires no argument to show that sin ought to be at once abandoned. Every thing, therefore, is conceded which the abolitionists need require, when it is granted that slaveholding is in itself a crime. But how can this assumption be reconciled with the conduct of Christ and the apostles? Did they shut their eyes to the enormities of a great offence against God and man? Did they temporize with a henious evil, because it was common and popular? Did they abstain from even exhorting masters to emancipate their slaves, though an imperative duty, from fear of consequences? Did they admit the perpetrators of the greatest crimes to the Christian communion? Who will undertake to charge the blessed Redeemer and his inspired followers with such connivance at sin, and such fellowship with iniquity? Were drunkards, murderers, liars, and adulterers thus treated? Were they passed over without even an exhortation to forsake their sins? Were they recognized as Christians? It can not be that slaveholding belongs to the same category with these crimes; and to assert the contrary, is to assert that Christ is the minister of sin.

This is a point of so much importance, lying as it does at the very foundation of the whole subject, that it deserves to be attentively considered. The grand mistake, as we apprehend, of those who maintain that slaveholding is itself a crime, is, that they do not discriminate between slaveholding in itself considered, and its accessories at any particular time or place. Because masters may treat their slaves unjustly, or governments make oppressive laws in relation to them, is no more a valid argument against the lawfulness of slaveholding, than the abuse of parental authority, or the unjust political laws of certain states, is an argument against the lawfulness of the parental relation, or of civil government. This confusion of points so widely distinct, appears to us to run through almost all the popular publications on slavery, and to vitiate their arguments. Mr. Jay, for example, quotes the second article of the constitution of the American Anti-Slavery Society, which declares that "slaveholding is a heinous crime in the sight of God," and then, to justify this declaration, makes large citations from the laws of the several Southern States, to show what the system of slavery is in this country, and concludes by saying, "This is the system which the American Anti-Slavery Society declares to be sinful, and ought therefore to be immediately abolished." There is, however, no necessary connection between his premises and conclusion. We may admit all those laws which forbid the instruction of slaves; which interfere with their marital or parental rights; which subject them to the insults and oppression of the whites, to be in the highest degree unjust, without at all admit-admitting that slaveholding itself is a crime. Slavery may exist without any one of these concomitants. In pronouncing on the moral character of an act, it is obviously necessary to have a clear idea of what it is; yet how few of those who denounce slavery, have any well-defined conception of its nature. They have a confused idea of chains and whips, of degradation and misery, of ignorance and vice, and to this complex conception they apply the name slavery, and denounce it as the aggregate of all moral and physical evil. Do such persons suppose that slavery, as it existed in the family of Abraham, was such as their imaginations thus picture to themselves? Might not that patriarch have had men purchased with his silver who were well clothed, well instructed, well compensated for their labor, and in all respects treated with parental kindness? Neither inadequate remuneration, physical discomfort, intellectual ignorance, moral degradation, is essential to the condition of a slave. Yet if all these ideas are removed from the commonly received notion of slavery, how little will remain. All the ideas which necessarily enter into the definition of slavery are deprivation of personal liberty, obligation of service at the discretion of another, and the transferable character of the authority and claim of service of the master.[263] The manner in which men are brought into this condition; its continuance, and the means adopted for securing the authority and claim of masters, are all incidental and variable. They may be reasonable or unreasonable, just or unjust, at different times and places. The question, therefore, which the abolitionists have undertaken to decide, is not whether the laws enacted in the slaveholding States in relation to this subject are just or not, but whether slaveholding, in itself considered, is a crime. The confusion of these two points has not only brought the abolitionists into conflict with the Scriptures, but it has, as a necessary consequence, prevented their gaining the confidence of the North, or power over the conscience of the South. When Southern Christians are told that they are guilty of a heinous crime, worse than piracy, robbery, or murder, because they hold slaves, when they know that Christ and his apostles never denounced slaveholding as a crime, never called upon men to renounce it as a condition of admission into the church, they are shocked and offended, without being convinced. They are sure that their accusers can not be wiser or better than their divine Master, and their consciences are untouched by denunciations which they know, if well founded, must affect not them only, but the authors of the religion of the Bible.

The argument from the conduct of Christ and his immediate followers, seems to us decisive on the point, that slaveholding, in itself considered, is not a crime. Let us see how this argument has been answered. In the able "Address to the Presbyterians of Kentucky, proposing a plan for the instruction and emancipation of their slaves, by a committee of the Synod of Kentucky," there is a strong and extended argument to prove the sinfulness of slavery, *as it exists among us*, to which we have little to object. When, however, the distinguished draughter of that address comes to answer the objection, "God's word sanctions slavery, and it can not, therefore, be sinful," he forgets the essential limitation of the proposition which he had undertaken to establish, and proceeds to prove that the Bible condemns slaveholding, and not merely the kind or system of slavery which prevails in this country. The argument drawn from the Scriptures, he says, needs no elaborate reply. If the Bible sanctions slavery, it sanctions the kind of slavery which then prevailed; the atrocious system which authorized masters to starve their slaves, to torture them, to beat them, to put them to death, and to throw them into their fish ponds. And he justly asks, whether a man could insult the God of heaven worse than by saying he does not disapprove of such a system? Dr. Channing presents strongly the same view, and says, that an infidel would be laboring in his vocation in asserting that the Bible does not condemn slavery. These gentlemen, however, are far too clear-sighted not to discover, on a moment's reflection, that they have allowed their benevolent feelings to blind them to the real point at issue. No one denies that the Bible condemns all injustice, cruelty, oppression, and violence. And just so far as the laws then existing authorized these crimes, the Bible condemned them. But what stronger argument can be presented, to prove that the sacred writers did not regard slaveholding as in itself sinful, than that while they condemn all unjust or unkind treatment (even threatening), on the part of masters towards their slaves, they did not condemn slavery itself? While they required the master to treat his slave according to the law of love, they did not command him to set him free. The very atrocity, therefore, of the system which then prevailed, instead of weakening the argument, gives it tenfold strength. Then, if ever, when the institution was so fearfully abused, we might expect to hear the interpreters of the divine will, saying that a system which leads to such results is the concentrated essence of all crimes, and must be instantly abandoned, on pain of eternal condemnation. This, however, they did not say, and we can not now force them to say it. They treated the subject precisely as they did the cruel despotism of the Roman emperors. The licentiousness, the injustice, the rapine and murders of those wicked men, they condemned with the full force of divine authority; but the mere extent of their power, though so liable to abuse, they left unnoticed.

Another answer to the argument in question is, that "The New Testament does condemn slaveholding, as *practiced among us*, in the most explicit terms furnished by the language in which the sacred penman wrote." This assertion is supported by saying that God has condemned slavery, because he has specified the parts which compose it and condemned them, one by one, in the most ample and unequivocal form.[264] It is to be remarked that the saving clause "slaveholding *as it exists among us*," is introduced into the statement, though it seems to be lost sight of in the illustration and confirmation of it which follow. We readily admit, that if God does condemn all the parts of which slavery consists, he condemns slavery itself. But the draughter of the address has made no attempt to prove that this is actually done in the sacred Scriptures. That many of the attributes of the system as established by law in this country, are condemned, is indeed very plain; but that slaveholding in itself is condemned, has not been and can not be proved. The writer, indeed, says, "The Greek language had a word corresponding exactly, in signification, with our word servant, but it had none which answered precisely to our term slave. How then was an apostle writing in Greek, to condemn our slavery? How can we expect to find in Scripture, the words 'slavery is sinful,' when the language in which it is written contained no term which expressed the meaning of our word slavery?" Does the gentleman mean to say the Greek language could not express the idea that slaveholding is sinful? Could not the apostles have communicated the thought that it was the duty of masters to set their slaves free? Were they obliged from paucity of words to admit slaveholders into the Church? We have no doubt the writer himself could, with all ease, pen a declaration in the Greek language void of all ambiguity, proclaiming freedom to every slave upon earth, and denouncing the vengeance of heaven upon every man who dared to hold a fellow creature in bondage. It is not words we care for. We want evidence that the sacred writers taught that it was incumbent on every slaveholder, as a matter of duty, to emancipate his slaves (which no Roman or Greek law forbade), and that his refusing to do so was a heinous crime in the sight of God. The Greek language must be poor indeed if it can not convey such ideas.

Another answer is given by Dr. Channing. "Slavery," he says, "in the age of the apostle, had so penetrated society, was so intimately interwoven with it, and the materials of servile war were so abundant, that a religion, preaching freedom to its victims, would have armed against itself the whole power of the State. Of consequence Paul did not assail it. He satisfied himself with spreading principles, which, however slowly, could not but work its destruction." To the same effect, Dr. Wayland says, "The gospel was designed, not for one race or one time, but for all men and for all times. It looked not at the abolition of this form of evil for that age alone, but for its universal abolition. Hence the important object of its author was to gain it a lodgment in every part of the known world; so that, by its universal diffusion among all classes of society, it might quietly and peacefully modify and subdue the evil passions of men; and thus, without violence, work a revolution in the whole mass of mankind. In this manner alone could its object, a universal moral revolution, be accomplished. For if it had forbidden the *evil* without subduing the *principle*, if it had proclaimed the unlawfulness of slavery, and taught slaves to *resist* the oppression of their masters, it would instantly have arrayed the two parties in deadly hostility throughout the civilized world; its announcement would have been the signal of a servile war; and the very name of the Christian religion would have been forgotten amidst the agitations of universal bloodshed. The fact, under these circumstances, that the gospel does not forbid slavery, affords no reason to suppose that it does not mean to prohibit it, much less does it afford ground for belief that Jesus Christ intended to authorize it."[265]

Before considering the force of this reasoning, it may be well to notice one or two important admissions contained in these extracts. First, then, it is admitted by these distinguished moralists, that the apostles did not preach a religion proclaiming freedom to slaves; that Paul did not assail slavery; that the gospel did not proclaim the unlawfulness of slaveholding; it did not forbid it. This is going the whole length that we have gone in our statement of the conduct of Christ and his apostles, Secondly, these writers admit that the course adopted by the authors of our religion was the only wise and proper one. Paul satisfied himself, says Dr. Channing, with spreading principles, which, however slowly, could not but work its destruction. Dr. Wayland says, that if the apostles had pursued the opposite plan of denouncing slavery as a crime, the Christian religion would have been ruined; its very name would have been forgotten. Then how can the course of the modern abolitionists, under circumstances so nearly similar, or even that of these reverend gentlemen themselves be right? Why do not they content themselves with doing what Christ and his apostles did? Why must they proclaim the unlawfulness of slavery? Is human nature so much altered, that a course, which would have produced universal bloodshed, and led to the very destruction of the Christian religion, in one age, wise and Christian in another?

Let us, however, consider the force of the argument as stated above. It amounts to this: Christ and his apostles thought slaveholding a great crime, but they abstained from saying so, for fear of the consequences. The very statement of the argument, in its naked form, is its refutation. These holy men did not refrain from condemning sin from a regard to consequences. They did not hesitate to array against the religion which they taught, the strongest passions of men. Nor did they content themselves with denouncing the general principles of evil; they condemned its special manifestations. They did not simply forbid intemperate sensual indulgence, and leave it to their hearers to decide what did or what did not come under that name. They declared that no fornicator, no adulterer, no drunkard could be admitted into the kingdom of heaven. They did not hesitate, even when a little band, a hundred and twenty souls, to place themselves in direct and irreconcilable opposition to the whole polity, civil and religious, of the Jewish State. It will hardly be maintained that slavery was, at that time, more intimately interwoven with the institutions of society than idolatry was. It entered into the arrangements of every family; of every city and province, and of the whole Roman empire. The emperor was the Pontifex Maximus; every department of the State, civil and military, was pervaded by it. It was so united with the fabric of the government that it could not be removed without effecting a revolution in all its parts. The apostles knew this. They knew that to denounce polytheism, was to array against them the whole power of the State. Their divine Master had distinctly apprized them of the result. He told them that it would set the father against the son, and the son against the father; the mother against the daughter, and the daughter against the mother; and that a man's enemies should be those of his own household. He said that he came not to bring peace, but a sword, and that such would be the opposition to his followers, that whosoever killed them, would think he did God service. Yet in view of these certain consequences, the apostles did denounce idolatry, not merely in principle, but by name. The result was precisely what Christ had foretold. The Romans, tolerant of every other religion, bent the whole force of their wisdom and arms to extirpate Christianity. The scenes of bloodshed, which century after century followed the introduction of the gospel, did not induce the followers of Christ to keep back or modify the truth. They adhered to their declaration, that idolatry was a heinous crime. And they were right. We expect similar conduct of our missionaries. We do not expect them to refrain from denouncing the institutions of the heathen, as sinful, because they are popular, or intimately interwoven with society. The Jesuits, who adopted this plan, forfeited the confidence of Christendom, without making converts of the heathen. It is, therefore, perfectly evident that the authors of our religion were not withheld by these considerations, from declaring slavery to be unlawful. If they did abstain from this declaration, as is admitted, it must have been because they did not consider it as in itself a crime. No other solution of their conduct is consistent with their truth or fidelity.

Another answer to the argument from Scripture is given by Dr. Channing and others. It is said that it proves too much; that it makes the Bible sanction despotism, even the despotism of Nero. Our reply to this objection shall be very brief. We have already pointed out the fallacy of confounding slaveholding itself with the particular system of slavery prevalent at the time of Christ, and shown that the recognition of slaveholders as Christians, though irreconcilable with the assumption that slavery is a heinous crime, gives no manner of sanction to the atrocious laws and customs of that age, in relation to that subject. Because the apostles admitted the masters of slaves to the communion of the church, it would be a strange inference that they would have given this testimony to the Christian character of the master who oppressed, starved, or murdered his slaves. Such a master would have been rejected as an oppressor, or murderer, however, not as a slaveholder. In like manner, the declaration that government is an ordinance of God, that magistrates are to be obeyed within the sphere of their lawful authority; that resistance to them, when in the exercise of that authority, is sinful,[266] gives no sanction to the oppression of the Roman emperors, or to the petty vexations of provincial officers. The argument urged from Scripture in favor of passive submission, is not so exactly parallel with the argument for slavery, as Dr. Channing supposes. They agree in some points, but they differ in others. The former is founded upon a false interpretation of Rom. xiii: 1-3; it supposes that passage to mean what it does not mean, whereas the latter is founded upon the sense which Dr. C. and other opponents of slavery, admit to be the true sense. This must be allowed to alter the case materially. Again, the argument for the lawfulness of slaveholding, is not founded on the mere injunction, "Slaves, obey your masters," analagous to the command, "Let every soul be subject to the higher powers," but on the fact that the apostles did not condemn slavery; that they did not require emancipation, and that they recognized slaveholders as Christian brethren. To make Dr. Channing's argument of any force, it must be shown that Paul not only enjoined obedience to a despotic monarch, but that he recognized Nero as a Christian. When this is done, then we shall admit that our argument is fairly met, and that it is just as true that he sanctioned the conduct of Nero, as that he acknowledged the lawfulness of slavery.

The two cases, however, are analogous as to one important point. The fact that Paul enjoins obedience under a despotic government, is a valid argument to prove, not that he sanctioned the conduct of the reigning Roman emperor, but that he did not consider the possession of despotic power a crime. The argument of Dr. C. would be far stronger, and the two cases more exactly parallel, had one of the emperors become a penitent believer during the apostolic age, and been admitted to the Christian church by inspired men, notwithstanding the fact that he retained his office and authority. But even without this latter decisive circumstance, we acknowledge that the mere holding of despotic power is proved not to be a crime by the fact that the apostles enjoined obedience to those who exercised it. Thus far the arguments are analogous; and they prove that both political despotism and domestic slavery, belong in morals to the *adiaphora*, to things indifferent. They may be expedient or inexpedient, right or wrong, according to circumstances. Belonging to the same class, they should be treated in the same way. Neither is to be denounced as necessarily sinful, and to be abolished immediately under all circumstances and at all hazards. Both should be left to the operation of those general principles of the gospel, which have peacefully ameliorated political institutions, and destroyed domestic slavery throughout the greater part of Christendom.

The truth on this subject is so obvious that it sometimes escapes unconsciously from the lips of the most strenuous abolitionists. Mr. Birney says: "He would have retained the power and authority of an emperor; yet his oppressions, his cruelties would have ceased; the very temper that prompted them, would have been suppressed; his power would have been put forth for good and not for evil."[267] Here every thing is conceded. The possession of despotic power is thus admitted not to be a crime, even when it extends over millions of men, and subjects their lives as well as their property and services to the will of an individual. What becomes then of the arguments and denunciations of slaveholding, which is despotism on a small scale? Would Mr. Birney continue in the deliberate practice of a crime worse than robbery, piracy, or murder? When he penned the above sentiment, he must have seen that neither by the law of God nor of reason is it necessarily sinful to sustain the relation of master over our fellow creatures; that if this unlimited authority be used for the good of those over whom it extends and for the glory of God, its possessor may be one of the best and most useful of men. It is the abuse of this power for base and selfish purposes which constitutes criminality, and not its simple possession. He may say that the tendency to abuse absolute power is so great that it ought never to be confided to the hands of men. This, as a general rule, is no doubt true, and establishes the inexpediency of all despotic governments, whether for the state or the family. But it leaves the morality of the question just where it was, and where it was seen to be, when Mr. Birney said he could with a good conscience be a Roman emperor, *i. e.* the master of millions of slaves.

The consideration of the Old Testament economy leads us to the same conclusion on this subject. It is not denied that slavery was tolerated among the ancient people of God. Abraham had servants in his family who were "bought with his money," Gen. xvii: 13. "Abimeleck took sheep and oxen and men servants and maid servants and gave them unto Abraham." Moses, finding this institution among the Hebrews and all surrounding nations, did not abolish it. He enacted laws directing how slaves were to be treated, on what conditions they were to be liberated, under what circumstances they might and might not be sold; he recognizes the distinction between slaves and hired servants, (Deut. xv: 18); he speaks of the way by which these bondmen might be procured; as by war, by purchase, by the right of creditorship, by the sentence of a judge, by birth; but not by seizing on those who were free, an offense punished by death.[268] The fact that the Mosaic institutions recognized the lawfulness of slavery is a point too plain to need proof, and is almost universally admitted. Our argument from this acknowledged fact is, that if God allowed slavery to exist, if he directed how slaves might be lawfully acquired, and how they were to be treated, it is in vain to contend that slaveholding is a sin, and yet profess reverence for the Scriptures. Every one must feel that if perjury, murder, or idolatry had been thus authorized, it would bring the Mosaic institutions into conflict with the eternal principles of morals, and that our faith in the divine origin of one or the other must be given up.

Dr. Channing says, of this argument also, that it proves too much. "If usages, sanctioned under the Old Testament and not forbidden under the New, are right, then our moral code will undergo a sad deterioration. Polygamy was allowed to the Israelites, was the practice of the holiest men, and was common and licensed in the age of the apostles. But the apostles no where condemn it, nor was the renunciation of it made an essential condition of admission into the Christian Church." To this we answer, that so far as polygamy and divorce were permitted under the old dispensation, they were lawful, and became so by that permission; and they ceased to be lawful when the permission was withdrawn, and a new law given. That Christ did give a new law on this subject is abundantly evident.[269] With regard to divorce, it is as explicit as language can make it; and with regard to polygamy it is so plain as to have secured the assent of every portion of the Christian churches in all ages. The very fact that there has been no diversity of opinion or practice among Christians with regard to polygamy, is itself decisive evidence that the will of Christ was clearly revealed on the subject. The temptation to continue the practice was as strong, both from the passions of men, and the sanction of prior ages, as in regard to slavery. Yet we find no traces of the toleration of polygamy in the Christian church, though slavery long continued to prevail. There is no evidence that the apostles admitted to the fellowship of Christians, those who were guilty of this infraction of the law of marriage. It is indeed possible that in cases where the converts had already more than one wife, the connection was not broken off. It is evident this must have occasioned great evil. It would lead to the breaking up of families, the separation of parents and children, as well as husbands and wives. Under these circumstances the connection may have been allowed to continue. It is however very doubtful whether even this was permitted. It is remarkable that among the numerous cases of conscience connected with marriage, submitted to the apostles, this never occurs.

Dr. Channing uses language much too strong when he says that polygamy was common and licensed in the days of the apostles. It was contrary both to Roman and Grecian laws and usages until the most degenerate periods of the history of those nations. It was very far from being customary among the Jews, though it might have been allowed. It is probable that it was, therefore, comparatively extremely rare in the apostolic age. This accounts for the fact that scarcely any notice is taken of, the practice in the New Testament. Wherever marriage is spoken of, it seems to be taken for granted, as a well understood fact, that it was a contract for life between one man and one woman; compare Rom. vii: 2, 3. 1 Cor. vii: 1, 2, 39. It is further to be remarked on this subject, that marriage is a positive institution. If God had ordained that every man should have two or more wives, instead of one, polygamy would have been lawful. But slaveholding is denounced as a *malum in se;* as essentially unjust and wicked. This being the case, it could at no period of the world receive the divine sanction, much less could it have continued in the Christian church under the direction of inspired men, when there was nothing to prevent its immediate abolition. The answer then of Dr. Channing is unsatisfactory, first, because polygamy does not belong to the same category in morals as that to which slaveholding is affirmed to belong; and secondly, because it was so plainly prohibited by Christ and his apostles as to secure the assent of all Christians in all ages of the church.

It is, however, argued that slavery must be sinful because it interferes with the inalienable rights of men. We have already remarked, that slavery, in itself considered, is a state of bondage, and nothing more. It is the condition of an individual who is deprived of his personal liberty, and is obliged to labor for another, who has the right to transfer this claim of service, at pleasure. That this condition involves the loss of many of the rights which are commonly and properly called natural, because belonging to men, as men, is readily admitted. It is, however, incumbent on those who maintain that slavery is, on this account, necessarily sinful, to show that it is criminal, under all circumstances, to deprive any set of men of a portion of their natural rights. That this broad proposition can not be maintained is evident. The very constitution of society supposes the forfeiture of a greater or less amount of these rights, according to its peculiar organization. That it is not only the privilege, but the duty of men to live together in a regularly organized society, is evident from the nature which God has given us; from the impossibility of every man living by and for himself, and from the express declarations of the word of God. The object of the formation of society is the promotion of human virtue and happiness; and the form in which it should be organized, is that which will best secure the attainment of this object.

As, however, the condition of men is so very various, it is impossible that the same form should be equally conducive to happiness and virtue under all circumstances. No one form, therefore, is prescribed in the Bible, or is universally obligatory. The question which form is, under given circumstances, to be adopted, is one of great practical difficulty, and must be left to the decision of those who have the power to decide, on their own responsibility. The question, however, does not depend upon the degree in which these several forms may encroach upon the natural rights of men. In the patriarchal age, the most natural, the most feasible, and perhaps the most beneficial form of government was by the head of the family. His power by the law of nature, and the necessity of the case, extended without any other limit than the general principles of morals, over his children, and in the absence of other regular authority, would not terminate when the children arrived at a particular age, but be continued during life. He was the natural umpire between his adult offspring, he was their lawgiver and leader. His authority would naturally extend over his more remote descendants, as they continued to increase, and on his death, might devolve on the next oldest of the family. There is surely nothing in this mode of constituting society which is necessarily immoral. If found to be conducive to the general good, it might be indefinitely continued. It would not suffice to render its abrogation obligatory, to say that all men are born free and equal; that the youth of twenty-one had as good a right to have a voice in the affairs of the family as the aged patriarch; that the right of self-government is indefeasible, etc. Unless it could be shown that the great end of society was not attainable by this mode of organization, and that it would be more securely promoted by some other, it would be an immorality to require or to effect the change. And if a change became, in the course of time, obviously desirable, its nature and extent would be questions to be determined by the peculiar circumstances of the case, and not by the rule of abstract rights. Under some circumstances it might be requisite to confine the legislative power to a single individual; under others to the hands of a few; and under others to commit it to the whole community. It would be absurd to maintain, on the ground of the natural equality of men, that a horde of ignorant and vicious savages, should be organized as a pure democracy, if experience taught that such a form of government was destructive to themselves and others. These different modes of constituting civil society are not necessarily either just or unjust, but become the one or the other according to circumstances; and their morality is not determined by the degree in which they encroach upon the natural rights of men, but on the degree in which they promote or retard the progress of human happiness and virtue. In this country we believe that the general good requires us to deprive the whole female sex of the right of self-government. They have no voice in the formation of the laws which dispose of their persons and property. When married, we despoil them almost entirely of a legal existence, and deny them some of the most essential rights of property. We treat all minors much in the same way, depriving them of many personal and almost all political rights, and that too though they may be far more competent to exercise them aright than many adults. We, moreover, decide that a majority of one may make laws for the whole community, no matter whether the numerical majority have more wisdom or virtue than the minority or not. Our plea for all this is, that the good of the whole is thereby most effectually promoted. This plea, if made out, justifies the case. In England and France they believe that the good of the whole requires that the right of governing, instead of being restricted, to all adult males, as we arbitrarily determine, should be confined to that portion of the male population who hold a given amount of property. In Prussia and Russia, they believe with equal confidence, that public security and happiness demand that all power should be in the hands of the king. If they are right in their opinion, they are right in their practice. The principle that social and political organizations are designed for the general good, of course requires they should be allowed to change, as the progress of society may demand. It is very possible that the feudal system may have been well adapted to the state of Europe in the middle ages. The change in the condition of the world, however, has gradually obliterated almost all its features. The villein has become the independent farmer; the lord of the manor, the simple landlord; and the sovereign leige, in whom, according to the fiction of the system, the fee of the whole country vested, has become a constitutional monarch. It may be that another series of changes may convert the tenant into an owner, the lord into a rich commoner, and the monarch into a president. Though these changes have resulted in giving the people the enjoyment of a larger amount of their rights than they formerly possessed, it is not hence to be inferred that they ought centuries ago to have been introduced suddenly or by violence. Christianity "operates as alterative." It was never designed to tear up the institutions of society by the roots. It produces equality not by prostrating trees of all sizes to the ground, but by securing to all the opportunity of growing, and by causing all to grow, until the original disparity is no longer perceptible. All attempts, by human wisdom, to frame society, of a sudden, after a pattern cut by the rule of abstract rights, have failed; and whether they had failed or not, they can never be urged as a matter of moral obligation. It is not enough, therefore, in order to prove the sinfulness of slaveholding, to show that it interferes with the natural rights of a portion of the community. It is in this respect analagous to all other social institutions. They are all of them encroachments on human rights, from the freest democracy to the most absolute despotism.

It is further to be remarked, that all these rights suppose corresponding duties, and where there is an incompetence for the duty, the claim to exercise the right ceases. No man can justly claim the exercise of any right to the injury of the community of which he is a member. It is because females and minors are judged (though for different reasons), incompetent to the proper discharge of the duties of citizenship, that they are deprived of the right of suffrage. It is on the same principle that a large portion of the inhabitants of France and England are deprived of the same privilege. As it is acknowledged that the slaves may be justly deprived of political rights, on the ground of their incompetency to exercise them without injury to the community, it must be admitted, by parity of reason, that they may be justly deprived of personal freedom, if incompetent to exercise it with safety to society. If this be so, then slavery is a question of circumstances, and not a *malum in se*. It must be borne in mind that the object of these remarks is not to prove that the American, the British, or the Russian form of society, is expedient or otherwise; much less to show that the slaves in this country are actually unfit for freedom, but simply to prove that the mere fact that slaveholding interferes with natural rights, is not enough to justify the conclusion that it is necessarily and universally sinful.

Another very common and plausible argument on this subject is, that a man can not be made a matter of property. He can not be degraded into a brute or chattel, without the grossest violation of duty and propriety; and that as slavery confers this right of property in human beings, it must, from its very nature, be a crime. We acknowledge the correctness of the principle on which this argument is founded, but deny that it is applicable to the case in hand. We admit that it is not only an enormity, but an impossibility, that a man should be made a thing, as distinguished from a rational and moral being. It is not within the compass of human law to alter the nature of God's creatures. A man must be regarded and treated as a rational being, even in his greatest degradation. That he is, in some countries and under some institutions, deprived of many of the rights and privileges of such a being, does not alter his nature. He must be viewed as a man under the most atrocious system of slavery that ever existed. Men do not arraign and try on evidence, and punish on conviction, either things or brutes. Yet slaves are under a regular system of laws which, however unjust they may be, recognize their character as accountable beings. When it is inferred from the fact that the slave is called the property of his master, that he is thereby degraded from his rank as a human being, the argument rests on the vagueness of the term *property*. Property is the right of possession and use, and must of necessity vary according to the nature of the objects to which it attaches. A man has property in his wife, in his children, in his domestic animals, in his fields and in his forests. That is, he has the right to the possession and use of these several objects, according to their nature. He has no more right to use a brute as a log of wood, in virtue of the right of property, than he has to use a man as a brute. There are general principles of rectitude, obligatory on all men, which require them to treat all the creatures of God according to the nature which he has given them. The man who should burn his horse because he was his property, would find no justification in that plea, either before God or man. When, therefore, it is said that one man is the property of another, it can only mean that the one has a right to use the other *as a man*, but not as a brute, or as a thing. He has no right to treat him as he may lawfully treat his ox, or a tree. He can convert his person to no use to which a human being may not, by the laws of God and nature, be properly applied. When this idea of property comes to be analyzed, it is found to be nothing more than a claim of service either for life or for a term of years. This claim is transferable, and is of the nature of property, and is consequently liable for the debts of the owner, and subject to his disposal by will or otherwise. It is probable that the slave is called the property of his master in the statute books, for the same reason that children are called the servants of the parents, or

675

that wives are said to be the same person with their husbands, and to have no separate existence of their own. These are mere technicalities, designed to facilitate certain legal processes. Calling a child a servant, does not alter his relation to his father; and a wife is still a woman, though the courts may rule her out of existence. In like manner, where the law declares, that a slave shall be deemed and adjudged to be a chattel personal in the hands of his master, it does not alter his nature, nor does it confer on the master any right to use him in a manner inconsistent with that nature. As there are certain moral principles which direct how brutes are to be used by those to whom they belong, so there are fixed principles which determine how a man may be used. These legal enactments, therefore, are not intended to legislate away the nature of the slave, as a human being; they serve to facilitate the transfer of the master's claim of service, and to render that claim the more readily liable for his debts. The transfer of authority and claim of service from one master to another, is, in principle, analogous to transfer of subjects from one sovereign to another. This is a matter of frequent occurrence. By the treaty of Vienna, for example, a large part of the inhabitants of central Europe changed masters. Nearly half of Saxony was transferred to Prussia; Belgium was annexed to Holland. In like manner, Louisiana was transferred from France to the United States. In none of these cases were the people consulted. Yet in all, a claim of service more or less extended, was made over from one power to another. There was a change of masters. The mere transferable character of the master's claim to the slave, does not convert the latter into a thing, or degrade him from his rank as a human being. Nor does the fact that he is bound to serve for life, produce this effect. It is only property in his time for life, instead of for a term of years. The nature of the relation is not determined by the period of its continuance.

It has, however, been argued that the slave is the property of his master, not only in the sense admitted above, but in the sense assumed in the objection, because his children are under the same obligation of service as the parent. The hereditary character of slavery, however, does not arise out of the idea of the slave as a chattel or thing, a mere matter of property, it depends on the organization of society. In England one man is born a peer, another a commoner; in Russia one man is born a noble, another a serf; here, one is born a free citizen, another a disfranchised outcast (the free colored man), and a third a slave. These forms of society, as before remarked, are not necessarily, or in themselves, either just or unjust; but become the one or the other, according to circumstances. Under a state of things in which the best interests of the community would be promoted by the British or Russian organization, they would be just and acceptable to God; but under circumstances in which they would be injurious, they would be unjust. It is absolutely necessary, however, to discriminate between an organization essentially vicious, and one which, being in itself indifferent, may be right or wrong, according to circumstances. On the same principle, therefore, that a human being in England is deprived, by the mere accident of birth, of the right of suffrage, and in Russia has the small portion of liberty which belongs to a commoner, or the still smaller belonging to a serf, in this country one class is by birth invested with all the rights of citizenship, another (females) is deprived all political and many personal rights, and a third of even their personal liberty. Whether this organization be right or wrong, is not now the question. We are simply showing that the fact that the children of slaves become by birth slaves, is not to be referred to the idea of the master's property in the body and soul of the parent, but results from the form of society, and is analagous to other social institutions, as far as the principle is concerned, that children take the rank, or the political or social condition of the parent.

We prefer being chargeable with the sin of wearisome repetition, to leaving any room for the misapprehension of our meaning. We, therefore, again remark that we are discussing the mere abstract morality of these forms of social organization, and not their expediency. We have in view the vindication of the character of the inspired writings and inspired men from the charge of having overlooked the blackest of human crimes, and of having recognized the worst of human beings as Christians. We say, therefore, that an institution which deprives a certain portion of the community of their personal liberty, places them under obligation of service to another portion, is no more necessarily sinful than one which invests an individual with despotic power (such as Mr. Birney would consent to hold); or than one which limits the right of government to a small portion of the people, or restricts it to the male part of the community. However inexpedient, under certain circumstances, any one of these arrangements may be, they are not necessarily immoral, nor do they become such, from the fact that the accident of birth determines the relation in which one part of the community is to stand to the other. In ancient Egypt, as in modern India, birth decided the position and profession of every individual. One was born a priest, another a merchant, another a laborer, another a soldier. As there must always be these classes, it is no more necessarily immoral, to have them all determined by hereditary descent, than it was among the Israelites to have all the officers of religion from generation to generation thus determined; or that birth should determine the individual who is to fill a throne, or occupy a seat in parliament.

Again, Dr. Wayland argues, if the right to hold slaves be conceded, "there is of course conceded all other rights necessary to insure its possession. Hence, inasmuch as the slave can be held in this condition only while he remains in the lowest state of mental imbecility, it supposes the master to have the right to control his intellectual development just as far as may be necessary to secure entire subjection."[270] He reasons in the same way, to show that the religious knowledge and even eternal happiness of the slave are as a matter of right conceded to the power of the master, if the right of slaveholding is admitted. The utmost force that can be allowed to this argument is, that the right to hold slaves includes the right to exercise all *proper* means to insure its possession. It is in this respect on a par with all other rights of the same kind. The right of parents to the service of their children, of husbands to the obedience of their wives, of masters over their apprentices, of creditors over their debtors, of rulers over their subjects, all suppose the right to adopt proper means for their secure enjoyment. They, however, give no sanction to the employment of any and every means which cruelty, suspicion, or jealousy may choose to deem necessary, nor of any which would be productive of greater general evil than the forfeiture of the rights themselves. According to the ancient law even among the Jews, the power of life and death was granted to the parent; we concede only the power of correction. The old law gave the same power to the husband over the wife. The Roman law confided the person and even life of the debtor to the mercy of the creditor. According to the reasoning of Dr. Wayland, all these laws must be sanctioned if the rights which they were deemed necessary to secure, are acknowledged. It is clear, however, that the most unrighteous means may be adopted to secure a proper end, under the plea of necessity. The justice of the plea must be made out on its own grounds, and can not be assumed on the mere admission of the propriety of the end aimed at. Whether the slaves of this country may be safely admitted to the enjoyments of personal liberty, is a matter of dispute; but that they could not, consistently with the public welfare, be intrusted with the exercise of political power, is in on all hands admitted. It is, then, the acknowledged right of the state to govern them by laws in the formation of which they have no voice. But it is the universal plea of the depositaries of irresponsible power, sustained too by almost universal experience, that men can be brought to submit to political despotism only by being kept in ignorance and poverty. Dr. Wayland, then, if he concedes the right of the state to legislate for the slaves, must, according to his own reasoning, acknowledge the right to adopt all the means necessary for the security of this irresponsible power, and of consequence, that the state has the right to keep the blacks in the lowest state of degradation. If he denies the validity of this argument in favor of political despotism, he must renounce his own against the lawfulness of domestic slavery. Dr. Wayland himself would admit the right of the Emperor of Russia to exercise a degree of power over his present half civilized subjects, which could not be maintained over an enlightened people, though he would be loth to acknowledge his right to adopt all the means necessary to keep them in their present condition. The acknowledgment, therefore, of the right to hold slaves, does not involve the acknowledgment of the right to adopt measures adapted and intended to perpetuate their present mental and physical degradation.

We have entered much more at length into the abstract argument on this subject than we intended. It was our purpose to confine our remarks to the scriptural view of the question. But the consideration of the objections derived from the general principles of morals, rendered it necessary to enlarge our plan. As it appears to us too clear to admit of either denial or doubt, that the Scriptures do sanction slaveholding; that under the old dispensation it was expressly permitted by divine command, and under the New Testament is nowhere forbidden or denounced, but on the contrary, acknowledged to be consistent with the Christian character and profession (that is, consistent with justice, mercy, holiness, love to God and love to man), to declare it to be a heinous crime, is a direct impeachment of the word of God. We, therefore, felt it incumbent upon us to prove, that the sacred Scriptures are not in conflict with the first principles of morals; that what they sanction is not the blackest and basest of all offenses in the sight of God. To do this, it was necessary to show what slavery is, to distinguish between the relation itself, and the various cruel or unjust laws which may be made either to bring men into it, or to secure its continuance; to show that it no more follows from the admission that the Scriptures sanction the right of slaveholding, that it, therefore, sanctions all the oppressive slave laws of any community, than it follows from the admission of the propriety of parental, conjugal, or political relations, that it sanctions all the conflicting codes by which these relations have at different periods and in different countries been regulated.

We have had another motive in the preparation of this article. The assumption that slaveholding is itself a crime, is not only an error, but it is an error fraught with evil consequences. It not merely brings its advocates into conflict with the Scriptures, but it does much to retard the progress of freedom; it embitters and divides the members of the community, and distracts the Christian church. Its operation in retarding the progress of freedom is obvious and manifold. In the first place, it directs the battery of the enemies of slavery to the wrong point. It might be easy for them to establish the injustice or cruelty of certain slave laws, where it is not in their power to establish the sinfulness of slavery itself.[271] They, therefore, waste their strength. Nor is this the least evil. They promote the cause of their opponents. If they do not discriminate between slaveholding and the slave laws, it gives the slaveholder not merely an excuse but an occasion and a reason for making no such distinction. He is thus led to feel the same conviction in the propriety of the one that he does in that of the other. His mind and conscience may be satisfied that the mere act of holding slaves is not a crime. This is the point, however, to which the abolitionist directs his attention. He examines their arguments, and becomes convinced of their inconclusiveness, and is not only thus rendered impervious to their attacks, but is exasperated by what he considers their unmerited abuse. In the mean time his attention is withdrawn from far more important points;—the manner in which he treats his slaves, and the laws enacted for the security of his possession. These are points on which his judgment might be much more readily convinced of error, and his conscience of sin.

In the second place, besides fortifying the position and strengthening the purpose of the slaveholder, the error in question divides and weakens the friends of freedom. To secure any valuable result by public sentiment, you must satisfy the public mind and rouse the public conscience. Their passions had better be allowed to rest in peace. As the anti-slavery societies declare it to be their object to convince their fellow-citizens that slaveholding is necessarily a heinous crime in the sight of God, we consider their attempt as desperate, so long as the Bible is regarded as the rule of right and wrong. They can hardly secure either the verdict of the public mind or of the public conscience in behalf of this proposition. Their success hitherto has not been very encouraging, and is certainly not very flattering, if Dr. Channing's account of the class of persons to whom they have principally addressed their arguments, is correct. The tendency of their exertions, be their success great or small, is not to unite, but to divide. They do not carry the judgment or conscience of the people with them. They form, therefore, a class by themselves. Thousands who earnestly desire to see the South convinced of the injustice and consequent impolicy of their slave laws, and under this conviction, of their own accord, adopting those principles which the Bible enjoins, and which tend to produce universal intelligence, virtue, liberty and equality, without violence and sudden change, and which thus secure private and public prosperity, stand aloof from the abolitionists, not merely because they disapprove of their spirit and mode of action, but because they do not admit their fundamental principle.

In the third place, the error in question prevents the adoption of the most effectual means of extinguishing slavery. These means are not the opinions or feelings of the non-slaveholding States, nor the denunciations of the holders of slaves, but the improvement, intellectual and moral, of the slaves themselves. Slavery has but two natural and peaceful modes of death. The one is the increase of the slave population until it reaches the point of being unproductive. When the number of slaves becomes so great that the master can not profitably employ them, he manumits them in self-defense. This point would probably have been reached long ago, in many of the Southern States, had not the boundless extent of the south-western section of the Union presented a constant demand for the surplus hands. Many planters in Virginia and Maryland, whose principles or feelings revolt at the idea of selling their slaves to the South, find that their servants are gradually reducing them to poverty, by consuming more than they produce. The number, however, of slaveholders who entertain these scruples is comparatively small. And as the demand for slave labor in the still unoccupied regions of the extreme south-west is so great, and is likely to be so long continued, it is hopeless to think of slavery dying out by becoming a public burden. The other natural and peaceful mode of extinction, is the gradual elevation of the slaves in knowledge, virtue, and property to the point at which it is no longer desirable or possible to keep them in bondage.[272] Their chains thus gradually relax, until they fall off entirely. It is in this way that Christianity has abolished both political and domestic bondage, whenever it has had free scope. It enjoins a fair compensation for labor; it insists on the moral and intellectual improvement of all classes of men; it condemns all infractions of marital or parental rights; in short, it requires not only that free scope should be allowed to human improvement, but that all suitable means should be employed for the attainment of that end. The feudal system, as before remarked, has, in a great measure, been thus outgrown in all the European states. The third estate, formerly hardly recognized as having an existence, is becoming the controlling power in most of those ancient communities. The gradual improvement of the people rendered it impossible, and undesirable to deprive them of their just share in the government. And it is precisely in those countries where this improvement is most advanced that the feudal institutions are the most completely obliterated, and the general prosperity the greatest. In like manner the gospel method of extinguishing slavery is by improving the condition of the slave. The grand question is, How is this to be done? The abolitionist answers, by immediate emancipation. Perhaps he is right, perhaps he is wrong; but whether right or wrong, it is not the practical question for the North. Among a community which have the power to emancipate, it would be perfectly proper to urge that measure on the ground of its being the best means of promoting the great object of the advancement of human happiness and virtue. But the error of the abolitionists is, that they urge this measure from the wrong quarter, and upon the wrong ground. They insist upon immediate abolition because slavery is a sin, and its extinction a duty. If, however, slaveholding is not in itself sinful, its abolition is not necessarily a duty. The question of duty depends upon the effects of the measure, about which men may honestly differ. Those who believe that it would advance the general good, are bound to promote it; while those who believe the reverse, are equally bound to resist it. The abolitionists, by insisting upon one means of improvement, and that on untenable ground, are most effectually working against the adoption of any other means, by destroying the disposition and power to employ them. It is in this way that the error to which we have referred throughout this article, is operating most disadvantageously for the cause of human liberty and happiness. The fact is, that the great duty of the South is not emancipation; but improvement.[273] The former is obligatory only as a means to an end, and, therefore, only under circumstances where it would promote that end. In like manner the great duty of despotic governments is not the immediate granting of free institutions, but the constant and assiduous cultivation of the best interests (knowledge, virtue, and happiness) of the people. Where free institutions would conduce to this object, they would be granted, and just so far and so fast as this becomes apparent.

Again, the opinion that slaveholding is itself a crime, must operate to produce the disunion of the States, and the division of all the ecclesiastical societies in this country. The feelings of the people may be excited violently for a time, but the transport soon passes away. But if the conscience is enlisted in the cause, and becomes the controlling principle, the alienation between the North and the South must become permanent. The opposition to Southern institutions will become calm, constant, and unappeasable. Just so far as this opinion operates, it will lead those who entertain it to submit to any sacrifices to carry it out, and give it effect. We shall become two nations in feeling, which must soon render us two nations in fact. With regard to the church, its operation will be more summary. If slaveholding is a heinous crime, slaveholders must be excluded from the church. Several of our judicatories have already taken this position. Should the General Assembly adopt it, the church is ipso facto, divided. If the opinion in question is correct, it must be maintained, whatever are the consequences. We are no advocates of expediency in morals. We have no more right to teach error in order to prevent evil, than we have a right to do evil to promote good. On the other hand, if the opinion is incorrect, its evil consequences render it a duty to prove and exhibit its unsoundness. It is under the deep impression that the primary assumption of the abolitionists is an error, that its adoption tends to the distraction of the country, and the division of the church; and that it will lead to the longer continuance and greater severity of slavery, that we have felt constrained to do what little we could towards its correction.

We have little apprehension that any one can so far mistake our object, or the purport of our remarks, as to suppose either that we regard slavery as a desirable institution, or that we approve of the slave laws of the Southern States. So far from this being the case, the extinction of slavery, and the amelioration of those laws are as sincerely desired by us, as by any of the abolitionists. The question is not about the continuance of slavery, and of the present system, but about the proper method of effecting the removal of the evil. We maintain, that it is not by denouncing slaveholding as a sin, or by universal agitation at the North, but by the improvement of the slaves. It no more follows that because the master has a right to hold slaves, he has a right to keep them in a state of degradation in order to perpetuate their bondage, than that the Emperor of Russia has a right to keep his subjects in ignorance and poverty, in order to secure the permanence and quiet possession of his power. We hold it to be the grand principle of the gospel, that every man is bound to promote the moral, intellectual, and physical improvement of his fellow men. Their civil or political relations are in themselves matters of indifference. Monarchy, aristocracy, democracy, domestic slavery, are right or wrong as they are, for the time being, conducive to this great end, or the reverse. They are not objects to which the improvement of society is to be sacrificed; nor are they strait-jackets to be placed upon the public body to prevent its free development. We think, therefore, that the true method for Christians to treat this subject, is to follow the example of Christ and his apostles in relation both to despotism and slavery. Let them enforce as moral duties the great principles of justice and mercy, and all the specific commands and precepts of the Scriptures. If any set of men have servants, bond or free, to whom they refuse a proper compensation for their labor, they violate a moral duty and an express command of Scripture. What that compensation should be, depends upon a variety of circumstances. In some cases the slaveholder would be glad to compound for the support of his slaves by giving the third or the half of the proceeds of his estate. Yet this at the North would be regarded as a full remuneration for the mere labor of production. Under other circumstances, however, a mere support, would be very inadequate compensation; and when inadequate, it is unjust. If the compensation be more than a support, the surplus is the property of the laborer, and can not morally, whatever the laws may be, be taken from him. The right to accumulate property is an incident to the right of reward for labor. And we believe there are few slaveholding countries in which the right is not practically acknowledged, since we hear so frequently of slaves purchasing their own freedom. It is very common for a certain moderate task[274] to be assigned as a day's work, which may be regarded as the compensation rendered by the slave for his support. The residue of the day is at his own disposal, and may be employed for his own profit. We are not now, however, concerned about details. The principle that "the laborer is worthy of his hire" and should enjoy it, is a plain principle of morals and command of the Bible, and can not be violated with impunity.

Again, if any man has servants or others whom he forbids to marry, or whom he separates after marriage, he breaks as clearly a revealed law as any written on the pages of inspiration, or on the human heart. If he interferes unnecessarily with the authority of parents over their children, he again brings himself into collision with his Maker. If any man has under his charge, children, apprentices, servants, or slaves, and does not teach them, or cause them to be taught, the will of God; if he deliberately opposes their intellectual, moral, or religious improvement, he makes himself a transgressor. That many of the laws of the slaveholding States are opposed to these simple principles of morals, we fully believe; and we do not doubt that they are sinful and ought to be rescinded. If it be asked what would be the consequence of thus acting on the principles of the gospel, of following the example and obeying the precepts of Christ? We answer, the gradual elevation of the slaves in intelligence, virtue, and wealth; the peaceable and speedy extinction of slavery; the improvement in general prosperity of all classes of society, and the consequent increase in the sum of human happiness and virtue. This has been the result of acting on these principles in all past ages; and just in proportion as they have been faithfully observed. The degradation of most eastern nations, and of Italy, Spain and Ireland, are not more striking examples of the consequences of their violation, than Scotland, England, and the non-slaveholding States are of the benefits, of their being even imperfectly obeyed. Men can not alter the laws of God. It would be as easy for them to arrest the action of the force of gravity, as to prevent the systematic violation of the principles of morals being productive of evil.

THE EDUCATION, LABOR, AND WEALTH OF THE SOUTH.
BY SAMUEL A. CARTWRIGHT, M.D.,
OF LOUISIANA.

NOTE.—This article of Dr. Cartwright's was designed by the Editor to follow "Cotton is King," but the copy was not received until the stereotyping had progressed nearly to completion.—PUBLISHER.

It has long been a favorite argument of the abolitionists to assert that slave labor is unproductive, that the prevalence of slavery tends to diminish not only the productions of a country, but also the value of the lands. On this ground, appeals are constantly made to the non-slaveholders of the South, to induce them to abolish slavery; assigning as a reason, that their lands would rise in value so as to more than compensate the loss of the slaves.

That we may be able to ascertain how much truth there is in this assertion, let us refer to *figures* and *facts*. The following deductions from the Report of the Auditor of Public Accounts of the State of Louisiana, speak in a language too plain to be misunderstood by any one, and prove conclusively, that, so far at least as the slave States are concerned, a dense slave population gives the highest value and greatest productiveness to every species of property. Similar deductions might he drawn from the Auditors' Reports of every slave State in the Union   EDITOR.

1. *Annual Report of the Auditor of Public Accounts of the State of Louisiana.* Baton Rouge, 1859.

2. *Annual Report of the Superintendent of Public Education.* Baton Rouge, 1859.

3. *Les Lois concernant, les Ecoles Publique dons l'Etat de la Louisiane*, 1849.

4. *Agricultural Productions of Louisiana.* By Edward J. Forstal, New Orleans, 1845.

5. *Address of the Commissioners for the Raising the Endowment of the University of the South.* New Orleans, 1859.

IT is much easier to acquire knowledge from things cognizable to the senses than from books. American civilization is founded upon the laws of nature and upon moral virue. "Honesty is the best policy," says Washington, its founder. The laws of nature are discovered by observation and experience. A practical direction is given to them by that species of knowedge, which is derived from handling the objects of sense and working upon the materials the earth produces. Moral virtue puts a bridle on the evil passions of the heart, and, at the same time, infuses into it an invincible courage in demanding what is right. A knowledge of nature enables its possessor to bridle the natural forces of air, earth, fire, and water—to hold the reins and drive ahead. With its rail-roads and telegraphs, American civilization is waging war with time and space, and, by its moral power and Christian example, with sin and evil. With its labor-saving machiney, its thirty millions do more work for God and man than three hundred millions of such people as inhabit Asia, Africa, Central, and South America, and Mexico. Its thirty millions are equal to any hundred millions of most of the governments of Europe. It is far ahead of the most enlightened nations of Europe, because its people are in the possession of all the blessings and comforts that heaven, through nature's laws, accord to earth's inhabitants, while three-fourths of the two hundred and fifty millions of Europe are writhing in an artificially created purgatory—deprived of all the good things of earth. Whoever would catch up with the annals of American progress, fall into line with American policy, and get within the influence of the guiding spirit of American policy, must not depend upon libraries for information, or he will be left far behind the age in which he lives; must look to the statistics of the churches, to the reports of legislative and commercial bodies, and to the monthly reviews recording the principal transactions of the busy world around him. If he wants to keep pace with the exploits of mankind under European civilization, in cutting one another's throats, sacking cities, destroying commerce, and laying waste the smiling fields of agriculture, the daily press will give the required information; but he can not rely upon it for these statistical details and stubborn facts which tell what the Caucasian in America, aided by his black man, Friday, is doing for Christianity, for liberty, for civilization, and for the good of the world. Some of these details are regarded as too dry and uninteresting, and others too long for admission in the daily press. Much is written and said about the benefits of education. The rudiments are alike important in both kinds of civilization, American and European. But after acquiring the rudimentary knowledge, the paths of education in the two hemispheres diverge from each other at right angles. The further the American travels in the labyrinths of that system of education, so fashionable in Europe, purposely designed to bury active minds in the rubbish of past ages, or tangle them in metaphysical abstractions and hide from them the beauty of truth and the matter-of-fact world around them, the less he is qualified to appreciate the blessings and benefits of republican institutions, and the more apt he is to be found in opposition to

American policy. By hard studies on subjects of no practical importance, physical or moral, the European system of education drives independence out of the mind, and virtue out of the heart, as a pre-requisite qualification for obedience to governments resting upon diplomacy, falsehood, artificial and unnatural distinctions among men. But in the United States, the various State governments being founded on moral truths and nature's laws, and not on the opinions of a privileged order, our system of education should be in harmony with our system of government; our youth should be taught to love virtue for virtue's sake; to study nature, bow to her truths, and to give all the homage that the crowned heads receive in Europe, to nature and to truth. Our government sets up no religious creed or standard of morals, but leaves every one perfectly free in religion and morals, to be governed by the Bible as *he understands it*, provided he does not trespass upon the rights of others. The principal books in our libraries give little or no aid in qualifying our youth for public office or to direct the legislation or policy of a government resting upon natural laws. The practical operation of our system is scarcely anywhere else recorded than in church history, gospel triumph, legislative reports, reviews, and pamphlets. There the facts may be found, but they are isolated and disconnected, teaching nothing; but could be made a most potent means, not only of instruction in the practical operation of our system of government, but of developing the human faculties, if introduced into our schools. They are full of objects for comparison. By comparison the mind is taught the difference between things; comparisons are at the bottom of all useful and practical knowledge. "They are suggestive," says Prof. Agassiz, "of further comparisons. When the objects of nature are the subjects of comparison, the mind is insensibly led to make new inquiries, is filled with delight at every step of progress it makes in nature's ever young and blooming fields, and study becomes a pleasure. No American knows what a good country he has got until he visits Europe and draws comparisons between the condition of the laboring classes there and those at home. Even in London, about half the people have neither church-room nor school-room."

The *Annual Report of the Auditor of Public accounts of the State of Louisiana* abounds with objects which have only to be compared in their various relations to one another to give the mind a clear perception of the operation and practical working of some of the most important natural laws and moral truths lying at the bottom of American civilization and progress. Without comparisons they are like hieroglyphical characters telling nothing. Comparisons will decipher them and make them speak a language full of instruction, which every one can understand.

The more thorough the education in European colleges, or in American schools on a similar model, the more there will be to *unlearn* before American institutions can be understood or their value appreciated, and the less will the American citizen be qualified to vote understandingly at the polls. The reason is, that the system of education which directs the policy of goverments founded upon artificial distinctions, is from necessity inimical to a government founded upon natural distinctions and moral truth. Education on the British model has set the North against the South, and has waylaid every step of American progress, from the acquisition of Louisiana to the last foot of land acquired from Mexico or the Indians, and it now stands across the path of the all-conquering march of American civilization into Cuba, Central America, and Mexico. The vicious system of education founded upon the European model has almost reconquered Massachusetts and several other Northern States, converting them, in many essential particulars, into British provinces. The people of the North are virtuous and democratic at heart; but they have been turned against their own country and the sentiments which experience teaches to be truths, the obvious benefits of negro slavery, for instance, by an education essentially monarchical. To sustain itself, American policy should have its own schools, to guide and direct it. Heretofore it has been guided and directed almost entirely by the light and knowledge derived from the great school of experience, in which the democratic masses are taught without the aid of other books than the Bible and hymn book. In that school they learned that the negro was not a white man with a black skin, but a different being, intended by nature to occupy a subordinate place in society; that school made known that the only place which nature has qualified him to fill was the place of a servant. That place was accordingly assigned him in the new order of civilization called American civilization, founded upon moral virtue and natural distinctions, and not upon artifice and fraud; upon nature's laws and God's truths, and not upon the fallacies of human reason, as that of Europe. They had not even the assistance of book education to tell them that the white man bore the name of Japheth in the Bible, and the negro that of Canaan; and that the negro's servile nature was expressed in his Hebrew name. American theologians had not paid sufficient attention to the Hebrew, and could not inform the American reader that both the Hebrew Bible and its Greek translation, called the Septuagint, plainly, and in direct terms, recognize two classes or races of mankind, one having a black skin, and the other being fair or white; and that, besides these two races, it recognizes a third race under the term Shem, a name which has no reference to color; but as the other two were plainly designated as *whites* and *blacks*, the inference is, that the third class was red or yellow, or of an intermediate color. In the Septuagint (the Bible which our Saviour quotes), Æthiop is the term used to designate the sons of Ham, a term synonymous with the Latin word *niger*, from which the Spanish word *negro* is derived. The Bible tells in unmistakable terms that Japheth, or the white race, was to be *enlarged*. The discovery of the western hemisphere opened a wide field for the *enlargement* of the white race, pent up for thousands of years in a little corner of the eastern hemisphere. The new hemisphere was found to be inhabited by nomads of the race of Shem, neither white nor black. The historical fact is, that the white race is every year *enlarging* itself by dispossessing the nomadic sons of Shem, found on the American continent, of their tents, and dwelling in them; and that the black race are its servants. Thus literally, in accordance with the prophecy, "*Japheth will be enlarged, he shall dwell in the tents of Shem, and Canaan* (the negro) *shall be his servant.*" The prophecy is not fulfilled, but only in process of fulfillment. It clearly points to a new order of civilization, in a wider world for enlargement than the old, in which the black race was to serve the white. The will of God that such a new order of civilization should be established, in which the negro and white man should mutually aid each other, and supply each other's deficiencies, is not only revealed in Hebrew words, written thousands of years ago, but revealed also in the laws of nature, and revealed by *Ethiop nowhere else but in our slave-holding States, stretching forth her arms to God.* American civilization, founded upon revealed truth and nature's laws, puts the negro in his natural position, that of subordination to the white man.

The observation and experience of those who founded a government resting on the basis of moral truth and natural, instead of artificial distinctions, revealed to them the necessity of consigning to the negro an inferior position, in order to carry out that democratic principle which demands a place for every thing, and every thing in its place. What are called the free States have provided no place for the poor negro. He is an outcast and a wanderer, hurtful instead of helpful to society. Mexico, Central and South America, in catching at the shadow, lost the substance of republicanism. Republican government has utterly failed with them, because they fell into the error of supposing that all men of all races are naturally equal to one another. The white race in those countries, acting upon that error, emancipated the inferior negro race, and amalgamated with that and with the Indian race. This disregard of the distinctions made by nature, between the white, black, and Indian races, was fatal to American civilization in those countries.

Mr. Jefferson never meant to say that negroes were equal to white men; but that white men, whether born in England or America were equal to one another. Our fathers contended for their own equality among Englishmen, which not being granted to them, they declared their independence. But scarcely had their swords won that independence, when the governing classes of Great Britain began to teach the rising generation, through the medium of books, schools, and colleges, that the democratic doctrine, which declared all white men equal to one another, *included negroes.* Thus making the learned world believe that democracy and negro slavery are incompatible—that there can be no such thing as a democracy, or a government where the people rule, so long as black people are held in slavery. The schools not only taught the doctrine that negro slavery is anti-republican, but that it is a moral, social and political evil, and soon it was denounced from the pulpit as *sin against God!*

Under the influence of such an education, imported from Europe, the American people, even in the South, began to regard negro slavery as an evil—not from any thing they saw, but from what they had been taught. Thence all manner of experiments were made with the negro to make his condition better out of slavery than in it. All of which proving a failure, the South took issue with Old and New England on the question of negro slavery being an evil, social, political, or moral, and called for the proof. No proof could be given except that drawn from England, from hearsay evidence, and from theoretical teaching of that system of education designed to support European despotisms, and to destroy American republicanism. This has opened the eyes of the South to the necessity of establishing schools and colleges of its own to uphold American civilization. The address of the commissioners for the raising of the endowment of the University of the South commends it to the attention of the American people, not as a sectional or Southern university, but as an American university, to be the house and home of the spirit of American civilization—a dwelling-place not lighted with fox-fire tapers or artificial lights to disguise nature, as the institutions of learning in Europe are, but with the light inherent in nature's truths and in the revealed word of God, honestly translated and interpreted. Some schools to aid American civilization have already been established, but there is a sad outcry for the proper kind of school books; those of Old and New England being rotten to the core with abolitionism and with that false democracy which would make the rising generation believe that the heroes of the American Revolution fought for ruining the negro by giving him liberty, fought to annul God's decrees, which made him a servant of servants, instead of fighting for the principle asserting their own equality with the lords of England and the crowned heads of Europe. Fortunately the work before us, the *Report of the Auditor of the Public Accounts of Louisiana*, will answer very well to supply the want of a proper kind of school book to indoctrinate beginners in the mysteries of the political institutions of their own country, and at the same time to discipline and expand their minds. It is only one of the numerous books of its class, which might be advantageously pressed into the service of the schools for a similar purpose. The statistics of the United States Census, and De Bow's *Industrial Resources*, and the *Minutes of the Progress of the American Churches*, would prove a very good beginning of a high school and college library. Comparisons being the basis of all useful and practical knowledge, in the works just referred to, and in the auditor's report and others of its class, will be found ample materials for comparison. Comparison will infuse a soul into the dry bones of the facts and figures of our religious and political institutions, and make them declare the hidden truths of nature which lie at the bottom of American republicanism, Christianity, prosperity, and progress. The task of comparing will be highly instructive to the youthful mind, and at the same time agreeable and interesting. As an example, here is the way a beginning is recommended, for a comparison in secular affairs.

LESSON NO. 1.—Let Lesson No. 1 consist in comparing the counties (or parishes, as they are called in Louisiana) having the largest white population and the fewest negroes, with those counties having the heaviest negro population and the fewest white people.

There are five parishes, or counties, found in the report of the auditor of public accounts, in which the white population exceeds the negro slaves three to one. Let these parishes be compared with five others in which the slave population exceeds the white seven to one.

Table I, represents the first class of parishes, and Table II, the second. Thus:

TABLE I.

| | Total acres of land owned. | Population | | |
		Whites.	Slaves.	Free Negroes.
Calcasieu,	35,486	2,367	947	280
Livingston,	60,885	3,998	1,297	7
Sabine,	85,446[275]	3,585	1,409	—
Vermillion,	73,654	3,260	1,378	19
Winn,	43,406	4,314	1,007	38
	298,877	17,524	6,038	343
			17,524	
Total whites and slaves,			23,562	
			343	
Aggregate population,			23,905	

TABLE II.

| | Total acres of land owned. | Population | | |
		Whites.	Slaves.	Free Negroes.
Carroll,	246,582	2,409	9,529	—
Concordia,	318,395	1,384	11,908	11
Madison,	304,494	1,293	9,863	—
Tensas,	323,797	1,255	13,285	328
W. Feliciana,	230,966	1,985	10,450	68
	1,224,234	8,326	55,035	407
			8,326	
Total whites and slaves,			63,361	
			407	
Aggregate population,			63,768	

It will be seen from the above, that the white population of the parishes in table I exceeds the slaves nearly three to one; while, in the parishes in table II, the slaves exceed the whites nearly seven to one.

If the land were divided equally among the aggregate population, each inhabitant of the parishes in table I would have 12 acres, and each inhabitant of the parishes in table II would have 22 acres. Here lesson 1 ends, by proving that there is not as great a demand for land, by nearly one half, where the population consists of one white man and seven negroes. By referring to a map of Louisiana, it will be seen that the territorial extent of the parishes in table I is much greater than those in table II. Hence it is not for the want of territory, that a population consisting of three whites to one negro, owns less land by nearly one half, than a population consisting of seven negroes to one white man.

LESSON NO. 2.—Lesson No. I requires the value of the land per acre, in tables I and II, to be ascertained and compared, with a view of solving the important problem: "*Which gives the most value to land, a dense white population with a few negroes, or a dense slave population with a few white people?*"

By referring to the report of the auditor of accounts of Louisiana, it will be seen that the assessed value of the lands of the parishes in table I amounts to $1,642,073, or $5 49 per acre; while that of table II amounts to $23,446,654, or $16 46 per acre. A population consisting of seven negro slaves to one white man, makes land three times as valuable as a population of three white men to one negro. The comparison drawn in this lesson, puts a soul in the dry bones of the facts and figures contained in the report of the auditor of public accounts, and makes them tell what it is which gives value to Southern land.

LESSON NO. 3.—Let this lesson be devoted to drawing comparisons to ascertain: "*Which pays the most taxes to the State, five parishes containing 17,524 whites with a few negroes, or five parishes containing less than half the whites (8,326) with a great many negroes?*" By referring to the report of the auditor it will be seen, that the 17,524 whites of the five parishes in table I pay the State only $25,487,93, or less than $1 50 each, while the 8,326 whites in the five parishes in table II pay the State $169,900 per annum, or upward of $20 each. The aggregate population of the parishes in table I pay only $1 06 each, while the aggregate population of the parishes in table II pay $2 66 each. Every three whites and twenty negroes pay the State $61 18. By making a calculation it will appear that it will require forty-three whites and fifteen negroes of the parishes in table I, to pay the State as much as three whites and twenty negroes pay in the parishes in table II.

COROLLARY.—Three white men with twenty negroes, financially considered, are worth as much to the State as forty-three white men with fifteen negroes.

This strange truth meets a steady explanation in the fact found in Lesson No. 2, that in those parishes where every three white inhabitants own twenty negroes, the land is more than three times as valuable as in the parishes, where every forty-three of the white population possess only fifteen negroes.

LESSON NO. 4.—In the last lesson the truth was brought out that forty-three white men and fifteen negroes are worth no more to the State, financially considered, than three white men and twenty negroes. Let this lesson examine the question: "*Whether forty-three white men in command of fifteen negroes are worth AS MUCH to the State, agriculturally and commercially considered, as three white men in command of twenty negroes?*" This is a bold question and requires some calculations. In making the calculations to base the comparisons upon, sugar will be estimated at $60 per hogshead; molasses at $7 per barrel; corn at $1 per bushel, and cotton at $40 dollars per bale. At these rates the value of the agricultural productions in the five parishes, where the white population is nearly three times as great as the negro, amounts to $446,550, in a population of 17,524 whites, 6,038 negro slaves, and 343 free negroes—the aggregate population 23,905, which gives to each inhabitant $18 68.

The value of the agricultural productions in the five parishes, viz: Carroll, Concordia, Madison, Tensas, and West Feliciana, where the negro slaves are nearly seven times as numerous as the white population, amounts to $8,854,770. In other words, 55,035 negroes under the command of 8,326 whites, in an aggregate population of 63,768 (407 being added for free negroes), produced $8,854,770 worth of agricultural products in one year, estimating cotton at $40 per bale, sugar $60 per hogshead, and corn at $1 a bushel; this amount divided by the aggregate population gives each individual, black and white, old and young, $138 87. Three whites in command of twenty negroes produce $3,194 worth of agricultral products. This lesson was to solve the question whether forty-three white men in command of fifteen negroes are worth as much to the State, agriculturally and commercially considered, as three white men in command of twenty negroes? It has been proved that in those five parishes where the whites nearly treble the negroes, each inhabitant only produces $18 68. This would give to forty-three white and fifteen negroes only $1,081 70 as their share of the value of the agricultural productions—whereas, the share of three whites and twenty negroes, in those parishes where the negro population is nearly seven to one of the white, has been ascertained to be $3,194. The student of political economy is now prepared to solve another question: "What number of inhabitants are required in those parishes where labor is isolated or disassociated, to produce as much as three white and twenty negroes produce in those parishes where labor is associated? The answer is 171; viz: 113 whites and 58 negroes. The question is proved to be correctly solved by multiplying 171 by $18.68 which gives $1,394 25, the exact amount and a quarter over, that twenty negroes and three whites produce in those parishes where labor is associated, or where the slave population is nearly seven times more numerous than the white.

Lesson No. 5.—Let two more lots of parishes be compared; one in which the white population is not quite double that of the negro slaves, and the other in which the negro slaves are not quite double the number of the whites.

TABLE III.
Parishes where whites exceed negroes less than two to one.

	Whites.	Slaves.	Free negroes.	Val. ag. prod.' 58.
Caldwell,	2,607	1,830	8	$121,920
St. Tammany,	2,588	1,945	—	67,170
Union,	7,191	4,154	5	691,641
Washington,	2,910	1,551	10	47,532
Jackson,	5,220	3,803	1	702,742
	20,516	13,283	24	$1,631,005

Dividing the total value of the agricultural products by the aggregate population, gives $48 22 to each individual, as the average in five parishes, where the negro slaves are somewhat more than half the whole population. This is a considerable improvement on the five parishes in table I, where the whites exceed the negroes nearly three to one, the average to each inhabitant being only $18 68, instead of $48 22.

TABLE IV.
Parishes where negroes exceed whites less than two to one.

	Whites.	Slaves.	Free negroes.	Val. ag. prod. '58.
Claiborne,	4,618	7,003	58	$857,675
De Soto,	4,459	7,301	29	739,945
Morehouse,	3,620	5,468	14	785,370
Nachitoches,	5,987	7,939	775	1,120,718
Caddo,	4,073	5,978	44	1,056,130
Bossier,	3,646	7,195	11	1,155,010
	26,403	40,784	931	5,674,848

The total value of the agricultural productions, divided by the aggregate population, 68,168, gives to each inhabitant $83 25. In table II the aggregate population was 63,768, nearly seven negroes to one white man; the value of the agricultural products divided, gave each $138 07, instead of $83 25. The parishes of table II, with an aggregate population of 63,768, seven sixths of whom were slaves, produced $8,854,770 worth of agricultural products; whereas, the parishes of table IV, containing a population of 68,168, the slaves being less than double the number of whites, produced three millions less of agricultural products than a smaller aggregate population produced in those parishes where the negroes outnumbered the whites nearly seven to one.

The report of the auditor of public accounts for the year 1859, does not contain the necessary data for making comparisons in the parishes on the lower stem of the Mississippi river, by reason of crevasses and other disastrous causes. The valuable pamphlet of Edward J. Forstale, on the agricultural products of Louisiana, will supply that deficiency, though of a much older date. It appears from Mr. Forstale, that, so far back as 1844, "on well conducted estates, the average value of sugar and molasses, per slave, was $237 50, estimating sugar at 4 cents, and molasses at 15 cents," while the general average in the sugar district, per slave, was, in the year 1844, only $150 31, from which he deducted $75 for expenses. By examining his Monograph, it will be seen that the great bulk of the sugar and molasses was produced in those parishes having the heaviest negro population in proportion to the white. Thus, St. Martin's, with a total population more than three times as large as St. Charles, and with a negro population more than twice as numerous, produced, in 1844, only 5,000 hogsheads, while St. Charles produced upward of 12,000. The white population of St. Charles is only 883, while that of the slaves is 3,769. The white population of St. Martin is 6,400, and the negro population 8,200. Assumption and Ascension are adjoining parishes. Assumption contains more than three thousand whites, and three hundred slaves over and above the population of Ascension. It has more land than Ascension, yet it pays $2,200 less taxes on lands than Ascension, and its gross taxes are $1,500 less than Ascension. The value of its agricultural products is likewise less.

These lessons by comparison might be indefinitely extended, by dropping the report of the auditor of public accounts of Louisiana, and taking up the statistics of the churches, and the last United States census. The statistics of the American churches prove that the slaveholding States contain more Christian communicants, in proportion to the population, including black and white, than the non-slaveholding—South Carolina more than Massachusetts, Virginia more than Pennsylvania, Kentucky more than Ohio. The report proves that in the cotton and sugar region, the white people who have few or no negroes, are poor and helpless, but when supplied with seven times their own number of negroes, they are the richest and most powerful agricultural people on the earth. The census will prove that the landed property of those who are thus supplied with from three to seven times their own number of negroes, if sold at its assessed value, and the proceeds of sales divided equally among all the inhabitants, black and white, each individual would have a larger sum than any Pennsylvanian, New Yorker, or New Englander, would have, if the land in the richest counties were sold at its assessed value, and the proceeds of sales divided equally among the inhabitants of the said county. For instance, if the land in some of the richest counties of Pennsylvania, say Adams, Berks, Centre, Chester, and Washington, were all sold, and the proceeds divided among the inhabitants, each individual would have only about half as much as each negro and white man would have, if the lands of Carroll, Madison, Concordia, and Tensas, where the negroes outnumber the whites seven to one, were all sold, and the proceeds equally divided among blacks and whites.

Comparisons, instituted upon the data furnished by the United States census, will show that what Virginia wants *is more negroes*, and what Pennsylvania wants is *more white laborers*. In some counties in Pennsylvania, Cambria and Carbon for instance, the land, if sold and proceeds divided, would not give each inhabitant $75 a piece, the most of the land being uncultivated for want of laborers. Ohio, Wyoming, and Nicholas counties, in Virginia, with an aggregate population exceeding thirty thousand, have only 222 negro slaves. The land, if sold and divided, would not give each inhabitant one hundred dollars. In Accomac, Albemarle, York, Prince Edward, and Prince George, the negro population is about equal to the white. The land, if sold and equally divided, would give each individual from $150 to $220, which is nearly as much as the inhabitants of the best counties of Pennsylvania would have from the proceeds of sales of these lands. Land, per acre, is cheaper in Virginia than in Pennsylvania, because much the largest portion of the Virginia lands are unimproved for the want of laborers, while the largest portion of the Pennsylvania lands are under cultivation. The cotton States and Louisiana are sucking the life-blood out of Virginia by draining that noble old State of her agricultural laborers. The high price of negroes is ruining Virginia. In Sussex, Southampton, Northampton, and many other counties, which send most negroes to the cotton States, the inhabitants have lost more in the fall in the price of their land, than they have gained in the high price they got for their negroes. The land, if sold and divided, would give each individual only fifty-seven dollars, less than three dollars an acre. Oxford is Great Britain's eye, or rather the telescope which is used to see afar off, to direct British policy. Mr. Jefferson saw the importance of a university of the first class, to be used as a telescope to look into the distance, to direct Virginia, or what ought to be the same thing, American policy, as Oxford directs British policy. Hence he devoted the latter years of his life to establishing an institution for that very purpose.

Long before the West India emancipation act was passed, it was known by the learned graduates and fellows of Oxford, that negroes would not work as free laborers; and that their emancipation would ruin the British West Indies. British policy, however, to build up India, imperatively demanded the sacrifice to be made, as Russian policy demanded the sacrifice of Moscow. The African race furnished the only laborers, who could compete with the Mongolian race in producing the rich products of tropical agriculture. Great Britain had a hundred and fifty millions of the bronze and yellow-skin Asiatics under her command, and only wanted the black-skin Africans out of the way, to monopolize tropical agriculture. To carry out the British policy of becoming, not only mistress of the seas, but mistress of the boundless wealth of tropical and tropicoid climates, the learned graduates of Oxford and Cambridge raised a hue and cry against the inhumanity of the *middle passage*. So little truth was there in it, that when the committee of the United States Senate, appointed to consider the causes of the mortality prevailing on emigrant ships from Europe to this country, and the means for the better protection of the health of the passengers, did me the honor in 1854 to request my views on the subject, I replied (see "*Report of the Select Committee of U. S. Senate on the Sickness and Mortality on Emigrant Ships*," pages 119-144—Washington, 1854), recommending certain rules to be adopted to preserve the health and ameliorate the condition of emigrants on shipboard, which appeared to me to be the best. But, subsequently, a little volume fell into my hands containing the rules of the African slave-traders, half a century ago, which were so much better than those I had recommended, I called the attention of the chairman of the Senate's committee, the Hon. Hamilton Fish, to them, advising him by all means to adopt the African slave-traders' rules, if he had any regard for the health and comfort of the European emigrants. In the latter part of the last century no one pretended, as now, that the negro lost any thing by exchanging slavery in Africa for the more benign system of slavery in America. But it was the imaginary sufferings on the middle passage, which brought humanity with her eyes shut to lend to British policy a helping hand to close Africa and prevent her sable sons from exchanging their barbarous masters for civilized ones. America consented to that policy. The Southern tobacco-planters, believing they had as many negroes as the cultivation of tobacco required, had petitioned the king before the Revolution, to close the African slave trade. He did not do it. After the Revolution it was not only closed, but declared to be piracy, by the federal government. The policy which closed it may have been good policy or bad at that time. It soon gave the non-slaveholding States the ascendency in the Union. The question, whether they shall retain that ascendency, will depend very much upon whether they continue to abuse the power they acquired over the South by cutting off the supply of Southern laborers. Having ascertained that the negro would not work as a free man, the next move of British policy was, to set those free who were already in America. All parties in England, some by one artifice and some by another, were ultimately led to promote the British policy of negro abolitionism. From England it was brought over to the United States, took root and grew so rapidly as soon to become a most disturbing element in both church and state. We had no colleges at the North, and scarcely any churches which knew the advantages humanity and Christianity derived from the mutual aid the black and white races afford each other. The most of them are and were virtually European colleges located in America. This has enabled those learned men in Great Britain, who guide and direct British policy, to make a nose of wax of the great body of the educated classes in the United States. The prominence given to the Latin language, to the neglect of the Greek and Hebrew, in our schools and colleges, has greatly tended to fill the heads of the students with monarchical ideas, and to prevent them from understanding and appreciating the institutions of their own country. The study of Homer and the Greek classics favors genuine republicanism, by fostering a high-toned moral virtue, and by creating a love for nature and for political institutions founded upon her laws; while the study of Virgil, and other Latin text-books, used in our schools and colleges, has a strong tendency to lead to a sickly sentimental admiration for nominal instead of real freedom, and for governments founded upon usurpations and artificial distinctions, as that of the Cæsars was, and as that of Great Britain is. There is as much difference between Homer and Virgil as between nature and art. The Latin, being a derivative language, and of very little use, would long since have been banished from the schools, but for the aid monarchy derives from its binding men of letters, as Virgil bound the Muses, to the footstool of thrones, to flatter the frail humanity thereon with the incense of divine honors. Homer's Muses, like true

Americans, pay no higher honors to the diadem on the king's head than to the gaudy plumage of the peacock's tail. Young America would derive great advantages from an intimate acquaintance with Homer. He wrote in a language which gives to all the arts and sciences their technical terms. Hence, the previous study of the Greek makes the acquaintance of the various sciences comparatively easy to the learner. The Greek and Hebrew being original languages, can be acquired in much less time than the Latin, which is a derivative language. It is to be hoped that the great University of the South, about to be established on the cool and salubrious plateau of the Cumberland Mountains, if it does not banish Latin, will at least give a greater degree of prominence to the Greek and Hebrew, the two languages in which the Scriptures were originally written. By comparing "*The Annual Report of the Superintendent of Public Education*, 1859, with "*Les Lois concernant les Ecoles Publique dans l'Etat de la Louisiane*, 1849," it will be perceived, that the New England system of public education is not adapted to Louisiana and the South. The laws are excellent, if the system itself was in conformity to the spirit of our political institutions. After ten years' trial, we learn from the Report of the Superintendent, that they can not be carried out, as no laws can be, which are theoretical, burdensome, troublesome, expensive, and void of practical benefits. If a law were passed by the State of Louisiana appropriating three hundred thousand dollars per annum to furnishing every family with a loaf of bread every day, it could not be executed. More than half the families would not accept the bread. The Report of the Superintendent of Public Education proves that more than half the families in Louisiana will not accept of the mental food the State offers to their children. Some parishes will not receive any of it. Tensas, for instance, which is taxed $16,000 for the support of public schools, has "not a single public school," says the Report, "in it, yet nearly every planter has a school in his own house." The truth is, that government does more harm than good by interfering with the domestic concerns of our people. If let alone, they would not need governmental aid in furnishing food for either the body or the mind. The South would have been far ahead in education, manufactures, and internal improvements, if the federal government had not interfered, to shut out the only kind of laborers who can labor in the cane and cotton field and live. The system of public education, all admit, has failed in the country, but, it is asserted, has succeeded very well in New Orleans. If the tree be judged by its fruits it is poisonous instead of salutary, to republican institutions, in our great cities. If the boys whom it has taught to read novels, had been put to trades, they could not have been driven away from the polls after they had grown to be men. There has been virtually no election in New Orleans, and in many of our large cities, for the last five or six years; whether from fear or indifference, it proves that the system of education is defective. America wants a University to raise the standard of morals, manners, and learning, so high, that every individual will be as secure from personal violence at the sacred ballot-box, as at the church altar. America wants schools to raise the standard of moral virtue so high, that every American citizen, naturalized or native, may confidently rely upon government putting forth its whole power to protect him in all the rights and privileges of an American citizen, both at home and abroad.

CONCLUDING REMARKS.
BY THE EDITOR.

HAVING thus finished our labors, and embodied in this work a range of discussion on slavery, occupying the whole ground, we have a word to say to those who are engaged in fomenting these mad schemes of the abolitionists. We ask you candidly and dispassionately to compare the spirit, tone, and style of argument in the work before you, with the writings and speeches of the anti-slavery propagandists, such as Cheever, Channing, Wendell Phillips, and *Sherman's protege*. In unsparing and vituperative denunciation they certainly excel; but are they not filled with the most gross exaggerations and misrepresentations, not to say willful falsehoods. Nowhere do you find that Christian candor and fairness of argument, that should characterize the search after truth, but in their stead only positive assertions, and inflammatory appeals to the most vindictive passions of human nature.

In this crusade of the North against the South, there is a most unwarrantable and impertinent interference with the concerns of others, that ought to be most sternly rebuked; and it is one of the encouraging signs of the times, that the Southern people are at last roused from their inaction, and are vigorously engaged in adopting means of self-protection. Many, however, in the North are engaged in this crusade in order to divert attention from their own plague-spot—AGRARIANISM. We all recollect the Patroon of Albany and the Van Rensellaer mobs,—the Fourerism and Socialism of the free States, and the ever-active antagonism of labor and capital. They are like the fleeing burglar, who, more loudly than his pursuers, cries stop thief! For the time perhaps they have succeeded in hounding on the rabble in full cry after the South, and in diverting attention from themselves. But how will they fare in the end? It is said of a certain animal, that when once it has tasted human blood it never relinquishes the chase; so when the mob shall have tasted the sweets of plunder and rapine in their raids upon the South, will they spare the hoarded millions of the money-princes and nabobs of the North? Are there not thousands of needy and thriftless adventurers, or of starving and vicious poor, in the free States and cities of the North, who look with ill-concealed envy, or with gloating rapacity, on the prosperity and wealth of the aristocrats, as they term them, of the spindle and loom, and of the counting-house? Ye capitalists, ye merchant princes, ye master manufacturers, you may excite to frenzy your Jacobin clubs, you may demoralize their minds of all ideas of right and wrong, but remember! the gullotine is suspended over your own necks!! The agrarian doctrines will ere long be applied to yourselves, for with whatsoever measure ye mete, it shall be measured to you again.

Ye who profess to be the ministers of the Prince of peace, yet are engaged in preaching Sharp's rifles, or Brown's pikes; who teach that murder is no crime, if committed by a slave upon his best friend, his master; that midnight incendiarism is meritorious; that the breach of every command in the decalogue is commendable, if perpetrated under the guise of abolition philanthropy; who claim to possess a "higher law" than the law of God; in fine, who preach every thing except Jesus Christ, and him crucified; how shall you escape the sentence of holy writ: "If any man shall add unto these things, God shall add unto him all the plagues that are written in this book; and if any man shall take away from the words of the book of this prophecy, God shall take away his part out of the book of life, and out of the holy city, and from the things which are written in this book."

Ye politicians, who, for the sake of place, power, and the spoils of office, are engaged in alienating the feelings of both sections of our Union; in producing division in our national councils; whose course is fast bringing about the dissolution of our Union; to whose skirts will cling the blood of the martyrs of liberty, so vainly shed?

Ye people of the North, our brothers by blood, by political associations, by a community of interest; why will ye be led away by a cruel and misguided philanthropy, or by designing demagogues? why will ye strive to inflict the most irreparable injury upon the objects of your misplaced sympathy? reduce to ruins this fair fabric of liberty, and this happy land to desolation? Your own leaders acknowledge that, hitherto, your agitation, far from bettering the condition of the slaves, has only made it worse; and in some respects this is true. So long as you confine yourselves to making or hearing abolition speeches, or forming among yourselves anti-slavery societies; so long as you confine the agitation to yourselves, you neither injure nor benefit the slaves; your exuberant philanthropy escapes through the safety-valve in the shape of gas. But when you attempt to circulate among them incendiary documents, intended to render them unhappy, and discontented with their lot, it becomes our duty to protect them against your machinations. This is the sole reason why most, if not all the slave States, have forbidden the slaves to be taught to read. But for your interference, most of our slaves would now have been able to read the word of God for themselves, instead of being dependent, as they now are, on that *oral* instruction, which is now so generally afforded them. When emissaries come among them, to give them *oral* instruction different from that contained in the word of God, instead of abridging the privileges of the slave, we deal directly with the emissary, and justly, too; for we are acting not only in self-defense, but we are guarding this dependent race, committed by God to our care, from those malign influences which would work evil, not only to us, but to themselves, also. Could you succeed in your efforts— which you will find to be impossible—as the red republicans did in St. Domingo, or as the English abolitionists did in Jamaica and Barbadoes, so far from having bettered the condition of the blacks, you would have inflicted on them an irreparable injury. But of this you will soon have an opportunity of satisfying yourselves. We have among us a few hundred thousand of this race, who have been emancipated through a mistaken philanthropy, and who, though not injurious, are almost useless to us; these we have concluded to colonize among you, that your lecturers, while lauding the black man as being far superior to the white race, may never be in want of a specimen of the genuine article, to point to, as a proof of the truth of their arguments. Some of the slave States—and most, if not all of them, will pursue the same policy—have already passed laws for the removal of the free blacks from their borders, but allowing them the option of remaining, by choosing their masters, and returning to a state of servitude; and strange as you may think it, many have already done so, in preference to going among their friends, the abolitionists. This is done, not so much because we wish to be rid of this heterogeneous element of our population, for at worst, they are, *with us*, only a kind of harmless dead weight, but because we wish to send them North as missionaries, to convert the abolitionists and free soilers. If we may judge from the census and votes in the different counties in Ohio, the experiment will be entirely successful, as those counties having the largest black population, voted, in 1859, against the anti-slavery ticket; whilst those which voted for it, possess but a meagre black population. Is this because an intimate acquaintance with the negro, convinces the community that freedom is not the normal or proper condition for him; or is it because he prefers to reside amongst those who make least pretensions of friendship for him? The anti-slavery men may take either horn of the dilemma.

PAPERS PRINTED IN AUGUSTA, GEORGIA.

SOUTHERN FIELD AND FIRESIDE,

A LITERARY AND AGRICULTURAL PAPER,

PUBLISHED WEEKLY, IN AUGUSTA, GEORGIA.
Dr. D. LEE, Agricultural Editor.
W. W. MANN, Literary Editor.
WM. N. WHITE, Horticultural Editor.

Devoted to Agriculture, Literature, and Art. It is in quarto form of eight pages—each issue containing forty columns of matter. In mechanical execution, it is in the best style of the typographic art. In utility, it is all that the best agricultural science and practical knowledge of the South can furnish. A weekly visitor to the homes of Southern Planters and Farmers, it will be more useful and acceptable to them than any monthly journal of equal merit.

In mental attractions, it will be all that a spirit of enterprise on my part, and a laudable emulation on the part of others, can evoke from Southern intellect and cultivation.

The Agricultural Editor is Dr. DANIEL LEE, the distinguished Professor of Agriculture in the University of Georgia—editor for many years past of the *Southern Cultivator*, and a leading contributor to many Northern agricultural journals of the highest reputation.

The Literary editor is Mr. W. W. MANN, of this city, an accomplished writer, of fine taste, and scholarly attainments, who, having retired from the active duties of the legal profession, spent many years in Europe, and was for several years the Paris Correspondent of the *National Intelligencer* and *Southern Literary Messenger*.

THE SOUTHERN FIELD AND FIRESIDE

Will combine the useful and the agreeable. It will furnish the Southern Farmer information useful in every field he cultivates, and the Southern family choice literature, the offspring of Southern intellect, worthy of welcome at every fireside. It will be, in all respects, a first class paper—on a scale of expenditure more liberal than has yet been attempted in the South, and designed to rival, in its merits, the most distinguished of the North.

TERMS.—*Two dollars per annum, in advance.*

A special appeal is made to the ladies of the South for their patronage and good wishes.

This paper will be entirely silent on politics.

On matters pertaining to their respective departments, address the Editors. On matters of business generally,

Address,   JAMES GARDNER.

Augusta Georgia, 1860.

THE
AUGUSTA EVENING DISPATCH,
PUBLISHED DAILY AND WEEKLY, BY
S. A. ATKINSON.
DAILY, per annum $4—WEEKLY, per annum $1.50; to clubs of five or more, $1.

CHEAPEST PAPER IN THE SOUTH.
It contains the latest general news; reliable commercial news; all the telegraphic news, a summary of congressional news; in short, it is made up of news from all quarters, derived from the mails, the wires, and through a large number of special correspondents.

The Telegraphic and Mail facilities of Augusta give it material advantage as a distributing point for the LATEST NEWS; and as an evening paper furnishes news to Georgia and the adjoining States twelve hours in advance of any other medium.

THE WEEKLY DISPATCH

Is issued every Tuesday; contains 36 columns of reading matter; and in addition to the Commercial and General News of the day and the Prices Current in Augusta, it contains an attractive variety of pleasing Miscellany, Tales, Sketches, Poetry, etc. The WEEKLY DISPATCH is emphatically a

---

COTTON IS KING

SOUTHERN PLANTER'S HOME NEWSPAPER.

Specimen copies sent when desired.   Address

S. A. ATKINSON, Prop., Augusta, Ga.

SOUTHERN MEDICAL AND SURGICAL JOURNAL:
DEVOTED EXCLUSIVELY TO THE SCIENCE OF MEDICINE.

Published monthly, in numbers of eighty pages each, handsomely bound in paper, at $3 a year, in advance.

ADDRESS,   W. S. JONES, AUGUSTA, GA.

CHRONICLE AND SENTINEL,
AUGUSTA, GA.

THE WEEKLY CHRONICLE AND SENTINEL (a mammoth sheet, thirty three by forty-seven inches—the largest paper in the State) is published every Wednesday throughout the year, at TWO DOLLARS per annum for a single copy, in advance; three copies, $5; six copies, $10; ten copies, $15.

The CHRONICLE AND SENTINEL is strictly conservative, Union-loving, and law-abiding in principle. Particular attention is devoted to the Commercial and News Departments of the paper; and its ample size affords facilities for complete and early details of all the interesting

POLITICAL, COMMERCIAL, AND GENERAL FOREIGN AND DOMESTIC
INTELLIGENCE
of the day, with an agreeable variety of miscellaneous reading.

THE COMMERCIAL DEPARTMENT

embraces the latest reports by Telegraph and Mail from all the leading markets of this country and Europe; together with a carefully-corrected "Prices Current" and Weekly Report of the

AUGUSTA COTTON, GRAIN, FLOUR, BACON, PRODUCE, AND GROCERY MARKET.

The latest intelligence received by Telegraph, up to 2 o'clock, P. M., Tuesday, may be found under the Telegraph head. As an advertising medium,

THE WEEKLY CHRONICLE AND SENTINEL

offers superior inducements, having a very extended circulation throughout the cotton and grain-growing sections of Georgia, Alabama, Mississippi, and Tennessee.

THE DAILY CHRONICLE AND SENTINEL

is published every morning (except Monday), its columns being kept open to the latest moment prior to the departure of the interior mails, for the reception of news by Telegraph. Its reputation as a *reliable* and *correct* Commercial Journal is well and favorably known. It will be mailed to subscribers at SIX DOLLARS per annum, in advance. ADDRESS,

W. S. JONES, AUGUSTA, GA.

THE CONSTITUTIONALIST,
PUBLISHED AT AUGUSTA, GA.,
AND DEVOTED TO POLITICS, COMMERCE AND NEWS;
ITS ISSUES ARE DAILY, TRI-WEEKLY AND WEEKLY.

In politics, it is Democratic. In its spirit and aims, Conservative. In its commercial tables and statements, accurate and reliable. In its news department, prompt, industrious, truthful. In its telegraphic arrangements, its facilities are unsurpassed. They are, in all respects, fully up to the requirements of the day.

THE CONSTITUTIONALIST belongs emphatically to the school of State Rights and Strict Construction. Its principles are those of the Democratic Party, as set forth by the National

Convention at Cincinnati. It is the advocate of the sovereignty of the State and the union of the States; but not one without the other. It is for the equal rights of the States, and of each section.

For the South it claims equality in the Union, or independence out of it.

A uniform, firm, and consistent course for the thirty-seven years of its existence, is a guarantee of fidelity to its principles.

TERMS.—Daily, $6.00.   Tri-Weekly, $4.00.   Weekly, $2.00.

CASH, INVARIABLY IN ADVANCE.

PAPER STOPPED AT THE END OF THE TIME PAID FOR.
JAMES GARDNER, Proprietor.

SOUTHERN CULTIVATOR;
A Monthly Journal, devoted exclusively to the Improvement of Southern Agriculture, Horticulture, Stock-Breeding, Poultry, General Farm Economy, etc.

The CULTIVATOR contains a much greater amount of reading matter than any other Agricultural Journal of the South—embracing, in addition to all the current agricultural topics of the day, valuable original contributions from many of the most intelligent and practical Planters, Farmers, and Horticulturists in every section of the South and Southwest.

D. REDMOND AND C. W. HOWARD, EDITORS.

TERMS:

One copy, one year, $1; six copies, $5; twenty-five copies, $20; one hundred copies, $75: always in advance.

ADDRESS,   W. S. JONES, AUGUSTA, GA.

FOOTNOTES

[1] Strange that we should be compelled to call those *border* States, which lie in the very midst of our Union.

[2] Randall's Life of Jefferson, vol. i. page 370.

[3] Randall's Life of Jefferson, vol. i. page 370, Note.

[4] That Mr. Jefferson was considered as having no settled plans or views in relation to the disposal of the blacks, and that he was disinclined to risk the disturbance of the harmony of the country for the sake of the negro, appears evident from the opinions entertained of him and his schemes by John Quincy Adams. After speaking of the zeal of Mr. Jefferson, and the strong manner in which, at times, he had spoken against slavery, Mr. Adams says: "But Jefferson had not the spirit of martyrdom. He would have introduced a flaming denunciation of slavery into the Declaration of Independence, but the discretion of his colleagues struck it out. He did insert a most eloquent and impassioned argument against it in his Notes on Virginia; but, on that very account, the book was published almost against his will. He projected a plan of general emancipation, in his revision of the Virginia laws, but finally presented a plan leaving slavery precisely where it was; and, in his Memoir, he leaves a posthumous warning to the planters that they must, at no distant day, emancipate their slaves, or that worse will follow; but he withheld the publication of his prophecy till he should himself be in the grave."—*Life of J. Q. Adams, page 177, 178.*

[5] See a more extended detail of the proceedings in relation to this subject, both in England and the colonies, in the Appendix.

[6] Providence, Rhode Island.

[7] See Table I, Appendix.

[8] The sentiment of the Colonization Society, was expressed in the following resolution, embraced in its annual report of 1826:

"*Resolved,*—That the society disclaims, in the most unqualified terms, the design attributed to it, of interfering, on the one hand, with the legal rights and obligations of slavery; and, on the other, of perpetuating its existence within the limits of the country."

On another occasion Mr. Clay, on behalf of the society, defined its position thus:

"It protested, from the commencement, and throughout all its progress, and it now protests, that it entertains no purpose, on its own authority, or by its own means, to attempt emancipation, partial or general; that it knows the General Government has no constitutional power to achieve such an object; that it believes that the States, and the States only, which tolerate slavery, can accomplish the work of emancipation; and that it ought to be left to them exclusively, absolutely, and voluntarily, to decide the question."—*Tenth Annual Report, p. 14, 1828.*

[9] Gerrit Smith, 1835.

[10] Lundy's Life.

[11] On the floor of an Ecclesiastical Assembly, one minister pronounced colonization "a dead horse;" while another claimed that his "old mare was giving freedom to more slaves, by trotting off with them to Canada, than the Colonization Society was sending of emigrants to Liberia."

[12] This portion of the work is left unchanged, and the statistics of the increase of slave labor products, up to 1859, introduced elsewhere.

[13] Deuteronomy, xxxii. 32, 33.

[14] See Appendix, Table I.

[15] It may be well here to illustrate this point, by an extract from McQueen, of England, in 1844, when this highly intelligent gentleman was urging upon his government the great necessity which existed for securing to itself, as speedily as possible, the control of the labor and the products of tropical Africa. In reference to the benefits which had been derived from her West India colonies, before the suppression of the slave trade and the emancipation of the slaves had rendered them comparatively unproductive, he said: "During the fearful struggle of a quarter of a century, for her existence as a nation, against the power and resources of Europe, directed by the most intelligent but remorseless military ambition against her, the command of the productions of the torrid zone, and the advantageous commerce which that afforded, gave to Great Britain the power and the resources which enabled her to meet, to combat, and to overcome, her numerous and reckless enemies in every battle-field, whether by sea or land, throughout the world. In her the world saw realized the fabled giant of antiquity. With her hundred hands she grasped her foes in every region under heaven, and crushed them with resistless energy."

In further presenting the considerations which he considered necessary to secure the adoption of the policy he was urging, Mr. McQueen referred to the difficulties which were then surrounding Great Britain, and the extent to which rival nations had surpassed her in tropical cultivation. He continued: "The increased cultivation and prosperity of foreign tropical possessions is become so great, and is advancing so rapidly the power and resources of other nations, that these are embarrassing this country, (England,) in all her commercial relations, in her pecuniary resources, and in all her political relations and negotiations." ...... "Instead of supplying her own wants with tropical productions, and next nearly all Europe, as she formerly did, she had scarcely enough, of some of the most important articles, for her own consumption, while her colonies were mostly supplied with foreign slave produce." ...... "In the mean time tropical productions had been increased from $75,000,000, to $300,000,000 annually. The English capital invested in tropical productions in the East and West Indies, had been, by emancipation in the latter, reduced from $750,000,000, to $650,000,000; while, since 1808, on the part of foreign nations $4,000,000,000 of fixed capital had been created in slaves and in cultivation wholly dependent upon the labor of slaves." The odds, therefore, in agricultural and commercial capital and interest, and consequently in political power and influence, arrayed against the British tropical possessions, were very fearful—six to one. This will be better understood by giving the figures on the subject. The contrast is very striking, and reveals the secret of England's untiring zeal about slavery and the slave trade. Indeed, Mr. McQueen frankly acknowledges, that "If the foreign slave trade be not extinguished, and the cultivation of the tropical territories of other powers opposed and checked by British tropical cultivation, then the interests and the power of such states will rise into a preponderance over those of Great Britain; and the power and the influence of the latter will cease to be felt, feared and respected, amongst the civilized and powerful nations of the world."

But here are the figures upon which this humiliating acknowledgement is made. The productions of the tropical possessions of Great Britain and foreign countries, respectively, at the period alluded to by Mr. McQueen, and as given by himself, stood as follows:

SUGAR—1842.

British Possessions.

West Indies, cwts. 2,508,552
East Indies, " 940,452
Mauritius,(1841) " 544,767
Total 3,993,771

Foreign countries.

Cuba, cwts. 5,800,000
Brazil, " 2,400,000
Java, " 1,105,757
Louisiana, " 1,400,000
Total 10,705,757

COFFEE—1842.

West Indies, lbs. 9,186,555
East Indies, " 18,206,448
Total 27,393,003

Java, lbs. 134,842,715
Brazil, " 135,000,800
Cuba, " 33,589,325
Venezuela, " 34,000,000
Total 337,432,840

COTTON—1840.

709

West Indies,	lbs.	427,529	United States,	lbs.	790,479,275
East Indies,	"	77,015,917	Java,	"	165,504,800
To China from do.	"	60,000,000	Brazil,	"	25,222,828
	Total	137,443,446		Total	981,206,903

[16] See Appendix, Table II.

[17] Table III. For Statistics up to 1859, see chapter VI. and Appendix.

[18] See Appendix, Table II.

[19] Paganism has, long since, attained its maximum in agricultural industry, and the introduction of Christian civilization, into India, can, alone, lead to an increase of its productions for export.

[20] 1839.

[21] ENGLAND AND SLAVERY.—In the *London Times* of October 7th, 1858, there is a long and very able and candid article on the subject of cotton. The proportions of the article used by different nations are thus stated:

Great Britain,	51.28
France,	13.24
Northern Europe,	6.84
Other foreign ports,	5.91
Consumption of the U. S.,	23.58

Thus it appears that England uses more of the raw material than all the rest of the world. After giving the great facts the writer uses the following language:

"An advance of one pence per pound on the price of American cotton is welcomed by the slave-owner of the Southern States as supplying him with the sinews of war for the struggle now waging with the Northern abolitionists. This mere advance of one pence on our present annual consumption is equivalent to an annual subscription of sixteen millions of dollars toward the maintainance of American slavery."—*American Missionary.*

[22] See the speech of the Hon. Gerrit Smith, on the "Kansas-Nebraska Bill," in which he asserts, that the invention of the *Cotton Gin* fastened slavery upon the country; and that, but for its invention, slavery would long since have disappeared.

[23] This is only the consumption north of Virginia.

[24] This estimate is probably too low, being taken from the census of 1850. The exports of cottons for 1850 were $4,734,424; and for 1353, $8,768,894; having nearly doubled in four years.

[25] These figures were taken from the official documents for the first edition. They vary a little from the revised documents from which Table VII is taken, but not so as to affect our argument.

[26] See Table VII, in Appendix.

[27] See Table VI, in Appendix; and in this connection it may be explained that the *crop year* ends August 31st.

[28] See Table II, in Appendix. We have of course to limit our statements in relation to some of these amounts to the figures used in the first edition, because they can only be ascertained from the census tables of 1850. While it will be found that the exports of bread-stuffs and provisions have increased considerably, it will be seen from Table VIII that it is not in a greater ratio than the exports of cotton and tobacco. To show that the statement as it stands was a fair one at the time, it is only necessary for the reader to look at the last named table to see that the three years preceding 1853 exported considerably less than that year.

[29] See Table III, Appendix.

[30] These estimates have not been recast and adapted to 1859, for the third edition, because, as will be seen from Tables VII, VIII and X, there has been no great change in the amount of these commodities consumed since 1853.

[31] This includes the period from 1806 to 1826, though the decline began a few years before the latter date.

[32] Benton's Thirty Year's View.

[33] The Tariff of 1846, under which our imports are now made, approximates the Free Trade principles very closely.

[34] These figures are taken from a part of the *Economist's* article not copied. For the difference between the imports from India, in the whole of the years 1850 to 1855, see Table I.

[35] The commercial year is five days shorter for 1855 than in former years.

[36] See Table VIII, in Appendix.

[37] Compendium of United States Census, 1850.

[38] Mr. C. Buxton, in *Edinburgh Review*, April, 1859.

[39] Parliamentary Papers, Population Returns for the West Indies, (of course the decrease by manumission is not included.)

[40] Mr. C. Buxton, in *Edinburgh Review*, April, 1859, from which these extracts are made.

[41] *North British Review*, August, 1848.

[42] This point will be examined more fully in a subsequent chapter.

[43] Mr. C. Buxton, in *Edinburgh Review*, April, 1859.

[44] *London Economist*, Feb. 12, 1859.

[45] See *African Repository*, October, 1859.

[46] See *African Repository*, October, 1859.

[47] The progressive increase is indicated by the following figures:

	1820.	1830.	1840.	1853.
Total slaves in United States,	1,538,098	2,009,043	2,487,356	3,296,408
Cotton exported, lbs.,	127,800,000	298,459,102	743,941,061	1,111,570,370
Average export to each slave, lbs.,	83	143	295	337

[48] The remarks in this chapter remain as they were in the first edition.

[49] Mr. Wilson, the Missionary at St. Catharines, still remained there, but not under the care of the Association.

[50] 11th Annual Report, pages 36, 37.

[51] *American Missionary*, October, 1858.

[52] *African Repository*, October, 1859.

[53] *African Repository*, January, 1858.

[54] Page 170.

[55] Extract from the report of a missionary, quoted in the Report, page 172.

[56] Extract from the report of another missionary, page 171, of the Report.

[57] The average exports from the Island of Jamaica, omitting cotton, during the three epochs referred to—that of the slave trade, of slavery alone, and of freedom—for periods of five years, during the first two, and for the three years separately, in the last, will give a full view of this point:

Years of Exports. lbs. Sugar. P. Rum. lbs. Coffee.

Annual average, 1803 to 1807,[A]	211,139,200	50,426	23,625,377
Annual average, 1829 to 1833,[A]	152,564,800	35,505	17,645,602
Annual average, 1839 to 1843,[A]	67,924,800	14,185	7,412,498
Annual exports, 1846,[B]	57,956,800	14,395	6,047,150
Annual exports, 1847,[B]	77,686,400	18,077	6,421,122
Annual exports, 1848.[B]	67,539,200	20,194	5,684,921

[A] *Blackwood's Magazine* 1848, p. 225.

[B] *Littel's Living Age*, 1850, No. 309, p. 125.—*Letter of Mr. Bigelow.*

[58] Macgregor, London ed., 1847.

[59] *De Bow's Review*, August, 1855.

[60] Macgregor, London ed., 1847.

[61] Ibid.

[62] *De Bow's Review*, 1855.

[63] 1800.

[64] 1840.

[65] 1847.

[66] American Missionary Association's Report, 1857, p. 32.

[67] The West Indies as they were and are—*Edinburgh Review*, April, 1859.—The article said to be by Mr. C. Buxton.

[68] The statement was made at a meeting which met to consider the evils of the Chinese and coolie system of immigration into the West Indies and Mauritius. It is not stated whether the amounts given are the whole production or only the exports.

[69] The reader will remember that the Emancipation Act, of 1833, left the West India blacks in the relation of apprentices to their masters, but that the system worked so badly that total emancipation was declared in 1838.

[70] They must refer to slavery in its later years, after the suppression of the slave trade. Previous to that event, the production of Jamaica was more than seventy-five per cent. greater than at present.

[71] See Table IV, Appendix.

[72] See Table V, Appendix.

[73] Rev. Mr. Phillippo, for twenty years a missionary in Jamaica, in his "Jamaica, its Past and Present Condition."

[74] *New York Evangelist*, 1858.

[75] *New York Observer*, March, 1856.

[76] *Lynchburgh* (Va.) *Courier*, quoted by *African Repository*, January, 1858.

[77] *Southern Monitor*, quoted by *African Repository*, January, 1858.

[78] *Express*—Ibid.

[79] Synod of Virginia, quoted by *African Repository*, 1858.

[80] Quoted in *African Repository*, April, 1858.

[81] The Methodist Episcopal Church North, in 1858, had a total of 22,326 of colored members, in all the States.

[82] Page 102.

[83] *American Missionary*, July, 1859.

[84] Matthew's Gospel, xv: 14.

[85] "A Subaltern's Furlough," by Lt. Coke, 45th Regiment, being a description of scenes in various parts of America, in 1833.

[86] Clarkson's History of the Slave Trade.

[87] Wadstrom, page 220.

[88] Memoirs of Granville Sharp.

[89] The testimony here offered is the more important, as the Western District is the center of emigration from the United States.

[90] The Hon. Mr. Harrison was one of the candidates at the time alluded to.

[91] See the resolution copied into the Preface to the present edition.

[92] This is the phrase, nearly verbatim, used by Mr. Sumner in his speech on the Fugitive Slave Bill. Language, a little more to the point, is used in "The Friendly Remonstrance of the People of Scotland, on the Subject of Slavery," published in the *American Missionary*, September, 1855. In depicting slavery it speaks of it as a system "which robs its victims of the fruits of their toil."

[93] An anecdote, illustrative of the pliability of some consciences, of this apparently rigid class, where interest or inclination demands it, has often been told by the late Governor Morrow, of Ohio. An old Scotch "Cameronian," in Eastern Pennsylvania, became a widower, shortly after the adoption of the Constitution of the United States. He refused to acknowledge either the National or State Government, but pronounced them both unlawful, unrighteous, and ungodly. Soon he began to feel the want of a wife, to care for his motherless children. The consent of a woman in his own Church was gained, because to take any other would have been like an Israelite marrying a daughter of the land of Canaan. On this point, as in refusing to swear allegiance to Government, he was controlled by conscience. But now a practical difficulty presented itself. There was no minister of his Church in the country—and those of other denominations, in his judgment, had no Divine warrant for exercising the functions of the sacred office. He repudiated the whole of them. But how to get married, that was the problem. He tried to persuade his intended to agree to a marriage contract, before witnesses, which could be confirmed whenever a proper minister should arrive from Scotland. But his "lady-love" would not consent to the plan. She must be married "like other folk," or not at all—because "people would talk so." The Scotchman for want of a wife, like Great Britain for want of cotton, saw very plainly that his children must suffer; and so he resolved to get married at all hazards, as England buys her cotton, but so as not to violate conscience. Proceeding with his intended to a magistrate's office, the ceremony was soon performed, and they twain pronounced "one flesh." But no sooner had he "kissed the bride," the sealing act of the contract at that day, than the good Cameronian drew a written document from his pocket, which he read aloud before the officer and witnesses; and in which he entered his solemn protest against the authority of the Government of the United States, against that of the State of Pennsylvania, and especially against the power, right, and lawfulness of the acts of the magistrate who had just married him. This done, he went his way, rejoicing that he had secured a wife without recognizing the lawfulness of ungodly governments, or violating his conscience.

[94] *National Intelligencer*, 1854.

[95] Psalm 1: 16, 18.

[96] See Table XII, in Appendix.

[97] See Speech of Edmund Burke, in Appendix.

[98] See Table VIII, in Appendix.

[99] It has been denied that "Cotton is King," and claimed that Hay is entitled to that royal appellation; because its estimated value exceeds that of Cotton. The imperial character of Cotton rests upon the fact, that it enters so largely into the manufactures, trade, and commerce of the world, while hay is only in demand at home.

[100] See Table XII in Appendix, for the statistics on this subject.

[101] See Table VIII, in Appendix.

[102] See Table XII.

[103] This paper is published at Kingston, Jamaica, and in confirmation of the views of the *London Economist*, quoted in the body of the work, the following extract is copied from its columns:

"Barbadoes, we all know, is prosperous because she possesses a native population almost as dense as that of China, with a very limited extent of superficial soil. In Barbadoes, therefore, population presses on the means of subsistence, in the same way, if not to the same extent, as in England, and the people are industrious from necessity. Trinidad and British Guiana, on the other hand, have taken steps to produce this pressure artificially, by large importations of foreign labor. The former colony, by the importation of eleven thousand coolies, has trebled her crops since 1854, while the latter has doubled hers by the introduction of twenty-three thousand immigrants.

"While Jamaica is the single instance of retrogression, she affords also the solitary example of non-immigration.

"Mauritius, by importing something like one hundred and seventy thousand laborers, has increased her exports of sugar from 70,000,000 lbs. in 1844, to 250,000,000 lbs. in 1858. Jamaica, by depending wholly on native labor, has fallen from an export of 69,000 hhds. in 1848, to one of 28,000 hhds. in 1859.

"It is believed that there are not at this moment above twenty thousand laborers who employ themselves in sugar cultivation for wages."

[104] Martin's British Colonies. See also Ethiopia, by the author, page 132, for full details on this question.

[105] The hhd. of sugar, as in Martin's tables, is here estimated at 1,600 lbs. See foot note on page 222.

[106] See American Archives, vol i. folio 1749.

[107] His estimates are in pounds sterling. It is here, for sake of uniformity, reduced to dollars, the pound being estimated at five dollars.

[108] Investigations before the Committee on the Petition of the West India Planters. See American Archives, vol i. folio 1736.

[109] American Archives, vol. i. folio 1519.

[110] American Archives, vol. i. folio 1531.

[111] Testimony of Geo. Walker, Esq, American Archives, vol. i. folios 1723-24.

[112] Testimony of Geo. Walker, Esq, American Archives, vol. i. folios 1728-29,

[113] Testimony of Geo. Walker, Esq, American Archives, vol. i. folio 1730.

[114] American Archives, vol i. folio 1737.

[115] American Archives, vol. i. folio 494.

[116] American Archives, vol. i. folio 523.

[117] American Archives, vol. i. folio 525.

[118] American Archives, vol. i. folio 530.

[119] American Archives, vol. i. folio 541.

[120] American Archives, vol. i. folio 593.

[121] American Archives, vol. i. folio 600.

[122] American Archives, vol. i. folio 616.

[123] American Archives, vol. i. folio 641.

[124] American Archives, vol. i. folio 687.

[125] American Archives, vol. i. folio 735.

[126] American Archives, vol. i. folio 914.

[127] American Archives, vol i. folio 573.

[128] American Archives, 4th series, vol. iii. folio 11.

[129] American Archives, 5th series, vol. i. folio 1178.

[130] American Archives, 5th series, vol. i. folio 192.

[131] American Archives, 4th series, vol. iii. folio 1385.

[132] DECREASE.

[133] Not organized in 1840.

[134] Not organized in 1850.

[135] The *London Economist*, from which we copy, observes, that the figures in this table differ slightly from some other estimates, as must be the case in all computations that are not official, but that from examination it has reason to think them as near the truth as any practical object can require. The quantities consumed in each country include the direct imports from the producing countries, as well as the indirect imports, chiefly from England. The consumption on the Continent, for 1858, was not known. January 15, 1859, the date of publication of the *Economist*. The bales are estimated at 400 lbs. each.

[136] Locke on Civil Government, chap. ii.

[137] Robert Hall.

[138] Political Philosophy, chap. v.

[139] Reflections on the Revolution in France.

[140] Locke on Civil Government, chap. ix.

[141] Chap. ii. § x.

[142] Channing's Works, vol. ii. p. 126.

[143] Elements of Moral Science, Part ii. chap. i. sec. 11.

[144] Moral Science, Part ii. chap. i. sec. 2.

[145] Letters on Slavery, p. 89.

[146] Ibid, p. 92.

[147] Letters, p. 50.

[148] Letters, p. 50.

[149] Letters, p. 50.

[150] Letters, p. 113.

[151] Moral Science, Part ii. chap. i. sec. 2.

[152] Letters, p. 119, 120.

[153] Moral Science Part ii. chap. i. sec. 2.

[154] Moral Science, Part ii. chap. i. sec. 2.

[155] Ibid.

[156] The *Italics* are our own.

[157] Lev. chap. xxv.

[158] Exod. chap. xxi.

[159] In the first chapter.

[160] Mr. Chase, of Ohio.

[161] "By nature," in the Original Bill of Rights.

[162] Mr. Seward, of New York.

[163] Lev. xxv. 44, 45, 56.

[164] Lev. xxv. 44, 45, 46.

[165] Exod. xxi. 20, 21.

[166] Exod. xxi. 7, 8.

[167] Deut. xxiii. 15, 16.

[168] Moses Stewart, a divine of Massachusetts, who had devoted a long and laborious life to the interpretation of Scripture, and who was by no means a friend to the institution of slavery.

[169] Speech in the Metropolitan Theatre, 1855.

[170] Speech at the Metropolitan Theatre, 1855.

[171] Fools may hope to escape responsibility by such a cry. But if there be any truth in moral science, than every man should examine and decide, or else forbear to act.

[172] The Italics are ours.

[173] The emphasis is ours.

[174] Elliott on Slavery, vol. i. p. 205.

[175] Life of Joseph John Gurney, vol. ii. p. 214.

[176] Bigelow's Notes on Jamaica in 1850, as quoted in Carey's "Slave Trade, Foreign and Domestic."

[177] Quoted by Mr. Carey.

[178] Carey's Slave Trade.

[179] "The West Indies and North America," by Robt. Baird, A. M., p. 145.

[180] "The West Indies and North America," by Robt. Baird, A. M., p. 143.

[181] The Corentyne.

[182] East bank of the Berbice River.

[183] West bank of the Berbice River.

[184] West coast of Berbice River.

[185] Quoted in Carey's Slave Trade.

[186] Gurney's Letters on the West Indies.

[187] Ibid.

[188] Ibid.

[189] Dr. Channing.

[190] We moot a higher question: Is he fit for the pulpit,—for that great conservative power by which religion, and morals, and freedom, must be maintained among us? "I do not believe," he declares, in one of his sermons, "the miraculous origin of the Hebrew church, or the Buddhist church, or of the Christian church, nor the miraculous character of Jesus. I take not the Bible for my master—nor yet the church—nor even Jesus of Na-zareth for my master. . . . . . He is my best historic ideal of human greatness; not without errors—not without the stain of his times, and I presume, of course, not without sins; for men without sins exist in the dreams of girls." Thus, the truth of all miracles is denied; and the faith of the Christian world, in regard to the sinless character of Jesus, is set down by this very modest *divine* as the dream of girls! Yet he believes that half a million of men were, by the British act of emancipation, turned from slaves into freemen! That is to say, he does not believe in the miracles of the gospel; he only believes in the miracles of abolitionism. Hence, we ask, is he fit for the pulpit,—for the sacred desk,—for any holy thing?

[191] See extract, p. 156.

[192] Spirit of Laws, vol. i. book xv. chap. vii.

[193] Spirit of Laws, vol. i. book xv. chap. viii.

[194] The emphasis is ours.

[195] See pages 155, and 159, 160.

[196] See chap. i. § 2.

[197] Works, vol. v. p. 63.

[198] See chap. i. § 2.

[199] We have in the above remark done Boston some injustice. For New York has furnished the Robespierre, and Massachusetts only the Brissot, of "les Amis des Noirs" in America.

[200] This reply is sometimes attributed to Robespierre and sometimes to Brissot; it is probable that in substance it was made by both of these bloody compeers in the cause of abolitionism.

[201] See Alison's History of Europe, vol. ii. p. 241.

[202] Encyclopædia of Geo. vol. iii. pp. 302, 303.

[203] Prov. xxx. 22.

[204] Encyc. of Geo., vol. iii. p. 303. Mackenzie's St. Domingo, vol. ii. pp. 260, 321.

[205] Franklin's Present State of Hayti, etc., p. 265.

[206] Dr. Channing's Works, vol. v. p. 47.

[207] April No., 1855.

[208] Dr. Channing's Works, vol. vi. p. 50, 51.

[209] On this point, see page 176.

[210] XIV. Wendell, Jack v. Martin, p. 528

[211] XIV. Wendell's Reports, Jack *v.* Martin.

[212] In asserting that freedom is national, Mr. Sumner may perhaps mean that it is the duty of the National Government to exclude slavery from all its territories, and to admit no new State in which there are slaves. If this be his meaning, we should reply, that it is as foreign from the merits of the Fugitive Slave Law, which he proposed to discuss, as it is from the truth. The National Government has, indeed, no more power to exclude, than it has to ordain, slavery; for slavery or no slavery is a question which belongs wholly and exclusively to the sovereign people of each and every State or territory. With our whole hearts we respond to the inspiring words of the President's Message: "If the friends of the Constitution are to have another struggle, its enemies could not present a more acceptable issue than that of a State, whose Constitution clearly embraces a republican form of government, being excluded from the Union because its domestic institutions may not,

in all respects, comport with the ideas of what is wise and expedient entertained in some other State."

[213] Chap. ii § x.

[214] Madison Papers, p. 1448.

[215] One member seems to have been absent from the House.

[216] Annals of Congress; 2d Congress, 1791-1793, p. 861.

[217] This error was by no means a capital one.

[218] Speech in the Senate, in 1855.

[219] Speech in Boston, October 3d, 1850.

[220] Mr. Sumner has a great deal to say, in his speech, about "the memory of the fathers." When their sentiments agree with his own, or only seem to him to do so, then they are "the demi-gods of history." But only let these demi-gods cross his path or come into contact with his fanatical notions, and instantly they sink into sordid knaves. The framers of the Constitution of the United States, says he, made "a compromise, which *cannot be mentioned without shame. It was that hateful bargain* by which Congress was restrained until 1808 from the prohibition of the foreign slave trade, thus securing, down to that period, *toleration for crime.*" . . . . "The effrontery of slaveholders was matched by *the sordidness of the Eastern members.*" . . . . "The bargain was struck, and at this price the Southern States gained the detestable indulgence. At a subsequent day, Congress branded the slave trade as piracy, and thus, by solemn legislative act, adjudged this compromise to be *felonious and wicked.*"

But for this compromise, as every one who has read the history of the times perfectly well knows, no union could have been formed, and the slave trade might have been carried on to the present day. By this compromise, then, the Convention did not tolerate crime nor the slave trade; they merely formed the Union, and, in forming it, *gained the power to abolish the slave trade in twenty years.* The gain of this power, which Congress had not before possessed, was considered by them as a great gain to the cause of humanity. If the Eastern members, from a blind and frantic hatred of slavery, had blasted all prospects of a union, and at the same time put the slave trade beyond their power forever, they would have imitated the wisdom of the abolitionists, who always promote the cause they seek to demolish.

If any one will read the history of the times, he will see that "the fathers," the framers of the Constitution, were, in making this very compromise, governed by the purest, the most patriotic, and the most humane, of motives. He who accuses them of corruption shows himself corrupt; especially if, like Mr. Sumner, he can laud them on one page as demi-gods, and on the very next denounce them as sordid knaves, who, for the sake of filthy lucre, could enter into a "felonious and wicked" bargain. Yet the very man who accuses them of having made so infamous and corrupt a bargain in regard to the slave trade can and does most eloquently declaim against the monstrous injustice of supposing them capable of the least act in favor of slavery!

[221] XII. Wendell, p. 314.

[222] XIV. Wendell, p. 530; XVI. Peters, p. 608.

[223] Indeed, if we had produced all the arguments in favor of the constitutionality of the Fugitive Slave Law, it would have carried us far beyond our limits, and swelled this single chapter into a volume.

[224] This decision of the Supreme Court, which authorizes the master to seize his fugitive slave *without process*, (see his speech, Appendix to Congressional Globe, vol. xxii., part 2, p. 1587,) is exceedingly offensive to Mr. Chase of Ohio; and no wonder, since the Legislature of his own State has passed a law, making it a penitentiary offense in the master who should thus prosecute his constitutional right as declared by this decision. But, in regard to this point, the Supreme Court of the United States does not stand alone. The Supreme Court of New York, in the case of Jack *v.* Martin, had previously said: "Whether the owner or agent might have made the arrest in the first instance without any process, we will not stop to examine; authorities of deserved respectability and weight have held the affirmative. 2 Pick. 11, 5 Serg. & Rawle, 62, and the case of Glen *v.* Hodges, in this court, before referred to, (in 9 Johnson,) seem to countenance the same conclusion. It would indeed appear to follow as a necessary consequence, from *the undoubted position, that under this clause of the Constitution the right and title of the owner to the service of the slave is as entire and perfect within the jurisdiction of the State to which he has fled as it was in the one from which he escaped. Such seizure would be at the peril of the party;* AND IF A FREEMAN WAS TAKEN, HE WOULD BE ANSWERABLE LIKE ANY OTHER TRESPASSER OR KIDNAPPER."

[225] Story on Constitution, vol. iii. book iii., chap. xl.

[226] The framers of the Constitution in that Congress were:—"John Langdon and Nicholas Gilmer, of New Hampshire; Caleb Strong and Elbridge Gerry, of Massachusetts; Roger Sherman and Oliver Elsworth, of Connecticut; Rufus King, of New York; Robert Morris and Thomas Fitzsimmons, of Pennsylvania; George Reid and Richard Basset, of Delaware; Jonathan Dayton, of New Jersey; Pierce Butler, of South Carolina; Hugh Williamson, of North Carolina; William Few and Abraham Baldwin, of Georgia; and last, but not least, James Madison, of Virginia." Yet from not one of these framers of the Constitution—from not one of these illustrious guardians of freedom—was a syllable

heard in regard to the right of trial by jury in connection with the Fugitive Slave Law then passed. The more pity it is, no doubt, the abolitionist will think, that neither Mr. Chase, nor Mr. Sumner, nor Mr. Seward, was there to enlighten them on the subject of trial by jury and to save the country from the infamy of such an Act. Alas! for the poor, blind fathers!

[227] This crime of kidnapping, says Mr. Chase, of Ohio, is "not unfrequent" in his section of country; that is, about Cincinnati.

[228] Appendix to Congressional Globe, vol. xxii., part ii., p. 1587.

[229] The property in slaves in the United States is their *service or labor*. The Constitution guarantees this property to its owner, both in apprentices and slaves. And the Supreme Court has decided, Judge Baldwin presiding, that all the means "necessary and proper" to secure this property, may be constitutionally used by the master, in the absence of all statute law. The Roman law made the slave of that law, to be, not a *personal chattel*, held to service or labor only, as is the American apprentice or slave, but to be a *mere thing;* and guaranteed to the master the right to do with that *mere thing*, just as he pleased. To cut it up, for instance, as the master sometimes did, to feed fishes.

Abolitionists are guilty of the inexcusable wickedness of holding up this ancient Roman slavery, as a model of American slavery; although they know that the personal rights of apprentices and slaves, are as well defined and secured, by judicial decisions and statute laws, as the rights of husband and wife, parent and child.

[230] These letters were first published in the *Religious Herald*, Richmond.

[231] This letter was addressed to ELDER JAMES FIFE.

[232] Texas and Michigan; see also, Arkansas and Indiana, Florida and Wisconsin.

[233] President Dew's Review of the Virginia Debates on the subject of Slavery.

[234] Paulding on Slavery.

[235] I refer to President Dew on this subject.

[236] It is not uncommon, especially in Charleston, to see slaves, after many descents and having mingled their blood with the Africans, possessing Indian hair and features.

[237] The author of "England and America." We do, however, most indignantly repudiate his conclusion, that we are bound to submit to a tariff of protection, as an expedient for retaining our slaves, "the force of the whole Union being required to preserve slavery, to keep down the slaves."

[238] Fourierites, Socialists.

[239] The Irish levee and rail-road laborers are driven by blows.

[240] English papers propose *this* for the West India negroes.

[241] Essays of Elia.

[242] *Southern Literary Messenger*, for January, 1835. *Note to Blackstone's Commentaries..*

[243] See Missionary reports, statistics; also, Prof. Christy's Ethiopia.—*Editor.*

[244] Journal of an officer employed in the expedition, under the command of Captain Owen, on the Western coast of Africa, 1822.

[245] The slaves of the "Wanderer" were returned to Africa against their wills.—*Editor.*

[246] In relation to the Missouri Controversy, J. Q. Adams said:—*Editor.*

"There is now every appearance that the slave question will be carried by the superior ability of the slavery party. For this much is certain, that if institutions are to be judged by their results in the composition of the councils of the Union, the slaveholders are much more ably represented than the simple freemen."—*Life of J. Q. Adams, by Josiah Quincy, p. 98."*

"Never, since human sentiment and human conduct were influenced by human speech, was there a theme for eloquence like the free side of this question, now before the Congress of the Union. By what fatality does it happen that all the most eloquent orators are on its slavish side?"—*Ibid. p. 103.*

"In the progress of this affair the distinctive character of the inhabitants of the several great divisions of this Union has been shown more in relief than perhaps in any national transaction since the establishment of the Constitution. It is, perhaps, accidental that the combination of talent and influence has been the greatest on the slave side."—*Ibid. p. 118.*

[247] The author of England and America thus speaks of the Colombian Republic:

"During some years, this colony has been an independent state; but the people dispersed over this vast and fertile plain, have almost ceased to cultivate the good land at their disposal; they subsist principally, many of them entirely, on the flesh of wild cattle; they have lost most of the arts of civilized life; not a few of them are in a state of deplorable misery; and if they should continue, as it seems probable they will, to retrograde as at present, the beautiful pampas of Buenos Ayres will soon be fit for another experiment in colonization. Slaves, black or yellow, would have cultivated those plains, would have kept together, would have been made to assist each other; would, by keeping together and assisting each other, have raised a surplus produce exchangeable in distant markets; would have kept their masters together for the sake of markets; would, by combination of labor, have preserved among their masters the arts and habits of civilized life." Yet this writer, the whole practical effect of whose work, whatever he may have thought or intended, is to show the absolute necessity, and immense benefits of slavery, finds it necessary to add, I suppose in deference to the general sentiment of his countrymen, "that slavery might have done all this, seems not more plain, than that so much good would have been bought too dear, if its price had been slavery." Well may we say that the word makes men mad.

[248] Johnson on Change of Air.

[249] Eight days in the Abruzzi.—*Blackwood's Magazine*, November, 1835.

[250] I do not use the word democracy in the Athenian sense, but to describe the government in which the slave and his master have an equal voice in public affairs.

[251] Example of St. Domingo.

[252] Effects in Mexico and South American republics among the mongrel races. See Prof. Christy's Ethiopia.

[253] On the abolition of slavery, Mr. Adams observed: "It is the only part of European democracy which will find no favor in the United States. It may aggravate the condition of slaves in the South, but the result of the Missouri question, and the attitude of parties, have silenced most of the declaimers on the subject. This state of things is not to continue forever. It is possible that the danger of the abolition doctrines, when brought home to Southern statesmen, may teach them the value of the Union, as the only means which can maintain their system of slavery."—Life of J. Q. Adams, page 177.—*Editor*.

[254] Invariably true.

[255] On this subject, J. Q. Adams, in his letter to the citizens of Bangor, Maine, July 4th, 1843, said: "It is only as *immortal* beings that all mankind can in any sense be said to be born equal; and when the Declaration of Independence affirms as a self-evident truth that all men are born equal, it is precisely the same as if the affirmation had been that all men are born with immortal souls."—Life of J. Q. Adams, page 395.—*Editor*.

[256] On these points, let me recommend you to consult a very able Essay on the Slave Trade and Right of Search, by M. Jollivet, recently published; and as you say, since writing your Circular Letter, that you "burn to try your hand on another little Essay, if a subject could be found," I propose to you to "try" to answer this question, put by M. Jol-

livet to England: "*Pourquoi sa philanthropie n'a pas daigne, jusqu' a present, doubler le cap de Bonne-Esperance?*"

[257] Monkey tribes.—*Editor.*

[258] In the *New York Independent* for January 2, 1851, there is a sermon delivered by Rev. Richard S. Storrs, Jr., of Brooklyn, Dec. 12, 1850, in which his opposition to the fugitive slave bill is expressly placed on the injustice of slavery. He argues the matter almost exclusively on that ground. "To what," he asks, "am I required to send this man [the slave] back? To a system which . . . no man can contemplate without shuddering." Again, "Why shall I send the man to this unjust bondage? The fact that he has suffered it so long already is a reason why I should NOT. . . . . Why shall I not HELP him, in his struggle for the rights which God gave him indelibly, when he made him a man? There is nothing to prevent, but the simple requirement of my equals in the State; the parchment of the law, which they have written." This is an argument against the Constitution and not against the fugitive slave law. It is an open refusal to comply with one of the stipulations of our national compact. If it has any force, it is in favor of the dissolution of the Union. Nay, if the argument is sound it makes the dissolution of the Union inevitable and obligatory. It should, therefore, in all fairness be presented in that light, and not as an argument against the law of Congress. Let it be understood that the ground now assumed is that the Constitution can not be complied with. Let it be seen that the moralists of our day have discovered that the compact framed by our fathers, which all our public men in the general and state governments have sworn to support, under which we have lived sixty years, and whose fruits we have so abundantly enjoyed, is an immoral compact, and must be repudiated out of duty to God. This is the real doctrine constantly presented in the abolition prints; and if properly understood we should soon see to what extent it commends itself to the judgment and conscience of the people.

[259] The doctrine that the executive officers of a government are not the responsible judges of the justice of its decisions, is perfectly consistent with the principle advanced above, viz: that every man has the right to judge for himself whether any law or command is obligatory. This latter principle relates to acts for which we are personally responsible. If a military officer is commanded to commit treason or murder, he is bound to refuse; because those acts are morally wrong. But if commanded to lead an army against an enemy he is bound to obey, for that is not morally wrong. He is the judge of his own act, but not of the act of the government in declaring the war. So a sheriff, if he thinks all capital punishment a violation of God's law, he can not carry a sentence of death into effect, because the act itself is sinful in his view. But he is not the judge of the justice of any particular sentence he is called on to execute. He may judge of his own part of the transaction: but he is not responsible for the act of the judge and the jury.

[260] See Cheever's "God against Slavery," and Wendell Phillips' Speech on Harper's Ferry, &c., &c.—ED.

[261] Their object, evidently, has been to prevent the free people of color from emigrating to Liberia, and to retain them in this country as a cat's paw to work out their own designs.—ED.

[262] But for this, a large proportion of our slaves, instead of being instructed orally, would have been taught to read the Scriptures for themselves.—ED.

[263] Paley's definition is still more simple, "I define," he says, "slavery to be an obligation to labor for the benefit of the master, without the contract or consent of the servant." Moral Philosophy, book iii, ch. 3.

[264] Address, etc., p. 20.

[265] Elements of Moral Science, p. 225.

[266] It need hardly be remarked, that the command to obey magistrates, as given in Rom. xiii: 1-3, is subject to the limitation stated above. They are to be obeyed as magistrates; precisely as parents are to be obeyed as parents, husbands as husbands. The command of obedience is expressed as generally, in the last two cases, as in the first. A magistrate beyond the limits of his lawful authority (whatever that may be), has, in virtue of this text, no more claim to obedience, than a parent who, on the strength of the passage "Children, obey your parents in all things," should command his son to obey him as a monarch or a pope.

[267] Quoted by Pres. Young, p. 45, of the Address, etc.

[268] On the manner in which slaves were acquired, compare Deut. xx: 14. xxi: 10, 11. Ex. xxii: 3. Neh. v: 4, 5. Gen. xiv: 14. xv: 3. xvii: 23. Num. xxxi: 18, 35. Deut. xxv: 44, 46.

As to the manner in which they were to be treated, see Lev. xxv: 39-53. Ex. xx: 10. xxii: 2-8. Deut. xxv: 4-6, etc. etc.

[269] "The word of Christ, (Matt. xix; 9), may be construed by an easy implication to prohibit polygamy: for if 'whoever putteth away his wife, and *marrieth* another committeth adultery' he who marrieth another *without* putting away the first, is no less guilty of adultery: because the adultery does not consist in the repudiation of the first wife, (for, however unjust and cruel that may be, it is not adultery), but in entering into a second marriage during the legal existence and obligation of the first. The several passages in St. Paul's writings, which speak of marriage, always suppose it to signify the union of one man with one woman."—PALEY'S Moral Phil., book iii, chap. 6.

[270] Elements of Moral Science, p. 221.

[271] Clarkson and Wilberforce were anxious, to have the slave trade speedily abolished, lest the force of their arguments should be weakened by its amelioration.—ED.

[272] If the negro is susceptible of this degree of improvement, he ought *then* to be free.—ED.

[273] Abolition has impeded this improvement.—ED.

[274] We heard the late Dr. Wisner, after his long visit to the South, say, that the usual task of a slave in South Carolina and Georgia, was about the third of a day's work for a Northern laborer.

[275] Report of 1857, for the land in this parish.

CPSIA information can be obtained
at www.ICGtesting.com
Printed in the USA
BVOW09s2243071217
502211BV00011B/162/P